Maritime Labour Convention, 2006 – UK and REG Implementation

Maritime Labour Convention, 2006 – UK and REG Implementation

Charles Boyle LLB (Hons), LLM, Barrister

Bloomsbury Professional

LONDON • DUBLIN • EDINBURGH • NEW YORK • NEW DELHI • SYDNEY

BLOOMSBURY PROFESSIONAL
Bloomsbury Publishing Plc 41–43 Boltro Road, Haywards Heath, RH16 1BJ, UK

British Library Cataloguing-in-Publication Data

A catalogue record for this book is available from the British Library.

ISBN:	HB	978 1 52650 537 8
	ePDF	978 1 52650 539 2
	ePub	978 1 52650 538 5

Typeset by Evolution Design & Digital Ltd (Kent)
Printed and bound by CPI Group (UK) Ltd, Croydon, CR0 4YY

Preface

Since the International Labour Organisation's Maritime Labour Convention, 2006 (MLC) came into force internationally on 20 August 2013, it has already been amended, and a further two sets of amendments have been agreed and are expected to come into force in 2019 and 2020. The MLC is indeed a living instrument, and the Special Tripartite Committee set up under Article XIII to keep the Convention under continuous review has proved to be responsive in agreeing changes in accordance with the needs of seafarers, shipowners and maritime administrations.

The purpose of this book is to set out in detail how the UK, Bermuda, Cayman Islands, Gibraltar and the Isle of Man (being the members of the Red Ensign Group (REG) which are subject to the MLC) have implemented the Convention. Specific references are given to the laws, merchant shipping notices and guidance, as well as identifying the areas where implementation is permitted by way of collective agreements.

As the MLC sits in the context of the wider international regulatory regime, it expressly endorses the application of other international instruments and standards, particularly those of the International Maritime Organisation – for example, the International Convention on Standards of Training, Certification and Watchkeeping of Seafarers, 1978 (as amended). Furthermore, many of the MLC's mandatory provisions have been incorporated into EU Directives, which are relevant to the UK and Gibraltar. These international and regional provisions are also referenced.

The idea for the book arose out of my work representing Nautilus International on the UK's MLC tripartite working group, which was instrumental in shaping policy and laws in this area. In conceiving the idea to write about the UK provisions, it seemed logical to go further and include those of the other REG members. The work of that group continues in its post-implementation role, which has proved necessary, as legislation continues to be reviewed, and MLC amendments must be implemented. It is also the consultative body for the consideration of applications from the other REG members for the adoption of implementation by way of 'substantial equivalence' measures (on which, see below), as they do not have seafarers' and shipowners' organisations based in their territories.

Chapter 1 sets out an introduction to the ILO and the MLC. Key Articles of the Convention are set out, as these explain its construction and the relative status of the Regulations and Code (which consists of mandatory Standards and non-mandatory Guidelines). The MLC's explanatory note is set out in full, and this is particularly helpful in describing the structure of the Convention and how its constituent parts interrelate. The Articles which permit ratifying states to apply flexibility, derogations or exemptions are also reproduced, including the concept of 'substantial equivalence' where implementation may be by way of means which are conducive to fully achieving the general object and purpose of a provision, which the state is not in a position to implement in the manner set out in the mandatory Code A. The REG applies the concept of substantial equivalence most notably in relation to the regulation of crew accommodation through the Large Commercial Yacht Code (LY3 Code – this has been merged into the Red Ensign Group Yacht Code, which comes into force on 1 January 2019).

Chapter 2 describes the general approach of how the UK applies its legislation to UK ships and, while they are in UK waters, non-UK ships without MLC documentation, and non-UK ships with MLC documentation. Those ships without MLC documentation must comply with the UK provisions, as these are the standards against which they will be assessed if they are inspected by UK port state control. Indeed, the MLC requires ILO member states to ensure that ships registered with non-MLC states do not receive more favourable treatment than ships which are registered with MLC states. Ships which carry MLC documentation are required to comply with the MLC itself. This general pattern of the application of MLC legislation is followed by the other REG members, with the occasional nuance, such as: reference to MLC standards as applied by the flag state; or, in the case of Gibraltar in relation to ships registered in the EEA, by reference to the EU Directives which incorporate the MLC into EU law.

Following those general issues, the UK and other REG members have their own dedicated chapters, which describe the specific implementation measures across the five Titles of the MLC, covering: minimum requirements for seafarers to work on a ship; conditions of employment; accommodation, recreational facilities, food and catering; health protection, medical care, welfare and social security protection; and compliance and enforcement. The UK provisions are described in more detail (Chapters 3 to 22) as the other REG members' laws are influenced by those to a significant extent. However, the specific provisions for Bermuda (Chapter 23), the Cayman Islands (Chapter 24), Gibraltar (Chapter 25) and the Isle of Man (Chapter 26) have been set out, with detailed references to the appropriate regulatory sources.

Due to the central role of the MLC's Title 5 on compliance and enforcement, it was decided to set that out in full (in Part VIII, Appendix 1), annotated with references to the relevant sections of the ILO's guidelines on flag state control and port state control. Title 5 sets out the MLC's provisions on flag state inspection and certification, the entitlement of flag states to delegate many functions to recognised organisations (classification societies), on-board complaints procedures, remedial powers, power to withdraw certification, port state inspections and onshore complaints procedures, and powers to detain ships.

The full text of the amendments to the MLC have been set out in Part VIII, Appendix 2. The 2014 amendments are already in force and require shipowners to provide financial security to cover: the costs of repatriation of abandoned seafarers; and shipowners' liabilities for contractual claims in the event of a seafarer's death or long-term disability due to occupational injury, illness or hazard. The REG provisions are also referenced, and those of the UK are described in detail. At this stage, promulgation of the REG provisions for the implementation of the 2016 and 2018 amendments is awaited.

In respect of seafarers' rights, the main enforcement and remedial provisions are also set out, and these include: the right of a seafarer to file complaints on board ship or with external authorities ashore, such as with the ship's flag state administration or with the authorities of the port that the ship is visiting; the right of a seafarer to commence legal action in courts and employment tribunals where their rights have been breached; REG flag state and port state powers of inspection and detention of ships; and reference to criminal offences for non-compliance and the associated sentencing powers of the courts (which include the imposition of fines and custodial sentences).

I would like to acknowledge and thank the following organisations and persons for responding to enquiries and reading and providing comments on draft chapters relevant to their jurisdiction: the UK Maritime and Coastguard Agency; Captain Pat Nawaratne, Director and Chief Marine Surveyor of the Bermuda Shipping and Maritime Authority; James Hatcher, Senior Maritime Policy Adviser and Shipping Master of the Cayman Islands Shipping Registry; Dina Suisi, Barrister-at-Law and Crown Counsel in Gibraltar; and the Isle of Man Ship Registry.

I would also like to acknowledge the work of my many colleagues, past and present, on the UK's MLC tripartite working group who, over many years, have contributed so much to the successful implementation of the MLC within the UK, and lent to it their unswerving support. These include officials of the Maritime and Coastguard Agency, Nautilus International, RMT, the UK Chamber of Shipping and the British Tugowners Association, and other industry bodies.

I express my gratitude to the publishing team at Bloomsbury Professional for agreeing to take up my proposal and providing me with support throughout the production process.

Finally, I would like to thank the International Labour Organisation for granting permission to reproduce sections of the MLC and other materials in this book.

Charles Boyle
London,
October 2018

Contents

About the Author

Charles Boyle has been the Director of Legal Services at Nautilus International (formerly Nautilus UK) since 2007. During that time, he has advised widely on British employment law, as it applies ashore and in a maritime context. He has worked extensively on MLC-related matters, which include: representing Nautilus International on the UK's MLC tripartite working group; attending ILO meetings as an adviser to the International Transport Workers' Federation, where he has served on drafting committees concerned with 2016 and 2018 amendments to the MLC; and supporting the European Transport Workers' Federation in lobbying and drafting issues in connection with implementing the MLC provisions on flag state control and port state control, and the 2014 MLC amendments, into EU law.

Table of UK Statutes

All references are to paragraph number.

Table of UK Statutory Instruments

All references are to paragraph number.

Table of REG Legislation

All references are to paragraph number.

CAYMAN ISLANDS

PRIMARY LEGISLATION

SECONDARY LEGISLATION

ISLE OF MAN

PRIMARY LEGISLATION

SECONDARY LEGISLATION

Table of International Conventions and Instruments

All references are to paragraph number; **bold text** *indicates where provisions are set out in full.*

Table of European Materials

All references are to paragraph number.

Table of Cases

All references are to paragraph number.

PART I

Introduction

CHAPTER 1

Introduction

1.1 The purpose of this book is to set out the laws, regulations and other measures (such as merchant shipping notices, marine guidance notes and scope for collective bargaining agreements) which implement the rights and obligations of the Maritime Labour Convention, 2006 (MLC) in the UK, Bermuda, Cayman Islands, Gibraltar and the Isle of Man.

RED ENSIGN GROUP

1.2 The Red Ensign Group (REG) comprises the international shipping registries operated by the UK and its Crown Dependencies (Isle of Man, Guernsey and Jersey) and Overseas Territories (Anguilla, Bermuda, British Virgin Islands, Cayman Islands, Falkland Islands, Gibraltar, Montserrat, St Helena and the Turks and Caicos Islands).[1] All ships registered with a REG member are British ships, entitled to fly the red ensign.[2]

The UK ratified the MLC on 7 August 2013 and, in accordance with Article VIII, para 4, it came into force for the UK on 7 August 2014. As the rest of the REG are not members of the ILO, they are not entitled to ratify the MLC in their own right, but the UK has extended it to Bermuda, Cayman Islands, Gibraltar and the Isle of Man, to which it now applies.[3] The UK and those four REG members each have their own domestic legislation and other measures (as described in para 1.1

1 Red Ensign Group: www.redensigngroup.org [Accessed 4 May 2018].
2 Merchant Shipping Act 1995, ss 1(1)(a), (c), 2.
3 Article 35 of the ILO Constitution requires states which ratify a Convention to apply it to its non-Metropolitan territories for whose international relations they are responsible.

above) which implement the MLC. The MLC has not been extended to the other REG members.

The REG has two categories of register. Under category 1, any ship of unlimited tonnage, type and length may be registered.[4] The REG members to which category 1 is open are the UK, Bermuda, Cayman Islands, Gibraltar and the Isle of Man, and the British Virgin Islands (the latter is the only category 1 registry to which the MLC has not been extended). The remaining REG members are only entitled to register category 2 ships, which are limited in type and size, and so exclude (1) all passenger ships, and (2) pleasure vessels and other vessels of more than 150 tons.[5]

INTERNATIONAL LABOUR ORGANISATION

1.3 The International Labour Organisation (ILO) (based in Geneva) is the only tripartite agency of the United Nations and brings together governments, employers and workers to set labour standards, develop policies and devise programmes promoting decent working conditions. During the meetings leading up to the adoption of the MLC, the shipowners were represented by the International Chamber of Shipping (ICS) and the seafarers were represented by the International Transport Workers' Federation (ITF).

The ILO came into being in 1919 through the Treaty of Versailles, which provided that the League of Nations 'will endeavour to secure and maintain fair and humane conditions of labour for men, women, and children, both in their own countries and in all countries to which their commercial and industrial relations extend, and for that purpose will establish and maintain the necessary international organisations'.[6] The ILO currently has 187 Member States.[7] It has full juridical personality, including the capacity to contract and to institute legal proceedings.[8]

The ILO's objectives are set out in the preamble to its constitution as follows:

> 'Whereas universal and lasting peace can be established only if it is based upon social justice;
>
> And whereas conditions of labour exist involving such injustice, hardship and privation to large numbers of people as to produce unrest so great that the peace and harmony of the world are imperilled; and an improvement of those conditions is urgently required; as, for example, by the regulation of the hours of work,

4 Merchant Shipping (Categorisation of Registries of Relevant British Possessions) Order 2003 (SI 2003/1248), Sch, as substituted by Merchant Shipping (Categorisation of Registries of Relevant British Possessions) (Amendment) Order 2008 (SI 2008/1243), art 2.

5 Merchant Shipping (Categorisation of Registries of Relevant British Possessions) Order 2003, Sch, as amended.

6 Treaty of Versailles, Article 23, para (a), 28 June 1919.

7 About the ILO: www.ilo.org/global/about-the-ilo/lang--en/index.htm [Accessed 29 April 2018].

8 ILO Constitution, Article 39, para 1(a), (c).

including the establishment of a maximum working day and week, the regulation of the labour supply, the prevention of unemployment, the provision of an adequate living wage, the protection of the worker against sickness, disease and injury arising out of his employment, the protection of children, young persons and women, provision for old age and injury, protection of the interests of workers when employed in countries other than their own, recognition of the principle of equal remuneration for work of equal value, recognition of the principle of freedom of association, the organization of vocational and technical education and other measures;

Whereas also the failure of any nation to adopt humane conditions of labour is an obstacle in the way of other nations which desire to improve the conditions in their own countries;

The High Contracting Parties, moved by sentiments of justice and humanity as well as by the desire to secure the permanent peace of the world, and with a view to attaining the objectives set forth in this Preamble, agree to the following Constitution of the International Labour Organization:'[9]

The aims and purposes of the ILO, and the principles which should inspire the policies of its Members, are set out in the Declaration of Philadelphia and include:

'(a) labour is not a commodity;

(b) freedom of expression and of association are essential to sustained progress;

(c) poverty anywhere constitutes a danger to prosperity everywhere;

(d) the war against want requires to be carried on with unrelenting vigour within each nation, and by continuous and concerted international effort in which the representatives of workers and employers, enjoying equal status with those of governments, join with them in free discussion and democratic decision with a view to the promotion of the common welfare.'[10]

The ILO accomplishes its work through three main tripartite organs:

'The International Labour Conference (ILC) sets the International labour standards and the broad policies of the ILO. It meets annually in Geneva. Often called an international parliament of labour, the Conference is also a forum for discussion of key social and labour questions.

The Governing body is the executive council of the ILO. It meets three times a year in Geneva. It takes decisions on ILO policy and establishes the programme and the budget, which it then submits to the Conference for adoption.

The International Labour Office is the permanent secretariat of the International Labour Organization. It is the focal point for the International Labour Organization's overall activities, which it prepares under the scrutiny of the Governing Body and under the leadership of the Director-General.'[11]

9 ILO Constitution, preamble.

10 ILO Constitution, Annex, Article I, paras (a)–(d), Declaration concerning the aims and purposes of the International Labour Organisation, adopted at the 26th Session of the ILC, Philadelphia, 10 May 1944.

11 ILO Constitution, Article 2, para 1(a)–(c): www.ilo.org/global/about-the-ilo/how-the-ilo-works/lang--en/index.htm [Accessed 19 April 2018].

MARITIME LABOUR CONVENTION, 2006

1.4 The ILO's Maritime Labour Convention, 2006 (MLC) was adopted by the International Labour Conference (ILC) at its 94th (Maritime) Session on 7 February 2006, and came into force on 20 August 2013. The date for entry into force was set to be 12 months after the date on which the MLC had been ratified by 30 member states with a total share in the world gross tonnage of ships of at least 33 per cent.[12] For those states which were not within the first 30 to ratify, the MLC came into force 12 months after the date on which their ratifications were filed with the ILO.[13]

The MLC revises the following Conventions:

- Minimum Age (Sea) Convention, 1920 (No. 7);
- Unemployment Indemnity (Shipwreck) Convention, 1920 (No. 8);
- Placing of Seamen Convention, 1920 (No. 9);
- Medical Examination of Young Persons (Sea) Convention, 1921 (No. 16);
- Seamen's Articles of Agreement Convention, 1926 (No. 22);
- Repatriation of Seamen Convention, 1926 (No. 23);
- Officers' Competency Certificates Convention, 1936 (No. 53);
- Holidays with Pay (Sea) Convention, 1936 (No. 54);
- Shipowners' Liability (Sick and Injured Seamen) Convention, 1936 (No. 55);
- Sickness Insurance (Sea) Convention, 1936 (No. 56);
- Hours of Work and Manning (Sea) Convention, 1936 (No. 57);
- Minimum Age (Sea) Convention (Revised), 1936 (No. 58);
- Food and Catering (Ships' Crews) Convention, 1946 (No. 68);
- Certification of Ships' Cooks Convention, 1946 (No. 69);
- Social Security (Seafarers) Convention, 1946 (No. 70);
- Paid Vacations (Seafarers) Convention, 1946 (No. 72);
- Medical Examination (Seafarers) Convention, 1946 (No. 73);
- Certification of Able Seamen Convention, 1946 (No. 74);
- Accommodation of Crews Convention, 1946 (No. 75);
- Wages, Hours of Work and Manning (Sea) Convention, 1946 (No. 76);
- Paid Vacations (Seafarers) Convention (Revised), 1949 (No. 91);
- Accommodation of Crews Convention (Revised), 1949 (No. 92);
- Wages, Hours of Work and Manning (Sea) Convention (Revised), 1949 (No. 93);

12 MLC, Article VIII, para 3.

13 MLC, Article VIII, para 4. The MLC has now been ratified by 88 states: www.ilo.org/dyn/normlex/en/f?p=1000:11300:0::NO::P11300_INSTRUMENT_ID:312331 [Accessed 4 November 2018].

- Wages, Hours of Work and Manning (Sea) Convention (Revised), 1958 (No. 109);
- Accommodation of Crews (Supplementary Provisions) Convention, 1970 (No. 133);
- Prevention of Accidents (Seafarers) Convention, 1970 (No. 134);
- Continuity of Employment (Seafarers) Convention, 1976 (No. 145);
- Seafarers' Annual Leave with Pay Convention, 1976 (No. 146);
- Merchant Shipping (Minimum Standards) Convention, 1976 (No. 147);
- Protocol of 1996 to the Merchant Shipping (Minimum Standards) Convention, 1976 (No. 147);
- Seafarers' Welfare Convention, 1987 (No. 163);
- Health Protection and Medical Care (Seafarers) Convention, 1987 (No. 164);
- Social Security (Seafarers) Convention (Revised), 1987 (No. 165);
- Repatriation of Seafarers Convention (Revised), 1987 (No. 166);
- Labour Inspection (Seafarers) Convention, 1996 (No. 178);
- Recruitment and Placement of Seafarers Convention, 1996 (No. 179);
- Seafarers' Hours of Work and the Manning of Ships Convention, 1996 (No. 180).[14]

A brief overview of the structure of the MLC and ratifying states' obligations

1.5 The MLC consists of Articles, Regulations, and the Code, which is divided into Part A (Standards) and Part B (Guidelines). The Article and Regulations set out the core rights and principles and the basic obligations of ratifying states.[15] The Code contains the details for the implementation of the Regulations.[16]

The Regulations and Standards are mandatory.[17] The Guidelines are non-mandatory, but ratifying states must give due consideration to implementing their responsibilities in the manner set out in those Guidelines.[18]

14 MLC, Article X. The status of many of these Conventions and other Recommendations was reviewed at the request of the Governing Body of the ILO at the Third Meeting of the Special Tripartite Committee (STC) in April 2018. The relevant Technical Notes and the STC's recommendations concerning the future of those instruments can be found at: www.ilo.org/global/standards/maritime-labour-convention/special-tripartite-committee/WCMS_622814/lang--en/index.htm [Accessed 17 September 2018].

15 Explanatory note to the Regulations and Code of the MLC, para 3.

16 Explanatory note to the Regulations and Code of the MLC, para 4.

17 MLC, Article VI, para 1.

18 MLC, Article VI, para 2. For a brief overview of the MLC, see Baatz, Y, *Maritime Law* (4th edition, Informa Law from Routledge, 2018, Abingdon, Oxon), 368–372, contributed by Filippo Lorenzon.

The Regulations and the Code are organised into general areas under five titles, as follows:

Title 1: Minimum requirements for seafarers to work on a ship;

Title 2: Conditions of employment;

Title 3: Accommodation, recreational facilities, food and catering;

Title 4: Health protection, medical care, welfare and social security protection; and

Title 5: Compliance and enforcement.[19]

Each title contains groups of related provisions; for instance, Title 1 sets out the conditions on minimum age (Regulation 1.1), medical certificate (Regulation 1.2), training and qualifications (Regulation 1.3), and recruitment and placement (Regulation 1.4).

Ratifying states are required to implement and enforce laws or regulations or other measures to fulfil their MLC obligations.[20] Unless otherwise stated, implementation can be by way of '... national laws or regulations, through applicable collective bargaining agreements or through other measures or in practice'.[21]

The Explanatory Note to the MLC is reproduced at para 1.14 below, and sets out the relative status and relationship between the Articles, Regulations and the Code.

The MLC in context

1.6 The MLC aspires to create a single, coherent instrument, embodying as far as possible all up-to-date standards of existing international maritime labour Conventions and Recommendations, as well as the fundamental principles to be found in other international labour Conventions, in particular:

- 'the Forced Labour Convention, 1930 (No. 29);
- the Freedom of Association and Protection of the Right to Organise Convention, 1948 (No. 87);
- the Right to Organise and Collective Bargaining Convention, 1949 (No. 98);
- the Equal Remuneration Convention, 1951 (No. 100);
- the Abolition of Forced Labour Convention, 1957 (No. 105);
- the Discrimination (Employment and Occupation) Convention, 1958 (No. 111);
- the Minimum Age Convention, 1973 (No. 138);

19 Explanatory note to the Regulations and Code of the MLC, para 5.
20 MLC, Article V, para 1.
21 MLC, Article IV, para 5.

- the Worst Forms of Child Labour Convention, 1999 (No. 182).'[22]

The UK has ratified all of the above Conventions.[23]

It has been noted that the lengthy preamble to the MLC, as well as what the ILO regards as 'fundamental' human rights conventions '... contextualizes the MLC, 2006 provisions and serves to firmly situate the Convention in the wider international law of the sea and international maritime legal regime'.[24] A legal opinion provided by the ILO legal adviser on the relevance of the preamble states:

> 'Preambles do not contain legal obligations ... [it] provides information as to the overall context and intention of the Convention in relation to other relevant international law and principles. In particular, it indicates a clear intention that the new Convention should, inter alia, embody the fundamental principles to be found in the ILO's "fundamental Conventions" ... and recalls the ILO Declaration of Fundamental Principles and Rights at Work, 1998.'[25]

The MLC recognises that, due to the global nature of the shipping industry, seafarers need special protection.[26] It has become known as the 'fourth pillar' of the international maritime regulatory regime, alongside the following IMO Conventions: the International Convention for the Safety of Life at Sea, 1974 (SOLAS); the International Convention for the Prevention of Pollution from Ships (MARPOL); and the International Convention on Standards of Training, Certification and Watchkeeping for Seafarers (STCW).

1.7 One of the purposes of the MLC is to create a level playing field in the context of seafarers' living and working conditions, helping to prevent good shipowners from being undercut by the less scrupulous. Helping to achieve this is the 'no more favourable treatment' clause which provides that '[e]ach Member shall implement its responsibilities under this Convention in such a way as to ensure that the ships that fly the flag of any State that has not ratified this Convention do not receive more favourable treatment than the ships that fly the flag of any State that has ratified it'.[27] In practice, this means that ships registered with non-ratifying states can be subject to port state inspections which require MLC standards to be met on board. Indeed the domestic legislation of the REG members which are subject to the MLC provides that such ships may be inspected against MLC standards, and may be detained for serious or repeated non-compliances. It therefore makes good commercial sense to be registered with a ratifying state, because ships which carry a maritime labour certificate, complemented by a declaration of maritime labour compliance (DMLC), are to

22 MLC, preamble, p 1.

23 ILO ratifications for the UK (fundamental conventions): www.ilo.org/dyn/normlex/en/f?p=NORMLEXPUB: 11200:0::NO::P11200_COUNTRY_ID:102651 [Accessed 4 May 2018].

24 McConnell, ML, Devlin, D, and Doumbia-Henry, C, *The Maritime Labour Convention, 2006: A Legal Primer to an Emerging International Regime* (1st edn, Martinus Nijhoff) 168.

25 Note 1 (Preamble), p 13, quoted in McConnell et al, p 170.

26 MLC, preamble, p 1.

27 MLC, Article V, para 7.

be treated as prima facie compliant, and so are less likely to encounter problems with port state control officers when visiting foreign ports.[28]

Central to the MLC is the flag state's jurisdiction over the ships which are registered with it. In this regard, the MLC refers to Article 94 of the United Nations Convention on the Law of the SEA, 1982 (UNCLOS), which establishes the duties and obligations of a flag State with regard to labour conditions, crewing and social matters on ships which fly its flag.[29]

The MLC was designed to secure the widest possible acceptability among governments, shipowners and seafarers committed to the principles of decent work, to be readily updateable and to lend itself to effective implementation and enforcement.[30] Ratifying states must, at the very least, meet the MLC requirements and may, of course, go beyond those minimum standards. The adoption of any ILO Convention or Recommendation is not to affect any law, award, custom or agreement which ensures more favourable conditions.[31]

Definitions and scope of application of the MLC

1.8 In general, the MLC applies to all seafarers serving on ships which are ordinarily engaged in commercial activities. It is convenient here to set out some key definitions,[32] some of which are important in determining the exact scope of application of the MLC, including the definitions of 'seafarer' and 'ship':

(a) *competent authority* means the minister, government department or other authority having power to issue and enforce regulations, orders or other instructions having the force of law in respect of the subject matter of the provision concerned;[33]

(b) *declaration of maritime labour compliance* means the declaration referred to in Regulation 5.1.3;[34]

(c) *gross tonnage* means the gross tonnage calculated in accordance with the tonnage measurement regulations contained in Annex I to the International Convention on Tonnage Measurement of Ships, 1969, or any successor Convention; for ships covered by the tonnage measurement interim scheme adopted by the

28 MLC, Regulation 5.1.1, para 4.
29 MLC, preamble, p 2.
30 MLC, preamble, p 2.
31 ILO Constitution, Article 19, para 8; MLC, preamble, p 2.
32 MLC, Article II, para 1(a)–(j).
33 In most cases, 'competent authority' will be the maritime administration or department of transport; however, in some cases, depending on the subject matter of the relevant provision, it will be other government departments, such as those which have responsibility for employment law or social security.
34 The declaration of maritime labour compliance consists of Part I (which lists the national implementing provisions and requirements for the key 16 areas of inspection set out in Appendix A5-I) and Part II (in which the shipowner must set out how it meets the requirements of Part I): MLC, Standard A5.1.3.10(a)–(b). It will be produced by the flag state and must be based on the model document set out in Appendix A5-II to the MLC.

International Maritime Organization, the gross tonnage is that which is included in the REMARKS column of the International Tonnage Certificate (1969);

(d) *maritime labour certificate* means the certificate referred to in Regulation 5.1.3;[35]

(e) *requirements of this Convention* refers to the requirements in these Articles and in the Regulations and Part A of the Code of this Convention;[36]

(f) *seafarer* means any person who is employed or engaged or works in any capacity on board a ship to which this Convention applies;[37]

(g) *seafarers' employment agreement* includes both a contract of employment and articles of agreement;[38]

(h) *seafarer recruitment and placement service* means any person, company, institution, agency or other organization, in the public or the private sector, which is engaged in recruiting seafarers on behalf of shipowners or placing seafarers with shipowners;[39]

(i) *ship* means a ship other than one which navigates exclusively in inland waters or waters within, or closely adjacent to, sheltered waters or areas where port regulations apply;

(j) *shipowner* means the owner of the ship or another organization or person, such as the manager, agent or bareboat charterer, who has assumed the responsibility for the operation of the ship from the owner and who, on assuming such responsibility, has agreed to take over the duties and responsibilities imposed on shipowners in accordance with this Convention, regardless of whether any other organization or persons fulfil certain of the duties or responsibilities on behalf of the shipowner.'[40]

35 The maritime labour certificate will be issued by the maritime administration (or recognised organisation acting on behalf of a flag state) to ships following a successful MLC inspection: the declaration of maritime labour compliance, Parts I and II, must be appended to it: MLC, Standard A5.1.3.1. It must be based on the model document set out Appendix A5-II to the MLC.

36 The 'requirements of this Convention' do not include the non-mandatory Code B (that is, the Guidelines); however, in accordance with Article VI, para 2, ratifying states '... shall give due consideration to implementing [their] responsibilities in the manner provided for in Part B of the Code'. McConnell et al (footnote 24 above, at pp 207–208) note that the term 'seafarers' rights' is not defined and that '... it is not entirely clear what the term refers to. It could refer to Article III and, in particular, Article IV as they are seen as cornerstones of the "seafarers' bill of rights"'. It is submitted that this view is generally accepted.

37 The master of the ship is also a 'seafarer' for the purposes of the MLC. For an account of the master's rights and obligations under the MLC, including the evolution in the 20th century which saw the master gain certain social welfare benefits of the seafarer (and not just be the commercial agent and custodian of the ship), see Lavelle J, *The Maritime Labour Convention, 2006, International Labour Law Redefined* (Informa Law from Routledge, Abingdon, Oxon), pp 47–68, contributed by John Cartner.

38 A seafarers' employment agreement may also include a collective bargaining agreement (MLC, Standard A2.1.2); furthermore, ratifying states may use collective bargaining agreements for many (but not all) aspects of national implementation (Article IV, para 5).

39 Ratifying states must require recruitment and placement organisations based in their territories to comply with the relevant provisions: MLC, Regulation 1.4.2, Standard A1.4.

40 The shipowner's name and address must be stated on various documents, including seafarers' employment agreements (Standard A2.1.4(b)) and the maritime labour certificate (Appendix A5-II).

Unless expressly provided otherwise, the MLC applies to all seafarers and all ships (as defined in sub-paras (f) and (i) above), whether the ship is publicly or privately owned, that are ordinarily engaged in commercial activities; however, it does not apply to ships engaged in fishing or in similar pursuits, ships of traditional build (such as dhows and junks), warships or naval auxiliaries.[41] For the fishing sector, there is the ILO Work in Fishing Convention, 2007 (No. 188) which provides minimum living and working conditions, and which came into force internationally on 16 November 2017.[42]

1.9 In the event of doubt as to whether any categories of persons are to be regarded as seafarers, or whether the MLC applies to a ship or particular category of ships, the question is to be determined by the competent authority in each member state after consultation with the shipowners' and seafarers' organisations concerned.[43]

There will be cases where there is doubt as to whether a certain category of worker is a seafarer for the purposes of the MLC – for instance, research scientists on survey ships or armed guards engaged to defend against attacks by pirates. To promote uniformity on the meaning of 'seafarer', the Annex to Resolution (VII) concerning information on occupational groups provides guidance for maritime administrations on this question, part of which is reproduced below:

> 'Categories
>
> An administration may have doubts about designating a particular category of persons working on board as a seafarer under Article II, paragraph 1(f), because:
>
> (i) the nature of their work is not part of the routine business of the ship (for example, scientists, researchers, divers, specialist offshore technicians, etc.);
>
> (ii) although trained and qualified in maritime skills, the persons concerned perform key specialist functions that are not part of the routine business of the ship (for example, harbour pilots, inspectors or superintendents);
>
> (iii) the work they perform is occasional and short term, with their principal place of employment being onshore (for example, guest entertainers, repair technicians, surveyors or portworkers).
>
> A person or category of persons should not automatically be excluded from the definition of seafarers solely on account of falling within one or more of the categories listed above. These lists are simply illustrative of situations where doubts may arise.

41 MLC, Article II, paras 2 and 4.

42 Convention 188 has been ratified by the following 12 states: Angola, Argentina, Bosnia and Herzegovina, Congo, Estonia, France, Lithuania, Morocco, Namibia, Norway, Senegal and South Africa: www.ilo.org/dyn/normlex/en/f?p=1000:11300:0:: NO:11300:P11300_INSTRUMENT_ID:312333 [Accessed 2 November 2018]. The UK is currently working on implementation for imminent ratification; its public consultation on the draft legislation closed on 12 January 2018: www.gov.uk/ government/consultations/implementation-of-the-ilo-work-in-fishing-convention-2007-ilo-188-into-uk-law [Accessed 30 April 2018].

43 MLC, Article II, paras 3 and 5.

Special factors in the situation may lead the administration to determine when a person is or is not a seafarer.

Criteria

In considering how to resolve such doubts, the following issues should be considered:

(i) the duration of the stay on board of the persons concerned;

(ii) the frequency of periods of work spent on board;

(iii) the location of the person's principal place of work;

(iv) the purpose of the person's work on board;

(v) the protection that would normally be available to the persons concerned with regard to their labour and social conditions to ensure they are comparable to that provided for under the Convention.'[44]

SHIPS UNDER 200 GT NOT ENGAGED ON INTERNATIONAL VOYAGES

1.10 In addition to the general provisions on flexibility within the MLC, there is the following specific provision relating to ships of less than 200 gross tonnage (GT):

> 'Where the competent authority determines that it would not be reasonable or practicable at the present time to apply certain details of the Code referred to in Article VI, paragraph 1, to a ship or particular categories of ships flying the flag of the Member, the relevant provisions of the Code shall not apply to the extent that the subject matter is dealt with differently by national laws or regulations or collective bargaining agreements or other measures. Such a determination may only be made in consultation with the shipowners' and seafarers' organizations concerned and may only be made with respect to ships of less than 200 gross tonnage not engaged in international voyages.'[45]

DETERMINATIONS TO BE NOTIFIED TO THE ILO

1.11 Any determination which a maritime administration makes (in consultation with shipowners' and seafarers' representatives) on whether a particular person is to be classified as a seafarer or a ship is one to which the MLC applies, or whether to make any exceptions for ships under 200 GT not engaged on international voyages, is to be communicated to the Director General of the ILO, who will notify the member states.[46]

44 Resolution (VII) concerning information on occupational groups, adopted by the International Labour Conference at its 94th (Maritime) Session on 22 February 2006, Geneva.

45 MLC, Article II, para 6.

46 MLC, Article II, para 7.

FUNDAMENTAL RIGHTS AND PRINCIPLES; EMPLOYMENT AND SOCIAL RIGHTS

1.12 The MLC sets out references to fundamental rights and principles, as follows:

> 'Each Member shall satisfy itself that the provisions of its law and regulations respect, in the context of this Convention, the fundamental rights to:
>
> (a) freedom of association and the effective recognition of the right to collective bargaining;
>
> (b) the elimination of all forms of forced or compulsory labour;
>
> (c) the effective abolition of child labour; and
>
> (d) the elimination of discrimination in respect of employment and occupation.'[47]

It also sets out the following seafarers' employment and social rights:

> '1. Every seafarer has the right to a safe and secure workplace that complies with safety standards.
>
> 2. Every seafarer has a right to fair terms of employment.
>
> 3. Every seafarer has a right to decent working and living conditions on board ship.
>
> 4. Every seafarer has a right to health protection, medical care, welfare measures and other forms of social protection.
>
> 5. Each Member shall ensure, within the limits of its jurisdiction, that the seafarers' employment and social rights set out in the preceding paragraphs of this Article are fully implemented in accordance with the requirements of this Convention. Unless specified otherwise in the Convention, such implementation may be achieved through national laws or regulations, through applicable collective bargaining agreements or through other measures or in practice.'[48]

The provisions of the preamble and Article III and IV caused concern for some states during the negotiations leading to the MLC.[49] Regarding Article III, the ILO has stated that the nature of the obligation on a state which ratifies the MLC '... is not to apply the provisions of the Conventions embodying those fundamental rights (which are referenced in the Preamble), but rather to satisfy itself that those fundamental rights are reflected in the relevant legislation'.[50] This obligation must be carried out in good faith and the measures taken must

47 MLC, Article III, paras (a)–(d). The UK applies its Equality Act 2010 to seafarers through the Equality Act 2010 (Work on Ships and Hovercraft) Regulations 2011 (SI 2011/1771).

48 MLC, Article IV.

49 McConnell et al, footnote 24 above, 168–172, 204–211.

50 Report I(1A) of the International Labour Conference, 94th (Maritime) Session, Pt II, Note 4 on Articles III and IV, para 1.

be included in MLC ratifying states' reports to the ILO under Article 22 of its Constitution.[51]

It has been noted that '[a]lthough the rights in Article IV, paragraphs 1–4 do not neatly correspond to the Titles of the Convention, taken together, they encompass all the provisions within those Titles'.[52] The ILC comments:

> 'Article IV can be seen as setting out the general rights and principles which are articulated, in greater detail, in the Regulations and Code, under the Titles. Paragraph 5 makes it clear that the "seafarers' employment and social rights", set out in paragraphs 1-4, are to be fully implemented, not in the abstract but, rather, "in accordance with the requirements of this Convention" – i.e. in accordance with the relevant provisions of the Articles, Regulations and Part A of the Code ...'[53]

IMPLEMENTATION AND ENFORCEMENT

1.13

> '1. Each Member shall implement and enforce laws or regulations or other measures that it has adopted to fulfil its commitments under this Convention with respect to ships and seafarers under its jurisdiction.
>
> 2. Each Member shall effectively exercise its jurisdiction and control over ships that fly its flag by establishing a system for ensuring compliance with the requirements of this Convention, including regular inspections, reporting, monitoring and legal proceedings under the applicable laws.
>
> 3. Each Member shall ensure that ships that fly its flag carry a maritime labour certificate and a declaration of maritime labour compliance as required by this Convention.
>
> 4. A ship to which this Convention applies may, in accordance with international law, be inspected by a Member other than the flag State, when the ship is in one of its ports, to determine whether the ship is in compliance with the requirements of this Convention.
>
> 5. Each Member shall effectively exercise its jurisdiction and control over seafarer recruitment and placement services, if these are established in its territory.
>
> 6. Each Member shall prohibit violations of the requirements of this Convention and shall, in accordance with international law, establish sanctions or require the adoption of corrective measures under its laws which are adequate to discourage such violations.[54]

51 Report I(1A) of the International Labour Conference, 94th (Maritime) Session, Pt II, Note 4 on Articles III and IV, para 1, citing the advice of the ILO Legal Adviser to the Preparatory Technical Maritime Conference (PTMC).

52 McConnell et al, footnote 24 above, p 208.

53 Report I(1A) of the International Labour Conference, 94th (Maritime) Session, Pt II, Note 4 on Articles III and IV, para 2; partially cited in McConnell et al, footnote 24 above, p 209.

54 The sanctions for non-compliances implemented by the REG members generally include: issue of an improvement notice; detention of ships; criminal offences and penalties; and the right for affected seafarers to commence legal claims.

7. Each Member shall implement its responsibilities under this Convention in such a way as to ensure that the ships that fly the flag of any State that has not ratified this Convention do not receive more favourable treatment than the ships that fly the flag of any State that has ratified it.'[55]

Regulations and Parts A and B of the Code

1.14

'1. The Regulations and the provisions of Part A of the Code are mandatory. The provisions of Part B of the Code are not mandatory.

2. Each Member undertakes to respect the rights and principles set out in the Regulations and to implement each Regulation in the manner set out in the corresponding provisions of Part A of the Code. In addition, the Member shall give due consideration to implementing its responsibilities in the manner provided for in Part B of the Code.

3. A Member which is not in a position to implement the rights and principles in the manner set out in Part A of the Code may, unless expressly provided otherwise in this Convention, implement Part A through provisions in its laws and regulations or other measures which are substantially equivalent to the provisions of Part A.[56]

4. For the sole purpose of paragraph 3 of this Article, any law, regulation, collective agreement or other implementing measure shall be considered to be substantially equivalent, in the context of this Convention, if the Member satisfies itself that:

   (a) it is conducive to the full achievement of the general object and purpose of the provision or provisions of Part A of the Code concerned; and

   (b) it gives effect to the provision or provisions of Part A of the Code concerned.'[57]

The explanatory note to the MLC provides useful guidance on its structure:

'EXPLANATORY NOTE TO THE REGULATIONS AND CODE OF THE MARITIME LABOUR CONVENTION

1. This explanatory note, which does not form part of the Maritime Labour Convention, is intended as a general guide to the Convention.

2. The Convention comprises three different but related parts: the Articles, the Regulations and the Code.

55 MLC, Article V. The REG members' laws generally require that ships registered with non-ratifying states must comply with MLC standards when in the ports or territorial waters of the particular REG member.

56 Ratifying states must ensure that any substantial equivalences that they adopt are reflected in the Pt I of their declaration of maritime labour compliance, which outlines the national implementation laws, regulations and other measures.

57 MLC, Article VI.

3. The Articles and Regulations set out the core rights and principles and the basic obligations of Members ratifying the Convention. The Articles and Regulations can only be changed by the Conference in the framework of article 19 of the Constitution of the International Labour Organisation (see Article XIV of the Convention).

4. The Code contains the details for the implementation of the Regulations. It comprises Part A (mandatory Standards) and Part B (non-mandatory Guidelines). The Code can be amended through the simplified procedure set out in Article XV of the Convention. Since the Code relates to detailed implementation, amendments to it must remain within the general scope of the Articles and Regulations.

5. The Regulations and the Code are organized into general areas under five Titles:

Title 1: Minimum requirements for seafarers to work on a ship

Title 2: Conditions of employment

Title 3: Accommodation, recreational facilities, food and catering

Title 4: Health protection, medical care, welfare and social security protection

Title 5: Compliance and enforcement

6. Each Title contains groups of provisions relating to a particular right or principle (or enforcement measure in Title 5), with connected numbering. The first group in Title 1, for example, consists of Regulation 1.1, Standard A1.1 and Guideline B1.1, relating to minimum age.

7. The Convention has three underlying purposes:

(a) to lay down, in its Articles and Regulations, a firm set of rights and principles;

(b) to allow, through the Code, a considerable degree of flexibility in the way Members implement those rights and principles; and

(c) to ensure, through Title 5, that the rights and principles are properly complied with and enforced.

8. There are two main areas for flexibility in implementation: one is the possibility for a Member, where necessary (see Article VI, paragraph 3), to give effect to the detailed requirements of Part A of the Code through substantial equivalence (as defined in Article VI, paragraph 4).

9. The second area of flexibility in implementation is provided by formulating the mandatory requirements of many provisions in Part A in a more general way, thus leaving a wider scope for discretion as to the precise action to be provided for at the national level. In such cases, guidance on implementation is given in the non-mandatory Part B of the Code. In this way, Members which have ratified this Convention can ascertain the kind of action that might be expected of them under the corresponding general obligation in Part A, as well as action that would not necessarily be required. For example, Standard A4.1 requires all ships to provide prompt access to the necessary medicines for medical care on board ship (paragraph 1(b)) and to "carry a medicine chest" (paragraph 4(a)). The fulfilment in good faith of this latter obligation clearly means something more than simply having a medicine chest on board each ship. A more precise indication of what is

involved is provided in the corresponding Guideline B4.1.1 (paragraph 4) so as to ensure that the contents of the chest are properly stored, used and maintained.

10. Members which have ratified this Convention are not bound by the guidance concerned and, as indicated in the provisions in Title 5 on port State control, inspections would deal only with the relevant requirements of this Convention (Articles, Regulations and the Standards in Part A). However, Members are required under paragraph 2 of Article VI to give due consideration to implementing their responsibilities under Part A of the Code in the manner provided for in Part B. If, having duly considered the relevant Guidelines, a Member decides to provide for different arrangements which ensure the proper storage, use and maintenance of the contents of the medicine chest, to take the example given above, as required by the Standard in Part A, then that is acceptable. On the other hand, by following the guidance provided in Part B, the Member concerned, as well as the ILO bodies responsible for reviewing implementation of international labour Conventions, can be sure without further consideration that the arrangements the Member has provided for are adequate to implement the responsibilities under Part A to which the Guideline relates.'[58]

SPECIAL TRIPARTITE COMMITTEE

1.15 A Special Tripartite Committee (STC), with special competence in maritime labour standards, has been established to keep the working of the MLC under continuous review.[59] It will also consider proposals to amendments to the Code under Article XV of the MLC.[60] It consists of two representatives nominated by each ratifying state, and representatives appointed by shipowners and seafarers appointed by the Governing Body of the ILO after consultation with the Joint Maritime Commission.[61]

Many of the MLC's provisions allowing derogations, exemptions and other flexibilities can only be adopted by ratifying states following consultation with shipowners' and seafarers' representatives. In cases where there are no such representatives situated in the relevant territory, the state must consult with the STC.[62] In the case of Bermuda, Cayman Islands, Gibraltar and the Isle of Man, where no such representatives are situated, they will consult the UK-based representatives through the MCA.[63]

58 Explanatory note to the Regulations and Code of the MLC, pp 12–13.

59 MLC, Article XIII, para 1. Standing Orders of the Special Tripartite Committee established for the Maritime Labour Convention, 2006 were adopted by the ILO Governing Body at its 313th Session (March 2012): www.ilo.org/wcmsp5/ groups/public/---ed_norm/---normes/documents/meetingdocument/wcms_183944.pdf [Accessed 3 May 2018].

60 STC Standing Orders, Article 2, para (b).

61 MLC, Article XIII, para 2.

62 MLC, Article VII.

63 The UK's MLC tripartite working group consists of the MCA, Nautilus International, RMT, UK Chamber of Shipping and some other industry bodies.

PROCEDURES FOR AMENDMENTS

1.16 The MLC has two procedures for amendments. Under Article XIV, amendments to the Articles and the Code may be adopted by the General Conference of the ILO in the framework of Article 19 of the ILO Constitution and its rules and procedures for the adoption of Conventions.[64] There is also a procedure under Article XV, which may only be used for amending the Code, but not the Articles [or the Regulations].[65]

For details of in force and future amendments to the MLC, see Appendix 2.

64 MLC, Article XIV, para 1.
65 MLC, Article XV, para 1.

CHAPTER 2

Application of the UK MLC Legislation

INTRODUCTION

2.1 The UK MLC legislation generally applies its substantive provisions to UK sea-going ships wherever they may be and (while they are in UK waters) non-UK ships which do not carry MLC documentation. A non-UK ship may fall within the latter category for any one of a number of reasons. For example, the ship may be registered in a non-MLC state; or, even if it is registered in an MLC state, it is under 500 gross tonnage (GT) and the shipowner has not chosen to carry MLC documentation on a voluntary basis.[1] Furthermore, the ship may be registered in an MLC state, is 500 GT or over, but is in serious breach of its flag state's laws in that it is not carrying MLC documentation. The MLC requires ratifying states to ensure that ships which are registered with a non-MLC state do not receive more favourable treatment than ships which are registered with MLC states, so widening the reach of the standards set by the Convention.[2] So UK port state control officers will generally inspect such ships against the UK provisions.

As regards ships which are registered with an MLC state, and which do carry MLC documentation, when they are in UK waters, the position is as follows. Rather than apply the UK's substantive provisions, the legislation requires the ship to be in compliance with the relevant parts of the MLC itself, and refers directly to the relevant provisions within the Convention.[3] This is because such ships are subject

1 A ship registered with an MLC state is only required to carry MLC documentation if it is 500 GT or over and is engaged in international voyages or operates from a foreign port or ports: MLC, Regulation 5.1.3, para 1(a)–(b). However, the owner of such ships may request MLC certification on a voluntary basis: MLC, Regulation 5.1.3, para 2.

2 MLC, Article V, para 7.

3 MLC, Article V, para 4. See, for example, Merchant Shipping (Maritime Labour Convention) (Minimum Requirements for Seafarers etc) Regulations 2014, SI 2014/1613, reg 6(1) ('Minimum Requirements Regulations').

to their own flag state's provisions (as set out in Pt I of that flag state's declaration of maritime labour compliance (DMLC)) which must, at the very least, meet the MLC's minimum standards.[4] If such ships are inspected by UK port state control, that inspection will be limited to a review of the ship's maritime labour certificate and DMLC, which is to be taken as prima facie evidence of compliance with the MLC.[5] However, there are specific circumstances which may give rise to a more detailed inspection and, in carrying this out, such ships are, again, to be inspected for compliance with MLC itself, not the UK substantive provisions.[6]

Unless otherwise stated, the following are excluded from the UK MLC legislation: pleasure vessels; fishing vessels; ships of traditional build; warships and naval auxiliaries; and vessels which are not ordinarily engaged in commercial activities.[7]

In addition to the UK's MLC legislation, the MCA produces Merchant Shipping Notices (MSNs) which, by virtue of being referenced in statutory instruments, contain mandatory standards; furthermore, detailed guidance is also provided in Marine Guidance Notes (MGNs). Although in need of update, MGN 470 provides a list of MSNs and MGNs relevant to MLC implementation.[8] Although not used much for MLC purposes, the MCA also issues Marine Information Notices (MINs), which tend to be valid for short periods of time and are addressed to a specific group of people.

In terms of implementation of the MLC, the UK had already met some of the requirements through legislation which pre-dated the Convention. This legislation implemented some older ILO Conventions (which the MLC has updated and consolidated) and EU law obligations. However, large gaps had to be filled by new statutory instruments, which are each made under section 2(2) of the European Communities Act 1972[9] and sections 85–86 of Merchant Shipping Act 1995.

Another EU dimension is that there are various EU Directives implementing the MLC into EU law, the main one being Directive 2009/13/EC, which has been followed by others on flag state control, port state control, and amendments to the MLC. The Directives do not add any substantive requirements to those in the MLC; however, they encourage EU member states to ratify the MLC, as they would, in any case, be subject to its provisions through EU law. Furthermore, the Directives facilitate enforcement of MLC obligations by virtue of: the availability of infringement proceedings against

4 MLC, Article V, para 1; Regulation 5.1.3, para 3.
5 MLC, Regulation 5.2.1, para 2.
6 MLC, Standard A5.2.1.
7 See, for example, Minimum Requirements Regulations, reg 3(5)(a)–(e).
8 MGN 470 (M): MLC, 2006 – List of Merchant Shipping Notes and Marine Guidance Notes.
9 The MLC is regarded as one of the 'EU Treaties' within the meaning of section 1(2) of the European Communities Act 1972 by virtue of the European Communities (Definition of Treaties) (Maritime Labour Convention) Order 2009 (SI 2009/1757).

a member state for any failure to fully implement its MLC obligations as expressed in the Directive; the doctrine of direct effect; and a uniform interpretation across the EU as expressed through any judgments of the Court of Justice of the European Union. It remains to be seen how the UK's exit from the European Union on 29 March 2019 will affect the relevance of the EU legal regime to the UK's MLC laws (and those of Gibraltar), and whether any changes will need to be made. When the European Union (Withdrawal) Act 2018 comes into force, statutory instruments made under section 2(2) of the 1972 Act will be saved.[10] In any event, the UK has ratified the MLC (and extended it to Gibraltar), so will remain bound to fully implement its provisions as a member of the ILO.

INSPECTION AND DETENTION OF SHIPS

2.2 The UK MLC legislation provides powers to inspect ships, require remedial action, and order detention for serious or repeated breaches of the legislation (although ships should not be detained unreasonably). The regulations also apply the powers contained in the Merchant Shipping Act 1995 in relation to the inspection and detention of ships.[11] To avoid repetition in each chapter covering the UK legislation, the powers generally take the following form:

> 'Inspection of United Kingdom ships and non-United Kingdom ships without MLC documentation
>
> (1) For the purpose of checking compliance with these Regulations, a relevant inspector (or, in the case of a United Kingdom ship, a proper officer) may at all reasonable times go on board a ship and inspect the ship, its equipment, any articles on it and any document carried on it.'
>
> 'Inspection of non-United Kingdom ships with MLC documentation
>
> (1) A relevant inspector may—
>
> (a) review a ship's Maritime Labour Certificate and Declaration of Maritime Labour Compliance or the ship's interim Maritime Labour Certificate; and
>
> (b) where Standard A5.2.1 of the MLC (inspections in port) applies, carry out a more detailed inspection in accordance with that Standard.'
>
> 'Detention of ships
>
> (1) Where a relevant inspector has clear grounds for believing that—
>
> (a) a ship does not comply with these Regulations; and

10 European Union (Withdrawal) Act 2018, s 2: www.legislation.gov.uk/ukpga/2018/16 [Accessed 26 October 2018]. For an account of the status of the MLC in the EU legal order, see Abel, A, 'The Maritime Labour Convention 2006 in the European Union', in Lavelle, J, *The Maritime Labour Convention 2006, International Labour Law Redefined* (Informa Law from Routledge), 1–17.

11 Merchant Shipping Act 1995, Pt X (Enforcement Officers and Powers).

(b) (i) the conditions on board are clearly hazardous to the safety, health or security of seafarers; or

(ii) the non-compliance represents a serious breach or the latest in a series of repeated breaches of these Regulations or the requirements of the MLC (including the rights of seafarers referred to in Articles III and IV of the MLC which are secured by it), that ship is liable to be detained.'[12]

The other REG members also adopt this approach within their legislation.

DEFINITIONS USED IN THIS BOOK

2.3 'MLC documentation' means either a valid maritime labour certificate with appended declaration of maritime labour compliance, Pts I and II, or an interim maritime labour certificate.

'MLC ship' means a ship to which the MLC applies[13] – see Chapter 1 at para 1.8.

'MLC state' means a state which has ratified the MLC and in which the MLC is in force.

'Non-MLC ship' means a ship to which the MLC does not apply – see Chapter 1 at para 1.8.

'Non-MLC state' means a state which has not ratified the MLC, or a state which has ratified the MLC, but the MLC is not yet in force for that state.[14]

DEFINITIONS USED BY UK LEGISLATION

2.4 'Declaration of Maritime Labour Compliance' means, in relation to a ship, the Part I and Part II documents drawn up and issued in accordance with the MLC, in the forms corresponding to the relevant models given in Appendix A5-II to the MLC and having the contents, duration and validity specified in Regulation 5.1.3 and Standard A5.1.3 of the MLC.[15]

'Maritime Labour Certificate' and 'interim Maritime Labour Certificate' mean, in relation to a ship, a certificate of that name issued in accordance with the

12 The above examples have been taken from Minimum Requirements Regulations, regs 54(1), 55(1) and 56(1). The wording of the power of detention follows that of MLC, Standard A5.2.1.6(a)–(b) (Inspections in port).

13 This includes ships which are registered with non-MLC states which are ordinarily engaged in commercial activities, as MLC states are required to apply MLC standards to them when being inspected in their ports: MLC, Article V, para 7.

14 The MLC comes into force for a state 12 months after the date that its ratification has been registered with the ILO: MLC, Article VIII, para 4.

15 Minimum Requirements Regulations, reg 2(1) and other UK MLC legislation.

MLC, in a form corresponding to the relevant model given in Appendix A5-II to the MLC and having the contents, duration and validity specified in Regulation 5.1.3 and Standard A5.1.3 of the MLC.[16]

'Fishing vessel' means a vessel for the time being used (or, in the context of an application for registration, intended to be used) for, or in connection with fishing for sea fish other than a vessel used (or intended to be used) for fishing otherwise than for profit; and for the purposes of this definition 'sea fish' includes shellfish, salmon and migratory trout (as defined by section 44 of the Fisheries Act 1981).[17]

'Pleasure vessel' means–

(a) any vessel which at the time it is being used is–

(i) (aa) in the case of a vessel wholly owned by an individual or individuals, used only for the sport or pleasure of the owner or the immediate family or friends of the owner; or

(bb) in the case of a vessel owned by a body corporate, used only for sport or pleasure and on which the persons on board are employees or officers of the body corporate, or their immediate family or friends; and

(ii) on a voyage or excursion which is one for which the owner does not receive money for or in connection with operating the vessel or carrying any person, other than as a contribution to the direct expenses of the operation of the vessel incurred during the voyage or excursion; or

(b) any vessel wholly owned by or on behalf of a members' club formed for the purpose of sport or pleasure which, at the time it is being used, is used only for the sport or pleasure of members of that club or their immediate family, and for the use of which any charges levied are paid into club funds and applied for the general use of the club,[18]

where, in the case of any vessel referred to in paragraphs (a) or (b), no other payments are made by or on behalf of users of the vessel, other than by the owner; and in this definition 'immediate family' means, in relation to an individual, the spouse or civil partner of the individual, and a relative of the individual or the individual's spouse or civil partner; and 'relative' means brother, sister, ancestor or lineal descendant.

16 Minimum Requirements Regulations, reg 2(1) and other UK MLC legislation.

17 Merchant Shipping Act 1995, s 313(1); Minimum Requirements Regulations, reg 2(1). Fishing vessels are excluded from the application of the MLC and UK MLC legislation: MLC, Article II, para 4; Minimum Requirements Regulations, reg 3(5)(b). However, the UK's ratification of the ILO's Work in Fishing Convention, 2007 (No. 188) is imminent: see Chapter 1 at footnote 42.

18 Minimum Requirements Regulations, reg 2(1) and other UK MLC legislation. Pleasure vessels are excluded from the application of the MLC (as they are not '... ordinarily engaged in commercial activities ...' and UK MLC legislation: MLC, Article II, para 4; Minimum Requirements Regulations, reg 3(5)(a)).

'Seafarer' means any person, including the master of a ship, who is employed or engaged or works in any capacity on board a ship and whose normal place of work is on board a ship.[19]

'Sea-going' in relation to a United Kingdom ship means–

(a) a ship which operates outside the waters specified as Category A, B, C and D waters in Merchant Shipping Notice 1837(M);[20]

(b) a ship to which the Merchant Shipping (Survey and Certification) Regulations 1995 apply and in respect of which no exemption granted under regulation 2(2) of those Regulations applies;

(c) a ship to which regulation 4 of the Merchant Shipping (Vessels in Commercial Use for Sport or Pleasure) Regulations 1998 applies and which falls within the description given in paragraph (3) of that regulation; or

(d) a high-speed craft in respect of which a permit to operate outside waters of Categories A, B, C or D has been issued in accordance with regulation 8 of the Merchant Shipping (High Speed Craft) Regulations 2004.[21]

'Shipowner' means–

(a) in relation to a ship which has a valid Maritime Labour Certificate or interim Maritime Labour Certificate, the person identified as the shipowner on that Certificate;

(b) in relation to any other ship, the owner of the ship or, if different, any other organisation or person such as the manager, or the bareboat charterer, that has assumed the responsibility for the operation of the ship from the owner.[22]

'UK ship' means a ship registered in the UK; or a ship which is not registered under the law of any country but which is wholly owned by citizens of British territories (as defined) or a company incorporated in the UK and having its principal place of business there; or a government ship (excluding navy ships)

19 Minimum Requirements Regulations, reg 2(1) and other MLC legislation. MGN 471, paras 2.1–2.4 and Annex 1 provide further guidance on the term 'seafarer' and note that it is intended to include: the master and crew, as well as cadets; other types of workers (for instance on a cruise ship), such as shopkeepers, resident entertainers, hairdressers and some self-employed persons working on the business of the ship. The following are excluded: those whose work is not part of the routine business of the ship (such as harbour pilots, inspectors, superintendents, scientists, researchers, divers and specialist offshore technicians); also excluded are those who work on board on an occasional and short-term basis, such as fitters, guest lecturers and entertainers, repair technicians, surveyors and port workers. Privately contracted armed security personnel are also excluded.

20 MSN 1837 (M) has been superseded by MSN 1837 (M) Amendment 2: Categorisation of Waters.

21 Minimum Requirements Regulations, reg 2(1).

22 Minimum Requirements Regulations, reg 2(1) and other MLC legislation. Unlike the MLC, in sub-paragraph (b) the UK's definition of 'shipowner' does not include 'agent' alongside manager and bareboat charterer: the MCA states that this is because the term 'agent' in the MLC has a different meaning from that term as it applies under English law, in that an agent would not accept personal liability for a shipowner's responsibilities; see MGN 471, paras 4.1–4.5.

ordinarily engaged in commercial maritime operations; or a hovercraft registered under the Hovercraft Act 1968.[23]

'UK waters' means the sea or other waters within the seaward limits of the territorial sea of the UK.[24]

For more information on the UK's definitions as regards MLC legislation, see MGN 471.[25]

23 Minimum Requirements Regulations, reg 2(1); Merchant Shipping Act 1995, ss 85(2)(a)–(b), 308(4). Note that the following are excluded: pleasure vessels; fishing vessels; ships of traditional build; warships and naval auxiliaries; and vessels which are not ordinarily engaged in commercial activities: Minimum Requirements Regulations, reg 3(5)(a)–(e). The MCA has produced guidance on when a Mobile Offshore Drilling Unit (MODU) will be considered to be a ship for the purposes of UK MLC legislation, see MGN 471, Annex 3.

24 Minimum Requirements Regulations, reg 2(1); Merchant Shipping Act 1995, s 313(2). The breadth of the UK 'territorial sea' is 12 nautical miles: Territorial Sea Act 1987, s 1(1).

25 MGN 471 (M): MLC, 2006: Definitions.

PART II

Title 1: Minimum Requirements to Work on a Ship

CHAPTER 3

Regulation 1.1: Minimum Requirements for Seafarers to Work on a Ship

INTRODUCTION

3.1 The purpose of Regulation 1.1 of the MLC is to ensure that no under-age persons work on a ship.[1] There are also further measures aimed at protecting the health and safety of 'young seafarers' under the age of 18, such as restrictions on night work and the prohibition of specific types of work, which is to be determined by the flag state in consultation with shipowners' and seafarers' organisations.[2]

The main provisions are set out in Pt 2 of the Merchant Shipping (Maritime Labour Convention) (Minimum Requirements for Seafarers etc) Regulations 2014[3] ('Minimum Requirements Regulations') and MSN 1838.[4]

MINIMUM AGE

UK ships wherever they may be and (while they are in UK waters) non-UK ships which do not carry MLC documentation[5]

3.2 A person under 16 years of age must not be employed, engaged or work on board a ship.[6]

1 MLC, Regulation 1.1 (Purpose).
2 MLC, Standard A1.1.2–4.
3 SI 2014/1613.
4 MSN 1838(M) – MLC, 2006: Minimum Age.
5 Minimum Requirements Regulations, reg 3(1)–(2)(a).
6 Minimum Requirements Regulations, reg 4(1).

A breach of the above provision amounts to an offence by the shipowner, master and employer, punishable (on summary conviction) to a fine not exceeding level 5 on the standard scale.[7] It is a defence for the accused to show that they took all reasonable steps to ensure compliance.[8] Therefore, original birth certificates or passport should be sighted, and copies retained.

A further provision on age applies to ship's cooks, who must be at least 18 years of age.

Additional measures applying to young seafarers (under the age of 18 years)

Restrictions on carrying out night work

3.3 Seafarers under 18 years of age (young seafarers) are, with some exceptions, prohibited from working on a ship at night.[9] For these purposes, 'night' means a period of nine consecutive hours, and must include the period from midnight to 5am (local time).[10]

The exceptions to the prohibition of young seafarers working at night apply where: the effective training of the seafarer, in accordance with established programmes and schedules, would otherwise be impaired; or the specific nature of the duty or recognised training programme requires night duties, and the work is specified in MSN 1838(M) as not being detrimental to their health and well-being,[11] which is any:

- Deck Officer training under STCW Regulations II/1, II/2 and II/3;
- Engineer Officer training under STCW Regulations III/1, III/2 and III/3;
- Navigational watch Rating training under STCW Regulation II/4;
- Engine Room watch Rating training under STCW Regulation III/4;
- Training of Ratings as able seamen (AB), Deck or Engine;
- Training of Electro-technical Officers under STCW Regulation III/6;
- Training of Electro-technical Ratings under STCW Regulation III/7;
- Training of Radio personnel under STCW Regulation IV/2;
- Training for alternative certification under STCW Regulation VII.[12]

7 Minimum Requirements Regulations, reg 59(1).
8 Minimum Requirements Regulations, reg 60.
9 Minimum Requirements Regulations, reg 5(1).
10 Minimum Requirements Regulations, reg 5(3)(a)–(b).
11 Minimum Requirements Regulations, reg 5(2)(a)–(b); MSN(M) 1838, para 4.1.
12 MSN 1838, para 4.3.

Risk assessments

3.4 There are special provisions for the health and safety of young seafarers.

As well as the general duties set out in the Merchant Shipping and Fishing Vessels (Health and Safety at Work) Regulations 1997 ('1997 H&S Regulations'),[13] which apply irrespective of age, the specific provisions in the Merchant Shipping and Fishing Vessels (Health and Safety at Work) (Employment of Young Persons) Regulations 1998 ('1998 H&S Regulations')[14] must also be followed in regard to young seafarers. Therefore, an assessment must be made, either separately or in addition to that under regulation 7 of the 1997 H&S Regulations, of the risks to young seafarers' health and safety during working time, taking into account their lack of experience, lack of awareness of risks, and immaturity, with particular reference to:

- the fitting out and layout of working areas;
- the nature, degree and duration of exposure to physical, biological and chemical agents;
- the form, range and use of work equipment and the way in which it is handled;
- the organisation of processes and activities;
- the extent of the health and safety training provided or to be provided to the young persons concerned; and
- risks from agents, processes and work listed in the Schedule to the Regulations.[15]

The Schedule sets out a non-exhaustive list of physical, biological and chemical agents, processes and work.[16] A detailed table, based on the Schedule, is contained in Annex 1 to MSN 1838, in three columns: (i) agents, processes and work; (ii) risk; and (iii) advice and steps to avoid the risk.

Young seafarers must be informed of any risks identified in the assessment and of all measures adopted for their protection.[17]

The duty to comply with the above measures is generally placed on the employer and, where the employer does not have control over the matter in question, it is, in addition, placed on the person who has such control,[18] who will invariably

13 SI 1997/2962, reg 7. These Regulations are the subject of MGN 20 (M+F), which set out detailed guidance on risk assessments and health surveillance.

14 SI 1998/2411, reg 5(1).

15 1998 H&S Regulations, reg 5(2).

16 These are taken from the Annex to Council Directive 94/33/EC of 22 June 1994 on the protection of young people at work.

17 1998 H&S Regulations, reg 5(3).

18 1997 H&S Regulations, reg 4; 1998 H&S Regulations, reg 4.

be the shipowner. In cases where the young seafarer is not a 'worker'[19] and, consequently, has no employer, the relevant duties under the 1998 H&S Regulations are imposed on the shipowner.[20]

Prohibited work

3.5 Subject to the exception referred to below, young seafarers are prohibited from being engaged in:

(a) work which is objectively beyond their physical or psychological capacity;

(b) work involving harmful exposure to agents which are toxic, carcinogenic, cause heritable genetic damage, or harm to the unborn child or which in any other way chronically affect human health;

(c) work involving harmful exposure to radiation;

(d) work involving the risk of accidents which it may be assumed cannot be recognised or avoided by young persons owing to their insufficient attention to safety or lack of experience or training; or

(e) work in which there is a risk to health from:

  (i) extreme cold or heat, or

  (ii) noise, or

  (iii) vibration.[21]

To the above list, MSN 1838(M) adds work from which there is a risk from optical radiation or electromagnetic fields.[22]

The exception is that seafarers may perform any of the above activities where they are indispensable for their vocational training, but they must be supervised by a competent person, and the duty is to ensure, so far as reasonably practicable, the health and safety of the young seafarer.[23]

Health surveillance

3.6 Where the risk assessment carried out under regulation 5(2) of the 1998 H&S Regulations shows that there is a risk to the safety, physical or mental health, or development of a young seafarer, or they are likely to be required

19 A 'worker' is any person who is 'employed by an employer under a contract of employment, including trainees or apprentices'; a 'contract of employment' is 'a contract of employment, whether express or implied, and if express, whether oral or in writing': 1997 H&S Regulations, reg 2(2); 1998 H&S Regulations, reg 2(2).

20 The Merchant Shipping (Maritime Labour Convention) (Health and Safety) (Amendment) Regulations 2014 (SI 2014/1616), which inserts regulation 13A and Schedule into the 1997 H&S Regulations.

21 1998 H&S Regulations, reg 5(4)(a)–(e)(i)–(iii).

22 MSN 1838, para 5.1.5.

23 1998 H&S Regulations, reg 5(6)(a)–(b); MSN 1838(M), para 5.1.8.

to work at night (other than in exceptional cases), they must be entitled to a free health assessment. This should be provided before commencing work, and involve an assessment of their health and capacities, and monitoring of their health at regular intervals.[24]

See also Regulation 4.3 (Health and safety protection and accident prevention) of the MLC for the generally applicable provisions on health and safety, as well as further specific measures relating to young seafarers.

Record of young persons

3.7 A record of young persons must be kept as part of the crew list, including their dates of birth and dates of engagement, together with a summary of the 1998 H&S Regulations.[25] For this purpose, the MCA has produced form MSF 4158 (contained in MGN 477), and it also summarises the 1998 H&S Regulations and other provisions relating to young seafarers.[26] Another form may be used, but it must replicate the wording of Form 4158.[27] Even if there are no young persons on board, Form 4158 must still be kept, marked with the entry 'NIL'.[28]

INSPECTION AND DETENTION OF SHIPS

3.8 Ships may be inspected to check for compliance with the Minimum Requirements Regulations.[29] Where the inspector has clear grounds for believing that (a) a ship does not comply with the Minimum Requirements Regulations, and (b) either the conditions on board are clearly hazardous to the safety, health or security of seafarers, or the non-compliance represents a serious breach or the latest in a series of repeated breaches of the Minimum Requirements Regulations or the requirements of the MLC (including fundamental rights and principles (Article III) and seafarers' employment and social rights (Article IV)), the ship is liable to be detained.[30] The power of detention applies to a UK ship wherever it may be, and to non-UK ships in or at a UK port, ship yard or offshore terminal.[31]

24 1998 H&S Regulations, reg 7(1)–(2). This entitlement is without prejudice to the right to health surveillance provided by 1997 H&S Regulations, reg 11; guidance is given in MGN 20, Annex 2.
25 1998 H&S Regulations, reg 9.
26 MGN 477 (M) – MLC, 2006: Seafarers' Employment Agreements, Annex 4, form MSF 4158 (Rev 11/13).
27 MSN 1838, para 10.2.
28 MGN 477, para 12.1.
29 Minimum Requirements Regulations, reg 54.
30 Minimum Requirements Regulations, reg 56.
31 Minimum Requirements Regulations, reg 58(1)(a)–(b).

Non-UK ships (while they are in UK waters) which do carry MLC documentation[32]

3.9 Such ships must not be operated in UK waters, unless they comply with paragraph 1 (minimum age of seafarers is 16 years) and paragraph 2 (prohibition against young seafarers carrying out night work) of MLC Standard A1.1.[33] This is subject to any permissible exceptions set by the flag state, which should be stated in Pt 1 of the ship's DMLC.[34] Non-compliance with either provision amounts to an offence by the shipowner, master and employer.[35] The same level of fine and the same defence (referred to at para 3.2 above) apply.[36]

3.10 Such ships are subject to an inspector reviewing their maritime labour documentation and, where Standard A5.2.1 of the MLC applies, carrying out a more detailed inspection in accordance with that Standard[37] (see 'Inspections in port'). Where the power to carry out a more detailed inspection arises, the power of inspection set out under regulation 54 applies to that ship.[38]

OFFENCES

3.11 A breach of the main provisions amounts to a criminal offence,[39] punishable on summary conviction by a fine not exceeding level 5 on the standard scale.[40] It is a defence for the accused to show that they took all reasonable steps to ensure compliance.[41]

CHECKLIST FOR COMPLIANCE

3.12

- Minimum age to be employed as a seafarer – 16 years.
- Minimum age to be employed as a ship's cook – 18 years.
- Keep a copy of original birth certificate or passport.
- Ensure that each seafarer's date of birth is entered on their seafarer's employment agreement – see Regulation 2.1 (Seafarers' employment agreements).[42]

32 Minimum Requirements Regulations, reg 3(3)–(4)(b)(i).
33 Minimum Requirements Regulations, reg 6(1).
34 Minimum Requirements Regulations, reg 6(1); flag state DMLC, Pt I, point 1.
35 Minimum Requirements Regulations, reg 6(2).
36 Minimum Requirements Regulations, regs 59(1), 60.
37 Minimum Requirements Regulations, reg 55(1)(a)–(b).
38 Minimum Requirements Regulations, reg 55(2)(a)–(b).
39 Minimum Requirements Regulations, regs 4(2), 5(4), 6(2).
40 Minimum Requirements Regulations, reg 59(1).
41 Minimum Requirements Regulations, reg 60.
42 Minimum Requirements Regulations, reg 10(1), Sch 1, Pt 1, point 1.

- Keep a record of young persons on form MSF 4158, or in a similar format containing the same information.
- Be aware of the special provisions applying to young seafarers, particularly: when night work can be carried out; specific risk assessment in addition to the general risk assessment; prohibited work; and health surveillance.
- Be aware of the further special provisions for young seafarers set out in: Regulation 1.2 (Medical certificate); Regulation 2.3 (Hours of work and hours of rest); Regulation 2.5 (Repatriation); and Regulation 4.3 (Health and safety protection and accident prevention).

DMLC: note the compliance provisions entered in Pt I, point 1, and enter implementing measures in Pt II, point 1.

CHAPTER 4

Regulation 1.2: Medical Certificate

INTRODUCTION

4.1 The purpose of Regulation 1.2 of the MLC is to ensure that all seafarers are medically fit to perform their duties at sea.[1] Medical certificates issued in accordance with the IMO's International Convention on Standards of Training, Certification and Watchkeeping for Seafarers, 1978 (as amended) (STCW Convention) are acceptable, as are those meeting the substance of that Convention.[2] The UK and the other REG members' provisions are consequently based on those of the STCW Convention.

The relevant provisions are set out in the Merchant Shipping (Maritime Labour Convention) (Medical Certification) Regulations 2010[3] ('Medical Certification Regulations') and MSN 1839[4] (published July 2014), which is subject to the changes set out in MSN 1839 (Corrigendum) (published January 2018). The changes relate to new procedures for colour vision testing, and some minor amendments have been made in connection with a few medical conditions, the most significant being to the standard for renal or uretic calculus, which should permit more affected seafarers to continue to work at sea.[5]

1 MLC, Regulation 1.2, purpose.
2 MLC, Standard A1.2, para 3.
3 SI 2010/737.
4 MSN 1839(M) – Seafarer Medical Examination System and Medical and Eyesight Standards: Application of the Merchant Shipping (Maritime Labour Convention) (Medical Certification) Regulations 2010, replaces the withdrawn MSN 1822(M): Consequential Amendments Regulations, reg 13(5).
5 MSN 1839, Corrigendum, paras 1.1–1.2; the Annexes contain the amendments to MSN 1839.

Some amendments have also been made to the Medical Certification Regulations by the Merchant Shipping (Maritime Labour Convention) (Consequential and Minor Amendments) Regulations 2014[6] ('Consequential Amendments Regulations') and the Merchant Shipping (Maritime Labour Convention) (Miscellaneous Amendments) Regulations 2018[7] ('Miscellaneous Amendments Regulations').

The most important changes are:

- 'medical practitioner' (taken together with criteria specified in MSN 1839) means that, to be an MCA-approved doctor, those based in the UK must be fully registered with the General Medical Council of Great Britain and hold a valid licence to practice; if based outside the UK they must: be qualified from one of the medical schools listed in the World Directory of Medical Schools; be entitled to practise in the country or territory in which they are based; satisfy the MCA that they are subject to a programme that ensures maintenance of their medical skills; and have a good command of the English language;[8] and
- 'seafarer' now means '... any person, including a master, who is employed or engaged or works in any capacity on board a ship and whose normal place of work is on a ship'.[9]

APPLICATION

4.2 The Medical Certification Regulations apply to UK sea-going ships wherever they may be.[10] The following are excluded: pleasure vessels; fishing vessels; warships or naval auxiliaries; offshore installations whilst on their working stations;[11] and any person whose work is not part of the routine business of the ship and whose principal place of work is ashore or who is subject to the various Working Time Regulations which apply to other sectors (shore, inland waterways or sea-fishing).[12]

REQUIREMENT FOR A MEDICAL FITNESS CERTIFICATE

4.3 The responsibility for ensuring that a seafarer possess a valid 'medical fitness certificate' is placed on both the seafarer (who must carry it on board

6 SI 2014/1614.
7 SI 2018/242.
8 Medical Certification Regulations, reg 2, as inserted by Consequential Amendments Regulations, reg 13(1)–(2)(a) and amended by Miscellaneous Amendments Regulations, reg 3(1)(b); MSN 1839, paras 13.1–13.12. Although MSN 1839 (at para 13.1.2(a)) refers to the Avicenna Directory, that, together with the International Medical Educational Directory, has now been merged into the World Directory of Medical Schools.
9 Medical Certification Regulations, reg 2 as inserted by Consequential Amendments Regulations, reg 13(1)–(2)(b).
10 Medical Certification Regulations, reg 5(1)(a).
11 Medical Certification Regulations, reg 5(2)(a)–(d).
12 Medical Certification Regulations, reg 5(3)(a)–(b).

throughout the voyage) and the shipowner.[13] The certificate must attest to the seafarer's fitness to carry out their duties at sea.[14]

There are some exceptions to the above requirements. Firstly, where the certificate has expired during the course of a voyage, the seafarer may continue to work until the next port of call at which it is possible to make an application for a certificate and be examined by a doctor, or up to a maximum of three months from the expiry of the certificate, whichever is the sooner.[15] Secondly, in cases of urgency, the MCA may permit a seafarer, without a valid certificate, to join a ship and work until the first port of call at which it is possible to apply for a certificate, but for no more than a period of three months. The latter exception is only applicable where the seafarer has held a valid certificate for at least 24 months (or at least 12 months for a seafarer aged under 18 when the certificate was issued) which has expired no earlier than one month before they join the ship.[16]

Examination and issue of medical fitness certificate

4.4 A UK certificate (form MSF 4104, known as the ENG1 medical certificate) must be issued by an MCA-approved doctor, following a successful examination, in accordance with the statutory medical and eyesight standards, which are set out in MSN 1839 (M).[17] The examination addresses medical conditions under the following main headings: infections; cancers; endocrine and metabolic; blood disorders; mental disorders; diseases of the nervous system; cardio-vascular system; respiratory system; digestive system; genito-urinary conditions; pregnancy; skin; musculo-skeletal; sensory; general; and physical fitness.[18] The eyesight test will examine visual acuity and colour vision (the latter of which applies to deck, engineer, electro-technical and radio personnel).[19] The approved doctor should be satisfied that the seafarer does not have a disease or condition which could be aggravated by working at sea, or represent an unacceptable health risk to the seafarer, other crew members or the safety of the ship.[20]

A person applying for a medical fitness certificate must disclose (with the application, or as soon as reasonably practicable afterwards) to the medical practitioner: (a) all existing medical conditions from which the person suffers

13 Medical Certification Regulations, regs 6(1)–(2) and 7(1), respectively.
14 Medical Certification Regulations, reg 2; MSN 1839, para 3.1.
15 Medical Certification Regulations, regs 6(3), 7(2).
16 Medical Certification Regulations, regs 6(4), 7(3).
17 Medical Certification Regulations, reg 8; MSN 1839(M), para 5.1.
18 MSN 1839, Annex A, as amended.
19 MSN 1839(M), para 5.3; detailed guidance is set out in Annex A, Appendix 1, as amended by MSN 1839, Corrigendum.
20 MSN 1839, para 5.2.1.

and of which the person is aware (if any); and (b) all medication which the person is taking (if any).[21]

In some prescribed cases, another type of medical certificate (known as the 'ML5') is acceptable for vessels operating under an MCA Code of Practice (that is, vessels which do not go further than 60 miles from a harbour or shelter) and domestic passenger vessels of Class VI or VI(A) (except, in the latter case, for anyone serving as the master).[22] The medical requirements for this type of certificate are set out in MGN 264.[23] An ML5 certificate may be issued for up to a maximum of five years.[24] The remainder of this chapter, however, is concerned with the ENG1 certificate (or an equivalent certificate issued by a UK-approved STCW Convention state).[25]

Categories of fitness, restrictions, conditions, refusal to issue certificate

4.5 The doctor may, if appropriate, restrict the certificate to a particular capacity of sea service or geographical areas, or issue it subject to conditions specified in MGN 1839.[26] By way of example, a seafarer who failed a colour vision test could be restricted from performing look-out duties.[27] A condition could be a measure which the seafarer must maintain (such as taking medication) to ensure that they remain fit for service.[28] The doctor should notify the seafarer in writing of any condition; however, it should not be written on the certificate; in some cases, it would be advisable for the seafarer to inform their employer and the master – for example, so that arrangements can be made for any necessary medication to be carried on board.[29]

The MCA uses four categories to denote the outcome of an examination: Category 1 – fit with no restrictions (in which case an ENG1 will be issued); Category 2 – fit but with restrictions (which will be recorded on the certificate);[30] Category

21 Medical Certification Regulations, reg 8(2A)–(2B), as inserted by Miscellaneous Amendments Regulations, reg 3(3).
22 Medical Certification Regulations, reg 10; MSN 1839, para 8.1(a). Ships of Class VI or Class VI(A) are defined in the Merchant Shipping (Life Saving Appliances for Passenger Ships of Classes III to VI(A)) Regulations 1999 (SI 1999/2721).
23 MGN 264(M) – Medical Fitness Requirements for Those Employed on Boats Certificated under MCA Codes of Practice, Crew of Seagoing Local Passenger Vessels and Non-seagoing Boatmasters.
24 MGN 264, para 5.2.
25 Advice on the application process for the ENG 1 and ML5 certificates can be found at: www.gov.uk/seafarer-medical-certificates [Accessed 21 June 2018].
26 Medical Certification Regulations, reg 8(2)(a)–(b), respectively.
27 MSN 1839, para 5.3.2.
28 MSN 1839, para 5.4.3.
29 MSN 1839, para 5.4.3.
30 MSN 1839(M), para 5.4.2. Note that any 'condition' set by the doctor will not, due to confidentiality, be recorded on the certificate. However, it may be necessary for the seafarer to report it to their employer and the master, for example, if they are required to take regular medication which they will need to carry on board (MSN 1839(M), para 5.4.3).

3 – temporarily unfit; and Category 4 – permanently unfit.[31] Where the doctor determines that a seafarer is temporarily unfit (for no more than three months), permanently unfit, or that the certificate should be subject to a restriction, they issue a notice of failure or restriction (form MSF 4106, known as the ENG3).[32]

Validity of certificate

4.6 UK certificates (including attestation to colour vision, where appropriate) are valid from the date of the examination (or consideration by a referee – see below) for up to a maximum period of two years for those who are 18 years and over, and one year for those under 18; in each case, they may be issued for shorter periods, where appropriate.[33] Seafarers who are required to demonstrate satisfactory colour vision are those who serve in the following departments: deck, engine, electro-technical and radio.[34]

Non-UK certificates accepted as equivalent

4.7 A 'certificate of medical fitness' issued by an authority empowered to issue such a certificate in any country or territory listed in MSN 1815 (M)[35] will, if it is in English (or in another language with an English version), be considered as equivalent to a UK certificate for most purposes.[36] Those countries and territories include: all EEA Member States (except Liechtenstein); Australia; Canada; Hong Kong; India; Jamaica; Mauritius; New Zealand; Pakistan; South Africa; Sri Lanka; and Ukraine.

Seafarer's duty to report significant medical conditions

4.8 A seafarer who possesses a UK medical certificate, who is (or is likely to be) absent from work for 30 days or more due to a medical condition, or who develops a significant medical condition, must report it to an MCA-approved doctor as soon as practicable.[37]. The same requirement is imposed on holders of non-UK certificates, in which case the report is to be made to the issuing

31 MSN 1839(M), para 5.4.1.
32 MSN 1839(M), para 6.2.
33 Medical Certification Regulations, reg 9. The MLC permits ratifying states to issue certificates of colour vision for a maximum period of six years (MLC Standard A1.2, para 7(b)); however, the UK has chosen to keep this in line with the period of validity of the main certificate.
34 MGN 1839, Appendix 1 to Annex A (as amended).
35 MSN 1815(M) (Amendment 1) – Countries whose Seafarer Medical Certificates are accepted as equivalent to the UK Seafarer Medical Certificate (ENG1), Annex 1.
36 Medical Certification Regulations, reg 11. Note that 'certificate of medical fitness' slightly differs from the UK 'medical fitness certificate'; both are referred to in reg 12(3) in connection with a seafarer's duty to report medical conditions (as described below), which makes it clear that that requirement applies to holders of a UK certificate or a non-UK certificate.
37 Medical Certification Regulations, reg 12(1)–(2)(b); MSN 1839(M), paras 9.1–9.2.

authority.[38] The term 'medical condition' includes both injury and illness, and a 'significant medical condition' is a medical condition which adversely affects or is reasonably likely to adversely affect the seafarer's ability to carry out his or her duties, including the seafarer's ability to undertake emergency duties.[39] In either case the seafarer's certificate is suspended from the date that it first became practicable for them to make the report (whether or not the report is actually made), until an MCA-approved doctor or (as the case may be) the non-UK issuing authority assesses the seafarer as being fit in accordance with the medical standards set out in MSN 1839(M).[40]

Suspension or cancellation of certificate

4.9 An MCA-approved doctor may suspend or cancel any medical certificate that they have issued on the grounds that: there has been a significant change in the holder's medical condition; the holder has not complied with an imposed condition; the doctor was in possession of incomplete health details at the time of issue; or the certificate was not issued in accordance with the Medical Certification Regulations.[41]

Seafarer's right to review

4.10 A seafarer who has been refused a medical certificate, disagrees with an imposed restriction or has had their certificate cancelled or suspended for more than three months has the right to have the matter reviewed by an independent medical referee, but must normally apply for the review within one month of the date of the decision being challenged.[42] There is, however, no right to a review of a 'condition' which has been imposed by the doctor under regulation 8(2)(b) of the Medical Certification Regulations.[43]

Transfer from night work

4.11 Where an MCA-approved doctor or referee has certified that a watchkeeper is suffering health problems due to night work, a duty is imposed on the employer to transfer the seafarer to duties which do not fall during night time,

38 Medical Certification Regulations, reg 12(2)(a).

39 Medical Certification Regulations, reg 2, as inserted by Miscellaneous Amendments Regulations, reg 3(2)(a).

40 Medical Certification Regulations, reg 12(3); MSN 1839(M), para 9.3.

41 Medical Certification Regulations, reg 13(1)–(2). Guidance is provided in MSN 1839, paras 11.1–11.8.

42 Medical Certification Regulations, reg 14(1)–(2). See MSN 1839, paras 11.1–11.8 for guidance on the review process.

43 MSN 1839(M), para 11.1; there is no reference in reg 14 to any review of an imposed condition.

if this is at all possible. Night work is defined as a period of nine consecutive hours that includes the period between midnight and 5am (local time).[44]

Approved doctors

4.12 The MCA has produced a list of approved UK doctors who are authorised to carry out statutory medical examinations on seafarers and issue ENG 1 certificates.[45] In addition, the MCA has approved some company doctors and may approve commercial healthcare providers to carry out examinations in respect of employees of the company.[46]

FEES

4.13 The doctor may charge a fee (the current statutory maximum is £80) for the examination leading to the issue of an ENG 1 certificate; however, this must be met by the employer, or any person who has offered to employ the seafarer, at the time that the application for the certificate is made.[47] Any charge of a fee for an examination leading to the issue of an ML5 certificate is a matter between the doctor and the seafarer.

OFFENCES

4.14 Any breaches of the main obligations imposed on the employers and seafarers amount to criminal offences, punishable on summary conviction by fines.[48] It is a defence for the accused to show that they had taken all reasonable steps to ensure compliance with the relevant provision.[49]

INSPECTION AND DETENTION OF SHIPS

4.15 The enforcement powers are more limited than those granted by other UK legislation implementing the MLC.

UK government ships may be inspected, applying the provisions of ss 258–266 (powers of inspection and the issue of improvement notices and prohibition notices) of the Merchant Shipping Act 1995.

44 Medical Certification Regulations, reg 15; MSN 1838(M), paras 12.1–12.2.
45 MCA-approved doctors in the UK (20 June 2018) – the list also includes the Isle of Man and Jersey: www.gov.uk/government/publications/mca-approved-doctors-uk-based [Accessed 21 June 2018].
46 MGN 1839, para 4.2.
47 Medical Certification Regulations, reg 8(3).
48 Medical Certification Regulations, reg 18(1)–(4).
49 Medical Certification Regulations, reg 18(5).

4.16 *Regulation 1.2: Medical Certificate*

An inspector may inspect a non-UK ships in UK waters, or a UK port, and require any seafarer on board that ship to produce any document, in order to ascertain compliance with the requirements of Regulation 1.2 and Standard A1.2 of the MLC.[50] Where the inspector is satisfied that a seafarer is unable to prove that they are working in accordance with the medical certification requirement of Regulation 1.2 and Standard A1.2 of the MLC, the inspector may send a report to the government of the flag state, and a copy of the report to the ILO.[51] In the exercise of these powers, a ship must not be unreasonably delayed.[52]

MAIN POINTS FOR COMPLIANCE

4.16

- Ensure that each seafarer on board has an original valid medical certificate issued by an MCA-approved doctor, or by an authority in a UK-approved state party to the STCW Convention (as set out in MSN 1815, Amendment 1)).
- Employer (or prospective employer) must pay medical examination fee.
- Record dates of validity to ensure that new certificates can be issued before expiry of existing certificates.
- Seafarers should comply with any restrictions or conditions imposed on the certificate.
- A seafarer who is absent from work due to a medical condition for 30 days or more, or who develops a significant medical condition, must report it to an MCA-approved doctor (or to the relevant issuing authority in the case of a certificate issued by another recognised STCW state).
- Shipowners should require seafarers to inform them of any suspension or cancellation of their certificate.
- If a seafarer is suffering from a health problem due to night work, they must be transferred to work at other times, if possible.

DMLC: note the compliance provisions entered in Pt I, point 2, and enter implementing measures in Pt II, point 2.

50 Medical Certification Regulations, reg 20(1).
51 Medical Certification Regulations, reg 20(2)(a)–(b), respectively.
52 Medical Certification Regulations, reg 20(3).

CHAPTER 5

Regulation 1.3: Training and Qualifications

INTRODUCTION

5.1 The purpose of Regulation 1.3 of the MLC is to ensure that seafarers are trained or qualified to carry out their duties on board ship.[1]

The MLC provides that, before commencing work on a ship, seafarers must be trained or certified as competent or otherwise qualified to perform their duties, and have successfully completed training for personal safety.[2] Training in accordance with the mandatory instruments of the IMO is deemed to meet those requirements.[3] The main instrument in this context is the IMO's International Convention on Standards of Training, Certification and Watchkeeping for Seafarers, 1978 (STCW Convention) (as amended, most recently by the 2010 'Manila amendments').

A detailed account of the STCW Convention is beyond the scope of this work. What is set out below is only intended to be a summary of the main UK provisions, which implement the STCW Convention in this area, for service on UK ships.

The relevant provisions are set out in the Merchant Shipping (Standards of Training, Certification and Watchkeeping) Regulations 2015,[4] which give effect to the STCW Convention (as amended) and, in part, implement Directive

1 MLC, Regulation 1.3, purpose.
2 MLC, Regulation 1.3, paras 1–2.
3 MLC, Regulation 1.3, para 3.
4 SI 2015/782.

2012/35/EU.[5] The 2015 Regulations also revoke earlier statutory instruments in this field, make some consequential amendments, and set out some transitional arrangements to preserve the certification and training carried out under the previous legislation.[6]

In this section, there are many references to the UK's '2015 Regulations' and the IMO's 'STCW Convention Regulations'. Those terms must be used consistently in referring to each, so as to avoid confusion between the two.

APPLICATION

5.2 The training and certification requirements for service on ships are set out in Pt 2 of the 2015 Regulations, which applies to seafarers serving on board sea-going UK ships, except the following: fishing vessels; pleasure vessels which are less than 80 GT under 24 metres in length; or wooden ships of primitive build.[7]

CERTIFICATION AND TRAINING

5.3 Deck officers and engineering officers must hold, in respect of the category and capacity in which they are serving, an appropriate certificate of competency (CoC) or an appropriate certificate of equivalent competency (CeC). Such certificates may only be issued by the MCA, where the applicant complies with the STCW Convention criteria in column 2 of the table in Schedule 3 (set out in Table 5.1 below), in relation to the category of service listed in column 1.[8] A CoC must be issued and endorsed in accordance with the STCW Convention Regulation I/2, and will entitle the holder to serve in the specified capacity and to perform the functions involved: (i) at the specified level of responsibility; (ii) on a ship of the type, GT or power and means of propulsion indicated by the endorsement; and (iii) while engaged on the particular voyage concerned.[9]

5 Directive 2012/35/EU of the European Parliament and of the Council, OJ L343, 14.12.2012, amending Directive 2008/106/EC on the minimum level of training for seafarers [to implement the Manila amendments].

6 2015 Regulations, regs 2, 56 and Schs 1–2. The previous provisions were mainly set out in the revoked Merchant Shipping (Training and Certification) Regulations 1997 (SI 1997/348).

7 2015 Regulations, reg 4.

8 2015 Regulations, reg 6(1)–(2).

9 2015 Regulations, egsr 6(3), 30.

Table 5.1: Categories of Certificates of Competency and Criteria for Issue (2015 Regulations, Sch 3)

(1) Categories and capacity	(2) STCW [Convention] Regulation in which the requirements for the issue of a certificate of competency are contained
Master and deck department	
Officer in charge of a navigational watch on any ship on voyages not limited to near-coastal voyages	Regulation II/1, paragraph 2
Master or chief mate on a ship of 3000 GT or more	Regulation II/2, paragraph 2
Master on a ship of between 500 GT and 2999 GT not engaged on near-coastal voyages	Regulation II/2, paragraph 4
Chief mate on a ship of between 500 GT and 2999 GT	Regulation II/2, paragraph 4
Officer in charge of a navigational watch on a ship of less than 500 GT engaged on near- coastal voyages	Regulation II/3, paragraph 4
Master on a ship of less than 500 GT engaged on near-coastal voyages	Regulation II/3, paragraph 6
Engine department	
Officer in charge of an engineering watch in a manned engine-room, or designated duty engineer officer in a periodically unmanned engine-room, on a ship powered by main propulsion machinery of 750 kilowatts propulsion power or more	Regulation III/1, paragraph 2
Chief engineer officer or second engineer officer on a ship powered by main propulsion machinery of 3000 kilowatts propulsion power or more	Regulation III/2, paragraph 2
Chief engineer officer and second engineer officer on a ship powered by main propulsion machinery of between 750 and 3000 kilowatts propulsion power	Regulation III/3, paragraph 2
Electro-technical officer on a ship powered by main propulsion machinery of 750 kilowatts propulsion power or more	Regulation III/6, paragraph 2

As an exception, the MCA may permit a seafarer who does not hold a UK CoC (or UK-issued CeC) to serve in the appropriate capacity for a maximum period of three months. This exception only applies to a seafarer who holds a valid certificate, of the appropriate capacity, issued by a non-EEA contracting state[10] to the STCW Convention, and the seafarer has submitted an application for a CeC.[11]

Training and qualifications required for specific duties and ship types

5.4 The 2015 Regulations also set out a range of duties and ship types, against which specified training, certification and qualifications are required for particular officers and ratings, and these have been summarised in Table 5.2 below. Some of these must also be endorsed by the MCA, in accordance with the STCW Convention Regulation I/2;[12] these have been indicated by the insertion of 'MCA endorsement required'.

Table 5.2: Requirements relating to specific duties and ship types

Specific duties and ship types	Training, certification and conditions
Engine-room watch duties, with main propulsion from 350 KW to less than 750KW in manned or periodically manned engine room.	Engineering certificate of competence (as in regulation 6 of the 2015 Regulations), or marine engine operator's licence compliant with section 10 of MSN 1857 (M+F).[13] MCA endorsement required only for a certificate of competency issued under regulation 6.
Radio duties on a Global Maritime Distress and Safety System (GMDSS) ship.	The seafarer must be at least 18 years old, have completed education and training, and meet the standards of section A-IV/2 of the STCW Code.[14] MCA endorsement required.
Oil or chemical tanker – basic training – for seafarers assigned specific duties and responsibilities related to cargo or cargo equipment.	Certificate of proficiency in basic training for such vessels – seafarer must meet the criteria specified in STCW Convention Regulation V/1-1, paragraph 2.[15] MCA endorsement required.

10 CoCs issued by EEA states are mutually recognised by other EEA states (see under 'Recognition of certificates issued by other states' below).
11 2015 Regulations, reg 6(4)–(5).
12 2015 Regulations, reg 30.
13 2015 Regulations, reg 7.
14 2015 Regulations, reg 8
15 2015 Regulations, reg 9.

Specific duties and ship types	Training, certification and conditions
Oil tanker – advanced training – requirements for: master, chief engineer, chief mate, second engineer and any other seafarer with immediate responsibility for loading, discharging, care in transit, handling of cargo, tank cleaning or other cargo-related operations.	Certificate of proficiency in advanced training for oil tanker cargo operations – seafarer must meet the criteria specified in STCW Convention Regulation V/1-1, paragraph 4.[16] MCA endorsement required.
Chemical tanker – advanced training – requirements for: master, chief engineer, chief mate, second engineer and any other seafarer with immediate responsibility for loading, discharging, care in transit, handling of cargo, tank cleaning or other cargo-related operations.	Certificate of proficiency in advanced training for chemical tanker cargo operations – seafarer must meet the criteria specified in STCW Convention Regulation V/1-1, paragraph 6.[17] MCA endorsement required.
Liquefied gas tanker – basic training – officer or rating assigned specific duties and responsibilities related to cargo or cargo equipment.	Certificate of proficiency in basic training for liquefied gas tanker cargo operations – seafarer must meet the criteria specified in STCW Convention Regulation V/1-2, paragraph 2.[18] MCA endorsement required.
Liquefied gas tanker – advanced training – requirements for: master, chief engineer, chief mate, second engineer and any other seafarer with immediate responsibility for loading, discharging, care in transit, handling of cargo, tank cleaning or other cargo-related operations.	Certificate of proficiency in advanced training for liquefied gas tanker cargo operations – seafarer must meet the criteria specified in STCW Convention Regulation V/1-2, paragraph 4.[19] MCA endorsement required.
Rating forming part of a navigational watch on a ship of 500 GT or more. Does not apply to a rating under training or a rating whose duties are of an unskilled nature.	Certificate of proficiency – seafarer must meet the criteria specified in STCW Convention Regulation II/4, paragraph 2.[20]
Rating forming part of an engine-room watch, or performing designated duties in a periodically manned engine-room, on a ship powered by propulsion of 750 KW or more.	Certificate of proficiency – seafarer must meet the criteria specified in STCW Convention Regulation III/4, paragraph 2.[21]

16 2015 Regulations, reg 10.
17 2015 Regulations, reg 11.
18 2015 Regulations, reg 12.
19 2015 Regulations, reg 13.
20 2015 Regulations, reg 14.
21 2015 Regulations, reg 15.

Specific duties and ship types	Training, certification and conditions
Rating – able seafarer in deck department – serving on ship of 500 GT or more.	Certificate of proficiency – seafarer must meet the criteria specified in STCW Convention Regulation II/5, paragraph 2.[22]
Rating – able seafarer in engine department – serving on ship powered by propulsion of 750KW or more.	Certificate of proficiency – seafarer must meet the criteria specified in STCW Convention Regulation III/5, paragraph 2 or 4.[23]
Seafarer designated to launch or take charge of a survival craft or a rescue boat (other than a fast rescue boat).	Certificate of proficiency – seafarer must meet the criteria set out in STCW Convention Regulation VI/2, paragraph 1.[24]
Seafarer designated to launch or take charge of a fast rescue boat.	Certificate of proficiency – seafarer must meet the criteria set out in STCW Convention Regulation VI/2, paragraph 2.[25]
Ship security officer.	Certificate of proficiency – seafarer must meet the criteria set out in STCW Convention Regulation VI/5, paragraph 1.[26]
Seafarer on a passenger ship engaged on international voyages (other than a high-speed craft).	The seafarer must complete the required training in accordance with their capacity, duties and responsibilities, as follows: • Training in crowd management, as specified in STCW Code, section A-V/2, must be completed by: the master, each officer and any other seafarer designated on muster lists to assist passengers in emergency situations.[27] • Safety training specified in STCW Code, section A-V/2, paragraph 2, must be completed by a seafarer providing direct service to passengers in passenger spaces.[28]

22 2015 Regulations, reg 16.
23 2015 Regulations, reg 17.
24 2015 Regulations, reg 19.
25 2015 Regulations, reg 20.
26 2015 Regulations, reg 21.
27 2015 Regulations, reg 22(1)–(3).
28 2015 Regulations, reg 22(1)–(2), (4).

Specific duties and ship types	Training, certification and conditions
	• Approved training in passenger safety, cargo safety and hull integrity, as specified in STCW Code, section A-V/2, paragraph 4, must be completed by: the master, chief engineer, chief mate, second engineer and any other seafarer assigned immediate responsibility for embarking and disembarking passengers, loading, discharging or securing cargo, or closing hull openings on board a ro-ro passenger ship.[29] • Approved training in crisis management and human behaviour, as specified in STCW Code, section A-V/2, paragraph 3, must be completed by: the master, chief engineer, chief mate, second engineer and any other seafarer designated on muster lists as having responsibility for the safety of passengers in emergency situations.[30]
High-speed craft, including hovercraft, constructed on or after 1 January 1996.	The seafarer must complete the training specified in section 18.3.3 of the International Code of Safety for High Speed Craft. The trainer must issue documentary evidence to each seafarer successfully completing the training and, for a master and officer, this must be an endorsed certificate in accordance with MSN 1740 (M).[31]
Safety familiarisation, basic training and instruction for all seafarers.	The seafarer must receive familiarisation and basic training or instruction, in accordance with the STCW Code, section A-VI/1, and meet that standard of competence.[32]

29 2015 Regulations, reg 22(1)–(2), (5).
30 2015 Regulations, reg 22(1)–(2), (6).
31 2015 Regulations, regs 23 and 42. MSN 1740(M) introduces revised requirements for the training and certification of officers and crew on all high-speed craft, including hovercraft.
32 2015 Regulations, reg 24.

Specific duties and ship types	Training, certification and conditions
Seafarer designated to control fire-fighting operations.	The seafarer must have successfully completed advanced training in techniques for fire-fighting, with particular emphasis on organisation, tactics and command, in accordance with the STCW Code, section A-VI/3, paragraphs 1 to 4, and meet that standard of competence.[33]
Seafarer designated as a provider of medical first aid or to take charge of medical care.	For medical first aid, the seafarer must meet the standards of competence set out in the STCW Code, section A-VI/4, paragraphs 1 to 3.[34] For taking charge of medical care, the seafarer must meet the standards set out in the STCW Code, section A-VI/4, paragraphs 4 to 6.[35]
Security-related familiarisation training for seafarers serving on a ship required to comply with the International Ship and Port Facility Security Code (ISPS Code).	The seafarer must receive security-awareness familiarisation and training or instruction, in accordance with the STCW Code, section A-VI/6, paragraphs 1 to 4.[36] A seafarer with designated security duties must meet the standards of competence specified in the STCW Code, section A-VI/6, paragraphs 6 to 8.[37]

Manila amendments – training

5.5 Following the entry into force of the Manila amendments to the STCW Convention on 1 January 2017, seafarers must have documentary evidence of either having completed a training course or having updated their training within the last five years in the following areas (as applicable to them):

- Personal Survival Techniques – STCW Code (Table A-VI/1-1);
- Fire Prevention and Fire Fighting – STCW Code (Table A-VI/1-2);
- Proficiency in Survival Craft and Rescue Boats other than fast rescue boats – STCW Code (Table A-VI/2-1);

33 2015 Regulations, reg 25.
34 2015 Regulations, reg 26(1).
35 2015 Regulations, reg 26(2).
36 2015 Regulations, reg 27(1)–(2).
37 2015 Regulations, reg 27(1), (3).

- Proficiency in Fast Rescue Boats – STCW Code (Table A-VI/2-2); and
- Advanced Fire Fighting – STCW Code (Table A-VI/3).[38]

Further information on training and certification can be found in MSN 1865[39] and MIN 535.[40] The latter provides guidance on the documentary evidence of STCW updating training which seafarers must submit from 1 January 2017 onwards, before applying for the issue, revalidation or upgrade of a CoC.

Recognition of certificates issued by other states

5.6 There are provisions for the UK to recognise certificates issued by EEA States and non-EEA states, but in each case the State in question must be a state party to the STCW Convention.

(i) EEA States

The MCA must recognise the following certificates, if they have been issued in accordance with the requirements of Directive 2008/106/EC,[41] by an EEA Member State: (a) certificate of competency issued to a master, officer or radio operator; (b) certificate of proficiency in training for tanker cargo operations; and (c) any other certificate of proficiency.[42]

In respect of (a) and (b) above, the MCA must, on application of the holder, and subject to the following conditions being met, issue a CeC, attesting to its recognition.[43] The conditions are that: the seafarer must meet the language standards set out in sections A-II/1, A-III/1, A-IV/2 and A-II/4 of the STCW Code;[44] and that any seafarer of the rank of master, chief mate, chief engineer or second engineer must either demonstrate sufficient knowledge of UK maritime legislation which is relevant to their management level functions, or undergo an adaptation period specified by the MCA (which must be no longer than three years).[45]

Following Brexit, in relation to the EU, the UK will be become a third-party state, and it remains to be seen if, or how, the current mutual recognition of CoCs may change. An academic report suggests that there are unlikely to be

38 How Manila amendments affect seafarer training and certificates: www.gov.uk/guidance/manila-amendments-and-how-they-affect-seafarer-training-and-certificates [Accessed 22 June 2018].

39 MSN 1865(M) – Seafarer Training and Certification Guidance: UK Requirements for Emergency, Occupational Safety, Security, Medical Care and Survival Functions.

40 MIN 535(M) – Final Clarification on the Requirements for Updating Ancillary & Safety Training and Completing Tanker Training.

41 Directive 2008/106/EC on the minimum level of training of seafarers.

42 2015 Regulations, reg 32(1)(a)–(c).

43 2015 Regulations, reg 32(2).

44 2015 Regulations, reg 32(4).

45 2015 Regulations, reg 32(3), (5)–(6), (8).

practical barriers to EU recognition, given that the UK is an STCW state party, with high credentials in the training of seafarers.[46]

(ii) Third-party states (non-EEA states)

In this scenario, the MCA may recognise the following certificates, if the specified conditions are met: (a) a CoC issued to a master or officer; (b) a CoC issued to a GMDSS radio operator; or (c) a certificate of proficiency in training for tanker cargo operations issued to a master or an officer.[47]

The conditions are that: (a) the certificate issued by the third-party state was recognised by an EEA State as at 14 June 2005 (and recognition has not been withdrawn by the EU Commission); (b) the third-party state is currently recognised by the EU Commission in accordance with Directive 2008/106/EC; or (c) where the third-party state is not recognised by the EU Commission, the UK has made a request to the Commission, under Article 19(2) of Directive 2008/106/EC, and three months have since passed without the Commission making a decision.[48] A subsequent refusal by the EU Commission to recognise the third-party state will lead to withdrawal of recognition, and cancellation of the certificate.[49]

Once the MCA recognises a certificate under any of those conditions, it must, on application of the holder, and subject to the following conditions being met, issue a CeC, attesting to its recognition.[50] The conditions are that: the seafarer must meet the language standards set out in sections A-II/1, A-III/1, A-IV/2 and A-II/4 of the STCW Code;[51] and, if the certificate issued by the non-EEA state only partially meets the UK standards, the MCA may specify additional standards that are to be attained.[52]

The MCA has published a list (last updated on 7 February 2018) of states whose CoCs are accepted for the issue of a UK CeC.[53]

Validity and revalidation of certificates and endorsements

5.7 Subject to some conditions, CoCs, CeCs and endorsements remain valid, provided that the holder complies with the standards and conditions: (a) as to medical fitness, as prescribed by the Merchant Shipping (Maritime Labour

46 'The UK maritime sectors beyond Brexit – A report on the impact of Brexit on UK shipping, maritime legal services, fisheries and trade' by the Institute of Maritime Law and the Southampton Marine and Maritime Institute of the University of Southampton, para 2.2.1, p 50, Syreloglou S, et al: https://cdn.southampton.ac.uk/assets/imported/transforms/content-block/UsefulDownloads_Download/AAF0B9E5B8B347F8B4F21089E3CE3FD4/Final%20Report%20Brexit.pdf [Accessed 22 June 2018].

47 2015 Regulations, reg 33(1)(a)–(c).

48 2015 Regulations, reg 33(2)(a)–(c).

49 2015 Regulations, reg 33(6)(a)–(b).

50 2015 Regulations, reg 33(3).

51 2015 Regulations, reg 33(4).

52 2015 Regulations, reg 33(5).

53 MCA list of recognised states: https://assets.publishing.service.gov.uk/government/uploads/system/uploads/attachment_ data/file/593162/CEC_Accepted_Countries_2017.pdf [Accessed 22 June 2018].

Convention) (Medical Certification) Regulations 2010 (on which, see Chapter 4); and (b) as to professional competency to act in the appropriate capacity, as required by the STCW Convention and Pt 2 of the 2015 Regulations.[54]

Regarding the conditions, all CoCs, CeCs and certificates of proficiency for training in tanker operations, held by a master or an officer, and any endorsement issued to any seafarer under regulation 30 of the 2015 Regulations, must be revalidated by the MCA at intervals not exceeding five years.[55] Before revalidation, the MCA must be satisfied that the holder of the certificate has established continued professional competence in accordance with section A-I/11 of the STCW Code.[56]

A seafarer who holds a certificate of proficiency in personal survival techniques, survival craft and rescue boats, advanced firefighting, fire prevention and firefighting, or fast rescue boats must carry out refresher training within every five-year period.[57] Relevant refresher training, within the same period, is also required for a master or a seafarer designated to take charge of medical care; and for a master and an officer serving on board a passenger ship engaged in international voyages or on board a high-speed craft.[58]

Hovercraft

5.8 Specific provisions apply to hovercraft, as set out in Pt 3 of the 2015 Regulations, which applies to UK sea-going hovercraft constructed on or after 1 January 1996.[59]

The owner of a hovercraft must ensure that the seafarers on board have completed the training specified in section 18.3.3 of the High Speed Craft Code, the provider of which must provide documentary evidence to those successfully completing the course.[60] In the case of the master, the evidence must be in the form of an endorsed certificate, as specified in MSN 1740.[61] This requires, amongst its detailed provisions, that the master and all officers having an operational role should possess a route- and craft-specific Type Rating Certificate issued by the MCA, and all other crew members should complete type rating training before being employed on a hovercraft.[62] The code references the following for further information: MSN 1740 (referred to above); and MGN 26.[63]

54 2015 Regulations, reg 34.
55 2015 Regulations, reg 35(1)–(2).
56 2015 Regulations, reg 35(3).
57 2015 Regulations, reg 36(1)–(2).
58 2015 Regulations, reg 36(3)–(4).
59 2015 Regulations, reg 42(1).
60 2015 Regulations, reg 42(2)–(3).
61 2015 Regulations, reg 42(4); MSN 1740 (M) – Training and certification of officers and crew on high-speed craft.
62 International Code of Safety for High Speed Craft (2000), 2008 edition, para 1.3.2.
63 MGN 26 (M): High Speed Craft Training – Further Guidance on Course Approval and Certification.

RESPONSIBILITIES, COMPLIANCE AND ENFORCEMENT

5.9 The responsibility for ensuring compliance with certification, training requirements, and the maintenance of relevant documentation and data (including that on medical fitness), falls on the 'company' which, for these purposes, is the owner of the ship, or any other person (such as the manager or bareboat charterer) who has agreed to be responsible for compliance with the STCW Convention Regulations.[64] The company will almost certainly be the same entity as the 'shipowner' under the MLC.[65]

The company is also responsible for providing written instructions to the master, in respect of policies and procedures, on ship familiarisation for new officers and ratings, which should include: (a) the allocation of a reasonable period of time during which each newly employed seafarer will have an opportunity to become acquainted with: (i) the specific equipment that they will be using or operating; and (ii) ship-specific watchkeeping, safety, environmental protection and emergency procedures and arrangements that the seafarer needs to know to perform the assigned duties properly; and (b) the designation of a knowledgeable crew member responsible for ensuring that an opportunity is provided to each newly employed seafarer to receive essential information in a language that the officer or rating understands.[66]

The company and the master are responsible for ensuring that the original certificates and other documents issued under the STCW Convention, and Part 2 of the 2015 Regulations, are carried on board at all times.[67]

Breaches of the obligations referred to above amount to offences by the company, master or designated crew member, triable summarily or on indictment.[68] It is a defence for the accused to show that they took all reasonable steps to avoid the commission of the offence.[69] Where applicable, it is for the accused to prove that it was not reasonably practicable to do more than was in fact done to satisfy the duty or requirement.[70]

INSPECTION AND DETENTION OF SHIPS

5.10 An inspector may detain a UK ship that does not comply with the 2015 Regulations.[71]

64 2015 Regulations, reg 51(2)(a)–(c).
65 The MLC definition of 'shipowner' is set out in Chapter 1 at para 1.8.
66 2015 Regulations, reg 51(4)–(5)(a)–(b).
67 2015 Regulations, reg 52.
68 2015 Regulations, reg 55(1)–(5).
69 2015 Regulations, reg 55(6).
70 2015 Regulations, reg 55(7).
71 2015 Regulations, reg 54(1)–(2); Merchant Shipping Act 1995, s 284.

Non-UK ships may be inspected to verify that relevant seafarers hold STCW certificates; any non-compliance in that regard must be reported to the nearest maritime, consular or diplomatic representative of the flag state.[72] If the defect is not remedied, and there is in consequence a danger to persons, property or the environment, the ship may be detained.[73]

KEY COMPLIANCE POINTS

5.11 The company and master should ensure the following:

- All seafarers are trained in accordance with the 2015 Regulations and hold the appropriate CoC, CeC or certificate of proficiency, revalidated as necessary, and that the originals are carried on board at all times; also ensure that seafarers carry their original valid medical certificate at all times (see Chapter 4).
- The endorsements on the certificates are appropriate in terms of: the level of responsibility that the seafarer is to take on; ship type, GT or power and means of propulsion; and the type of voyage concerned.
- Seafarers are instructed to inform the master and company/shipowner if their certificate is lost or cancelled.
- Before any seafarer joins a ship, they receive familiarisation and basic training or instruction, in accordance with the STCW Code, section A-VI/1, and meet that standard of competence.
- Necessary refresher training is carried out in accordance with the Manila amendments, as well as other training that is required at five-yearly intervals, and that documentary evidence of this is maintained.

DMLC: note the compliance provisions entered in Pt I, point 3, and enter implementing measures in Pt II, point 3.

Seafarers should ensure the following:

- They keep their original CoC, CeC and certificates of proficiency on board at all times.
- They are certified to carry out any tasks they are expected to perform.

72 2015 Regulations, reg 53(1)(a), (2), (3)(a).
73 2015 Regulations, reg 54(1)(b)(iii), (2); Merchant Shipping Act 1995, s 284.

CHAPTER 6

Regulation 1.4: Recruitment and Placement

INTRODUCTION

6.1 The purpose of Regulation 1.4 of the MLC is to ensure that seafarers have access to an efficient and well-regulated seafarer recruitment and placement system.[1]

Seafarers are to have access to an efficient, adequate and accountable system for finding employment on board ship without charge.[2] Ratifying states must ensure that seafarer recruitment and placement services ('RPS') operating in their territory conform to the standards of Regulation 1.4 and the Code.[3] Ratifying states are also required to ensure, in respect of ships which are registered with them, that the shipowners who use seafarer RPS which are situated in a non-MLC state are satisfied that those services also meet the standards set in the Code.[4]

Whereas most MLC obligations are directed at shipowners, this is an area in which they are mainly directed at seafarer RPS. Some of the UK's general laws

1 MLC, Regulation 1.4, purpose.
2 MLC, Regulation 1.4, para 1.
3 MLC, Regulation 1.4, para 2.
4 MLC, Regulation 1.4, para 3.

relating to recruitment partially fulfil its MLC obligations in this area, such as the Employment Agencies Act 1973 and the Conduct of Employment Agencies and Employment Businesses Regulations 2003[5] (as amended) ('Conduct Regulations'). Seafarer RPS must comply with those general laws, as well as, and subject to, the specific laws introduced to implement Regulation 1.4 of the MLC.[6] Those are mainly set out in the Merchant Shipping (Maritime Labour Convention) (Recruitment and Placement) Regulations 2014[7] ('RPS Regulations'), the Merchant Shipping (Maritime Labour Convention) (Minimum Requirements for Seafarers etc) Regulations 2014[8] ('Minimum Requirements Regulations'), and MGN (M) 475.[9]

The RPS Regulations define two types of business model for the way in which seafarers are recruited for and supplied to shipowners. An 'employment agency' is a business, carried on in the UK, which provides services, for the purposes of finding persons ('work-seekers') employment with employers ('hirers'), or of supplying hirers with work-seekers for employment by the hirer, except where the service provided is limited exclusively to the provision of information. An 'employment business' is a business, carried on in the UK, which employs persons, whom it supplies to hirers to perform services for, and under the control of, the hirers.[10] The main difference between the two is that: (a) when introduced by an agency, the seafarer will enter into a contract with the hirer (not the agency); and (b) when supplied by an employment business, the seafarer will be in contract with the latter, but not with the hirer.

The term 'seafarer RPS' will be used to refer to employment agencies and employment businesses collectively. Occasionally, it may be necessary to refer to just one or the other, due to their differing business models, as described above.

The RPS Regulations apply in relation to the introduction or supply of seafarers to sea-going ships, regardless of which state the ship is registered in, except: pleasure vessels; fishing vessels; ships of traditional build; warships or naval auxiliaries; and vessels which are not ordinarily engaged in commercial activities.[11]

5 SI 2003/3319.
6 MGN 475 – MLC, 2006: Recruitment and placement, paras 4.1–4.2.
7 SI 2014/1615.
8 SI 2014/1613.
9 MGN 475 (M): Maritime Labour Convention 2006: Recruitment and Placement.
10 RPS Regulations, reg 2(1).
11 RPS Regulations, reg 2(4). For more information on the UK's MLC recruitment provisions, see M Egan and M Smith, *Employment Agencies, Recruitment Agencies and Agency Workers* (Lexis Nexis, Bristol, 2017, 1st edition), pp 67–78.

OBLIGATIONS OF SEAFARER RPS

Seafarer employment checks

6.2 Before introducing or supplying a work-seeker to a hirer, for the purposes of employment as a seafarer on a sea-going ship, seafarer RPS must first verify:

(a) the identity of the worker-seeker; and

(b) that the work-seeker has the experience, training, qualifications and any authorisation, which the hirer considers are necessary, or which are required by law, or by any professional body, for the work in question.[12]

As regards (a), the seafarer's identity can be checked by requesting their passport or seafarer identity document.

Regarding (b), see Chapter 5 for a summary of the UK's requirements in connection with the STCW Convention standards. If the ship is registered in another MLC state, Pt I of the DMLC,[13] at point 3, should list the qualifications which the flag state requires on that ship for deck, engine and radio officers and ratings (which will usually be based on STCW Convention standards, although there may be other standards applying to smaller ships). As regards 'authorisation', it will be necessary to establish if the seafarer has the right to work on the particular ship, so steps should be taken to confirm this, and whether they need a work permit or other document. However, UK-based seafarer RPS should make themselves aware of the situations in which a non-EEA seafarer would require a work permit, which is when they are to join:

- ferries operating between two UK ports, including ports in Northern Ireland, but not the Channel Islands or Isle of Man;
- 'ro-ro' services between UK ports which carry 12 or more lorry drivers;
- dredgers operating wholly or largely within UK waters; or
- scheduled domestic freight services between UK ports.

However, seafarers who are under contract to join a ship which is due to leave UK waters do not require a work permit.[14]

The UK government provides advice on how to carry out proper checks on original documents, recording the date of the check and keeping copies.[15]

12 RPS Regulations, reg 4(a)–(b) (employment agencies); Conduct Regulations, reg 19(1)(a)–(b) (employment businesses).

13 DMLCs are generally readily available on the websites of major maritime authorities.

14 Immigration Rules, para 128; Government guidance: www.gov.uk/government/publications/seafarers-crm01/ seafarers-crm01#crm18-seafarers-and-work-permits [Accessed 22 June 2018].

15 UK government guidance on checking a job applicant's right to work documents: www.gov.uk/check-job-applicant-right-to-work [Accessed 22 June 2018].

An example of other authorisations could relate to those granted by professional bodies for doctors or nurses working on a cruise ship. Seafarer RPS should liaise with the shipowner, flag state and the relevant professional body to satisfy themselves that those workers are qualified accordingly.

Seafarer employment agreements

6.3 There are also obligations in relation to seafarer employment agreements (SEAs) which, for these purposes, are defined as: (a) for service on a UK ship, the written agreement required under r 9 of the Minimum Requirements Regulations (see Regulation 2.1); and (b) for non-UK ships, the agreement governing the seafarer's work on the ship (and, in both cases, an unsigned draft of the agreement).[16]

The seafarer RPS must ensure that:

(a) the seafarer is informed of their rights and duties under the SEA, prior to, or in the process, of engagement;

(b) arrangements are made for the seafarer to have the opportunity to examine the SEA, before and after they sign it; and

(c) arrangements are made for the seafarer to receive a copy of the SEA, after they sign it.[17]

Shipowners have similar duties in respect of seafarers' understanding of their SEAs[18] which are not intended to be diminished by the obligations imposed on seafarer RPS.[19]

For more information on the minimum information which must be included in a SEA, see Regulation 2.1.

Prohibition against blacklisting

6.4 The MLC prohibits seafarer RPS from using means, mechanisms or lists for the purpose of preventing or deterring seafarers from gaining employment for which they are qualified.[20] Such practices are known to occur in some seafarer-supplying countries, resulting in seafarers often feeling inhibited from making legitimate complaints about their working or living conditions, for fear of being blacklisted from further employment opportunities.

16 RPS Regulations, reg 3.
17 RPS Regulations, reg 5(a)–(c).
18 Minimum Requirements Regulations, regs 9, 10(4)(a)–(c).
19 MLC, Standard A1.4.10.
20 MLC, Standard A1.4.5(a).

At this stage, for implementation purposes, the UK is relying on the Employment Relations Act 1999 (Blacklists) Regulations 2010[21] and the Employment Relations (Northern Ireland) Order 1999 (Blacklists) Regulations (Northern Ireland) 2014.[22] These Regulations prohibit the compilation, use, sale or supply of 'prohibited lists', which are those containing details of past or present members of trade unions, or persons who are, or have been, taking part in trade union activities, which are compiled for the purposes of discrimination in recruitment or the treatment of workers (a contravention is actionable as a breach of statutory duty).[23] Claims for breaches can be made to the employment tribunal[24] (following the ACAS early conciliation procedure)[25] or to court.[26]

The processing of such data, without the consent of the data subject and for such unlawful purposes, would also breach the Data Protection Act 2018[27] and the General Data Protection Regulation's principles on lawful processing.[28]

The UK's legislation only goes some way to implementing the MLC's prohibition against blacklisting, as it is targeted at such practices due to trade union membership or activities, whereas the MLC simply prohibits blacklisting for any reason. The UK provisions are important, though, given that seafarers often act as union representatives and are involved in collective bargaining negotiations on MLC rights and other industrial relations matters. It remains to be seen if the UK will legislate to broaden its prohibition against blacklisting accordingly.

PROHIBITION AGAINST CHARGING SEAFARERS RECRUITMENT FEES

6.5 The MLC requires ratifying states to prohibit domestic seafarer RPS from charging seafarers fees for recruitment, placement or providing employment. The MLC's prohibition against fees does not apply to the costs of obtaining a national statutory medical certificate (but see reference to the UK

21 SI 2010/493.

22 SR 2014/88.

23 Employment Relations Act 1999 (Blacklists) Regulations 2010, reg 3(1)–(3); Employment Relations (Northern Ireland) Order 1999 (Blacklists) Regulations (Northern Ireland) 2014, regs 3(1)–(3). In each set of Regulations, there are some lawful exceptions, set out in reg 4 (eg compiling, using or supplying a prohibited list to bring a contravention to light).

24 2010 Blacklists Regulations, reg 5 (refusal of employment), reg 6 (refusal of employment agency services), reg 9 (detriment); Northern Ireland Blacklists Regulations 2014, regs 5–6, 9, respectively.

25 These are 'relevant proceedings' under Employment Tribunals Act 1996, s 18(1)(z2). The mandatory ACAS early conciliation procedure only applies to Scotland, England and Wales; it does not apply to Northern Ireland.

26 2010 Blacklists Regulations, reg 13 (action for breach of statutory duty); Northern Ireland Blacklists Regulations 2014, reg 13.

27 Data Protection Act 2018, s 2(1)(a).

28 Regulation (EU) 2016/679 of the European Parliament and of the Council of 27 April 2016 on the protection of natural persons with regard to the processing of personal data and on the free movement of such data, and repealing Directive 95/46/EC (General Data Protection Regulation), Arts 5–6, 4.5.2016, OJ L 119/1.

position below), national seafarer's book or a passport or other similar personal travel documents; however, shipowners must meet the costs of visas.[29]

In the UK, recruitment services are (with some exceptions) prohibited from requesting or receiving any fee, directly or indirectly, for their work-finding services, or for providing information.[30] Many of the exceptions apply to the entertainment sector, to workers such as musicians, singers, dancers and other performers, in respect of whom the recruitment service may charge commission or a fee out of the worker's earnings (but not an upfront fee).[31] This lacuna could be problematic in respect of such entertainers working on cruise ships as, under the MLC and UK implementing legislation, they would be categorised as seafarers if '... their normal place of work is on a ship'.[32] Entertainers who work regularly or for substantial periods on cruise ships would likely fall within the definition of 'seafarer', whereas those appearing on an ad hoc basis, of short-term duration, may not.[33] Although it would not be unlawful for a UK-based seafarer RPS to receive commission from entertainers on cruise ships, if the matter came to light during 'a more detailed inspection' in another MLC state, the ship could be delayed or even detained, as port state control would be applying MLC standards to the ship, and not UK laws.[34]

DUTY TO ENSURE SHIPOWNERS HAVE FINANCIAL SECURITY FOR REPATRIATION

6.6 The MLC requires ratifying states to require seafarer RPS based in their territory to ensure, as far as practicable, that shipowners to whom they supply seafarers have the '... means to protect seafarers from being stranded in a foreign port'.[35] This requirement did not find its way into the RPS Regulations, although it is contained within the MCA's non-mandatory certification scheme (referred to below).[36]

All owners of MLC ships are required to carry on board a certificate or other documentary evidence of financial security, to cover the costs of the repatriation of seafarers.[37] Therefore, seafarer RPS should ensure that such provision

29 MLC, Standard A1.4.5(b).
30 Employment Agencies Act 1973, s 6; Employment (Miscellaneous Provisions) (Northern Ireland) Order 1981, s 7.
31 Conduct Regulations, reg 26, Sch 3 (for Great Britain); Conduct of Employment Agencies and Employment Businesses Regulations (Northern Ireland) 2005 (SI 2005/395), reg 26, Sch 3.
32 RPS Regulations, reg 2(1).
33 For further guidance, see: ILO Resolution on categories of workers at para 1.9; ILO's MLC, 2006 – Frequently asked questions (4th ed 2015): question 2B, relating to entertainers and hotel staff: www.ilo.org/wcmsp5/groups/public/---ed_norm/---normes/documents/publication/wcms_238010.pdf [Accessed 23 June 2018].
34 MLC, Standard A5.2.1.
35 MLC, Standard 1.4, para 5(c)(iv).
36 MGN 475, para 7.1.
37 MLC, Standard A1.4.5(c)(iv); Standard A2.5.2.

is in place for each MLC ship to which they supply seafarers. There must be individual documentation for each ship, which will contain the ship's name and other identifying features. See Chapter 11 on repatriation and, in particular, the provisions on financial security and the specific requirements which shipowners are required to meet in this regard.

This is particularly important, as seafarer RPS are required to establish a system of protection to cover not just their own liabilities towards seafarers, but also those of the shipowner[38] (which could include the cost of repatriation if the latter fails in this respect), as explained below.

ESTABLISH A SYSTEM OF PROTECTION

6.7 Seafarer RPS are required to establish a system of protection, 'by way of insurance or an equivalent appropriate measure', to compensate seafarers (whom they have placed with shipowners on sea-going ships) for any monetary loss they may incur as a result of a failure:

(a) of the seafarer RPS to meet their obligations to the seafarer; and

(b) of the shipowner, which is party to the SEA, to meet its obligations to the seafarer.[39]

The reference to 'obligations' includes both contractual and statutory obligations.[40] Together, such obligations would apply to wages, holiday pay, repatriation, shipowners' liabilities for medical care, and payment during periods of sickness. Therefore, RPS are advised, in respect of each ship to which they supply seafarers, to ensure that there is in force a certificate or documentary evidence of financial security to cover repatriation and contractual claims for death or long-term disability due to an occupational injury, illness or hazard.[41]

In implementing this provision, the UK has adopted almost the same wording as the MLC.[42] The exact measures which ratifying states are required to take to comply with this provision have been the subject of much debate, and the UK raised its concerns at the ILO during the first meeting of the Special Tripartite Committee in 2014.

Although the RPS Regulations do not set any limitations on the extent of the mandatory system of protection, the MCA has provided some criteria which applies to its non-mandatory audit scheme. It requires a commercial insurance

38 MLC, Standard A1.4.5(c)(vi).

39 RPS Regulations, reg 6(1)–(2). The 'obligations' include contractual and statutory obligations (reg 6(3)).

40 RPS Regulations, reg 6(3).

41 MLC, Standard A4.2.2.

42 MLC, Standard A1.4.5(c)(vi).

policy to be in place, or 'some other appropriate measure' will be considered. The scheme requires:

- employment agencies to cover liabilities arising within two months of them placing the seafarer with the shipowner; and
- employment businesses to cover liabilities arising at any point while the seafarer remains in their employment.

In each case, the liability is limited to a maximum of two months in respect of each seafarer that they have placed.[43]

Whether or not seafarer RPS apply for voluntary certification under the scheme, they are still legally obliged to establish such a system of protection. The scheme, at the very least, offers some guidance on what may be found to be acceptable.

COMPLAINTS ABOUT RECRUITMENT SERVICES

6.8 The MLC requires ratifying states to require seafarer RPS to examine and respond to complaints concerning their activities, and to advise the appropriate government department about any unresolved complaints.[44] As its means of implementation, the UK refers to the MLC on-board and onshore complaints procedures required under regulation 13 of the Merchant Shipping (Maritime Labour Convention) (Survey and Certification) Regulations 2013.[45] However, the effectiveness of this would depend on the complaint actually reaching the relevant seafarer RPS, which are unlike to be the first recipient of any complaint through those procedures. See Regulation 5.1.5 (On-board complaint procedures) and Regulation 5.2.2 (Onshore seafarer complaint handling procedures) in Chapter 22.

In the UK, complaints about recruitment services can be made to the Employment Agency Standards Inspectorate (EAS), which is part of the Department for Business, Energy and Industrial Strategy (BEIS). As well as investigating complaints, EAS also carries out targeted inspections on a pro-active basis, although these are likely to be rare due to the reduction in resources in recent years.[46]

If the recruitment service is a member of the UK professional body, the Recruitment and Employment Confederation (REC), it is required to have its

43 MGN 475, paras 8.1–8.7.

44 MLC, Standard A1.4.5(c)(v).

45 SI 2013/1785; MGN 475, para 7.1, table.

46 EAS has published its 'Enforcement Policy Statement' (2017), which contains helpful information for complainants: www.gov.uk/government/uploads/system/uploads/attachment_data/file/615442/employment-agency-standards-inspectorate-enforcement-statement.pdf [Accessed 23 June 2018].

own complaints procedure. If such a recruitment service fails to resolve the issue, a complaint can be made to the REC.[47]

RECORD-KEEPING

6.9 Seafarer RPS are required to keep records which are sufficient to show whether the RPS Regulations are being complied with.[48]

The particulars to be included in relation to every application received by a work-seeker are set out below:

'(a) the date on which the application was received;

(b) the work-seeker's name, address and, if under 22 on the date the application was received, the date of birth;

(c) any terms which apply or will apply between the employment agency or employment business and the work-seeker, and any document recording any variation of the terms;

(d) details of the work-seeker's training, experience, qualifications, and any authorisation to undertake particular work (and copies of any documentary evidence of the same obtained by the employment agency or employment business);

(e) details of any requirements specified by the work-seeker in relation to taking up employment;

(f) the names of hirers to whom the work-seeker is introduced or supplied;

(g) details of any resulting engagement and date from which it takes effect;

(h) a copy of any contract between the work-seeker and any hirer entered into by the employment agency on the work-seeker's behalf;

(i) the date on which the application was withdrawn or the contract terminated (where applicable);

(j) in the case of an employment agency that is permitted by the Conduct Regulations to charge fees to work-seekers–[49]

    (i) the dates of the requests by the employment agency for fees from the work-seeker and of receipt of such fees, with copy statements or invoices, numbers and amounts; or

    (ii) statements of dates and amounts of sums deducted from money received by the employment agency on the work-seeker's behalf in accordance with regulation 25 of the Conduct Regulations, to the extent that these are not required to be comprised in records

47 See www.rec.uk.com/membership/compliance/complaints [Accessed 23 June 2018].

48 RPS Regulations, reg 7 (as substituted by Conduct of Employment Agencies and Employment Businesses (Amendments) Regulations 2016 (SI 2016/510), reg 3(2)).

49 See Conduct Regulations, reg 26, Sch 3 in relation to entertainers, etc.

maintained in respect of a client account in accordance with paragraph 12 of Schedule 2[50] to the Conduct Regulations;

(k) details of enquiries made under regulation 4[51] about the work-seeker and the position concerned with copies of all relevant documents and dates they were received or sent as the case may be.'[52]

In addition, in relation to every application received by the seafarer RPS from a hirer, the particulars outlined below must be kept; for these purposes, the hirer could be a shipowner, employer, or even another employment business which supplies seafarers to shipowners (eg a manning agency):

'(a) the date on which the application was received;

(b) the hirer's name and address, and location of the work to be done for the hirer;

(c) details of the position the hirer seeks to fill;

(d) the duration or likely duration of work;

(e) any experience, training, ability, qualifications, and authorisation required by the hirer, by law, or by any professional body and any other conditions attaching to the position the hirer seeks to fill;

(f) the terms offered in respect of the position the hirer seeks to fill;

(g) a copy of the terms between the employment agency or employment business and the hirer, and any document recording any variation of the terms;

(h) the names of work-seekers introduced or supplied;

(i) details of each resulting engagement and date from which it takes effect;

(j) the dates of requests by the employment agency or employment business for fees or other payment from the hirer and of receipt of such fees or other payments, and copies of statements or invoices.'[53]

The records may be kept in electronic form, provided that they can be reproduced in legible form.[54]

50 The provisions in the Conduct Regulations relate to client accounts.

51 These will be the details relating to the identity, experience, training, qualifications and any necessary authorisations relating to the work-seeker.

52 RPS Regulations, reg 7(2)(a)–(k) (as substituted by Conduct of Employment Agencies and Employment Businesses (Amendments) Regulations 2016 (SI 2016/510), reg 3(2)).

53 RPS Regulations, reg 7(3)(a)–(j) (as substituted by Conduct of Employment Agencies and Employment Businesses (Amendments) Regulations 2016 (SI 2016/510), reg 3(2)).

54 RPS Regulations, reg 7(7) (as substituted by Conduct of Employment Agencies and Employment Businesses (Amendments) Regulations 2016 (SI 2016/510), reg 3(2)).

SEAFARER RPS WHICH SHIPOWNERS ARE PERMITTED TO USE

6.10 As regards seafarer RPS, the RPS Regulations only apply to those situated in the UK. However, many owners of UK ships will use such services based in other countries. So, to ensure compliance with the MLC recruitment provisions, owners of UK ships are only permitted to use recruitment and placement services based in:

(a) the UK;

(b) a country which has ratified the MLC;

(c) a country to which another country's ratification of the MLC has been extended;

(d) another country, in which the service conforms to the requirements of MLC, Standard A1.4, paragraph 5 (which sets out many of the requirements referred to above), whether or not those requirements are part of the law of that country.[55]

This requirement comes, of course, from the MLC,[56] and its purpose is to ensure that its recruitment standards are not circumvented by using seafarer RPS in a non-MLC state. When using seafarer RPS falling within paragraphs (b) and (c), it is reasonable for the shipowner to assume that they comply with the MLC standards implemented in that state.[57]

However, any owner of a UK ship who chooses to use a seafarer RPS situated in a non-MLC state should first satisfy itself that it complies with MLC, Standard A1.4.5. The MCA advises that shipowners will be required to provide evidence that they have taken all reasonable steps to ensure that the recruitment service is compliant, such as by carrying out their own audit or relying on evidence of a suitable third-party audit,[58] perhaps carried out by a reputable classification society.

As an example of a response to this provision, Guernsey (which has many entities involved in seafarer recruitment, employment and payroll processes and has not had the MLC extended to it by the UK) enacted the Seafarer Recruitment and Placement Services (Maritime Labour Convention 2006) (Guernsey and Alderney) Ordinance, 2013. The Ordinance prohibits domestic seafarer RPS from introducing or supplying seafarers to shipowners, unless they are registered with the responsible government department, following a successful inspection or recent audit showing compliance with Regulation 1.4 of the MLC.[59] Shipowners using Guernsey-based recruitment services are entitled to see their certificate of registration,[60] to ensure compliance.

55 Minimum Requirements Regulations, reg 8(1)–(2)(a)–(b).
56 MLC, Standard A1.4.9.
57 MGN 475, para 3.3.
58 MGN 475, para 3.4.
59 Seafarer Recruitment and Placement Services (Maritime Labour Convention 2006) (Guernsey and Alderney) Ordinance, 2013, ss 2–4.
60 Seafarer Recruitment and Placement Services (Maritime Labour Convention 2006) (Guernsey and Alderney) Ordinance, 2013, s 5(3).

MCA'S NON-MANDATORY AUDIT SCHEME

6.11 To assist seafarer RPS in becoming compliant with MLC recruitment standards, the MCA has introduced a non-mandatory audit scheme, under which a certificate will be issued following a successful audit.[61] Such a certificate will enable RPS to demonstrate compliance to shipowners.

OFFENCES

6.12 Non-compliance with many of the above provisions, as well as making a false record, will amount to a criminal offence, punishable on summary conviction by a fine not exceeding level 5 on the standard scale.[62] The RPS Regulations do not provide a statutory defence. However, in respect of the offence under regulation 8 of the Minimum Requirements Regulations (shipowner using a seafarer RPS in a non-MLC state in a case where the RPS does not conform with Standard A1.4.5 of the MLC), it is a defence for the accused to show that they took all reasonable steps to ensure compliance.[63]

Extensions of time to commence summary proceedings (beyond the usual period of six months) are given in all three UK jurisdictions. Proceedings may be commenced within three years of the commission of the offence, but within six months of the appropriate prosecution authority being presented with sufficient evidence.[64]

CHECKLIST FOR COMPLIANCE

6.13 Seafarer RPS should:

- Check seafarer's identity, training, qualifications, and any applicable authorisation etc.
- In relation to SEAs, inform seafarers of their rights, give them a chance to examine the agreement and provide them with signed original.
- Not charge seafarers prohibited fees.
- Ensure shipowner has financial security, particularly to cover repatriation costs.
- Establish a system of protection to ensure the seafarer RPS can meet its own, and the shipowners', liabilities to seafarers.
- Keep proper records of dealing with seafarers and clients.

61 MGN 475, paras 6–9. Enquiries about the non-mandatory audit scheme should be made to the MCA's Inspection Branch (tel: 023 8083 9628).
62 RPS Regulations, reg 8; Minimum Requirements Regulations, regs 8(3), 59(1).
63 Minimum Requirements Regulations, reg 60.
64 RPS Regulations, reg 9.

- Consider applying for certification through the MCA's non-mandatory audit scheme.
- Check the DMLC, Part I, to find out information on flag state's laws, particularly point 3 (qualifications of seafarers) and point 5 (use of any licensed or certified or regulated private recruitment and placement services).

Shipowners should:

- Only use RPS in an MLC state or those which can demonstrate compliance with MLC Standard A1.4.5.

DMLC: note the compliance provisions entered in Pt I, point 5, and enter implementing measures in Pt II, point 5.

PART III

Title 2: Conditions of Employment

CHAPTER 7

Regulation 2.1: Seafarers' Employment Agreements

INTRODUCTION

7.1 The purpose of Regulation 2.1 of the MLC is to ensure that seafarers have a fair employment agreement.[1]

The terms and conditions of a seafarer employment agreement (SEA) must be set out or referred to in a clear, written and legally enforceable agreement, consistent with Standard A2.1 of the MLC.[2] The SEA must be agreed by the seafarer under conditions which ensure that they have an opportunity to review and seek advice

1 MLC, Regulation 2.1, purpose.
2 MLC, Regulation 2.1, para 1.

on the terms and conditions and freely accept them before signing.[3] To the extent compatible with ratifying states' laws, SEAs will be understood to incorporate applicable collective bargaining agreements.[4]

The main provisions relating to the issuing and contents of SEAs, for seafarers serving on UK MLC ships, are set out in Pt 4 of the Merchant Shipping (Maritime Labour Convention) (Minimum Requirements for Seafarers etc) Regulations 2014[5] ('Minimum Requirements Regulations'), supplemented by MGN 477 (M).[6] Since 7 August 2014, there has been a requirement to issue every seafarer (including the master) serving on board a UK MLC ship with an individual SEA.[7] Previously, the names of the seafarers serving on board such ships (except the master) were entered into a single 'crew agreement', which was kept and displayed on board, in accordance with the Merchant Shipping (Crew Agreements, Lists of Crew and Discharge of Seamen) Regulations 1991[8] ('the 1991 Regulations') and MGN 474(M).[9] Crew agreements are now only used on pleasure vessels (which are exempt from the MLC), although shipowners may voluntary apply to the MCA for an exemption, so that they can issue individual SEAs instead.[10]

On the application of UK MLC legislation, see Chapter 2.[11]

ISSUE OF SEAs TO SEAFARERS

7.2 Every seafarer serving on a UK MLC ship must be issued with an original SEA, by the shipowner, as soon as practicable after it is signed by each party.[12] The ultimate responsibility to issue a compliant SEA is therefore on the shipowner, whether or not it is the employer of the seafarer, and also in cases where the seafarer is self-employed or is a trainee.[13] Of course, a seafarer recruitment and placement service may issue a SEA on behalf of the shipowner, but the latter is ultimately responsible for ensuring that it is done[14] (see Chapter 6).

3 MLC, Regulation 2.1, para 2.
4 MLC, Regulation 2.1, para 3.
5 SI 2014/1613.
6 MGN 477 (M) 'Maritime Labour Convention 2006: Seafarers' Employment Agreements'. The previous MGNs 148(M) 'Approval of Crew Agreements – Merchant Ships' and 149(M) 'Approval of Crew Agreements – Yachts' were withdrawn on 23 July 2014.
7 Minimum Requirements Regulations, reg 9(1).
8 SI 1991/2144.
9 MGN 474 (M) – 'Retention of Crew Agreements for Vessels not subject to the Maritime Labour Convention requirement to have Seafarer Employment Agreement'.
10 1991 Regulations, reg 25(5); MGN 474, paras 9.1–9.2.
11 The relevant application provision is Minimum Requirements Regulations, reg 3.
12 Minimum Requirements Regulations, reg 12(1).
13 Note that the term 'trainee' is generally used instead of 'cadet', although sometimes the MCA still uses the latter term in its publications.
14 MLC, Standard A1.4.10.

The shipowner must also hold a signed original of each SEA (which may be kept on board or ashore); however, as a minimum, a hard copy or electronic copy of each SEA must be held on board and be available for inspection by the seafarer, the MCA and other specified authorities.[15]

In a case where the seafarer is an employee, but not that of the shipowner: (a) the employer must be a party to the SEA; and (b) there must be provision within the SEA under which the shipowner guarantees to the seafarer the performance of specified obligations of the employer.[16] As a guide, the MCA has provided the following wording in its model SEA, which requires that the shipowner will:

> 'hereby guarantee that in the event of the employer named at (2) above failing, for whatever reason, to meet its obligations to the seafarer named at (1) above under the terms of this Seafarer Employment Agreement I / We* as shipowner(s) undertake to meet those obligations to that seafarer [and at no cost to that seafarer].'[17]

Although the shipowner is already responsible to pay the seafarer their wages under statute, under which a statutory claim for arrears can be brought in the UK (see Chapter 8), this guarantee gives the seafarer the option of suing the shipowner in contract which, depending on any applicable law and jurisdiction clause, could be in a country outside the UK. On UK ships, the guarantee is not required in a case where the seafarer is on board mainly to receive training, and where there subsists a SEA between the seafarer and an approved training provider.[18] In the case of trainees, the shipowner need not be party to such an agreement, which will, if it complies with MGN 485(M),[19] be considered to be substantially equivalent to a SEA.[20]

Where the seafarer is either an employee of the shipowner, or is self-employed, the shipowner must be a party to the SEA.[21] In respect of the latter, the MLC requires self-employed seafarers to have '… evidence of contractual or similar arrangements …' signed by the shipowner or its representative.[22]

15 Minimum Requirements Regulations, regs 12(3)(a)–(b), 14(1); MGN 477, paras 7.1–7.2. The other specified parties are the Registrar-General of Shipping and Seamen, and HMRC (reg 14(1)).
16 Minimum Requirements Regulations, reg 9(2)(a)–(b); the obligations are specified in Sch 1, Pt 1, paras 5–11; Pt 2.
17 MGN 477, Annex 2 'Model Format for a Seafarer Employment Agreement'.
18 Minimum Requirements Regulations, reg 9(4)(a)–(b). An 'approved training provider' 'means a person who provides or secures the provision of seafarer training pursuant to an agreement with the Secretary of State (reg 9(6)).
19 MGN 485(M) 'Maritime Labour Convention, 2006: Seafarer Employment Agreements – Application to Trainees'.
20 The concept of 'substantial equivalence' is set out in MLC, Article VI, paras 3–4; see Chapter 1 at para 1.14.
21 Minimum Requirements Regulations, reg 9(3).
22 MLC, Standard A2.1.1(a).

The shipowner must, as soon as practicable after entering into a SEA, provide the seafarer with an original, signed by each party, together with any documents referred to therein.[23] The SEA must be signed either by the shipowner or its authorised signatory (who should be named in Pt 2, point 4, of the Declaration of Maritime Labour Compliance).[24] Copies must be kept on board for each seafarer, which they are entitled to see on request.[25] If the SEA (or any associated document) is not in the English language, the shipowner must ensure that an English translation is held on board.[26]

CONTENT OF THE SEA

7.3 The matters which the SEA must address, as a minimum, depend on whether the seafarer is an employee, is self-employed, or is a trainee. An 'employee' means 'an individual who is employed under a contract of employment'; and an 'employer' means 'a person by whom the seafarer is employed under a contract of employment'.[27]

Where the seafarer is an employee of the shipowner, or any other person, the SEA must include provision for the matters listed in Pts 1 and 2 of Sch 1.[28] For this scenario, the MCA has provided a model SEA which, although not mandatory, will be helpful as a guide to compliance.[29] Where the seafarer is self-employed, or is a trainee, the SEA must include provision for the matters listed in Pts 1 and 3 of Sch 1.[30] The SEA may include all required matters within one document, or make reference to other documents in which they are contained[31] such as a collective bargaining agreement (CBA). The MLC (and UK legislation) requires that CBAs are incorporated into SEAs to the extent compatible with national law and applicable CBAs must be referenced in the SEA.[32] Indeed, incorporation is most effectively achieved if the SEA contains an express clause incorporating any present or future CBA, rather than asserting that there has been incorporation through an implied term or by operation of custom and practice.[33]

23 Minimum Requirements Regulations, reg 12(1).
24 MGN 477, para 4.2.
25 Minimum Requirements Regulations, reg 12(3)(a)–(b).
26 Minimum Requirements Regulations, reg 13.
27 Minimum Requirements Regulations, regs 2(1), 9(6).
28 Minimum Requirements Regulations, reg 10(1)(a).
29 MGN 477, Annex 2 'Model Format for a Seafarer Employment Agreement'.
30 Minimum Requirements Regulations, reg 10(1)(b); in the case of a trainee, the name and address of the approved training provider must also be set out in the SEA.
31 Minimum Requirements Regulations, reg 10(2).
32 MLC, Regulation 2.1, para 3; MLC, Standard A2.1.4(j); Minimum Requirements Regulations, reg 10(1)–(2), Sch 1, Pt 1, para 14.
33 On the incorporation of collective agreements into individual contracts of employment, see Tolley's *Employment Handbook* (32nd edn, Lexis Nexis, 2018) 49–53 (contributed by Peter Wallington QC). The collective agreement is presumed not to be legally enforceable between the parties to it, unless it is in writing, and it contains a provision (however expressed) stating that the parties intend it to be legally enforceable (Trade Union and Labour Relations (Consolidation) Act 1992, s 179).

Schedule 1 to the Minimum Requirements Regulations provides as follows:

'Schedule 1

Provision to be included in a Seafarer Employment Agreement

PART 1 Provision to be included in all agreements

1. The full name, birthplace and date of birth (or age at the time of entering into the agreement) of the seafarer.

2. The name and address of the shipowner.

3. The place where the agreement is entered into.[34]

4. The date on which the agreement is entered into.

5. The capacity in which the seafarer is to work.

6. If the agreement has been made for a definite period, the termination date.

7. If the agreement has been made for an indefinite period, the period of notice of termination required and the circumstances in which such notice may be given.

8. If the agreement has been made for a particular voyage, the destination port and the period following arrival after which the agreement terminates.

9. The health and social security protection benefits to be provided to the seafarer under the agreement.[35]

10. The maximum period of service on board following which the seafarer is entitled to repatriation (which must not exceed a period of 12 months less the number of days statutory paid leave to which the seafarer is entitled).[36]

11. The seafarer's entitlement to repatriation (including the mode of transport and destination of repatriation).

12. The circumstances in which the seafarer is required to meet or reimburse the shipowner for the costs of repatriation.[37]

13. The maximum sum which the shipowner will pay to the seafarer in respect of compensation for any loss of personal property arising from the loss or foundering of the ship.[38]

14. Details of any collective bargaining agreement which is incorporated (in whole or in part) into the agreement or is otherwise relevant to it.[39]

34 This could be important for determining jurisdictional issues and other matters, such as liability for NI contributions.

35 See Chapters 17 (Medical care on board ship and ashore), 18 (Shipowners' liability) and 21 (Social security).

36 For points 10–12, see Chapter 11 (Repatriation).

37 See Chapters 8 (Wages) and 11 (Repatriation).

38 See Regulation 2.6 (Seafarer compensation for the ship's loss or foundering).

39 For British seafarers, the relevant unions party to any CBA will mainly be Nautilus International (for officers, ratings and other grades) and the RMT for ratings. On UK ships, there are also seafarers of many nationalities, who may be covered by a CBA of the International Transport Workers' Federation.

PART 2 Provision to be included where seafarer is an employee

1. The wages (either the amount or the formula to be used in determining them).[40]
2. The manner in which wages must be paid, including payment dates (the first of which must be no more than one month after the date on which the agreement is entered into, with all subsequent dates being no more than one month apart) and the circumstances (if any) in which wages may or must be paid in a different currency.
3. The hours of work.[41]
4. The paid leave (either the amount or the formula to be used in determining it).[42]
5. Any pension arrangements, including any entitlement to participate in a pension scheme.[43]
6. The grievance and disciplinary procedures.[44]

PART 3 Provision to be included where seafarer is not an employee

1. The remuneration (either the amount or the formula to be used in determining it).
2. The manner in which the remuneration must be paid, including payment dates (the first of which must be no more than one month after the date on which the agreement is entered into, with all subsequent dates being no more than one month apart) and the circumstances (if any) in which the remuneration may or must be paid in a different currency.'[45]

40 For points 1–2, see Regulation 2.2 (Wages).

41 See Regulation 2.3 (Hours of work and rest).

42 See Regulation 2.4 (Entitlement to annual leave).

43 There are no mandatory requirements in the MLC in respect of occupational pension provision. However, as a minimum, the UK requires employers to enter 'eligible employees' into an 'auto-enrolment' scheme under Pensions Act 2008, s 3: www.thepensionsregulator.gov.uk [Accessed 24 June 2018]. It has been held that the scheme applies to an employer based in Bermuda in regard to seafarers 'who ordinarily work in Great Britain' (s 1(1)(a)), which includes seafarers who: (i) work from a base in GB even if the ship spends most of its time outside GB; and (ii) reside in GB and habitually embark and disembark their ship there, even if the ship spends most of its time outside GB. However, (iii) the scheme does not apply to seafarers who reside in GB who work on a ship which spends all or most of its time outside GB and where the seafarers do not habitually embark and disembark their ship in GB. This case concerned seafarers working on Carnival's cruise ships, most of which were registered in Bermuda. See *Fleet Maritime Services (Bermuda) Ltd v The Pension Regulator*; High Court, QBDiv, Case No. CO/5667/2014, paras 3 and 77(i)–(iii). The two main industry-wide pension schemes are: the Ensign Retirement plan: www.ensignpensions.com [Accessed 25 June 2018]; and the Merchant Navy Ratings Pension scheme: www.rmt.org.uk/about/pensions/pensions-news/merchant-navy-ratings-pension-fund-mnrpf--rmt7116/ [Accessed 25 June 2018].

44 Shipowners may choose to adopt the Code of Conduct for the Merchant Navy (2013) (covering disciplinary procedures), agreed between Nautilus International, RMT, the UK Chamber of Shipping, and approved by the MCA: www.alphamarine.ie/assets/PDFs/Code-of-Conduct-for-the-Merchant-Navy.pdf [Accessed 24 June 2018]. Guidance on both disciplinary and grievance procedures, as well as a Code of Practice, can be obtained from ACAS: www.acas.org.uk/index.aspx?articleid=1878 [Accessed 24 June 2018].

45 Minimum Requirements Regulations, reg 10(1), Sch 1.

PARTICULAR PROVISIONS FOR TRAINEES

7.4 In recognising that some aspects of SEAs are not easily applicable to trainees (who are also 'seafarers' under UK MLC legislation), as most of them will be subject to a training agreement with their training provider or sponsor, rather than a SEA with the shipowner, so MGN 485 makes special provision for them.[46] So long as the trainee is provided with a training agreement, which complies with MGN 485, it will be treated as being 'substantially equivalent'[47] to a SEA (but note that 'employed apprentices' will still be required to be issued with a SEA).[48]

To comply, the training agreement between an approved training provider and a (trainee) seafarer will need to provide that:

- either through the training agreement itself; or
- through a combination of the training agreement and another agreement between the approved training provider and the shipowner (and, in such a case, the seafarer is to be informed and given a copy of relevant arrangements),

there are contractual arrangements in place to ensure that the seafarer has the equivalent information and protection in respect of employment conditions as would be the case under a UK SEA.[49]

The training agreement must, as a minimum, include:

1. the seafarer's full name, date of birth or age, and birthplace;
2. the training provider's name and address;
3. the place where, and date when, the training agreement was entered into;
4. the capacity in which the seafarer is to be engaged on the ship;
5. the amount and arrangements for payment of the training bursary, including information about charges for transfer of funds, and exchange rates, if applicable;
6. the provisions for the termination of the agreement, including the date fixed for its expiry, and the conditions entitling either party to terminate it, as well as the required notice period, which should not be less for the shipowner than for the seafarer;
7. the health and social security protection benefits to be provided to the seafarer;[50]
8. the seafarer's entitlement to repatriation;[51]

46 MGN 485 (M) 'Maritime Labour Convention, 2006: Seafarer Employment Agreements – Application to Trainees', para 1.1.

47 The concept of 'substantial equivalence' comes from MLC, Article VI, paras 3–4.

48 MGN 485, para 1.3.

49 MGN 485, paras 2.1–2.2.

50 See Chapters 17 (Medical care on board ship and ashore), 18 (Shipowners' liability) and 21 (Social security).

51 See Chapter 11 (Repatriation).

9. reference to any collective bargaining agreement that may be applicable;[52]
10. information about hours of work;[53]
11. information about the disciplinary and grievance procedures available to the seafarer;
12. information about any pension arrangements in place.[54]

If the training agreement contains a clause for the recovery of training costs, in the event that the seafarer fails to complete their training, then the clause must be equitable and transparent, and specify the nature of the costs purported to be recoverable. The following costs cannot be recovered: accommodation, food, catering, repatriation (unless arising out of the seafarer being in serious breach of their SEA obligations), medical expenses (unless the treatment is in connection with an injury or illness incurred otherwise than in the service of the ship, due to wilful misconduct, or intentionally concealed at the point of engagement).[55] Any such clause will have to be carefully drafted for it to be enforceable and, if applying in the case of a breach of contract by the trainee, could be struck out as a 'penalty clause' unless the amount set for recovery represents a genuine pre-estimate of loss suffered by the employer.[56]

JURISDICTION AND APPLICABLE LAW

7.5 It will be noted that, amongst the matters which must be addressed in SEAs, there is no express requirement for a jurisdiction and applicable law clause. The MLC and the UK have left this to be decided by the parties, although the SEA must be legally enforceable.[57] The only reference in the MLC to this issue is in connection with its Title 5 compliance and enforcement measures, which '... do not determine legal jurisdiction or a legal venue'.[58] An interesting analysis on the jurisdictional issues which may arise out of a SEA has been written by Jennifer Lavelle, who advises that the parties to a SEA give careful consideration to including provision on these matters.[59]

52 See footnote 32 above.
53 See Chapter 9 (Hours of work and hours of rest).
54 MGN 485, sub-paras 2.3.1–2.3.12.
55 MGN 485, para 2.6.
56 See Tolley's *Employment Handbook* (32nd edn, Lexis Nexis, 2018) 392, citing *Giraud UK Ltd v Smith* [2000] IRLR 763, and other cases.
57 MLC, Regulation 2.1, para 1.
58 MLC, Regulation 5, para 4.
59 Lavelle, J *The Maritime Labour Convention 2006: International Labour Law Redefined* (Informa Law from Routledge), 181–213, ch 9 'How to determine jurisdiction and governing law in disputes arising out of a seafarer's employment agreement'. Lavelle bases her analysis on the following EU instruments: Regulation (EU) 1215/2012 of the European Parliament and of the Council of 12 December 2012 on jurisdiction and the recognition and enforcement of judgments in civil and commercial matters (recast), 20.12.2012 L 351/1; Regulation (EC) 593/2008 of the European Parliament and of the Council of 17 June 2008 on the law applicable to contractual obligations (Rome I), 4.7.2008 L 177/6; and Regulation (EC) 864/2007 of the European Parliament and of the Council of 11 July 2007 on the law applicable to non-contractual obligations (Rome II), 31.7.2007 L 199/40.

THE LANGUAGE OF SEAs

7.6 For seafarers on UK ships, SEAs and supporting documentation, such as collective bargaining agreements, should normally be in English. However, in cases where these documents are written in other another language, English translations must be kept on board, and be available for inspection by the authorities.[60] It is not necessary to hold a translation of every individual SEA which is written in a foreign language; it will be sufficient to hold an English translation of each type of SEA (bearing in mind that there may be differences in form, terms and conditions, for particular groups of seafarers).[61]

SEAFARER TO HAVE OPPORTUNITY TO REVIEW THE SEA

7.7 Before a seafarer enters into their SEA, the shipowner (or, in the case of a trainee, approved training provider) must take reasonable steps to satisfy itself that, in respect of the SEA, the seafarer:

(a) had sufficient opportunity to review and take advice on the terms and conditions;

(b) received an explanation of their rights and responsibilities; and

(c) is entering into it freely.[62]

The SEA must contain a declaration, by the seafarer and the shipowner (or, where relevant, approved training provider), that the above requirements have been met.[63]

MINIMUM NOTICE PERIODS

7.8 The minimum period of notice, to terminate a SEA, is seven days (subject to exceptions on compassionate grounds or dismissals for gross misconduct), or any longer period specified in the SEA, but not so long as to be unduly restrictive.[64] The period of notice to be given by the seafarer must be no longer than that which the shipowner (or, in the case of trainee, the training provider) is required to give.[65]

For these purposes, the SEA should state what amounts to 'compassionate grounds' and 'gross misconduct'. The MCA leaves this for the parties to the SEA to decide, but gives examples of the death or serious illness of a close family member, or a serious breach or ongoing breaches of the Merchant Navy Code of Conduct if it is applicable.[66]

60 Minimum Requirements Regulations, regs 13, 14.
61 MGN 477, paras 8.1–8.3.
62 Minimum Requirements Regulations, reg 10(4)(a)–(c).
63 Minimum Requirements Regulations, reg 10(6).
64 Minimum Requirements Regulations, reg 11(1), (3). MGN 477, paras 6.1–6.4.
65 Minimum Requirements Regulations, reg 11(2).
66 MGN 477, para 6.3.

CONTINUATION OF SEA IF SEAFARER HELD CAPTIVE

7.9 Some forthcoming amendments to the MLC are relevant here, although they are not expected to come into force until 26 December 2020. In April 2018, the MLC Special Tripartite Committee agreed that, in the event of a seafarer being held in captivity by pirates or armed robbers, their SEA should continue to have effect, regardless of whether the date fixed for its expiry has passed or either party has given notice to suspend or terminate it. Furthermore, wages and other entitlements under the SEA, relevant CBA, applicable national laws, including the remittance of any allotments, must continue to be paid during the entire period of captivity. When in force, these provisions will be: MLC Standard A2.1, para 7(a)–(c); MLC Standard A2.2, para 7, and Guideline B2.5.1, para 8. The UK must have national provisions in place to implement these amendments by the date they come into force. See the full text of the amendments in Appendix 2.[67]

RECORD OF EMPLOYMENT

7.10 As soon as practicable after a seafarer's work on board comes to an end, the shipowner must provide the seafarer with a written record of their work.[68] The record must address the following matters:[69]

> 'Schedule 2
>
> Provision to be included in a written record of work on a ship
>
> 1. Name, port of registry, gross or registered tonnage and official number of the ship.
> 2. Description of voyage.
> 3. Capacity in which seafarer worked on the ship.
> 4. Date on which seafarer started work on the ship.
> 5. Date and location of seafarer's discharge from the ship.'[70]

The record must not contain any information about the quality of the seafarer's work, their wages or conduct.[71] The record may be entered in the seafarer's discharge book, or by the issue of a certificate of discharge, if the former is not produced.[72]

67 Third meeting of the Special Tripartite Committee established by the Governing Body in accordance with Article XIII of the Maritime Labour Convention, 2006, as amended (MLC, 2006): Text of the amendments adopted on 27 April 2018: www.ilo.org/wcmsp5/groups/public/---ed_norm/---normes/documents/meetingdocument/wcms_627161.pdf [Accessed 25 June 2018].
68 Minimum Requirements Regulations, reg 12(5).
69 Minimum Requirements Regulations, reg 12(5)–(6)(a).
70 Minimum Requirements Regulations, reg 12(6)(a), Sch 2.
71 Minimum Requirements Regulations, reg 6(b)–(c).
72 MGN 477, para 7.3.1.

LIST OF CREW AND YOUNG PERSONS

7.11 The requirement to maintain an up-to-date list of crew (a copy of which must be kept by the shipowner at an address in the UK) still applies, even if the seafarers have been issued with SEAs and are serving on a UK MLC ship.[73] For the list of crew, the MCA has produced Form MSF 4157, and its associated cover, Form 4156, which are contained at Annex 4 to MGN 477 (these supersede Forms ALC 1, ALC 1(a), and ALC 1(b)).

As stated in Chapter 3, a record of young persons (under the age of 18) is to be kept, using Form MSF 4158 (which supersedes Form ALC 1(c)) or similar form, with the list of crew, with a summary of the Merchant Shipping and Fishing Vessels (Health and Safety at Work) (Employment of Young Persons) Regulations 1998 (which is conveniently contained on Form 4158).[74]

The list of crew remains in force until all the persons entered thereon have been discharged.[75] The shipowner is required to submit the list to the Registrar-General of Shipping and Seamen, within seven days of the expiry of each period of six months after it is made.[76] The address is: Anchor Court, Keen Road, Cardiff CF24 5JW; email: seafarer_registry@mcga.gov.uk.

DISPUTES ARISING OUT OF SEAs

7.12 A seafarer who has a dispute in connection with their SEA may, in the first instance, lodge a complaint under the MLC on-board complaints procedure.[77] If that fails to resolve the issue, a complaint under the MLC on-shore complaints procedure may be made, if the ship is in a port of an MLC state.[78] Failing resolution, the seafarer should take legal advice on their contractual and statutory rights.

73 Merchant Shipping (Crew Agreements, Lists of Crew and Discharge of Seamen) Regulations 1991 (SI 1991/2144), regs 14, 15(1).

74 SI 1998/2411.

75 Merchant Shipping (Crew Agreements, Lists of Crew and Discharge of Seamen) Regulations 1991, r 19 (as amended by Merchant Shipping (Maritime Labour Convention) (Consequential and Minor Amendments) Regulations 2014 (SI 2014/1614), r 8(7)).

76 Merchant Shipping (Crew Agreements, Lists of Crew and Discharge of Seamen) Regulations 1991, r 20(2) (as amended by Merchant Shipping (Maritime Labour Convention) (Consequential and Minor Amendments) Regulations 2014 (SI 2014/1614), r 8(8)).

77 MGN 477, para 16.1. See MSN 1849 (M) 'Maritime Labour Convention, 2006: On-board Complaints Procedure'; MLC, Regulation 5.1.5 and Code.

78 MGN 477, para 16.2. See MGN 487 (M) 'Maritime Labour Convention, 2006: On-shore Complaints'. In foreign ports, it is recommended that the national maritime authority is contacted for details of their on-shore complaints procedure, which is required to be established under MLC, Regulation 5.2.2 and Code.

HARASSMENT AND BULLYING

7.13 The MCA recommends that shipowners should put in place procedures to deal with harassment and bullying, in accordance with the ECSA–ETF guidelines 'Eliminating Workplace Harassment and Bullying'.[79] Amendments to the non-mandatory Code B of the MLC are due to come into force on 8 January 2019, addressing harassment and bullying in a health and safety context, and are explained in Chapter 19 at para 19.43. The text of the amendments is set out in Appendix 2.

PROVISIONS IN RESPECT OF NON-UK SHIPS

7.14 Non-UK ships with MLC documentation, while they are in UK waters, must not operate unless they comply with MLC Standard A2.1, paragraphs 1 and 4.[80] In summary, paragraph 1 requires seafarers to be provided with a signed original of their SEA, and given the opportunity to examine it, and to be provided with a record of their employment. Paragraph 4 sets out the minimum particulars which the SEA must address, which are the same as those listed in Sch 1, Pt 1, paragraphs 1–12 and 14, and Pt 2, paragraphs 1 and 4 (see para 7.3 above).

OFFENCES

7.15 Any breach of the main provisions amounts to a criminal offence,[81] punishable on summary conviction by fines of up to level 3 to level 5 on the standard scale.[82] It is a defence for the accused to show that they took all reasonable steps to ensure compliance with the relevant provision.[83]

INSPECTION AND DETENTION OF UK SHIPS AND NON-UK SHIPS

7.16 The same powers of inspection and detention apply as described in Chapter 2.[84]

FUTURE AMENDMENTS TO THE MLC

7.17 When the 2018 amendments to the MLC come into force (which is likely to be 26 December 2020), ratifying states will be required to provide that:

79 MGN 477, paras 15.1–15.2; www.etf-europe.org/files/seealsodocs/41923/Guidelines%20 to%20shipping% 20 companies % 20EN.pdf [Accessed 25 June 2018].
80 Minimum Requirements Regulations, regs 3(3)–(4)(b)(ii), 15(1)(a)–(b).
81 Minimum Requirements Regulations, regs 10(3), (7), 12(2), 12(4), (8), 13(3), 14(2), 15(2)–(3).
82 Minimum Requirements Regulations, reg 59(1), (2)(a)–(c), (3)(a)–(b).
83 Minimum Requirements Regulations, reg 60.
84 Minimum Requirements Regulations, regs 54–56.

(a) SEAs continue for the entirety of any period in which a seafarer is held in captivity as a result of an act of piracy or armed robbery at sea; and (b) seafarers' wages, allotments and other entitlements must be fully paid during the entirety of any such period. These amendments will be inserted as Standard A2.1.7 and A2.2.7 and to Guideline B2.5.1.8. The full text of the amendments is set out in Appendix 2.

CHECKLIST FOR COMPLIANCE

7.18 Shipowner and employer:

- Every seafarer must be given an original signed SEA containing at least the mandatory information described above.
- Any representative who signs on behalf of the shipowner must be named in the DMLC, Pt II.
- The seafarer must: have an opportunity to review and take advice on the contents of the SEA; be given an explanation of their rights under the SEA; and have entered into their SEA freely. The SEA must contain a declaration to the effect that these requirements have been met.
- Ensure that a copy of the SEA and any applicable CBA is kept on board.
- Issue each seafarer with a written record of their employment at the end of the engagement – do not make any reference to the quality of the seafarer's work or their wages.
- Maintain an up-to-date list of crew – the shipowner must keep a copy at an address in the UK.
- Maintain a record of young persons on board.
- DMLC: observe the compliance provisions entered in Pt I, point 4, and enter details of compliance measures in Pt II, point 4.

Seafarer:

- Only enter into SEA freely with a clear understanding of its provisions. If in doubt, seek advice from a trade union or lawyer.

CHAPTER 8

Regulation 2.2: Wages

INTRODUCTION

8.1 The purpose of Regulation 2.2 of the MLC is to ensure that seafarers are paid for their services.[1]

The main provisions are set out in: the Merchant Shipping (Maritime Labour Convention) (Minimum Requirements for Seafarers etc) Regulations 2014[2] ('Minimum Requirements Regulations'); the Merchant Shipping (Seaman's Allotments) Regulations 1972[3] ('Allotment Regulations 1972'); and the Merchant Shipping (Seaman's Wages and Accounts) Regulations 1972[4] ('Wages and Accounts Regulations 1972'), the latter two of which have been amended by the Merchant Shipping (Maritime Labour Convention) (Consequential and Minor Amendments) Regulations 2014[5] ('Consequential Amendments Regulations'). MCA guidance is provided in MGN 478.[6]

1 MLC, Regulation 2.2, purpose.
2 SI 2014/1613.
3 SI 1972/1698.
4 SI 1972/1700.
5 SI 2014/1614.
6 MGN 478 (M) – MLC, 2006: Seafarers' Wages.

PAYMENT OF WAGES AND ACCOUNT OF WAGES

8.2 Each seafarer must be paid at no greater than monthly intervals, and the manner in which they will be paid, the amount (or formula used for calculating it) and the payment dates must be set out in their seafarer employment agreement (SEA).[7]

If any amount of wages or other remuneration payable under a SEA is not paid on the due date, interest must be paid on the unpaid amount at the rate of 20% per annum from the date on which the amount was due until the date of payment.[8] This penalty does not apply to the extent that the delay was due to: a mistake; a reasonable dispute as to liability; the act or default of the seafarer; or any other cause not being the wrongful act or default of the persons liable to make the payment or of their servants or agents.[9]

Account of seafarer's wages

8.3 The shipowner must ensure that an account of wages or other remuneration under a SEA is prepared and delivered to the seafarer, periodically at intervals not exceeding one month during the term of the SEA, and within one month of the SEA terminating.[10]

The account must include the following information:

- For employed seafarers:
  - (a) the name of the seafarer;
  - (b) the date of birth of the seafarer (if known);
  - (c) the number of the seafarer's current discharge book (if any);
  - (d) the capacity in which the seafarer worked on board the ship;
  - (e) the period covered by the account;
  - (f) the amounts payable for the period covered by the account; and
  - (g) the type and amount of any deductions made during the period covered by the account.[11]

  If any amounts have been determined by reference to a currency exchange rate, the details of the relevant exchange rate and any commission paid must be stated.[12]

7 Minimum Requirements Regulations, reg 10(1), Sch 1, Pt 2, paras 1–2, Pt 3, paras 1–2.
8 Minimum Requirements Regulations, reg 16(1).
9 Minimum Requirements Regulations, reg 16(2).
10 Minimum Requirements Regulations, reg 17(1)(a)–(b).
11 Minimum Requirements Regulations, reg 17(2)(a)–(g).
12 Minimum Requirements Regulations, reg 17(3).

- For self-employed seafarers:
  - (a) payments due;
  - (b) payments made (including any not falling within sub-paragraph (a)); and
  - (c) any rates of exchange and any commissions paid which are relevant to those payments.[13]

DEDUCTIONS

8.4 The employer may make deductions in respect of the following expenses already incurred by a seafarer: canteen bills (although note that meals are to be provided free of charge – see Chapter 16); goods supplies; radio or telephone calls (which may include access to the internet or emails); postage expenses; cash advances; and allotments.[14]

Furthermore, deductions may be made, at the request of the seafarer, for payments to be made to a: pension fund; charity; trade union; or friendly society.[15]

Subject to some conditions and limitations, the employer may also make a deduction of the actual expense or pecuniary loss incurred in consequence of:

(i) the seafarer's absence without leave which amounts to a breach of their SEA;[16]

(ii) any other breach or breaches of the seafarer's obligations as set out in their SEA;[17] and

(iii) dismissal from the ship for serious misconduct.[18]

The deduction in respect of paras (i) and (ii) is limited to £200.[19] As regards para (iii), there is now no set limit, and any such costs are likely to arise out of repatriating a seafarer who has been dismissed overseas for gross misconduct – see Chapter 11 on how a shipowner may recover repatriation and relief and maintenance costs in these circumstances.[20]

No deduction may be made (for absence without leave) where the seafarer satisfies the master that: their absence was due to an accident or mistake or some

13 Minimum Requirements Regulations, reg 17(4)(a)–(c).

14 Wages and Accounts Regulations 1972, regs 4(1), 5(a)(i)–(iv) (reg 4(1) has been amended by Consequential Amendments Regulations, reg 5(4); MGN 478, para 5.3(A)(i)–(vi).

15 Wages and Accounts Regulations 1972, reg 5(b); MGN 478, para 5.3(B)(vii)–(ix)(a)–(b).

16 Wages and Accounts Regulations 1972, reg 5(c), as amended by Consequential Amendments Regulations, reg 5(4).

17 Wages and Accounts Regulations 1972, reg 5(d), as amended by r 5(4) of the Consequential Amendments Regulations, reg 5(4).

18 Wages and Accounts Regulations 1972, reg 5(e), as inserted by Merchant Shipping (Seaman's Wages and Accounts) (Amendment) Regulations 1978 (SI 1978/1757), reg 2(2).

19 Wages and Accounts Regulations 1972, reg 6(a)–(b), as amended by Merchant Shipping (Seaman's Wages and Accounts) (Amendment) Regulations 1985 (SI 1985/340), reg 2(a).

20 MGN 478, para 5.6.

other cause beyond their control; and they took all reasonable precautions to avoid being absent.[21]

No deduction may be made in any of the scenarios (i) and (ii) above[22] unless the employer (or master) has complied with the provisions relating to giving the seafarer a notice of deduction and inviting the seafarer to make representations. The notice must be provided to the seafarer: at least 24 hours before their wages are due to be paid; or, if that is not possible, then before their wages are due to be paid (if possible).[23] If the latter is not possible, the notice most be sent by registered post to the seafarer's last known address.[24]

The notice must state that the employer is satisfied on reasonable grounds that there has been a breach or breaches, as the case may be, of the seafarer's obligations under their SEA and that, subject to the provisions of regulations 4 to 7 of the Merchant Shipping (Seamen's Wages and Accounts) Regulations 1972, the deduction specified in the notice appears to the employer to be authorised to be made from the wages due, and:

(i) identifies the relevant breaches of the SEA;

(ii) states the grounds for believing that such breaches have taken place;

(iii) specifies, with sufficient particulars to show how it is calculated, the amount of the actual expense or pecuniary loss incurred or sustained by the employer (and, if applicable, how it exceeds the maximum of the £200 which may be deducted); and

(iv) specifies the total amount of the deduction proposed to be made.[25]

Claims by an authority for maintenance of a seafarer's dependants

8.5 Subject to conditions, a 'responsible authority' has power to present a notice on the employer ordering it to retain a proportion of the seafarer's wages, which the authority has incurred in maintaining the seafarer's dependants, being their spouse and any person under the age of 19 in respect of whom they are liable to maintain or in respect of whom they are liable to make contributions to a local authority.[26] The amount of net wages that may be retained (in respect of one or more notices) is limited to: one half if the notice relates to one dependant only; or two-thirds if the notice relates to two or more dependants.[27] A 'responsible authority' means the Secretary of State, the Department of Health and Social

21 Wages and Accounts Regulations 1972, reg 7(a)–(b), respectively.

22 The notice provisions only apply to reg 5(c) or (d) and not to (e); Wages and Accounts Regulations 1972, reg 8(1).

23 Wages and Accounts Regulations 1972, reg 8(1)–(3)(a)(i)–(ii).

24 Wages and Accounts Regulations 1972, reg 8(3)(b).

25 Wages and Accounts Regulations 1972, reg 8(4)(i)–(iv), respectively, as amended by Merchant Shipping (Seaman's Wages and Accounts) (Amendment) Regulations 1985, reg 2(b).

26 Merchant Shipping Act 1995, s 40(1)–(2).

27 Merchant Shipping Act 1995, s 40(3)(a)–(b), respectively.

Services for Northern Ireland, a Health and Social Services Board acting on behalf of that Department, or (except in Northern Ireland) any local authority.[28]

Repatriation

8.6 As regards the limited circumstances in which the shipowner may recover the costs of repatriation when the seafarer is in serious default of their SEA obligations, see Chapter 11.

Allotments

8.7 Previously, seafarers were only entitled to allot a maximum of one half of their wages to no more than two persons; now there is no such limit on the amounts they may allot or the number of beneficiaries.[29] Allotments must be made promptly and directly to the person nominated by the seafarer.[30] The employer may recover the costs incurred in making payments by allotment but may not otherwise impose a charge for providing the service; costs which are ordinarily incurred in making payments to the seaman may not be recovered.[31] Any necessary currency exchanges must be made at a reasonable rate.[32] A model allotment note is set out at Annex 2 to MGN 478.

Continuation of SEA and payment of wages if seafarer held captive as a result of piracy or armed robbery at sea

8.8 Some future amendments to the MLC are relevant here, although they are not expected to come into force until 26 December 2020. In April 2018, the MLC Special Tripartite Committee agreed that, in the event of a seafarer being held in captivity by pirates or armed robbers, their SEA must continue to have effect, regardless of whether the date fixed for its expiry has passed or either party has given notice to suspend or terminate it.[33] Furthermore, wages and other entitlements under the SEA, relevant CBA, applicable national laws, including the remittance of any allotments, must continue to be paid during the entire

28 Merchant Shipping Act 1995, s 40(10).

29 Allotment Regulations 1972, regs 2(1)-(2), 3(1), as amended by Consequential Amendments Regulations, reg 4(2)–(3).

30 Allotment Regulations 1972, reg 6, as inserted by Consequential Amendments Regulations, reg 4(4).

31 Allotment Regulations 1972, reg 7(1)–(2), as inserted by Consequential Amendments Regulations, reg 4(4).

32 Allotment Regulations 1972, reg 7(3), as inserted by Consequential Amendments Regulations, reg 4(4).

33 Third meeting of the Special Tripartite Committee established by the Governing Body in accordance with Article XIII of the Maritime Labour Convention, 2006, as amended (MLC, 2006): Text of the amendments adopted on 27 April 2018: www.ilo.org/wcmsp5/groups/public/---ed_norm/---normes/documents/meetingdocument/wcms_627161.pdf [Accessed 25 June 2018].

period of captivity. When in force, these provisions will be: MLC Standard A2.1, para 7(a)–(c); MLC Standard A2.2, para 7, and Guideline B2.5.1, para 8. The UK is obliged to have national provisions in place to implement these amendments by the date they come into force. See the full text of the amendments in Appendix 2,[34] and Chapter 7 at para 7.17 on the effect that the amendments will have on SEAs.

MINIMUM WAGE LEVELS

8.9 Seafarers of many different nationalities work on UK ships, so the international context and agreements that set minimum wage levels should be kept in mind. A SEA may incorporate a collective bargaining agreement which sets wage levels.[35]

The MLC guidelines recommend that ratifying states should establish procedures for determining minimum wages for seafarers, in consultation with shipowners' and seafarers' representatives.[36] Furthermore, they recommend that the basic wages for a calendar month for an able seafarer should not be less than the rate set by the Joint Maritime Commission (JMC) or other body recognised by the ILO.[37] The current minimum level set by the JMC remains at US $614 per month; the next meeting of the JMC on this issue is in November 2018.

Other negotiations take place through the International Bargaining Forum (IBF), between the International Transport Workers' Federation (ITF) and the Joint Negotiating Group (which is made up of the International Maritime Employers' Council, the International Mariners Management Association of Japan and the Korean Shipowners' Association).[38] Negotiations take place every two years, following which ITF-affiliated unions negotiate with shipowners in their own country, which can result in national or company-level IBF agreements, the terms of which must be within the agreed IBF framework.

UK national minimum wage

8.10 The National Minimum Wage Act 1998 (NMWA) expressly applies to seafarers on UK ships, unless their employment is wholly outside the UK, or they are not ordinarily resident in the UK.[39] The requirement for UK residence will exclude

34 Third meeting of the Special Tripartite Committee established by the Governing Body in accordance with Article XIII of the Maritime Labour Convention, 2006, as amended (MLC, 2006): Text of the amendments adopted on 27 April 2018: www.ilo.org/wcmsp5/groups/public/---ed_norm/---normes/documents/meetingdocument/wcms_627161.pdf [Accessed 25 June 2018].

35 Minimum Requirements Regulations, reg 10(1)(a), (2); Sch 1, Pt 1, para 4.

36 MLC, Guideline B2.2.3.

37 MLC, Guideline B2.2.4.

38 ITF – About the IBF: www.itfseafarers.org/about-IBF.cfm [Accessed 30 June 2018].

39 NMWA 1998, s 40.

many seafarers who ordinarily reside in low-cost labour-supplying countries, such as the Philippines and India, who are often paid at rates well below the UK NMW level.

The NMWA makes no express reference to the position of seafarers on non-UK ships; however, the government has recently issued guidance on how section 1 (which sets out the conditions on applicability for workers in general) can be interpreted to include seafarers who do not fall within section 40.[40] Section 1 provides that the NMW will apply to a worker who 'is working, or ordinarily works, in the United Kingdom under his contract',[41] and the guidance sets out the circumstances in which a seafarer should be treated as working in the UK, and provides:

> '• All seafarers working on ships within the UK internal waters and ports are entitled to be paid at least the NMW.
>
> • This is regardless of where the ship is registered, or where the worker ordinarily works or resides.
>
> ...
>
> Seafarers on a non-UK flagged ship will be entitled to the NMW for work performed outside the UK if they "ordinarily work" in the UK.
>
> It will be necessary to consider the circumstances of the employment to ascertain whether the seafarer has a sufficiently strong connection to the UK. Criteria considered when deciding whether someone ordinarily works in the UK might include:
>
> • where the seafarer's tour of duty begins and ends;
>
> • where the seafarer is subject to income tax and National Insurance Contributions;
>
> • the currency that the seafarer is paid in.'[42]

40 Over recent years, several cases have come before the courts and tribunals on the issue of the extra-territorial application of British employment law to seafarers: (1) *Diggins v Condor Marine Crewing Services Ltd* [2010] ICR 213 (CA), Elias LJ (as he then was) approving the judgment of HHJ Burke in the EAT; seafarer on Bahamian-flagged ship held to have the right not to be unfairly dismissed under s 94 of the Employment Rights 1996; the relevant issue is where the seafarer is based, not the employer; (2) *Windstar Management Services Ltd v Harris* (UKEAT/0001//16/LA) (seafarer's tour of duty starting in London airport: UK held to be the base, even though work did not commence until joining a cruise ship overseas (see paras 44–47); (3) *Seahorse Maritime Ltd v Nautilus International* ((UKEAT/0281/16/LA): UK-based seafarers who travelled to perform work on stationary ships held to be akin to international commuters, to which the collective consultation provisions of s 188 of the Trade Union and Labour Relations (Consolidation) Act 1992 applied; the factors showing that they had a sufficiently strong connection with Great Britain and British employment law were: English law governed their contracts; their contracts were administered by an agency based in England (albeit the employer was based in Guernsey); the seafarers lived in England, which is where they started and finished their work, as travel to and from the ships was within their employment duties; Seahorse appealed the EAT's ruling to the Court of Appeal, where the hearing was held on 26 July 2018 – judgment is awaited. See also the leading (non-seafarer) cases on the territorial extent of British employment law: *Lawson v Serco Ltd* [2006] IRLR 289 (HL); and *Ravat v Halliburton Manufacturing & Services Ltd* [2012] IRLR 315.

41 NMWA, s 1(2)(b).

42 Guide to the application of the Equality Act 2010 and the National Minimum Wage for Seafarers (published January 2018): assets.publishing.service.gov.uk/government/uploads/system/uploads/attachment_data/file/674596/seafarers-employment-rights-minimum-wage.pdf [Accessed 19 September 2018].

The effect of the Equality Act 2010 should also be taken into account. The Equality Act is applied to seafarers on UK ships in prescribed circumstances by the Equality Act 2010 (Work on Ships and Hovercraft) Regulations 2011.[43] The Regulations contain specific provisions on pay, which permits employers to pay lower wages to seafarers who applied for work, or were recruited, outside Great Britain, but only if they are not a British citizen, a national of another EEA State, or a national of a designated state.[44] The Regulations permit discrimination, to that extent, on the basis of nationality. Identical provisions apply in Northern Ireland, which has its own equality legislation.

Before the Regulations came into force, this issue was regulated by section 9 of the Race Relations Act 1976, which allowed discrimination on the grounds of nationality in respect of seafarers serving on UK ships, if they had been recruited outside the UK, regardless of their nationality, so even EEA seafarers were adversely affected. The EU Commission considered this to be an infringement of EU law on the free movement of workers within the EU and similar agreements with non-EU countries which prohibit discrimination.[45] This led to the changes made by the 2011 Regulations, which extend protection against discrimination to wider categories of seafarers than did the repealed section 9.

REMEDIES FOR A CLAIM FOR UNPAID WAGES

8.11 Seafarers may make a contractual claim for unpaid wages in a court or tribunal in a country which has jurisdiction to hear their claim. This will depend on, amongst other things, the jurisdiction and applicable law clause in their SEA.[46]

A statutory claim for deduction of wages may be made to the UK employment tribunal during or after employment.[47] However, this remedy only applies to a seafarer who: (1) is serving on a UK ship, does not work wholly outside the UK, and ordinarily resides in the UK;[48] or (2) is based in the UK or has a sufficiently close connection to Great Britain and British employment law.[49] A three-

43 SI 2011/1771.

44 Equality Act 2010 (Work on Ships and Hovercraft) Regulations 2011, reg 5. A 'designated state' means the countries of the African, Caribbean and Pacific Group of States, the Kingdom of Morocco, Montenegro, the Most Serene Republic of San Marino, the People's Democratic Republic of Algeria, the Principality of Andorra, the Republic of Albania, the Republic of Croatia, the Republic of Macedonia, the Republic of Tunisia, the Republic of Turkey, the Russian Federation or the Swiss Confederation: reg 2(1).

45 Free movement of workers: Commission requests United Kingdom to end pay discrimination of non-UK seafarers: http://europa.eu/rapid/press-release_IP-11-82_en.htm [Accessed 19 September 2018].

46 See the article 'How to determine jurisdiction and governing law in disputes arising out of a seafarer's employment agreement' by J Lavelle (referred to in Chapter 7).

47 Employment Rights Act 1996, s 23.

48 Employment Rights Act 1996, s 199(7)–(8)(b).

49 See footnote 40 above on the relevant case law.

month time limit applies, which is 'paused' during the mandatory ACAS early conciliation procedure.[50]

After employment has ended, a contractual claim can also be made to the employment tribunal.[51] This is subject to a three-month time limit beginning with the effective date of termination of the contract.[52] Again, time is 'paused' during the mandatory ACAS early conciliation procedure.[53]

NON-UK SHIPS, WITH MLC DOCUMENTATION, IN UK WATERS

8.12 When a non-UK ship, with MLC documentation, is in UK waters, it must comply with MLC Standard A2.2, paragraph 2 (seafarers to be given a monthly account of payments due and amounts paid).[54]

OFFENCES

8.13 Non-compliances with the main provisions amount to criminal offences, punishable on summary conviction to a fine not exceeding level 2 on the standard scale.[55] In respect of offences under the Minimum Requirements Regulations, it is a defence for the accused to show that they took all reasonable steps to comply with the relevant provision.[56] There is no statutory defence in respect of the offences under regulation 7(4) (on charges and exchange rates in connection with making allotments) of the Allotment Regulations 1972.

INSPECTION AND DETENTION OF SHIPS

8.14 The inspection and detention powers, as set out in Chapter 2, apply to the obligations set out in the Minimum Requirements Regulations, as detailed above.[57]

50 Employment Tribunals Act 1996, s 18(a) (see Regulation 2.4 where the ACAS early conciliation procedure is discussed).
51 Employment Tribunals Extension of Jurisdiction (England and Wales) Order 1994 (SI 1994/1623), arts 3(c), 6; Employment Tribunals Extension of Jurisdiction (Scotland) Order 1994 (SI 1994/1624), arts 3(c), 6.
52 Employment Tribunals Extension of Jurisdiction (England and Wales) Order 1994, art 7; Employment Tribunals Extension of Jurisdiction (Scotland) Order 1994, art 7.
53 Employment Tribunals Act 1996, s 18(1)(g)–(h), in respect of: England and Wales; and Scotland, respectively. See Regulation 2.4 where the ACAS early conciliation procedure is discussed.
54 Minimum Requirements Regulations, reg 18.
55 Allotment Regulations 1972, reg 7(4)–(5), as inserted by Consequential Amendments Regulations, reg 4(4); Minimum Requirements Regulations, regs 17(5), 18(2) and 59(4)(a)–(b).
56 Minimum Requirements Regulations, reg 60.
57 Minimum Requirements Regulations, regs 54–56.

CHECKLIST FOR COMPLIANCE

8.15

- Seafarers must be paid at least on a monthly basis and given an account of their wages showing the amount due and deductions to be made.
- Enter details of wages (or formula used for calculating them) in SEA.
- Note the provisions on deductions and circumstances in which a notice of deduction must be given to the seafarer.
- Set up an allotment for any seafarer who requests one. Any exchange rates must be made at a reasonable rate. Only the costs incurred in making an allotment may be recovered by the shipowner, who may not impose its own charge for providing the service.
- DMLC: observe UK requirements in Pt I, point 14, and note compliance measures in Pt II, point 14.

CHAPTER 9

Regulation 2.3: Hours of Work and Hours of Rest

INTRODUCTION

9.1 The purpose of Regulation 2.3 of the MLC is to ensure that seafarers have regulated hours of work or hours of rest. The provisions are set out in the Merchant Shipping (Maritime Labour Convention) (Hours of Work) Regulations 2018[1] ('the 2018 Regulations'), which came into force on 6 April 2018 and revoke most of the Merchant Shipping (Maritime Labour Convention) (Hours of Work) (Amendments) Regulations 2014[2] ('the 2014 Regulations').[3]

The 2018 Regulations also implement most of the provisions of Council Directive 1999/63/EC,[4] as amended by Council Directive 2009/13/EC,[5] as well as the relevant articles of EU Directives concerning port state control and flag state control.

Guidance on UK implementation is provided in MSN 1877.[6]

1 SI 2018/58.
2 SI 2014/308.
3 2014 Regulations, reg 30(c).
4 Council Directive 1999/63/EC of 21 June 1999 concerning the Agreement on the organisation of working time of seafarers concluded by the European Community Shipowners' Associations (ECSA) and the Federation of Transport Workers' Unions in the European Union (FST) (now known as the European Transport Workers' Federation (ETF), OJ, L 167/33, 2.7.1999.
5 Council Directive 1999/63/EC of 16 February 2009 implementing the Agreement concluded by the ECSA and the ETF on the Maritime Labour Convention, 2006, and amending Directive 1999/63/EC, OJ, L 124/30, 20.5.2009.
6 MSN 1877(M) – MLC, 2006: Hours of Work and Entitlement to Leave.

APPLICATION

9.2 The 2018 Regulations apply one set of specified provisions to UK ships, wherever they may be, and to 'non-MLC ships' while they are in UK waters;[7] they also apply some of their other provisions to 'MLC ships' while they are in UK waters.[8] The following definitions are therefore important:

> '"MLC ship" means a sea-going ship which is not a United Kingdom ship if–
>
> (a) the Maritime Labour Convention has come into force for the State whose flag the ship is entitled to fly; and
>
> (b) the ship carries–
>
> (i) a Maritime Labour Certificate to which a Declaration of Maritime Labour Compliance is attached; or
>
> (ii) an interim Maritime Labour Certificate;
>
> "non-MLC ship" means a sea-going ship which is neither a United Kingdom ship nor an MLC ship;'[9]

It should be noted that a 'non-MLC ship' could still include a ship which is registered with an MLC-ratifying state, as ships which are under 500 GT and not operating internationally are not required to carry a Maritime Labour Certificate (although the owner may apply for voluntary certification).[10]

The 2018 Regulations do not apply to: (a) pleasure vessels; (b) fishing vessels; (c) warships or naval auxiliaries; or (d) vessels which are not ordinarily engaged in commercial activities.[11] However, unusually for MLC legislation, they do apply to 'ships of traditional build' (except reg 17 on the right to shore leave).[12]

For these purposes, 'seafarer' means 'any person, including a master, who is employed or engaged or who works in any capacity on board a ship and whose normal place of work is on a ship, other than a seafarer who is subject to any requirement contained in the Merchant Shipping (Working Time: Inland Waterways) Regulations 2003 [SI 2003/3049]'.[13]

UK SHIPS; AND NON-MLC SHIPS IN UK WATERS

9.3 This section sets out the provisions which apply to UK ships, wherever they may be, and to 'non-MLC ships' while they are in UK waters.

7 2018 Regulations, reg 3(1)(a)–(j).
8 2018 Regulations, reg 3(2)(a)–(i).
9 2018 Regulations, reg 2(1).
10 MLC, Regulation 5.1.3.1(a)–(b).
11 2018 Regulations, reg 3(4)(a)–(d).
12 2018 Regulations, reg 3(3).
13 2018 Regulations, reg 2(2)(a), recently amended by the Merchant Shipping (Working Time: Inland Waterways) (Amendment) Regulations 2017 (SI 2017/1149).

Minimum hours of rest

9.4 Under the MLC, ratifying states must establish a system of maximum hours of work or minimum hours of rest.[14] The UK has chosen the latter, which provides that the minimum hours of rest are:

(a) 10 hours in any 24-hour period; and

(b) 77 hours in any seven-day period.

Subject to any authorised exception being granted by the MCA (as set out below), the 10 hours of rest may be divided into no more than two periods, one of which is to be at least six hours in length.[15] For these purposes, '"hours of rest" means time outside hours of work and does not include short breaks', and '"hours of work" means time during which a seafarer is required to do work on the business of the ship'.[16]

The persons responsible for ensuring that a seafarer gets the minimum hours of rest are the shipowner, the employer (where different), and the master.[17]

Seafarers may still be required to participate during their hours of rest in a muster, drill or training session held under the Merchant Shipping (Musters, Training and Decision Support Systems) Regulations 1999, but this must be conducted in a way which minimises disturbance of hours of rest and does not induce fatigue.[18] Furthermore, a seafarer who is on-call may be required to do call-outs during hours of rest, but must be provided with an adequate compensatory rest period for any call-out work during such hours.[19] However, on-call time in itself does not count as working time, unless the seafarer actually performs work.[20]

The master may require a seafarer to work any hours of work necessary for the immediate safety of the ship, persons on board or cargo, or for the purpose of giving assistance to another ship or to a person in distress at sea.[21] The master must ensure that any such seafarer is provided with an adequate rest period as soon as practicable after the normal situation has been restored.[22]

Authorised exceptions

9.5 The MCA may authorise collective agreements or workforce agreements which provide for some exceptions.[23] However, the relevant provisions do not

14 MLC, Standard A2.3.1.
15 2018 Regulations, reg 6(1)–(2).
16 2018 Regulations, reg 2(1).
17 2018 Regulations, reg 5(1)–(2).
18 2018 Regulations, reg 5(3)(a)–(b).
19 2018 Regulations, reg 5(4)(a)–(b).
20 MSN 1877, para 4.1.
21 2018 Regulations, reg 11(1).
22 2018 Regulations, reg 11(2).
23 2018 Regulations, reg 7(1)(a)–(b).

permit any exceptions to the requirement for seafarers to have a minimum 10 hours of rest in any 24-hour period.

Exceptions to the minimum 77 hours rest in any seven-day period

9.6 The authorised agreement must require that:

(a) there are at least 70 hours total rest in any period of seven days;

(b) the exceptions do not apply in relation to a period of more than two consecutive weeks; and

(c) the interval between any two periods of exceptions is at least twice the duration of the longer of the two periods.[24]

Exceptions to the requirement that the rest break cannot be divided into more than two periods

9.7 The authorised agreement must require that the minimum 10 hours of rest are divided into three periods:

(a) one of the three periods is at least six hours long, and neither of the two other periods are less than one hour long;

(b) intervals between consecutive periods do not exceed 14 hours each; and

(c) the exceptions do not apply to more than two 24-hour periods in any seven-day period.[25]

Other exceptions

9.8 The MCA may also authorise other exceptions in such an agreement, which are not subject to the conditions set out in paragraphs 9.6 and 9.7 above, for ships which: (a) operate only within 60 miles of a safe haven; (b) are not engaged in the transport of cargo or passengers; and (c) do not operate to or from, or call at, any port in a country other than the UK.[26] A 'safe haven' is a harbour or shelter of any kind which affords entry and protection from the weather.[27]

For these purposes, any 'collective agreement' must be between an independent trade union and an employer or employers' association.[28] For a trade union to be 'independent', it must be free from any dominance, control, interference (arising

24 2018 Regulations, reg 7(2)(a)–(c).

25 2018 Regulations, reg 7(3)(a)–(c).

26 2018 Regulations, reg 7(4)(a)–(c).

27 2018 Regulations, reg 7(5).

28 2018 Regulations, reg 2(1); Trade Union and Labour Relations (Consolidation) Act 1992 ('the 1992 Act'), s 178; 2018 Regulations, reg 4(a)(i): a collective agreement within the meaning of Industrial Relations (Northern Ireland) Order 1992 (SI 1992/807) (NI 5), art 2(2).

from financial, material or other support) from an employer or employers' association.[29]

A 'workforce agreement' is one between an employer and its employees or their representatives, which meets the conditions in Schedule 1 to the 2018 Regulations.[30] Amongst other things, it must be in writing, it can only be valid for a maximum period of five years, and it must apply to all of the relevant members of the workforce, or to all of the relevant members of the workforce who belong to a particular group.[31]

Records

9.9 The master (or authorised person) must maintain records (in English and in the working language of the ship, if different) of each seafarer's daily hours of rest in accordance with the format (at Annex B) and other requirements of MSN 1877.[32] The records must be endorsed by the master (or authorised person) and the relevant seafarer, and endorsed by a relevant inspector at appropriate intervals; a copy of the endorsed record must be given to the seafarer.[33] On ships with many departments, such as cruise ships, the master may delegate the heads of each department to maintain records relating to their staff, although the shipowner, employer and master are ultimately responsible for ensuring that seafarers are provided with at least the minimum hours of rest.[34] The records must be retained for a period of at least one year.[35]

Posting up of tables

9.10 The master (or authorised person) must ensure that the following tables are posted in a prominent place in the ship: a table of scheduled watchkeeping; and a table of scheduled hours of rest.[36] The tables must: contain the information specified in MSN 1877; be in the format specified in that MSN, or in a format substantially like it; and be in English and in the working language of the ship.[37] A model format for a table of shipboard working arrangements is set out at

29 1992 Act, s 5.
30 2018 Regulations, reg 2(1).
31 2018 Regulations, Sch 1, para 1(a)–(c)(i)–(ii).
32 2018 Regulations, reg 12(1)–(3); MSN 1877(M) Amendment 1, MLC, 2006: Hours of Work and Entitlement to Leave – Application of the Merchant Shipping (Maritime Labour Convention) (Hours of Work) Regulations 2018.
33 2018 Regulations, reg 12(4)–(6). For these purposes, reg 2(1) provides that a 'relevant inspector' means any person mention in Merchant Shipping Act 1995, s 258(1), being a surveyor of ships, superintendent, or any person appointed by the Secretary of State to exercise powers under that section.
34 2018 Regulations, reg 5(1)–(2)(a)–(c); MSN 1877, para 3.3.
35 MSN 1877, para 8.2.
36 2018 Regulations, reg 9(1)(a)–(b), respectively.
37 2018 Regulations, reg 9(2)(a)–(c), respectively.

Annex A(i) to MSN 1877; selected texts setting out the requirements of the hours of work and rest regimes of the MLC and the STCW Convention are set out at Annex A(ii).

The MCA advises that, in producing the tables, account should be taken of the following factors: trade and type of operation; type and size of ship; construction and technical equipment of the ship; manning levels and changes in crew numbers due to crew changes and sickness; the maximum period of continuous watchkeeping; minimum rest periods; total workload; the seriousness of irregular working hours and their contribution to causing fatigue; and the importance of scheduling reasonably stable working hours over a voyage.[38] Reference should also be made to MGN 505.[39]

Carriage of documents and duty to supply information

9.11 It is the responsibility of the shipowner and the master to ensure that a copy of the 2018 Regulations, MSN 1877, and any collective agreements or workforce agreements authorised under reg 7 (exceptions to minimum hours of rest) of the 2018 Regulations are carried at all times on board ship in an easily accessible place.[40]

The shipowner must supply the MCA with any information it requests in relation to watchkeepers and other seafarers working at night.[41] This may include records of hours of rest, any health assessment requested or carried out, and any measures taken to protect their health and safety; such a request is most likely following a complaint from a seafarer or report of an accident or incident.[42]

MLC SHIPS IN UK WATERS

9.12 This section sets out the UK provisions which apply to non-UK ships carrying valid MLC certification while they are in UK waters.[43] These are the standards to which they will be subject, if inspected by UK port state control.

Maximum hours of work or minimum hours of rest

9.13 The shipowner, master and employer must ensure that seafarers are provided with hours of work or hours of rest in accordance with Standard A2.3

38 MSN 1877, paras 6.4(a)–(h), respectively.
39 MGN 505 (M): Human element guidance – Part 1; Fatigue and fitness for duty: Statutory duties, causes of fatigue and guidance on good practice.
40 2018 Regulations, reg 12(7).
41 2018 Regulations, reg 14.
42 MSN 1877, para 9.1.
43 2018 Regulations, regs 2(1), 3(2)(a)–(i).

of the MLC.[44] The ship's declaration of maritime labour compliance, Pt I (at point 6), will state whether the flag state has chosen the maximum hours of work or minimum hours of rest regime, which must comply with the following:

- maximum hours of work:
  - (i) 14 hours in any 24-hour period; and
  - (ii) 72 hours in any seven-day period;

  or
- minimum hours of rest:
  - (i) 10 hours in any 24-hour period; and
  - (ii) 77 hours in any seven-day period.[45]

Table of working arrangements

9.14 The master (or authorised person) must post a table of the working shipboard arrangements in accordance with paragraphs 10 and 11 of Standard A2.3 of the MLC.[46]

The table must be posted in an easily accessible place and contain, for every seafarer, their schedule of service at sea and in port, and the maximum hours of work or the minimum hours of rest required by the flag state or in any applicable collective agreement.[47] It must be in a standardised format, in the working language of the ship and in English.[48]

Exceptions for emergencies

9.15 The usual exception allowing work during an emergency, followed by an adequate rest period for seafarers who perform work during a scheduled rest period, applies – as set out at paragraph 9.4 above.[49]

Records of hours of work or rest

9.16 The master (or authorised person) must maintain records of seafarers' daily hours of rest or work and provide copies to seafarers in accordance with the provisions of MLC, Standard A2.3, paragraph 12.[50] The records must be: in

44 2018 Regulations, reg 8(1)–(2).
45 MLC, Standard A2.3, para 5(a)–(b).
46 2018 Regulations, reg 10.
47 MLC, Standard, A2.3, para 10(a)–(b).
48 MLC, Standard, A2.3, para 11.
49 2018 Regulations, reg 11.
50 2018 Regulations, reg 13.

a standardised format; in the working language of the ship and in English; and endorsed by the master (or authorised person) and the seafarer.[51]

COMPLIANCE AND ENFORCEMENT

9.17 For details of the powers of inspection and detention, criminal offences, seafarers' remedies and the restriction against contracting out, see Chapter 10, which covers entitlement to annual leave which is also implemented by the 2018 Regulations.

DMLC: observe UK provisions as entered in Pt I, point 6, and enter implementing provisions in Pt II, point 6.

RESTRICTION AGAINST CONTRACTING OUT

9.18 Other than the permissible exceptions which the MCA may authorise if incorporated in a collective agreement or a workforce agreement, any agreement is void to the extent that it purports to exclude or limit the operation of the 2018 Regulations, or to preclude a claim. However, there are some exceptions to the general prohibition against contracting out. The exceptions relate to an agreement to refrain from instituting or continuing proceedings where ACAS has taken conciliation action under sections 18A to 18C of the Employment Tribunals Act 1996 (the agreement is set out in a 'COT 3 Form'), or where the prescribed conditions are met, including that the seafarer must obtain advice from an independent adviser on the terms and effect of the agreement (which are the same as those in the general employment law applying to settlement agreements).[52]

51 MLC, Standard A2.3, para 12.
52 2018 Regulations, reg 28.

CHAPTER 10

Regulation 2.4: Entitlement to Leave

INTRODUCTION

10.1 The purpose of Regulation 2.4 of the MLC is to ensure that seafarers have adequate leave.[1] This must be paid leave and granted under appropriate conditions.[2] In addition, seafarers are to be granted shore leave to benefit their health and well-being and consistent with the operational requirements of their positions.[3]

UK SHIPS; AND NON-MLC SHIPS IN UK WATERS

10.2 The provisions are set out in the Merchant Shipping (Maritime Labour Convention) (Hours of Work) Regulations 2018[4] ('2018 Regulations'), which came into force on 6 April 2018 and revoke most of the Merchant Shipping (Maritime Labour Convention) (Hours of Work) (Amendments) Regulations 2014[5] ('2014 Regulations').

The right to paid leave applies to employed seafarers and to those who are 'engaged'.[6] An employed seafarer is one who is serving (or has served) under a contract of employment.[7] A seafarer who is engaged means one who is serving:

1 MLC, Regulation 2.4, purpose.
2 MLC, Regulation 2.4, para 1.
3 MLC, Regulation 2.4, para 2.
4 SI 2018/58.
5 SI 2014/308.
6 2018 Regulations, reg 15(1).
7 2018 Regulations, reg 2(2)(c).

> '... under a contract, whether express or implied, and (if it is express) whether oral or in writing, whereby the seafarer undertakes to do or perform personally any work or services for another party to the contract whose status is not by virtue of the contract that of a client or customer of any profession or business undertaking carried out by the seafarer;'.[8]

An 'engaged' seafarer would be serving under a 'contract for services' and entitled to paid leave.[9] However, a genuinely self-employed seafarer who is in business on their own account would be excluded from this right.[10]

The entitlement is to: paid annual leave of two and a half days for each month of employment in the leave year and pro rata for incomplete months; and additional paid leave of eight days in each leave year and pro rata for incomplete years.[11] This implements into UK law the mandatory MLC Standard 2.4.2 (which provides for a minimum of two and a half days' paid leave per month) and the non-mandatory Guideline B2.4.1.4(a) (which recommends that public holidays, of which there are eight in the UK, should not be counted as part of paid annual leave). Therefore, the UK has chosen to make it compulsory for eight additional days' paid leave to be granted in lieu of public holidays. During the leave period, seafarers should be paid at their normal level of remuneration.[12]

The leave may be taken in instalments; it may not be replaced by payment in lieu, except where the seafarer's employment is terminated.[13] Seafarers should be permitted to take their paid annual leave in a place with which they have a substantial connection, which will normally be their repatriation destination.[14] Unlike the Working Time Regulations 1998,[15] the 2018 Regulations do not contain provisions requiring the employee or employer to give notice to take or cancel leave, respectively.[16] The practical arrangements for, and the time for, taking leave are for agreement between the employer and the seafarer,[17] and may be set out in the seafarers' employment agreements or a collective agreement.

The prohibition against justified absences from work being counted as annual leave only applies to the compulsory MLC-derived leave of two and a half days per

8 2018 Regulations, reg 2(2)(b).
9 MSN 1877, para 2.1.
10 The definitions of 'employed' and 'engaged' are virtually the same as those set out in Employment Rights Act 1996, s 230(1), (3)(a) for 'employee' and 'worker', respectively. For a discussion on the distinction and legal consequences which flow from those terms and that of 'self-employment' as regards the applicability of rights enshrined in British employment law, see Tolley's *Employment Handbook* (32nd edn, Lexis Nexis, 2018), 401–417 (contributed by Joseph Barrett).
11 2018 Regulations, reg 15(1)(a)–(b), respectively.
12 MSN 1877, para 10.9.
13 2018 Regulations, reg 15(2)(a)–(b), respectively.
14 MSN 1877, para 10.14.
15 SI 1998/1833.
16 Working Time Regulations 1998, reg 15.
17 MSN 1877, paras 10.8, 10.13.

month (and not to the additional eight days' leave per year).[18] Justified absences from work include any absence authorised by: any enactment; any contract between the seafarer's employer and the seafarer; any collective agreement or workplace agreement; or custom and practice.[19]

The MCA also sets out the following as examples of justified absences which should not be counted as part of paid annual leave:

- 'absence from work to attend an approved maritime vocational training course, or any course which the employer requires to be undertaken;

  "approved maritime vocational training course" means any training course approved by the MCA (or another competent authority) for seafarer training required for the role currently undertaken or, in the case of a cadet, for the completion of a cadetship or for the seafarer's next certificate of competency;
- periods of absence as a result of sickness or injury (unless, in the case of a seafarer on sick leave, the seafarer chooses to take paid annual leave);
- leave arising as a result of any statutory entitlement applicable to the individual seafarer, such as maternity or paternity leave;
- temporary shore leave, other than in cases where the seafarer requests annual leave while the ship is in port;
- compensatory leave;'[20]

Young seafarers

10.3 Consideration should be given to the need to facilitate leave for young seafarers under the age of 18 years who have served for six months (or other shorter agreed period) on foreign-going ships, where the seafarer has not returned to their country of residence in that time and will not do so in the subsequent three months of the voyage; the MCA recommends that the shipowner should offer to repatriate the seafarer so that they can take any leave earned during the voyage.[21]

Emergency recall from leave

10.4 A seafarer who is taking paid annual leave should be recalled only in cases of extreme emergency and with their consent.[22]

18 2018 Regulations, reg 15(3); MLC, Standard A2.4, para 2.
19 2018 Regulations, reg 15(4)(a)–(b), respectively.
20 MSN 1877, para 10.10.
21 MSN 1877, para 10.15. This follows MLC, Guideline B2.4.4.1.
22 MSN 1877, para 10.16.

Leave year

10.5 The date for the commencement of the leave year is to be agreed by the employer and the seafarer. However, if there is no such agreement, the following provisions apply: if the employment began on or before 30 June 2002, the leave year should be treated as beginning on that date and each anniversary thereafter; where the employment commenced after 30 June 2002, the leave year begins on the date on which employment begins and each subsequent anniversary.[23]

Shore leave

10.6 The shipowner and the master must ensure that shore leave is granted to seafarers, to benefit their health and well-being, where consistent with the operational requirements of their positions.[24]

Inspection and detention

10.7 There is power to inspect a ship[25] and detain it where there are clear grounds for believing that there are clearly hazardous conditions on board, or serious or repeated breaches of the 2018 Regulations (which apply to it) or the MLC.[26]

There are provisions on release of ships, arbitration and compensation for an invalid detention.[27]

The MCA is required to publish, at least every month, information concerning ships which have been detained under regulation 21 of the 2018 Regulations in a UK port in the previous month, which it does through the Paris MoU on port state control.[28] The reporting form used by the MCA is at Annex C to MSN 1877.

MLC SHIPS IN UK WATERS

Entitlement to paid leave

10.8 The employer must ensure that the seafarer is given paid annual leave in accordance with Regulation 2.4 of the MLC.[29] This is a reference to mandatory paid leave of a minimum of two and a half days per month, under Standard A2.4.2.

23 MSN 1877, para 10.17.
24 2018 Regulations, reg 17.
25 2018 Regulations, reg 19.
26 2018 Regulations, reg 21.
27 2018 Regulations, regs 22–23.
28 2018 Regulations, reg 24; MSN 1877, para 13.1.
29 2018 Regulations, reg 17.

The 2018 Regulations do not require seafarers on such ships to be granted the additional eight days' leave; that is a matter for flag state law, and any entitlement to additional days must be set out in the seafarers' employment agreement.[30]

Shore leave

10.9 The shipowner and the master must ensure that shore leave is granted to seafarers, to benefit their health and well-being, where consistent with the operational requirements of their positions.[31]

INSPECTION AND DETENTION

10.10 Authorised inspectors may review a ship's MLC documentation and, if there are grounds to do so under MLC Standard A5.2.1, carry out a more detailed inspection[32] (see Chapter 22). The same provisions (as those set out above) on detention, arbitration and compensation apply.[33] Details of any detention must be included in the MCA's monthly report.[34]

OFFENCES

10.11 Breaches of the 2018 Regulations amount to criminal offences that may be committed by the shipowner, employer, master (or designate), a summary of which are set out at Annex D to MSN 1877.[35] They are all summary offences, punishable in England and Wales by a fine and, in Scotland or Northern Ireland, to a fine not exceeding level 5 on the standard scale.[36] It is a defence for the accused to show that they took all reasonable steps to ensure compliance with the relevant provision.[37]

REMEDIES

10.12 If a seafarer is denied their right to take statutory leave or is not fully paid during such a period of leave, they have the right to present a claim to the employment tribunal.[38] Where the tribunal finds a complaint well-founded, it must make a declaration to that effect, and it may make an award of compensation.[39]

30 MLC, Standard A2.1.4(f).
31 2018 Regulations, reg 17.
32 2018 Regulations, reg 20.
33 2018 Regulations, regs 21–23.
34 2018 Regulations, reg 24.
35 2018 Regulations, reg 25(1)–(2).
36 2018 Regulations, reg 25(3)(a)–(b), respectively.
37 2018 Regulations, reg 25(4).
38 2018 Regulations, reg 26(1)(a)–(b).
39 2018 Regulations, reg 26(3)(1)–(b).

The level of compensation is to be based on just and equitable principles in all the circumstances, having regard to the employer's default in refusing to permit the seafarer to exercise their right, and any loss sustained by the seafarer which is attributable to the matters complained of.[40]

The claim must be presented to the tribunal within three months from the date that it is alleged that the exercise of the right to take leave should have been permitted (or permitted to begin, in the case of two or more successive days of leave) or, in a pay claim, payment should have been made.[41]

However, in Great Britain a claim under regulation 26 of the 2018 Regulations is to be treated as 'relevant proceedings';[42] before proceedings can be instituted, the claimant must first notify ACAS about the matter to which the proceedings relate, and the latter will offer to conduct 'early conciliation' with the employer.[43] The three-month time limit is paused during the conciliation period; when that ends, the claimant will be given an early conciliation certificate and, from that time, will have at least one month to present their claim to the tribunal.[44]

In Northern Ireland, claims should be submitted directly to the industrial tribunal (within the primary three-month time limit) as there is no mandatory conciliation scheme, although non-mandatory conciliation services are available through the Labour Relations Agency.[45]

If the claim is submitted late (in Great Britain or Norther Ireland), the tribunal has discretion to hear it if it has been submitted within such further period as the tribunal considers reasonable, in a case where it is satisfied that it was not reasonably practicable for the complaint to be presented on time.[46]

Other remedies

10.13 In connection with their right to rest hours and the taking of annual leave, seafarers have the following protections under the Employment Rights Act 1996:

40 2018 Regulations, reg 26(4)(a)–(b).

41 2018 Regulations, reg 26(6).

42 Employment Tribunals Act 1996, s 18(1)(n), as inserted by 2018 Regulations, reg 31, Sch 2, para 1(a).

43 Employment Tribunals Act 1996, ss 18A–18B; ACAS early conciliation: www.acas.org.uk/index.aspx?articleid=4028 [Accessed 31 May 2018].

44 2018 Regulations, reg 27.

45 Industrial Tribunals (Northern Ireland) Order 1996 (SI 1996/1921 (NI 18)) ('the 1996 Order'), art 20(1)(u), as amended by 2018 Regulations, reg 31, Sch 2, para 4.

46 2018 Regulations, reg 26(2)(b) For guidance on the employment tribunal's discretion to extend time for late claims, see Tolley's *Employment Handbook* (32nd edn, Lexis Nexis, 2018), 496–501 (contributed by Marcus Pilgerstorfer).

- the right not to be subject to any detriment for refusing to contravene or forgo their rights, or failing to sign a work force agreement or performing activities as a representative under the 2018 Regulations;[47]
- a seafarer will be considered to be unfairly dismissed if the principal reason is due to any of the above actions or omissions;[48]
- a seafarer will be considered to be unfairly dismissed if the principal reason is because they brought proceedings to enforce their rights under the 2018 Regulations or alleged that their employer had breached their rights under those Regulations.[49]

The same rights apply under arts 68A, 132A and 135 (respectively) of the Employment Rights (Northern Ireland) Order 1996.[50]

RESTRICTION AGAINST CONTRACTING OUT

10.14 With some exceptions, any agreement is void to the extent that it purports to exclude or limit the operation of the 2018 Regulations, or preclude a claim. The exceptions are:

- those which the MCA may authorise if incorporated in a collective agreement or a workforce agreement (see Chapter 9 at para 9.5 onwards);[51]
- an agreement to refrain from instituting or continuing proceedings where ACAS has taken conciliation action under sections 18A to 18C of the Employment Tribunals Act 1996 (the agreement is set out in a 'COT 3 Form'), or where the prescribed conditions are met, including that the seafarer must obtain advice from an independent adviser on the terms and effect of the agreement (which are the same as those in the general employment law applying to settlement agreements).[52] This provision is also applied to Northern Ireland.[53]

47 ERA 1996, s 45A, as amended by 2018 Regulations, reg 31, Sch 2, para 2(a).
48 ERA 1996, s 101A, as amended by 2018 Regulations, reg 31, Sch 2, para 2(b).
49 ERA 1996, s 104, as amended by 2018 Regulations, reg 31, Sch 2, para 2(c).
50 SI 1996/1919 (NI 16); 2018 Regulations, reg 31, Sch 2, para 3(a)–(c), amending 1996 Order, arts 68A(5)(d), 132A(2)(d) and 135(4)(d).
51 2018 Regulations, reg 7.
52 2018 Regulations, reg 28.
53 2018 Regulations, reg 4(d)(i)–(ii), referencing conciliation carried out by the Labour Relations Agency under 1996 Order, art 20.

CHAPTER 11

Regulation 2.5: Repatriation

INTRODUCTION

11.1 The purpose of Regulation 2.5 of the MLC is to ensure that seafarers are able to return home.[1] Seafarers have a right to be repatriated at no cost to themselves in the circumstances and under the conditions specified in the Code.[2] Ratifying states must ensure that ships that fly their flag provide financial security to ensure that seafarers are duly repatriated in accordance with the Code.[3]

The repatriation provisions (together with those in Regulation 4.2 on shipowners' liability for contractual claims in respect of compensation for death or long-term disability of seafarers) were the first parts of the MLC to be amended, by the insertion of the detailed requirements, which MLC states were to implement, in respect of the financial security provisions (the amendments are set out in full

1 MLC, Regulation 2.5, purpose.
2 MLC, Regulation 2.5, para 1; 'the Code' is the associated Standards and Guidelines.
3 MLC, Regulation 2.5, para 2.

in Appendix 2). Like most other MLC requirements, the amendments have been incorporated into EU law, by Directive 2018/131/EU inserting the provisions into Directive 2009/13/EC (which contains many of the mandatory MLC requirements of titles 1 to 4).[4]

The carrying of financial security provision was already a general requirement of Regulations 2.5 and 4.2 as originally drafted; however, the amendments set out precise detail on the extent of the liabilities to be covered. These amendments were agreed by the MLC's Special Tripartite Committee in February 2014, approved by the ILO's International Labour Conference on 11 June 2014, and came into force on 18 January 2017.[5]

The first UK MLC repatriation provisions are contained in Pts 6 and 10B of the Merchant Shipping (Maritime Labour Convention) (Minimum Requirements for Seafarers) Regulations 2014[6] ('Minimum Requirements Regulations') and MGN 479.[7] They apply to UK sea-going ships wherever they may be and (while they are in UK waters) non-UK ships which do not carry MLC documentation.[8]

However, to implement the MLC financial security amendments on repatriation (and in respect of Regulation 4.2 (Shipowners' liability)), the Merchant Shipping (Maritime Labour Convention) (Compulsory Financial Security) (Amendment) Regulations 2018[9] ('Financial Security Amendment Regulations') came into force on 12 July 2018, and insert the relevant provisions (Pt 10B) into the Minimum Requirements Regulations.[10] As regards those amendments, Part 10B applies to UK MLC ships, and (while they are in UK waters) to non-UK MLC ships that do not carry MLC documentation.[11] The only requirement that applies to non-UK

4 Council Directive (EU) 2018 of 23 January 2018 implementing the Agreement concluded by the European Community Shipowners' Associations (ECSA) and the European Transport Workers' Federation (ETF) to amend Directive 2009/13/EC in accordance with the amendments of 2014 to the Maritime Labour Convention, 2006, as approved by the International Labour Conference on 11 June 2014, OJ 26.1.2018 L 22/28.

5 Amendments of 2014 to the Maritime Labour Convention, 2006, approved by the Conference at its One Hundred and Third Session, Geneva, 11 June 2014: www.ilo.org/wcmsp5/groups/public/---ed_norm/---relconf/documents/meetingdocument/wcms_248905.pdf [Accessed 27 December 2017].

6 SI 2014/1613. The previous provisions were the Merchant Shipping (Repatriation) Regulations 1979 (SI 1979/97) which, although still in force, have been superseded by the Minimum Requirements Regulations in respect of MLC ships: 1979 Regulations, reg 2(1A), inserted by Merchant Shipping (Maritime Labour Convention) (Consequential and Minor Amendments) Regulations 2014 (SI 2014/1614), reg 6(3).

7 MGN 479 (M) – Maritime Labour Convention, 2006: Repatriation.

8 Minimum Requirements Regulations, reg 3(1)–(2). The following are excluded: pleasure vessels; fishing vessels; ships of traditional build; warships and naval auxiliaries; and vessels which are not ordinarily engaged in commercial activities: reg 3(5)(a)–(e), respectively.

9 SI 2018/667.

10 Minimum Requirements Regulations, Pt 10A (Security against shipowner's liability for death or long-term disability of seafarers); Pt 10B (Security against the abandonment of seafarers), as inserted by Financial Security Amendment Regulations, reg 2(7).

11 Minimum Requirements Regulations, reg 3(1)–(2)(a), as amended by Financial Security Amendment Regulations, reg 2(3)(a).

MLC ships, which carry MLC documentation while they are in UK waters, is to carry MLC documentation in accordance with MLC, Standard A2.5.2 (financial security for abandoned seafarers).[12]

Guidance on financial security is also provided in MGN 480 (M).[13]

DUTY TO REPATRIATE SEAFARERS

11.2 A shipowner of a UK ship, or (while it is in UK waters) a non-UK ship which does not carry MLC documentation, must make provision for repatriation, as soon as is practicable, where:

(a) the seafarers' employment agreement (SEA) expires;

(b) the SEA is terminated by the shipowner;

(c) the SEA is terminated by the seafarer, in accordance with its terms;

(d) the seafarer is no longer able to carry out their duties under their SEA, or cannot be expected to carry them out in the specific circumstances, including the following circumstances:[14]

  (i) illness, injury or medical condition, which requires repatriation when medically fit to travel;

  (ii) shipwreck;

  (iii) the shipowner is not able to fulfil its legal or contractual obligations to the seafarer, following insolvency, the sale of the ship or a change in its registration;

  (iv) the ship is bound for a war zone to which the seafarer does not consent to go;[15]

(e) the seafarer has completed the maximum period of service on board, following which the seafarer is entitled to repatriation, in accordance with their SEA;[16]

(f) the SEA is terminated pursuant to an order of a court or tribunal.[17]

12 Minimum Requirements Regulations, reg 3(3)–(4)(b)(ix), as amended by Financial Security Amendment Regulations, reg 2(3)(c)(ii). The requirement to carry such financial security is contained in the new reg 53M(1)(b).

13 MGN 480 (M) Amendment 2 – MLC, 2006: Shipowners' liabilities including seafarer compensation, paras 2.1–2.8.2.

14 By using 'including', it implies that the list (i)–(iv) is non-exhaustive.

15 What constitutes a 'war zone' may be defined in the SEA, or by the UK's Warlike Operations Area Committee (WOAK): MGN 479, para 3.2(d). WOAK includes representatives of Nautilus International and the UK Chamber of Shipping: www.ukchamberofshipping.com/events/warlike-operations-area-committee-18-january-2017/ [Accessed 26 June 2018].

16 This period must be less than 12 months (MLC, Standard A2.5.1.2(b)). In accordance with UK implementation, it is left for agreement between the parties, but must not exceed 327 days (arrived at by subtracting the 38 days' statutory paid leave entitlement from 365 days): MGN 79, para 3.3. This means that a seafarer will be entitled to repatriation at this point, although they are not legally compelled to accept it.

17 Minimum Requirements Regulations, reg 19(1)(a)–(f).

REPATRIATION DESTINATION

11.3 The repatriation destination is that provided for in the SEA,[18] or other place (if any) subsequently agreed, between the seafarer and the shipowner.[19] If there is no such provision, the seafarer is entitled to choose to be repatriated to: (a) the place where they entered into their SEA; or (b) their country of residence.[20]

SCOPE OF THE DUTY TO REPATRIATE

11.4 The duty to repatriate ends where:

(a) the seafarer has been returned to their repatriation destination;

(b) the shipowner makes reasonable arrangements for repatriation, which are unsuccessful because of the seafarer's unreasonable conduct;

(c) the shipowner has made reasonable, but unsuccessful, endeavours to contact the seafarer for at least three months;

(d) the seafarer confirms in writing that repatriation is not required; or

(e) the seafarer is dead.[21]

Where a seafarer dies on board, or while on shore leave outside their country of residence, the shipowner must meet the reasonable costs of burial or cremation, except to any extent that they are met by a public authority.[22] If the seafarer's personal representatives incur such costs, due to the shipowner's failure in this respect, the former may make recovery against the latter as a civil debt.[23] Alternatively, the shipowner and the next of kin may agree on terms, such as costs, for the return of the body for burial or cremation.[24]

RELIEF AND MAINTENANCE PENDING REPATRIATION

11.5 The shipowner must make provision for the necessary relief and maintenance pending repatriation, with regard to the seafarer's personal circumstances and requirements, which must include:

(a) food;

(b) clothing;

(c) accommodation;

18 The repatriation destination must be stated in the SEA: Minimum Requirements Regulations, Sch 1, Pt 1, para 11.
19 Minimum Requirements Regulations, reg 20(1).
20 Minimum Requirements Regulations, reg 20(2)(a)–(b).
21 Minimum Requirements Regulations, reg 21(a)–(e).
22 Minimum Requirements Regulations, reg 52(1)–(2).
23 Minimum Requirements Regulations, reg 52(3).
24 MGN 479, para 5.3.

(d) toiletries and other personal necessaries;

(e) surgical, medical, dental or optical treatment (including the repair or replacement of any appliance) for any condition requiring immediate care; and

(f) in cases where legal aid is unavailable or insufficient, reasonable costs for the defence of the seafarer, in any criminal proceedings, in respect of any act or omission, within the scope of the seafarer's employment, being proceedings where neither the shipowner (nor its agent) is the complainant.[25]

PROHIBITION ON RECOVERING REPATRIATION COSTS FROM SEAFARERS

11.6 Shipowners are prohibited from entering into an agreement with seafarers which would require the latter to make payment towards 'repatriation costs' or 'relief and maintenance costs', and any such agreement will be void to that extent.[26] There is one exception, in that it is permissible to include a reimbursement term in a SEA in respect of repatriation costs (but this exception does not apply to relief and maintenance costs), but only where the agreement is terminated due to the seafarer's serious misconduct, allowing the shipowner to deduct such costs from the seafarer's wages.[27] Where no provision is made in the SEA, the shipowner can only recover the costs of repatriation and relief and maintenance costs (or damages) by a civil claim (and only where the SEA is terminated due to the seafarer's serious misconduct).[28] In such misconduct cases, the shipowner must still repatriate the seafarer, but may recover the costs by way of deduction or a civil claim, as described.

MODE OF TRAVEL

11.7 The mode of travel by which repatriation is to take place is a matter for agreement between the shipowner and the seafarer, and must be stated in the SEA.[29] Although the MLC states that it should normally be by air,[30] there may be circumstances where other modes of transport are more expeditious or necessary (for example, where air travel is not readily available, or the seafarer cannot fly due to illness).[31]

25 Minimum Requirements Regulations, reg 22(1)–(3)(a)–(f).
26 Minimum Requirements Regulations, reg 23(1)(a)–(b), (6).
27 Minimum Requirements Regulations, reg 23(2)–(3). Note that subsection (2) only refers to the reimbursement of 'repatriation costs' and makes no reference to 'relief and maintenance costs'.
28 Minimum Requirements Regulations, reg 23(4). In contrast to reg 23(2), recovery under reg 23(4) extends to '... the costs described in paragraph (1) ...', which includes repatriation costs and relief and maintenance costs.
29 Minimum Requirements Regulations, Sch 1, Pt 1, para 11.
30 MLC, Guideline B2.5.1, para 6.
31 MGN 479, para 6.1.

The MCA recommends that shipowners meet the costs of transportation of 30kg of the seafarer's personal luggage to their repatriation destination.[32]

RETURN OF SEAFARER'S PROPERTY

11.8 When the duty to repatriate arises, the master must take charge of any of the seafarer's property left on board and enter a description of each item in the official log book.[33] The master and the shipowner must ensure that reasonable care is taken of the property, and the shipowner must ensure that it is returned to the seafarer or (if the latter has died) their next of kin.[34]

The master may sell any perishable property (the proceeds of sale will belong to the seafarer), and destroy or dispose of any property which is considered to be a potential health or safety risk; in both cases, details must be entered in the official log book.[35]

The seafarer, or their next of kin, must reimburse the shipowner the reasonable costs of delivery to them, if demanded.[36]

FINANCIAL SECURITY

11.9 The original provisions in the Minimum Requirements Regulations provide that, in respect of every UK MLC ship, and every non-UK ship which is not carrying MLC documentation while it is in UK waters, there must be in force a contract of insurance or other financial security, adequate to ensure that the shipowner will be able to meet any liabilities arising in respect of repatriation (under reg 19) and relief and maintenance pending repatriation (under reg 22).[37] Those provisions are still in force; however, there have been significant additions made by the Financial Security Amendment Regulations (which came into force on 12 July 2018) to implement the MLC amendments on financial security, which are triggered when a seafarer becomes 'abandoned'.

The full text of the MLC amendments, which are closely followed by UK law, is set out in Appendix 2, and the following is intended to be only a summary of the UK provisions.

32 MLC, Guideline B2.5.3(d); MGN 479, para 7.4.1.

33 Minimum Requirements Regulations, reg 24(1)–(2).

34 Minimum Requirements Regulations, reg 24(4), (10); MGN 479, para 10.1. The duty is satisfied if the delivery is made to the last known address of the relevant party: reg 24(11).

35 Minimum Requirements Regulations, reg 24(6)–(8). The shipowner must ensure that a document containing the details entered in the official log book relating to any such sale or destruction is delivered to the seafarer or their next of kin (delivery to their last known address is sufficient): reg 24(10)–(11).

36 Minimum Requirements Regulations, reg 24(13).

37 Minimum Requirements Regulations, reg 26(1)(a).

Abandonment security

11.10 The ships referred to above must carry 'abandonment security', which means a contract of insurance or other form of security relating to a ship that: (a) provides financial assurance of an amount which the shipowner reasonably considers adequate to cover specified items for any seafarer who is abandoned in relation to the ship; and (b) provides that any seafarer who is abandoned in relation to the ship is entitled to: (i) make an abandonment claim; and (ii) receive financial assistance in respect of those items.[38] An 'abandonment claim' is one submitted directly to the abandonment security provider by an abandoned seafarer or their authorised representative, being supported by evidence showing that the seafarer is abandoned.[39] The financial security cover will usually be provided by the P&I Club with which the ship is entered, even though some of the liabilities are beyond traditional P&I cover.[40]

The abandonment security certificate must contain the following information:

'(a) the name of the ship to which the abandonment security relates;

(b) the port of registry of the ship;

(c) the call sign of the ship;

(d) the International Maritime Organisation number of the ship;

(e) the name and address of the abandonment security provider;

(f) the contact details of the point of contact at the abandonment security provider responsible for handling seafarers' abandonment claims;

(g) the name of the owner of the ship;

(h) the period of validity of the abandonment security;

(i) a declaration from the abandonment security provider that the abandonment security meets the requirements of standard A2.5.2 of the MLC.'[41]

The right of a seafarer to make an abandonment claim only arises once they have become 'abandoned', which is when the shipowner:

'(a) fails to make the provision required under regulation 19 (duty to repatriate seafarers);

38 Minimum Requirements Regulations, regs 53M(1)(a), 53N(1), as inserted by Financial Security Amendment Regulations, reg 2(7).

39 Minimum Requirements Regulations, reg 53N(3), as inserted by Financial Security Amendment Regulations, reg 2(7).

40 Circular issued by the International Group of P&I Clubs: www.skuld.com/topics/people/mlc-2006/maritime-labour-convention-2006-as-amended-financial-security-requirements/. There are also insurance products which cover the MLC financial security provisions, an example being CrewSEACURE: https://crewseacure.com/ [Accessed 4 November 2018].

41 Minimum Requirements Regulations, reg 53Q(1), Sch 4, as inserted by Financial Security Amendment Regulations, reg 2(7).

(b) having regard to the seafarer's personal circumstances and requirements, leaves the seafarer without necessary maintenance and support, including leaving the seafarer without–

  (i) adequate food;

  (ii) drinking water supplies;

  (iii) accommodation;

  (iv) essential fuel for survival on board the ship; or

  (v) necessary medical care; or

(c) otherwise unilaterally severs ties with the seafarer, including failing to pay any amount in respect of wages payable to the seafarer under the seafarer's seafarer employment agreement for a period of at least two months.'[42]

The items to be covered are:

'(a) up to four months' unpaid wages relating to work undertaken by the seafarer before the end of the relevant period;

(b) the cost during the relevant period of–

  (i) adequate food;

  (ii) drinking water supplies;

  (iii) clothing, where necessary;

  (iv) accommodation;

  (v) essential fuel for survival on board the ship;

  (vi) necessary medical care;

(c) the cost of repatriation, including–

  (i) the cost of appropriate travel arrangements and any related costs of passage, but this may be limited to travel or passage that is completed before the seafarer ceases to be abandoned; and

  (ii) the cost of transport of the seafarer's personal effects; and

(d) all other expenses reasonably incurred by the seafarer before the end of the relevant period as a result of being abandoned.'[43]

The 'relevant period' commences on the day the seafarer is abandoned and ends on the earliest of the seafarer's arrival in or at: their country of residence; the repatriation destination as stated in the SEA; or such place as the seafarer has agreed in advance with the abandonment security provider, or any person who has made provision for the seafarer's repatriation.[44]

42 Minimum Requirements Regulations, reg 53L(1)(a)–(c), as inserted by Financial Security Amendment Regulations, reg 2(7).

43 Minimum Requirements Regulations, reg 53N(2)(a)–(d), as inserted by Financial Security Amendment Regulations, reg 2(7).

44 Minimum Requirements Regulations, reg 53L(3), as inserted by Financial Security Amendment Regulations, reg 2(7).

11.11 The financial security certificate must be displayed on board the ship in a conspicuous place; there must be an English translation if it is not in that language, containing the information set out in Schedule 4 to the Minimum Requirements Regulations, which is the same as that contained in MLC, Appendix A2-I (which is set out at para 11.10 above).[45]

The termination by an abandonment security provider of an abandonment security before the end of its period of validity is only effective if the provider gives at least 30 days' prior written notice, together with a copy of the financial security certificate, to the MCA.[46]

The shipowner must give written notification of early termination to the seafarers, stating the date on which the security was, or is to be, terminated.[47]

The financial security provisions provide a welcome safety net for seafarers caught up in such situations, which still occur frequently, many of which are logged on the ILO's database of abandoned seafarers.[48] The seafarer (or their representative) can claim directly through the financial security provider, and should provide evidence to substantiate their claim, including their SEA and past wage slips. As far as arrears of wages are concerned, there must first be two months' worth outstanding, and any payment from the provider is limited to four months of wages. The provider must determine whether the seafarer is entitled to their claim within seven days of receipt, and make payment of the entitlement within 14 days of receipt.[49] A penalty of 20% interest per annum applies to late payments.[50] The provisions are without prejudice to a seafarer's other legal rights, so any excess may be claimed by other means, the most realistic being (in an abandonment situation when the shipowner is often insolvent) the enforcement of a maritime lien against the ship. Under UK implementation, if the final security provider makes a payment, they acquire the rights of the seafarer through subrogation, and may arrest the ship to enforce the maritime lien.[51] A recent entry in the ILO database, in connection with the IOM-registered yacht 'Indian Empress', provides an example of the crew's wages being paid by the MLC financial security provider Skuld, and

45 Minimum Requirements Regulations, reg 53Q, as inserted by Financial Security Amendment Regulations, reg 2(7).

46 Minimum Requirements Regulations, reg 53R, as inserted by Financial Security Amendment Regulations, reg 2(7).

47 Minimum Requirements Regulations, reg 53S, as inserted by Financial Security Amendment Regulations, reg 2(7).

48 ILO database on reported incidents of abandoned seafarers: www.ilo.org/dyn/seafarers/seafarersbrowse.home [Accessed 26 June 2018]. A recent abandonment in the UK was the Indian-owned and flagged 'Malaviya 20': www.birketts.co.uk/insights/latest-news/malaviya-twenty-abandonment-ordeal-finally-comes-t [Accessed 21 September 2018].

49 Minimum Requirements Regulations, reg 53O, as inserted by Financial Security Amendment Regulations, reg 2(7).

50 Minimum Requirements Regulations, reg 53O(5), as inserted by Financial Security Amendment Regulations, reg 2(7).

51 Minimum Requirements Regulations, reg 53P, as inserted by Financial Security Amendment Regulations, reg 2(7).

reference to the latter's *in rem* action against the yacht to recover the monies paid out.[52]

SECRETARY OF STATE FUNCTIONS IF SHIPOWNER FAILS TO REPATRIATE SEAFARERS

11.12 In the event that shipowners default in their duty to repatriate, the MLC provides that the flag state must do so (and may recover the costs from the shipowner); if the flag state also fails to repatriate, the port state or the state of which the seafarer is a national, may do so (and recover the costs from the flag state which, in turn, may recover such costs from the shipowner); in no circumstances should a charge be imposed on the seafarer unless they are in serious default of their employment obligations.[53]

The Secretary of State:

- must make any provision which the shipowner of a UK ship is required to make under regulation 19 or 22 (repatriation and duty pending repatriation, respectively) (or secure that it is made), if (a) the shipowner fails to make the required provision, and (b) the seafarer is not entitled to receive financial assistance under an abandonment security;[54]
- may make any provision which the shipowner of a UK ship is required to make under regulation 19 or 22 (or secure that it is made), if (a) the shipowner fails to make the required provision, and (b) the seafarer is entitled to receive financial assistance under an abandonment security.[55]

The effect of those provisions is that the Secretary of State will be liable to make such provision on the failure of the shipowner to do so, whether or not the seafarer is entitled to receive assistance under an abandonment security. Where the Secretary of State does incur costs in either case, it may recover them (including the costs incurred by another person) from the shipowner as a civil debt.[56]

11.13 To the extent that a seafarer on a UK ship may be out of pocket, by having personally incurred any such expenses, they may also make recovery against the shipowner as a civil debt.[57] Neither the Secretary of State or the

52 ILO abandonment database: www.ilo.org/dyn/seafarers/seafarersbrowse.details?p_lang=en&p_abandonment_ id=343&p_search_id=180626165833 [Accessed 26 June 2018].

53 MLC, Standard A2.5.5(a)–(c).

54 Minimum Requirements Regulations, reg 27(1)(a)–(b), as substituted by Financial Security Amendment Regulations, reg 2(4)(a).

55 Minimum Requirements Regulations, reg 27(1A)(a)–(b), as substituted by Financial Security Amendment Regulations, reg 2(4)(a).

56 Minimum Requirements Regulations, reg 27(1B)(a)–(b) (as substituted by Financial Security Amendment Regulations, reg 2(4)(a)) and reg 27(3).

57 Minimum Requirements Regulations, reg 27(4).

seafarer is permitted to recover monies which have already been recovered by the other, in regard to any particular expense, so protecting the shipowner from reimbursing twice in respect of such items.[58]

Where a shipowner of a non-UK ship fails to make provision for repatriation, the Secretary of State may do so,[59] and recover the costs from the shipowner as a civil debt.[60] In this scenario, the MLC permits ratifying states to recover their costs from the flag state; however, the UK has instead made provision for recovery directly against the shipowner.[61] This latter provision is likely to be used (as anticipated by the MLC) where the shipowner of a non-UK ship has failed to return (a) seafarers from a UK port to their repatriation destination, and (b) UK-resident seafarers from a foreign port to the UK.

Furthermore, the Secretary of State has power to detain a non-UK MLC ship, at the request of representatives of the flag state, on the provision of evidence that the latter has incurred costs due to the shipowner failing in its repatriation duties; the ship may be detained until the shipowner has reimbursed the flag state.[62] In implementing this provision, the MLC provides that international instruments are to be taken into account, including the International Convention on Arrest of Ships, 1999.[63]

Now that the financial security provisions are in force internationally, it remains to be seen if incidents of abandonment will fall and the duration of such incidents will be reduced.

YOUNG SEAFARERS

11.14 Although not a legal duty, shipowners are recommended to offer and pay for the repatriation of young seafarers under the age of 18 who, after four months into their first foreign-going voyage, are not suited to life at sea. Notification of such a repatriation, with reasons, should be made to the manning agent, training provider, or any national authority which issued the documentation which enabled the seafarer to take up sea-going employment.[64]

58 Minimum Requirements Regulations, reg 27(5)(a)–(b), as amended by Financial Security Amendment Regulations, reg 2(4)(d).

59 This provision of assistance in the case of a non-UK ship will be at the discretion of the Secretary of State. The primary duty is placed on the shipowner and then the flag state: MLC, Standard A2.5.1.5(a)–(c).

60 Minimum Requirements Regulations, reg 27(2), (3)(a)–(b).

61 MLC, Standard A2.5.1.5(a).

62 Minimum Requirements Regulations, reg 57.

63 MLC, Standard A2.5.1.6; the 1999 Convention is the successor to the International Convention for the Unification of Certain Rules Relating to the Arrest of Sea-going Ships, 1952. See generally Berlingieri, F, *Berlingieri on Arrest of Ships*, Volume II (Informa Law from Routledge, 6th edition, Abingdon, Oxon).

64 MGN 479, para 14.1, which implements the non-mandatory MLC, Guideline B2.5.2.3.

NON-UK SHIPS CARRYING MLC DOCUMENTATION

11.15 The UK provisions also impose repatriation duties on owners of non-UK ships (which carry MLC documentation) while they are in UK waters.[65] Shipowners must provide for repatriation, as soon as practicable, in the circumstances described in MLC, Standard A2.5.1 (which are broadly in line with the circumstances set out in reg 19(1)(a)–(d) of the Minimum Requirements Regulations – see para 11.2 above) subject to any national provisions which the flag state has adopted pursuant to MLC, Standard A2.5.1.2.[66] There may be reference to such national provisions in the SEAs, as these are required to contain details of the seafarer's entitlement to repatriation.[67] The flag state's financial security requirements will also be referenced in the DMLC, Pt I, point 15, and the shipowner's compliance measures should be set out in the DMLC, Pt II, point 15.

Shipowners must comply with MLC, Standard A2.5.1.3 (prohibition against advance payment towards repatriation/deduction of wages – except, in the latter case, where the seafarer is in serious default of their employment obligations) and MLC, Standard A2.5.1.9 (duty to make available to seafarers the flag state provisions on repatriation in an appropriate language), whether or not the ship's flag state imposes such requirements.[68]

Shipowners must be covered by financial security for repatriation in accordance with MLC, Regulation 2.5.2 and Standard A2.5.2.3 (for abandoned seafarers).[69]

OTHER DOCUMENTS TO BE CARRIED ON BOARD

11.16 Shipowners of UK ships and (while they are in UK waters) non-UK ships which do not carry MLC documentation must ensure that a copy of Pt 6 (Repatriation) of the Minimum Requirements Regulations and MGN 479 are carried on board and available to seafarers.[70] Unless the shipowner reasonably considers that all seafarers on board understand English sufficiently, the duty extends to carrying and making available translated version(s), so that all seafarers on board can understand at least one version.[71]

65 Minimum Requirements Regulations, regs 3(3)(a)–(b)(i)–(ii), (4)(b)(iv), 28.

66 Minimum Requirements Regulations, reg 28(1), as amended by Financial Security Amendment Regulations, reg 2(5). MLC, Standard A2.5.2 requires ratifying states to ensure that there are provisions in their laws, regulations or other measures, or in collective bargaining agreements, prescribing: (a) the circumstances in which seafarers are entitled to repatriation; (b) the maximum duration of service on board after which the entitlement arises (which must not exceed 12 months); and (c) the precise entitlements, including destination, mode of transport, items of expense to be covered, and any other arrangements.

67 MLC, Standard A2.1.4(i).

68 Minimum Requirements Regulations, reg 28(3)(a)–(b), respectively.

69 Minimum Requirements Regulations, reg 26(1)(b); 53M(1)(b), as inserted by Financial Security Amendment Regulations, reg 2(7).

70 Minimum Requirements Regulations, reg 25(1).

71 Minimum Requirements Regulations, reg 25(2).

CRIMINAL OFFENCES FOR NON-COMPLIANCE

11.17 Failure by the relevant person to comply with the main provisions, in connection with UK ships, amounts to a criminal offence.[72] Most offences are punishable on summary conviction by a fine, most of which are limited to level 3 or level 5 on the standard scale.[73]

In particular, it should be noted that it is an offence: for UK ships and (while they are in UK waters) non-UK ships without MLC documentation to be operated without having in place 'abandonment security' (in accordance with the Minimum Requirements Regulations, as amended); and for non-UK ships (while they are in UK waters) to be operated without having in place financial security in accordance with MLC, Standard A2.5.2, paragraph 3.[74]

It is a defence for the defendant to show that they had taken all reasonable steps to ensure compliance.[75]

INSPECTION AND DETENTION OF SHIPS

11.18 The powers of inspection and detention of UK and (while they are in UK waters) non-UK ships apply, as described in Chapter 2 at paragraph 2.2.[76]

CHECKLIST FOR COMPLIANCE

11.19

- Shipowner to make provision to repatriate seafarers.
- Shipowner to make provision for relief and maintenance pending repatriation.
- Shipowner prohibited from entering into agreement with seafarer in respect of which the latter is to make payment for repatriation or relief and maintenance.
- Master to take charge of property left behind and enter description thereof in official log book.
- Shipowner and master to take reasonable care of property left behind, pending delivery to the seafarer or (if appropriate) their next of kin.
- Master to enter details of the sale of any perishable or deteriorating property in official log book.

72 Minimum Requirements Regulations, regs 19(2), 22(5), 23(5), 24(3), (5), (9), (12), 25(3), 26(2), 28(2), (4), 53M(2), 53Q(3), (5), 53S(3) (the latter three regulations have been inserted by Financial Security Amendment Regulations, reg 2(7)).

73 Minimum Requirements Regulations, reg 59(1), (3)(c)–(d), 59A(1)–(2)(b)–(c).

74 Minimum Requirements Regulations, reg 53M, as inserted by Financial Security Amendment Regulations, reg 2(7).

75 Minimum Requirements Regulations, reg 60.

76 Minimum Requirements Regulations, regs 54–56.

- Master to enter the details of any destruction or disposal of perishable or deteriorating property in official log book.
- Shipowner to cause any property left behind, and (if applicable) a document containing the information in the official log book relating to any sale, destruction or disposal of property, to be delivered to the seafarer or (if appropriate) their next of kin.
- Shipowner to ensure Pt 6 of the Minimum Requirements Regulations and MGN 479, with any necessary versions translated into other language(s) are carried on board.
- UK MLC ships wherever they may be, and non-UK ships without MLC documentation, while they are in UK waters, to have in force a contract of insurance or financial security to cover repatriation and relief and maintenance costs.
- Ensure that details of seafarers' repatriation entitlements are entered in their SEA.
- Non-UK ships, with MLC documentation, while they are in UK waters, to have to have in force a contract of insurance or financial security to cover repatriation and relief and maintenance costs.
- Non-UK ships, with MLC documentation, while they are in UK waters, to arrange for any necessary repatriation of seafarers, in the circumstances described in MLC, Standard A2.5.1.1, subject to any provisions adopted by the flag sate, pursuant to MLC, Standard A2.5.1.2.

  However, the shipowner must comply with MLC, Standard A2.5.1.3 (prohibition against seafarer making an advanced payment towards repatriation, etc.) and Standard A2.5.1.9 (duty to carry flag state provisions on repatriation (with any necessary translations)), whether or not the flag state has imposed such a prohibition or requirement, respectively.

DMLC: comply with the UK requirements in Pt I, point 15, on abandonment financial security, and enter compliance measure in Pt II, point 15.

Ensure that the financial security certificate is displayed in a conspicuous place on board the ship.

CHAPTER 12

Regulation 2.6: Seafarer Compensation for the Ship's Loss or Foundering

INTRODUCTION

12.1 The purpose of Regulation 2.6 of the MLC is to ensure that seafarers are compensated when a ship is lost or has foundered.[1] Seafarers are entitled to adequate compensation in the case of injury, loss or unemployment arising from the ship's loss or foundering.[2]

12.2 This chapter outlines the UK provisions in respect of the relatively brief Regulation 2.6 of the MLC and its associated Code. It requires shipowners to pay to seafarers an indemnity against unemployment, resulting from the loss or foundering of the ship, which is to be without prejudice to any other rights, under flag state laws, for losses or injuries arising from the same incident.[3]

The UK provisions are contained in Pt 10 of the Merchant Shipping (Maritime Labour Convention) (Minimum Requirements for Seafarers) Regulations 2014[4] ('Minimum Requirements Regulations') and MGN 480.[5] Those provisions also cover the UK's implementation of Regulation 4.2 and associated Code of the MLC on 'Shipowners' liability',[6] which is dealt with in Chapter 18.

1 MLC, Regulation 2.6, purpose.
2 MLC, Regulation 2.6, para 1.
3 MLC, Regulation 2.6, Standard A2.6.1–2.
4 SI 2014/1613.
5 MGN 480 (M) Amendment 2 – Maritime Labour Convention, 2006: Shipowners' Liabilities including Seafarer Compensation.
6 MLC, Regulation 4.2: 'Purpose: To ensure that seafarers are protected from the financial consequences of sickness, injury or death occurring in connection with their employment'.

SHIPOWNERS' LIABILITY FOLLOWING SHIP'S LOSS OR FOUNDERING

12.3 The following provisions apply to UK MLC ships wherever they may be, and non-UK ships (without MLC documentation) while they are in UK waters.[7]

If the loss or foundering of such a ship results in a seafarer being unemployed, the shipowner must pay an indemnity against lost wages. The amount payable will be what would have been due under the seafarers' employment agreement (SEA), for every day on which the seafarer is unemployed, in the two-month period commencing on the day after the loss or foundering.[8]

If the loss or foundering of the ship causes the seafarer to suffer injury or loss[9] (other than the two months' wages referred to above), the shipowner must pay compensation to the seafarer which, other than for cases of death or personal injury, may be limited by a clause in the SEA.[10] Liability under this provision is not dependent on the injury or loss being caused by the negligence or fault of the shipowner. There is, however, a requirement for the ship to be covered by financial security (by way of a contract of insurance or other form of security) which the shipowner reasonably believes is adequate to cover potential liabilities which may arise, including those under SEAs, in the event of death or long-term disability, arising from occupational injury, illness or hazard (see Chapter 18).[11] A failure to do so amounts to a criminal offence by the shipowner.[12]

Any compensation referred to above may be recoverable by the seafarer as a civil debt.[13]

7 Minimum Requirements Regulations, reg 3(3)(1)(a)–(b).
8 Minimum Requirements Regulations, reg 48(1)–(2). This provision supersedes Merchant Shipping Act 1995, s 38 in respect of MLC ships: MGN 480, para 1.2.1.
9 Likely to be seafarers' possessions kept on board: MGN 480 Amendment 2, para 1.2.2.
10 Minimum Requirements Regulations, reg 48(3)–(4).
11 Minimum Requirements Regulations, reg 49(1)–(2).
12 Minimum Requirements Regulations, reg 49(3). The offence is punishable, on summary conviction, by a fine not exceeding level 5 on the standard scale; and, on indictment, by a maximum of two years' imprisonment, or a fine, or both (Minimum Requirements Regulations, reg 59(5)). It is a defence to show that all reasonable steps had been taken to ensure compliance (Minimum Requirements Regulations, reg 60).
13 Minimum Requirements Regulations, reg 48(5).

CHAPTER 13

Regulation 2.7: Manning Levels

INTRODUCTION

13.1 The purpose of Regulation 2.7 of the MLC is to ensure that seafarers work on board ships with sufficient personnel for the safe, efficient and secure operation of the ship.[1]

Ratifying states must require their ships to be sufficiently manned to ensure that they are operated safely, efficiently and with due regard to security under all conditions, taking into account concerns about seafarer fatigue and the nature and conditions of the voyage.[2] The crew must be adequate in terms of its size and qualifications, to ensure the safety and security of the ship and its personnel, under all operating conditions, in accordance with the minimum safe manning document (SMD), and to comply with the MLC.[3] Account must be taken of the need to avoid or minimise excessive working hours, and to ensure sufficient rest and limit fatigue, as well as the principles laid down in applicable international instruments, especially those of the IMO.[4] Account must be taken of all the requirements of Regulation 3.2 and Standard A3.2 of the MLC concerning food and catering (see Chapter 16).[5]

1 MLC, Regulation 2.7, purpose.
2 MLC, Regulation 2.7.1, Standard A2.7.1.
3 MLC, Standard A2.7.1.
4 MLC, Standard A2.7.2.
5 MLC, Standard A2.7.3.

UK PROVISIONS

13.2 The main provisions are set out in Pt 4 of the Merchant Shipping (Standards of Training, Certification and Watchkeeping) Regulations 2015[6] ('the 2015 Regulations'), which implement the IMO's International Convention on Standards of Training, Certification and Watchkeeping for Seafarers 1978 (as amended) ('STCW Convention'), MSN 1868[7]and MSN 1846.[8]

Subject to some exceptions, Pt 4 of the 2015 Regulations applies to sea-going ships, being UK ships wherever they may be, and to non-UK ships in UK waters.[9] It does not apply to fishing vessels, pleasure vessels or small commercial 'code' vessels.[10]

A detailed account of safe manning on ships is beyond the scope of this work, as it is regulated mainly by the STCW Convention. What is set out below is therefore more by way of introduction to some of the main points and principles.[11]

SAFE MANNING DOCUMENT

13.3 In respect of ships of 500 GT or more, the shipowner[12] must ensure that: (a) an SMD is in force in respect of the ship and the manning of the ship; (b) the SMD is kept on board at all times; and (c) the manning levels on board are maintained at least to the levels specified in the SMD.[13] The master must ensure

6 SI 2015/782. The MCA has power to grant, amend or cancel exemptions from any or all of the requirements of Pt 4 (reg 50). The Merchant Shipping (Safe Manning, Hours of Work and Watchkeeping) Regulations 1997 (SI 1997/1320) have been revoked by 2015 Regulations, reg 2(1), Sch 1.

7 MSN 1868 (M) – Standards of Training, Certification & Watchkeeping Convention: UK Requirements for Safe Manning and Watchkeeping.

8 MSN 1846 (M) – Maritime Labour Convention, 2006: Food and Catering: Ship's Cooks and Catering Staff.

9 2015 Regulations, reg 45(1): 'ship' includes 'hovercraft' (reg 45(3)).

10 2015 Regulations, reg 45(2): small commercial 'code' vessels are those referred to in Merchant Shipping (Vessels in Commercial Use for Sport or Pleasure) Regulations 1998 (SI 1998/2771), reg 5(3).

11 For a fuller account, see MSN 1868.

12 Whereas the UK MLC legislation applies to the 'shipowner', the 2015 Regulations (implementing part of the STCW Convention) applies to the 'company', which is similarly defined as '... the owner of the ship or any other person, such as the manager or the bareboat charterer, who has assumed the responsibility for the operation of the ship from the owner and who, on assuming such responsibility, has agreed to take over all the duties and responsibilities imposed on the company by the STCW Regulations;'. MSN 1868 is addressed to the 'owner and operator'. To remain consistent, the terms 'company' and 'owner and operator' will be used in connection with reference to the 2015 Regulations and MSN 1868 respectively.

13 2015 Regulations, reg 46(1). An SMD issued under the revoked 1997 Regulations remains valid, subject to surviving any review under 2015 Regulations, reg 45(6) (reg 56(6)). A ship under 500 GT may also apply for an SMD as a matter of good practice: MSN 1868, para 1.2.

that the ship does not proceed to sea without a valid SMD on board, and that the manning of the ship complies at least with the levels set out in the SMD.[14]

To obtain an SMD, the company must submit proposals to the MCA on the numbers and grade of seafarers it considers necessary, for safely manning the ship for an intended voyage.[15] Once the SMD has been issued, the company must inform the MCA of any pertinent changes of circumstances, upon which the MCA may review the continuing validity or approve fresh proposals from the company.[16]

Application to the MCA for an SMD is by way of Form MSF 4227,[17] together with a statement as to how the proposed manning level has been determined, and how it takes account of the guidance in MSN 1868 and the provisions of the Merchant Shipping (Maritime Labour Convention) (Hours of Work) Regulations 2018[18] (see Chapter 9).[19]

In determining safe manning proposals, the owner or operator should consult with other interested parties, such as the master, seafarers, their unions and the MCA; the records of the consultation process and the agreed safe manning schedule (a copy of which must be displayed prominently in the crew accommodation) should be retained for five years.[20]

RESPONSIBILITIES OF OWNERS AND OPERATORS: GENERAL PRINCIPLES

13.4 The owner or operator must ensure that the ship is safely and adequately manned.[21] In preparing a proposal for an SMD, MSN 1868 sets out the following general principles for the owner or operator:

- ‘Make an assessment of the tasks, duties and responsibilities of the ship's complement as required for its safe operation, for the protection of the marine environment and for dealing with emergency situations;
- Prepare and submit a proposal for the minimum safe manning level based upon an assessment of the numbers and grades/capacities in the ship's complement required for the safe operation and for the protection of the marine environment, justifying the proposal by explaining how the proposed ship's complement will deal with emergency situations, including the evacuation of passengers where applicable;

14 2015 Regulations, reg 46(2): this provision refers to the Merchant Shipping (Hours of Work) Regulations 2002 (SI 2002/2125), which have now been superseded by the 2018 Regulations.
15 2015 Regulations, reg 46(3).
16 2015 Regulations, reg 46(5)–(6). For instance, any change of equipment, construction or use of the ship, which may affect the safe manning level: MSN 1868, para 6.3.
17 See www.gov.uk/government/uploads/system/uploads/attachment_data/file/294949/msf_4227_safe_manning_doc-2.pdf [Accessed 21 January 2018].
18 SI 2018/58.
19 MSN 1868, paras 9.1–9.2.
20 MSN 1868, paras 6.1, 6.7, 7.1 and 7.4.
21 MSN 1868, para 2.1.

- Ensure that the minimum safe manning level is adequate at all times and in all respects, including meeting peak workload situations, conditions and requirements, and is in accordance with the principles, recommendations and guidelines contained in this MSN;
- In case of changes in trading area(s), operations, construction, machinery, equipment or operation and maintenance of the ship, which may affect the safe manning level, prepare and submit a new proposal for the minimum safe manning level.'[22]

The owner and operator must, in ensuring that working hours are kept to a safe limit, identify the functions to be undertaken, and the number of personnel and skills and experience required.[23] Working arrangements, which provide for sufficient rest periods, must be established, taking into account the obligations under the Merchant Shipping (International Safety Management (ISM) Code) Regulations 2014[24] to ensure that the master and crew are capable of undertaking concurrent and continuing operations at the appropriate levels of their responsibilities.[25] On passenger ships, a working language is to be established, in accordance with Regulation 14, Ch V, of the IMO's International Convention for the Safety of Life at Sea (SOLAS).[26]

Proper account must also be taken of IMO Resolution A1047 (27)[27] which, in turn, requires maritime administrations to take account of existing instruments in force of the IMO, ILO, International Trade Union Confederation (ITUC) and World Health Organisation (WHO) which deal with: watchkeeping; hours of work or rest; safety management; certification of seafarers; training of seafarers; occupational safety, health and hygiene; crew accommodation and food; security; and radio communications.[28]

ESTABLISHING WATCHKEEPING ARRANGEMENTS: SPECIFIC PROVISIONS

At sea

13.5 The master must:

- ensure that the watchkeeping arrangements are at all times adequate for maintaining safe navigational, engineering and radio watches: (a) in accordance with STCW Regulation VIII/2, paragraph 2; and (b) taking into account (i)

22 MSN 1868, para 2.2.
23 MSN 1868, para 2.3.
24 SI 2014/1512.
25 MSN 1868, para 2.3.
26 MSN 1868, para 2.3.
27 IMO Resolution A.1047(27), 'Principles of Minimum Safe Manning', adopted on 30 November 2011 (recital 6 of which revokes IMO Resolution A.890(21), 'Principles of Safe Manning', adopted on 25 November 1999).
28 IMO Resolution A.1047(27), para 2.2; MSN 1868, para 2.4.

the prevailing circumstances and conditions, and (ii) section A-VIII/2 of the STCW Code;[29]

- give directions to the deck watchkeeping officers responsible for navigating the ship safely during their periods of duty, in accordance with: (a) section A-VIII/2, Pt 4-1, of the STCW Code; and (b) MSN 1868.[30]

The chief engineer must:

- ensure that the engineering watchkeeping arrangements are at all times adequate for maintaining a safe watch, in accordance with: (a) section A-VIII/2, Pt 4-2, of the STCW Code; and (b) MSN 1868.[31]

In port

13.6 The master must:

- where the ship is safely moored or safely anchored under normal circumstances in port, arrange for an appropriate and effective watch to be maintained for the purposes of safety, in accordance with: (a) section A-VIII/2, Pt 5, of the STCW Code; and (b) MSN 1868.[32]

Ships carrying hazardous cargo in port

13.7 In addition to the duties under regulation 48 of the 2015 Regulations, the master must:

- in respect of a ship carrying hazardous cargo[33] in bulk, ensure that (a) a safe deck watch and safe engineering watch are maintained by the ready availability of a duly qualified officer(s) and (if appropriate) ratings, and (b) the principles and requirements of MSN 1868 are taken into account;[34]
- in respect of a ship carrying hazardous cargo other than in bulk, ensure that (a) account is taken of the nature, quantity, packing and stowage of the hazardous cargo, and of any special conditions on board, afloat and ashore, and (b) the principles and requirements of MSN 1868 are taken into account.[35]

Annexes A and B to MSN 1868 provide tables and guidance on the number of deck and engineering officers required for different sizes of ship by gross tonnage, registered power (KW) and also relating to their trading areas (near-coastal or

29 2015 Regulations, reg 47(1).
30 2015 Regulations, reg 47(2).
31 2015 Regulations, reg 47(3).
32 2015 Regulations, reg 48.
33 For these purposes, 'hazardous cargo' (whether in bulk or otherwise) means any cargo which is, or may be, explosive, flammable, toxic, health-threatening or environment-polluting (reg 49(3)).
34 2015 Regulations, reg 49(1)(a), (2).
35 2015 Regulations, reg 49(1)(b), (2).

unlimited). As the tables only provide guidance, owners and operators must take all relevant factors into account before finalising their manning proposals.[36]

SHIP'S DOCTOR

13.8 A ship carrying 100 or more persons, on an international voyage lasting more than 72 hours, must carry a doctor.[37] For further details about medical care on board, see Chapter 17.

SHIP'S COOK

13.9 There is a requirement to carry a qualified ship's cook for ships which ordinarily operate with 10 or more seafarers, unless the ship only operates within 60 miles of a safe haven and does not call at a port outside the UK.[38] For further details of the requirements, qualifications and exceptions relating to ship's cooks, see Chapter 16.

NATIONALITY RESTRICTIONS

13.10 The only nationality restrictions are those imposed by the Merchant Shipping (Officer Nationality) Regulations 1995 ('the 1995 Regulations').[39] These require a master of every 'strategic ship' to be a: (a) a Commonwealth citizen; (b) an EEA national; or (c) a national of a state (other than a EEA State) which is a member of the North Atlantic Treaty Organisation (NATO).[40] A 'strategic ship' means a: (a) a British-registered fishing vessel of over 24 metres; or (b) a UK ship of 500 tons or more, which is a cruise ship, product tanker or ro-ro ship.[41]

OFFENCES

13.11 The 2015 Regulations set out various offences, which can be committed for non-compliance, as set out in the table below. With one exception, all offences are punishable as follows: on summary conviction in England and Wales, a fine; in Scotland and Northern Ireland, a fine not exceeding the statutory maximum; on indictment in any of those countries, imprisonment (in the case of an individual) not exceeding six months, or a fine, or both.[42] The exception relates to an offence

36 MSN 1868, para 4.3.
37 Merchant Shipping (Maritime Labour Convention) (Minimum Requirements for Seafarers) Regulations 2014 (SI 2014/1613) ('Minimum Requirements Regulations'), regs 44, 46(3)–(4).
38 Minimum Requirements Regulations, reg 37.
39 SI 1995/1427; MSN 1868, para 5.1.
40 1995 Regulations, reg 3.
41 1995 Regulations, reg 2.
42 2015 Regulations, reg 55(2)–(3).

under reg 55(5) by the chief engineer, which can only be tried summarily, with a maximum sentence: in England and Wales, a fine; in Scotland or Northern Ireland, a fine not exceeding level 5 on the standard scale.[43] In all cases, it is a defence if all reasonable steps had been taken; the onus is on the defendant to show, where relevant, that it was not reasonably practicable to do more.[44]

This table may also be used as a checklist for compliance.

Regulation imposing duty/ creating offence	**Summary of duty, contravention of which amounts to an offence**	**Liable party**
Reg 46(1)(a)/ reg 55(2)	SMD to be in force.	Company
Reg 46(1)(b)/ reg 55(2)	SMD to be kept on board.	Company
Reg 46(1)(c)/ reg 55(2)	Ship to be manned at least to SMD levels.	Company
Reg 46(2)/ reg 55(3)	Ship not to proceed to sea without valid SMD/manning to at least SMD levels.	Master
Reg 47(1)/ reg 55(3)	Master to ensure that adequate watchkeeping arrangements are made.	Master
Reg 47(2)/ reg 55(3)	Master to give directions to deck watchkeeping officers.	Master
Reg 47(3)/ reg 55(5)	Chief engineer to ensure that adequate watchkeeping arrangements are made.	Chief engineer
Reg 48/reg 55(3)	Master to ensure appropriate watch is maintained for ship safely moored or anchored in port.	Master
Reg 49/reg 55(3)	In respect of a ship in port carrying hazardous cargo, master to ensure a safe deck watch/take account of nature and packaging of cargo, etc.	Master

INSPECTION AND DETENTION OF SHIPS

13.12 A non-UK ship may be inspected to verify that seafarers on board hold valid STCW certificates, and to assess the ability of a seafarer to maintain the watchkeeping standards set out in Pt 4 of the 2015 Regulations, following the ship being involved in a maritime incident (such as a collision or grounding) or being operated dangerously, etc.[45] UK ships may be detained for any breach of

43 2015 Regulations, reg 55(5).
44 2015 Regulations, reg 55(6)–(7).
45 2015 Regulations, reg 53.

the 2015 Regulations.[46] Non-UK ships may be detained for a breach of regulation 47, 48 or 49 (see above), breach of the terms of any exemption granted under regulation 50 or a failure to rectify any deficiency set out in regulation 53(3) (failure of a seafarer to hold an STCW certificate, a failure to comply with the SMD, etc) after notification to the master, and there is in consequence a danger to persons, property or the environment.[47]

Compliance

DMLC: comply with the UK provisions as set out in Pt I, point 7, and enter details of measures taken to comply in Pt II, point 7.

46 2015 Regulations, reg 54(1)(a).
47 2015 Regulations, reg 54(1)(b)(i)–(iii).

CHAPTER 14

Regulation 2.8: Careers and Skill Development and Opportunities for Seafarers' Employment

INTRODUCTION

14.1 The purpose of Regulation 2.8 of the MLC is to promote career and skill development and employment opportunities for seafarers.[1]

Ratifying states are required to establish national policies which encourage career and skill development and employment opportunities for seafarers, in order that the maritime sector is provided with a stable and competent work force.[2] These policies should assist seafarers to develop their competencies, qualifications and employment opportunities.[3] As regards seafarers whose primary duties relate to the safe operation and navigation of ships, ratifying states are required to consult with shipowners' and seafarers' organisations, for the purposes of establishing clear objectives for vocational guidance, education and ongoing training.[4]

The UK fulfils these requirements by measures which pre-date the entry into force of the MLC. Prominent amongst them are the government's support for maritime training ('SMarT') and the tonnage tax regime.

1 MLC, Regulation 2.8, p 39.
2 MLC, Regulation 2.8, para 1; Standard A2.8.1.
3 MLC, Standard A2.8.2.
4 MLC, Standard A2.8.3.

SMarT

14.2 The SMarT scheme has been running since April 1998, and supports courses approved by the Maritime and Coastguard Agency (MCA) and Merchant Navy Training Board (MNTB), for officers, trainee officers and ratings. The Government's principal objective in supporting this training is to facilitate an adequate supply of UK maritime expertise to meet the UK's economic and strategic requirements.

The most recent MCA publications are MGN 455,[5] MIN 466[6] and MIN 486.[7]

In February 2018, the government announced that SmarT funding is to be increased to £30 million per annum, which will enable the annual intake of cadets to increase from 750 to 1,200.[8]

SMarT is currently administered on behalf of the MCA by MaTSU, which is an independent unit of Ricardo-AEA. MaTSU approves the payment of public funding to approved training providers (sponsoring companies) to support the costs (up to 50%) of approved training.

Originally there were five areas of training supported by SMarT, as set out below; however, SMarT 4 has been withdrawn, but the others remain in place:

- SMarT 1: trainee officers – first Certificate of Competency (CoC);[9]
- SMarT 2: officers training towards their second CoC (this has been reintroduced following earlier withdrawal);[10]
- SMarT 3: ratings training, rating-to-officer conversion training, adult entry engineer leading to engineer officer;[11]
- SMarT 4: for officers to revalidate their CoCs from STCW[12] 1978 to the STCW 1995 amendments (no longer available);[13]
- SMarT 5: second route for ratings training and parts of the rating-to-officer conversion.[14]

5 MGN 455: The Government Support for Maritime Training Scheme (SMarT) – Revised Arrangements from 1 August 2012 to 31 March 2015.
6 MIN 466 (M): The Government Support for Maritime Training (SMarT) – Additional Guidance.
7 MIN 486 (M): Support for Maritime Training (SMarT) – Additional Funds of up to £3 Million.
8 See www.gov.uk/government/news/government-doubles-trainee-funding-in-smart-move-to-boost-uk-maritime-sector [Accessed 4 November 2018].
9 MGN 455, para 3.1.
10 MGN 455, para 4.1.
11 MGN 455, para 5.1.
12 The IMO's International Convention on Standards of Training, Certification and Watchkeeping for Seafarers 1978 (as amended, most recently by the Manila Amendments 2010).
13 MGN 455, para 6.1.
14 MGN 455, para 7.1.

CONDITIONS OF ELIGIBILITY FOR TRAINEES AND REGISTERED TRAINING PROVIDERS

14.3 A trainee must be: (a) an EEA national or a Channel Islands or Isle of Man passport holder; (b) ordinarily resident in the UK; and (c) proficient in the English language (written and oral).[15]

A registered training provider must: (a) be based in or incorporated in the EEA, the Channel Islands or Isle of Man; (b) have entered into a training provider's agreement with the MCA; and (c) be able to provide and monitor the relevant training.[16]

Further information can be obtained from:

The SMarT Administrator
MaTSU
The Gemini Building
Fermi Avenue
Harwell
Didcot
OX11 0QR

Tel: 01235 753244
Email: SMarT.enquiries@ricardo.com

or

SMarT Team
Seafarer Training and Certification
Maritime and Coastguard Agency
105 Commercial Road
Southampton
SO15 1EG

Tel: 02380 329183/381/280
Email: smart@mcga.gov.uk

TONNAGE TAX

14.4 Election into the tonnage tax regime requires a commitment by a company to train or underwrite the training of sufficient UK or EEA seafarers to meet a 'minimum training obligation' (MTO). The MTO falls into two parts: one for officers, and the other for ratings.[17]

15 MGN 455, para 8.1.
16 MGN 455, para 13.5.
17 Tonnage Tax Minimum Training Commitment – Overview: https://assets.publishing.service.gov.uk/government/uploads/system/uploads/attachment_data/file/447685/tonnage-tax-minimum-training-commitment-overview.pdf [Accessed 27 June 2018].

PART IV

Title 3: Accommodation, Recreational Facilities, Food and Catering

CHAPTER 15

Regulation 3.1: Crew Accommodation and Recreational Facilities

INTRODUCTION

15.1 The purpose of Regulation 3.1 of the MLC is ensure that seafarers have decent accommodation and recreational facilities on board.[1] Ratifying states are required to ensure that their ships provide and maintain decent accommodation and recreational facilities consistent with supporting seafarers' health and well-being.[2] It should be noted that the requirements in the Code of Regulation 3.1 which relate to ship construction and equipment apply to ships constructed on or after the date the MLC came into force, which was 20 August 2013.[3] For ships constructed before that date, the requirements relating to ship construction and equipment that are set out in the Accommodation of Crews Convention (Revised), 1949 (No. 92) and the Accommodation of Crews (Supplementary Provisions) Convention, 1970 (No. 133) must continue to apply to the extent that they were applicable, prior to that date, under the law or practice of the relevant country.[4] For these purposes, a ship is deemed to be constructed on the date when its keel is laid or when it is at a similar stage of construction.[5]

1 MLC, Regulation 3.1, purpose.
2 MLC, Regulation 3.1, para 1.
3 MLC, Regulation 3.1, para 2.
4 MLC, Regulation 3.1, para 2.
5 MLC, Regulation 3.1, para 2.

15.2 The provisions relating to accommodation and recreational facilities are set out in Pt 7 of the Merchant Shipping (Maritime Labour Convention) (Minimum Requirements) Regulations 2014[6] ('Minimum Requirements Regulations') and MSN 1844 (M),[7] which is supplemented by MGN 481 (M).[8] These apply to UK ships wherever they may be, and to non-UK ships without MLC documentation, while they are in UK waters.[9] In Pt 7 of the Minimum Requirements Regulations, only reg 33 applies to non-UK ships with MLC documentation, while they are in UK waters (as outlined below).[10]

The term 'crew accommodation' is defined as '... accommodation, including the construction, machinery, fittings and equipment of that accommodation, intended for or used by seafarers'.[11]

TRANSITIONAL PROVISIONS AND EXCEPTIONS

15.3 The MLC provisions on ship board construction and equipment only apply to ships which were constructed on or after the date the Convention came into force for the relevant flag state.[12] For the UK, that date was 7 August 2014, which is also the date on which the Minimum Requirements Regulations came into force.[13]

The UK's MLC provisions on crew accommodation are set out in MSN 1844.[14] There are exceptions to these provisions, in respect of: (i) certain older ships; (ii) those ships to which the Secretary of State has granted an exemption; or (iii) approved substantial equivalence arrangements.[15] Before outlining the provisions of MSN 1844, the extent to which the exemptions apply will be set out.

Provisions for certain older ships

15.4 As regards ships, the keels of which were laid, or which were at a similar stage of construction, before 11 July 1997, the position is as follows:

- if the crew accommodation has not been substantially reconstructed or altered on or after 11 July 1997, such ships must comply with the requirements set

6 SI 2014/2013.
7 MSN 1844 (M): Maritime Labour Convention, 2006 – Crew Accommodation.
8 MGN 481 (M) Amendment 1: Maritime Labour Convention, 2006 – Crew Accommodation, Supplementary Guidance.
9 Minimum Requirements Regulations, reg 3(1).
10 Minimum Requirements Regulations, regs 3(3)–(4)(b)(v), 33.
11 Minimum Requirements Regulations, reg 29(1).
12 MLC, Regulation 3.2.
13 The UK ratified the MLC on 7 August 2013; in accordance with MLC Article VIII, para 4, the Convention comes into force 12 months after the date on which its ratification is registered.
14 Minimum Requirements Regulations, reg 29(2).
15 Minimum Requirements Regulations, regs 29(2), 30–32.

out in Sch 6 to the Merchant Shipping (Crew Accommodation) Regulations 1978,[16] as if they had not been revoked;[17]

- If the crew accommodation has been substantially reconstructed or altered on or after 11 July 1997, but before 7 August 2014, such ships must comply with the requirements set out in the Merchant Shipping (Crew Accommodation) Regulations 1997.[18]

Exemptions

15.5 The Secretary of State may grant, in respect of a ship, a written exemption from some or all of the requirements of MSN 1844, where (a) this is expressly permitted by the corresponding MLC Standard A3.1, and (b) the Secretary of State has fulfilled any obligation imposed by MLC Standard A3.1 in respect of the exemption.[19]

Substantial equivalence

15.6 This form of exemption derives from the flexibility permitted by MLC Article VI, paragraphs 3 and 4, under which (unless otherwise provided) ratifying states, which are not in a position to implement rights and principles in the manner set out in Part A of the Code, may do so through laws, regulations or other measures, which are 'substantially equivalent' to Part A (see Chapter 1 at para 1.14). Therefore the Secretary of State may approve arrangements which, in respect of a particular ship, or ships of a particular description, when taken together with conditions to which the approval is subject, are considered to be substantially equivalent to the requirements set out in MSN 1844.[20] This flexibility has been used in relation to certain workboats and large commercial yachts.

Workboats

15.7 Subject to the foregoing, workboats constructed (or substantially reconstructed or altered) on or after 7 August 2014 are subject to all MLC accommodation standards, as set out in Pt 7 of the Minimum Requirements Regulations and MSN 1844. However, MGN 491[21] provides that such workboats which are 200 GT to less than 500 GT may instead adopt a set of 'substantial equivalence' measures set out in its Annex 1 (reproduced below), which allow the accommodation to be placed below the load line.[22] Workboats must comply

16 SI 1978/795, revoked on 11 July 1997 by Merchant Shipping (Crew Accommodation) Regulations 1997 (SI 1997/1508), reg 1(2)(a).
17 Minimum Requirements Regulations, reg 30(1)(a).
18 Minimum Requirements Regulations, reg 30(1)(b); SI 1997/1508.
19 Minimum Requirements Regulations, reg 31(1)(a)–(b).
20 Minimum Requirements Regulations, reg 32(1).
21 MGN 491 (M) Amendment 1: MLC, 2006 – Application to workboats of 200GT to less than 500GT.
22 MGN 491, para 5.2.

with either one regime or the other; it is not permitted to 'cherry pick' between the two.[23] In all other respects, those workboats must comply with Pt 7 of the Minimum Requirements Regulations and MSN 1844.

For those concerned with the application of the MLC to commercial vessels of less than 200 GT, there are yet further substantial equivalence provisions and guidance set out in MGN 490.[24] Such vessels built after the MLC came into force must comply with either MSN 1844 or the substantial equivalence standards set out in Annex 1; it is not permitted to 'cherry pick' between the two.[25]

Workboats constructed before 7 August 2014 (which have not been substantially reconstructed or altered on or after that date) are not required to comply with the standards set out in Pt 7 of the Minimum Requirements Regulations or MGN 1844: they are subject to the standards which applied before that date.[26]

As stated, the MLC provides that a ship is deemed to have been constructed on the date when its keel is laid or when it is at a similar stage of construction; the UK provides that workboats which are constructed of fibre reinforced plastic, or similar materials, '... will be considered to be at a similar stage of construction to having their keel laid if they have had more than 5% of the hull resin and reinforcement laid'.[27]

Annex 1 to MGN 491

15.8 Annex 1 to MGN 491 provides that workboats of 200 GT to less than 500 GT must comply with the seafarer accommodation requirements of the MLC, as set out in Pt 7 of the Minimum Requirements Regulations and MSN 1844, except as permitted below:

> '1. Sleeping rooms may be provided below the reference load line if it can be shown that compliance with Standard A3.1, paragraph 6(c) of the MLC would compromise the functionality, safety or stability of the ship.
>
> 2. The floor of the sleeping room may be up to 2000 mm below the reference load line provided that:
>
> .1 Adequate continuous climate control is provided, partly aimed at controlling of condensation and moisture related odours;
>
> .2 At least two adequate escape routes are present;
>
> .3 A bilge alarm which has its audible alarm in the watertight compartment of the sleeping room is available;

23 MGN 491, para 5.2.

24 MGN 490 (M) Amendment 1 – Maritime Labour Convention, 2006: Application to small vessels of less than 200GT that are ordinarily engaged in commercial activities.

25 MGN 490, para 5.2; Annex 1 – Accommodation and recreational facilities – substantially equivalent standards – new vessels of less than 200GT. Annex 2 provides guidance on the UK MLC legislation, and Annex 3 sets out a checklist and model 'Document of Compliance'.

26 MGN 491, para 5.4.

27 MGN 491, para 5.3.

.4 Adequate, adjustable lighting is provided; the lack of daylight shall be compensated according to the needs of the seafarer;

.5 Appropriate materials and colours for wall and floor coverings are applied, which provide improved space perception;

.6 A minimum of 203 cm headroom in the accommodation must be provided.

Further notes:

The reference load line is defined as follows:

- For ships to which an International Load Line Certificate is issued: the minimum assignable summer freeboard as defined in the Load Line Convention, Annex 1, Regulation 6.2.a.
- For ships to which no International Load Line Certificate is issued: a line parallel to the designed load waterline located at a distance of 20% of the depth of the ship, as defined in the International Load Line Convention Annex I, Regulation 3(5), with a maximum of 1000 mm below the freeboard deck as defined in the International Load Line Convention, Annex I, Regulation 3(9).'

Large commercial yachts

Constructed after the MLC came into force

15.9 There are 'substantially equivalent' crew accommodation and recreational provisions for commercial yachts which are certified under the Large Commercial Yacht Code[28] ('LY3 Code') and constructed on or after the date the MLC came into force internationally (20 August 2013). These apply to: (i) yachts of less than 200 GT, which trade internationally;[29] and (ii) yachts of 200 GT or over (whether or not they trade internationally).[30]

It should be noted that the LY3 Code and the Passenger Yacht Code[31] (PYC) are being merged into the 'Red Ensign Group Yacht Code'[32] (REG YC), which comes

28 The LY3 Code applies to yachts which are 24 metres and over in load line length, are in commercial use for sport or pleasure, do not carry cargo and do not carry more than 12 passengers. It was developed by the UK, its overseas territories (Anguilla, Bermuda, British Virgin Islands, Cayman Islands, Falkland Islands, Gibraltar, Montserrat, St Helena and the Turks & Caicos Islands) and crown dependencies (Isle of Man, Guernsey and Jersey) and international industry representatives (listed at Annex 1): LY3 Code, paras 1, 1.6. LY3 Code: https://assets.publishing.service.gov.uk/government/uploads/system/uploads/attachment_data/file/444652/LY3_-_Final_Version.pdf [Accessed 26 September 2018].

29 LY3 Code, Chapter 21A.

30 LY3 Code, Chapter 21B. For an account of the application of the MLC to yachts, including its accommodation provisions, see Lorenzon, F and Coles, R, *The Law of Yachts and Yachting* (Informa Law from Routledge, 2nd edition, Abingdon, Oxon, 2018), 129–156.

31 A Code of Practice for Yachts Carrying 13 to 36 Passengers (4th edn, January 2014): https://assets.publishing.service.gov.uk/government/uploads/system/uploads/attachment_data/file/295098/py_code__3rd_edition___final-2__march_2013_.pdf [Accessed 26 September 2018].

32 Red Ensign Group Yacht Code (January 2019): www.redensigngroup.org/reg-yacht-code.aspx [Accessed 26 September 2018].

into force on 1 January 2019. The LY3 Code will become Part A of the REG YC and, although the crew accommodation provisions will be mostly unchanged, there will be some updates (and those on crew accommodation are referred to below). The PYC will become Part B of the REG YC, and provides that ships will be constructed, certified and operated under the MLC provisions for passenger ships.[33] There will be a number of annexes common to Parts A and B.

Those concerned with yachts (constructed after the MLC came into force) certified under the LY3 Code, soon to become Part A of the REG YC, should note that the substantially equivalent provisions on crew accommodation and recreational facilities are set out as follows:

- Yachts of less than 200 GT – Chapter 21A of the LY3 Code/Chapter 21A of Part A of the REG YC;
- Yachts of 200 GT and over – Chapter 21B of the LY3 Code/Chapter 21B of Part A of the REG YC.

There are also specific substantial equivalence provisions on sleeping accommodation for yachts within the following GT ranges: up to 3000 GT;[34] from 200 GT to less than 500 GT;[35] and from 500 GT to less than 1250 GT.[36]

Furthermore, under the LY3 Code, yachts of 3000 GT or more were originally required to comply with the provisions for sleeping accommodation set out in MLC, Standard A3.1.[37] However, following concerns raised by builders about applying those provisions to yachts of 3000 GT but less than 5000 GT, the MCA issued MGN 517, which permitted the option to adopt the substantial equivalence provisions in its Annex 1.[38] Those substantial equivalence provisions have been incorporated into Part A of the REG YC, and may be applied to yachts of 3000 GT but less than 5000 GT.[39] Yachts of 5000 GT and over must comply with the provisions of Standard A3.1 of the MLC,[40] which is incorporated into UK laws by Part 7 of the Minimum Requirements Regulations, and MSN 1844, which is supplemented by MGN 481.

With some limited scope for exceptions, the provisions referred to above apply to sailing vessels in the same way that they apply to motor vessels.[41]

33 REG YC, Part B, Chapter 9.1.
34 LY3 Code, section 21B.8.2/REG YC, Part A, section 21B.8.2.
35 LY3 Code, section 21B.8.3/REG YC, Part A, section 21B.8.3.
36 LY3 Code, section 21B.8.4/REG YC, Part A, section 21B.8.4.
37 LY3 Code, section 21B.8.5.
38 MGN 517 (M): MLC, 2006 – Substantially equivalent accommodation standards for Large Commercial Yachts of 3000GT to less than 5000GT.
39 REG YC, Part A, section 21B.8.5(a)(i)–(vii).
40 LY3 Code, section 21B.8.5 (which applies to yachts of 3000 GT and over but there is a substantial equivalence option for yachts of 3000 GT to less than 5000 GT set out in MGN 517, Annex 1); REG YC, Part A, section 21B.8.6(a).
41 LY3 Code, Chapter 21B.20; REG YC, Part A, Chapter 21B.20.

Provisions for other yachts

15.10 As for yachts to which the MLC substantially equivalent standards do not apply (eg because they were built pre-MLC, or post-MLC but are less than 200 GT and do not trade internationally), they are subject to other requirements within the LY3 Code/Part A of the REG YC.[42] These yachts are not subject to the MLC, but to the standards set out in other ILO Conventions for merchant vessels, emphasising that such standards should be practicable for vessels greater than 500 GT, and that for vessels under 500 GT (particularly sailing vessels) such standards should be applied 'where possible'.[43]

INSPECTIONS AND RECORDS

15.11 The master (or authorised officer), accompanied by at least one member of the crew, must, at least every seven days, carry out inspections of the crew accommodation, to ensure that it is clean, decently habitable, and maintained in a good state of repair.[44] The findings must be recorded in the official log book, specifying: the date and time of inspection; name and rank of persons inspecting; and particulars of any non-compliances with the Minimum Requirements Regulations.[45]

Similarly, frequent inspections must be carried out on yachts and include, in addition to the crew accommodation: supplies of food and drinking water; spaces and equipment used for the storage and handling of food and drinking water; and the galley and other equipment used for the preparation and service of meals. The results of each inspection must be recorded and available for review.[46]

NON-UK SHIPS WITH MLC DOCUMENTATION

15.12 As for non-UK ships with MLC documentation, while they are in UK waters, they must comply with the minimum standards for on-board accommodation and recreational facilities, set out in MLC, Standard A3.1, paragraphs 6 to 17.[47] The foregoing is subject to the following exceptions: (i) the MLC provisions on ship construction and equipment do not apply to ships constructed before the date the MLC came into force, which was 20 August 2013; and (ii) any permissions, exemptions or variations granted by the flag state

42 LY3 Code, Chapter 21; REG YC, Part A, Chapter 21.
43 LY3 Code, Chapter 21, para 1.4; REG YC, Part A, Chapter 21, para (3).
44 Minimum Requirements Regulations, reg 29(4).
45 Minimum Requirements Regulations, reg 29(6).
46 LY3 Code, Chapter 21B.17; REG YC, Part A, Chapter 21B.17.
47 Minimum Requirements Regulations, regs 3(3)–(4)(v), 33(1).

(so far as permissible under the MLC).[48] In accordance with MLC, Standard A3.1.18, the master (or authorised person) must carry out frequent inspections (to ensure cleanliness, habitability and good maintenance), record the results and make them available for review, whether or not these are requirements of the flag state.[49]

OFFENCES

15.13 Various offences are created, under the Minimum Requirements Regulations, which are set out in the table below. Unless otherwise indicated (by showing the potential penalty on indictment), they are summary offences only. It is a defence for a person charged to show that they took all reasonable steps to comply with the relevant provision.[50]

Regulation imposing duty/creating offence	Summary of duty failure of which amounts to an offence	Potentially liable parties/ penalty
Reg 29(2)/ reg 29(3)	To comply with the requirements of MSN 1844.	Shipowner/ Summary: Level 5/ Indictment: maximum 2 years' imprisonment and/or fine
Reg 29(4)/ reg 29(5)	Master or authorised person to inspect accommodation at intervals not exceeding seven days.	Master/ Level 3
Reg 29(6)/ reg 29(7)	Master or authorised person to enter record of inspection in official log book.	Master/ Level 5
Reg 30(1)–(2)/ reg 30(4)	In accordance with the transitional provisions, pre-MLC ships to comply with the Merchant Shipping (Crew Accommodation) Regulations 1978 or the Merchant Shipping (Crew Accommodation) Regulations 1997 (whichever is applicable).	Shipowner/ Summary: Level 5/ Indictment: maximum 2 years' imprisonment and/or fine

48 MLC, Regulation 3.1.2; Minimum Requirements Regulations, reg 33(2). MLC, Regulation 3.1.2 further provides that ships constructed before 20 August 2013 are subject to the Accommodation of Crews Convention (Revised), 1949 (No. 92) and the Accommodation of Crews (Supplementary Provisions) Convention, 1970 (No. 33), to the extent that they were applicable prior to that date for the flag state concerned.

49 Minimum Requirements Regulations, reg 33(4).

50 Minimum Requirements Regulations, reg 60.

Regulation imposing duty/creating offence	**Summary of duty failure of which amounts to an offence**	**Potentially liable parties/ penalty**
Reg 31(1)–(2)/ reg 31(3)	To comply with the terms of an exemption from some or all of the requirements in MSN 1844.	Shipowner/ Summary: Level 5/ Indictment: maximum 2 years' imprisonment and/or fine
Reg 32(1)–(3)/ reg 32(4)	To comply with the condition(s) applicable to the approval of substantial equivalence arrangements.	Shipowner/ Summary: Level 5/ Indictment: maximum 2 years' imprisonment and/or fine
Reg 33(1)/ reg 33(3)	Non-UK MLC ship in UK waters to comply with MLC, Standard A3.1, paras 6 to 17 (recreational and accommodation facilities).	Shipowner/ Summary: Level 5/ Indictment: maximum 2 years' imprisonment and/or fine
Reg 33(4)(a)/ reg 33(5)	Master of a non-UK MLC ship in UK waters to comply with MLC, Standard A3.1, para 18 (frequent inspections).	Master/ Level 3
Reg 33(4)(b)/ reg 33(5)	Master of a non-UK MLC ship in UK waters to comply with MLC, Standard A3.1, para 18 (record and make available results of inspections).	Master/ Level 2

ENFORCEMENT

15.14 For the provisions on MLC certification and enforcement, see Chapter 22.

MSN 1844 (M): MARITIME LABOUR CONVENTION, 2006 – CREW ACCOMMODATION

15.15 A summarised version of MSN 1844 is set out below, retaining original paragraph numbers.

General

15.16

2.1 Crew accommodation (except store rooms) must be situated:

(a) amidships or aft (where practicable) and must not be situated forward of the collision bulkhead; and

(b) wholly above the Summer Load Line (if any) marked on the ship in accordance with the provisions of rules made or treated as made under the Merchant Shipping Act (Load Line) Regulations 1998.

2.2 Crew accommodation must be situated, constructed and arranged to exclude, so far as reasonably practicable, noise coming from other parts of the ship and other parts of the crew accommodation.

2.3 Crew sleeping rooms on a passenger ship must not be situated immediately beneath a working passageway.

2.4 Any bulkhead, casing or deck separating a sleeping room from: (a) a machinery space; (b) a mess room; (c) a recreation room; (d) a room in which films or television are shown; (e) a games room; and (f) a public room, must be acoustically insulated.

2.5 All parts of the crew accommodation (except cold store rooms) must have a clear headroom of at least 203 centimetres at every point where free movement is necessary (an exception may be permitted if it is reasonable to do so and does not result in discomfort to the crew).

2.6 With the exception of hospitals on passenger ships, no part of the crew accommodation may be shared with or used by passengers.

2.7 Inside panelling of crew accommodation must be constructed of a material suitable for the purpose and conducive to ensuring a healthy environment.

2.8 Crew accommodation must be so situated, constructed and arranged as to ensure the exclusion of effluvia originating in other spaces.

2.9 and 2.10 concern the granting of exemptions and substantial equivalence under regs 31 and 32 of the Minimum Requirements Regulations respectively (see paras 15.3–15.10 above).

2.11 Ships of less than 200 gross tonnage may be exempted after consultation with the shipowners' and seafarers' organisations, where it is reasonable to do so, taking into account the size of the ship and the number of persons on board in relation to the requirements of the following parts of MSN 1844:(a) paragraphs 7.1 (heating) and 20.1 to 20.4 (washing and drying facilities); and (b) paragraph 11 with respect to floor area only.

2.12 Where there is need to take account, without discrimination, of the interests of seafarers having differing and distinctive religious and social practices, the MCA may, after consultation with the seafarers' and shipowners' organisation, permit fairly applied variations on condition that they do not result in overall facilities less favourable for seafarers.

Divisions between the crew accommodation and other parts of the ship

15.17

3.1 (and 3.2) Bulkheads which enclose any part of the crew accommodation and are exposed to the weather must be properly constructed of steel or other suitable material and must be of watertight construction; any openings in them must be provided with means of a weathertight closure which, for any entrance, must be a hinged door. Such bulkheads, and any part of the side of the ship which forms a wall or part of a wall of the crew accommodation, must be so insulated as to prevent overheating or condensation unless the crew accommodation is so protected by its situation and ventilation that overheating and condensation are unlikely to occur.

3.3 Every bulkhead, casing or deck separating any part of the crew accommodation from any space (including a cold store room) which is subject to abnormal heat or cold must be so insulated as to prevent condensation or discomfort to the crew.

3.4 Every bulkhead which separates any part of the crew accommodation (other than recreation deck space) from a space used as: (a) a machinery space; (b) a bunker; (c) a room for storing fire-extinguishing gases; (d) a chain locker; (e) a cofferdam; (f) a cargo space; (g) a store room; (h) a lamp room or a paint room; or (i) a battery locker, must be of gastight construction, and must be of watertight construction where necessary to protect the crew accommodation.

3.5 There must be no opening in any of the bulkheads referred to in paragraph 3.4 except that, where sanitary accommodation or changing rooms provided for the exclusive use of engine room officers and ratings are sited adjacent to the propelling machinery space, there may be an opening in the propelling machinery space bulkhead to the sanitary accommodation or changing rooms and an opening from the sanitary accommodation to a passageway forming part of the crew accommodation provided that a hinged, steel self-closing gastight door is fitted to one of such openings.

3.6 No batteries of a type which emit gases must be stored in the crew accommodation and there must be no opening from the crew accommodation into a space where such batteries are stored. Precautions must be taken to ensure that fumes from batteries cannot be discharged into the crew accommodation.

3.7 No manhole or other opening to a fuel tank must be situated in the crew accommodation.

Interior bulkheads

15.18

4.1 All bulkheads within the crew accommodation must be properly constructed of steel or other suitable material.

4.2 Subject to sub-paragraph (c):

(a) every bulkhead which separates any part of crew accommodation from: (i) sanitary accommodation; (ii) a laundry; (iii) a drying room; (iv) a galley; (v) a cold store room; or (vi) a dry provision store room, must be of gastight construction, and

(b) every bulkhead which separates any part of the crew accommodation from any of the spaces specified in subparagraphs (a)(i) to (v) inclusive must be watertight to a height of not less than 23 centimetres, except in the case of doorways situated in bulkheads when the bulkheads must be watertight to a height of not less than 10 centimetres.

(c) The requirements of sub-paragraphs (a) and (b) do not apply to bulkheads separating: (i) spaces that are used for the same purpose; (ii) a laundry from a drying room; and (iii) a private bathroom from the sleeping room if there is direct access from the sleeping room to the private bathroom.

4.3 There must be no openings in any bulkhead separating any sanitary accommodation, laundry or drying room from any part of the crew accommodation except a passageway, recreation deck space or other sanitary accommodation, laundry or drying room; nor in a bulkhead separating a galley from a sleeping room.

Floor decks

15.19

5.1 Every floor deck which forms the floor of any part of the crew accommodation must be properly constructed. If it is directly over an oil tank or permanent coal bunker it must be oiltight or gastight respectively. Every floor deck must have a surface which provides a good foothold and can be easily kept clean. Any floor covering must be impervious to water and, if the deck is directly over an oil tank, impervious to oil.

5.2 (and 5.3) Every floor deck made of metal, except floor decks in sanitary accommodation, galleys, laundries and store rooms, must be covered with material suitable to its purpose. Every floor deck in sanitary accommodation, galleys and laundries must be covered with terrazzo tiles or other hard material which is impervious to liquids and provides a good foothold.

In each case, the material or covering must be properly laid and joins where the floor meets the walls must be rounded in such a way as to avoid crevices.

Pipes in crew accommodation

15.20

6.1 Hawse pipes must not pass through crew accommodation.

Heating

15.21

7.1 Except in ships employed solely within the Tropics or the Gulfs area, all sleeping rooms, mess rooms, day rooms, recreation rooms, rooms for watching films and television, hobbies and games rooms, offices, studies, sanitary accommodation and hospitals must be installed with a main heating system capable of ensuring that:

(a) the ventilation system provided for the room or crew accommodation is working so as to supply at least 25 cubic metres of fresh air per hour for each person which the room or crew accommodation is designed to accommodate at any one time; and

(b) the temperature of the ambient air is –1°C.

The temperature in the room or crew accommodation can be maintained at 21°C.

7.2 The main heating system must be operated by either steam, hot water or electricity, or must be a system which supplies warm air.

7.3 Means for turning on or off or varying the heat emitted by a radiator or other heating device without using a tool or key must be provided, wherever reasonably practicable, in the space in which that radiator or other device is fitted. All heating equipment must be constructed so that its operation is not affected by the use or non-use of propelling machinery, steering gear, deck machinery, calorifiers or cooking appliances.

7.4 (a) Subject to subparagraph (b) below, the crew accommodation must be heated by means of the main heating system at all times when any members of the crew are living or working on board and the circumstances are such that heating is required.

(b) Heating by means of the main heating system need not be provided when the vessel is in port if such parts of the crew accommodation as are then in use are provided with a safe and efficient temporary means of heating capable of ensuring the standard required by paragraph 7.1.

7.5 Heating equipment must be so constructed and installed, and if necessary shielded, as to avoid risk of fire or of danger of discomfort to the crew.

Lighting

15.22

8.1 In passenger ships all parts of the crew accommodation, except galleys, pantries, laundries, drying room, lockers, private and semi-private bathrooms and store rooms, must wherever reasonably practicable be adequately lit by natural light.

8.2 In all other ships other than passenger ships:

(a) subject to paragraph (b) below, all parts of the crew accommodation except galleys, pantries, laundries, drying room, lockers, private and semi-private bathrooms and store rooms must be adequately lit by natural light;[51] and

(b) sanitary accommodation and passageways must wherever practicable be adequately lit by natural light.

8.3 An electric lighting system must be installed which is capable of supplying adequate light in all parts of the crew accommodation. Electric lights must be so arranged as to give maximum benefit to the crew and must include an

51 Paragraph 8.2(a) requires that natural light is compulsory in these circumstances, whereas paragraphs 8.1 and 8.2(b) require it where it is 'reasonably practicable' and 'practicable', respectively.

electric reading lamp for each bed with a controlling switch at the head of the bed.

Ventilation

15.23

9.1 Every enclosed space in the crew accommodation, except a cold store room, must be provided with a ventilation system capable of maintaining the air in that space in a sufficiently pure condition for the health and comfort of the crew in all conditions of weather and climate which the ship is likely to encounter during the voyages on which she is intended to be engaged, and capable of being controlled as necessary for that purpose.

9.2 Without prejudice to the generality of paragraph 9.1:

(a) in all foreign going ships of 1000 tons or over except those regularly engaged in latitudes north of latitude 50° North or south of latitude 45° South; and

(b) in all ships of under 1000 tons regularly engaged on voyages solely within the area of the Tropics or the Gulfs area;

the ventilation system provided pursuant to paragraph 9.1 must be an air-conditioning system which must be designed:

(i) to maintain the air at a satisfactory temperature and relative humidity as compared with the outside air conditions, and to ensure a sufficiency of air changes in all air-conditioned spaces; and

(ii) to take account of the particular characteristics of operations at sea and not produce objectionable noises and vibrations.

9.3 In ships provided with an air-conditioning system, sanitary accommodation, laundries, drying rooms, changing rooms and pantries must be provided with mechanical exhaust ventilation capable of ensuring rates of air changes sufficient for the type of accommodation for which it is provided.

9.4 In every ship of 3,000 tons or over, every sidescuttle must be at least 300 millimetres in diameter.

Drainage

15.24

10.1 The crew accommodation must have efficient drainage. In particular:

(a) drainage pipes and channels must be provided wherever necessary to clear water shipped from the sea; and

(b) in order to preclude effluvia from the crew accommodation, the soil and other waste water drainage system must be so arranged and fitted with such water seals, air vents and storm valves as are necessary to prevent siphonage or blow-back.

10.2 Each space in the sanitary accommodation (except private bathrooms) and each laundry must be served by one or more scuppers which only serve those spaces.

10.3 There must be no drainage into sanitary accommodation from any source outside that accommodation except other sanitary accommodation.

Sleeping rooms

15.25

11.1 When sleeping accommodation on board ships is required, the following requirements for sleeping rooms apply:[52]

(a) in ships other than passenger ships, an individual sleeping room must be provided for each seafarer; in case of ships less than 3000 gross tonnage or special purpose ships, exemptions from this requirement may be granted after consultation with the shipowners' and seafarers' organisations concerned;

(b) in single berth seafarers' sleeping rooms, the floor area should be not less than:

(i) 4.5 square metres in ships of less than 3000 gross tonnage;

(ii) 5.5 square metres in ships of 3000 gross tonnage or over but less than 10,000 gross tonnage;

(iii) 7 square metres in ships of 10,000 gross tonnage or over.

11.2 However, in order to provide single berth sleeping rooms on ships of less than 3000 gross tonnage, passenger ships and special purpose ships, a reduced floor area may be permitted.

11.3 In ships of less than 3000 gross tonnage, other than passenger ships and special purpose ships, sleeping rooms may be occupied by a maximum of two seafarers; the floor area of such sleeping rooms must not be less than 7 square metres.

11.4 On passenger ships and special purpose ships, the floor area of sleeping rooms for seafarers not performing the duties of ships' officer must be not less than:

(i) 7.5 square metres in rooms accommodating two persons;

(ii) 11.5 square metres in rooms accommodating three persons;

(iii) 14.5 square metres in rooms accommodating four persons.

11.5 On special purpose ships, sleeping rooms may accommodate more than four persons and, in such cases, the floor area must not be less than 3.6 square metres per person.

11.6 In the case of seafarers performing the duty of petty officers, there should be not more than two persons per sleeping room.

52 See also MGN 481 Amendment 1, para 10.1 providing supplementary guidance on the separation of sleeping rooms for different groups of officers and ratings.

11.7 On passenger ships and special purpose ships, the floor area per person of sleeping rooms for seafarers performing the duties of ships' officers, where no private sitting room or day room is provided, for junior officers must not be less than 7.5 square metres and for senior officers must not less than 8.5 square metres; junior officers are understood to be at operational level and senior officers at the management level.

11.8 On ships other than passenger ships and special purpose ships, the floor area per person of sleeping rooms for seafarers who perform the duties of ships' officers, where no private sitting room or day room is provided, must be not less than:

(i) 7.5 square metres in ships of less than 3000 gross tonnage;

(ii) 8.5 square metres in ships of 3000 gross tonnage or over but less than 10,000 gross tonnage;

(iii) 10 square metres in ships of 10,000 gross tonnage or over.

11.9 The master, chief engineer and chief navigating officer must have, in addition to their sleeping rooms, an adjoining sitting room, day room or equivalent additional space; ships of less than 3000 gross tonnage may be exempted from this requirement after consultation with the shipowners' and seafarers' organisations.

11.10 In determining the floor area of a room, spaces occupied by berths, lockers, seats or chests of drawers and other furniture must be included in the measurement of the floor area, but spaces which, by reason of their small size or irregular shape, cannot accommodate furniture, and do not contribute to the area available for free movement, must not be so included.

11.11 Where sleeping rooms are shared, separate sleeping rooms must be provided for male and female persons.

Beds

15.26

12.1 Every sleeping room must be fitted with a bed for each person accommodated in the room.

12.2 Beds must not be fitted fore and aft along the ship's side unless the size of the room is such that it would be impracticable to fit them elsewhere. Where beds are fitted along the ship's side, they must be in single-tier, except in a room where there is no sidescuttle fitted or in which any sidescuttle fitted is clear of the beds.

12.3 The minimum inside dimension of beds must be adequate to accommodate mattresses of a size not less than 198 centimetres by 80 centimetres.

12.4 Every bed must be fitted with either: (a) a spring bottom or spring under-mattress and a top mattress of a material which will resist damp and is unlikely to harbour vermin; or (b) a suitable resilient mattress on a suitably ventilated base.

12.5 Leeboards or lee-rails must be fitted to the upper berth of every double-tier bed.

12.6 Where a double-tier bed is fitted, a suitable portable ladder must be supplied for access to the upper berth. The ladder must be so constructed that it hooks on to the lee rail to prevent any slipping when in use. Suitable provision must be made for its safe stowage when not in use.

Furniture and fittings in sleeping rooms

15.27

13.1 Every sleeping room must be so planned and equipped as to ensure reasonable comfort for the occupants and to facilitate tidiness.

13.2 For each occupant, the furniture must include a clothes locker of ample space (minimum 475 litres) and a drawer or equivalent space of not less than 56 litres; if the drawer is incorporated in the clothes locker, the combined minimum volume of the clothes locker must be 500 litres; it must be fitted with a shelf and be able to be locked by the occupant so as to ensure privacy.

13.3 Each sleeping room must be provided with a table or desk, which may be of the fixed, drop-leaf or slide-out type, and with comfortable seating accommodation.

13.4 Sleeping rooms must be fitted with curtains or equivalent for the sidelights.

13.5 Sleeping rooms must be fitted with a mirror, small cabinets for toilet requisites, a book rack and a sufficient number of coat hooks.

13.6 With the exception of passenger ships, each sleeping room must be provided with a washbasin having hot and cold running fresh water, except where a private bathroom with such a washbasin is provided.

Mess rooms

15.28

14.1 Unless the circumstances are such that no members of the crew are required to mess on board, mess rooms must be provided for the crew; each mess room must be large enough to accommodate the greatest number of persons likely to use it at any one time.

14.2 Mess rooms must be located away from sleeping rooms and as close as practicable to the galley. Ships of less than 3000 gross tonnage may be exempted from this requirement, after consultation with the shipowners' and seafarers' organisations concerned.

14.3 Mess rooms should be of adequate size and comfort and properly furnished and equipped (including facilities for refreshment), taking account of the number of seafarers likely to use them at any one time.

14.4 Mess room facilities may be either common or separate. The decision in this respect should be taken after consultation with seafarers' and shipowners' representatives and subject to the agreement of the MCA. Account should be taken of factors such as the size of the ship and the distinctive cultural, religious and social needs of the seafarers.

14.5 Where separate mess rooms are provided, separate provision must be made for: (a) master and officers; and (b) petty officers and other seafarers.

14.6 On ships other than passenger ships, the floor area of mess rooms for seafarers should be not less than 1.5 square metres per person of the planned seating capacity.

Furniture and fittings in mess rooms

15.29

15.1 In all ships, mess rooms should be equipped with tables, appropriate seats, fixed or moveable, sufficient to accommodate the greatest number of seafarers likely to use them at any one time.

15.2 Every mess room provided for persons who do not provide their own food must be provided with adequate stowage space for mess utensils in a sideboard, dresser or in separate lockers.

15.3 Every mess room provided for persons who do provide their own food must be fitted with a stowage locker for each person likely to use the room. Each such stowage locker must be:

(i) large enough to contain one person's mess utensils and supply of food;

(ii) fitted with a secure lock or hasp for a padlock;

(iii) so fitted as to be clear of the floor by at least 300 millimetres; and

(iv) adequately ventilated.

Lockers provided in pursuance of this paragraph may be fitted together in the mess room or in a suitable place readily accessible from it.

15.4 There must be available at all times when seafarers are on board: (a) a refrigerator, which must be conveniently situated and of sufficient capacity for the number of persons using the mess room or mess rooms; (b) facilities for hot beverages; and (c) cool water facilities.

15.5 Where available pantries are not accessible to mess rooms, adequate lockers for mess utensils and proper facilities for washing utensils must be provided.

Recreation spaces

15.30

16.1 Recreation rooms, conveniently situated and appropriately furnished, must be provided for officers and ratings. Where these are not provided separately from the mess rooms, the latter must be planned, furnished and equipped to give recreational facilities. Furnishings for recreation accommodation must, as a minimum, include a bookcase and facilities for reading, writing and, where practicable, for games.

16.2 Appropriate seafarers' recreational facilities, amenities and services, as adapted to meet the special needs of seafarers who must live and work on ships, must be provided on board for the benefit of all seafarers, taking into account provisions on health and safety protection and accident prevention.

16.3 In every ship, deck space permanently reserved for the use of the crew for recreational purposes must be provided on an open deck. The space must be adequate in area having regard to the number of persons in the crew and the size of the ship.

Offices

15.31

17.1 All ships must be provided with separate offices or a common ship's office for use by deck and engineering departments; ships of less than 3,000 gross tonnage may be exempted from this requirement after consultation with the shipowners' and seafarers' organisations concerned.

Sanitary accommodation

15.32

18.1 The following private and semi-private bathrooms, ie., a bathroom provided for the exclusive use of two persons, must be provided for officers:

(a) in ships of 5,000 tons or over but less than 15,000 tons, at least five officers' sleeping rooms must be provided with adjoining private bathrooms for the use of the officers occupying those sleeping rooms;

(b) in ships of 15,000 tons or over, every officer's sleeping room must be provided with an adjoining private bathroom for the use of the officer using that sleeping room;

(c) without prejudice to (a), in ships of 10,000 tons or over but less than 15,000 tons, every officer's sleeping room which is not provided with an adjoining private bathroom must have a semi-private bathroom appropriated to it.[53]

18.2 In ships of 25,000 tons or over, other than passenger ships, every rating's sleeping room which is not provided with a private bathroom must have a semi-private bathroom appropriated to it. These semi-private bathrooms must not be shared by petty officers and other ratings.

18.3 All seafarers must have convenient access on the ship to sanitary facilities meeting minimum standards of health and hygiene and reasonable standards of comfort, with separate sanitary facilities being provided for men and women.

18.4 In all ships, a minimum of one toilet, one washbasin and one tub or shower or both for every six persons or less who do not have personal facilities must be provided at a convenient location.

53 For guidance on semi-private bathrooms for officers, see MSN 481 (M) – Maritime Labour Convention, 2006: Crew Accommodation, Supplementary Guidance, paras 14.1–14.8.

18.5 Every bath and shower must be provided with a handrail, grating or mat. Except in private or semi-private bathrooms, the showers must be provided with kerbs and individual drainage.

18.6 Hot and cold fresh running water must be available in all wash places.

18.7 The hot water must be at a constant temperature of at least 66°C and must be heated by thermostatically controlled calorifiers of adequate capacity or by some equally safe and efficient means.

18.8 Every shower must be provided with an anti-scalding mixing valve which must be set in such a way that the temperature of the shower water can be varied by the person using it to any temperature between the ambient temperature and a temperature of at least: (i) in the case of a thermostatically controlled mixing valve, 38°C but not more than 43°C; or (ii) in the case of any other mixing valve, 35°C but not more than 40°C.

18.9 All sanitary spaces must have ventilation to the open air, independently of any other part of the accommodation.

18.10 Every water closet must be provided with the following:

(a) (i) a water closet pedestal of a single type with a pan of white vitreous china or other suitable material;

(ii) a hinged seat of a suitable hard smooth impervious material;

(iii) a trap with a metal inspection plate; and

(iv) an efficient ventilator connected to the outlet;

(b) an adequate flush of water which must always be available and supplied through self-closing non-concussive supply valves with a portable seating of metal which is not likely to become corroded.

18.11 Where water closets specified in paragraph (18.10) would be unsuitable for use by some members of the crew because of distinctive national habits or customs, those water closets may be suitably adapted or other suitable closets must be provided, so long as the sanitary accommodation does not result in overall facilities less favourable than those which would result from the application of paragraph 18.10.

18.12 In ships of 1,600 tons or over, the following additional sanitary accommodation must be provided – a separate room containing a water closet and a washbasin:

(a) easily accessible from the navigating bridge for the use of those working in that area;

(b) within or near to the engine room control compartment or, in ships not fitted with such a compartment, within easy access of the propelling machinery space;

(c) easily accessible from the galley for the use of those working in that area; and

(d) except in ships in which single-berth sleeping rooms and private or semi-private bathrooms are provided for the use of all engine room personnel, washing accommodation fitted with showers, washbasins and mirrors in sufficient number (having regard to the number of such personnel not provided with single-berth sleeping rooms and private or semi-private bathrooms) situated in a place outside but conveniently close to the propelling machinery space.[54]

Supply of drinking water and fresh water

15.33

19.1 Cold drinking water for the purposes of drinking, cooking and dishwashing must be laid on to taps in galleys, bars and pantries and, in the case of any mess room provided for members of the crew for whom no pantry is provided, a tap to the mess room.

19.2 The tanks from which the drinking water and the fresh water laid on to the washbasins, baths and showers is supplied and any plant installed on board ship from which drinking water and/or fresh water is produced must be of a capacity to ensure an adequate supply of such water at all times for all members of the crew, provided that, as a minimum, the tanks must be sufficient to provide at least 2 days' supply of such water.

19.3 Where drinking water and/or fresh water is produced by plant on board, the water so produced must be treated by suitable automatic means of disinfection.

Washing/drying facilities

15.34

20.1 In all ships, except where, due to the nature of the service, the crew are not accommodated overnight, facilities for washing, drying and ironing clothes must be provided for officers and ratings on a scale appropriate to the size of the crew and the normal duration of the voyage. These facilities must, wherever possible, be located within easy reach of their accommodation and arrangements must be made to ensure separate availability of the facilities to officers and ratings.

20.2 The facilities to be provided must include:

(a) suitable sinks and washing machines which may be installed in wash rooms if provision of a separate laundry facility is not reasonably practicable, with an adequate supply of hot and cold fresh water or by means of heating water;

(b) drying machines and adequately heated and ventilated drying rooms unless drying machines are of a type which dry clothes completely; and

(c) electric irons and ironing boards or their equivalent.

20.3 Adequately ventilated compartments or lockers for use solely for hanging oilskins and other working clothes must be provided in a place outside, but

54 See para 20.4 regarding the provision of clothes lockers for the seafarers to whom para 18.12(d) applies.

conveniently near to, the sleeping rooms. Separate compartments or lockers must be provided for officers and ratings.

20.4 Where washing accommodation is provided in accordance with paragraph 18.12(d), such accommodation must be provided with a clothes locker for each member of the engine room department not provided with a single-berth sleeping room and a private or a semi-private bathroom. Clothes lockers so provided must comply with the requirements of paragraph 20.3 in respect of lockers for working clothes.

Galleys[55]

15.35

21.1 Except in ships in which no member of the crew will be required to mess on board, a galley suitably positioned clear of working areas and situated as close as practicable to the mess rooms must be provided for the preparation of food for the crew.

21.2 Every galley must be provided with all equipment necessary to enable food in sufficient quantity to be properly and readily prepared for all persons whom the galley is intended to serve, and to be served hot to them in the mess room in all weathers.

21.3 Every galley must be provided with facilities for washing up. Hot fresh water and cold drinking water must be laid on to any sink or other washing-up facility in the galley. In ships of 3,000 tons or over, there must, in addition, be provided a washbasin supplied with hot and cold fresh water.

21.4 The ventilation in the galley must be so arranged as to ensure an adequate supply of fresh air and the efficient discharge of fumes into the open air.

Dry provision store rooms

15.36

22.1 In every ship, except one in which each member of the crew provides their own food, one or more store rooms must be provided for the storage of provisions for the crew. The rooms must be fitted with sufficient shelves, cupboards and bins, having regard to the maximum period likely to elapse between successive replenishment of stores and to the maximum number of persons for whom food is to be provided. Shelves, cupboards and bins must be so constructed as to enable them to be effectively cleaned.

22.2 Access to every dry provision store room must be obtained from a passageway, galley, pantry or other dry provision store room.

55 For further guidance on the design, construction, equipment and maintenance of galley areas, see MSN 1845 (M) – MLC, 2006: Food and catering; Provisions of food and fresh water, paras 4.1–4.4 and Annex 1, section 1.

Cold store rooms and refrigerating equipment

15.37

23.1 Subject to paragraph 22:

(a) in every foreign-going ship of 1,000 tons or over, cold store rooms must be provided for the storage of perishable provisions;

(b) in every foreign-going ship of under 1,000 tons and in every home trade ship, there must be provided, for the storage of perishable provisions for the crew, either cold store rooms or adequate alternative cold store room facilities;

(c) if the door to such a room or facility opens into any part of the crew accommodation, the door must be of steel, gastight and self-closing.

23.2 A red warning light outside every cold store room or group of cold store rooms must be included in the lighting circuit of each such room or groups of rooms. Every cold store room must be fitted with an internal means of sounding an external alarm and with a means of releasing the door fastenings from the inside.

Hospitals

15.38

24.1 Ships carrying 15 or more seafarers and engaged on voyages of more than three days' duration must provide separate hospital accommodation to be used exclusively for medical purposes. Vessels that remain within 60 miles of the coast are not bound by this. The hospital accommodation must be easy to access in all weathers, provide comfortable housing for the occupants, and be conducive to their receiving prompt and proper attention.

24.2 Every hospital, whether permanent or temporary, must be situated so that it is as quiet and comfortable as possible and is readily accessible in all weathers: (a) from the sleeping room of a member of the crew who is, and is employed as, a duly qualified doctor or nurse; and (b) if no such doctor or nurse is carried, from the master's accommodation.

24.3 At least one bed in every permanent hospital must be a single-tier bed and must, wherever practicable, be placed so that it is accessible from both sides and from the foot.

Medical cabinet[56]

15.39

25.1 A cabinet or other suitable facility for storing medicines and other medical stores, which the ship is required by regulations made under section 85 of the

56 See Chapter 17.

Merchant Shipping Act 1995 to carry for the crew, must be well-ventilated and fitted in the crew area of the ship which is:

(a) always dry;

(b) readily accessible from (but not sited in) the permanent or temporary hospital; and

(c) not subject to abnormal heat.

25.2 Where a medical cabinet is required, it must be provided with the following:

(a) an outer door with an efficient lock;

(b) where controlled drugs are to be stored, an inner cupboard fitted with a door and a lock which cannot be opened by the same key as the lock to the outer door;

(c) suitable arrangements for the storage of these medicines, medical stores and associated measuring devices, all as required by the regulations referred to in paragraph 25.1;[57] and

(d) a dispensing counter with a surface that can be easily kept clean.

Protection from mosquitoes

15.40

26.1 Ships regularly trading in mosquito-infested ports must be fitted with the appropriate devices as required by the competent authority.[58]

Cleaning, maintenance and inspection of crew accommodation

15.41

27.1 The crew accommodation must be maintained in a clean and habitable condition, and all equipment and installations must be maintained in good working order.

27.2 Every part of the crew accommodation, except store rooms, must be kept free from stores and other property not belonging to or provided for the use of persons for whom that part of the accommodation is appropriated, and in particular no cargo must be kept in any part of the crew accommodation.

27.3 The requirements for inspection, and the recording of such inspections, are set out in reg 29 of the Minimum Requirements Regulations.[59]

57 The relevant legislation is the Merchant Shipping and Fishing Vessels (Medical Stores) Regulations 1995 (SI 1995/1802), which were made under Merchant Shipping Act 1979, ss 21(1)(a), (3)–(4), (6) and 22(1), so the reference in para 25.1 to Merchant Shipping Act 1985, s 85 appears to be an error.

58 See Chapter 17 on precautions against malaria.

59 See para 15.11 above.

MGN 481 (M) AMENDMENT 1 – MARITIME LABOUR CONVENTION, 2006: CREW ACCOMMODATION, SUPPLEMENTARY GUIDANCE

15.42 The requirements of MGN 481 (M) Amendment 1 are set out below (except paras 1.1–1.2, which contain introductory texts already set out in this chapter):

'2. General

2.1 In the crew accommodation:

a) all structures, furniture and fittings and means of access to and egress from the crew accommodation should be so situated, constructed and arranged as to minimise any risk of injury to the crew;

b) to afford protection to the crew in rough sea conditions;

i. handrails should be provided in passageways and stairways where necessary and should be of robust construction and strongly secured to the bulkheads;

ii. fixed furniture should be strongly secured;

iii. means should be provided to secure portable furniture;

iv. doors, including those to cupboards and other items of furniture, should be so secured as not to open accidentally;

v. drawers should be so designed as not to slide open and fall out accidentally;

vi. tables, shelves, stowage racks, and other similar fittings should be fitted with retaining lips or bars or with non-slip surfaces so that objects placed on them will not slide off.

2.2 The arrangements for the storage, distribution and utilisation of gaseous fuel should reduce to a minimum the risk of fire or explosion within the crew accommodation.

2.3 Entrance to crew accommodation from the open deck should be protected against the weather and sea to the greatest possible extent practicable.

3. Divisions between the crew accommodation and other parts of the ship

3.1 Where no other arrangements are practicable, an opening in a bulkhead separating a passageway in the crew accommodation from any of the spaces specified in MSN 1844 (M) paragraph 3.4 (d) and (e) or from a store room other than an engine room or deck store room may be accepted, if that opening is sealed in any way which is effective having regard to the use of the space.

3.2 Where crew accommodation adjoins an oil tank then the two should be separated by either a gastight steel division additional to the division which retains the oil; or by an all-welded steel division capable of withstanding a head of water at least 1.5 metres greater than the maximum service head.

4. Overhead decks

4.1 External bulkheads of sleeping rooms and mess rooms should be adequately insulated. All machinery casings and boundary bulkheads of galleys and other spaces in which heat is produced should be adequately insulated where there is a possibility of resulting heat effects in adjoining accommodation or passageways.

4.2 Protection should be provided from the effects of heat resulting from steam or hot-water service pipes.

5. Pipes in Crew Accommodation

5.1 Unless no other arrangement is reasonably practicable, steam supply and exhaust pipes for steering gear, winches and similar equipment should not pass through crew accommodation but where this is unavoidable they should pass through passageways and be properly encased.

5.2 Steam pipes that do pass through crew accommodation should be constructed of solid drawn steel or other suitable [material] to be able to withstand the maximum pressure from the ship's boiler system. Be fitted with connections made by faced flanges, properly jointed and have adequate drainage arrangements.

5.3 Where necessary for the protection of the crew calorifiers, steam and hot water pipes in the crew accommodation should be lagged. Cold water pipes in the crew accommodation should be lagged where necessary to prevent condensation.

5.4 Pipes used for crew accommodation service should be fit for purpose. Soil and waste pipes should be constructed in order to minimise the risk of obstruction and to facilitate cleaning.

5.5 Soil pipes should not pass overhead in mess rooms, sleeping rooms, dry provision store rooms, galleys or the hospital, unless it is impracticable to place them elsewhere.

5.6 Soil or waste pipes should not pass through drinking water tanks or other fresh water tanks.

5.7 The scuppers serving sanitary accommodation and laundries should be at least 50 millimetres in diameter and must be placed wherever water is likely to collect on the floor.

6. Heating

6.1 In all ships in which a heating system is required, the heating should be by means of hot water, warm air, electricity, steam or equivalent. However, within the accommodation area, steam should not be used as a medium for heat transmission.

6.2 The heating system should be capable of maintaining the temperature in the seafarer accommodation at a satisfactory level under normal conditions of weather and climate likely to be met to within the trade in which the ship is engaged.

6.3 Radiators or other heaters should be provided with a means for turning on and off or varying the temperature.

6.4 Heating equipment should be constructed so that its operation is not affected by propelling machinery, steering gear, deck machinery calorifiers or cooking appliances.

6.5 The system of heating the seafarer accommodation should be in operation at all times when seafarers are living or working on board and conditions require its use.

6.6 Radiators and heating apparatus should be placed and where necessary shielded so as to avoid risk of fire, danger, or discomfort to the occupants.

7. Lighting

7.1 If a reading light is fitted in a sleeping room, then it should be fitted with a lamp capable of emitting at least 200 lumens.

7.2 The electric lighting in sleeping rooms, day rooms, recreation rooms, rooms for watching films and television, hobbies and games rooms, mess rooms, hospital wards, offices, studies, sanitary accommodation, laundries, drying rooms, dry provision store rooms, cold store rooms, galleys, passageways, companionways and covered deck recreation spaces should be treated as adequate if:

(a) the lamps, paintwork and other surface finishes are new, the illuminance in the horizontal plane when measured at points specified in respect of that space in the attached Annex is steady and maintained, subject to a tolerance of 10%, at a value stated in the Annex in respect of those points; and

(b) it complies with any other specifications within the Annex in respect of that space.

8. Ventilation

8.1 Air-conditioning systems whether of a centralised or individual unit type should:

8.1.1 maintain the air at a satisfactory temperature and relative humidity as compared to outside air conditions, ensure sufficiency of air changes in all air-conditioned spaces, take account of the particular characteristics of operations at sea and not produce excessive noise or vibrations; and

8.1.2 facilitate easy cleaning and disinfection to prevent or control the spread of disease.

8.2 Power for the operation of the air-conditioning and other ventilation units should be available at all times.

9. Interior finishes

9.1 Upholstered parts of furniture and fittings should be made from either polished hardwood or a rust-proof material, impervious to dirt and moisture, and which is not likely to warp, crack or become corroded.

9.2 Any wooden surfaces within crew accommodation such as panelling should be either painted, varnished or coated with another suitable product.

9.3 All paints, varnish and other surface finishes in the crew accommodation should be easily kept clean.

9.4 The interior of the crew accommodation and all furniture and fittings within it should not be able to harbour dirt or vermin.

10. Sleeping Rooms

10.1 Where practicable, the following groups of persons should be provided with sleeping rooms separate from those provided for the other groups:

10.1.1 officers;

10.1.2 petty officers;

10.1.3 cadets;

10.1.4 ratings of the deck department other than petty officers;

10.1.5 ratings of the engine room department other than petty officers;

10.1.6 ratings of the catering department other than petty officers;

(Unless general purpose ratings are employed, the ratings in those two groups in subparagraphs [10.1.4 and 10.1.5] should be counted as one group).

10.2 When calculating the floor area of a sleeping room occupied by berths and lockers, chests of drawers and seats should be included. But small or irregularly shaped spaces which do not effectively add to the space available for free movement and cannot be used for installing furniture and should be excluded.

11. Beds

11.1 The framework and lee-board, if any, of a berth should be of approved material, hard, smooth and not likely to corrode or to harbour vermin.

11.2 If tubular frames are used for the construction of berths, they should be completely sealed and without perforations, which would give access to vermin.

11.3 Where beds abut each other, they should be separated by rigid screens made of wood or other suitable opaque material.

11.4 Berths should not be arranged in tiers of more than two and the lower berth in a double tier should be not less than 30cm above the floor. The upper berth should be placed approximately midway between the bottom of the lower berth and the lower side of the deckhead beams.

11.5 In case of berths placed alongside the ship's side, there should be only a single tier where a sidelight is situated above a berth.

11.6 Where one berth is placed over another, a dust proof bottom should be fitted beneath the bottom mattress or spring bottom of the upper berth.

12. Mess Rooms

12.1 Mess room facilities may be either common or separate. The decision in this respect should be taken after consultation with seafarers' and shipowners' representatives and subject to the approval of the MCA. Account should be taken of factors such as size of the ship and the distinctive cultural, religious and social needs of the seafarers.

12.2 Where separate mess rooms facilities are to be provided to seafarers, then separate mess rooms should be provided for:

12.2.1 master and officers; and

12.2.2 petty officers and other seafarers.

12.3 On ships other than passenger ships, the floor area of mess rooms for seafarers should be not less than 1.5 square metres per person of the planned seating capacity.

13. Recreation Spaces

13.1 Where practicable consideration should be given to including the following facilities at no extra cost to the seafarer:

13.1.1 a smoking room;

13.1.2 television viewing and the reception of radio broadcasts;

13.1.3 showing of films, the stock of which should be adequate for the duration of the voyage and where necessary changed at reasonable intervals;

13.1.4 sports equipment including exercise equipment, table games and deck games;

13.1.5 where possible, facilities for swimming;

13.1.6 a library containing vocational and other books, the stock of which should be adequate for the duration of the voyage and changed at reasonable intervals;

13.1.7 facilities for handicrafts;

13.1.8 electronic equipment such as a radio, television, video recorders, DVD/CD player, personal computer and software and cassette player/recorder;

13.1.9 where appropriate, the provision of bars on board for seafarers unless these are contrary to national, religious or social customs; and

13.1.10 reasonable access to ship-to-shore telephone communications, email, internet facilities, where available, with any charges for use of these services being reasonable in amount.

14. Sanitary Accommodation

14.1 Semi-private bathrooms are to be situated on an inter-communicating compartment between two adjoining sleeping rooms or, if the bathroom is for ratings, it may be situated opposite or approximately opposite the entrance or entrances to their sleeping room or rooms.

14.2 (a) Semi-private bathrooms should contain a bath or shower, a water closet pedestal and other items as specified in MSN 1844 (M) paragraph 18.10 and, unless a washbasin is provided in each sleeping room for which the bathroom is appropriate, with a washbasin.

(b) Private bathrooms should contain a bath or shower, a water closet pedestal, a washbasin and other items specified in MSN 1844 (M) paragraph 18.10.

14.3 Toilets should be situated convenient to, but separate from sleeping rooms and wash rooms, without direct access from the sleeping rooms or from a passage between sleeping rooms or from a passage between sleeping rooms and toilets to which there is no other access. This does not apply where a toilet is located in a compartment between tow sleeping rooms having a total of not more than four seafarers.

14.4 Washbasins and tub baths should be of adequate size and constructed with a smooth surface not liable to crack, flake or corrode.

14.5 Where there is more than one toilet in a compartment they should be screened to ensure privacy wherever reasonably practicable the space screened should be large enough for one person to undress comfortably.

14.6 (a) Subject to sub-paragraph (b) below, if access to a water closet is from a passageway other than a passageway leading only to water closets, a lobby, where practicable, [should] be provided at the entrance to the water closet. If that is not practicable, the water closet should be provided with a self-closing door which is close fitting and has no apertures.

(b) The above need not be complied with where adequate mechanical exhaust ventilation arrangements are provided in those spaces.

14.7 Subject to paragraph 14.8 below every water closet pedestal should be fitted in a closet separated from other parts of the crew accommodation by bulkheads which comply with requirements of paragraphs 4.1 and 4.2 of MSN 1844 (M).

14.8 A water closet need not be separated by bulkheads from:

14.8.1 another water closet;

14.8.2 a urinal or:

14.8.3 if the water closet is served by a trunked mechanical exhaust ventilation system which effectively removes odours from it, washing accommodation if it is separated from that other water closet, urinal or washing accommodation by a steel partition or another suitable material and open at the top and bottom. This is not necessary in a private or semi-private bathroom.

15. Supply of Drinking Water and Fresh Water

15.1 Any manholes leading into drinking and fresh water storage tanks, and all pipes and other parts of the distribution systems should be constructed to allow for efficient maintenance and prevention of contamination.

16. Galleys

16.1 All spaces surrounding and behind fixed galley equipment should be easy to keep clean.

16.2 All galley furniture and fittings should be made of a material which is impervious to dirt and moisture. Any metal parts should be rustproof. The bottoms of all fitted furniture should be either flush with the deck or fitted high enough to enable the deck space beneath to be easily kept clean.

16.3 Sufficient gutters and scuppers should be fitted in the galley to ensure that it drains efficiently. Traps should be fitted to scuppers which should be led either overboard or to an enclosed tank which has a mechanical suction pump.

17. Dry Provision Store Rooms

17.1 Dry provision store rooms should be situated, constructed and ventilated in order to minimise the risk of deterioration of the stores through heat, draught, condensation or infestation by insects or vermin. In particular a dry provision store should not:

17.1.1 be situated over propelling machinery space, boiler room or any other space which is subject to abnormal heat; or

17.1.2 adjoin a galley, propelling machinery space or other space which is subject to abnormal heat, unless the division between the store room and that space is adequately insulated.

17.2 Dry provision store rooms are only to be used for the storage of dry provisions.

18. Cold Store Rooms and Refrigerating Equipment

18.1 It should be possible to effectively clean cold stores rooms and domestic style deep freezers and refrigerators. They should be large enough taking into account the size of the crew and the duration of the voyages.

18.2 Access to every cold store rooms should be [by] a passageway, galley or pantry or from another cold store room.

18.3 Cold storage facilities should be served by refrigerating machinery which may be either independent of the facility or self-contained.

18.4 If independent machinery is fitted, then it should be separated from all other parts of the crew accommodation by bulkheads complying with the requirements of paragraphs 4.1 and 4.2 of MSN 1844 (M). [Access to the] refrigeration machinery space should be by means of a hinged door from an open deck.

19. Hospitals

19.1 The arrangement of the entrance, berths, lighting, ventilation, heating and water supply should be designed to ensure the comfort and facilitate the treatment of the occupants.

19.2 Ideally the minimum width of the entrance to any permanent hospital should be 760 millimetres and the access arrangements should be such that a stretcher can be easily carried into it and placed alongside at least one single tier bed.

19.3 Sufficient beds should be provided in permanent hospitals on a ratio of one bed per 50 (or fraction of) seafarers up to a maximum of 4 beds.

19.4 Any sidescuttles or windows in the ward which are exposed to the direct sunlight, should have curtains or blinds fitted.

19.5 Permanent hospitals, even if they are air-conditioned or have a trunked mechanical ventilation system should have a natural system of inlet and exhaust ventilation to the open air which is independent of any ventilators provided for other parts of the ship.

19.6 A portable electrical lamp in addition to the lighting fitted in a permanent hospital should be provided and should be capable of emitting 600 lumens. If it is in a hospital ward, the lamp should be capable of emitting 400 lumens.

19.7 Each bed in the hospital ward should be provided with:

(a) a locker approximately 305 millimetres square by 610 millimetres high fitted with a flat top and a shelf;

(b) a water bottle;

(c) a tumbler; and

(d) an electric bell push communicating with the sleeping room of the doctor, nurse or other person in charge of the patient.

19.8 Hospital wards should have:

(a) sufficient seats taking into account the number of beds in the ward;

(b) a clothes locker (additional to any lockers provided in accordance with paragraph 19.7); and

(c) a box cover to conceal a bed pan.

19.9 Sanitary accommodation should be provided for the exclusive use of the occupants of the hospital either as part of the accommodation or in close proximity. Such sanitary accommodation should comprise a minimum of one toilet, one washbasin and one tub or shower and in ships of 5,000 tons or over a bath at least 1.3 metres in internal length shall be fitted.

19.10 Washbasins and baths in a permanent hospital should be in accordance with the contents of paragraph 14.4 of this guidance note. Furthermore, unless the ship has a collecting tank or sewage plant the discharge system, where practicable should be separate from any other discharge system in the ship.

19.11 A scupper at least 50 millimetres in diameter should be fitted in the lowest part of any room in a hospital where a bath is fitted unless that room is the ward.

19.12 Any water closet or other room in which the water closet pedestal is fitted should have a gastight self-closing door, unless it is served by a trunked mechanical exhaust ventilation system, which effectively removes odours from it.

19.13 In passenger ships, one hospital may be provided to serve both crew and passengers. In such a case separate male and, except where there are no female members of crew, female wards and sanitary accommodation should be provided for the exclusive use of the crew.

19.14 The floor covering in every permanent hospital should, so far as practicable, be free from joints.

20. Exemptions

20.1 Regulation 31 of the Merchant Shipping (Maritime Labour Convention) (Minimum Requirements for Seafarers etc.) Regulations 2014 states that vessels of less than 200 Gross Tonnes[60] (as determined under the Merchant Shipping (Tonnage) Regulations 1997) may be exempt by the Secretary of State (this is normally via the Maritime and Coastguard Agency) of all or some of the requirements of the crew accommodation provisions provided in the exemption [if]:

20.1.1 [it] is reasonable taking account of the size of the ship and the number of persons on board

20.1.2 [it] does not result in overall facilities less favourable than which would result if no exemption had been given; and

20.1.3 [it] relates to Standard A3.1.7(b), 11(d), and 13 of the Maritime Labour Convention or as respects floor area only, Standard A3.1.9 (f) and (h) and to (l) of the Maritime Labour Convention, or

20.1.4 the exemption is otherwise expressly permitted in Standard A3.1 of the Maritime Labour Convention, 2006.

20.2 It goes on the say that such an exemption:

20.2.1 is valid only if given in writing;

20.2.2 may be given subject to such conditions and limitations as the Secretary of State may specify; and

20.2.3 may be altered or cancelled by the Secretary of State, giving written notice to the shipowner.

20.3 The process to be followed to obtain such an exemption is the same as the process laid down in MGN 472 (M)[61] Guidance Procedure of applying for a Substantial Equivalence.

ANNEX

In this Annex "general measurement" points mean in relation to any space, those points which, measured at a height of 850 millimetres above the floor, fall on an imaginary line drawn vertically through the following points:

(a) every point mid-way between every 2 adjacent lamps in that space;

(b) every point mid-way between any lamp and any position on the boundary or that space to which that lamp is nearer than any other lamp; and

(c) where any part of the space available for free movement is shielded from the direct rays of lamp by a re-entrant angle formed in the boundary of that space, the central point of the space so shielded.

60 It should be noted that reg 31 does not expressly mention ships of less than 200 GT or the MLC provisions referred to in MGN 481, para 20.1.3. Regulation 31 permits the Secretary of State to grant a written exemption to 'a ship' (there is no reference to gross tonnage) from some or all of the requirements in MSN 1844, so long as the exemption is permitted by Standard A3.1 of the MLC, including anything permitted in accordance with paragraphs 6(a), (d) or 9(g) of that Standard.

61 MGN 472 (M) – Maritime Labour Convention, 2006: Guidance on the procedure for applying for a Substantial Equivalence.

		Value
Sleeping Rooms and Day Rooms		
1.	All general measurement points	50 lux
2.	At every mirror	200 lux
3.	At every seat at a writing desk or table	150 lux
4.	At not less than half the seats (other than those mentioned in 3 above in a sleeping room provided for use of more than one person	150 lux
Mess rooms		
5.	At measurement points	100 lux
6.	At every table and sink	150 lux
Recreation Rooms (including rooms for watching films and television, hobbies and games rooms)		
7.	At measuring points	50 lux
8.	At every recreational table	100 lux
9.	At every seat at a writing table or desk	150 lux
10.	At not less than half the seats other than those mentioned in 3 above	150 lux
Hospital wards		
11.	At general measurement points	50 lux
12.	At any washbasin	100 lux
13.	At least one fixed lamp shall be installed in addition to the electric reading lamp required by regulation 13(4)[62] to be provided at the head of each bed	
Offices and studies		
14.	At general measurement points	100 lux
15.	At every seat at a writing desk or table	200 lux
Sanitary Accommodation (including sanitary accommodation in hospitals)		
16.	At general measurement points	100 lux
17.	At any mirror	200 lux
Laundries		
18.	At general measurement points	100 lux
Drying rooms		
19.	At the centre of the space	50 lux

62 It is not clear what the reference to 'regulation 13(4)' relates to; this may be a drafting error and it may be that it should refer to MGN 481, para 19.6 above.

		Value
Galleys (including bakeries and pantries)		
20.	At working positions	300 lux
21.	The lights shall be so disposed as to ensure that food preparation tables, range tops, serving tables and washing up sinks receive the maximum amount of light	
Dry provision store rooms and cold store rooms		
22.	At general measurement points	100 lux
23.	The lights shall be so disposed as to ensure that shelves and cupboards receive the maximum amount of light	
Passageways, companionways and covered deck recreation spaces		
24.	At general measurement points	50 lux
25.	A light shall be placed: 1. At the head of each stairway, ladder and hatchway and 2. At or near the doors of lockers provided for oilskins or working clothes'	

Compliance: Check the DMLC, Pt I, point 8, and enter details of how compliance is achieved in the DMLC, Pt II, point 8.

CHAPTER 16

Regulation 3.2: Food and Catering

INTRODUCTION

16.1 The provisions on food and catering are set out in Regulation 3.2 of the MLC and its associated Code, the purpose of which is: '[t]o ensure that seafarers have access to good quality food and drinking water provided under regulated hygienic conditions'.[1]

Ratifying states are required to ensure, in respect of ships registered with them, that: they carry and serve food (which is to be provided free of charge) and drinking water of appropriate quality, nutritional value and quantity that adequately covers the requirements of the ship and takes into account the differing cultural and religious backgrounds of the crew;[2] and seafarers employed as ship's cooks with responsibility for food preparation are trained and qualified for their positions.[3]

UK PROVISIONS

16.2 The main UK provisions are set out in Part 8 of the Merchant Shipping (Maritime Labour Convention) (Minimum Requirements for Seafarers)

1 MLC, Regulation 3.2.
2 MLC, Regulation 3.2.1–3.2.2.
3 MLC, Regulation 3.2.3.

Regulations 2014[4] ('Minimum Requirements Regulations'), MSN 1845[5] and MSN 1846.[6]

Application of Part 8

16.3 Part 8 of the Minimum Requirements Regulations applies to MLC ships as follows:

- subject to reg 37(1) (on which, see para 16.6 below), all provisions apply to UK ships wherever they may be and to non-UK ships which do not carry MLC documentation,[7] while they are in UK waters;[8]
- only reg 41 applies to non-UK ships carrying MLC documentation, while they are in UK waters.[9]

The following are excluded as they are not ships to which the MLC applies: (a) pleasure vessels; (b) fishing vessels; (c) ships of traditional build; (d) warships or naval auxiliaries; and (e) vessels which are not ordinarily engaged in commercial activities.[10]

FOOD, DRINKING WATER AND CATERING DEPARTMENT

16.4 The shipowner and master must ensure that:

- food and drinking water are provided, free of charge, which: (a) are suitable in respect of quantity, quality and, in relation to food, nutritional value and variety, taking account of (i) the number of seafarers on board and the character, nature and duration of the voyage, and (ii) the seafarers' differing religious requirements and cultural practices in relation to food; (b) do not contain anything which is likely to cause sickness or injury to health or which renders any food or drinking water unpalatable; and (c) are otherwise fit for consumption.[11] See MSN 1845, paras 3.1–3.3, and Annex 1, section 3 'Diet and nutrition';
- food and drinking water is stored and handled, and the catering department is organised and equipped, in accordance with the requirements of MSN 1845[12] (see, in particular, paras 4.1–4.4 and Annex 1, section 1, 'Design, construction, equipment and maintenance of galley areas', section 7 'Stores' and Annex 2 on

4 SI 2014/1613.
5 MSN 1845 (M): MLC – Food and Catering: Provision of Food and Fresh Water.
6 MSN 1846 (M): MLC – Food and Catering: Ship's Cooks and Catering Staff.
7 Because they are registered with a state in respect of which the MLC (i) has not come into force; or (ii) has come into force but, even so, the ship (for whatever reason) is non-compliant and does not carry the required MLC documentation.
8 Minimum Requirements Regulations, reg 3(1), (2)(a).
9 Minimum Requirements Regulations, reg 3(3)–(4)(vi).
10 Minimum Requirements Regulations, reg 3(1), (3), (5)(a)–(e).
11 Minimum Requirements Regulations, reg 34(1)–(2).
12 Minimum Requirements Regulations, reg 35(1)(a)–(b). MSN 1845 (M): MLC, 2006 – Food and Catering: Provision of Food and Fresh Water.

fresh water loading and supply arrangements, disinfection, storage, distribution systems and maintenance).

The 'catering department' means the galley, mess rooms and any other areas on board intended or used for the storage or preparation of food for seafarers or the service of meals to seafarers.[13]

Inspections

16.5 The master is obliged to ensure that, not less than once a week, inspections are carried out to check that: (a) the supplies of food and drinking water comply with regs 34–35; and (b) the catering department and its equipment comply with reg 35, and the results of the inspection are to be recorded in the official log book.[14] These inspections must be carried out by the master (or person authorised by the master), together with a member of the catering staff.[15]

REQUIREMENT TO CARRY A QUALIFIED SHIP'S COOK

16.6 Before discussing the requirement relating to ships, it should be noted that it does not apply to: (a) a ship which normally operates with only 10 seafarers on board; or (b) a ship which operates only within 60 miles of a safe haven (which is a harbour or shelter which provides protection from the weather) and which does not operate to or from, or call at, a port in a country other than the UK.[16] Otherwise (unless one of the exceptions set out below applies), ships must not be operated unless they carry a qualified ship's cook.[17]

Exceptions

16.7 In circumstances of exceptional necessity, the MCA may grant an exemption from requiring a qualified ship's cook: (a) until the next port of call; or (b) for a period not exceeding one month, but only if there is a person on board who is trained or instructed in areas including food and personal hygiene and safe handling and storage of food in accordance with the requirements set out in Annex 1 to MSN 1846.[18] Such an exemption: (a) must be given in writing; (b) may be granted on terms specified by the MCA; and (c) may be altered or cancelled by the MCA on giving written notice to the shipowner.[19] The MCA advises that 'exceptional circumstances' will include cases of illness or injury

13 Minimum Requirements Regulations, reg 42.
14 Minimum Requirements Regulations, reg 36(1)(a)–(b), (4).
15 Minimum Requirements Regulations, reg 36(2)(a)–(b).
16 Minimum Requirements Regulations, reg 37(1)(a)–(b).
17 Minimum Requirements Regulations, reg 37(2).
18 Minimum Requirements Regulations, reg 37(3)(a)–(b); MSN 1846, para 9.1.
19 Minimum Requirements Regulations, reg 37(4)(a)–(c).

to the ship's cook, or a close family relative, requiring the ship's cook to be repatriated; however, they will not include situations where the relieving ship's cook has not arrived on board, problems relating to visas or other commercial problems.[20]

Furthermore, there is a power for the MCA to give written approval, in respect of a particular ship, or ships of a particular description, to arrangements which are considered to be substantially equivalent to the requirement to carry a qualified ship's cook.[21] The MCA advises that such arrangements may be approved on passenger ships, mobile offshore drilling units (MODUs) or special purpose ships, which have large catering departments and may carry specialist chefs, cooks and managers who individually are not trained in all of the competencies required by ship's cooks, but they do so collectively.[22]

CERTIFICATES OF COMPETENCY FOR SHIP'S COOK

16.8 Applications for a certificate of competency (CoC) as a ship's cook should be made to the MCA (on Form 4395),[23] which may request certificates of discharge and the necessary documentary evidence, to establish that the applicant is an eligible person, before issuing a CoC.[24] An 'eligible person' means a seafarer who: is at least 18 years of age; has completed training in accordance with MSN 1846 (Annex 1 (food safety in catering) and Annex 2 (health and safety in catering in the maritime industry)); has served for not less than one month at sea in any capacity (confirmed by discharge book entries or certificates of discharge); has completed training with a White List STCW signatory state on personal survival techniques (STCW Code A-VI/1-1), fire prevention and firefighting (STCW Code A-VI/1-2), elementary first aid (STCW Code A-VI/1-3), personal safety and social responsibility (STCW Code A-VI/1-4) and security awareness; and holds a current seafarer medical fitness certificate 'ENG 1' or equivalent (see Chapter 4).[25]

Where prior training has not been designed to meet the requirements in Annexes 1 and 2 to MSN 1846, an application can be made for accreditation to the International Association of Marine Institutes.[26] MIN 559[27] contains a list

20 MSN 1846, Guidance, p 3; applications for an exemption can be made to: safemanning@mcga.gov.uk.
21 Minimum Requirements Regulations, reg 37(5)–(7).
22 MSN 1846, Guidance, p 3.
23 Form 4395 Rev 07/14 – Application for a Ships' Cook's Certificate of Competency: www.gov.uk/government/uploads/system/uploads/attachment_data/file/657494/140715__ships__cooks_application_form.pdf. The form also contains useful guidance and details of the documents that should be submitted.
24 Minimum Requirements Regulations, reg 38(1)–(2).
25 Minimum Requirements Regulations, reg 42; MSN 1846, paras 3.1–3.5, Guidance p 4.
26 MSN 1846, Guidance, p 4; https://iami.info/.
27 MIN 559(M): MLC, 2006 – Food and Catering: recognised qualifications in food hygiene or food safety in catering for ship's cooks and others processing food in the galley.

of qualifications and awarding bodies that are recognised and accepted in the UK as meeting the learning outcomes and assessment criteria of Annex 1 to MSN 1846.[28]

Recognition of existing CoCs

16.9 Any CoCs which were: (a) issued under the Merchant Shipping (Certification of Ships' Cooks) Regulations 1981; (b) treated as equivalent under reg 8 of those Regulations; or (c) deemed under reg 9 of those Regulations to be issued pursuant to s 43 of the Merchant Shipping Act 1970, which are still in force on 7 August 2014, are to be treated as if they were issued under reg 38 of the Minimum Requirements Regulations; however, a CoC recognised under these transitional provisions will only remain valid until 13 August 2019 (giving the holder time to upgrade their skills and training to obtain a certificate issued under the Minimum Requirements Regulations).

For a holder of a CoC issued under the 1981 Regulations, or an equivalent which has been issued by a UK training establishment, to update their certificate to one issued under the Minimum Requirements Regulations, they must complete the following training set out in MSN 1846: food safety in catering (Annex 1); cultural and religious catering requirements (Annex 2); dietary requirements of shift workers (Annex 2); and the STCW basic safety courses and security awareness referred to above. As an alternative to completing the training referred to in MSN 1846, the master may sign a testimonial to the effect that the cook is competent in those areas and requires no further training.

Certificates of equivalent competency

16.10 The MCA also accepts, as equivalent, ship's cook certificates issued by an EU member state, or those which have been issued by another state after it has ratified the MLC.[29] Certificates issued by other states may only be accepted if it is shown that the training approved by that state's maritime administration is equivalent to the UK requirements and a memorandum of understanding exists between the UK and that administration.[30] The holder would also have had to complete the STCW basic safety courses and security awareness referred to above.[31]

Suspension or cancellation of certificates

16.11 Ship's cooks holding UK CoCs are now subject to the disciplinary provisions contained within ss 62–69 of the Merchant Shipping Act 1995,

28 MSN 1846, Guidance, p 4.
29 MSN 1846, para 5.1.
30 MSN 1846, para 5.2.
31 MSN 1846, para 5.3.

under which their CoC is subject to suspension or cancellation, following an official inquiry finding that they are unfit to hold the position because they are incompetent, have been guilty of misconduct, or for any other reason.[32] These provisions are very rarely used in the UK against officers or ratings.

Lost, destroyed or stolen CoCs will be replaced by the MCA; the replacement copy must be certified by the MCA or designated person.[33] The MCA is obliged to keep records relating to the issue, suspension, cancellation or alteration and any other matters affecting ship's cooks' CoCs.[34]

TRAINING REQUIREMENTS FOR CATERING STAFF AND PERSONS PROCESSING FOOD IN THE GALLEY

16.12 The shipowner must ensure that: (a) every member of the catering staff is properly trained or instructed in accordance with Annex 1 to MSN 1846; and (b) any person processing food in the galley is properly trained or instructed in areas including food and personal hygiene and handling in accordance with Annex 1 to MSN 1846.[35] A member of the 'catering staff' is any seafarer whose normal duties include the preparation and storage of food, the service of meals to seafarers on board, or other work in the galley or in areas where food is stored or handled.[36] The MCA advises that this includes cooks, cooks' assistants, stewards and stewardesses.[37]

REQUIREMENTS FOR NON-UK SHIPS WITH MLC DOCUMENTATION

16.13 While a non-UK ship with MLC documentation is in UK waters, it must comply with:

- MLC, Regulation 3.2.1–3.2.2, being (1) the supply of adequate food and drinking water of appropriate quality, nutritional value and quantity, which takes into account the differing cultural and religious backgrounds of the crew; and (2) seafarers are to be provided with food free of charge during the period of their engagement.[38]
- MLC, Standard A3.2.7 – frequent documented inspections by, or under the authority of, the master with respect to: (a) supplies of food and drinking water; (b) all spaces and equipment used for the storage and handling of food and drinking water; and (c) galley and other equipment for the preparation and service of meals.[39]

32 Minimum Requirements Regulations, reg 38(3)–(5).
33 Minimum Requirements Regulations, reg 38(6)–(8).
34 Minimum Requirements Regulations, reg 38(8).
35 Minimum Requirements Regulations, reg 40(1)(a)–(b); MSN 1846, para 9.1.
36 Minimum Requirements Regulations, reg 42.
37 MSN 1846, para 8.3.
38 Minimum Requirements Regulations, reg 41(1).
39 Minimum Requirements Regulations, reg 41(3)(a)–(b).

- MLC, Standard A3.2.2(b)–(c) – the organisation and equipment of the catering department must be such as to permit the provision to the seafarers of adequate, varied and nutritious meals prepared and served in hygienic conditions; and catering staff are to be properly trained or instructed for their positions.[40]
- MLC, Standard A3.2.3–A3.2.4 – shipowners to ensure that ship's cooks are trained, qualified and competent, in accordance with flag state laws and regulations; this must include the completion of a training course, approved or recognised by the maritime authority, which covers practical cookery, food and personal hygiene, food storage, stock control, and environmental protection and catering health and safety. These requirements are subject to any dispensation issued by the flag state in accordance with MLC, Standard A3.2.6 which provides that, under circumstances of exceptional necessity, the maritime authority may issue a dispensation permitting a non-fully qualified cook to serve in a specified ship for a specified limited period, until the next convenient port of call or for a period not exceeding one month, so long as the person holding the dispensation is trained or instructed in areas including food and personal hygiene and the handling and storage of food on board.[41]

OFFENCES

16.14 Various offences are created, under the Minimum Requirements Regulations, which are set out in the table below. Unless otherwise indicated (by showing the potential penalty on indictment), they are summary offences only. It is a defence for a person charged to show that they took all reasonable steps to comply with the relevant provision.[42]

Regulation creating requirement/ offence	**Description of duty, failure of which gives rise to offence**	**Liable parties/ Maximum fine**
Reg 34(1)–(2)/ reg 34(3)	Shipowner and master to ensure that: (1) suitable food and drinking water are provided; (2) free of charge.	Shipowner and/or master Level 5 (reg 59(1))
Reg 35(1)(a)–(b)/ reg 35(2)	Food and drinking water to be stored and handled, and catering department to be organised, in accordance with MSN 1845.	Shipowner and/or master Level 5 (reg 59(1))

40 Minimum Requirements Regulations, reg 41(5)(a)–(b).
41 Minimum Requirements Regulations, reg 41(8).
42 Minimum Requirements Regulations, reg 60.

Regulation creating requirement/ offence	Description of duty, failure of which gives rise to offence	Liable parties/ Maximum fine
Reg 36(1)(a)–(b)/ reg 36(3)	Master to ensure through weekly inspections that (a) food and drinking water comply with regs 34–35 and MSN 1845; and (b) catering department and equipment comply with reg 35 and MSN 1845.	Master Level 4 (reg 59(2)(d))
Reg 36(4)/ reg 36(5)	Master to ensure that the results of inspections of the food, drinking water, catering department and equipment are recorded in the official log book.	Master Level 3 (reg 59(3)(h))
Reg 37(2)/ reg 37(8)(a)	No ship to be operated without a qualified ship's cook (unless an exemption applies).	Shipowner and master Punishable on summary conviction by a fine not exceeding level 5 on the standard scale or, on conviction on indictment, by imprisonment for a maximum of two years or a fine or both (reg 59(5)(f))
Reg 37(3)(a)–(b)/ reg 37(8)(b)	The terms of any exemption from the requirement to carry a ship's cook must be observed, being: (a) until the next port of call; and (b) not exceeding one month.	Shipowner and master Punishable on summary conviction by a fine not exceeding level 5 on the standard scale or, on conviction on indictment, by imprisonment for a maximum of two years or a fine or both (reg 59(5)(f))
Reg 37(8)(c)	Breach of a condition on which the MCA has granted permission to apply a substantial equivalence provision instead of carrying a qualified ship's cook.	Shipowner and master Punishable on summary conviction by a fine not exceeding level 5 on the standard scale or, on conviction on indictment, by imprisonment for a maximum of two years or a fine or both (reg 59(5)(f))

Regulation creating requirement/ offence	**Description of duty, failure of which gives rise to offence**	**Liable parties/ Maximum fine**
Reg 40(1)(a)–(b)/ reg 40(2)	Shipowner to ensure that the following persons are trained in accordance with MSN 1846: (a) catering staff; and (b) any person processing food in the galley.	Shipowner Level 5 (reg 59(1))
The offences below only apply to non-UK ships carrying MLC documentation while they are in UK waters:		
Reg 41(1)/ reg 41(2)	Ship must not operate in UK waters unless MLC, Regulation 3.2, paras 1–2, are complied with: (1) the supply of adequate food and drinking water of appropriate quality, nutritional value and quantity, taking into account differing cultural and religious backgrounds of the crew; and (2) seafarers are to be provided with food free of charge.	Shipowner and master Level 5 (reg 59(1))
Reg 41(3)(a)–(b)/ reg 41(4)	Master or authorised person to: (a) carry out frequent inspections; and (b) document them, with respect to: supplies of food and drinking water; all spaces and equipment used for the storage and handling of food and drinking water; and galley and other equipment for the preparation and service of meals.	Master Reg 41(3)(a) – Level 5 (reg 59(1)) Reg 41(3)(b) – Level 3 (reg 59(3)(i))
Reg 41(5)(a)/ reg 41(6)	The organisation and equipment of the catering department must be such as to permit the provision to the seafarers of adequate, varied and nutritious meals prepared and served in hygienic conditions.	Shipowner and master Level 5 (reg 59(1))
Reg 41(5)(b)/ reg 41(7)	Catering staff to be properly trained or instructed.	Shipowner Level 5 (reg 59(1))

Regulation creating requirement/ offence	**Description of duty, failure of which gives rise to offence**	**Liable parties/ Maximum fine**
Reg 41(8)/ reg 41(9)	Shipowners to ensure that ship's cooks are trained, qualified and competent, in accordance with flag state laws and regulations, which must include the completion of a training course, approved or recognised by the maritime authority.	Shipowner Punishable on summary conviction by a fine not exceeding level 5 on the standard scale or, on conviction on indictment, by imprisonment for a maximum of two years or a fine or both (reg 59(5)(g))

Compliance

DMLC: observe national provisions as set out in Pt I, point 8, and enter implementing measures in Pt II, point 8.

PART V

Title 4: Health Protection, Medical Care, Welfare and Social Security Protection

CHAPTER 17

Regulation 4.1: Medical Care On Board Ship and Ashore

INTRODUCTION

17.1 The purpose of Regulation 4.1 of the MLC and its associated Code is to protect the health of seafarers and ensure their prompt access to medical care on board ship and ashore.[1]

Ratifying states are required to allow seafarers on ships in its territorial waters to have access to their medical facilities ashore.[2] The objective is to ensure that seafarers are provided with health protection and medical care that is as comparable as possible to that which is generally available to workers ashore and, to the extent consistent with national law and practice, that it is provided free of charge.[3]

The main UK provisions are the Merchant Shipping and Fishing Vessel (Medical Stores) Regulations 1995,[4] Pt 9 of the Merchant Shipping (Maritime

1 MLC, Regulation 4.1, purpose.
2 MLC, Regulation 4.1.3; Standard A4.1(c).
3 MLC, Regulation 4.1.4; Standard A4.1(b), (d).
4 SI 1995/1802.

Labour Convention) Minimum Requirements for Seafarers) Regulations 2014[5] ('Minimum Requirements Regulations'), MSN 1768[6] and MGN 482.[7] The duties in Pt 9 apply to UK MLC ships wherever they may be, and to non-UK ships, which do not carry MLC documentation, while they are in UK waters.[8] The Minimum Requirements Regulations provide that, in Pt 9, only reg 46 applies to non-UK ships, carrying MLC documentation, while they are in UK waters.[9]

DUTIES IN RESPECT OF SEAFARERS' MEDICAL CARE

17.2 Shipowners must ensure that seafarers, who become sick or injured during their tour of duty, are provided with medical care on board, so far as practicable, and they must meet the expenses reasonably incurred in connection with their treatment.[10] This is subject to the sickness or injury first occurring (i) between the date their seafarer employment agreement (SEA) commences, and the date the shipowner's duty to repatriate ends (in accordance with reg 21 of the Minimum Requirements Regulations – see Chapter 11), or (ii) after that period, but being caused by circumstances or events arising during it.[11]

The shipowner is required to meet the expenses of surgical, medical, dental or optical treatment (including the supply, repair or replacement of any appliance) and board and lodging (except to the extent that they are met by a public authority). The duty is limited to meeting such expenses incurred during the period of 16 weeks from the date the sickness or injury first occurs, or until the date, if sooner, on which the seafarer is notified, by a person authorised to issue seafarer medical certificates,[12] that they are unfit to carry out their duties and are unlikely to be fit to carry them out in future.[13] However, these limitations are without prejudice to the shipowner's duty, under reg 22 of the Minimum Requirements Regulations, to provide for relief and maintenance (which includes medical care) pending repatriation.[14] So, in respect of an infirm seafarer who is too ill to travel, the

5 SI 2014/1613.
6 MSN 1768 (M+F): Application of the Merchant Shipping and Fishing Vessels (Medical Stores) Regulations 1995 (SI 1995/1802) and Merchant Shipping and Fishing Vessels (Medical Stores) (Amendment) Regulations 1996 (SI 1996/2821).
7 MGN 482 (M) – Maritime Labour Convention, 2006: Medical Care.
8 Minimum Requirements Regulations, reg 3(1)(a)–(b).
9 Minimum Requirements Regulations, reg 3(3)–(4)(b)(vii).
10 Minimum Requirements Regulations, reg 43(3)(a)–(b), superseding Merchant Shipping Act 1995, s 45(1) for MLC ships.
11 Minimum Requirements Regulations, reg 43(1)–(2)(a)–(b).
12 Defined in Minimum Requirements Regulations, reg 47, to mean a person authorised by, or on behalf of, the Secretary of State, or other national maritime administration, for the purposes of Regulation 1.2 (medical certificate) of the MLC, or Regulation I/9 of the IMO's International Convention on Standards of Training, Certification and Watchkeeping for Seafarers, 1978 (as amended) ('STCW Convention'); see Chapter 4.
13 Minimum Requirements Regulations, reg 43(6). If the notification in either respect is subsequently revoked, the shipowner has a duty to meet the expenses incurred within the period of 16 weeks from the date the sickness or injury first occurs: reg 43(7).
14 Minimum Requirements Regulations, reg 43(5)(b).

shipowner is obliged to meet the costs of medical care until their repatriation, even if this takes place beyond 16 weeks, or if the seafarer has been declared to be permanently unfit.[15]

When a ship is in a port of call, where reasonably practicable, the shipowner must permit a seafarer to go ashore for medical attention, if it is not available on board.[16]

Shipowners or employers (if different) are required to set out the details of the medical care they are to provide to seafarers, in their SEAs, as part of the health and social security benefits.[17] As well as providing clarity, this provides seafarers with contractual remedies against the shipowner or employer (if different) for any non-compliance, in addition to the statutory remedy in reg 43(9) of the Minimum Requirements Regulations (see para 17.4 below).[18]

The Dreadnought Unit

17.3 The Dreadnought Unit provides priority medical treatment to eligible seafarers (which includes active seafarers resident in the UK) through Guy's and St Thomas' NHS Foundation Trust, based at the sites of those respective hospitals in London. Details of the service, eligibility and how to access it are provided in MGN 370.[19]

RECOVERY OF EXPENSES

17.4 The shipowner may recover from the seafarer, as a civil debt, any expenses that it has met, in connection with:

(a) injury suffered otherwise than in the service of the ship;

(b) injury or sickness arising from the wilful misconduct of the seafarer; or

(c) injury or sickness intentionally concealed by the seafarer prior to entering into their SEA.[20]

A seafarer may also recover any expenses they have incurred (except in the circumstances set out in paragraphs (a)–(c) above), which were for the account of the shipowner, as a civil debt.[21]

15 MGN 482, para 3.2. See Chapter 11.
16 Minimum Requirements Regulations, reg 45(1).
17 Minimum Requirements Regulations, Sch 1, Pt 1, para 9.
18 In a case where the employer is not the shipowner, the employer must be a party to the SEA and, in addition, the shipowner must guarantee the performance of the employer's obligations thereunder: Minimum Requirements Regulations, reg 9(2)–(3).
19 MGN 370 (M+F): The Dreadnought Medical Service, St Thomas' Hospital, London.
20 Minimum Requirements Regulations, reg 43(8)(a)–(c).
21 Minimum Requirements Regulations, reg 43(9).

DUTY TO CARRY A MEDICAL PRACTITIONER

17.5 Ships carrying 100 or more persons, which are engaged in international voyages lasting more than 72 hours, must carry a medical practitioner on board.[22]

SEAFARER IN CHARGE OF MEDICAL CARE

17.6 The MLC provides that ships that do not carry a doctor must have at least one seafarer on board who is (i) in charge of medical care and administering medicine, as part of their regular duties, or (ii) competent to provide medical first aid, and is trained to the requirements set out in the STCW Convention.[23]

Where a UK ship does not employ a doctor, it is the master's duty to administer medical attention, or to ensure that it is given by someone appointed by and under the supervision of the master.[24] The Merchant Shipping (Training and Certification) Regulations 2015, in turn, provide that a seafarer designated to provide medical first aid, or medical care, must meet the standard of competence set out in section A-VI/4 paragraphs 1–3, or section A-VI/4, paragraphs 4–6, of the STCW Code, respectively.[25]

Deck officers (including those with boatmaster or yachtmaster qualifications) are all trained in medical first aid or, at more senior levels, in medical care.[26] The master and officer in charge of first aid or medical care are required to attend refresher training at least every five years.[27]

In designating such officers, the shipowner should take account of the number of seafarers on board, and the availability of medical care ashore, and should ensure that there are sufficient competent seafarers to support the designated officer, and (as far as possible) that such duties do not interfere with their scheduled hours of rest.[28]

22 Minimum Requirements Regulations, reg 44(1)–(2). A 'medical practitioner' means (i) a person ordinarily resident in the UK who is a 'fully registered person' (in accordance with Medical Act 1983, s 55(1)) who (a) holds a licence to practise, or (b) meets the criteria specified in MSN 1841; or (ii) a practitioner not ordinarily resident in the UK, who meets the criteria specified in MSN 1841.

23 MLC, Standard A4.1.4(c).

24 Merchant Shipping Act 1995, s 53.

25 SI 2015/782, reg 26(1)–(2), respectively. The syllabus, for smaller vessels not covered by the STCW Convention, is set out in MGN 147 (M+F): Training in First Aid and Medical Care for Fishing Vessel Personnel, Boatmaster's Licence Holders and Small Commercial Vessel Personnel.

26 MGN 482, para 5.1.

27 MGN 482, para 5.3.

28 MGN 482, para 5.5.

MEDICAL STORES, EQUIPMENT AND GUIDES

17.7 The relevant provisions are the Merchant Shipping and Fishing Vessel (Medical Stores) Regulations 1995 ('1995 Regulations'),[29] the guidance for which is set out in MSN 1768 (M+F).[30] The 1995 Regulations implement Council Directive 92/29/EEC,[31] as far as the latter relates to the carriage of medicines and other medical stores, and apply to all UK MLC ships.[32]

All UK MLC ships are required to carry medical stores in accordance with MSN 1768,[33] which sets out the definitions of categories of vessel to which it applies, and the requirements for each category in Annexes 1–9, which have been summarised below.

The categories of vessel for the purposes of the 1995 Regulations

17.8 There are three categories: A, B and C. As far as relevant, they include: category A (seagoing vessels with no limitation on length of trips); category B (seagoing vessels making trips of less than 150 nautical miles from the nearest port with adequate medical equipment, and seagoing vessels making trips of less than 175 nautical miles from the nearest port that has adequate medical equipment and which remain continuously within range of helicopter rescue services); and category C (harbour vessels, boats and craft staying very close to shore[34] – lifeboats and life-rafts are also required to carry category C stores).[35]

Medical stores required and recommended additional equipment (Annex 1)

17.9 This is divided into four columns, showing the stores which are required to be carried on category A, B and C vessels.

29 SI 1995/1802, as amended by the Merchant Shipping and Fishing Vessel (Medical Stores) (Amendment) Regulations 1996 (SI 1996/2821).

30 MSN 1768 (M+F): Application of the Merchant Shipping and Fishing Vessels (Medical Stores) Regulations 1995 (SI 1995/1802) and the Merchant Shipping and Fishing Vessels (Medical Stores) (Amendment) Regulations 1996 (SI 1996/2821).

31 Council Directive 92/29/EEC of 31 March 1992 on the minimum safety and health requirements for improved medical treatment on board vessels (OJ L 113, 30.4.92, p 19).

32 1995 Regulations, regs 2–3.

33 1995 Regulations, reg 4 (which refers to MSN 1607 and MSN 1608, which are no longer in force). Reference should therefore be made to MSN 1768 (M+F): Ships' Medical Stores – Application of the Merchant Shipping and Fishing Vessels (Medical Stores) Regulations 1995.

34 For the purposes of the 1995 Regulations, the absolute limit is 60 nautical miles out to sea, but the shipowner and skipper should assess, in respect of voyages less than 60 nautical miles, whether the vessel is 'very close to shore': MSN 1768, para 2.1.

35 MSN 1768, para 2.1.

Column 1: this shows the reference number in Council Directive 92/29/EEC, which is included for the identification of treatments, when seeking or receiving radio medical advice from any Member State.

Column 2: this shows the statutorily required treatment which must be available to comply with the 1995 Regulations.

Column 3: this shows the recommended medicine and dosage strength which the MCA considers best complies with the statutorily required treatment. Shipowners and operators may substitute exact equivalents, on the advice of a qualified medical practitioner or pharmacist, provided they are satisfied that an equivalent level of treatment is assured.

Column 4: this shows the recommended quantity of medicine and equipment which the MCA considers sufficient to provide treatment for 10 workers or for the crew of a lifeboat or life-raft.[36]

Additional requirements for passenger vessels: Doctor's Bag (Annex 2)

17.10 A Doctor's Bag is required for seagoing ships (excluding Class VI and VI(A) vessels) carrying more than 12 passengers (where there is no qualified medical practitioner among the crew).[37] There is a list of all the statutory medicines and treatments which must be kept in the bag, which should be locked and kept in a locked cabinet, with the key held by the master or nominated person.[38] The bag must contain a label stating:

> 'The medicines in this case are only to be used by a qualified medical practitioner, registered general nurse, qualified paramedic, or someone under the direct supervision of a medical practitioner on board the ship.'[39]

Those persons should be made aware that radio medical advice may be obtained and, if necessary, medical evacuation arranged, by contacting HM Coastguard.[40]

First aid kits (Annex 3)

17.11 A seagoing ship with a crew of more than 10 must carry first aid kits (the required contents are listed in Annex 3), distributed in appropriate places (such as the galley and engine room). Passenger vessels must carry one first aid kit for every 100 passengers (or fraction of that number), up to a maximum of three kits. A first aid kit is to be kept in the Doctor's Bag.[41]

36 MSN 1768, Annex 1, pp 5–18.
37 MSN 1768, para 1.
38 MSN 1768, Annex 2, para 2, pp 19–21.
39 MSN 1768, Annex 2, para 2.
40 MSN 1768, para 5.
41 MSN 1768, Annex 3, p 22.

Advice on medicines to be carried on ships (including ferries) transporting dangerous substances (Annex 4)

17.12 When a UK ship is carrying a dangerous substance or substances, in quantities in excess of those defined in Vol 1, s 18 of the IMDG Code, the master must ensure that the correct antidote can be found in the IMO Medical First Aid Guide for Ships; account should be taken of any updates of the IMO IMDG Code, when preparing the list of medicines to be carried.[42]

The following substances are to be taken into account, in whichever form they are carried on board (including waste or cargo residues): explosive substances and objects; gases (compressed, liquefied or dissolved under pressure); inflammable liquids and solids; substances which are liable to spontaneous combustion or which, on contact with water, give off inflammable gases; combustible, toxic, infectious, radioactive, corrosive or various dangerous substances; and organic peroxides.[43]

The quantities of medicines that need to be carried on board should be based on a risk assessment, taking into account crew numbers, length of voyage and the risk of accidental exposure.[44]

There is a specific provision for ferries, which must carry the following antidotes and equipment:[45]

- Antidotes: general; cardio-vascular; gastro-intestinal system; nervous system; anti-infective; for external use.
- Equipment: for the administration of oxygen.

Medical guides to be carried and radio medical advice (Annex 5)

17.13 Each category of ship must carry the medical guides shown below:

- Category A: Ship Captain's Medical Guide; the Controlled Drugs Register; MSN 1768;
- Category B: Ship Captain's Medical Guide; MSN 1768;
- Category C: First Aid Manual (St John's, Red Cross or St Andrew's); MSN 1768; or First Aid Instructions in English on waterproof paper (lifeboats and life-rafts only).[46]

Ships (including ferries) carrying dangerous cargoes (or residue) should comply with the IMO's International Maritime Dangerous Goods (IMDG) Code[47] and

42 MSN 1768, Annex 4, para 1.
43 MSN 1768, Annex 4, para 2.
44 MSN 1768, Annex 4, para 3.
45 MSN 1768, Annex 4, para 4.
46 MSN 1768, Annex 5, p 24.
47 The 2016 Edition (as amended) is the most current, which came into force on 1 January 2018; www.imo.org/en/Publications/IMDGCode/Pages/Default.aspx [Accessed 4 January 2018].

the guidance in the IMO/WHO/ILO Medical First Aid Guide for use in accidents involving Dangerous Goods (MFAG 1994), and Annex 4 to MSN 1768.[48]

Radio medical advice is available to all ships at sea, by contacting HM Coastguard, as explained in MGN 225.[49] Contact should be made on either MF DSC, VHF DSC, VHF Channel 16 or INMARSAT (mobile phones should be avoided).[50] The advice is provided by two UK designated centres: Aberdeen Royal Infirmary; and Queen Alexandra Hospital, Portsmouth.[51]

In addition, shipowners should ensure that up-to-date complete lists of the following are carried on board: telemedicine services; and coast earth stations (for ships equipped with satellite communication). All national and international radio services are entered in the Admiralty List of Radio Signals, particularly Volume 5. Seafarers with responsibility for medical care or first aid should be instructed in the use of the ship's medical guide and the medical section of the most recent edition of the International Code of Signals, to enable them to understand the type of information needed by the advising doctor and the advice received.[52]

Precautions against malaria (Annex 6)

17.14 Some advice on preventive measures on board ship, and when in malarial areas, is provided.[53] The advice is that anyone who has been treated for malaria or suspected malaria must have a medical examination at the next port of call, accompanied by a blood slide; serious cases need urgent hospitalisation.[54]

More detailed guidance is provided in MGN 399(M)[55] on the following issues: Anti-Malaria Medication; Summary of Needs for Malaria Medication; and Malaria Emergency Standby Medication.[56]

Guide to use of medicines (Annex 7)

17.15 Advice is given on: medicine supplies; controlled drugs (and register); storage and security of medicines; and record-keeping.

48 MSN 1768, para 1.1.
49 MGN 225 (M+F): Radio Medical Advice for Ships at Sea.
50 MGN 225, para 3; for urgent calls, the words 'PAN PAN' should be repeated three times.
51 MSN 1768, Annex 5.
52 MGN 482, paras 8.2–8.3.
53 MSN 1768, Annex 6, p 25.
54 MSN 1768, Annex 6, para 4.
55 MGN 399 (M): Prevention of Infectious Disease at Sea by Immunisations and Anti-Malaria Medication (prophylaxis), which replaces MGN 257 (M).
56 MGN 399: paras 7.1–7.6; Annexes 4 and 5 respectively.

Where no specific storage temperature is given, drugs should be stored at room temperature between 15 and 25° centigrade. Some of the drugs should be kept under refrigeration, at 2 to 5° centigrade, but care must be taken not to freeze them.[57]

A detailed table shows references, drug types, uses and dosages, to be used in conjunction with the Ship Captain's Medical Guide.[58]

Specimen requisition form for obtaining controlled drugs (Annex 8)

17.16 This form is to be used when applying for controlled drugs, which can only be supplied by a retail pharmacist or other licensed person. The form should state: '[t]he above drugs are required for the medical stores of the above vessel in compliance with the Merchant Shipping (Medical Stores) Regulations 1995', and must be signed by the shipowner or master.[59]

Completion of the controlled drugs register (Annex 9)

17.17 Examples are shown on how to complete the register, which is divided into two sections recording: (1) drugs obtained from an authorised supplier or confiscated from seafarers; and (2) how the drug was dispensed or disposed of.

MEDICAL REPORT FORM

17.18 The MCA has produced a model form (MSF 4155),[60] to be used in respect of a seafarer going ashore for medical treatment. The form will provide the receiving doctor with details of the illness or injury and treatment administered. The doctor ashore will enter details of their diagnosis, treatment given, together with any further recommended treatment. The completed form is to be returned to the master and treated as confidential.[61]

NON-UK SHIPS CARRYING MLC DOCUMENTATION

17.19 The only requirements in Pt 9 of the Minimum Requirements Regulations applying to non-UK ships, carrying MLC documentation while they are in UK waters, are as follows.

57 MSN 1768, Annex 7.
58 MSN 1768, Annex, pp 26–35.
59 MSN 1768, Annex 8.
60 MSF 4155: Confidential Medical Report: www.gov.uk/government/uploads/system/uploads/attachment_data/file/294953/MSF4155_REV1213.pdf [Accessed 7 January 2018].
61 MGN 482, para 9.1.

Seafarers must be given access to prompt and adequate medical care, at no cost to themselves, while working on board.[62] Where practicable, they must be permitted, without delay, to visit a doctor or dentist in ports of call.[63]

Ships must also carry a qualified medical doctor, if they are carrying 100 or more persons and are engaged in international voyages lasting more than 72 hours.[64]

OFFENCES

17.20 Any breaches by the shipowner, of the requirements set out in regulations 4 to 11 of the 1995 Regulations, are punishable on summary conviction by a fine not exceeding level 5 on the standard scale.[65] Where the offence is in respect of failing to carry the medical stores required by regulation 4, it is a defence to show that the deficiency was caused by the medicines and medical stores being used for their proper purpose, and it has not been practicable to replace them.[66] It is a defence (in respect of any of the offences under the 1995 Regulations) for the person charged to show that they took all reasonable precautions and exercised all due diligence.[67]

The 1995 Regulations also provide power for the inspection and detention of UK ships for breaches of the following regulations: reg 4 (carriage of medical stores); reg 6 (standards of medical stores); and reg 7 (packaging and labelling of containers).[68]

The Minimum Requirements Regulations also introduce a number of offences, as set out in the table below. It is a defence for the person charged to show that they had taken all reasonable steps to ensure compliance.[69] This table can be used as a checklist for the main compliance points.

62 Minimum Requirements Regulations, reg 46(1)(a).
63 Minimum Requirements Regulations, reg 46(1)(b).
64 Minimum Requirements Regulations, reg 46(4). The doctor must be qualified in accordance with the flag state requirements: reg 46(6).
65 1995 Regulations, regs 12(1), 13.
66 1995 Regulations, reg 12(2).
67 1995 Regulations, reg 12(3).
68 1995 Regulations, regs 14–15.
69 Minimum Requirements Regulations, reg 60.

Regulation creating duty/ offence	Description of duty	Liable person/ level of fine
Reg 43(3)(a)–(b)/ reg 43(10)	Shipowner: (a) to ensure seafarer is provided with medical care on board; and (b) to meet expenses relating to seafarer's medical care.	Shipowner/ Level 5
Reg 44(1)–(2)/ reg 44(3)	Medical practitioner to be carried on board ships carrying 100 or more persons engaged in international voyages lasting more than 72 hours.	Shipowner/ Level 5
Reg 45(1)/ reg 45(2)	Shipowner to permit seafarer to go ashore for medical attention.	Shipowner/ Level 4
Reg 46(1)(a)–(b)/ reg 46(2)	Non-UK MLC ships in UK waters: (a) seafarer to be given free medical care on board ship; and (b) seafarer to be permitted to visit a doctor or dentist in ports of call.	Shipowner/ Level 4
Reg 46(3)–(4)/ reg 46(5)	Non-UK MLC ships in UK waters: medical practitioner to be carried on board ships carrying 100 or more persons engaged in international voyages lasting more than 72 hours.	Shipowner/ Level 5

INSPECTION AND DETENTION OF SHIPS

17.21 The powers of inspection and detention, as they apply to UK ships and non-UK ships while they are in UK waters, are set out in Chapter 2 at para 2.2.[70]

COMPLIANCE POINTS

17.22 DMLC: see the UK provisions in Pt I, point 12, and enter compliance measures in Pt II, point 12.

See Chapter 18 on shipowners' responsibilities in meeting the costs of seafarers' medical treatment and paying seafarers' wages during periods of incapacity due to work-related illness or injury.

70 Minimum Requirements Regulations, regs 54–56.

CHAPTER 18

Regulation 4.2: Shipowners' Liability

INTRODUCTION

18.1 The purpose of Regulation 4.2 of the MLC and its associated Code is to ensure that seafarers are protected from the financial consequences of sickness, injury or death occurring in connection with their employment.[1] There is some overlap with MLC Regulation 4.1 and its associated Code, as far as it relates to shipowners' duties to provide and meet the expenses for medical care.[2]

The shipowners' liability provisions of the MLC were (together with those in Regulation 2.5 and its associated Code on repatriation) the first parts of the MLC to be amended, by the insertion of the detailed requirements on how the financial security provision was to operate in relation to shipowners' liability for contractual claims in respect of compensation for death or long-term disability of seafarers.[3] These amendments were agreed by the Special Tripartite Committee (set up under Article XIII of the MLC) in February 2014, approved by the ILO's International Labour Conference on 11 June 2014, and came into force on 18 January 2017.[4] Like most other MLC requirements, the amendments

1 MLC, Regulation 4.2, p 58.
2 MLC, Standard A4.2.1(a) and (c).
3 The MLC required, in its original form, financial security to be in place to cover repatriation (Regulation 2.5.2) and shipowners' liabilities (Standard A4.2.1(b)), but did not set out the framework within which it was to operate; this has now been provided by the amendments.
4 Amendments of 2014 to the Maritime Labour Convention, 2006, approved by the Conference at its One Hundred and Third Session, Geneva, 11 June 2014: www.ilo.org/wcmsp5/groups/public/---ed_norm/---relconf/documents/meetingdocument/wcms_248905.pdf [Accessed 27 December 2017].

have been incorporated into EU law, by Directive 2018/131/EU inserting the provisions into Directive 2009/13/EC (which contains many of the mandatory MLC requirements of titles 1–4).[5]

The main UK provisions are set out in Pts 10 and 10A of the Merchant Shipping (Maritime Labour Convention) (Minimum Requirements for Seafarers etc) Regulations 2014[6] ('Minimum Requirements Regulations'), as amended by the Merchant Shipping (Maritime Labour Convention) (Compulsory Financial Security) (Amendment) Regulations 2018[7] ('Financial Security Amendment Regulations') (which insert Pt 10A into the Minimum Requirements Regulations), and MGN 480.[8] All of the provisions of Pts 10 and 10A apply to UK MLC ships wherever they may be, and to non-UK ships without MLC documentation when they are in UK waters.[9]

As regards non-UK ships, carrying MLC documentation while they are in UK waters, Pt 10 does not apply, and only reg 53B(1)(b) of Pt 10A applies (requirement to carry financial security in accordance with the provisions of MLC, Standard A4.2.1.1).[10]

SHIPOWNERS TO PROVIDE MEDICAL CARE

18.2 As explained above, MLC, Standard A4.2.1(a) and (c), which requires shipowners to provide medical care and treatment for sick or injured seafarers, overlaps with MLC Regulation 4.1. An account of those obligations is provided in Chapter 17.

FINANCIAL SECURITY

18.3 The full text of the MLC amendments on financial security are set out in Appendix 2. Set out below is a summary of the UK provisions which follow those of the MLC.

5 Council Directive (EU) 2018 of 23 January 2018 implementing the Agreement concluded by the European Community Shipowners' Associations (ECSA) and the European Transport Workers' Federation (ETF) to amend Directive 2009/13/EC in accordance with the amendments of 2014 to the Maritime Labour Convention, 2006, as approved by the International Labour Conference on 11 June 2014, OJ 26.1.2018 L 22/28.
6 SI 2014/1613.
7 SI 2018/667.
8 MGN 480 (M) Amendment 2 – Maritime Labour Convention, 2006: Shipowners' Liabilities including Seafarer Compensation.
9 Minimum Requirements Regulations, reg 3(1)(2)(a).
10 Minimum Requirements Regulations, reg 3(3)–(4)(b)(viii), as amended by Financial Security Amendment Regulations, reg 2(3)(c)(ii), (6).

UK MLC ships and, while they are in UK waters, non-UK MLC ships which do not carry MLC documentation

18.4 All such ships must have 'shipowner's security' in force.[11] In many cases, the security will be provided by the P&I Club with which the ship is entered, although there are other providers offering specific insurance to cover these liabilities.[12]

The shipowner's security must:

- provide financial assurance of an amount which the shipowner reasonably considers adequate to ensure that the shipowner will be able to meet any liabilities that the shipowner may have, including liabilities under seafarer employment agreements, to provide compensation in the event of death or long-term disability to seafarers arising from occupational injury, illness or hazard; and
- provide that a claim for compensation may be submitted directly to the shipowner's security provider by: any relevant seafarer who sustains a long-term disability arising from a relevant occupational injury, illness or hazard; and the personal representatives of any deceased relevant seafarer, the death of whom arose from a relevant occupational injury, illness or hazard.[13]

'Relevant occupational injury, illness or hazard' means an occupational injury, illness or hazard: occurring during the period of validity of the shipowner's security; and in relation to which the shipowner is, or may be, liable to provide compensation to the seafarer or, as the case may be, the seafarer's estate.[14]

The security document must contain the following information:

'(a) the name of the ship to which the shipowner's security relates;

(b) the port of registry of the ship;

(c) the call sign of the ship;

(d) the International Maritime Organisation number of the ship;

(e) the name and address of the shipowner's security provider;

(f) the contact details of the point of contact at the shipowner's security provider responsible for handling claims made by seafarers;

(g) the name of the owner of the ship;

(h) the period of validity of the shipowner's security;

11 Minimum Requirements Regulations, reg 53B(1)(a), as inserted by Financial Security Amendment Regulations, reg 2(7).

12 For example, CrewSEACURE: https://crewseacure.com/ [Accessed 27 September 2018].

13 Minimum Requirements Regulations, reg 53C(2)–(3), as inserted by Financial Security Amendment Regulations, reg 2(7).

14 Minimum Requirements Regulations, reg 53C(4), as inserted by Financial Security Amendment Regulations, reg 2(7).

(i) a declaration from the shipowner's security provider that the shipowner's security meets the requirements of standard A4.2.1 of the MLC.'[15]

The provider must pay the contractual compensation to the seafarer, or the seafarer's personal representative, within seven days beginning with the date on which it is established that the shipowner is liable for the contractual compensation either: (a) by agreement between (i) the shipowner's security provider, and (ii) the seafarer or the seafarer's personal representative; or (b) by order of a court or tribunal which is not subject to appeal.[16] A penalty of 20% is imposed on arrears beginning with the date that the shipowner's security provider became satisfied of the shipowner's liability.[17] For these purposes, a 'claim for contractual compensation' means 'a claim for compensation in the event of death or long term disability of a seafarer arising from occupational injury, illness or hazard where the compensation payable in respect of the claim is set out in the [SEA], and "contractual compensation" is to be construed accordingly'.[18] The SEA includes any incorporated collective bargaining agreements.[19] The financial security does not extend to personal injury claims in negligence or for breach of statutory duty.

18.5 It is an offence for any person to induce another to accept less than the full amount of compensation payable, as set out in the SEA, in respect of the death or long-term disability of a seafarer arising from occupational injury, illness or hazard.[20]

There are provisions requiring an interim payment to be made under specified conditions, including when the full amount payable has not yet been determined and the seafarer is suffering hardship.[21]

The 'shipowner's security document' (certificate or other documentary evidence of a shipowner's security issued by the shipowner's security provider) must be displayed in a conspicuous place on board the ship; if it is not in English, it must be accompanied by an English translation.[22]

15 Minimum Requirements Regulations, reg 53G(1), Sch 3, as inserted by Financial Security Amendment Regulations, reg 2(7).
16 Minimum Requirements Regulations, reg 53D(1)–(2)(a)–(b), as inserted by Financial Security Amendment Regulations, reg 2(7).
17 Minimum Requirements Regulations, reg 53D(3), as inserted by Financial Security Amendment Regulations, reg 2(7).
18 Minimum Requirements Regulations, reg 53D(4), as inserted by Financial Security Amendment Regulations, reg 2(7).
19 Minimum Requirements Regulations, reg 10(1)(a), (2), Sch 1, Pt 1, para 14.
20 Minimum Requirements Regulations, reg 53F, as inserted by Financial Security Amendment Regulations, reg 2(7).
21 Minimum Requirements Regulations, reg 53E, as inserted by Financial Security Amendment Regulations, reg 2(7).
22 Minimum Requirements Regulations, reg 53G, as inserted by Financial Security Amendment Regulations, reg 2(7).

The security provider may only terminate the security before its expiry date by giving 30 days' notice in writing to the MCA, accompanied by a copy of the shipowner's security document; otherwise, any attempt to terminate will be invalid.[23]

Where a shipowner becomes aware that any shipowner's security is to be, or has been, terminated before the end of its period of validity, the shipowner must, as soon as reasonably practicable, give written notice to that effect to all seafarers.[24]

Non-UK MLC ships carrying MLC documentation while they are in UK waters

18.6 Such ships must carry financial security to assure that compensation in the event of death or long-term disability of seafarers arising from occupational illness, injury or hazard is provided in relation to the ship in accordance with MLC, Standard A4.2.1.1.[25]

SICK PAY

18.7 Shipowners are obliged to ensure that seafarers are paid in accordance with their SEA during periods of incapacity, due to sickness or injury, although this is subject to some conditions, limitations and exceptions. For the duty to arise, the sickness or injury must first occur: (i) during the seafarer's employment on board (until repatriation), or (ii) after that period, but where it is caused by circumstances or events arising during it.[26] The sickness or injury must not first occur during a period of leave (other than shore leave) and must result in the seafarer's incapacity for work.[27] The extent of the duty is greater up until the point of repatriation than it is afterwards.

The purported termination of a SEA is to have no effect if it is solely or mainly for the purpose of avoiding liability to pay sick pay arising under the provisions described in paragraphs 18.8 and 18.9 below.[28]

23 Minimum Requirements Regulations, reg 53H–53I, as inserted by Financial Security Amendment Regulations, reg 2(7).
24 Minimum Requirements Regulations, reg 53J, as inserted by Financial Security Amendment Regulations, reg 2(7).
25 Minimum Requirements Regulations, reg 53B(1)(b), as inserted by Financial Security Amendment Regulations, reg 2(7).
26 Minimum Requirements Regulations, reg 50(1)(a). If the illness or injury occurs during a leave period (except shore leave), the duty does not arise: reg 50(1)(b).
27 Minimum Requirements Regulations, reg 50(b)–(c).
28 Minimum Requirements Regulations, reg 50(15), as inserted by Merchant Shipping (Maritime Labour Convention) (Miscellaneous Amendments) Regulations 2018 (SI 2018/242) ('Miscellaneous Amendments Regulations'), reg 5(4)(e).

The duty does not apply if the injury was not sustained at work, the injury or sickness arose out of the seafarer's wilful misconduct, or the seafarer deliberately concealed the sickness or incapacity from the shipowner at the time of entering into their SEA.[29]

Until repatriation

18.8 If the sickness or injury occurs on board, or during repatriation, the duty is to ensure that the seafarer receives the 'wages' to which they would have been entitled, up until the point at which the duty to repatriate ends,[30] had they remained fit for work during that period, and even if the SEA expires during that period.[31] In many cases, the employer of the seafarer will not be the shipowner, and the former will still be required to pay wages in accordance with the terms of the SEA. However, the shipowner is obliged to make good any shortfall. In this context, the definition of 'wages' means the pay for the seafarer's normal hours of work, including overtime, allowances and other remuneration, excluding bonuses (post repatriation, the shipowner must pay 'basic wages' as set out in para 18.9 below).[32]

Post repatriation

18.9 If a seafarer, who has become sick or injured (occurring as described in para 18.7 above), is consequently unable to work once they have been repatriated, and is not paid their 'basic wages' in accordance with their SEA during the 'period of incapacity', the shipowner must make good any shortfall.[33]

In this context, 'basic wages' means the pay for the seafarer's normal hours of work, but excludes '… overtime, bonuses, allowances, paid leave and other remuneration'.[34] The 'period of incapacity' begins with the day after the date of injury or the first day of sickness ('the start day') and ends on the earliest of the following: the date that the seafarer is again fit for work; the termination date set in the SEA; the date that the SEA is actually terminated in accordance with its terms (although note that, as stated in para 18.7 above, any purported termination will have no effect if it is solely or mainly for the purpose of avoiding liability to pay sick pay); or the expiry of 16 weeks beginning with the start day.[35] The MLC permits ratifying states to limit the liability of a shipowner to pay wages in whole or in part, in respect of a seafarer no longer on board, to a period of 16

29 Minimum Requirements Regulations, reg 50(11)(a)–(c) respectively.
30 See Chapter 11 for the circumstances in which the duty to repatriate ends under Minimum Requirements Regulations, reg 21.
31 Minimum Requirements Regulations, reg 50(2)–(3), (9).
32 Minimum Requirements Regulations, reg 53.
33 Minimum Requirements Regulations, reg 50(4)(a)–(b), as amended by Miscellaneous Amendments Regulations, reg 5(4)(a)(i)–(iii).
34 Minimum Requirements Regulations, reg 53.
35 Minimum Requirements Regulations, reg 50(5), as substituted by Miscellaneous Amendments Regulations, reg 5(4)(b); MGN 480 Amendment 2, para 3.2.2.

weeks from the day of the injury or the commencement of the sickness,[36] and the UK has adopted this.

The above obligations may be overridden by a collective agreement on condition that it requires the person responsible for paying the incapacitated seafarer 'the relevant amount', which means the whole or a specified percentage of the basic wages that would have been payable under the SEA if: (a) the seafarer had remained fit for work; and (b) where the SEA would otherwise have terminated during the period that the seafarer was not fit for work, the SEA had continued on the same terms during that period.[37] Before the changes were made by the Miscellaneous Amendments Regulations on 6 April 2018, the seafarer was entitled to be paid basic wages if they remained sick throughout the 16-week period, even if their SEA terminated before the expiry of that period.[38] Since the amendment, the only circumstances in which an incapacitated seafarer will be entitled to be paid after the expiry of their SEA is where there is an applicable collective agreement meeting the conditions set out in sub-paragraphs (a) and(b) above. This facilitates the regulation of sick pay by collective agreement, and is likely to benefit a seafarer in a case where they are paid their full basic wages, but not necessarily so where they are paid a reduced 'specified percentage' of their basic wages.[39] The duration of the period for which a seafarer would be entitled to sick pay under such a collective agreement should be set by the agreement itself, but it must cover the period for which they remain incapacitated for a minimum of 16 weeks from the day of the injury or commencement of the sickness.[40]

The post-repatriation duty is subject to the seafarer applying for all relevant social security benefits (in consequence of the seafarer's incapacity to work and the sickness or injury which resulted in the incapacity), under the laws of the UK or the laws or arrangements in the country to which they are repatriated; the shipowner may reduce their liability by any amounts received for the period during which the obligation applies.[41] The shipowner may recover as a civil debt any amounts already paid to the seafarer to the extent that they exceed any such reduced amounts.[42]

Remedies

18.10 The seafarer is entitled to recover from the shipowner any outstanding amounts as a civil debt.[43] The shipowner has recourse to civil action to recover

36 MLC, Standard A4.2.1, para 4.

37 Minimum Requirements Regulations, reg 50(12)–(14), as inserted by Miscellaneous Amendments Regulations, reg 5(4)(e).

38 Minimum Requirements Regulations, reg 50(4)(b), before it was amended by Miscellaneous Amendments Regulations, reg 5(4)(a)(iii), (5)(a)–(b).

39 For more information on sick pay, see MGN 480 (M) Amendment 2, paras 3.1–3.5.

40 MLC, Standard A4.2.1, para 4.

41 Minimum Requirements Regulations, reg 50(6)–(7)(a). The seafarer is obliged to inform the shipowner, if requested, of any amounts of social security received: reg 50(8).

42 Minimum Requirements Regulations, reg 50(7)(b).

43 Minimum Requirements Regulations, reg 50(1).

any amounts paid which exceed the seafarer's entitlement, when taken together with any social security benefits they have received.[44]

PROPERTY LEFT BEHIND

18.11 The shipowner and master must take reasonable care of a sick or injured seafarer's property left behind, pending delivery. These duties are the same as those which arise in the context of repatriation.[45]

SHIPOWNERS' LIABILITY IN RESPECT OF BURIAL OR CREMATION

18.12 If a seafarer dies on board or during shore leave (except in their country of residence), the shipowner must meet the expenses of burial or cremation, except to the extent that these are met by a public authority.[46] Where the seafarer's personal representatives incur costs in meeting expenses which should be met by the shipowner under regulation 52(1), whether by incurring such costs directly or by reimbursing another person who has incurred those costs, those representatives may recover those costs from the shipowner as a civil debt.[47]

OFFENCES

18.13 A failure to provide financial security on a UK ship, or a non-UK ship while it is in UK waters, is an offence, punishable by a fine on summary conviction or, on conviction on indictment, by imprisonment for a term not exceeding two years or a fine, or both.[48]

It is an offence for any person to induce another to accept less than the full amount of compensation payable, as set out in the SEA, in respect of the death or long-term disability of a seafarer arising from occupational injury, illness or hazard (this only applies in connection with seafarers who are or were on a UK ship), punishable by a fine on summary conviction or, on conviction on indictment, by imprisonment for a term not exceeding two years or a fine, or both.[49]

A failure by the shipowner of a UK ship to give notice to seafarers that the shipowner's security has been or is to be terminated before its expiry date

44 Minimum Requirements Regulations, reg 50(7)(b).

45 Minimum Requirements Regulations, reg 50(1), which applies the provisions of reg 24(2), (4), (6)–(8), (10), (11) and (13) in Pt 6 (repatriation). See Chapter 11 at para 11.8.

46 Minimum Requirements Regulations, reg 52(1)–(2). See Chapter 11 at para 11.4.

47 Minimum Requirements Regulations, reg 52(3).

48 Minimum Requirements Regulations, regs 53B(2), 59A(3)–(4)(a), as inserted by Financial Security Amendment Regulations, reg 2(7).

49 Minimum Requirements Regulations, regs 53F, 59A(4)(b), as inserted by Financial Security Amendment Regulations, reg 2(7).

amounts to an offence punishable on summary conviction to a fine (in Scotland and Northern Ireland, the fine must not exceed level 5 on the standard scale).[50]

It is a defence for the accused to show that they took all reasonable steps to ensure compliance with the provision concerned.

INSPECTION AND DETENTION

18.14 The powers to inspect and detain UK ships (and, while they are in UK waters, non-UK ships) apply, as set out in Chapter 2 at paragraph 2.2.[51]

COMPLIANCE

18.15 DMLC: Comply with the UK provisions in Pt I, point 16 on the provision of financial security, and enter details of compliance measures in Pt II, point 16.

50 Minimum Requirements Regulations, reg 59A(1)–(2)(a), as inserted by Financial Security Amendment Regulations, reg 2(7).

51 Minimum Requirements Regulations, regs 54–56.

CHAPTER 19

Regulation 4.3: Health and Safety Protection and Accident Prevention

INTRODUCTION

19.1 The provisions on health and safety are set out in Regulation 4.3 of the MLC and its associated Code, the purpose of which is '[t]o ensure that seafarers' work environment on board ships promotes occupational safety and health'.[1]

1 MLC, Regulation 4.3, p 64.

19.1 *Regulation 4.3: Health and Safety Protection and Accident Prevention*

Ratifying states are required, in respect of ships which fly their flag, to: ensure that seafarers are provided with occupational health protection and live, work and train on board in a safe and hygienic environment;[2] develop and promulgate national guidelines for the management of occupational safety and health on board, after consultation with representative shipowners' and seafarers' organisations, taking into account applicable codes, guidelines, and standards recommended by international organisations, national administrations and maritime industry organisations;[3] and adopt laws, regulations and other measures addressing matters specified in the Code to Regulation 4.3, taking into account relevant international instruments, and set standards for occupational safety and health protection and accident prevention.[4]

The MLC Code in this area is lengthy and detailed. The mandatory Code A explains the types of pro-active measures which ratifying states are required to implement, such as: the promotion of occupational safety and health policies and programmes, including risk evaluation and the training and instruction of seafarers;[5] reasonable precautions to prevent occupational accidents, injuries and diseases;[6] specifying the obligations of shipowners, seafarers and other concerned persons to comply with the applicable standards and with the ship's occupational safety and health policy and programme, with special attention being paid in respect of seafarers under the age of 18;[7] and the establishment of a safety committee on board ships on which there are five or more seafarers.[8] The non-mandatory Code B then sets out guidelines to be observed on many specific matters, such as: structural features of the ship, including means of access and asbestos-related risks;[9] anchors, chains and lines;[10] work in enclosed spaces;[11] exposure to noise[12] and vibration;[13] reporting and collection of statistics;[14] investigations into the causes and circumstances of all occupational accidents, injuries and diseases resulting in loss of life or serious injury;[15] and safety and health education of young seafarers.[16]

2 MLC, Regulation 4.3.1.
3 MLC, Regulation 4.3.2.
4 MLC, Regulation 4.3.3.
5 MLC, Standard A4.3.1(a).
6 MLC, Standard A4.3.1(b).
7 MLC, Standard A4.3.2(b).
8 MLC, Standard A4.3.2(d).
9 MLC, Guideline B4.3.1.2(b).
10 MLC, Guideline B4.3.1.2(k).
11 MLC, Guideline B4.3.1.2(n).
12 MLC, Guideline B4.3.2.
13 MLC, Guideline B4.3.3.
14 MLC, Guideline B4.3.5.
15 MLC, Guideline B4.3.6.
16 MLC, Guideline B4.3.10.

UK PROVISIONS

19.2 The main provisions are contained in the Merchant Shipping and Fishing Vessels (Health and Safety at Work) Regulations 1997[17] ('the 1997 Regulations'), as substantially amended by the Merchant Shipping (Maritime Labour Convention) (Health and Safety) (Amendment) Regulations 2014 ('MLC H&S Regulations').[18]

Other relevant provisions are: the MCA's Code of Safe Working Practices for Merchant Seafarers ('COSWP'),[19] endorsed by the UK's National Maritime Occupational Health and Safety Committee ('NMOHSC') as setting out best practice guidance for improving health and safety, which is addressed to seafarers on UK ships and those ashore with relevant responsibilities;[20] the Merchant Shipping and Fishing Vessels (Health and Safety at Work) (Employment of Young Persons) Regulations 1998;[21] and the Merchant Shipping (Accident Reporting and Investigation) Regulations 2012.[22]

AMENDMENTS TO THE 1997 REGULATIONS

19.3 The MLC H&S Regulations make significant amendments to the 1997 Regulations.

Definitions

19.4 The usual definitions which UK MLC legislation uses for 'seafarer' and 'shipowner' have been introduced:

> '"seafarer" means any person, including a master, who is employed or engaged or works in any capacity on board a ship which is not a fishing vessel and whose normal place of work is on such a ship;[23]
>
> ...

17 SI 1997/2962. The 1997 Regulations give effect, as regards shipping activities in the UK, to: Council Directive 89/391/EEC on the introduction of measures to encourage improvements in the safety and health of workers at work (OJ No. L 183, 29.6.89, p. 1); Council Directive 91/383/EEC supplementing the measures to encourage improvements in the safety and health at work of workers with a fixed duration employment relationship or a temporary employment relationship (OJ No. L206 29.7.91 p. 19); and Council Directive 92/85/EEC on the introduction of measures to encourage improvements in the safety and health at work of pregnant workers and workers who have recently given birth or are breastfeeding (OJ No. L 348 28.11.92, p. 1).

18 SI 2014/1616.

19 The latest version is the '2015 edition – Amendment 2, December 2017', available at: www.gov.uk/government/uploads/system/uploads/attachment_data/file/671403/CSWPMS_GOV_UK_2017.pdf [Accessed 28 January 2018].

20 COSWP, introductory section 'About this Code', paras 1–2.

21 SI 1998/2411.

22 SI 2012/1743. For an account of UK health and safety statutes as they apply to ships, see Aldous, G and Nelson, L, *Work Accidents at Sea* (2nd edition, 9 Gough Square, London), pp 11–22.

23 1997 Regulations, reg 2(2), as inserted by MLC H&S Regulations, reg 2(2)(f).

"shipowner" means–

(a) in relation to a ship which has a valid Maritime Labour Certificate or interim Maritime Labour Certificate, the person identified as the shipowner on that Certificate;

(b) in relation to any other ship, the owner of the ship or, if different, any other organisation or person such as the manager, or the bareboat charterer, that has assumed the responsibility for the operation of the ship from the owner;'[24]

Group A to E ships

19.5 The amendments introduce five groups of ships (A to E) and set out the provisions which apply to each group:

- Group A: a UK ship (which is not a fishing vessel) wherever it may be;
- Group B: a non-UK sea-going ship (which is not a fishing vessel) which is in UK waters and which carries MLC documentation;
- Group C: a non-UK sea-going ship (which is not a fishing vessel) which is in UK waters and which does not carry MLC documentation;
- Group D: a UK fishing vessel wherever it may be;
- Group E: a non-UK fishing vessel which is in UK waters.[25]

The above definitions are subject to the following qualifications: pleasure vessels, ships of traditional build, warships and naval auxiliaries are not Group A, B or C ships;[26] vessels which are not ordinarily engaged in commercial activities are not Group B or C ships.[27] So, although the MLC does not apply to vessels which are not ordinarily engaged in commercial activities,[28] the 1997 Regulations will apply to Group A ships (as they do not fall within the aforementioned exclusion).

It should be noted that, although some of the provisions of the 1997 Regulations, even as amended by the MLC H&S Regulations, apply to fishing vessels, the MLC does not apply to such vessels.[29] The fishing sector is covered by the ILO's Work in Fishing Convention (No. 188), 2007, which came into force on 16 November 2017 and contains provisions on occupational safety and health and accident prevention.[30]

24 1997 Regulations, reg 2(2), as inserted by MLC H&S Regulations, reg 2(2)(f).
25 1997 Regulations, reg 3(7)(a)–(e) (respectively), as inserted by MLC H&S Regulations, reg 2(5).
26 1997 Regulations, reg 7(a)–(c), (8), as inserted by MLC H&S Regulations, reg 2(5).
27 1997 Regulations, reg 7(b)–(c), (9), as inserted by MLC H&S Regulations, reg 2(5).
28 MLC, Article II, para 4.
29 MLC, Article II, para 4.
30 ILO Work in Fishing Convention (No. 188), 2007, Pt VI, Articles 31–33. The convention has been ratified by: Angola; Argentina; Bosnia and Herzegovina; Congo; Estonia; France; Lithuania; Morocco; Namibia; Norway; Senegal; and South Africa. The UK is expected to ratify the Convention soon, having carried out a public consultation on the draft implementation legislation. See Chapter 1 at footnote 42.

The meaning of 'sea-going'

19.6

(a) The term 'sea-going' means, in relation to a UK ship (which is not a fishing vessel), that the ship is:[31]

(i) a UK ship which operate outside category A, B, C and D waters (which are rivers, canals, estuaries, deep lakes and lochs), as set out in MSN 1837;[32]

(ii) a ship to which the Merchant Shipping (Survey and Certification) Regulations 1995[33] apply (and in respect of which no exemption has been granted under reg 2(2) of those Regulations), being UK ships wherever they may be and non-UK ships whilst they are in UK waters (except that the following are excluded: fishing vessels; pleasure vessels; high-speed craft which comply with the requirements of the Merchant Shipping (High Speed Craft) Regulations 2004;[34] passenger ships to which the Merchant Shipping (Passenger Ships) (Safety Code for UK Categorised Waters) Regulations 2010[35] apply; and vessels to which the Merchant Shipping (Technical Requirements for Inland Waterways Vessels) Regulations 2010[36] apply);

(iii) a ship to which reg 4 of the Merchant Shipping (Vessels in Commercial Use for Sport or Pleasure) Regulations 1998[37] applies (which are 'large vessels' (of 24 metres in load line length or, in the case a vessel the keel of which was laid or was at a similar stage of construction before 21 July 1968, less than 150 tons) to which the Large Commercial Yacht Code (known as the 'LY3 Code')[38] applies);[39]

(iv) a high-speed craft in respect of which a permit to operate outside waters of category A, B, C or D has been issued in accordance with reg 8 of the Merchant Shipping (High Speed Craft) Regulations 2004.[40]

31 1997 Regulations, reg 2(2), as inserted by MLC H&S Regulations, reg 2(2)(f).

32 MSN 1837 (M) Amendment 2: Categorisation of Waters, paras 3.1–3.4. The categorisations are given force by Merchant Shipping (Categorisation of Waters) Regulations 1992, reg 2 and determine which UK waters are not 'sea' for regulations made, or treated as made, under Merchant Shipping Act 1995, s 85 (MSN 1837, paras 1.1 and 4.1). The MLC does not apply to ships which navigate exclusively in inland waters (Article II, para 1(h)).

33 SI 1995/1210, reg 2(1), as amended by Merchant Shipping (Technical Requirements for Inland Waterway Vessels) Regulations 2010 (SI 2010/1075), reg 14 and Sch 2.

34 SI 2004/302.

35 SI 2010/680.

36 SI 2010/1075.

37 SI 1998/2771.

38 The LY3 Code has been updated and consolidated into the Red Ensign Group Yacht Code, and will come into force on 1 January 2019 (see Chapter 15 at para 15.9).

39 The LY3 Code supersedes the Code of Practice for Safety of Large Commercial Sailing and Motor Vessels, which is referred to in 1998 Regulations, reg 4. The LY3 Code applies to large commercial yachts which are 24 metres and over in load line length or, if built before 21 July 1968, 150 gross tons and over, are in commercial use for sport or pleasure, and do not carry cargo and do not carry more than 12 passengers (sail training vessels are included); LY3 Code, para 3.1.

40 SI 2004/302. Under reg 8 the permit must state the maximum number of passengers the craft is allowed to carry, and any operating restrictions to which it is subject under reg 7 in relation to potentially hazardous wash.

(b) The term 'sea-going' means, in relation to a UK fishing vessel, or a ship which is not a UK ship, that the ship operates outside category A, B, C and D waters, as set out in MSN 1837.

Application of the 1997 Regulations

19.7 There have been significant amendments to the application provision in reg 3 of the 1997 Regulations. The resulting effect is that the 1997 Regulations apply as follows:

(1) To all activities of workers on ships, except when (a) a worker is on a public service vessel or a vessel engaged in search and rescue activity, and (b) characteristics of that activity inevitably conflict with a provision of the Regulations.[41]

(2) As regards Group A, B and C ships, specific provisions of the 1997 Regulations, insofar as far as they apply to workers, also apply to seafarers who are not workers and, insofar as they apply to employers, also apply to shipowners (except that, in relation to seafarers who are not workers, the relevant obligation is only imposed on the shipowner).[42] The provisions of the 1997 Regulations which are so applied are: regs 4(1)(a), 5(1), 7, 12(1)–(2), 16(1)(b)(iii), 18(b)–(c), 19(1)(b)(ii) and 20.

The reason for this change is that those categories of ships are MLC ships (whereas Groups D and E are fishing vessels) and MLC rights apply to all seafarers (whether they are employed or self-employed)[43] and, furthermore, MLC obligations on health and safety are imposed on shipowners (whether or not they are the employer of the seafarers on board).[44] Seafarers who are not workers, and so are self-employed, do not have an employer upon whom an obligation can be imposed, so in those cases the duty can only be imposed on the shipowner.

(3) Pt II (general duties) – (a) all of the provisions apply to Group A ships and, with the exception of regs 7(4A) and 11A, to Group D ships; and (b) regs 4, 5, 7 and 12 apply to Group C ships.[45]

(4) Pt III (duties of the company) – (a) reg 13 applies to ships in Groups A, C and D; and (b) reg 13A applies only to Group A ships.[46]

41 1997 Regulations, reg 3(1), as amended by MLC H&S Regulations, reg 2(3) (which omits 'United Kingdom' so that reg 3(1) is widened to apply to 'ships' (previously it only applied to 'United Kingdom ships').

42 1997 Regulations, reg 3(1A), as inserted by MLC H&S Regulations, reg 2(4).

43 MLC, Article II, para (f).

44 MLC, Standard A4.3.2(b).

45 1997 Regulations, reg 3(2)(a)–(b) respectively, as amended by MLC H&S Regulations, reg 2(5).

46 1997 Regulations, reg 3(3)(a)–(b) respectively, as amended by MLC H&S Regulations, reg 2(5).

(5) Pt IV (special responsibility for health and safety and consultation with workers) – (a) all of the provisions apply to Group A ships; (b) regs 15 and 19 apply to Group C ships; and (c) regs 14, 19–20 apply to Group D ships.[47]

(6) Pt V (general duties of workers) – all of the provisions apply to ships in Groups A and D only.[48]

(7) Pt VI (prohibitions, penalties, inspections and detentions) – (a) all of the provisions other than regs 27, 28, 28A–28B and 29 apply to Group A ships; (b) regs 28A–28B and 30 apply to Group B ships; (c) regs 22, 24–26, 27A–27B apply to Group C ships; (d) all of the provisions other than regs 27A–28B apply to Group D ships; and (e) regs 28–30 apply to Group E ships.[49]

As each Part of the Regulations is described below, it is also stated which provisions of that Part apply to particular groups of ships.

OBLIGATIONS IN THE 1997 REGULATIONS

Part II: General duties

19.8 Application of Pt II: (a) all of the provisions apply to Group A ships and, with the exception of regs 7(4A) and 11A, to Group D ships; and (b) regs 4, 5, 7 and 12 apply to Group C ships.[50]

Persons on whom duties are imposed

19.9 The duty to comply with the provisions of the 1997 Regulations is imposed on (a) the employer and the shipowner,[51] and (b) any other person upon whom a duty is imposed by those Regulations.[52] Where such a person does not have control of the matter to which the particular regulation applies, because they do not have responsibility for the operation of the ship, the duty is also extended to any natural or legal person who has control of that matter (but the persons described in paragraphs (a) and (b) also remain responsible).[53] The other persons who could potentially have such control include the manager, or the agent or bareboat charterer (either of which could also be the 'shipowner' for the purposes of the MLC).[54]

47 1997 Regulations, reg 3(4)(a)–(c) respectively, as amended by MLC H&S Regulations, reg 2(5).
48 1997 Regulations, reg 3(5), as amended by MLC H&S Regulations, reg 2(5).
49 1997 Regulations, reg 3(6)(a)–(e) respectively, as amended by MLC H&S Regulations, reg 2(5).
50 1997 Regulations, reg 3(2)(a)–(b), as amended by MLC H&S Regulations, reg 2(5).
51 Although the shipowner may be the employer, seafarers are often employed by other parties, such as manning agents and offshore companies. The name of the employer and (where different) the shipowner, will be stated on the seafarers' employment agreement (SEA) (see Chapter 7).
52 1997 Regulations, regs 3(1A)(i), 4(1)(a)–(b), as amended by MLC H&S Regulations, reg 2(4)(a)(i).
53 1997 Regulations, reg 4(2).
54 MLC, Article II, para 1(j).

Content of the general duties

19.10 Employers and shipowners are required to ensure the health and safety of workers and other persons (including self-employed seafarers), so far as reasonably practicable, having regard to the following principles:[55]

'(a) the avoidance of risks, which among other things include the combating of risks at source and the replacement of dangerous practices, substances or equipment by non-dangerous or less dangerous practices, substances or equipment;

(b) the evaluation of unavoidable risks and the taking of action to reduce them;

(c) adoption of work patterns and procedures which take account of the capacity of the individual, especially in respect of the design of the workplace and the choice of work equipment, with a view in particular to alleviating monotonous work and to reducing any consequent adverse effect on workers' health and safety;

(d) adaptation of procedures to take account of new technology and other changes in working practices, equipment, the working environment and any other factors which may affect health and safety;

(e) adoption of a coherent approach to management of the vessel or undertaking, taking account of health and safety at every level of the organisation;

(f) giving collective protective measures priority over individual protective measures; and

(g) the provision of appropriate and relevant information and instruction for workers.

(2) Without prejudice to the generality of the duties under paragraph (1), the matters to which those duties extend shall include in particular–

(a) provision and maintenance of plant, machinery and equipment and systems of work that are, so far as is reasonably practicable, safe and without risk to health;

(b) arrangements for ensuring, so far as is reasonably practicable, safety and absence of risk to health in connection with the use, handling, stowage and transport of articles and substances;

(c) such arrangements as are appropriate, having regard to the nature of, and the substances used in, the activities and size of the operation, for the effective planning, organisation, control, monitoring and review of preventive and protective measures;

(d) provision of such information, instruction, training and supervision as is necessary to ensure the health and safety of workers and that of other persons aboard ship who may be affected by their acts or omissions;

(e) maintenance of all places of work in the ship in a condition that is, so far as is reasonably practicable, safe and without risk to health;

55 The duty has been expressly extended to shipowners in regard to workers and self-employed seafarers by reg 3(1A)(a)(i)–(ii) of the 1997 Regulations, as inserted by MLC H&S Regulations, reg 2(4).

(f) arrangements to ensure, so far as is reasonably practicable, that no person has access to any area of the ship to which it is necessary to restrict access on grounds of health and safety unless the individual concerned has received adequate and appropriate health and safety instruction;

(g) provision and maintenance of an environment for persons aboard ship that is, so far as is reasonably practicable, safe and without risk to health;

(h) collaboration with any other persons covered by regulation 4 to protect, so far as is reasonably practicable, the health and safety of all authorised persons aboard the ship or engaged in loading or unloading activities in relation to that ship.'[56]

HEALTH AND SAFETY POLICY

19.11 A written general health and safety policy, revised as appropriate, must be prepared by the employer and the shipowner, as well as the organisation and arrangements for carrying out that policy, all of which must be brought to the notice of workers.[57] However, the policy will not apply where five or less workers in aggregate are employed by the same employer, or associated employers, in a UK ship.[58] For these purposes, 'associated employers' means: (a) one is a company of which the other (directly or indirectly) has control; or (b) both are companies of which a third person (directly or indirectly) has control.[59]

RISK ASSESSMENT

19.12 The employer and the shipowner must make a suitable and sufficient assessment of the risks to the health and safety of workers (and the shipowner must also do so in regard to self-employed seafarers) and other persons who may be affected by the acts or omissions of the employer or shipowner, arising in the normal course of their activities and duties, to identify: (a) groups of workers and self-employed seafarers at particular risk in the performance of their duties; and (b) the measures to be taken to comply with the employer's and shipowner's duties under the 1997 Regulations; any significant findings or revision of the assessment is to be brought to the notice of workers and self-employed seafarers.[60]

56 1997 Regulations, reg 5(1)–(2).

57 1997 Regulations, reg 6(1). The duty has been imposed on shipowners by reg 3(1A)(a)(i) of the 1997 Regulations, as amended by MLC H&S Regulations, reg 2(4)(i)–(ii).

58 1997 Regulations, reg 6(2); those who are not 'workers' (eg self-employed seafarers) do not count towards the aggregate.

59 1997 Regulations, reg 6(3), applying ERA 1996, s 231.

60 1997 Regulations, reg 7(1)–(2). The duty has also been imposed on shipowners towards self-employed seafarers by reg 3(1A)(a)(i), (iii), (b) of the 1997 Regulations, as inserted by MLC H&S Regulations, reg 2(4).

The risk assessment must be reviewed if there is reason to suspect that it is no longer valid, or there has been a significant change in the matters to which it relates, and any necessary changes to procedures or practices should be made.[61]

Every employer and every self-employed person on board must inform the company of any risks arising out of, or in connection with, their own undertaking.[62] Measures are to be taken, including, if necessary, the supply of protective equipment, to ensure an improvement in health and safety in respect of the risks identified, and workers are to be informed of the measures taken for their protection.[63]

When conducting the risk assessment, or a review of it, there is now a requirement for the shipowner to have regard to the statistical information and associated advice contained in MGN 484.[64]

Statistical information

19.13 The Marine Accident Investigation Branch (MAIB) publishes annual reports summarising statistics of accidents reported during the year.[65] The latest report is that of 2016,[66] and contains an overview of the reports for that year, details of investigations started, recommendations for that year, and progress reports on recommendations made in previous years.

Safety alerts

19.14 There are several sources of safety alerts:[67]

- MAIB Safety Bulletins[68] – relating to urgent safety issues emerging during the course of an investigation.
- MAIB Safety Digests[69] – which draw attention to some of the lessons arising out of investigations in relation to recent accidents and incidents.

61 1997 Regulations, reg 7(3).
62 1997 Regulations, reg 7(4). The 'company' is most likely to be the same person as the MLC 'shipowner': see the definitions of each in reg 2(2) of the 1997 Regulations, the latter definition having been inserted by MLC H&S Regulations, reg 2(2)(f).
63 1997 Regulations, reg 7(5)–(6).
64 1997 Regulations, reg 7(4A), as inserted by MLC H&S Regulations, reg 2(6); MGN 484 (M) – MLC, 2006: Health and Safety, Published accident statistics – information and advice.
65 MGN 484, para 2.1.
66 MAIB Annual Report 2016: www.gov.uk/government/uploads/system/uploads/attachment_data/file/634809/MAIB _AnnualReport2016.pdf [Accessed 10 February 2018].
67 MGN 484, paras 3.1–3.6.
68 MAIB Safety Bulletins: www.gov.uk/maibreports?keywords=&report_type%5B%5D=safety-bulletin&date_of_occurrence%5Bfrom%5D=&date_of_occurrence%5Bto%5D= [Accessed 10 February 2018].
69 MAIB Safety Digests: www.gov.uk/government/collections/maib-safety-digests [Accessed 10 February 2018].

- Confidential Hazardous Incident Reporting Programme (CHIRP)[70] – publishes quarterly 'FEEDBACK' newsletters containing a selection of accident reports.
- MCA Safety Alerts[71] – produced by the MCA, other maritime authorities and industry bodies to raise awareness of recent safety issues.

For more information about risk assessments, see the Code of Safe Working Practices for Merchant Seafarers, chapter 1, and MGN 20, Annex 1 and Appendix.[72]

NEW OR EXPECTANT MOTHERS

19.15 Where the workers include a woman with the potential for child-bearing, and the work could involve a risk to the new or expectant mother or her baby, from any processes or working conditions, or physical, biological or chemical agents, including those specified in Annexes I and II to Council Directive 92/85/EEC,[73] the risk assessment carried out under reg 7(1) must include the assessment of such risks.[74]

If any other action required to be taken by the employer under the 1997 Regulations would not avoid the risk identified in the assessment then, if it is reasonable to do so, and would avoid such risks, the woman's working conditions or hours of work must be altered.[75] If it is not reasonable to make such alterations, or they would not avoid the risk, the employer must suspend the worker from work for so long as is necessary to avoid the risk: such suspension is to be with pay (unless she has unreasonably refused to perform suitable alternative work) and without prejudice to the worker's rights under ss 66–68 of the Employment Rights Act 1996 ('ERA 1996') (suspension on maternity grounds).[76] In the aforementioned provisions, reference to risk, in relation to any risk of infectious or contagious disease, refers only to any such level of risk at work which is in addition to the level to which a new or expectant mother would be expected to be exposed outside the workplace.[77] These obligations only apply if the worker has notified the employer or the company, in writing, that she is pregnant (and, if requested to

70 CHIRP Maritime: www.chirpmaritime.org [Accessed 10 February 2018].

71 MCA Safety Alerts: www.gov.uk/government/collections/maritime-and-coastguard-agency-mca-marine-safety-alerts [Accessed 10 February 2018].

72 MGN 20 (M+F) – Merchant Shipping and Fishing Vessels (Health and Safety at Work) Regulations 1997.

73 Council Directive 92/85/EEC of 19 October 1992 on the introduction of measures to encourage improvements in the safety and health at work of pregnant workers and workers who have recently given birth or are breastfeeding (tenth individual Directive within the meaning of Article 16(1) of Directive 89/391/EEC (OJ 28.11.92, No L 348/1). To see the Annexes, visit: http://eur-lex.europa.eu/legalcontent/EN/TXT/HTML/?uri=CELEX:31992L0085&from=en [Accessed 6 February 2018].

74 1997 Regulations, reg 8(1).

75 1997 Regulations, reg 8(2).

76 1997 Regulations, reg 8(3).

77 1997 Regulations, reg 8(4).

do so, produced within a reasonable time a certificate from a registered medical practitioner or registered midwife showing that she is pregnant), has given birth within the previous six months, or is breast-feeding.[78]

New or expectant mothers who work at night, on producing a certificate from a registered medical practitioner or registered midwife, showing that it is necessary for her health and safety that she should not be at work for any stated period, should be offered suitable alternative daytime work, if available.[79] If daytime work is not available, she must be suspended from work on pay (again, the provisions of ss 66–68 of ERA 1996 apply) for as long as is necessary for her health or safety.[80]

The employer's obligations to make the alterations referred to above cease when they know that the worker is no longer a new or expectant mother, or cannot establish that she remains so.[81] It is therefore important that workers comply with the notice provisions.

HEALTH SURVEILLANCE

19.16 Workers are to be provided with appropriate health surveillance, having regard to the risks to their health and safety, which are identified through the risk assessment undertaken under reg 7.[82]

Reporting of occupational diseases

19.17 There is a new requirement for employers to report occupational diseases to the MCA, where an employer receives a written report from a medical practitioner, stating that a seafarer who works (or who has worked) on a ship has (or has had) a disease which is listed in Annex 1 to MSN 1850, as set out below.[83] The duty to make the report only applies if the seafarer is (or was) involved in the activity or exposed to carcinogens, mutagens or biological agents (as stated in the Annex) while working on the ship.[84]

78 1997 Regulations, reg 10(1)–(2)(a).
79 1997 Regulations, reg 9(1).
80 1997 Regulations, reg 9(2).
81 1997 Regulations, reg 10(2).
82 The 1997 Regulations, reg 11.
83 1997 Regulations, reg 11A(1), (3)–(4) as inserted by MLC H&S Regulations, reg 2(7); MSN 1850 (M) – MLC, 2006: Health and Safety Reporting of Occupational Diseases.
84 1997 Regulations, reg 11A(2), as inserted by MLC H&S Regulations, reg 2(7).

> **'Occupational diseases**
>
> (a) Carpal Tunnel Syndrome, where the person's work involves regular use of percussive or vibrating tools
>
> (b) Cramp in the hand or forearm, where the person's work involves prolonged periods of repetitive movement of the fingers, hand or arm
>
> (c) Occupational dermatitis, where the person's work involves significant or regular exposure to a known skin sensitizer or irritant
>
> (d) Hand Arm Vibration Syndrome, where the person's work involves regular use of percussive or vibrating tools, or the holding of materials which are subject to percussive processes, or processes causing vibration
>
> (e) Occupational asthma, where the person's work involves significant or regular exposure to a known respiratory sensitizer
>
> (f) Tendonitis or tenosynovitis in the hand or forearm, where the person's work is physically demanding and involves frequent, repetitive movements
>
> **Exposure to carcinogens, mutagens and biological agents**
>
> (a) Any cancer attributed to an occupational exposure to a known human carcinogen or mutagen (including ionising radiation)
>
> (b) Any disease attributed to an occupational exposure to a biological agent'

In making the report, the employer must: (a) have regard to the ILO's guidance concerning the protection of workers' personal data,[85] referred to in paragraph 3.2 of MSN 1850; (b) complete form MSF 4159;[86] and (c) send the completed form to the MCA (the address on form MSF 4159).[87] Copies of form MSF 4159 and the medical practitioner's report should be retained by the employer, as these may be needed for insurance or social security purposes or for inspection by the MCA.[88]

Although the obligation to report such a disease rests with the employer in respect of their employees, the MCA recommends that self-employed persons

85 The ILO guidance on the 'Protection of workers' personal data': www.ilo.org/wcmsp5/groups/public/---ed_protect/---protrav/---safework/documents/normativeinstrument/wcms_107797.pdf [Accessed 10 February 2018].

86 MSF 4159 – occupational disease report form for UK registered merchant ships: www.gov.uk/government/uploads/system/uploads/attachment_data/file/442263/MSF_4159_logo_free.pdf [Accessed 10 February 2018].

87 1997 Regulations, reg 11A(3)(a)–(c) respectively, as inserted by MLC H&S Regulations, reg 2(7).

88 MSN 1850, para 3.3.

also report a listed disease, or request another person to do so on their behalf.[89]

For more information on health surveillance, see the Code of Safe Working Practices for Merchant Seafarers, chapter 7, and MGN 20, Annex 2.

CAPABILITIES AND TRAINING

19.18 Employers and shipowners are required, in entrusting tasks to workers (and shipowners in regard to self-employed seafarers) to take account of their capabilities, and ensure that they are provided with adequate and appropriate health and safety training and instruction: (a) before being assigned to shipboard duties; and (b) on being exposed to new or increased risk because of (i) being transferred or given a change of responsibilities, (ii) the introduction of new equipment or a change to the equipment already in use, (iii) the introduction of new technology, or (iv) the introduction of new shipboard practices, a new system of work, or a change to a system of work already in use.[90] This training is: (a) to be repeated periodically as appropriate; (b) to be adapted to take account of any new or changed risks; and (c) to take place during the working hours of the concerned workers.[91]

Employment agencies supplying workers

19.19 As regards a worker who is employed by an employment agency, who is to carry out work on a ship, the company must supply the agency with information on: (a) any special occupational qualifications required to carry out the work safely; (b) the specific features of the jobs to be filled by those workers (insofar as those features are likely to affect their health and safety); and (c) any health surveillance required to be provided to workers under the 1997 Regulations or other relevant regulations; and the employment agency must ensure that the information provided is given to the workers.[92] The words 'is to carry out' imply that the information is to be supplied to the workers before the work commences. This provision does not apply to self-employed persons, as they will not be employed by an employment agency or any other person.

For information on the obligations of seafarer recruitment and placement services, see Chapter 6.

89 MSN 1850, para 2.2.
90 1997 Regulations, reg 12(1)–(2), as applied by reg 3(1A)(a)(iv), (b) of the 1997 Regulations, as inserted by MLC H&S Regulations, reg 2(4).
91 1997 Regulations, reg 12(3).
92 1997 Regulations, reg 12(4).

Part III: Duties of the company

19.20 Application of Pt III: (a) reg 13 applies to ships in Groups A, C and D; and (b) reg 13A applies only to Group A ships.[93]

CO-ORDINATION OF HEALTH AND SAFETY

19.21 Where there are workers on board a UK ship who are not employed by the company (which will often be the case), the latter is required to: (a) consult every other employer of those workers regarding the arrangements for health and safety required under reg 5(2)(c) (eg appropriate arrangements, having regard to the nature of, and the substances used in, the activities and the size of the operation, for the effective planning, organisation, control, monitoring and review of preventative and protective measures); (b) co-ordinate arrangements for the protection of all workers and the prevention of risk to their health and safety; and (c) ensure that all workers are informed of the significant and relevant findings of the risk assessment carried out under reg 7, and of the arrangements for their protection referred to in paragraph (b).[94]

A further new provision (reg 13A) has been inserted to protect self-employed seafarers. It applies (a) where there is a duty owed by an employer to a worker on a ship, in respect of a risk concerning workplace health and safety, by virtue of one or more of the provisions in the Regulations listed in the new Schedule (shown below); and (b) where at least one seafarer who is not a worker is exposed to that risk.[95] In such a case, the shipowner must, as far as reasonably practicable and appropriate, ensure that any action taken in respect of that risk as regards workers is also taken as regards self-employed seafarers.[96]

> **'Schedule**[97]
>
> **Merchant Shipping Health and Safety Regulations containing duties in respect of workers which regulation 13A extends to all seafarers**
>
> The Merchant Shipping and Fishing Vessels (Health and Safety at Work) (Electromagnetic Fields) Regulations 2016[98]
>
> The Merchant Shipping and Fishing Vessels (Health and Safety at Work) (Artificial Optical Radiation) Regulations 2010[99]
>
> The Merchant Shipping and Fishing Vessels (Health and Safety at Work) (Asbestos) Regulations 2010[100]

93 1997 Regulations, reg 3(3)(a)–(b), as amended by MLC H&S Regulations, reg 2(5).
94 1997 Regulations, reg 13(a)–(c), respectively.
95 1997 Regulations, reg 13A(1)(a)–(b) respectively, as inserted by MLC H&S Regulations, reg 2(8).
96 1997 Regulations, reg 13A(2), as inserted MLC H&S Regulations, reg 2(8).
97 1997 Regulations, Sch, as inserted by MLC H&S Regulations, reg 2(23).
98 SI 2016/1026, as inserted by reg 24(1)–(2) of those Regulations.
99 SI 2010/2987.
100 SI 2010/2984, as amended by SI 2012/632 and SI 2013/1473.

The Merchant Shipping and Fishing Vessels (Health and Safety at Work) (Work at Height) Regulations 2010[101]

The Merchant Shipping and Fishing Vessels (Health and Safety at Work) (Chemical Agents) Regulations 2010[102]

The Merchant Shipping and Fishing Vessels (Health and Safety at Work) (Biological Agents) Regulations 2010[103]

The Merchant Shipping and Fishing Vessels (Health and Safety at Work) (Carcinogens and Mutagens) Regulations 2007[104]

The Merchant Shipping and Fishing Vessels (Control of Vibration at Work) Regulations 2007[105]

The Merchant Shipping and Fishing Vessels (Control of Noise at Work) Regulations 2007[106]

The Merchant Shipping and Fishing Vessels (Lifting Operations and Lifting Equipment) Regulations 2006[107]

The Merchant Shipping and Fishing Vessels (Provision and Use of Work Equipment) Regulations 2006[108]

The Merchant Shipping and Fishing Vessels (Safety Signs and Signals) Regulations 2001[109]

The Merchant Shipping and Fishing Vessels (Personal Protective Equipment) Regulations 1999[110]

The Merchant Shipping and Fishing Vessels (Manual Handling Operations) Regulations 1998[111]

The Merchant Shipping and Fishing Vessels (Health and Safety at Work) (Employment of Young Persons) Regulations 1998'[112]

Part IV: Special responsibility for health and safety and consultation with workers

19.22 Application of Pt IV: (a) all of the provisions apply to Group A ships; (b) regs 15 and 19 apply to Group C ships; and (c) regs 14, 19–20 apply to Group D ships.[113]

101 SI 2010/332.
102 SI 2010/330, as amended by SI 2010/1110, SI 2011/1043 and SI 2012/1844.
103 SI 2010/323.
104 SI 2007/3100.
105 SI 2007/3077.
106 SI 2007/3075.
107 SI 2006/2184, as amended by SI 2008/2166.
108 SI 2006/2183, as amended by SI 2008/2165.
109 SI 2001/3444.
110 SI 1999/2205.
111 SI 1998/2857.
112 SI 1998/2411, as amended by SI 2002/2125 and SI 2002/3135.
113 1997 Regulations, reg 3(4)(a)–(c), as inserted by MLC H&S Regulations, reg 2(5).

The employer is required to appoint a competent person (or persons) to provide the necessary protective and preventative services to enable compliance with the 1997 Regulations; a sufficient number of persons should be appointed and provided with the necessary time, resources and means to carry out their duties.[114] The appointment of the competent person is to be recorded in writing by the employer.[115]

The following provisions (in paras 19.23–19.24 below) apply to sea-going ships (except fishing vessels) in which five or more seafarers are working.[116]

Duties of safety officers

19.23 The company must appoint a competent person as safety officer and record the appointment in writing.[117] The safety officer has the following duties:

> '(1) Subject to paragraph (2), it shall be the duty of the safety officer [having had regard to the International Labour Organization guidance concerning the protection of workers' personal data specified in Merchant Shipping Notice 1850 (M)] to use his best endeavours to–
>
> (a) improve the standard of safety consciousness among the crew and ensure that the provisions of the Code[118] and safety instructions, rules and guidance for the ship relating to health and safety are complied with;
>
> (b) investigate, so far as is reasonably practicable:
>
> (i) every accident involving death [or serious injury, as defined in the Merchant Shipping (Accident Reporting and Investigation) Regulations 2012],[119]
>
> (ii) all potential hazards to health and safety, and
>
> (iii) all reasonable complaints by workers about health and safety,[120]
>
> and making recommendations to the master to prevent the recurrence of such an accident or to remove any hazard, provided that the duty to investigate shall not extend to accidents arising from a casualty to the ship;
>
> (c) ensure that health and safety inspections of each accessible part of the ship are carried out at least once every three months and more frequently if there have been substantial changes in the conditions of work;

114 1997 Regulations, reg 14.

115 1997 Regulations, reg 17(5).

116 1997 Regulations, reg 15(1), as amended by MLC H&S Regulations, reg 2(9), which lowered the threshold to 'five or more seafarers' from 'more than five workers'.

117 1997 Regulations, reg 15(2), (5). There is a power for the Secretary of State to grant exemptions from appointing a safety officer for classes of cases or individual cases (reg 15(3)).

118 The Code of Safe Working Practices for Merchant Seamen: the latest the '2015 edition, Amendment 2 – December 2017'.

119 SI 2012/1743, as amended by the Merchant Shipping (Accident Reporting and Investigation) Regulations 2013 (SI 2013/2882).

120 Sub-paragraph (iii) also applies with regard to complaints made by self-employed seafarers: reg 3(1A)(a)(v), as inserted by MLC H&S Regulations, reg 2(4).

(d) make representations and, where appropriate, recommendations to the master, about any deficiency in the ship in respect of–

(i) any legislative requirement relating to health and safety,

(ii) any relevant Merchant Shipping Notice, or

(iii) any provision of the Code,[121]

and also suggest whether those representations and recommendations should be passed by the master on to the employer or other person who has control of the matter;

(e) maintain a record of every accident involving death, major or serious injury and every dangerous occurrence, and make it available on request to any elected representative, to the master and to any person duly authorised by the Secretary of State;

(f) stop any work which he observes in progress and reasonably believes may cause a serious accident, and immediately inform the master or the master's deputy who shall decide when work can safety be resumed.

(2) Nothing in this regulation shall require a safety officer to take any action at a time when emergency action to safeguard life or the ship is being taken.'[122]

Safety representatives and safety committees

19.24 The company is obliged to make rules for the election and appointment of a safety representative; the candidate receiving the most votes will be appointed, provided that: (a) they have two years' consecutive sea service since attaining the age of 18; and (b) for the position of safety representative on board a tanker, they have at least six months' service on board such a ship.[123] The company must also appoint a safety committee, which must include the master as chairman, the safety officer and every safety representative, and may also include any other person appointed under reg 14(1) to provide the necessary protective and preventative services for the undertaking; those appointments must be recorded in writing.[124] Safety representatives and safety committees may–

'(a) participate, subject to the concurrence of the safety officer, in any of the investigations or inspections carried out by the safety officer under regulation 16 [which are set out above] or, after notification to the master or his deputy, undertake similar investigations or inspections themselves, whether or not such investigations or inspections have already been carried out by the safety officer;

121 The Code of Safe Working Practices for Merchant Seamen: the latest the '2015 edition, Amendment 2 – December 2017'.

122 1997 Regulations, reg 16(1)(a)–(f), (2). The words in square brackets are amendments made by MLC H&S Regulations reg 2(10)–(11), respectively.

123 1997 Regulations, reg 17(1)–(2).

124 1997 Regulations, reg 17(4)–(5).

(b) make representations to the employer on potential hazards and dangerous occurrences at the workplace which affect, or could affect, workers on the ship;[125]

(c) make representations to the master and the employer on general matters affecting the health and safety of workers on the ship and, in particular, on such matters as those on which the employer carries out consultation under regulation 20[126] [which are set out below];

(d) request the safety officer to carry out any occupational health and safety inspection they consider necessary and to report the findings to them.'[127]

Duties of the company and master

19.25 The company and the master must, in co-ordination with the employer, facilitate the work of the person appointed to provide the necessary protective and preventative services for the undertaking, the safety officer and safety representatives, in carrying out their health and safety function, and in particular to:

'(a) provide for use by them a copy of the Code[128] (where appropriate), and access to any necessary information, documents and similar material including relevant legislation and Merchant Shipping Notices;

(b) provide them with relevant information about–

(i) the risks and measures for protection identified under regulation 7,[129]

(ii) factors known, or suspected, by them to affect the health and safety of the workers[130] on board the ship, and

(iii) arrangements for fire-fighting, first aid and other emergency procedures;

(c) ensure that those persons have the necessary resources and means to carry out their functions and duties;

(d) allow any of those persons such absence from ship duties without loss of pay as may be necessary to enable them to fulfil their functions, or to undertake any necessary training in health and safety matters;

(e) receive, at any reasonable time, representations about health and safety from the safety officer, safety representatives or the safety committee,

125 Paragraph (b) also applies to shipowners (as well as to employers) and to self-employed seafarers (as well as to workers): reg 3(1A)(a)(vi), as inserted by MLC H&S Regulations, reg 2(4).

126 Paragraph (c) also applies to shipowners (as well as to employers) and to self-employed seafarers (as well as to workers): reg 3(1A)(a)(vi), as inserted by MLC H&S Regulations, reg 2(4).

127 1997 Regulations, reg 18(a)–(d).

128 The Code of Safe Working Practices for Merchant Seamen: the latest the '2015 edition, Amendment 2 – December 2017'.

129 Risk assessments.

130 Sub-paragraph (ii) also applies in respect of self-employed seafarers: reg 3(1A)(a)(vii), as inserted by MLC H&S Regulations, reg 2(4).

discuss their representations with them and implement any agreed measures as soon as may be reasonable and practicable.'[131]

Where no safety officer is appointed under reg 15 (which only requires such an appointment where there are five or more seafarers working on board), the company must (having had regard to the ILO's guidance concerning the protection of workers' personal data specified in MSN 1850) maintain a record of every accident involving death, major or serious injury, and every dangerous occurrence, and make it available on request to any worker and any person duly authorised by the Secretary of State.[132]

Consultation with workers

19.26 The employer is required, in advance and in good time, to consult with workers or their elected representatives and, in the case of sub-paragraphs (c) and (d) below, where applicable, with the company, in all matters relating to their health and safety, and in particular on:

'(a) the arrangements for appointing a competent person under regulation 14 to provide protective and preventive services for the undertaking;

(b) the findings of the risk assessment;

(c) arrangements for health and safety training under regulation 12;

(d) the introduction of new technology.'[133]

Employers and shipowner must allow workers, or their elected representatives, to make representations about health and safety, and must implement any agreed measures as soon as may be reasonable and practical.[134] The employer and shipowner and, where applicable, the company must also give them access to any relevant information about: (a) health and safety matters from inspection agencies and health and safety authorities; and (b) every accident involving death, major or serious injury, and every dangerous occurrence.[135] Elected representatives are to be given training and adequate time off work, with pay, to perform their roles.[136]

The obligations referred to above, which are imposed on employers towards their employees, are also imposed on shipowners in regards to those persons; the shipowner (but not an employer supplying seafarers to the ship) is also obliged to carry out the above obligations towards self-employed seafarers.[137]

131 1997 Regulations, reg 19(1)(a)–(e).
132 1997 Regulations, reg 19(2), as amended by MLC H&S Regulations, reg 2(13).
133 1997 Regulations, reg 20(1)(a)–(d).
134 1997 Regulations, reg 20(2).
135 1997 Regulations, reg 20(3)(a)–(b).
136 1997 Regulations, reg 20(4).
137 1997 Regulations, reg 3(1A)(a)(viii), as inserted by MLC H&S Regulations, reg 2(4).

Part V: General duties of workers and seafarers

19.27 Application of Pt V: all of the provisions apply to ships in Groups A and D only.[138]

Duties are also imposed on workers and seafarers (whether or not they are employed or self-employed): (a) to take reasonable care of their own health and safety and that of others on board, who may be affected by their acts or omissions; and (b) to co-operate with the company, the employer, the shipowner and any other person on whom a health and safety duty is imposed, to enable that duty to be performed or complied with.[139] No worker or seafarer is permitted to:

> '(a) use any machinery, equipment, dangerous substance, transport equipment, means of production or safety device provided by his employer or the Company other than in accordance with any relevant training or instructions which have been received or provided by the employer or the Company in compliance with these Regulations; or
>
> (b) disconnect, change or remove or otherwise interfere with any safety device provided by the employer or the Company.'[140]

There is also a duty on workers and seafarers to immediately inform the master, safety officer or another competent person (appointed to provide preventative and protective services under reg 14) of any deficiencies in the company's health and safety arrangements.[141] Furthermore, workers and seafarers must immediately inform their employer, safety officer or other competent person of:

> '(a) any work situation which he reasonably considers to represent a serious and immediate danger to health and safety; and
>
> (b) any matter which he reasonably considers to represent a deficiency in the employer's protection arrangements for health and safety.'[142]

Part VI: Prohibitions, penalties, inspections and detentions

19.28 Application of Pt VI: (a) all of the provisions other than regs 27, 28, 28A–28B and 29 apply to Group A ships; (b) regs 28A–28B and 30 apply to Group B ships; (c) regs 22, 24–26, 27A–27B apply to Group C ships; (d) all of the provisions other than regs 27A–28B apply to Group D ships; and (e) regs 28–30 apply to Group E ships.[143]

138 1997 Regulations, reg 3(5), as inserted by MLC H&S Regulations, reg 2(5).
139 1997 Regulations, reg 21(1)(a)–(b), as amended by MLC H&S Regulations, reg 2(14).
140 1997 Regulations, reg 21(2)(a)–(b), as amended by MLC H&S Regulations, reg 2(14).
141 1997 Regulations, reg 21(3), as amended by MLC H&S Regulations, reg 2(14).
142 1997 Regulations, reg 21(4)(a)–(b), as amended by MLC H&S Regulations, reg 2(14).
143 1997 Regulations, reg 3(6)(a)–(e), as inserted by MLC H&S Regulations, reg 3(5).

Prohibition on levy

19.29 It is provided that no charge is to be levied on any worker, in respect of anything done or pursued, in regard to the specific requirements under the 1997 Regulations.[144]

Duty not to interfere with or misuse certain things

19.30 It is prohibited for any person to intentionally or recklessly interfere with, or misuse, anything provided in the interest of health and safety on board a UK ship.[145]

Offences under the 1997 Regulations

19.31 The 1997 Regulations contain a number of offences and penalties for breaches of various provisions, as set out in the table below. All offences (except for a breach of reg 5) are summary only, and the level of maximum fine on the standard scale is shown for each. Where a body corporate is guilty of any offence, any director, manager, secretary, officer, person purporting to act as such, and (in a case where it is managed by its members) member, is also guilty where the offence has been committed with their consent, connivance or neglect.[146] Where a Scottish partnership is guilty of an offence and it is proved to have been with the consent of, connivance with, or attributable to any neglect of, a partner, they are also guilty.[147] In regard to any offences where the failure is to do something as far as reasonably practicable, it is for the defendant to show that it was not reasonably practicable to do more than was done to satisfy the requirement.[148]

This will also serve as a checklist to aid compliance.

144 The 1997 Regulations, reg 22.
145 1997 Regulations, reg 23.
146 1997 Regulations, reg 25(1)–(2).
147 1997 Regulations, reg 25(3), as inserted by Merchant Shipping and Fishing Vessels (Health and Safety at Work) (Employment of Young Persons) Regulations 1998 (SI 1998/2411), reg 17(g).
148 1997 Regulations, reg 26.

Provision creating duty/offence	Duty, failure of which gives rise to offence	Liable party/ maximum fine or penalty
Reg 5/ reg 24(1)	To observe specific principles and matters in ensuring health and safety of workers and other persons.	Employer and shipowner Summary conviction – a fine not exceeding the statutory maximum Conviction on indictment – maximum 2 years' imprisonment, or a fine, or both
Reg 6/ reg 24(3)	Employer to prepare written general policy on health and safety (unless only employs five or less workers).	Employer Level 4
Reg 7/ reg 24(3)	Employer and shipowner to prepare risk assessment.	Employer and shipowner Level 4
Reg 8/ reg 24(4)	Employer to take certain steps to protect a new or expectant mother and their baby.	Employer Level 3
Reg 9/ reg 24(4)	Employer to make adjustments for new or expectant mother performing night work.	Employer Level 3
Reg 11/ reg 24(4)	Employer to provide with health surveillance.	Employer Level 3
Reg 11A/ reg 24(4)[149]	Employer to file report with the MCA (form MSF 4159) in respect of a seafarer with a disease listed in MSN 1850.	Employer Level 3
Reg 12/ reg 24(4)	Employer and shipowner to provide workers with health and safety training.	Employer and shipowner Level 3
	Shipowner to provide self-employed seafarers with health and safety training.	Shipowner Level 3
	Employer and shipowner to provide specific information to employment agency, which then must provide it to the workers it supplies.	Employment agency Level 3

149 1997 Regulations, reg 24(4), as amended by MLC H&S Regulations, reg 2(16).

Provision creating duty/offence	Duty, failure of which gives rise to offence	Liable party/ maximum fine or penalty
Reg 13/ reg 24(4)	Company to consult all employer(s) of workers on arrangements for preventative and protective measures under reg 5(2)(c), and to ensure workers are informed of any significant finding arising from the risk assessment carried out under reg 7.	Company (which is likely also to be shipowner) Level 3
Reg 13A/ reg 24(1)[150]	Shipowner to discharge obligations contained in the statutory instruments listed in the schedule (which apply to workers) to self-employed seafarers.	Shipowner Summary conviction – a fine not exceeding the statutory maximum Conviction on indictment – maximum 2 years' imprisonment, or a fine, or both
Reg 14/ reg 24(2)	The employer to appoint a competent person(s) to provide the necessary protective and preventative services to enable the employer to comply with the 1997 Regulations.	Employer Level 5
Reg 15/ reg 24(5)(a)(i)	In ships with five or more workers, the company is to appoint a competent person as safety officer.	Company Level 5
Reg 16/ reg 24(3)	Specific duties of the appointed safety officer.	Safety officer Level 4
Reg 17/ reg 24(3)	Company to make arrangements for the election and appointment of safety representatives. Company to ensure that the following appointments are recorded in writing: – competent person to provide protective and preventative services under reg 14(1); – safety officer under reg 15(2); – elected safety representatives under reg 17(1); and – the appointment of any of those persons onto the safety committee.	Company Level 4

150 1997 Regulations, reg 24(1), as amended by MLC H&S Regulations, reg 2(15).

Provision creating duty/offence	**Duty, failure of which gives rise to offence**	**Liable party/ maximum fine or penalty**
Reg 19(1)/ reg 24(5) (a)(ii) (company)/ reg 24(5)(b) (master)	Company and master, in co-ordination with the employer, to facilitate the work of any person appointed under regs 14(1), 15(2) and 17(1) (as set out above) in carrying out their health and safety functions.	Company – Level 5 Master – Level 3
Reg 19(2)/ reg 24(5)(a) (ii)	Where no safety officer is appointed under reg 15(2) (because there are less than five workers on board), the company must maintain records of every accident involving death, major or serious injury and every dangerous occurrence.	Company Level 5
Reg 20/ reg 24(3)	Workers or their elected representatives to be consulted on health and safety matters by the employer, company and shipowner.	Employer, company shipowner Level 4
	Self-employed seafarers or their elected representatives to be consulted on health and safety matters by the shipowner.	Shipowner Level 4
Reg 21/ reg 24(3)	Duties on workers to take reasonable care for their health and safety and that of others, and to co-operate and inform on certain matters.	Workers Level 4
Reg 22/ reg 24(4)	No charge to be levied on any worker.	Employer, company and shipowner Level 3
Reg 23/ reg 24(4)	No person is permitted to intentionally or recklessly interfere with or misuse anything provided in the interests of health and safety.	Any person Level 3

ENFORCEMENT OF THE 1997 REGULATIONS

19.32 When the 1997 Regulations came into force, they contained their own inspection and detention provisions in regs 27–29.[151] These still remain, but the MLC H&S Regulations have made some substantial additions by the insertion of regs 27A, 27B, 28A and 28B, which provide MLC inspection and detention powers.

151 The scope of reg 27 has been narrowed to now only apply to fishing vessels: MLC H&S Regulations, reg 2(17)(a)–(b).

Inspection and detention of UK ships and non-UK ships without MLC documentation

19.33 The new powers provide that a UK ship, or a non-UK ship without MLC documentation, may be inspected to check for compliance with the 1997 Regulations.[152] The inspector has power to detain the ship (but, for a non-UK ship, only when it is in a UK port, shipyard or at an offshore terminal in UK waters) where they have clear grounds to believe:

'(a) one or more of the requirements of Regulation 4.3 and Standard A4.3 of the MLC (health and safety protection and accident prevention) have not been complied with; and

(b) (i) the conditions on board are clearly hazardous to the safety, health or security of seafarers; or

(ii) the non-compliance represents a serious breach or the latest in a series of repeated breaches of the requirements of the MLC (including the rights of seafarers referred to in Articles III and IV of the MLC which are secured by it).'[153]

Inspection and detention of non-UK ships with MLC documentation

19.34 Non-UK ships with MLC documentation may be subject to a review of their MLC documentation and, where appropriate, a more detailed inspection under MLC, Standard A5.2.1 (which is set out in Appendix 1).[154] Such a ship may be detained on the same grounds and in the same place as set out above.[155]

PARTICULAR DUTIES APPLYING TO YOUNG PERSONS

19.35 The Merchant Shipping and Fishing Vessels (Health and Safety at Work) (Employment of Young Persons) Regulations 1998 ('the 1998 Regulations')[156] contain specific provisions in respect of young persons. For these purposes, a young person is: for employment on a UK sea-going ship, any person who is of the age of 16 or 17; or, for employment on any other UK ship, any person who is under the age of 18 and is over school-leaving age.[157]

152 1997 Regulations, reg 27A, as inserted by MLC H&S Regulations, reg 2(18).
153 1997 Regulations, reg 27B(1)–(2), as inserted by MLC H&S Regulations, reg 2(18).
154 1997 Regulations, reg 28A(1)(a)–(b), as inserted by MLC H&S Regulations, reg 2(18).
155 1997 Regulations, reg 28B(1)–(2), as inserted by MLC H&S Regulations, reg 2(18).
156 SI 1998/2411.
157 1998 Regulations, reg 2(2)(a)–(b), as substituted by Merchant Shipping (Hours of Work) Regulations 2002 (SI 2002/2125), reg 21, Sch 2, para 4(a).

The 1998 Regulations apply to all activities of young persons engaged as workers on UK ships;[158] some provisions (regs 1–3, 14–16) also apply to such workers on non-UK ships which are in UK waters.[159]

The duties are imposed on the employer (unless they are imposed on any other person).[160] Where that person does not have control of the matter in question (because they do not have responsibility for the operation of the ship), the duty is also extended to the person who does have control of that matter.[161]

ADDITIONAL GENERAL DUTIES

19.36 The 1998 Regulations require, in addition to the duties contained in the 1997 Regulations, that measures must be taken to protect young workers at work from the risks to their health and safety, which are a consequence of their lack of experience, absence of awareness of existing or potential risks, or the fact that young persons have not yet fully matured.[162]

Before a young person begins work on a ship, a risk assessment is to be carried out, either separately, or in addition to that carried out under reg 7 of the 1997 Regulations, taking into account the inexperience, lack of awareness of risks and immaturity of young persons, paying particular attention to:

'(a) the fitting out and layout of working areas;

(b) the nature, degree and duration of exposure to physical, biological and chemical agents;

(c) the form, range and use of work equipment and the way in which it is handled;

(d) the organisation of processes and activities;

(e) the extent of the health and safety training provided or to be provided to the young persons concerned; and

(f) risks from agents, processes and work listed in the Schedule to these Regulations.'[163]

Regarding sub-paragraph (f), the Schedule sets out a detailed and non-exhaustive list of physical, biological and chemical agents, many of which (in the latter two categories) are contained in various EU Directives, which are referred to therein. The 'processes' referred to are:

158 1998 Regulations, reg 3(1), (3).
159 1998 Regulations, reg 3(2)–(3).
160 1998 Regulations, reg 4(1).
161 1998 Regulations, reg 4(2).
162 1998 Regulations, reg 5(1).
163 1998 Regulations, reg 5(2)(a)–(f).

'Processes and work

1. Processes at work referred to in Annex I to Directive 90/394/EEC.[164]
2. Manufacture and handling of devices, fireworks or other objects containing explosives.
3. Work with fierce or poisonous animals.
4. Animal slaughtering on an industrial scale.
5. Work involving the handling or equipment for the production, storage or application of compressed, liquefied or dissolved gases.
6. Work with vats, tanks, reservoirs or carboys containing chemical agents referred to in paragraph 1.3.[165]
7. Work involving a risk of structural collapse.
8. Work involving high-voltage electrical hazards.
9. Work the pace of which is determined by machinery and involving payment by results.'[166]

The list of substances, preparations and processes referred to in Annex I to Directive 90/394/EEC are:

'1. Manufacture of auramine.

2. Work involving exposure to aromatic polycyclic hydrocarbons present in coal soots, tar, pitch, fumes or dust.

3. Work involving exposure to dusts, fumes and sprays produced during the roasting and electro-refining of cupro-nickel mattes.

4. Strong acid process in the manufacture of isopropyl alcohol.'

Young persons are to be informed of possible risks to their health and safety, identified by the assessment carried out under reg 5(2), and of all measures adopted for their protection.[167]

Subject to what follows, young persons are not to be engaged in the following types of work:

'(a) work which is objectively beyond their physical or psychological capacity;

(b) work involving harmful exposure to agents which are toxic, carcinogenic, cause heritable genetic damage, or harm to the unborn child or which in any other way chronically affect human health;

(c) work involving harmful exposure to radiation;

164 Council Directive of 28 June 1990 on the protection of workers from the risks related to exposure to carcinogens at work (Sixth individual Directive within the meaning of Article 16 (1) of Directive 89/391/EEC), OJ, 26.7.90, L 196/1.
165 1998 Regulations, reg 5(2)(f), Sch.
166 1998 Regulations, reg 5(2)(f), Sch, processes and work.
167 1998 Regulations, reg 5(3).

(d) work involving the risk of accidents which it may be assumed cannot be recognised or avoided by young persons owing to their insufficient attention to safety or lack of experience or training; or

(e) work in which there is a risk to health from–

(i) extreme cold or heat, or

(ii) noise, or

(iii) vibration.'[168]

However, the restriction referred to above does not prohibit the employment of a young person in such an activity where: (a) it is indispensable for their vocational training; and (b) it is performed under the supervision of a competent person, and in such circumstances the duty will be to ensure, as far as reasonably practicable, the young person's health and safety.[169]

REST PERIODS

19.37 Young persons must be provided with: (a) a rest period of at least 12 consecutive hours in every 24-hour period; and (b) a rest period of at least two days, which is, if possible, to be consecutive, in every week.[170] If their daily working time is more than four and a half hours, they should also be provided with a rest break of at least 30 minutes, which is, if possible, to be consecutive.[171] Those are the legal requirements applying to UK ships, but it is worth noting that non-mandatory guidelines in MLC recommend more favourable provisions for young persons as follows: working hours should not exceed more than eight hours per day and 40 hours per week; a one-hour break for the main meal of the day; and a 15-minute rest period as soon as possible following each two hours of continuous work.[172]

The following provisions apply:

- training time is included in the calculation of working time;[173]
- if work is done for more than one employer, working hours days are cumulative;[174]
- some scope for derogation is permitted, the main provisions being: the 12-hour daily rest and the two-day rest per week may be interrupted in cases of activities involving work periods that are split up over the day or are of short duration; the two-day rest per week may be reduced to 36 hours where this is justified by technical or operational reasons;[175]

168 1998 Regulations, reg 5(4)(a)–(e).
169 1998 Regulations, reg 5(6)(a)–(b).
170 1998 Regulations, reg 6(1)(a)–(b).
171 1998 Regulations, reg 6(2).
172 MLC, Guideline B2.3.1.1(a)–(c).
173 1998 Regulations, reg 6(3).
174 1998 Regulations, reg 6(4).
175 1998 Regulations, reg 6(5)(a)–(b)(i)–(ii).

- in connection with rest periods, the company is obliged to ensure that the employer, or other person in control of the matter, complies with the relevant provisions.[176] For these purposes, the 'company' is '... the owner of the ship or any other organisation or person such as the manager, or bareboat charterer, who has assumed the responsibility for operation of the ship from the owner',[177] which is almost identical to the definition of the 'shipowner' under both the MLC and relevant UK legislation.[178]

Prohibition against night work

19.38 See Chapter 3 on the MLC-derived prohibition (and exceptions) on night work for young persons.

HEALTH ASSESSMENT

19.39 Without prejudice to the employer's duty to provide for health surveillance under reg 11 of the 1997 Regulations, the following obligation also applies: (a) where the risk assessment carried out under reg 5(2) of the 1998 Regulations shows that there is a risk to the safety, physical or mental health or development of young people; or (b) where a young person is likely to be required to work at night (unless such work is exceptional), no young person is to be engaged as a worker unless they have been provided with a free assessment of their health capacities, and monitoring of their health at regular intervals.[179]

OTHER PROVISIONS RELATING TO YOUNG PERSONS

19.40 There are other specific requirements relating to young persons, which are set out elsewhere in this book as follows: prohibition against night work and the obligation to maintain a record (see Chapter 3); and medical records (see Chapter 4).

OFFENCES UNDER THE 1998 REGULATIONS

19.41 Any contravention of the 1998 Regulations is punishable, on summary conviction, by a fine not exceeding level 3 on the standard scale.[180] Where a

176 1998 Regulations, reg 6(8).
177 1998 Regulations, reg 2(2).
178 For these definitions of 'shipowner' see MLC, Article II, para I(j); and, for a UK example, Merchant Shipping (Maritime Labour Convention) (Minimum Requirements for Seafarers) Regulations 2014 (SI 2014/1613), reg 2(1).
179 1998 Regulations, reg 7(1)–(2).
180 1998 Regulations, reg 10(1).

body corporate is guilty of any offence, any director, manager, secretary, similar officer, or person purporting to act as such, and (in a case where it is managed by its members) member, is also guilty where the offence has been committed with their consent, connivance or neglect.[181] Where a Scottish partnership is guilty of an offence and it is proved to have been committed with the consent of, connivance with or attributable to any neglect of, a partner, they are also guilty.[182] In regard to any offences where the failure is to do something so far as reasonably practicable, it is for the defendant to show that it was not reasonably practicable to do more than was done to satisfy the requirement.[183]

The table below shows the main obligations, a breach of which gives rise to an offence, together with the primary party on whom the duty is imposed. However, in many cases the employer (when only a supplier of seafarers to the company) will not have control over the matter to which the duty relates because it does not have responsibility for the operation of the ship. In such cases, the 'company' will also be responsible jointly with the employer for ensuring compliance.[184] And, in many cases, the company will be the same party as the 'shipowner' as defined in the UK's legislation implementing the MLC.

This will also serve as a checklist to aid compliance.

Provision creating duty	**Duty, failure of which gives rise to offence**	**Party primarily liable**
Reg 5(1)	Appropriate measures to be taken to protect young persons from risks to their health and safety.	Employer
Reg 5(2)	Risk assessment to be carried out before young person begins work on board a ship.	Employer
Reg 5(3)	Young persons to be informed of possible risks identified as a result of the assessment, and the steps taken for their protection.	Employer
Reg 5(4)	Young persons not to be engaged in specified types of dangerous work.	Employer
Reg 5(5)	In assessing risk, regard is to be had to: (a) the findings of the risk assessment carried out under reg 5(2); and (b) the list of agents, processes and work contained in the Schedule to the 1998 Regulations.	Employer

181 1998 Regulations, reg 11(1)–(2).
182 1998 Regulations, reg 11(3).
183 1998 Regulations, reg 12.
184 1998 Regulations, reg 4(1)–(2).

Provision creating duty	**Duty, failure of which gives rise to offence**	**Party primarily liable**
Reg 6(1)(a)–(b), (2)	Young person to be provided with a rest period of: (1)(a) at least 12 consecutive hours in each 24-hour period; and (b) two days (consecutively if possible) in every week; and (2) 30 minutes (consecutively if possible) after four and a half hours' work.	Employer
Reg 6(8)	Company to ensure that the employer, or any other person having control of the matter relating to rest periods, complies with the relevant duty.	Company
Reg 7(1)(a)–(b), (2)	Young person to be provided with a free health assessment before starting work, and ongoing monitoring of their health at regular intervals, if: (1)(a) the risk assessment carried out under reg 5(2) shows that there is a risk to their safety, physical or mental health or development; or (b) they are likely to be required to work at night (unless, in relation to (b), night work is of an exceptional nature).	Employer
Reg 9(1)–(3)	(1) A list of young persons, with their dates of birth, must be kept; (2) a summary of the 1998 Regulations must be kept; and (3) the master must keep a register of young persons, together with their dates of birth and dates of engagement. Note: reg 9 has not been updated to reflect the MLC change from the old 'crew agreement' to the new 'seafarer employment agreement' (SEA), and references to the former have been removed from the above summary to avoid confusion. To comply with reg 9 in the context of SEAs, see Chapter 3 at para 3.7, which refers to the new list of young persons in MSF 4158 (contained in MGN 477),[185] which also summarises the 1998 H&S Regulations and other provisions relating to young seafarers.	Employer, company, master

INSPECTION AND DETENTION OF SHIPS

19.42 A relevant inspector may inspect a UK ship and, if satisfied that the 1998 Regulations have not been complied with, may detain the ship until the health

185 MGN 477 (M): Maritime Labour Convention, 2006 – Seafarer Employment Agreements.

and safety of all young persons aboard is secured.[186] A 'relevant inspector' for these purposes is: (a) a surveyor; (b) a superintendent; or (c) any other person authorised by the Secretary of State.[187]

In relation to such non-compliances by non-UK ships, which have called at a UK port in the normal course of business, such an inspector may:

(a) send a report to the flag state and a copy to the ILO;

(b) where conditions on board are clearly hazardous to health and safety:

  (i) take the necessary measures to rectify those conditions, or

  (ii) detain the ship.[188]

Where action under paragraphs (i) or (ii) is taken, the inspector must notify the nearest maritime consular or diplomatic representative of the flag state.[189]

Neither UK or non-UK ships should be detained or delayed unreasonably.[190] The shipowner or master can refer the detention to arbitration (on giving notice within 21 days from the service of the detention notice) and, if successful, the Secretary of State may be ordered to pay compensation to cover losses.[191]

See also the MLC-derived powers of inspection and detention inserted into the 1997 Regulations, as summarised in paragraph 19.32 above. These have not been replicated in the 1998 Regulations, although there will be situations where dangerous or repeated breaches of the 1998 Regulations also fall within the general grounds for detention set out in the 1997 Regulations.

See Chapter 22 for an account of the MLC-derived provisions on these issues.

FUTURE AMENDMENTS TO THE MLC

19.43 On 8 January 2019 the 2016 amendments come into force, and these are set out in full in Appendix 2. The amendments will be to Code B of Regulation 4.3 and address the problems caused by harassment and bullying in the context of health and safety on board ships, as follows:

(i) At the end of Guideline B4.3.1, which provides that ratifying states should take account of international provisions regarding occupational safety and health protection, there is to be inserted: 'Account should also be taken of the latest version of the *Guidance on eliminating shipboard harassment and*

186 1998 Regulations, reg 13.
187 1998 Regulations, reg 2(2), referring to Merchant Shipping Act 1995, s 258(1)(a)–(c).
188 1998 Regulations, reg 14(1)–(2).
189 1998 Regulations, reg 14(3).
190 1998 Regulations, regs 13, 14(4).
191 1998 Regulations, reg 16; Merchant Shipping Act 1995, ss 96–97.

bullying[192] jointly published by the International Chamber of Shipping and the International Transport Workers' Federation'.

(ii) In Guideline B4.3.1.4, which sets out various matters on which ratifying states should take account of in terms of their implications for health and safety, there is to be inserted: '(d) harassment and bullying'.

(iii) In Guideline B4.3.6.2, which lists subjects which ratifying states should consider investigating, there is to be inserted: '(g) problems arising from harassment and bullying'.

The UK has yet to promulgate how it will implement these amendments.

COMPLIANCE

19.44 See the DMLC, Pt I, point 11 which sets out the UK provisions, and enter details of how compliance is implemented in the DMLC, Pt II, point 11.

192 ICS/ITF Guidance on eliminating shipboard harassment and bullying (published 2016): www.ics-shipping.org/docs/default-source/Other-documents/guidance-on-eliminating-shipboard-harassment-and-bullying.pdf?sfvrsn=4 [Accessed 20 October 2018].

CHAPTER 20

Regulation 4.4: Access to Shore-based Welfare Facilities

INTRODUCTION

20.1 The purpose of Regulation 4.4 of the MLC is to ensure that seafarers working on board a ship have access to shore-based facilities and services to secure their health and well-being.[1]

Ratifying states must ensure that shore-based welfare facilities, where they exist, are easily accessible, and they must promote the development of welfare facilities, such as those listed in the Code to Regulation 4.4, in designated ports to provide seafarers on ships that are in its ports with access to adequate welfare facilities and services.[2] The responsibilities of ratifying states with respect to shore-based facilities, such as welfare, cultural, recreational and information facilities and services, are set out in the Code.[3]

Ratifying states are required to ensure that, in respect of welfare services situated in their territories, they are easily accessible, and available for the use of all seafarers without discrimination based on nationality, race, colour, sex, religion, political opinion or social origin, and irrespective of the flag state of the ship on which they work.[4] The development of welfare facilities is to be promoted in appropriate ports, and the establishment of welfare boards is to be encouraged, to regularly review welfare facilities and services, to ensure that they are appropriate in the light of changes to the needs of seafarers resulting from technical, operational and other developments in the shipping industry.[5]

The MLC provides detailed guidance on the level of implementation that is expected, on issues such as: ratifying states' responsibilities; welfare facilities and

1 MLC, Regulation 4.4, purpose.
2 MLC, Regulation 4.4, para 1.
3 MLC, Regulation 4.4, para 2.
4 MLC, Regulation 4.4.1, Standard A4.4.1.
5 MLC, Standard A4.4.2–A4.4.3.

services in ports; welfare boards; financing of welfare facilities; dissemination of information and facilitation measures; and seafarers in a foreign port.[6]

ORGANISATION OF UK WELFARE SERVICES

20.2 The UK has not introduced any MLC-specific legislation in this area, but it has produced MGN 486,[7] describing the roles of the Merchant Navy Welfare Board (MNWB) and Port Welfare Committees (PWCs).

The MNWB is the umbrella charity[8] in the maritime sector, and promotes co-operation between organisations which provide welfare services to merchant seafarers and their dependants within the UK.[9] Its key objectives are:

- 'To help improve the effectiveness of all those charities caring for merchant seafarers, fishermen and their dependants and this is done irrespective of nationality, religion or ethnic background.
- Strive to ensure that all welfare needs are met through the most effective deployment of resources.
- Facilitate the work of Constituent organisations through the provision of grants and specialist support services.
- Provide a dedicated welfare support and referral service for UK seafarers and their dependants.
- Manage and support Port Welfare Committees to develop local welfare services.
- Encourage and enable closer collaboration amongst both Constituent organisations and Port Welfare Committees.
- Represent and raise awareness of seafarers' welfare issues at national level.'[10]

The MNWB has over 40 constituent member charities and maintains 15 PWCs throughout the UK in major port areas (as well as a Seafarers' Welfare Board in Gibraltar).

Maritime charities

20.3 The Maritime Charities Group (MCG) was established in 2003 and comprises: Seafarers UK; MNWB; Trinity House; Nautilus International; Seafarers Hospital Society; and the Royal Navy & Royal Marines Charity. The MCG's mission '... is to promote the best use of resources among the maritime charities'. Its objectives include: to encourage best practice, share information

6 MLC, Guidelines 4.4.1–4.4.6, respectively.
7 MGN 486 (M) – Maritime Labour Convention, 2006: Access to shore-based welfare services.
8 The MNWB is a registered charity in England and Wales (No. 212799), based in Southampton.
9 MGN 486, para 2.1.
10 MNWB website: www.mnwb.org/Objects [Accessed 13 January 2018].

and harmonise procedures in respect of grant applications; and to fund projects and research for the benefit of maritime charities.[11]

The extensive list of constituent charities includes: Apostleship of the Sea; Honourable Company of Master Mariners Charities; Merchant Navy Association; Mission to Seafarers; Nautilus Welfare Fund;[12] Sailors' Society; Seamen's Christian Friend Society; Soldiers, Sailors, Airmen and Families Association (SSAFA); and Seafarers UK.[13]

Port Welfare Committees

20.4 Many of the PWCs have more than one branch in their respective regions,[14] holding at least three meetings per annum, which facilitate a forum for involved agencies to meet regularly, share information, provide mutual support and to network.[15] The MCA is represented by a surveyor or coastguard on about 13 PWCs, and the other involved parties are maritime trade unions, shipowners' representatives, port authorities, port health authorities and maritime charities.[16]

The PWCs produce informative port information leaflets,[17] providing details of local: welfare facilities; seafarers' centres; ship welfare visiting organisations;[18] hospitals; telephone helpline and internet access facilities; places of worship; port chaplains; transport and tourist information; entertainment venues and attractions; sports facilities; libraries, and much more.

International Seafarers' Welfare and Assistance Network (ISWAN)

20.5 The port information leaflets refer to 'SeafarerHelp', which is a free 24/7 multi-lingual helpline service (available to all seafarers and accessible via

11 See www.mnwb.org/MCG [Accessed 15 January 2018].

12 Nautilus Welfare (base in Wallasey, Merseyside) offers a range of specialist services to support retired seafarers and their dependants, including a care home, independent living accommodation and grants: www.nautiluswelfarefund.org [Accessed 29 September 2018].

13 Many of the constituent charities have their own websites, and the full list of them can be accessed by visiting: www.mnwb.org/Constituent_Members [Accessed 29 September 2018]. SSAFA extends its assistance to veterans of the armed forces, some of whom work in the merchant navy.

14 For example, the South West has welfare services in Falmouth, Fowey and Plymouth.

15 Port Welfare Authorities Terms of Reference, para 4.4.

16 MGN 486, paras 1, 3.2–3.3.

17 These are produced pursuant to MLC, Guideline B4.4.5.1, '[i]nformation should be disseminated among seafarers concerning facilities open to the general public in ports of call, particularly transport, welfare, entertainment and educational facilities and places of worship, as well as facilities provided specifically for seafarers'.

18 These include religious organisations (such as the Apostleship of the Sea) and maritime trade unions (including the International Transport Workers' Federation (ITF), Nautilus International and RMT).

telephone and various online methods) provided by ISWAN's specialist staff.[19] It also provides an advice and referral service, 'Nautilus 24/7',[20] for members of Nautilus International and seafarers who are members of unions affiliated to the Nautilus Federation.[21]

ISWAN plays an important role in promoting seafarers' welfare internationally, administers an emergency welfare fund for seafarers in dire need, and produces health information.

Seafarer unions

20.6 The seafarer unions in the UK are Nautilus International[22] and the RMT,[23] both of which are members, with the MCA, of the UK's tripartite working party which fed into the policy and law-making processes to implement the MLC into UK law. Both unions provide a wide range of services to their members, including: representation at work; collective bargaining; and support of employment and personal injury claims.

Furthermore, there is the Nautilus Federation,[24] which has many constituent members around the globe, which provides a collective voice in response to the challenges and opportunities presented by the maritime industry. It provides a 'Joint Assistance and Support Network' (JASON), which facilitates reciprocal assistance and support between the unions in respect of their members who have become involved with investigative authorities following their involvement in a maritime incident, such as a collision, grounding or pollution, etc. Major objectives involve fighting against the criminalisation of seafarers and ensuring, in such situations, the observance of the IMO/ILO Guidelines on Fair Treatment of Seafarers in the Event of a Maritime Accident.

19 See http://seafarerswelfare.org [Accessed 14 January 2018].
20 See https://nautilusint.org/en/need-help/nautilus-247/ [Accessed 14 January 2018].
21 To see the affiliated unions, visit: https://nautilusfederation.org/unions/ [Accessed 14 January 2018].
22 Nautilus International: www.nautilusint.org [Accessed 29 September 2018].
23 National Union of Rail, Maritime and Transport Workers: www.rmt.org.uk [Accessed 29 September 2018].
24 Nautilus Federation: https://nautilusfederation.org/ [Accessed 29 September 2018].

CHAPTER 21

Regulation 4.5: Social Security

INTRODUCTION

21.1 The purpose of Regulation 4.5 of the MLC is to ensure that measures are taken with a view to providing seafarers with access to social security protection.[1]

Ratifying states are required to ensure that all seafarers (and, to the extent provided for in national laws, their dependants) have access to social security protection in accordance with the MLC Code[2] (without prejudice to any more favourable conditions which apply nationally).[3] Such states are required to take steps, according to their national circumstances, individually and through international co-operation, to achieve progressively comprehensive social security protection for seafarers.[4] Furthermore, states are required to ensure that seafarers who are subject to their social security legislation (and, again, to the extent provided for by their national law, their dependants) are entitled to social security protection which is no less favourable than that enjoyed by shore workers.[5]

The nine branches to be considered, with a view to achieving progressively comprehensive social security protection, for all seafarers ordinarily resident in the relevant state's territory, are: medical care, sickness benefit, unemployment benefit, old-age benefit, employment injury benefit, family benefit, maternity

1 MLC, Regulation 4.5, p 70.
2 At some points, the MLC Code distinguishes between, on the one hand, seafarers who are ordinarily resident in the state's territory (Standard A4.5.3) and, on the other, those who are serving on a ship registered with the state (Standard A4.5.5).
3 MLC, Regulation 4.5.1. Under Article 19, para 8, of the ILO Constitution, the adoption of any Convention or Recommendation, or the ratification of any Convention by a member, is not deemed to affect any law, award, custom or agreement, which ensures more favourable conditions to the workers concerned.
4 MLC, Regulation 4.5.2.
5 MLC, Regulation 4.5.3.

benefit, invalidity benefit and survivor's benefit, complementing the protection which shipowners are required to provide under MLC, Regulations 4.1 (medical care) and 4.2 (shipowners' liability), and other titles of the MLC.[6]

Such coverage may be achieved through appropriate bilateral or multilateral agreements or contribution-based systems.[7] At the time of ratification, states are required to provide at least three of those nine branches of social security.[8] The MLC's guidelines advise that those three branches should include medical care, sickness benefit and employment injury benefit.[9] Ratifying states are required to inform the ILO, at the time of ratification, which of those benefits they provide, and they are shown on the MLC 'ratifications' page for each state.

The obligations in respect of seafarers serving on a ship registered with a particular state, whether or not they ordinarily reside in that state, include those provided through Regulations 4.1 (medical care on board ships and ashore) and 4.2 (shipowners' liability), as well as those that are inherent in its general obligations under international law.[10] Ratifying states will require shipowners to provide those benefits to seafarers serving on their ships.[11] However, under Regulation 4.1, ratifying states must also allow visiting seafarers, who are in need of immediate medical care, access to their medical facilities; shipowners must permit this and, to the extent permitted by the flag state's law, it should be provided at no cost to the seafarer, which means that the shipowner must meet any costs.[12]

The health and social security protection benefits which the shipowner provides to seafarers serving on their ships must be set out in the seafarers' employment agreement (SEA).[13]

UK SOCIAL SECURITY

21.2 A detailed account of UK social security law is beyond the scope of this work, and the following only sets out the general position on benefits and National Insurance contribution (NIC) deductions.

6 MLC, Standards A4.5.1, A4.5.3.
7 MLC, Standard A4.5.3.
8 MLC, Standard A4.5.2.
9 MLC, Guideline B4.5.1.
10 MLC, Standard A4.5.5.
11 Merchant Shipping (Maritime Labour Convention) (Minimum Requirements for Seafarers etc) Regulations 2014 (SI 2014/1613) ('Minimum Requirements Regulations'), regs 43–47 (medical care), 48–53 (shipowners' liability).
12 MLC, Regulation 4.1, para 3; Standard A4.1.1(d); Minimum Requirements Regulations, regs 43(3)(b), (4)(a)–(b), 45.
13 MLC, Standard A2.1.4(h); Minimum Requirements Regulations, reg 10(1), Sch 1, Pt 1, para 9.

Benefits for resident seafarers

21.3 The UK has not implemented any specific legislation in connection with its MLC obligations, and relies on the general body of social security laws, which are mainly set out in the Social Security Contributions and Benefits Act 1992 and various sets of regulations made thereunder.

The following benefits are available to resident seafarers, subject to detailed qualifying criteria (some are contributory benefits and others are income-related): medical care (free to access through the NHS), sickness benefit,[14] unemployment benefit,[15] old-age benefit,[16] employment injury benefit,[17] family benefit,[18] invalidity benefit[19] and survivor's benefit.[20]

National Insurance contributions

21.4 There is a dedicated 'Mariners Unit' within HMRC, which provides specialist advice on NIC deductions and also has a questionnaire which can be completed so that the seafarer's situation can be assessed.[21]

NICs should be deducted from UK resident seafarers' wages by their employer if they work:

- for, or are paid by, a company based in the UK;
- on a vessel registered in the UK for an employer based in the European Economic Area (EEA) or in a country that has a reciprocal agreement[22] with the UK;
- in the designated sector of the UK continental shelf on a vessel engaged in any activity in connection with the exploration and exploitation of natural resources.[23]

14 Social Security Contributions and Benefit Act 1992, s 31, Pt XI.
15 Social Security Contributions and Benefit Act 1992, s 25.
16 Social Security Contributions and Benefit Act 1992, ss 78–79.
17 Social Security Contributions and Benefit Act 1992, Pt V.
18 Social Security Contributions and Benefit Act 1992, s 128 (working family tax credit).
19 Social Security Contributions and Benefit Act 1992, ss 33–34, 103.
20 Social Security Contributions and Benefit Act 1992, ss 36–41.
21 HMRC Mariners Unit: www.gov.uk/government/publications/mariners-national-insurance-questionnaire [Accessed 28 June 2018].
22 The UK has agreements about National Insurance and benefit entitlement with the following non-EEA countries: Barbados; Bermuda; Canada; Chile; Israel; Jamaica; Japan; Jersey and Guernsey; Korea; Mauritius; Philippines; Turkey; USA. Furthermore, the 1958 Agreement with the former Yugoslavia continues to apply in respect of Bosnia-Herzegovina; Kosovo; Montenegro; Serbia and the former Republic of Macedonia; it also applies to Croatia and Slovenia, although it has been superseded by EU law. Reciprocal agreements: www.gov.uk/government/publications/reciprocal-agreements [Accessed 28 June 2018].
23 HMRC – NIC if you work at sea: www.gov.uk/guidance/national-insurance-if-you-work-on-a-ship [Accessed 28 June 2018].

Even if seafarers are not liable to pay NICs, they may be entitled to pay voluntary contributions towards benefits and the state pension. Again, the Mariners Unit at HMRC should be contacted for advice.

ARRANGEMENTS WITHIN THE EEA

21.5 Article 11 of EC Regulation 883/2004[24] sets out the general rules in determining the applicable legislation. In relation to seafarers, Article 11(4) provides:

> 'For the purposes of this Title, an activity as an employed or self-employed person normally pursued on board a vessel at sea flying the flag of a Member State shall be deemed to be an activity pursued in the said Member State. However, a person employed on board a vessel flying the flag of a Member State and remunerated for such activity by an undertaking or a person whose registered office or place of business is in another Member State shall be subject to the legislation of the latter Member State if he resides in that State. The undertaking or person paying the remuneration shall be considered as the employer for the purposes of the said legislation.'

Compliance point: although Regulation 4.5 of the MLC relates more specifically to the ratifying states' responsibilities to provide social security to resident seafarers, shipowners must include details in the SEA[25] of the health and social security benefits they provide (for instance, at least those deriving from MLC, Regulations 4.1 and 4.2).

24 Regulation (EC) 883/2004 of the European Parliament and of the Council of 29 April 2004 on the coordination of social security systems, OJ 30.4.2004, L 166/1.

25 Minimum Requirements Regulations, reg 10(1)(a), Sch 1, Pt 1, para 9.

PART VI

Title 5: Compliance and Enforcement

CHAPTER 22

Title 5: Compliance and Enforcement – UK

INTRODUCTION

22.1 In the MLC, the Regulations specify ratifying states' responsibility to fully implement and enforce the principles and rights set out in the Articles, as well as particular obligations provided for under Titles 1 to 4.[1] The flexibility to implement Part A of the Code by substantially equivalent provisions does not apply to Title 5, which must be implemented in the manner set out in the corresponding Standards of Part A, giving due consideration to the corresponding Guidelines in Part B.[2] In implementing Title 5, ratifying states must be mindful that seafarers and shipowners are equal before the law and must not be subject to discrimination in their access to courts, tribunals or other dispute resolution mechanisms.[3] The provisions of Title 5 do not determine legal jurisdiction or a legal venue.[4]

Due to its importance to the implementation and enforcement of the MLC through flag state control and port state control, the whole of Title 5 has been reproduced in Appendix 1, annotated with notes covering issues relating to flag state inspections, the issue of MLC documentation, port state control inspections,

1 MLC, Title 5, para 1.
2 MLC, Title 5, paras 2–3.
3 MLC, Title 5, para 4.
4 MLC, Title 5, para 4.

detention of ships and other remedial action, on-board complaints procedures and onshore complaints procedures. What follows is intended to highlight where the main UK sources of law and materials can be found.

The main provisions are set out in the Merchant Shipping (Maritime Labour Convention) (Survey and Certification) Regulations 2013[5] ('the S&C Regulations') and MSN 1848.[6]

FLAG STATE RESPONSIBILITIES, ETC

22.2 The purpose of Regulation 5.1 is to ensure that each ratifying state implements its responsibilities under the MLC with respect to ships which fly its flag.[7]

SURVEY AND INSPECTION OF SHIPS

22.3 With the following exception, the S&C Regulations apply to UK MLC ships, wherever they may be. The exception is that they do not apply at all to UK MLC ships which (i) operate only within 60 miles of a safe haven, and (ii) do not operate to or from, or call at, a port in a country other than the UK ('safe haven' means a harbour or shelter of any kind which affords safe entry and protection from the weather).[8] However, even though the latter are excepted from an MLC survey or inspection regime under the S&C Regulations, they are still subject to, and must comply with, the UK MLC legislation as described in Regulations 1.1 to 4.5. Furthermore, they are subject to the inspection and detention provisions contained within that legislation to ensure compliance with the particular provisions set out therein.

Another point to note is that, although the S&C Regulations use the term 'survey' throughout, MSN 1848 makes a distinction between, on the one hand, 'survey' and, on the other, 'inspection'. This MSN usage is adopted here, in that 'survey' applies in the case where a Maritime Labour Certificate ('MLCert') will be issued on a successful outcome, and 'inspection' applies when this is undertaken in a situation where no certificate is required or requested (on a voluntary basis).

If a party is dissatisfied about the outcome of a survey, they may serve a written notice on the responsible party within 21 days of receiving notification of the outcome, stating that there is a dispute and requesting that the matter be referred to a single arbitrator.[9]

5 SI 2013/1785.
6 MSN 1848 (M) Amendment 2 – MLC, 2006: Survey and Certification of UK Ships.
7 MLC, Regulation 5.1, purpose.
8 S&C Regulations, reg 4(3)(f)(i)–(ii).
9 S&C Regulations, reg 14.

Survey for the issue of an MLCert

22.4 The MCA uses the term 'survey' in a case where a certificate is required to be issued (such as a MLCert), and the term 'inspection' in a case where no certificate is required to be issued and is not requested.[10]

A ship meeting the following criterion, that it is of 500 GT or more operating on international voyages or out of a foreign port or between foreign ports, is subject to a mandatory 'survey' in accordance with MSN 1848 for the issue or renewal of an MLCert;[11] it then must undergo an intermediate survey as set out in MSN 1848 in the period between anniversary dates of an MLCert in its second and third years of validity.[12]

A ship which does not meet the criterion above may request a voluntary 'survey' in accordance with MSN 1848 for the issue of an MLCert;[13] once issued with an MLCert the ship becomes subject to the renewal and intermediate survey regime referred to above.[14]

Inspection to confirm compliance with the UK MLC standards

22.5 A ship which does not meet the criterion and which does not seek a voluntary survey and certification will be subject to a mandatory 'inspection', at least twice in each five-year period, to ensure it meets UK MLC standards.[15]

Survey for the issue of an interim MLCert

22.6 Alternatively, in specific circumstances, a ship may be subject to a survey for the issue of an interim MLCert, valid for a period of six months.[16]

Those circumstances are that it is:

- the first registration of the ship with any flag state; or
- a transfer of the ship from another flag state; or
- where an MLCert has been issued by a certifying authority in respect of the ship, upon a person taking responsibility for the operation of the ship who (i) is not the person named as the shipowner in that MLCert, and (ii) has not been named as the shipowner in any MLCert previously issued in respect of that ship.[17]

10 MSN 1848, para 3.1.
11 S&C Regulations, reg 5.
12 S&C Regulations, reg 5(1)(c).
13 MSN 1848, para 3.2.2.
14 MSN 1848, paras 3.2.1–3.2.2.
15 S&C Regulations, reg 5(3); MSN 1848, para 3.2.3.
16 S&C Regulations, reg 8.
17 S&C Regulations, reg 8(1)(a)–(b).

Where a certifying authority or the government of an MLC state has verified that:

(a) a ship has been subjected to a survey, so far as reasonable and practicable, as set out in MSN 1848,

(b) the shipowner has demonstrated that the ship has adequate procedures to comply with the UK MLC standards,

(c) the master of the ship is familiar with:

 (i) the requirements of the MLC, and

 (ii) the responsibilities which people have in connection with the implementation of the MLC as respects a UK ship, and

(d) the MCA or the government of the MLC state has the information which would be necessary for it to produce Part 1 of the DMLC as respects the ship,

the certifying authority or the government of the MLC state may issue an interim MLCert.[18]

For a ship that is subject to a survey, the shipowner must provide the certifying authority with the information necessary for it to draw up the DMLC, Pt I, and the shipowner must draw up Pt II and provide it to the certifying authority.[19]

A model interim MLCert is set out in MSN 1848, Annex 2.

MLCert and DMLC Pts I and II

22.7 An MLCert and certified DMLC Pts I and II will be issued when the certifying authority is satisfied that the UK MLC standards set out in Annex 1 and Schedules 1 and 2 to MSN 1848 are being complied with;[20] it will be valid for a period not exceeding five years from the date of completion of the survey.[21] A renewal survey must take place no more than five years after the initial survey and thereafter at such intervals; an intermediate survey must be carried out between the second and third anniversary date of the MLCert.[22] Where an interim MLCert has been issued, there will be no accompanying DMLC Pt I or Pt II.

A model MLCert and DMLC, Pts I and II, are set out in MSN 1848, Annexes 3 to 5 (respectively).

18 S&C Regulations, reg 8(2)(a)–(d).
19 S&C Regulations, reg 11.
20 S&C Regulations, regs 6, 11.
21 S&C Regulations, reg 10(1)(a)–(b).
22 S&C Regulations, reg 5(1)(b)–(c).

NON-UK SHIPS

22.8 There is provision for the MCA (or an organisation with which it has an agreement pursuant to Article 5(2) of Directive 2009/15/EC)[23] to inspect a foreign ship at the request of its flag state, against the MLC standards set by the foreign flag state, and issue and endorse MLC documentation having the effect as if issued and endorsed by the foreign flag state.[24]

DOCUMENTS TO BE CARRIED ON BOARD

22.9 The shipowner and master must ensure that there is carried on board at all times:

- a copy of the MLC;
- an MLCert or interim MLCert; and
- if the ship has an MLCert (as opposed to an interim MLCert), the DMLC.[25]

ON-BOARD COMPLAINT PROCEDURE

22.10 The shipowner and the master must ensure that there is a procedure to lodge a complaint alleging a breach of the requirements of the MLC and for that complaint to be resolved fairly, effectively and expeditiously.[26] The UK on-board complaint procedure is set out in MSN 1849.[27] The procedure must:

(a) seek to resolve the complaint at the lowest level possible,

(b) enable a seafarer to complain directly to the master of the ship and appropriate external authorities (including the MCA and other port state authorities),

(c) include the right of the seafarer to be accompanied or represented during any hearing which takes place under that procedure, and

(d) comply with the requirements of Merchant Shipping Notice 1849(M).[28]

The on-board complaints procedure may be set out in a collective agreement, provided its provisions do not conflict with those in MSN 1849.[29]

The shipowner and the master must ensure that a seafarer joining the ship is or has been provided with:

23 Directive 2009/15/EC of the European Parliament and of the Council of 23 April 2009 on common rules and standards for ship inspection and survey organisations and for the relative activities of maritime administrations, OJ 28.5.2009 L 131/47.

24 S&C Regulations, reg 9.

25 S&C Regulations, reg 12.

26 S&C Regulations, reg 13(1).

27 MSN 1849 (M) – MLC, 2006: On-board complaints procedure.

28 S&C Regulations, reg 13(2)(a)–(d), (4); MSN 1849, para 3.1.5.

29 MSN 1849, para 4.1.

(a) a copy of the on-board complaint procedure;

(b) contact information for the certifying authority for the ship,

(c) where applicable, contact information for the authority which is the competent authority for the purposes of the MLC in the seafarer's country of residence, and

(d) the name of a person on board the ship who can confidentially provide the seafarer with impartial advice on their complaint and otherwise assist them in following the procedure.[30]

A seafarer alleging a breach of the requirements of the MLC may lodge a complaint with the MCA, which must treat its source as confidential.[31] The shipowner and the master must ensure that a seafarer is not subjected to any detriment on the grounds that they have lodged a complaint, whether through an on-board procedure or to the MCA.[32] That provision is only engaged if the complaint alleges a breach of the requirements of the MLC.[33] In *Wilson* the claimant alleged that the MCA had failed to investigate his complaint fairly and without bias. Mr Wilson had alleged, in his complaint to the MCA, that the termination amounted to detriment (retaliation) under reg 13(5) for raising various complaints about his employment on board a UK cruise ship. However, the MCA held that, as the subject matter of his complaints did not amount to breaches of the MLC, reg 13(5) was not engaged, and this approach was approved by the court.[34]

The complaint and resulting decision must be recorded, and a copy provided to the seafarer.[35]

OFFENCES

22.11 Breaches of any of the main provisions amount to a criminal offence:

- Against the shipowner and master for proceeding to sea without carrying valid and endorsed MLC certification, a copy of the MLC or for non-compliance with the on-board complaint procedure requirements;[36]
- Against any person for acts relating to MLCerts (such as altering, falsely producing, lending, failing to surrender, (in Scotland) forging) or recklessly or falsely providing information for a survey.[37]

30 S&C Regulations, reg 13(3)(a)–(d).
31 S&C Regulations, reg 13(4).
32 S&C Regulations, reg 13(5).
33 *Wilson v Secretary of State for Transport and (joined as interested parties) (1) Princess Cruise Lines Ltd (2) International Labour Organisation* Case No: CO/19/2015, QBD.
34 *Wilson*, para 47.
35 MSN 1849, para 3.1.2.
36 S&C Regulations, reg 13(1)–(2), (4).
37 S&C Regulations, reg 15(3)(a)–(f).

The offences are punishable, on summary conviction, by fines not exceeding the statutory maximum or, on indictment, to imprisonment or a fine or both.[38] The maximum term of imprisonment is: for offences under reg 15(1)–(2), (4), two years; and, for offences under reg 15(3)(a)–(f), six months.[39] It is a defence for the accused to prove that they had taken all reasonable steps to ensure compliance with the relevant provisions.[40]

INSPECTION AND DETENTION OF SHIPS

UK ships

Inspection

22.12 A relevant inspector or proper officer may at all reasonable times go on board a ship and inspect the ship, its equipment, any article and any document carried on it, for the purposes of checking compliance with the S&C Regulations.[41] During such an inspection the Regulations apply the following provisions of the Merchant Shipping Act 1995: powers of inspector (s 259); and improvement notices and prohibition notices (ss 261–266).[42]

Detention

22.13 When a relevant inspector has clear grounds for believing that: (a) a ship does not comply with the S&C Regulations; and (b) (i) the conditions on board are clearly hazardous to the safety, health or security of seafarers, or (ii) the non-compliance represents a serious breach or the latest in a series of repeated breaches of the S&C Regulations or the requirements of the MLC (including the rights of seafarers referred to in Articles III and IV of the MLC which are secured by it), the ship is liable to be detained.[43]

Further provisions relate to: power to let the ship proceed to sea for the purpose of proceeding to the nearest appropriate repair yard available;[44] the application of s 284 (enforcing the detention of a ship) of the MSA 1995;[45] service of a detention notice on the master, stating the grounds of detention and requiring them to be remedied before the ship can be released;[46] the conditions for releasing the ship once the non-compliance no longer applies; and the payment and refund of any security (which must not exceed £30,000).[47]

38 S&C Regulations, reg 15(1)–(4).
39 S&C Regulations, reg 15(1)–(4), respectively.
40 S&C Regulations, reg 15(5).
41 S&C Regulations, reg 16.
42 S&C Regulations, reg 16.
43 S&C Regulations, reg 17(1)(a)–(b).
44 S&C Regulations, reg 17(2).
45 S&C Regulations, reg 17(3).
46 S&C Regulations, reg 17(4)(a)–(b).
47 S&C Regulations, reg 17(5)–(7).

PORT STATE RESPONSIBILITIES

22.14 The purpose of Regulation 5.2 is to enable member states to implement their responsibilities under the MLC regarding international co-operation in the implementation and enforcement of the MLC standards on foreign ships.[48]

Regulations 5.2.1 and 5.2.2

22.15 The following provisions apply to non-UK sea-going ships while the ship is in UK waters, except where it is exercising the right of innocent passage or the right of transit passage through straits used for international navigation.[49]

Documentation and complaint procedure requirements

22.16 Such ships must comply with the following provisions of the MLC:

- Standard A5.1.1.2 (requirement to have copy of MLC on board),
- Regulation 5.1.3, at paragraphs 3 and 4, and Standard A5.1.3.12 (MLCert and DMLC to be carried on board ship),
- Regulation 5.1.5 and Standard A5.1.5 (on-board complaint procedures), and
- Regulation 5.2.2 and Standard A5.2.2 (onshore seafarer complaint-handling procedures).[50]

If such a ship proceeds, or attempts to proceed, to sea without complying, the shipowner and the master commit an offence punishable, on summary conviction, to a fine not exceeding the statutory maximum or, on conviction on indictment, to imprisonment for a term not exceeding two years, or a fine, or both.[51] It is a defence for the accused to prove that they had taken all reasonable steps to ensure compliance with the relevant provisions.[52]

In relation to a ship which is registered with a non-MLC state, it is a defence for the accused to prove that substantially similar documents (to those referred to above) were carried on board.[53]

48 MLC, Regulation 5.2, purpose.

49 S&C Regulations, reg 4(2); on innocent passage and transit, see generally Pts II and III of the United Nations Convention on the Law of the Sea, 1982. For an account of transit passage through international straits, see R Churchill and A Lowe, *The Law of the Sea* (Manchester University Press, Manchester, 3rd edition, 2017), pp 104–110.

50 S&C Regulations, reg 18(1)(a)–(d), respectively.

51 S&C Regulations, reg 18)2).

52 S&C Regulations, reg 18(3).

53 S&C Regulations, reg 18(4).

Inspection of non-UK ships

22.17 Where the ship is registered with an MLC state, a relevant inspector may inspect the ship's MLCert and DMLC or the ship's interim MLCert and, where MLC Standard A5.2.1 (inspections in port) applies (which is set out in Appendix 1), may carry out a more detailed inspection in accordance with that Standard.[54]

Where the ship is registered with a non-MLC state, a relevant inspector may carry out an inspection as set out in MLC Standard A5.2.1.[55] The MLC requires ratifying states to ensure that ships registered with non-MLC states do not receive more favourable treatment than those which are registered with MLC states.[56]

Detention of ships

22.18 Where the relevant inspector has clear grounds for believing that: (a) the ship does not comply with the requirements of the MLC, and (b) (i) the conditions on board are clearly hazardous to the safety, health or security of seafarers, or (ii) the non-compliance represents a serious breach or the latest in a series of repeated breaches of the requirements of the MLC (including the rights of seafarers referred to in Articles III and IV of the MLC which are secured by it), the ship is liable to be detained.[57] A relevant inspector may permit the ship to proceed to sea for the nearest appropriate repair yard.[58] The powers set out in s 284 (enforcing detention of a ship) of the MSA 1995 apply.[59]

If a ship is detained, the MCA must immediately inform the consul or diplomatic representative of the flag state or the appropriate maritime authorities of that state, and invite them to send a representative to attend the ship.[60]

Where a ship is detained under regulation 20 but the failure to comply has ceased, a person having power to detain the ship must, at the request of the shipowner or master, immediately release the ship.[61]

54 S&C Regulations, reg 19(1).
55 S&C Regulations, reg 19(2).
56 MLC, Article V, para 7.
57 S&C Regulations, reg 20(1)(a)–(b).
58 S&C Regulations, reg 20(2).
59 S&C Regulations, reg 20(4)(a)–(b); except that reg 20(4)(c) provides that s 284(7) (regarding ships detained until a document is produced to a customs officer) will not apply.
60 S&C Regulations, reg 20(5).
61 S&C Regulations, reg 20(6).

PART VII

Implementation of Titles 1 to 5 in the Four REG Members

CHAPTER 23

Bermuda

INTRODUCTION

23.1 The Bermuda Register of Ships was set up in 1789 as a port of registry for Great Britain. In 2016 it became known as the Bermuda Shipping and Maritime Authority (BSMA), succeeding the Government Department of

Maritime Administration. The BSMA is a Category 1 Red Ensign Register, entitled to register British ships of unrestricted type or tonnage. The BSMA has an extensive passenger ship fleet, a large proportion of gas carriers and tankers, and it has expertise in container ships, bulk carriers and ro-ro ships.[1]

In Bermuda, the Merchant Shipping Act 2002[2] ('2002 Act') consolidates the Merchant Shipping Acts 1894 to 1988. The 2002 Act, like the UK's Merchant Shipping Act 1995, covers a wide range of matters, including seafarers' working and living conditions. The Merchant Shipping (ILO) Amendment Act 2012[3] ('2012 Act') amends many of the sections of the 2002 Act to implement MLC changes. In many cases, provisions are also inserted into sections which are relevant to specific areas of the MLC, empowering the Minister responsible for maritime administration to make regulations in connection with those matters. There is also a more general power for the Minister to make regulations for the purpose of making other enactments compliant with the MLC.[4]

Application

23.2 The Bermuda MLC legislation generally applies to:

- Bermuda ships wherever they may be, except: (i) fishing vessels; (ii) vessels owned and operated by a Government Department or Agency for non-commercial purposes; (iii) pleasure vessels in which no seafarers are employed; or (iv) harbour tugs operating in Bermuda waters;[5] and
- non-Bermuda ships, when in a port in Bermuda, except: (i) fishing vessels; (ii) pleasure vessels (in this case, there is no application even when seafarers are employed on such vessels); warships, naval auxiliaries and other ships owned or operated by a state and not engaged on commercial activity.[6]

The following definitions are used within the main legislative instruments:

- 'Bermuda ship' is a ship registered in Bermuda under Part IV of the Merchant Shipping Act 2002;[7]
- 'collective bargaining agreement' means a written agreement, valid for not more than five years, between a shipowner and an independent trade union which is recognised in its country of domicile;[8]

1 BSMA: www.bermudashipping.bm [Accessed 5 October 2018].
2 2002: 35.
3 2012: 30, s 1. The 2012 Act came into force on 30 June 2014 by virtue of Merchant Shipping (ILO) Amendment Act 2012 Commencement Day Notice 2014 (BR 51/2014), s 2.
4 2012 Act, s 26.
5 See, for example, Merchant Shipping (Repatriation) Regulations 2013 (BR 108/2013), reg 3(1)(a)(i)–(iv).
6 See, for example, Merchant Shipping (Repatriation) Regulations 2013, reg 3(1)(b)(i)–(iii).
7 Merchant Shipping Act 2002, ss 2(1), 16(3).
8 See, for example, Merchant Shipping (Repatriation) Regulations 2013, reg 2.

- 'commercial activity' means any activity or employment of the vessel for which a contract or charter party is in force and includes the carriage of any cargo or persons for reward;[9]
- 'independent', in relation to a trade union, means not under the influence or control of an employer, group of employers, or one or more employers' associations, and not subject to interference or control, by way of financial or material support, or by any other means, from an employer or any such group or association;[10]
- 'fishing vessel' means a vessel for the time being used, or intended to be used, for, or in connection with, fishing for sea fish other than a vessel used for fishing otherwise than for profit or a vessel for the time being used (or intended to be used) wholly for the purpose of conveying persons wishing to fish for pleasure; and for the purposes of this definition 'sea fish' includes shellfish;[11]
- 'Non-Bermuda ship' means a ship which is not registered in Bermuda;[12]
- 'pleasure vessel' is drafted in almost identical terms to that definition used by the UK, except that Bermuda does not include a reference to a 'civil partner'[13] (see Chapter 2 at para 2.4);
- 'seafarer' means any person, including a master, who is employed or engaged or works in any capacity on board a ship, on the business of the ship; and where there is doubt as to whether a person working or engaged on a ship is a seafarer [and subject to Bermuda's MLC laws], the Minister must make a determination and, in doing so, he is guided by the advice and guidance provided by the International Labour Organization;[14]
- 'shipowner' means the owner of the ship, or another organisation or person, such as a manager, agent, or bareboat charterer, who has assumed the responsibility for the operation of the ship from the owner.[15]

Some general changes

23.3 The 2002 Act is amended to replace the terms 'seaman' and 'seamen' throughout with the terms used in the MLC, namely 'seafarer' and 'seafarers'.[16]

9 See, for example, Merchant Shipping (Repatriation) Regulations 2013, reg 2.
10 See, for example, Merchant Shipping (Repatriation) Regulations 2013, reg 2.
11 Merchant Shipping Act 2002, s 2(1).
12 Merchant Shipping Act 2002, s 2(1). The Act uses the term 'foreign ship'; however, in this chapter, the term 'non-Bermuda ship' is used for the sake of consistency with the terminology in this book.
13 See, for example, Merchant Shipping (Repatriation) Regulations 2013, reg 2.
14 See, for example, Merchant Shipping (Repatriation) Regulations 2013, reg 2. See also Chapter 1 at para 1.9 regarding Resolution (VII) concerning information on occupational groups, adopted by the International Labour Conference at its 94th (Maritime) Session on 22 February 2006, Geneva.
15 See, for example, Merchant Shipping (Repatriation) Regulations 2013, reg 2.
16 2012 Act, s 3(a)–(b).

REGULATION 1.1: MINIMUM AGE

23.4 The relevant provisions are set out in the Merchant Shipping (Minimum Age at Sea and Employment of Young Persons at Sea) Regulations 2013[17] ('Minimum Age Regulations').

No person under the age of 16 is to be employed or engaged on board a ship.[18]

The following provisions apply to young persons, who are persons under 18 years of age.[19]

The master of a Bermuda ship must maintain a list showing the names and capacities of any young persons employed, the dates on which they became employed, and their dates of birth, and they must transmit a copy of that list to the BSMA, and keep the list up to date upon changes being made, and make it available to an authorised officer.[20]

Subject to the following exceptions, young persons are not permitted to work at night, which is defined as a period of nine consecutive hours, including the period between midnight and 5am local time.[21] The exceptions are: (a) when the work is part of a training course recognised by the BSMA (or Minister for Education), and when experience of night work is an essential part of that training and its effectiveness would be impaired without night work; and (b) when the specific nature of the duty or the recognised training programme requires night duties, and the BSMA is satisfied, after consultation with concerned shipowners' and seafarers' representatives, that the work will not be detrimental to the health or well-being of the young persons.[22] When a young person is permitted to work at night under any of those exceptions, they must not work alone.[23] Furthermore, young persons are not to be employed as a ship's cook, or the operator of any lifting appliance or cargo-handling equipment.[24]

Young persons are prohibited from work which is likely to jeopardise their health or safety, unless their participation is supervised and it is an essential part of a training course referred to in reg 6(2).[25] A detailed non-exhaustive list of examples is set out in reg 7(2)(a)-(j), and is summarised in Pt 1 of the Declaration of Maritime Labour Compliance (DMLC) as work involving: stoking, trimming, work in dangerous enclosed spaces, work with dangerous chemicals requiring

17 BR 104/2013.
18 2002 Act, s 67(1), as substituted by 2012 Act, s 15; Minimum Age Regulations, reg 4.
19 Minimum Age Regulations, reg 2.
20 Minimum Age Regulations, reg 5.
21 Minimum Age Regulations, regs 2, 6(1).
22 Minimum Age Regulations, reg 6(2)(a)–(b).
23 Minimum Age Regulations, reg 6(3).
24 Minimum Age Regulations, reg 6(4)(a)–(b).
25 Minimum Age Regulations, reg 7(1)–(4).

special protective equipment, operators of lifting equipment, and work in breathing apparatus.[26]

Young persons are not to be employed on a Bermuda ship unless they hold a valid certificate of medical fitness ('young person's medical certificate') in accordance with the Merchant Shipping (Medical Certification of Seafarers) Regulations 2013.[27]

Non-compliances amount to criminal offences by the shipowner and/or master, which are punishable with a fine not exceeding $10,000.[28] It is a defence for the person charged to show that they took all reasonable precautions and exercised due diligence to avoid the commission of the offence.[29]

There is power for an authorised person to inspect non-Bermuda ships in Bermuda ports who, if satisfied that the arrangements for young persons are not in accordance with that ship's DMLC Pt I or, in respect of a ship which does not carry a Maritime Labour Certificate (MLCert), the requirements of Regulation 1.1 of the MLC, the inspector may detain the ship until the deficiency is rectified.[30]

If the BSMA discovers that a Bermuda ship does not comply with the Minimum Age Regulations, it may: (a) withdraw the MLCert until the deficiency is rectified; or (b) if the vessel is in a port outside Bermuda, inform the port state authority of that port of the deficiency.[31]

Compliance

23.5 DMLC: implement Bermuda requirements as set out in Pt I, point 1, and record details of compliance measures in DMLC, Pt II, point 1.

REGULATION 1.2: MEDICAL CERTIFICATE

23.6 The Minister is empowered to make regulations specifying the standards of medical fitness for seafarers, to give effect to the requirements of Regulation 1.2 of the MLC.[32] The detail is set out in the Merchant Shipping (Medical Certification of Seafarers) Regulations 2013,[33] ('Medical Certification Regulations').

26 DMLC Pt 1, (1) Minimum age.
27 Minimum Age Regulations, reg 7A, inserted by BR 52/2014, reg 2.
28 Minimum Age Regulations, reg 8(1)–(2); reg 8(2) was amended by BR 52/2014, reg 3.
29 Minimum Age Regulations, reg 8(3).
30 Minimum Age Regulations, reg 9(1).
31 Minimum Age Regulations, reg 9(2)(a)–(b).
32 2002 Act, s 59(1)(c), as inserted by 2012 Act, s 13(c).
33 BR 122/2013.

The shipowner and master must ensure that a seafarer has a valid medical fitness certificate before and on (respectively) commencing work on board.[34] An extension of up to three months applies if the certificate expires during the course of employment.[35] The certificate will cease to be valid if the seafarer works in a capacity or geographical area precluded by any stated restriction.[36]

The certificate is valid for one year in respect of seafarers under the age of 18, and two years for seafarers over that age.[37] The certification for colour vision is valid for a maximum period of six years. The certificate must be written in English but may contain a translation in the language of the issuing country.[38] A model certificate is set out in the Schedule to the Regulations.[39]

There are provisions setting out classes of approved doctors, which include those in the UK authorised to issue an ENG 1 medical certificate.[40] Bermuda Shipping Notice 2012-007[41] sets out a list of countries whose certificates are accepted and provides that certificates issued by company medical departments authorised by the BSMA or the UK's MCA are acceptable. Examinations must follow the Guidelines on the medical examination of seafarers, jointly published by the ILO and the IMO,[42] and STCW standards apply.[43]

The certificate must attest to: (a) satisfactory hearing and eyesight; (b) the colour vision of seafarers employed in navigational and engineering watchkeeping roles; and (c) the seafarer not suffering from any medical condition likely to be aggravated by service at sea or to render the seafarer unfit for such service or to endanger the health of other persons on board; furthermore the certificate must state the minimum information set out in section A-I/9 of the STCW Convention.[44]

Further provision is made for the suspension and cancellation of certificates,[45] and review of an examining doctor's refusal to issue a certificate, impose a restriction, or suspend it for more than three months.[46]

34 Medical Certification Regulations, reg 4(1)–(2); for young persons, Minimum Age Regulations, reg 7A.
35 Medical Certification Regulations, reg 4(3).
36 Medical Certification Regulations, reg 4(4).
37 Medical Certification Regulations, regs 5(1)(a)–(b), 6(4)(a)–(b).
38 Medical Certification Regulations, reg 5(2).
39 Medical Certification Regulations, reg 7(1), Sch.
40 Medical Certification Regulations, reg 6(1)(a)–(c).
41 BSN 2012-007: Countries whose Seafarer Medical Certificates are accepted for service in Bermuda ships.
42 Guidelines on the medical examination of seafarers, 2013, published by the ILO and the IMO: www.ilo.org/wcmsp5/groups/public/---ed_dialogue/---sector/documents/normativeinstrument/wcms_174794.pdf [Accessed 1 March 2018].
43 Medical Certification Regulations, reg 7(1)–(2).
44 Medical Certification Regulations, reg 6(2)(a)–(c), (3).
45 Medical Certification Regulations, reg 7A(1)–(4).
46 Medical Certification Regulations, regs 7B–8.

Offences apply for non-compliances by the shipowner and master, as well as any seafarer who falsifies a certificate or is otherwise dishonest in connection with the application process; fines on summary conviction may not exceed $10,000 in respect of the shipowner, and $5,000 in respect of the master or seafarer.[47] It is a defence for the person charged to show that they took all reasonable precautions and exercised due diligence to avoid the commission of the offence.[48]

There are powers of inspection, enforcement and detention (for non-compliances).[49]

For further information, see Bermuda Shipping Notice 2012-007 – Medical Certification Requirements.

Compliance

23.7 DMLC: implement Bermuda requirements as set out in Pt I, point 2, and record details of compliance measures in DMLC, Pt II, point 2.

REGULATION 1.3: TRAINING AND QUALIFICATION

23.8 The Merchant Shipping Act 2002 empowers the Minister to make regulations specifying standards of competence on Bermuda ships.[50] The relevant provisions are set out in Pt I of the Merchant Shipping (Training, Certification, Manning and Watchkeeping) Regulations 2005[51] ('the TCMW Regulations').

Although Bermuda is subject to the STCW Convention through extension by the UK, it does not issue its own certificates of competency ('CoCs'). The approach it adopts is to accept a CoC issued by the UK MCA (on which, see Chapter 5), or by endorsing CoCs issued by certain countries and issuing a certificate of equivalent competency (CeC) to the holder.

A person will be qualified as an officer in the capacity of master, chief mate, officer in charge of a navigational watch, chief engineer officer, second engineer officer, officer in charge of an engineering watch, or radio operator, if they hold for such capacity: (a) a CoC issued by the BSMA (however, as stated above, the BSMA does not currently issue CoCs); (b) a CoC issued by the UK MCA (which is acceptable without requiring endorsement by the BSMA);[52] or (c) a

47 Medical Examination Regulations, reg 9(1)–(3).
48 Medical Examination Regulations, reg 9(4).
49 Medical Examination Regulations, reg 10(1)–(2)(a)–(b).
50 2002 Act, s 59(1)(b).
51 BR 44/2005.
52 TCMW Regulations, reg 7(2).

CoC issued by a signatory state to the STCW Convention which is on the IMO white list, so long as the BSMA issues an endorsement in respect of it.[53]

The procedure for applying for a BSMA endorsement and the list of countries whose CoCs are acceptable are set out in BSN 2016-015.[54] The application must be made by the shipowner or ship operator (not the seafarer); evidence of the application kept on board will be acceptable for a maximum period of three months whilst awaiting the endorsement.[55]

Other provisions include: ratings forming part of a navigational watch or engineering watch (except those under training or performing unskilled duties) must be certified in accordance with Regulations II/4.2 or III/4.2 of the Annex to the STCW Convention respectively (by any STCW state and without the need for a Bermuda endorsement);[56] however, a person performing duties in a manned or periodically unmanned engine room on a ship powered by main propulsion machinery of 350KW–750KW must hold a Bermuda endorsement or an acceptable maritime operator's licence;[57] a GMDSS[58] radio operator must be at least 18 years old and must hold a CoC from the UK MCA or IMO white list country (in the latter case, it must be accompanied by a Bermuda endorsement);[59] mandatory minimum training and qualifications for masters, officers and ratings on tankers,[60] ro-ro passenger ships,[61] and other passenger ships;[62] basic safety training;[63] and familiarisation training in accordance with section A-VI/1 of the STCW Convention. Specific requirement apply to commercial and privately operated large commercial yachts (those which are 24 metres and over in length).[64]

Further requirements apply for those concerned with: high-speed craft,[65] survival craft, rescue boats and fast rescue boats;[66] advanced firefighting;[67] and medical first aid and medical care.[68]

In terms of enforcement, there are powers of inspection and detention.[69]

53 TCMW Regulations, regs 4–5, 7, Sch 1.
54 BSN 2016-015: Officer certification and issue of endorsements.
55 BSN 2016-015; Statement of Receipt of Application for a Bermuda Endorsement (citing STCW Convention, Regulation I/10.5).
56 TCMW Regulations, reg 8(1)–(2).
57 TCMW Regulations, reg 8(3).
58 GMDSS is the Global Maritime Distress and Safety System.
59 TCMW Regulations, reg 9(a)–(c).
60 TCMW Regulations, reg 10.
61 TCMW Regulations, reg 11.
62 TCMW Regulations, reg 12.
63 TCMW Regulations, reg 16.
64 TCMW Regulations, regs 14–15, Schs 2–3.
65 TCMW Regulations, reg 13.
66 TCMW Regulations, reg 17.
67 TCMW Regulations, reg 18.
68 TCMW Regulations, reg 19.
69 TCMW Regulations, regs 34–35 respectively.

Compliance

23.9 DMLC: implement Bermuda requirements as set out in Pt I, point 3, and record details of compliance measures in DMLC, Pt II, point 3.

REGULATION 1.4: RECRUITMENT AND PLACEMENT

23.10 The only MLC implementing provision is that shipowners are prohibited from using recruitment and placement services which are based in a country which has not ratified the MLC.[70] However, even so, the BSMA has indicated that it permits shipowners to recruit from seafarer recruitment and placement services based in non-MLC states on condition that they ensure, as far as practicable, that they meet the standards set out in Standard A1.4 of the MLC.[71]

Bermuda is not a seafarer-supplying territory, and this probably accounts for the limited implementation measures under Regulation 1.4 of the MLC.

Compliance

23.11 DMLC: implement Bermuda requirements as set out in Pt I, point 5, and record details of compliance measures in DMLC, Pt II, point 5 (noting which country any recruitment and placement service used is situated in – which should be an MLC state).

REGULATION 2.1: SEAFARERS' EMPLOYMENT AGREEMENTS

23.12 A seafarer employment agreement ('SEA') is to be made between every seafarer and the shipowner or their authorised representative, and must be signed by the seafarer and the shipowner or their authorised representative.[72] The detail is set out in the Merchant Shipping (Seafarer's Employment) Regulations 2013[73] ('Employment Regulations').

Issue of SEA

23.13 The shipowner is to ensure that every seafarer has a written SEA, which complies with the Employment Regulations, and which may be: (a) for a single voyage; (b) for a determinate period covering more than one voyage; or (c) continuous for an indeterminate period covering multiple voyages.[74] A 'voyage'

70 Merchant Shipping (Seafarer's Employment) Regulations 2013 (BR 107/2013), reg 18.
71 And this is indeed permitted by MLC, Standard A1.4.9.
72 2002 Act, s 38, as substituted by 2012 Act, ss 6–7.
73 BR 107/2013.
74 Employment Regulations, reg 4(a)–(c), respectively.

means the time beginning when a seafarer starts work on board a ship until the time when (a) their SEA is terminated, or (b) the seafarer goes on leave.[75]

Seafarers must be given a copy of their SEA in advance, so that they have an opportunity to examine it and, if necessary, seek advice before signing it.[76]

Each seafarer must (a) carry a copy of the signed original SEA, or (b) have access to an electronic copy of it.[77] The SEA must make reference to any other applicable terms of employment or collective bargaining agreement ('CBA') which become incorporated into the SEA, and those documents must also be available on board to seafarers (if not in English, then an English translation must be available covering most of the areas covered by the MLC).[78]

Duration of SEA

23.14 The maximum length of a single-voyage SEA is nine months, and it must state the expected voyage commencement and SEA termination dates; however, once the seafarer has been repatriated, the SEA may be terminated by either party one month before or after the stated termination date, if the nature of the voyage places an unnecessary burden on the shipowner to terminate the SEA on the termination date stated therein.[79] A SEA for a determinate or indeterminate period must state the maximum time of any voyage that the seafarer is expected to undertake, which is not to exceed six months, provided that, where it is not readily possible for the shipowner to repatriate the seafarer at the end of the stated period, the voyage period may be extended by up to one month.[80]

Termination of SEA

23.15 Every SEA must state the conditions for early termination by either party. The minimum notice periods are: seven days in respect of a single-voyage SEA, and in respect of a first voyage under a determinate or continuous SEA; and one calendar month for subsequent voyages under a determinate or continuous SEA.[81] Furthermore, every SEA must specify the circumstances (set out in reg 11) in which the SEA may be terminated by mutual consent and without penalty by giving shorter notice or without notice, unless these matters are set out in an applicable CBA.[82] Such circumstances include: death or serious injury

75 Employment Regulations, reg 2(1)(a)–(b).
76 Employment Regulations, reg 17.
77 Employment Regulations, reg 8(1)(a)–(b).
78 Employment Regulations, regs 8(2), 9(1)–(2)(a)–(m).
79 Employment Regulations, reg 5(1)–(2).
80 Employment Regulations, reg 5(3).
81 Employment Regulations, reg 10(1)–(2)(a)–(c).
82 Employment Regulations, reg 10(3).

of specified close relatives; detention of the ship for breaches of international conventions; and where the ship is lost, sold, or heading for a warlike zone to which the seafarer does not consent to go.[83]

A shipowner may terminate a SEA without notice if it is established, through an agreed disciplinary process, that the seafarer has been involved in any of the following matters:

(a) smuggling;

(b) possession of narcotics, explosives, weapons or similar items;

(c) desertion;

(d) assault on a passenger or another seafarer;

(e) inability of the seafarer to perform his duties on board through misuse of alcohol or drugs;

(f) failure of a drugs test;

(g) theft, or wilful damage to the ship or its equipment;

(h) smoking in an area where smoking is prohibited;

(i) failure to comply with a public health requirement;

(j) the provision of any assistance to stowaways, or other persons attempting to breach the ship's security arrangements;

(k) a refusal of the seafarer to obey a lawful order, provided that a refusal to sail must not be serious misconduct where the circumstances in regulation 11(3)(a)[84] or 11(3)(b)[85] apply; or

(l) the seafarer is unable to perform their duties through incompetence.[86]

The shipowner may include additional matters that are to be regarded as serious misconduct, but they must be specified in the SEA (or a connected document, such as a CBA) and in the approved DMLC, Pt II.[87]

When a SEA is terminated in accordance with the Employment Regulations, the seafarer will not be entitled to the compensatory wages under regulation 10 (notice periods) and may be liable to the costs of repatriation in accordance with the Merchant Shipping (Repatriation) Regulations 2013 and the Merchant Shipping (Seafarer's Wages) Regulations 2013.[88]

83 Employment Regulations, reg 11.

84 When the ship is detained for a period of 30 days for non-compliance with any of the provisions of the International Convention for the Safety of Life at Sea 1974 (SOLAS), the International Convention on Load Lines 1966, the STCW Convention, the International Convention for the Prevention of Pollution from Ships 1973 (MARPOL), or the MLC.

85 When the ship remains under arrest for a period of 30 days.

86 Employment Regulations, reg 12(1)(a)-(l).

87 Employment Regulations, reg 12(2).

88 Employment Regulations, reg 12(3).

Content of SEA

23.16 The SEA must be written in English and contain all the matters specified below:[89]

‘(a) seafarer’s full name, date of birth or age, and nationality;

(b) shipowner’s name and address;

(c) place where the seafarer’s employment agreement is entered into and the date on which it is entered into;

(d) capacity in which the seafarer is to be employed;[90]

(e) amount of wages to be paid under the agreement and, where overtime is separate from basic pay, the rate for overtime payments;[91]

(f) amount of annual leave, or paid leave due under the employment agreement or the method to be used to calculate it;[92]

(g) hours of work to be undertaken by the seafarer;[93]

(h) in the case of a single voyage, agreement on the intended port of destination where this is known and the date on which the agreement is to terminate;

(i) in the case of an agreement for a determinate time, the date on which it is agreed the agreement will terminate;

(j) the conditions under which either party may terminate the agreement and the required notice period which shall be not less than that specified in regulation 9;[94] or

(k) where a separate set of terms and conditions or a collective bargaining agreement form part of the employment agreement a reference to the fact that those terms and conditions or collective bargaining agreement are to be read as forming part of the employment agreement;

(l) the health and social security protection benefits to be provided to the seafarer by the shipowner;[95] and

(m) details of the seafarer’s right to repatriation.’[96]

Other requirements

23.17 Other provisions include: seafarers to be given a record of their employment on leaving the ship (without reference to the quality of their work or

89 Employment Regulations, reg 13(1)–(3).
90 See Regulation 1.3; seafarers should be trained and certified accordingly.
91 See Regulation 2.2.
92 See Regulation 2.4.
93 See Regulation 2.3.
94 The reference to ‘regulation 9’ appears to be a drafting error, as the provisions on notice periods are set out in reg 10.
95 See Regulations 4.1–4.2.
96 See Regulation 2.5.

wages earned);[97] and the maintenance of a crew list (which may be in electronic form if also duplicated ashore), to be kept for at least three years following the departure of the last seafarer entered thereon.[98]

Future amendments to the MLC

23.18 When the 2018 amendments to the MLC come into force (which is likely to be 26 December 2020), ratifying states will be required to provide that: (a) SEAs continue for the entirety of any period in which a seafarer is held in captivity as a result of an act of piracy or armed robbery at sea; and (b) seafarers' wages, allotments and other entitlements must be fully paid during the entirety of any such period. The full text of the amendments is set out in Appendix 2.

Compliance

23.19 DMLC: implement Bermuda requirements as set out in Pt I, point 4, and record details of compliance measures in DMLC, Pt II, point 4.

REGULATION 2.2: WAGES

23.20 The provisions on the payment of wages, deductions, overtime, etc, are set out in the Merchant Shipping (Seafarers' Wages) Regulations 2013[99] ('Wages Regulations').

Every seafarer must be paid regularly, in full, in accordance with the terms of their SEA, at intervals that do not exceed one month, and be provided with a statement of monthly payments due and amounts paid, and showing additions and deductions.[100] If payment is made in a currency other than that agreed in the SEA, or at a different exchange rate than that agreed in the SEA, the applied exchange rate must be stated.[101]

Where the SEA includes separate compensation for overtime worked, the normal hours of work must be (a) eight hours per day, and (b) a maximum of 48 hours per week (unless, in the latter case, a CBA provides differently); and the overtime rate is to be that specified in any CBA but must be at least 1.25 times the basic rate.[102]

Where the SEA provides a consolidated or partially consolidated wage, it must specify the number of hours of work that are expected for the agreed

97 Employment Regulations, reg 6(1)–(3).
98 Employment Regulations, reg 7(1)–(3).
99 BR 105/2013.
100 2002 Act, s 39(1), as substituted by 2012 Act, ss 6–7; Wages Regulations, reg 4(1)–(2).
101 Wages Regulations, reg 4(2).
102 Wages Regulations, reg 4(3)(a)–(c).

remuneration and any additional allowances that may become due in particular circumstances.[103]

A 'consolidated wage' means a salary or a wage that includes: (a) basic pay; and (b) all other pay-related benefits (including overtime pay).[104] A 'partially consolidated wage' means a salary or a wage that includes the basic pay and some, but not all, of any additional pay-related benefits.[105] 'Basic pay' means the wages, however composed, paid for normal hours of work and does not include payments for overtime worked, bonuses, allowances, paid leave, or any other additional remuneration.[106]

Any overtime applicable to a partially consolidated wage must be at least 1.25 times the basic rate.[107] Wages are normally to be paid by bank transfer to the seafarer's nominated account or similar arrangement; no deduction is to be made for any cost of the transfer.[108] Exceptionally, where it is not practicable to pay by bank transfer, payment may be made by bank cheque or money order.[109]

The master (or authorised person) must keep monthly records of overtime (in paper or electronic format), which must be endorsed as a true copy by the seafarer and be available to a Bermuda surveyor or auditor.[110] The seafarer must be given a copy of any paper records, or access to electronic records and has a right to obtain paper copies on request.[111]

At the end of a seafarer's employment, all outstanding wages must be paid, at the latest, by the end of the month in which the seafarer leaves the ship.[112] If the balance is not so paid (and the SEA or any CBA does not provide for payment of wages during the seafarer's leave), a serious penalty is imposed, in that the seafarer will be entitled to an additional payment of wages, at the SEA rate, for each day the balance remains outstanding, for up to 56 days; and, after that point, the outstanding balance will be subject to interest at 20% until paid.[113] This penalty does not apply where the failure to pay outstanding wages is due to: (a) mistake; (b) delay due to a reasonable dispute; (c) an act or default by the seafarer; or (d) any other cause not being the act or default of the person liable to pay the wages.[114]

Seafarers must be given the opportunity to transmit by bank transfer a proportion or fixed amount of their wages (known as an 'allotment') to nominated persons,

103 Wages Regulations, reg 4(4).
104 Wages Regulations, reg 2; 'consolidated wage' inserted by BR 56/2014, reg 3.
105 Wages Regulations, reg 2.
106 Wages Regulations, reg 2.
107 Wages Regulations, reg 4(5).
108 Wages Regulations, reg 4(6).
109 Wages Regulations, reg 4(7).
110 Wages Regulations, reg 5(1)–(2), (4).
111 Wages Regulations, reg 5(3)(a)–(b).
112 Wages Regulations, reg 6(1).
113 Wages Regulations, reg 6(2).
114 Wages Regulations, reg 6(3)(a)–(d).

and the allotment must state the frequency of such payments which should be no more frequently than monthly.[115] The 'proportion' may be all of the monthly amount due, less any deductions that are reasonably anticipated.[116] In operating such an arrangement: any charge imposed by the shipowner must be reasonable; if the wages are in a different currency than that of the transferee's account, the exchange rate must be set at the official published rate; and details of the transmission must be shown on the monthly account of wages.[117]

The only permissible deductions are those set out in a CBA and: statutory deductions for tax, social security, national insurance, court orders, and the statutory deductions required by the seafarer's country of domicile; telephone calls; necessities purchased; cash advances; contributions to a pension or saving scheme; allotments; repatriation where the seafarer has been dismissed for serious misconduct; and, subject to a limit of one month's wages, expense or loss incurred by the shipowner due to the seafarer's misconduct.[118]

In respect of non-compliances, there are criminal offences punishable by fines,[119] and powers to inspect and detain ships, and to withdraw the Maritime Labour Certificate.[120]

Future amendments to the MLC

23.21 See paragraph 23.18 above regarding the 2018 amendments to the MLC, which are likely to come into force on 26 December 2020.

Compliance

23.22 DMLC: implement Bermuda requirements as set out in Pt I, point 14, and record details of compliance measures in DMLC, Pt II, point 14.

REGULATION 2.3: HOURS OF WORK AND HOURS OF REST

23.23 The relevant provisions are contained in the Merchant Shipping (Hours of Rest) Regulations 2011[121] ('Hours of Rest Regulations').

The following definitions apply: 'hours of rest' means time outside hours of work and does not include short breaks from work;[122] 'hours of work' means time

115 Wages Regulations, reg 7(1)–(2)(a)–(c).
116 Wages Regulations, reg 7(2)(c); MLC, Standard A2.2, para 3.
117 Wages Regulations, reg 7(3)(a)–(c).
118 Wages Regulations, reg 8(1)–(4).
119 Wages Regulations, reg 8A(1)–(2), inserted by BR 56/2014, reg 4.
120 Wages Regulations, reg 9(1)–(2); reg 9(1) was amended by BR 56/2014, reg 5.
121 BR 51/2011, amended by BR 120/2013.
122 Hours of Rest Regulations, reg 2.

during which the seafarer is required to do work on the business of the ship;[123] 'on call' means time when a seafarer is available on board the vessel and nominated to answer any alarm or other call but not otherwise required to be working.[124]

The shipowner and master must ensure that each seafarer is provided with at least the minimum hours of rest as follows: (a) not less than 10 hours in any 24-hour period; (b) not less than 77 hours in any seven-day period.[125] Hours of rest may be divided into no more than two periods, one of which must be of six hours' duration, and the interval between the two periods must not exceed 14 hours.[126] The Minister responsible for maritime administration may authorise a CBA permitting exceptions to reg 4, provided that reg 4 is followed so far as possible.[127]

In addition to ensuring the observance of the minimum hours of rest, the master must ensure that every watchkeeping officer has sufficient rest before commencing each watch.[128]

Time spent on call is not to be counted as working time; however, a seafarer who is on call and who is required to answer call outs is entitled to a compensatory rest period, commensurate with the number of times they have been called out.[129] Musters, fire-fighting and lifeboat drills should be conducted in a way that minimises disturbance of rest periods, and compensatory rest should be granted to seafarers whose normal rest is disturbed.[130] The master may require any seafarer (who cannot unreasonably refuse) to work any hours that are necessary for the immediate safety of the ship, persons on board, or for giving assistance to another ship in distress; following restoration of normality, an adequate compensatory rest period should be provided to any seafarer who has not had the rest periods defined in reg 4.[131]

The master is to ensure that a table of scheduled hours of work at sea and in port is created (in English) and made available to seafarers, any port state authority officer or Bermuda surveyor; it must show the minimum hours of rest required under the Hours of Rest Regulations or any approved CBA.[132] A contravention will amount to an offence by the master, punishable on summary conviction to a fine not exceeding $5,000.[133]

The master (or authorised person) is to maintain monthly records of each seafarer's hours of work and rest in English, showing the daily and weekly totals

123 Hours of Rest Regulations, reg 2.
124 Hours of Rest Regulations, reg 2.
125 Hours of Rest Regulations, reg 4(1)–(2)(a)–(b).
126 Hours of Rest Regulations, reg 4(3).
127 Hours of Rest Regulations, reg 6(3).
128 Hours of Rest Regulations, reg 5.
129 Hours of Rest Regulations, reg 6(1).
130 Hours of Rest Regulations, reg 6(2)(a)–(c), as substituted by BR 120/2013, reg 2.
131 Hours of Rest Regulations, reg 8(1)–(2).
132 Hours of Rest Regulations, reg 7(1)–(3).
133 Hours of Rest Regulations, reg 10(1).

of hours of rest; there must be a note, in respect of any day in which the hours of rest were less than the minimum.[134] The record must be in the format set out in a Bermuda Shipping Notice (the current one is 2011-002, Annex 1),[135] or commercially produced (in a format prepared by the ILO), and may be kept electronically, provided that all seafarers have access to their own records at any reasonable time during working hours.[136] Each record is to be endorsed at the end of each month by the master (or authorised person) and the seafarer, and seafarers are to be given a copy or, alternatively, access to their records.[137] Steps must be taken by the master to remedy any persistent deviations from the minimum hours of rest, by amending the table of scheduled hours of work (made under reg 7).[138] A contravention will amount to an offence by the master, punishable on summary conviction to a fine not exceeding $5,000.[139]

An authorised inspector may inspect a Bermuda or non-Bermuda ship in a port in Bermuda to ensure that the minimum hours of rest specified in Regulation 2.3 of the MLC are being observed and, if they are not, may detain the ship.[140] Any authorised officer who discovers that a Bermuda ship does not comply with the Hours of Rest Regulations may: (a) withdraw the Maritime Labour Certificate until the deficiency is rectified; or (b) if the ship is outside Bermuda, report the deficiency to the port state authority in that port.[141]

Compliance

23.24 DMLC: implement Bermuda requirements as set out in Pt I, point 6, and record details of compliance measures in DMLC, Pt II, point 6.

REGULATION 2.4: ENTITLEMENT TO LEAVE

23.25 The relevant provision are mainly set out in the Employment Regulations.

Every seafarer is entitled to two and a half days' paid leave for every calendar month of service, and pro-rata for an incomplete month, where an incomplete day of service is to be treated as a whole day.[142] Where there is no CBA, seafarers are entitled to an additional one and a half days' per month of paid leave, to take account of public holidays.[143] Where there is a CBA, any additional leave will be in accordance with its terms.

134 Hours of Rest Regulations, reg 9(1)(a)–(e).
135 Bermuda Shipping Notice 2011-002 – Hours of Rest Requirements.
136 Hours of Rest Regulations, reg 9(2)–(3).
137 Hours of Rest Regulations, reg 9(4).
138 Hours of Rest Regulations, reg 9(5).
139 Hours of Rest Regulations, reg 10(2).
140 Hours of Rest Regulations, reg 11(1).
141 Hours of Rest Regulations, reg 11(2)(a)–(b).
142 Employment Regulations, reg 14(1)–(2).
143 Employment Regulations, reg 14(3).

Leave may be taken in instalments, but is not to be replaced by a payment in lieu, except where the seafarer's employment is terminated.[144] Temporary shore leave is to be granted to seafarers whenever practicable, but is not to be counted as paid leave.[145] Furthermore, absences from work due to any of the following reasons are not to be counted as leave: attending a maritime training course with the shipowner's agreement; illness; maternity; or injury.[146]

Compliance

23.26 Seafarers' entitlement to annual leave does not have a specific entry in the DMLC; however, it must be entered in their SEA.[147]

REGULATION 2.5: REPATRIATION

23.27 The Merchant Shipping (Repatriation) Regulations 2013[148] ('Repatriation Regulations'), which are made under a power in s 84(2) of the 2002 Act, set out the detail of repatriation obligations and rights.

Right to repatriation

23.28 A seafarer is entitled to repatriation when their SEA ends in a place outside their repatriation destination.[149] Additionally, the right to repatriation arises where:

(a) the seafarer gives notice in accordance with their SEA when the ship has ceased to hold valid safety certificates as required by SOLAS or the Loadline Convention, or is arrested and remains so for a period of 30 days;

(b) the seafarer's SEA is terminated on the loss or sale of the ship, or its change in registration;

(c) the shipowner is no longer able to fulfil his legal or contractual obligations to the seafarer as a consequence of insolvency, sale of the ship, change in registry or similar cause;

(d) the seafarer is unable, as a result of illness or injury arising from their work on board the ship, to continue to perform their duties on board; or

(e) the SEA is terminated by the seafarer, after giving notice in accordance with its terms, in the event that the ship is bound for a war zone to which the seafarer does not consent to go.[150]

144 Employment Regulations, reg 14(4).
145 Employment Regulations, reg 14(5).
146 Employment Regulations, reg 14(6).
147 Employment Regulations, reg 13(2)(f).
148 BR 108/2013.
149 Repatriation Regulations, reg 5(1).
150 Repatriation Regulations, reg 5(2)(a)–(e), as amended by BR 54/2014, reg 3.

Subject to the following exception, a shipowner is prohibited from requiring a seafarer to make a contribution towards their repatriation before, during or after their employment.[151] A shipowner may make a deduction towards the costs of repatriation from the seafarer's wages if the seafarer is justifiably dismissed for serious misconduct, as defined in the Employment Regulations [152] (set out in paragraph 23.15 above). The obligation to repatriate expires, in respect of any seafarer, three months after the obligation arose unless, before the end of that period, the shipowner became subject to an obligation imposed by Regulations made under s 84 of the 2002 Act towards the seafarer.[153] As the Repatriation Regulations are made under s 84, the three-month period would be extended if the shipowner was already subject to any other obligation (beyond the right to repatriation) imposed under those Regulations.

If the shipowner of a Bermuda ship fails in its repatriation duties, the Minister must make the necessary arrangements, and is entitled to recover costs (including those of the port state or home state of the seafarer which has arranged the repatriation) from the shipowner.[154] The Minister may request the arrest of any or all of the shipowners' ships until reimbursement is made.[155] If the owner of a non-Bermuda ship fails in its repatriation duties while the ship is in Bermuda waters, the Minister must arrange for the seafarer's repatriation and may recover the costs from the flag state of the ship.[156]

Repatriation destination

23.29 The repatriation destination means: (a) the place the seafarer entered their SEA; (b) a place stipulated in an applicable CBA; (c) the seafarer's country of residence; or (d) a place which is mutually agreed between the seafarer and the employer at the time of entering the SEA.[157]

Liabilities of shipowner in connection with repatriation

23.30 The costs which the shipowner must meet in connection with repatriation are as follows:

(a) passage by air from the place where the SEA is terminated (or from the nearest airport);

(b) any necessary accommodation and food from the time a seafarer leaves the ship until the time they start travelling on the transport for repatriation arranged by the shipowner;

151 2002 Act, s 84, as substituted by 2012 Act, s 21; Repatriation Regulations, reg 7(1).
152 Repatriation Regulations, reg 7(4); Employment Regulations, reg 12(3); Wages Regulations, reg 8(3)(g).
153 2002 Act, s 85, as amended by 2012 Act, s 3; Repatriation Regulations, reg 5(3).
154 Repatriation Regulations, reg 8(1).
155 Repatriation Regulations, reg 8(2), as amended by BR 54/2014, reg 4.
156 Repatriation Regulations, reg 8(3), as inserted by BR 54/2014, reg 4.
157 Repatriation Regulations, reg 2.

(c) the seafarer's pay and allowances in accordance with their SEA or CBA until they reach their repatriation destination, except to the extent that this goes beyond the minimum period set by the shipowner; time spent waiting for repatriation must not be deducted from paid leave periods earned in accordance with the SEA;

(d) transport of up to 30kg of personal baggage from the ship to the repatriation destination; and

(e) in the case of a seafarer whose SEA is terminated through injury or illness, medical treatment when necessary until the seafarer is medically fit to travel.[158]

As regards sub-paragraph (e) above, it is not clear why Bermuda makes such treatment contingent on the SEA being 'terminated' as, under the MLC, a sick or injured seafarer would be entitled to such treatment whether or not the SEA had been terminated.[159]

See also the 2014 MLC amendments on financial security (referred to in para 23.31 below), which set out further rights and liabilities in this area in connection with seafarers who have been abandoned.

Requirement to carry evidence of financial security

23.31 The MLC provisions on financial security for repatriation (and for shipowners' liability) were the first Parts of the MLC to be amended. Before the amendments, the MLC already required ratifying states to ensure that their ships carried financial security for repatriation.[160] The amendments came into force on 18 January 2017[161] and introduce much more detailed requirements for the financial security system, as well as further rights for seafarers and liabilities for shipowners. To meet the pre-amendment requirements, Bermuda provided that shipowners must provide financial security to cover the costs of repatriation, which may be a policy of insurance or other arrangements; evidence of such cover must be carried on board, which may be a copy of an insurance policy or other certification,[162] and this requirement remains in force. In most cases, the financial security will be provided by the P&I Club, although there are also other commercial organisations offering such cover.

Bermuda has not yet brought into force any new laws to implement the amendments. For the time being, it has issued BMGN 2017-01 – Guidance on

158 Repatriation Regulations, reg 6(1)(a)–(e), respectively.

159 MLC, Standard A4.2.1, para 1(a), (c); and more recently under the MLC amendments in connection with 'abandoned' seafarers who need medical treatment, MLC, Standard A2.5.2.9(c).

160 MLC, Regulation 2.5, para 2.

161 Amendments to the Code implementing Regulation 2.5 – Repatriation of the MLC, 2006 (and appendices): www.ilo.org/wcmsp5/groups/public/---ed_norm/---relconf/documents/meetingdocument/wcms_248905.pdf [Accessed 18 March 2018].

162 Repatriation Regulations, reg 4.

implementation of 2014 Amendments to MLC 2006 on Bermuda Ships, which should be followed. Bermuda shipowners must comply with the requirements of the 2014 amendments themselves,[163] which are set out in Appendix 2, until the specific national provisions come into force. It should be noted that, under the amendments, a copy of the financial security certificate (or other documentary evidence) must be displayed in a conspicuous place on board the ship where it is available to seafarers.[164]

The UK has already implemented the amendments into law (see Chapter 11 at paras 11.9–11.11), which closely follow the MLC amendments and may be indicative of the approach that Bermuda will take.

Other provisions

23.32 The shipowner must ensure that information on the entitlement to repatriation under the Repatriation Regulations is available to every seafarer on board the ship.[165]

If a seafarer dies in the course of their employment on board a ship, or leaves a ship due to injury or illness, the master must arrange for the property belonging to that seafarer to be collected and for a full list of the property to be prepared, which should be signed by the master and another seafarer.[166] In the case of a deceased seafarer, the property and a copy of the signed list should be returned to the seafarer's next of kin (unless the property is perishable, illegal or prohibited).[167] In the case of a sick or injured seafarer, the master should (as appropriate in the circumstances): (a) retain the property on board until the seafarer returns; (b) deliver the property to the seafarer's accommodation ashore; or (c) deliver the property to the seafarer's country of domicile.[168]

Criminal offences exist for specified non-compliances by the shipowner and master, punishable on summary conviction by fines not exceeding $10,000 and $3,000, respectively.[169]

There is a power of inspection when any ship to which the Repatriation Regulations apply is in a Bermuda port, and to detain the ship if the inspector is satisfied that its repatriation arrangements are not in accordance with the ship's DMLC, Part I or, where the ship does not carry a Maritime Labour Certificate, it does not comply with Regulation 2.5 of the MLC.[170] Any authorised officer of the

163 BMGN 2017-01, conclusion, para 4(a)–(b).
164 MLC, Standard A2.5.2.6.
165 Repatriation Regulations, reg 9.
166 Employment Regulations, reg 19(1)–(2).
167 Employment Regulations, reg 2(3).
168 Employment Regulations, reg 19(4)(a)–(c), respectively.
169 Repatriation Regulations, reg 9A(1)–(2), as inserted by BR 54/2014, reg 5.
170 Repatriation Regulations, reg 10(1). Note that the text of reg 10(1) refers to 'Regulation 2.3' which, it is submitted, must be a drafting error, and should refer to 'Regulation 2.5'.

BSMA who discovers that a Bermuda ship does not comply with the Repatriation Regulations may: withdraw the vessel's Maritime Labour Certificate until such time as the deficiency is rectified; or, if the vessel is in a port outside Bermuda, report the deficiency to the port state authority in that port.[171]

Compliance

23.33 DMLC: implement Bermuda requirements as set out in Pt I, point 15 (financial security for repatriation), and record details of compliance measures in DMLC, Pt II, point 15. Ensure that the details of the seafarer's entitlement to repatriation are set out in the SEA.

REGULATION 2.6: SEAFARER COMPENSATION FOR THE SHIP'S LOSS OR FOUNDERING

23.34 The relevant provisions are set out in the Employment Regulations.

In the event of a ship being lost or foundering, the shipowner is obliged to pay to each seafarer on board an indemnity against any resulting unemployment, which is to be without prejudice to any other rights the seafarer may have.[172] The indemnity is to be paid for each day the seafarer remains unemployed, at the applicable rate in the SEA, but may be limited to two months' wages.[173] If payment is not made, the seafarer may take the same legal action that applies to the recovery of arrears of wages.[174]

REGULATION 2.7: MANNING LEVELS

23.35 The relevant provisions are the Merchant Shipping (Training, Certification, Manning and Watchkeeping) Regulations 2005[175] ('TCMW Regulations') and the Merchant Shipping (Manning Levels) Regulations 2011[176] ('Manning Regulations'), made under ss 59 and 93 (respectively) of the Merchant Shipping Act 2002.

The Manning Regulations provide that the shipowner must, regarding ships for which it is responsible, ensure that: (a) every officer is qualified in accordance with the STCW Convention; (b) all seafarers are trained in accordance with the STCW Convention (see Chapter 5, which refers to many aspects of the of the

171 Repatriation Regulations, reg 10(2)(a)–(b).
172 Employment Regulations, reg 18A(1)–(2). Regulation 18A was inserted by Merchant Shipping (Seafarer's Employment) Amendment Regulations 2014 (BR 53/2014), reg 3.
173 Employment Regulations, reg 18A(3).
174 Employment Regulations, reg 18A(4).
175 BR 44/2005.
176 BR 52/2011.

STCW Convention in the context of the UK provisions); (c) documentation and data relevant to all seafarers on board are maintained and available for inspection; (d) every master and officer is proficient in the English language; (e) when more than one language is spoken on board, a common working language is established for safety procedures; and (f) every master, chief mate, chief engineer and second engineer is fully conversant with the Bermuda legal and administrative processes to the extent appropriate to their role on board.[177]

The shipowner must also provide written instructions to the master setting out policies and procedures to ensure that newly employed seafarers on board get the opportunity to familiarise themselves with equipment, operating procedures and other arrangements for the proper performance of their duties;[178] and ensure that a knowledgeable crew member is designated to ensure that new seafarers receive essential information in a language they understand.[179]

The shipowner must ensure that, in respect of every ship of over 500 GT (except pleasure vessels) for which they are responsible, there is in force a safe manning document (SMD) that complies with the IMO's principles of safe manning (as set out in Assembly Resolutions A.890(21)[180] and A.955(23)),[181] although owners of ships of less than 500 GT and pleasure vessels may apply for an SMD on a voluntary basis.[182] The shipowner must also ensure that the manning levels are: maintained in accordance with the SMD; and regularly reviewed in accordance with the principles of safe manning, and that the BSMA is informed of any changes in the construction, operation, employment or status of the ship that may lead to a change in the minimum safe manning.[183] Particular provisions for deck and engineering officers apply to commercially and privately operated motor, sailing and square-rigged sailing vessels of 24 metres and over in load line length and under 3000 GT.[184]

The master must not proceed to sea, on a ship of over 500 GT, without an SMD and compliant manning.[185] However, if a seafarer (whose position is a requirement for the SMD) becomes incapacitated through accident or illness, or is unable to perform their duties due to other unforeseen circumstances, the ship may proceed to sea, at the master's discretion, provided that: (a) the voyage will be no more than 21 days; (b) if it is the master who is unavailable, there is a seafarer on board

177 Manning Regulations, reg 4(1)(a)–(f).
178 TCMW Regulations, reg 23(4)–(6).
179 TCMW Regulations, reg 23(5)(b).
180 IMO Assembly Resolution A.890(21) adopted on 25 November 1999 on the Principles of Safe Manning: www.imo.org/en/OurWork/HumanElement/VisionPrinciplesGoals/Documents/890.pdf [Accessed 5 March 2018].
181 IMO Assembly Resolution A.955(23) adopted on 5 December 2003 on Amendments to the Principles of Safe Manning (Resolution A.890(21)): www.imo.org/en/OurWork/HumanElement/VisionPrinciplesGoals/Documents/955.pdf [Accessed 5 March 2018].
182 Manning Regulations, reg 5(1)–(2)(a).
183 Manning Regulations, reg 5(2)(b)–(c).
184 TCMW Regulations, regs 14–15, Schs 2–3.
185 Manning Regulations, reg 5(3).

who holds a master's CoC; (c) suitable arrangements for watchkeeping are made so that the minimum rest periods can be complied with (see para 23.23 above); (d) necessary adjustments are made to the ship's emergency plans; and (e) the master informs the BSMA before sailing, and when a replacement seafarer joins the ship.[186]

Where there is no doctor on board (see para 23.50 below regarding the circumstances in which a doctor must be carried on board), the shipowner must ensure that there is at least one seafarer on board (who may be the master) who is nominated to be in charge of medical care and the administration of medicines, and who is qualified in accordance with the STCW Code, Section A-VI/4.[187]

There are provisions creating criminal offences against the shipowner and the master, for breach of their duties in connection with maintaining the SMD and proceeding to sea without one, respectively (the penalties are fines not exceeding $20,000 and $15,000, respectively).[188] There are powers of inspection and detention for non-compliances in respect of Bermuda ships and non-Bermuda ships in Bermuda ports, and for the withdrawal of the Maritime Labour Certificate in connection with Bermuda ships anywhere.[189]

Compliance

23.36 DMLC: implement Bermuda requirements as set out in Pt I, point 7, and record details of compliance measures in DMLC, Pt II, point 7.

REGULATION 2.8: CAREER AND SKILL DEVELOPMENT AND OPPORTUNITIES FOR SEAFARERS' EMPLOYMENT

23.37 There are no specific provisions, Bermuda not being a significant seafarer-supplying country.

REGULATION 3.1: ACCOMMODATION AND RECREATIONAL FACILITIES

23.38 The relevant provisions are set out in the Merchant Shipping (Seafarers' Accommodation) Regulations 2013[190] ('Accommodation Regulations'), which are made under s 56 of the Merchant Shipping Act 2002. The Accommodation Regulations supersede the UK's Merchant Shipping (Crew Accommodation) Regulations 1997, which had been incorporated by Bermuda into Sch 5 to its

186 Manning Regulations, reg 7(a)–(e).
187 Manning Regulations, reg 6.
188 Manning Regulations, reg 8(1)–(2).
189 Manning Regulations, reg 9(1)–(2)(a)–(b).
190 BR 123/2013.

Merchant Shipping Act 1979.[191] The Accommodation Regulations set out in detail the provisions relating to: lighting; ventilation; heating; port lights and windows; drainage; sleeping rooms; mess rooms, sanitary accommodation; recreation spaces; and many other matters covered by the MLC in this area.

The MLC provisions on ship board construction and equipment only apply to ships which were constructed on or after the date the Convention came into force for the relevant flag state.[192] The MLC, through extension from the UK, has applied to Bermuda since 2 May 2014. Accordingly, the Accommodation Regulations, in connection with the right to single occupancy and the sizes of floor spaces in sleeping accommodation, apply MLC-derived standards to new ships than they do to existing ships.[193] However, other provisions apply to existing ships as well as new ships.[194] A 'new ship' is one whose keel was laid, or which was at a similar stage of construction, on or after the date the MLC was extended to Bermuda; an 'existing ship' is a ship which is not a new ship.[195]

The Accommodation Regulations do not apply to ships which are certified as complying with the UK MCA's Large Commercial Yacht Code[196] ('LY3 Code'). It should be noted that the LY3 Code and the Passenger Yacht Code ('PYC') are being merged into the 'Red Ensign Group Yacht Code' (REG YC), which comes into force on 1 January 2019 – see Chapter 15 at para 15.9 for further details, including references to the alternative 'substantially equivalent' provisions on accommodation.

The Accommodation Regulations closely follow the UK provisions, which are set out in Pt 7 of the Merchant Shipping (Maritime Labour Convention) (Minimum Requirements for Seafarers etc) Regulations 2014,[197] MSN 1844[198] and MGN 481,[199] which can be used as a guide, although there are occasionally some differences in detail (see Chapter 15). For instance, on Bermuda ships, noise levels in working and living spaces are to be in conformity with the ILO Code of Practice 'Ambient factors in the workplace, 2001'[200] and with IMO Resolution A.468(XII) 'Code on Noise Levels on board Ships, 1981' (this has now been updated by a new code annexed to IMO Resolution MSC.337(91), adopted in

191 Accommodation Regulations, reg 40.
192 MLC, Regulation 3.1.2.
193 Accommodation Regulations, regs 16–17, 19 (existing ships); regs 18, 20 (new ships).
194 For example, the provisions on materials and surface finishes (reg 5), heating (reg 12), and drainage (reg 14).
195 Accommodation Regulations, reg 2.
196 Accommodation Regulations, reg 3(1)(a)(ii). The LY3 Code (published in 2012) applies to yachts which are 24 metres and over in load line length, are in commercial use for sport or pleasure, do not carry cargo and do not carry more than 12 passengers.
197 SI 2014/1613.
198 MSN 1844(M) – MLC, 2006: Crew Accommodation.
199 MGN 481(M) Amendment 1 – MLC, 2006: Crew Accommodation, Supplementary Guidance.
200 ILO Code of Practice 'Ambient factors in the workplace': www.ilo.org/wcmsp5/groups/public/---ed_protect/---protrav/---safework/documents/normativeinstrument/wcms_107729.pdf [Accessed 10 March 2018].

2012).[201] The UK provisions do not expressly refer to those instruments, but instead they provide that crew accommodation is to be situated, constructed and arranged to exclude, so far as reasonably practicable, (a) noise coming from other parts of the ship, and (b) noise coming from other parts of the crew accommodation.[202]

However, both Bermuda and the UK faithfully apply the minimum requirements of MLC, Standard A3.1.9 on occupancy levels and floor space in sleeping rooms (these are set out in Chapter 15 relating to the UK's MSN 1844, paras 11.1–11.11).

Another difference applies to the procedure for seeking exemptions from some of the provisions. For instance, for many of the derogations, exemptions, or flexible application (such as substantial equivalence) which the MLC permits, it requires the maritime authority to first consult the relevant shipowners' and seafarers' organisations[203] or, where they do not exist, the consultation must be made with the ILO Special Tripartite Committee (STC).[204] The Accommodation Regulations[205] reflect these processes but, as there are no such consultative organisations in Bermuda, the maritime authority may approach the UK MCA to carry out the relevant consultation on its behalf with the UK shipowners' and seafarers' organisations, or resort directly to the STC. The UK's MSN 1844 requires the MCA to consult with the shipowners' and seafarers' organisations, and does not refer to the STC, as this is unnecessary due to the presence of the consultative organisations.[206]

The shipowner and the master are responsible for ensuring that the accommodation is kept clean, habitable, and that the relevant equipment is kept in working order.[207] The master (or authorised person) must carry out (at least monthly) compliance inspections of the seafarers' accommodation, galleys and mess rooms; however, if there are more than 250 crew members, the monthly inspections need not cover every area, but must do so every three months.[208] The date and details of any defect, together with any remedial action, are to be recorded and signed by the master following each inspection; the record is to be kept on board for at least three years and be available to seafarers and any authorised persons.[209] Breaches of these provisions amount to criminal offences by the shipowner or master, punishable on summary conviction by fines of up to $3,000 to $10,000.[210]

201 IMO Resolution MSC. 337(91) 'Adoption of the Code on Noise Levels on board Ships' (adopted on 30 November 2012): www.imo.org/en/KnowledgeCentre/IndexofIMOResolutions/Documents/MSC%20-%20Maritime%20Safety/337(91).pdf [Accessed 8 October 2018].
202 MSN 1844, para 2.2(a)–(b).
203 MLC, Standards A3.1.9(a), A3.1.9(m), A3.1.10(a), A3.1.11(b), A3.1.15.
204 MLC, Articles VII, XIII.
205 Accommodation Regulations, regs 20(8), 24(3), 25(2), 28(2).
206 MSN 1844, paras 11.1(a), 11.9, 14.2, 17.1.
207 Accommodation Regulations, reg 36(1)–(2).
208 Accommodation Regulations, reg 36(3)(a)–(c).
209 Accommodation Regulations, reg 36(4).
210 Accommodation Regulations, reg 38(1)–(3).

There are powers to inspect and detain Bermuda or non-Bermuda ships in a port in Bermuda for non-compliance.[211] Authorised officers, on discovering that a Bermuda ship does not comply with the Accommodation Regulations, are empowered: (a) to withdraw the ship's Maritime Labour Certificate until the matter is rectified; or (b) if the ship is in a port outside Bermuda, to report the deficiency to the local port state control authority.[212]

Compliance

23.39 DMLC: implement Bermuda requirements as set out in Pt I, points 8–9, and record details of compliance measures in DMLC, Pt II, points 8–9.[213]

REGULATION 3.2: FOOD AND CATERING

23.40 The relevant provisions are set out in the Merchant Shipping (Provisions, Catering and Ship's Cooks) Regulations 2013[214] ('PCS Regulations'), which contain some minor amendments made by the Merchant Shipping (Provisions, Catering and Ship's Cooks) Amendment Regulations 2014.[215] Guidance on training, experience and certification requirements is also provided in BSN 2017-026.[216]

Supply of food and water

23.41 Every shipowner is to ensure that seafarers are supplied, free of charge, with food and drinking water, of appropriate quality, nutritional value and quantity, that adequately covers the requirements of the ship, and takes into account the differing cultural and religious backgrounds of the crew, and the nature and duration of the voyage.[217]

The shipowner should not knowingly provide food and water that contain anything known to cause, or likely to cause, sickness or injury to health and must ensure that supplies are of satisfactory quality.[218] Except when impracticable, food should only be sourced from reputable suppliers and, when fresh supplies

211 Accommodation Regulations, reg 37(1).
212 Accommodation Regulations, reg 37(2)(a)–(b).
213 Merchant Shipping (Inspections of Ships and Issue of Maritime Labour Certificates) Regulations 2013, Sch.
214 BR 106/2013.
215 BR 55/2014.
216 BSN 2017-026 – Certification as Ship's Cooks.
217 2012 Act, s 56A(1), as inserted by 2012 Act, s 10; PCS Regulations, regs 4(1), 5(1). As regards a ship which has restaurants, a shipowner may charge a seafarer for the use of such a restaurant, if they choose to use it instead of the facilities provided for seafarers: PCS Regulations , reg 4(2).
218 PCS Regulations, reg 5(2).

are purchased locally, this should only be done by or under the direct supervision of the cook, or by qualified purchasing departments where they exist.[219]

Storage of food, maintenance and hygiene

23.42 The arrangements for the maintenance of hygiene, storage of food, control of fresh water supplies and the preparation of food must take into account any guidance provided in a Bermuda Shipping Notice (BSN) and be in accordance with the Accommodation Regulations. There is currently no relevant BSN; however, the most relevant provisions in the Accommodation Regulations are set out below:

- Storage of food: there must be adequate cold store rooms, with sufficient shelves and other arrangements fitted so that they can be easily cleaned and with ready access to the galley; they must be situated, constructed and ventilated so as to minimise the possibility of the deterioration of the stores through heat, condensation, infestation or other cause; they must not be situated directly over or directly adjoining a machinery space or galley that is subject to abnormal heat, unless the division between them is adequately insulated; and they must be for the exclusive purpose of storing dry provisions.[220]
- Control of fresh water supplies: tanks should be sufficient to provide two days' supply;[221] tanks, manholes leading to them and distribution pipes must be constructed to prevent any risk of contamination and allow for ease of maintenance and cleaning;[222] where potable and fresh water is produced on board, it is to be treated by suitably automated means of disinfection.[223]
- Preparation of food: every ship (except those on which no seafarer is required to eat on board) must be provided with a galley which is suitable for the preparation of seafarers' meals, positioned clear of the working areas and be as close as practicable to the mess rooms;[224] every galley must be provided with: a washbasin supplied with hot and cold fresh water; a supply of cold drinking water; sufficient scuppers and drains; effective ventilation and extraction systems; a suitable means of washing down and cleaning with fresh water; and facilities to easily access the ventilation system.[225]

Carriage of ship's cooks

23.43 Every ship must carry a qualified ship's cook; however, there is an exception to this requirement for ships that have a safe manning certificate for fewer than 10 seafarers and which are engaged on voyages of less than 24

219 PCS Regulations, reg 5(2).
220 Accommodation Regulations, reg 34(1).
221 Accommodation Regulations, reg 32(2).
222 Accommodation Regulations, reg 32(3).
223 Accommodation Regulations, reg 32(4).
224 Accommodation Regulations, reg 33(1).
225 Accommodation Regulations, reg 33(5)(a)–(f).

hours where the seafarers have an opportunity to obtain meals ashore.[226] If this exception applies, every person who works in the ship's galley or is involved in the handling or preparation of food must be trained or instructed in the essential aspects of food hygiene and safety, which also applies to catering staff[227] (as set out below). Where no qualified ship's cook is available, the BSMA may grant a temporary dispensation for a maximum period of one month or until the next port of call where a replacement can be obtained.[228] Ship's cook certificates issued before the PCS Regulations came into force were acceptable until 20 August 20183 (five years after the MLC came into force internationally).[229]

Ship's cooks must be over 18 years of age and have attended a recognised training course (and be certified accordingly), covering at least: practical cookery; food and personal hygiene; food storage; stock control; environmental protection; and catering health and safety; and they must have served at sea for at least two years.[230]

A recognised training course is one: (a) recognised by the BSMA; or (b) in another MLC ratifying state and recognised by its maritime authority as meeting the requirements set out above.[231] There is also discretion to accept cooks whose training in shore-based establishments is considered to be equivalent.[232]

In respect of ships which carry a large number of seafarers, such as cruise ships, the shipowner may, in addition to carrying a qualified ship's cook, engage other cooks as necessary in order to provide an efficient service.[233] The requirements and procedure for applying for a 'Certificate of Equivalency as a Ship's Cook' are set out in BSN 2017-026.[234]

Catering staff

23.44 Seafarers whose work involves the preparation or handling of food must also receive training and instruction before (or on) joining the ship covering: (a) personal hygiene; (b) practices in maintaining hygienic conditions; and (c) safe practices in handling food, display and storage.[235] The details of the training is to be recorded and the records must be kept on board for as long as the relevant seafarers remain on board.[236]

226 PCS Regulations, reg 9(1), as amended by BR 55/2014, reg 3.
227 PCS Regulations, regs 7, 10(4).
228 PCS Regulations, reg 10(5).
229 PCS Regulations, reg 10(6).
230 PCS Regulations, reg 10(1)(a)–(d).
231 PCS Regulations, reg 10(2)(a)–(b).
232 PCS Regulations, reg 10(3).
233 PCS Regulations, reg 9(2), as amended by BR 55/2014, reg 3.
234 BSN 2017-026, paras 4.1–5.4.
235 PCS Regulations, reg 7(1)(a)–(c).
236 PCS Regulations, reg 7(2).

On-board inspections

23.45 The master must ensure that the quality of the drinking water for seafarers is checked regularly, and that at least monthly inspections are carried out of: (a) every store room and its contents; (b) every refrigerated store and its contents; (c) every galley and its equipment; and (d) other spaces used for the preparation or serving of food and associated equipment.[237] The date of the inspection, any deficiencies and proposed remedial action (with timescale for completion), and the status of previous deficiencies are to be recorded.[238] If any deficiency is likely to cause sickness or injury, the master must take immediate steps to stop the use of the concerned area, stores or equipment until it is restored to a safe condition.[239]

Inspections in a Bermuda port

23.46 Authorised persons may inspect Bermuda and non-Bermuda ships in a port in Bermuda and, if satisfied that the provision of food and water or the qualifications of ship's cooks do not comply with the ship's Declaration of Maritime Labour Compliance, Part I or, where none is carried, the requirements of Regulation 3.2 and Standard A3.2 of the MLC, they may detain the ship until the deficiency is rectified.[240]

Enforcement action by the BSMA

23.47 Authorised officers, on discovering that a Bermuda ship does not comply with the PCS Regulations, are empowered: (a) to withdraw the ship's Maritime Labour Certificate until the matter is rectified; or (b) if the ship is in a port outside Bermuda, to report the deficiency to the local port state control authority.[241]

Compliance

23.48 DMLC: implement Bermuda requirements as set out in Pt I, point 10, and record details of compliance measures in DMLC, Pt II, point 10.[242]

237 PCS Regulations, reg 8(1)(a)–(d).
238 PCS Regulations, reg 8(2).
239 PCS Regulations, reg 8(4).
240 PCS Regulations, reg 11(1).
241 PCS Regulations, reg 11(2)(a)–(b).
242 Merchant Shipping (Inspections of Ships and Issue of Maritime Labour Certificates) Regulations 2013, Sch.

REGULATION 4.1: MEDICAL CARE ON BOARD SHIP AND ASHORE

23.49 The main provisions are set out in the Merchant Shipping (Ship's Doctors) Regulations 2004[243] ('Ship's Doctors Regulations') and the Merchant Shipping (Medical Stores) Regulations 2005.[244]

Access to medical care

23.50 Seafarers are entitled to visit a doctor or dentist without delay and, where practicable, in ports of call at no cost to the seafarer.[245]

Seafarers are to be covered by adequate measures for the protection of their health and must have access to prompt and adequate medical care, while working on board, and at no cost to themselves.[246]

The shipowner must ensure that a qualified doctor is carried on board a ship which carries 100 or more persons and which is engaged on an international voyage of more than three days, or on a voyage which is more than one and a half day's sailing time from a port with adequate medical equipment.[247] A 'qualified doctor' is one which is registered to practise medicine in any of the following: Australia; Bermuda; Canada; an EU Member State; Hong Kong; New Zealand; Singapore; South Africa; USA; or West Indies.[248] A contravention amounts to an offence, punishable on summary conviction by a fine not exceeding $10,000.[249] It is a defence for the person charged to show that they took all reasonable precautions and exercised all due diligence to avoid the commission of the offence.[250]

If no doctor is carried on board, the shipowner must ensure that at least one seafarer on board (who may be the master) is nominated to be in charge of medical care and the administration of medicines, and who is qualified in accordance with section A-VI/4 of the SCTW Convention.[251]

Every ship carrying 15 or more seafarers, engaged on a voyage of more than three days' duration, must be provided with hospital accommodation to be used exclusively for medical purposes.[252] In all other ships, except those where every seafarer is provided with a single berth sleeping room, a suitable room is to be nominated as a temporary hospital and, when used as such, must not be used

243 BR 68/2004.
244 BR 46/2005, as amended by the Merchant Shipping (Medical Stores) Amendment Regulations 2011 (BR 53/2011).
245 Employment Regulations, r 14A, as inserted by BR 53/2014, r 2.
246 2002 Act, s 58(1), as substituted by 2012 Act, s 12.
247 Ship's Doctors Regulations, reg 3, as amended by BR 49/2011, reg 2.
248 Ship's Doctors Regulations, reg 2, Sch.
249 Ship's Doctors Regulations, reg 5(1).
250 Ship's Doctors Regulations, reg 5(2).
251 Merchant Shipping (Manning of Ships) Regulations 2011 (BR 52/2011), reg 6.
252 Accommodation Regulations, reg 30(1).

for any other purpose.[253] A medical cabinet for the storage of supplies must be provided on all ships.[254]

Carriage of medical stores

23.51 The Medical Stores Regulations adopt the UK MCA's MSN 1768[255] (on which, see Chapter 17). They apply not only to ships to which the MLC applies, but to all ships except pleasure vessels and tugs operating in a harbour area.[256] Ships must carry medicines and medical stores as follows:

(1) A sea-going ship with no limitation on the length of voyage – MSN 1768, Category A.

(2) A sea-going ship making a voyage during which it is no more than 150 nautical miles from the nearest port with adequate medical equipment (or no more than 175 nautical miles from the nearest port with adequate medical equipment if it remains within the range of helicopter rescue services) – MSN 1768, Category B.

(3) A sea-going ship carrying a dangerous substance in its cargo, or any residue from an earlier cargo – as specified in MSN 1768 in relation to such ships.

(4) A sea-going ship carrying more than 12 passengers but not a doctor as a member of the crew – MSN 1768, Annex 2.

Note that the requirements in sub-paragraphs (3) and (4) are in addition to those entries in sub-paragraph (1), (2) or (3), as the case may be.[257] On passenger ships in which a doctor is always employed, the medicines referred to above can be varied in accordance with current medical practice.[258]

A standard medical report must be used in connection with the treatment of seafarers, and the contents must be confidential; the form should be that used in the UK MCA's Ship Captain's Medical Guide,[259] or similar.[260]

Appropriate medical guides should be carried on board, including instructions for the use of antidotes.[261] MSN 1768, Annex 5, refers to the Ship Captain's Medical Guide, other guides, as well as radio medical advice.[262] The latter is

253 Accommodation Regulations, reg 30(2).
254 Accommodation Regulations, reg 31.
255 MSN 1768 (M+F) – Application of the Merchant Shipping and Fishing Vessels (Medical Stores) Regulations 1995 (SI 1995/1802) and the Merchant Shipping and Fishing Vessels (Medical Stores) (Amendment) Regulations 1996 (SI 1996/2821).
256 Medical Stores Regulations, reg 3(1)(a)–(b), as amended by BR 53/2011, reg 3.
257 Medical Stores Regulations, reg 4(1)–(2).
258 Medical Stores Regulations, reg 5(1).
259 The Ship Captain's Medical Guide (6 May 2014): www.gov.uk/government/publications/the-ship-captains-medical-guide [Accessed 8 October 2018]. Note that the guide is currently under review.
260 Medical Stores Regulations, reg 5A(1)–(2), as inserted by BR 53/2011, reg 5.
261 Medical Stores Regulations, reg 10.
262 Medical Stores Regulations, reg 10.

provided through the UK service, as explained in MGN 225,[263] and is accessible to all ships at sea by contacting HM Coastguard on MF DSC, VHF DSC, VHF Channel 16 or INMARSAT.[264]

There are also other provisions on: the standards of medical stores;[265] packaging and labelling of containers;[266] storage of medicines;[267] replenishment of dated medicines;[268] and inspections (yearly) of medicines and medical stores.[269]

In terms of enforcement, non-compliances with any of regulations 4–11 amount to an offence by the shipowner (and/or other person in default), punishable on summary conviction by a fine not exceeding $10,000.[270] Authorised inspectors may inspect the vessel and issue an improvement notice or exercise a power of detention in respect of a non-compliance.[271]

Compliance

23.52 DMLC: implement Bermuda requirements as set out in Pt I, point 12, and record details of compliance measures in DMLC, Pt II, point 12.

REGULATION 4.2: SHIPOWNERS' LIABILITY

23.53 Seafarers are also entitled to material assistance and support from the shipowner with respect to the financial consequences of sickness, injury or death occurring while the seafarer is employed under a SEA or arising from their employment under a SEA.[272]

The main provisions are set out in the Employment Regulations.

Shipowners are liable for the costs of medical care arising from sickness or injury from the date the seafarer commences work on board a ship until repatriation.[273] The shipowner must meet the costs of medical care, medical treatment, medications, therapeutic appliances and accommodation away from domicile, until the seafarer has recovered, or until the sickness or incapacity has been established to be of a permanent nature, or until the seafarer is able to claim medical benefits through insurance or other scheme in their country of

263 MGN 225 (M+F) – Radio Medical Advice for Ships at Sea.
264 MGN 225, para 3.
265 Medical Stores Regulations, reg 6.
266 Medical Stores Regulations, reg 7.
267 Medical Stores Regulations, reg 8.
268 Medical Stores Regulations, reg 9.
269 Medical Stores Regulations, regs 5(2), 11.
270 Medical Stores Regulations, reg 12(1)–(4).
271 Medical Stores Regulations, reg 13(1)–(2).
272 2002 Act, s 58(3), as substituted by 2012 Act, s 12.
273 Employment Regulations, reg 15(1).

domicile.[274] However, the liability to meet these expenses is limited to a period of 16 weeks from the date of the injury or the commencement of the illness.[275]

When the liability under the above provisions for the costs of sickness or injury arises, the shipowner must also pay the seafarer's wages at the basic rate as set out under any applicable CBA or the SEA: (a) while the seafarer remains on board or until they have been repatriated (see para 23.27 above); and (b) from the time the seafarer has been repatriated until the time they have recovered.[276] The liability to pay wages is also capped at a period of 16 weeks from the date of the injury or the commencement of the illness.[277]

Exceptions

23.54 The MLC permits ratifying states to exclude liability for sickness and injury in three circumstances.[278] The Employment Regulations set out those circumstances as when: (a) the injury has occurred other than in the service of the ship; (b) the injury or illness is the result of the misconduct of the seafarer; or (c) the injury or illness is deliberately and intentionally concealed by the seafarer when entering into their SEA.[279]

In the chapeau of reg 15(5) it states that the '... liabilities set out in paragraphs (1), (2) and (3) shall not arise when ...' any of those circumstances apply. It is submitted that there has been a drafting error here, and that the reference to 'paragraph (3)' should instead be a reference to 'paragraph (4)'. The reason for this contention is that paragraph (3) states that the ship must carry financial security (it imposes an obligation, not a liability) and this is mandatory under the MLC, not conditional;[280] on the other hand, paragraph (4) imposes a liability on the shipowner to pay for medical care and treatment. It is submitted that only such a reading as contended for would comply with MLC, Standard A4.2.1, paragraph 5(a)–(c).

Costs of burial

23.55 The shipowner is also liable for the costs of burial of a seafarer who dies aboard the ship or ashore during a period of employment on board.[281] This liability is not subject to any of the exceptions referred to above.

274 Employment Regulations, reg 15(4).
275 Employment Regulations, reg 16(1).
276 Employment Regulations, reg 15(7)(a)–(b).
277 Employment Regulations, reg 16(2).
278 MLC, Standard A4.2.1.5(a)–(c).
279 Employment Regulations, reg 15(5)(a)–(c).
280 MLC, Standard A4.2.1.1(b).
281 Employment Regulations, reg 15(6).

Return of seafarer's property

23.56 Whenever a seafarer leaves the ship due to sickness or injury, or dies during employment, the master must arrange for their property to be collected, listed and returned to the seafarer or their next of kin.[282] See paragraph 23.32 for further details.

Requirement to carry evidence of financial security

23.57 The shipowner must provide financial security which is sufficient to ensure compensation to any seafarer in the event of death or long-term disability as a result of an occupational illness, injury or hazard.[283] The extent of the compensation should be at least that set out in the SEA or applicable CBA, and must not be less than the current terms agreed by the International Bargaining Forum.[284] The financial security must also cover any other liabilities which may arise under reg 15, all of which have been set out above.[285] Evidence of the financial security (which may be a policy of insurance) must be carried on board and be available to seafarers, authorised officials and port state control officers.[286]

The MLC provisions on shipowners' liabilities were (together with those on repatriation) the first Part of the MLC to be amended.[287] The amendments came into force on 18 January 2017, and add much more detail to the original requirement (as set out in MLC, Standard A4.2, paragraph 1(b)) to carry financial security, as implemented by Bermuda by reg 15, which remains in force. In most cases, the financial security will be provided by the P&I Club, although there are also other commercial organisations offering such cover.

Bermuda has not yet brought into force any new laws to implement the amendments. For the time being, it has issued BMGN 2017-01 – Guidance on implementation of 2014 Amendments to MLC 2006 on Bermuda Ships, which should be followed. Bermuda shipowners must comply with the requirements of the 2014 amendments themselves, which are set out in Appendix 2, until the specific national provisions come into force.[288] It should be noted that, under the amendments, a copy of the financial security certificate (or other documentary

282 Employment Regulations, reg 19.
283 Employment Regulations, reg 15(2).
284 Employment Regulations, reg 15(2). The IBF is the negotiating body consisting of the International Transport Workers' Federation (ITF) (representing seafarers) and the Joint Negotiating Group (JNG) (representing employers). See: www.itfseafarers.org/about-IBF.cfm [Accessed 15 March 2018].
285 Employment Regulations, reg 15(8).
286 Employment Regulations, reg 15(3), (8).
287 Amendments to the Code implementing Regulation 4.2 – Shipowners' liability of the MLC, 2006 (and appendices): www.ilo.org/wcmsp5/groups/public/---ed_norm/---relconf/documents/meetingdocument/wcms_248905.pdf [Accessed 16 March 2018].
288 BMGN 2017-01, conclusion, para 4(a)–(b).

evidence) must be displayed in a conspicuous place on board the ship where it is available to seafarers.[289]

The UK has already implemented the amendments into law (see Chapter 18 at paras 18.3–18.6), which closely follow the MLC amendments and may be indicative of the approach that Bermuda will take.

Enforcement

23.58 In terms of enforcement, non-compliances with any of regulations 15–16 amount to an offence by the shipowner, punishable on summary conviction by a fine not exceeding $10,000.[290] There are powers of inspection and detention over Bermuda and non-Bermuda ships in a port in Bermuda for non-compliances with the Declaration of Maritime Labour Compliance, Pt I, and with the MLC.[291] Where the BSMA is informed of a Bermuda ship which does not comply with the Employment Regulations, it may: (a) withdraw its Maritime Labour Certificate, or (b) inform the port state control authority of the port that it is in.[292]

Compliance

23.59 DMLC: implement Bermuda requirements as set out in Pt I, point 16 (financial security for shipowners' liability), and record details of compliance measures in DMLC, Pt II, point 16.

REGULATION 4.3: HEALTH AND SAFETY PROTECTION AND ACCIDENT PREVENTION

23.60 The main provisions are set out in the Merchant Shipping (Health and Safety at Work) Regulations 2004[293] ('H&S Regulations 2004') (as amended),[294] which are made under s 93 of the Merchant Shipping Act 2002. The relevant aspects of the H&S Regulations 2004 very much follow the UK's Merchant Shipping and Fishing Vessels (Health and Safety at Work) Regulations 1997[295] ('1997 Regulations'), which are described in detail in Chapter 19 and can be used as a general guide.

289 MLC, Standard A4.2.1, para 11.
290 Employment Regulations, reg 22(1).
291 Employment Regulations, reg 23(1).
292 Employment Regulations, reg 23(2)(a)–(b).
293 BR 52/2004.
294 The amendments have been made by the Merchant Shipping (Health and Safety at Work) Amendments Regulations 2011 (BR 50/2011) and the Merchant Shipping (Health and Safety at Work) Amendments Regulations 2013 (BR 119/2013).
295 SI 1997/2962.

The H&S Regulations 2004 apply to the activities of workers on Bermuda ships, except that they do not apply to public service vessels and vessels engaged in search and rescue, when the characteristics of the work inevitably conflict with the provisions; in the latter case, the employer still has a duty, so far as reasonably practicable, to ensure the health and safety of the relevant workers.[296] However, as regards non-Bermuda ships in a Bermuda port, there are powers of inspection and detention (for failing to meet the standards of Bermuda ships as set by the Regulations).[297]

The duties are imposed on: (a) the employer; and (b) any other natural or legal person upon whom a duty is imposed[298] (for example, the company, master, safety officer and seafarers all have specific duties imposed upon them). Furthermore, where the aforementioned parties do not have control of the relevant matter to which the regulation relates, because they do not have responsibility for the operation of the ship, that duty also extends to any natural or legal person who has control of that matter.[299] In many cases, that duty will be extended to the company, in addition to the specific duties referred to above. The 'company' is defined as: 'the owner of the ship or any other organisation or person such as the manager, or bareboat charterer, who has assumed the responsibility for operation of the ship from the owner',[300] being very similar to the definition of 'shipowner' under the MLC.[301]

The main points of focus, to comply with the Declaration of Maritime Labour Compliance Pt I (DMLC Pt I), are set out below. Unless otherwise stated, the approach taken by Bermuda is virtually the same as that set out in the UK's 1997 Regulations, so references are made to Chapter 19 where these provisions are set out or described.

Part II: General duties

23.61

- The general duties imposed on employers for the health and safety of workers:[302] these are virtually identical to those set out under reg 5(1)–(2) of the UK's 1997 Regulations, which have been set out in Chapter 19.
- Health and safety policy:[303] this adopts the approach taken by reg 6(1)–(2) of the 1997 Regulations, see Chapter 19.

296 H&S Regulations 2004, reg 3(1)(a)–(b).
297 H&S Regulations 2004, reg 3(2), applying regs 28–30.
298 H&S Regulations 2004, reg 4(1)(a)–(b).
299 H&S Regulations 2004, reg 4(2).
300 H&S Regulations 2004, reg 2.
301 MLC, Article II, para 1(j).
302 H&S Regulations 2004, reg 5(1)–(2).
303 H&S Regulations 2004, reg 6(1)–(2).

- Risk assessment:[304] this follows reg 7(1)–(6) of the 1997 Regulations, see Chapter 19.
- Provisions on new or expectant mothers:[305] these follow the provisions in reg 8(1)–(4) of the 1997 Regulations, except that there is no reference to Annexes I and II to Council Directive 92/85/EEC or ss 66–68 of the UK's Employment Rights Act 1996, see Chapter 19.
- Avoidance of night work for new or expectant mothers:[306] this follows reg 9(1)–(2) of the 1997 Regulations, see Chapter 19.
- For the employer or company to be obliged to comply with regs 8–9, the new or expectant mother must notify the employer or company that she is pregnant, has given birth within the previous six months or that she is breastfeeding;[307] this follows reg 10(1)–(2) of the 1997 Regulations, see Chapter 19.
- Health surveillance:[308] this follows reg 11 of the 1997 Regulations, see Chapter 19.
- Capabilities and training:[309] this follows reg 12(1)–(4) of the 1997 Regulations, see Chapter 19.

Part III: Duties of the company

23.62

- Co-ordination of health and safety:[310] this follows reg 13 of the 1997 Regulations, see Chapter 19.
- Reporting of occupational diseases:[311] see Bermuda Shipping Notice 2013–023,[312] set out in the Schedule to the H&S Regulations 2004. The employer must report a reportable disease (a list of which is set out in Annex 1 to the BSN) on receiving notification from a registered medical practitioner; the report form is set out in Annex 2.[313] The report is to be made to: Bermuda Shipping and Maritime Authority, 4th Floor Mintflower Place, 8 Par-La-Ville Road, Hamilton HM08, Bermuda; email: registry@bermudashipping.bm.
- The employer must keep a copy of the report for 40 years.[314]

304 H&S Regulations 2004, reg 7(1)–(6).
305 H&S Regulations 2004, reg 8(1)–(4).
306 H&S Regulations 2004, reg 9(1)–(2).
307 H&S Regulations 2004, reg 10(1)–(2).
308 H&S Regulations 2004, reg 11.
309 H&S Regulations 2004, reg 12(1)–(4).
310 H&S Regulations 2004, reg 13.
311 H&S Regulations 2004, reg 13A, as inserted by Merchant Shipping (Health and Safety at Work) (Amendment) Regulations 2013, reg 2.
312 BSN 2013-023 – Reporting of Occupational Diseases, as required by the Merchant Shipping (Health and Safety at Work) (Amendment) Regulations 2013.
313 BSN 2013-023, para 1.1.
314 BSN 2013-023, para 3.2.

Part IV: Special responsibility for health and safety and consultation with workers

23.63

- The appointment of a person(s) to provide protective and preventative services:[315] this follows reg 14(1)–(4) of the 1997 Regulations, see Chapter 19.
- There must be appointed a safety officer and safety committee on sea-going ships on which five or more seafarers are employed.[316]
- Duty of safety officers:[317] this replicates reg 16 of the 1997 Regulations and, like that provision, adopts the UK's Code of Safe Working Practices for Merchant Seafarers[318] ('COSWP'). The only difference is the reference to Bermuda's Merchant Shipping (Safety Officials and Reporting of Accidents and Dangerous Occurrences) Regulations 1986,[319] instead of the UK equivalent.
- Appointment of safety representatives and safety committees:[320] this follows reg 17(1)–(5) of the 1997 Regulations, see Chapter 19.
- Powers of safety representatives and safety committees:[321] this follows reg 18(a)–(d) of the 1997 Regulations, see Chapter 19.
- Duties of the company and master:[322] these follow reg 19(1)–(2) of the 1997 Regulations and refer to the UK's COSWP, see Chapter 19.
- Consultation with workers:[323] this follows reg 20(1)–(5) of the 1997 Regulations, see Chapter 19.

Part V: General duties of workers

23.64

- General duties of workers to take care of themselves and others who may be affected by their acts or omissions, etc:[324] this follows reg 21(1)–(4) of the 1997 Regulations, except that Bermuda's Merchant Shipping Act 2002[325] is referred to instead of the UK's Merchant Shipping Act 1995.

315 H&S Regulations 2004, reg 14(1)–(4).
316 H&S Regulations 2004, reg 15(1)–(2), as amended by Merchant Shipping (Health and Safety at Work) Amendment Regulations 2011, reg 2.
317 H&S Regulations 2004, reg 16(1)–(2).
318 H&S Regulations 2004, reg 2; COSWP, 2015 ed. Amendment 1: www.gov.uk/government/uploads/system/uploads/attachment_data/file/671403/CSWPMS_GOV_UK_2017.pdf [Accessed 17 March 2018].
319 BR 50/1986.
320 H&S Regulations 2004, reg 17(1)–(5).
321 H&S Regulations 2004, reg 18(a)–(d).
322 H&S Regulations 2004, reg 19(1)–(2).
323 H&S Regulations 2004, 20(1)–(5).
324 H&S Regulations 2004, reg 21(1)–(4).
325 H&S Regulations 2004, reg 2.

Pt VI: Prohibitions, penalties, inspections and detentions

23.65 The prohibitions on imposing a levy on a worker and against interfering or misusing anything provided in the interests of health and safety[326] follow the same pattern as regs 22–23 of the 1997 Regulations.

There are offences and penalties for non-compliances,[327] the pattern of which is similar to that in regs 24–25 of the 1997 Regulations. The monetary levels of maximum fines range from $2,000 to $20,000. On the statutory defence, whereas the UK imposes on the defendant the burden of showing that it was not reasonably practicable to do more than was done,[328] Bermuda reverses the burden of proof and requires the prosecution to establish that it was reasonably practicable to do more.[329]

There are powers to inspect Bermuda ships, and non-Bermuda ships which are in a port in Bermuda, and to detain the former for non-compliances, and the latter where they do not conform to 'the standards' required of Bermuda ships by the H&S Regulations 2004.[330]

A detention can be referred to arbitration within 21 days of service of the detention notice, and compensation (based on resulting loss) can be awarded by the government on a successful challenge.[331]

Forthcoming amendments to the MLC

23.66 The 2016 amendments to the MLC come into force on 8 January 2019 and will amend Code B of Regulation 4.5 addressing harassment and bullying in a health and safety context. See Chapter 19 for a more detailed commentary, and the full text of the amendments is set out in Appendix 2.

Compliance

23.67 DMLC: implement Bermuda requirements as set out in Pt I, point 11, and record details of compliance measures in DMLC, Pt II, point 11.

326 H&S Regulations 2004, regs 22–23.
327 H&S Regulations 2004, regs 24, 25; reg 24 was amended by the Merchant Shipping (Health and Safety at Work) (Amendment) Regulations 2013.
328 1997 Regulations, reg 26.
329 H&S Regulations 2004, reg 26.
330 H&S Regulations 2004, regs 27–29.
331 H&S Regulations 2004, reg 30; 2002 Act, ss 104–105.

REGULATION 4.4: ACCESS TO SHORE-BASED WELFARE FACILITIES

23.68 The Bermuda Sailors Home is based in Hamilton and its mission is '[t] o principally provide centers of rest and recreation for seafarers and additionally the operation of the Bermuda Jubilee Sailing Trust Fund'. It was founded in 1927, and since 1963 has been based at 22 Richmond Road, Pembroke, HM 08 (tel (441) 295-5598). It is affiliated with the British Sailors' Society and the Mission to Seamen.

The Home is popularly known as 'The Mariners' Club' and provides seafarers with assistance, social events (restaurant, bar, games, television, library, telephone, a letter-writing service and bus tours). It will, on request, assist seafarers who are in disputes with shipowners and send provisions when not supplied by the latter. It also provides marine disaster emergency accommodation.[332]

REGULATION 4.5: SOCIAL SECURITY

23.69 Bermuda has not introduced any particular state-funded social security provisions for seafarers who may be resident in the territory. The law imposes social security obligations on shipowners, as set out below. The law aspires to seafarers being provided with the nine areas of social security, in accordance with MLC, Standard A4.5.1 'in a progressive manner', those areas being: (a) medical care benefit; (b) sickness benefit; (c) unemployment benefit; (d) old-age benefit; (e) employment injury benefit; (f) family benefit; (g) maternity benefit; (h) invalidity benefit; and (i) survivors benefit.[333]

However, such a level of social security provision for seafarers has not yet been implemented on a mandatory basis. Shipowners are required to provide, as a minimum, three of those nine branches, two of which must be (i) medical care benefit, and (ii) protection from the financial consequences of sickness, injury or death; the third may be any of the other seven branches set out above.[334] This partially follows MLC guidance, which recommends that, at the time of ratification, states should provide, as a minimum, social security in the areas of medical care, sickness benefit, with the third being employment injury benefit.[335]

The health and social security benefits provided by the shipowner must be set out in the SEA.[336]

332 Bermuda Sailors' Home: www.centreonphilanthropy.org/directory_companies/view/177 [Accessed 19 March 2018].

333 Employment Regulations, reg 14B(1)(a)–(i), inserted by BR 53/2014, reg 2.

334 Employment Regulations, reg 14B(2)(a)–(b)(i)–(iii), inserted by BR 53/2014, reg 2.

335 MLC, Guideline B4.5.1.

336 Employment Regulations, reg 13(3)(a).

INTRODUCTION TO TITLE 5

23.70 The complete Title 5 of the MLC is set out at Appendix 1, which fully explains MLC flag state and port state responsibilities. It has been annotated with references to the ILO Guidelines on flag state control[337] and port state control.[338]

The UK's Title 5 provisions are described in more detail in Chapter 22. Those provisions may be used as a guide to flag state and port state implementation.

Set out below are reference to the main Bermuda provisions, with references to their sources, for those who need to know the precise requirements.

REGULATION 5.1: FLAG STATE RESPONSIBILITIES

23.71 The main provisions are set out in the Merchant Shipping (Inspection of Ships and Issue of Maritime Labour Certificates) Regulations 2013[339] ('Inspection Regulations').

Documents to be carried

23.72 All Bermuda ships of 500 GT and over must carry:

- a valid maritime labour certificate (MLCert) and a declaration of maritime labour compliance (DMLC), which must be posted in a conspicuous place on board the ship; and
- a copy of the MLC, including any amendments.[340]

Under the MLC, ships which do not meet the mandatory criteria for certification may be put forward for voluntary certification.[341] The Bermuda MLC legislation still applies to MLC ships below 500 GT, even if they are not put forward for voluntary certification.

337 Guidelines for flag State inspections under the Maritime Labour Convention, 2006 (published 2009): www.ilo.org/global/standards/maritime-labour-convention/monitoring-implementation-tools/WCMS_101788/lang--en/index.htm [Accessed 5 July 2018].

338 Guidelines for port State control officers carrying out inspections under the Maritime Labour Convention, 2006: www.ilo.org/global/standards/maritime-labour-convention/monitoring-implementation-tools/WCMS_101787/lang--en/index.htm [Accessed 5 July 2018].

339 BR 121/2013.

340 Inspection Regulations, regs 3(a), 4.

341 MLC, Regulation 5.1.3, para 2.

Inspection

23.73 The inspection for the issue of an MLCert will cover the 16 areas as set out in MLC, Appendix A5-I.[342]

A one-off interim MLCert (valid for a maximum period of six months) may be applied for in the case of new-builds, change of flag or ownership, so long as the prescribed conditions are met.[343]

Validity of MLCert

23.74 The MLCert will be valid for a maximum period of five years, on condition that an intermediate inspection is carried out between the second and third anniversaries; a renewal inspection must be carried out for the issue of a new MLCert.[344]

MLCert and DMLC

23.75 The MLCert format to be used is that issued by the BSMA; the DMLC Pt I (which shows the flag state requirements) will be drawn up by the BSMA, and Pt II (which shows the shipowner's measures to comply with the flag state requirements) and the declaration must be completed by the shipowner.[345]

The model MLCert and DMLC, Pt I, are contained in the Schedule to the Inspection Regulations.

Record of deficiencies

23.76 The inspector will keep a record of every inspection, including a note of any significant deficiencies that are found and the date when such deficiencies are found to be remedied, and this record must be retained with the ship's MLCert, and be available to authorities and seafarers.[346]

On-board complaint procedure

23.77 An on-board complaint procedure must be made available to seafarers so that they can lodge a complaint alleging a breach of the requirements

342 Inspection Regulations, reg 5(1)–(2) (only the original 14 areas of inspection are referred to, but the amendments to the MLC have added areas 15 and 16 for financial security for repatriation and shipowners' liabilities, respectively).
343 Inspection Regulations, reg 5(3)(a)–(d).
344 Inspection Regulations, reg 6.
345 Inspection Regulations, reg 7.
346 Inspection Regulations, reg 8.

of the MLCert and for that complaint to be resolved fairly, effectively and expeditiously.[347]

Offences

23.78 A failure to comply with the certification provisions amounts to a criminal offence by the shipowner and master, punishable by fines of up to $5,000 to $10,000.[348]

REGULATION 5.2: PORT STATE RESPONSIBILITIES

23.79 See also the ILO Guidelines on port state control.[349]

Inspections of non-Bermuda ships

Inspection

23.80 Non-Bermuda ships may be the subject of inspection under Regulation 5.2.1 (Inspections in port) of the MLC for the purpose of reviewing compliance.[350]

Where the inspection discloses clear grounds for believing that the working and living conditions on the ship do not conform to the requirements of the MLC, a more detailed inspection may be carried out as provided in MLC, Regulation 5.2.1 and Code, to ascertain the working and living conditions on board.[351]

Detention

23.81 Where, following the more detailed inspection, the ship is found not to conform to the requirements of the MLC, and:

(a) the conditions on board are hazardous to the safety, health or security of seafarers; or

(b) the non-conformity constitutes a repeated breach of the requirements of the MLC (including seafarers' rights),

347 Inspection Regulations, reg 11.
348 Inspection Regulations, reg 12.
349 Guidelines for port State control officers carrying out inspections under the Maritime Labour Convention, 2006: www.ilo.org/global/standards/maritime-labour-convention/monitoring-implementation-tools/WCMS_101787/lang--en/index.htm [Accessed 5 July 2018].
350 Inspection Regulations, reg 13(1)–(2).
351 Inspection Regulations, reg 13(3).

the authorised officer must take steps to ensure that the ship does not proceed to sea until the non-conformities identified during the detailed inspection have been rectified.[352]

All possible efforts must be taken to avoid a ship being unduly detained or delayed.[353]

On-shore seafarer complaint-handling procedures

23.82 The BSMA is responsible for handling complaints from seafarers on ships visiting Bermuda, and must keep the source of the complaint confidential.[354] The BSMA must record the complaint and refer it to the Mercantile Marine Superintendent to arrange for an investigation under MLC, Standard A5.2.2 and Guideline B5.2.2, to facilitate a prompt and practical means of address.[355]

352 Inspection Regulations, reg 13(4)(a)–(b).
353 Inspection Regulations, reg 13(5).
354 Inspection Regulations, reg 14(1), (5).
355 Inspection Regulations, reg 14(2)–(3).

CHAPTER 24

Cayman Islands

INTRODUCTION

24.1 The Cayman Islands Shipping Registry was established in 1903 when George Town was first recognised as a British Port of Registry, and is now a division of the Maritime Authority of the Cayman Islands (MACI).[1] The MACI Annual Report for 2015–16 (the most recent one on its website) shows that, as a percentage of gross tonnage, the five main categories of vessel types are: oil/chemical tankers; car carriers; bulk carriers; oil tankers; and yachts.[2]

DEFINITIONS

24.2 Set out below are some important definitions generally used for the purposes of the CI implementing statutes:

- 'Cayman Islands ship' means a ship registered in the Islands under this Law [Merchant Shipping Law (2016 Revision)], and 'Cayman Islands vessel' and 'Cayman Islands fishing vessel' must be construed accordingly;[3]
- 'Cayman Islands waters' mean the sea or other waters within the seaward limits of the territorial sea of the Islands;[4]
- 'Declaration of Maritime Labour Compliance' means, in relation to a ship, the valid Part I and Part II documents drawn up and issued in accordance with the Maritime Labour Convention, in the forms corresponding to the relevant models given in Appendix A5-II to the Convention and having the contents, duration and validity specified in Regulation 5.1.3 and Standard A5.1.3 of the Convention;[5]
- 'Maritime Labour Certificate' and 'interim Maritime Labour Certificate' mean a Certificate issued in accordance with the Maritime Labour Convention;[6]
- 'Non-Cayman Island ship' is a ship which is not a Cayman Islands ship (as defined above);
- 'seafarer' means any person, including a master, who is employed or engages or works in any capacity on board a ship and whose normal place of work is on a ship;[7]
- 'seafarer employment agreement' means, in relation to a seafarer, the agreement between a seafarer and a shipowner required by regulation 5 [of the SEA Regulations];[8] and

1 MACI is a statutory corporation formed as a separate legal entity under the Maritime Authority of the Cayman Islands Law, 2005.
2 MACI Annual Report 2015–16: www.cishipping.com/system/files/reports/documents/Annual%20Report%202015-2016%2008JAN18.pdf [Accessed 13 October 2018].
3 Merchant Shipping Law (2016 Revision), s 2.
4 Merchant Shipping Law (2016 Revision), s 2.
5 Merchant Shipping (Maritime Labour Convention) (Seafarer Employment Agreement, Shipowners' Liabilities and Wages) Regulations, 2014 ('SEA Regulations'), reg 2.
6 SEA Regulations, reg 2.
7 SEA Regulations, reg 2.
8 SEA Regulations, reg 2.

- 'shipowner' means:
  - (a) in relation to a ship which has a valid Maritime Labour Certificate, the person identified as the shipowner on that Certificate; or
  - (b) in relation to any other ship, the owner of the ship or, if different, any other organisation or person such as the manager, or the bareboat charterer, that has assumed the responsibility for the operation of the ship from the owner.[9]

REGULATION 1.1: MINIMUM AGE

24.3 The provisions are set out in the Merchant Shipping (Certification, Safe Manning, Hours of Work and Watchkeeping) Regulations (2004 Revision),[10] which implement the STCW Convention and so will be referred to below as the 'STCW Regulations', and the Merchant Shipping (Maritime Labour Convention) (Health and Safety) Regulations, 2014 ('H&S Regulations').

The STCW Regulations apply to: (a) sea-going CI ships wherever they may be and non-CI ships when in CI waters; (b) masters and seamen employed in sea-going CI ships; and (c) seafarers employed in pleasure vessels to the extent provided for in regulation 6(7), (8) and (9) (which cover the recognition of certificates).[11] They do not apply to: warships and naval auxiliaries or other ships owned or operated by a State and engaged only on Government non-commercial service; (b) fishing vessels; (c) wooden ships of primitive build; or (d) seafarers employed in such ships as are referred to in paragraphs (a) to (c).[12]

The H&S Regulations apply to: (a) CI ships, wherever they may be; and (b) non-CI ships, which do not carry MLC documentation, while they are in CI waters.[13] The only provisions which apply to non-CI ships, which do carry MLC documentation, while they are in CI waters, are regulations 25 and 26 on port state inspection and detention, respectively.[14] The following vessels are excluded: pleasure vessels; fishing vessels; warships or naval auxiliaries; and offshore installations whilst on their working stations.[15]

A person under the age of 16 must not be employed or engaged on a Cayman Islands ('CI') ship.[16]

9 SEA Regulations, reg 2.
10 Supplement No 6 published with Gazette No 16 of 9 August 2004.
11 STCW Regulations, reg 3(1)(a)–(c), respectively.
12 STCW Regulations, reg 3(2)(a)–(d), respectively.
13 H&S Regulations, reg 3(1)(a)–(b).
14 H&S Regulations, reg 3(2)(a)–(b)(i)–(ii).
15 H&S Regulations, reg 3(3)(a)–(d).
16 STCW Regulations, reg 37(1).

There are also special health and safety provisions for 'young seafarers'; a young seafarer is one under the age of 18.[17] A young seafarer must not work at night (unless the exception set out below applies) or be employed as a ship's stoker, trimmer, or ship's cook.[18]

In this context, 'night' means a period of at least nine consecutive hours, including the period from midnight to 5am.[19]

A young seafarer must not carry out a 'restricted task' without being supervised and having received appropriate instruction, unless they are recognised as fully qualified to perform that task.[20] A 'restricted task' is one involving any agents, processes or work specified in Sch 1 (agents, processes and work), or is identified by the specific risk assessment required for the young seafarer by reg 16 as presenting a special risk of accident or of detrimental effect on their health or physical development.[21]

There are also 'prohibited tasks', so (subject to the following exception) young seafarers must not perform work:

(a) which is likely to jeopardise their health or safety, as determined by the MACI after consultation with shipowners' and seafarers' organisations (see below regarding types of prohibited work specified in the DMLC Pt I);

(b) which is objectively beyond their physical or psychological capacity;

(c) involving harmful exposure to agents which are toxic, carcinogenic, cause heritable genetic damage, or harm the unborn child, or that in any other way chronically affect human health;

(d) involving harmful exposure to radiation;

(e) involving the risk of accidents that may be assumed cannot be recognised or avoided by the young seafarer owing to their insufficient attention to safety or lack of experience or training;

(f) in which there is a risk to health from extreme cold, heat, noise or vibration;

(g) requiring entry into an enclosed space (including boilers, tanks and cofferdams); or

(h) at night.[22]

Furthermore, the DMLC Pt I lists the following as being prohibited: working in enclosed spaces; working adjacent to open holds or tanks; working over the ship's side; working aloft such as on masts, mast tables or samson posts, etc; operating machinery, winches or lifting equipment with heavy tools; work in the

17 STCW Regulations, reg 2.
18 STCW Regulations, reg 37(2)–(3); CISN 07/2014 – Requirements and guidance for the provision of food and fresh water and training requirements for catering staff on ships, para 6.1.
19 STCW Regulations, reg 37(4); H&S Regulations, reg 2.
20 H&S Regulations, reg 18(1), (3).
21 H&S Regulations, reg 18(2)(a)–(b), respectively.
22 STCW Regulations, reg 37(3); H&S Regulations, reg 19(1)(a)–(h).

vicinity of cargo operations; mooring operations or other such similar work; or employment as a ship's cook.[23]

The exception (and this also applies to night work) is that a young seafarer may carry out a task which is an indispensable part of an established training programme, provided the task is performed under the supervision of a competent person, and is carried out so that the young seafarer's health and safety is ensured as far as reasonably practicable.[24]

See also paragraph 24.140 onwards below, which sets out details of the offences for non-compliances and powers of inspection and detention of ships.

Compliance

24.4 DMLC: implement CI requirements as set out in Pt I, point 1, and record details of compliance measures in DMLC, Pt II, point 1.

REGULATION 1.2: MEDICAL CERTIFICATE

24.5 The MACI does not issue its own medical certificates and does not have its own procedures for directly approving medical practitioners to do so. The system adopted is that of recognising certificates issued by other countries listed in CISN 05/2011.[25] The relevant provisions are set out in the Merchant Shipping (Maritime Labour Convention) (Medical Certification) Regulations, 2014 ('Medical Certification Regulations').[26]

Application

24.6 The Medical Certification Regulations apply to CI ships wherever they may be; only reg 12 (port state inspections of non-CI ships) applies to non-CI ships while they are in a CI port or waters.[27]

The following vessels and persons are excluded: pleasure vessels; fishing vessels; warships or naval auxiliaries;[28] offshore installations whilst on their working stations; and any person whose work is not part of the routine business of the ship and whose principal place of work is ashore.[29]

23 DMLC, Pt I, point 1.
24 H&S Regulations, reg 19(2)(a)–(b).
25 CISN 05/2011 (Rev 6) – Issue of endorsements attesting to the recognition of a certificate of competency.
26 Supplement No 3 published with Extraordinary Gazette No 64 dated 29 August 2014.
27 Medical Certification Regulations, reg 3(1)(a)–(b).
28 Medical Certification Regulations, reg 3(2)(a)–(d), respectively.
29 Medical Certification Regulations, reg 3(3).

Requirement for a medical fitness certificate

24.7 A 'medical fitness certificate' is one issued in accordance with Regulation I/9 of the STCW Convention by or under the authority of a country (and this must be clearly stated) listed in the Schedule to CISN 05/2011; it must be written in English (or in English and some other language).[30] The MACI also has discretion to approve certificates issued by other countries.[31] See Chapter 4regarding the attestation which certificates must contain in relation to hearing, sight (and colour vision, where relevant) and health.

Subject to some exceptions, seafarers must not work on a ship, and a person must not employ a seafarer on a ship, unless the seafarer has been issued with a valid medical fitness certificate, which they must keep on board their ship at all times.[32] Furthermore, seafarers are prohibited from working, and employers are prohibited from employing seafarers, in a capacity of sea service or in a geographical area precluded by any restriction in their certificate, or in breach of a condition of their certificate.[33]

Exceptions

24.8 Where the certificate has expired during the course of a voyage, the seafarer may continue to work until the first port at which it is possible to make an application for a medical fitness certificate and be examined by a medical practitioner, or three months from the expiry of the certificate.[34]

In urgent cases, with the MACI's approval, if a person does not hold a valid medical fitness certificate, but has held a medical fitness certificate for a period of not less than 24 months (or for 12 months for a young seafarer aged under 18 years) and that certificate has expired within one month of the seafarer joining a ship, the seafarer may work on that ship until the first port at which it is possible for an application for a medical fitness certificate to be made and to be examined by a medical practitioner, but this exception only applies for a maximum period of three months.[35]

A medical fitness certificate is valid from the date of the medical examination (or the date of consideration by a medical referee) for a maximum period of two years (or one year in the case of a young seafarer aged under 18 years).[36] Any contravention of the above requirements by the seafarer or the employer amounts

30 Medical Certification Regulations, reg 7(1), (3); CISN 05/2011, paras 3.2–3.4.
31 Medical Certification Regulations, reg 7(2).
32 Medical Certification Regulations, regs 4(1)–(2), 5(1), respectively.
33 Medical Certification Regulations, regs 4(5)–(6), 5(4)–(5), respectively.
34 Medical Certification Regulations, regs 4(3)(a)–(b), 5(2)(a)–(b), respectively.
35 Medical Certification Regulations, regs 4(4), 5(3)(a)–(b), respectively.
36 Medical Certification Regulations, reg 6(a)–(b).

to an offence punishable, on summary conviction, by a fine of $10,000 or, on conviction on indictment, by a fine of $20,000.[37]

There are reporting requirements imposed on any seafarer who is, or is likely to be, absent from work for 30 days due to a medical condition, or who has a significant injury or illness.[38] The report must be made to the authority which issued their certificate or, in any other case, to a medical practitioner; the seafarer's certificate will be suspended until they have been assessed as fit in accordance with the UK's MSN 1839 (which replaces MSN 1822).[39]

If a medical practitioner has certified that a seafarer engaged on watchkeeping duties is suffering from health problems due to night work, and it is possible for the shipowner to transfer the seafarer to suitable work outside of night hours, then the shipowner must do so.[40] For these purposes, 'night' means a period the duration of which is not less than nine consecutive hours and which includes the period between midnight and 5am local time.[41] A failure by the shipowner to comply amounts to an offence punishable, on summary conviction, by a fine of $10,000 or, on conviction on indictment, by a fine of $20,000.[42]

Inspection and detention of CI ships

24.9 Where an inspector is satisfied that a seafarer is unable to produce a medical fitness certificate and, due to the seafarer's health, the ship cannot sail without serious risk to the safety and health of those on board, the ship may be detained.[43]

Inspection of non-CI ships

24.10 In respect of a non-CI ship in Cayman Islands waters (or in one of its ports), an inspector may require the seafarers on board to produce their medical fitness certificates (or any related document) to ascertain if the ship complies with Regulation 1.2 and Standard A1.2 of the MLC.[44] The inspector may report any non-compliances to the flag state and send a copy to the ILO.[45]

37 Medical Certification Regulations, reg 10(1)(a)–(b), respectively.
38 Medical Certification Regulations, reg 8(1)(a)–(b), (4).
39 Medical Certification Regulations, reg 8(2)–(3); MSN 1839(M) – Seafarer Medical Examination System and Medical Eyesight Standards.
40 Medical Certification Regulations, reg 9(1)(a)–(b).
41 Medical Certification Regulations, reg 9(2)(a)–(b).
42 Medical Certification Regulations, reg 10(2)(a)–(b); note that reg 10(2) refers in error to the relevant duty being contained in reg 8 (which only imposes a duty on seafarers) instead of the (correct) reg 9.
43 Medical Certification Regulations, reg 11.
44 Medical Certification Regulations, reg 12(1).
45 Medical Certification Regulations, reg 13(2)(a)–(b).

It is an offence for any person to obstruct an inspector in the exercise of their powers, or for a seafarer on a non-CI ship, without reasonable excuse, to fail to produce their medical certificate (or any related document), punishable, on summary conviction, by a fine of $10,000 or, on conviction on indictment, by a fine of $50,000.

Defence

24.11 It is a defence for a person charged with any of the above offences to show that they took all reasonable precautions and exercised all due diligence to avoid the commission of the offence.[46]

Compliance

24.12 DMLC: implement CI requirements as set out in Pt I, point 2, and record details of compliance measures in DMLC, Pt II, point 2.

REGULATION 1.3: TRAINING AND QUALIFICATIONS

24.13 The main provisions are set out in the STCW Regulations. Also relevant is CISN 05/2011, which sets out the STCW Convention signatory states whose Certificates of Competency (CoCs) are accepted by the CI.[47]

Application

24.14 On the application of the STCW Regulations, see paragraph 24.3 above.

The STCW Regulations use the term 'company', which '…includes an individual, and in relation to a ship means the owner of the ship or any other organisation or person such as the manager, or the demise charterer, who has assumed the responsibility for the operation of the ship from the owner and who, on assuming such responsibility, has agreed to take over all the duties and responsibilities imposed on the company by the Regulations annexed to the STCW Convention'.[48] In most cases the 'company' will be the same party as the 'shipowner', which is the term used in the MLC and the CI implementing legislation.[49]

46 Medical Certification Regulations, reg 10(4).
47 CISN 05/2011 (Rev 6) – Issue of endorsements attesting to the recognition of a certificate of competency, para 2.1.
48 STCW Regulations, reg 2(1).
49 MLC, Article II(1)(j); see, for example, Merchant Shipping (Maritime Labour Convention) (Health and Safety) Regulations, 2014, reg 2.

Officers

24.15 The MACI does not issue its own Certificates of Competency (CoCs). Instead, officers must hold a CoC for the capacity in which they serve, which has been issued by or under the authority of a CI-recognised STCW state (listed in CISN 05/2011) and apply for it to be endorsed (using form CISR 504) by the MACI.[50] The endorsement will be in the form set out in the first Schedule to the STCW Regulations and will be valid for the period for which the underlying CoC remains valid (without being withdrawn, suspended or cancelled), limited to a maximum period of five years.[51] The MACI may allow an officer (except a radio operator), who holds a valid CoC issued by an STCW state, to work for a maximum period of three months on a ship, without an endorsement, so long as they possess evidence that an application for endorsement has been submitted.[52]

As regards pleasure vessels only, the MACI has discretion to recognise certificates issued by STCW states which are not listed in CISN 05/2011, in which case a licence (instead of an endorsement) will be issued to attest to its recognition.[53] In no case will a certificate issued by a non-STCW signatory be recognised.[54]

Officers serving at the management level (master, chief mate, chief engineer or second engineer) must have appropriate knowledge of the CI maritime legislation and proficiency in the English language relative to the functions which they are permitted to perform, in accordance with the requirements set out in the second Schedule to the STCW Regulations.[55]

The MACI may, in exceptional circumstances, issue a dispensation from the requirement to hold an appropriate CoC, and such a dispensation may only be granted to a person who is properly certified to fill the post immediately below the position to which the dispensation relates.[56]

Ratings

24.16 Except for ratings under training, or those carrying out unskilled duties, deck and engine-room ratings are required to hold a certificate as follows:

- those forming part of a navigational watch on a ship of 500 GT or more must hold a 'Navigational Watch Rating Certificate', issued in accordance with Regulation II/4 of the Annex to the STCW Convention; and

50 STCW Regulations, regs 4–6, 7A; CISN 05/2011, para 2.1.
51 STCW Regulations, reg 6(2)–(3).
52 STCW Regulations, reg 6(4).
53 STCW Regulations, regs 3(1)(c), 6(7)–(9).
54 STCW Regulations, reg 5(6).
55 STCW Regulations, reg 5(4); Second Schedule.
56 STCW Regulations, reg 26.

- those forming part of an engine-room watch or designated to perform duties in a periodically unmanned engine-room on a ship powered by main propulsion machinery of 750 KW propulsion power or more must hold an 'Engine Room Watch Rating Certificate', issued in accordance with Regulation III/4 of the Annex to the STCW Convention,

in each case issued by the MACI or by or under the authority of another STCW state.[57]

Any person performing watchkeeping duties in a manned or periodically unmanned engine-room on a ship powered by main propulsion machinery of 350 KW power or more, but less than 750 KW, must hold an engineering certificate or an appropriate certificate complying with the requirements specified by the MACI.[58]

All seafarers

24.17 All seafarers must receive familiarisation, basic safety training or instruction in accordance with Section A-VI/1 of the Annex to the STCW Code, and meet the appropriate standard of competence.[59] The company must provide written instructions to the master setting out the policies and procedures to be followed, so that newly joining seafarers are given a reasonable opportunity to familiarise themselves with shipboard equipment, operating procedures and other arrangements in advance of taking up relevant duties.[60] A master or other seafarer who fails to carry out an obligation arising under this requirement commits an offence punishable as follows: in respect of a master, on summary conviction, by a fine of $15,000 or, on indictment, by a fine of $25,000 and imprisonment for 12 months; and, in respect of any other seafarer, a fine not exceeding level 3 on the standard scale.[61] A 'reasonable steps' defence is available[62] (see below).

Specific duties

24.18 There are specific requirements relating to radio communications and radio personnel,[63] and training and qualifications of masters and seamen on tankers, ro-ro passenger ships, other passenger ships, and high-speed craft.[64]

57 STCW Regulations, reg 8(1)–(2).
58 STCW Regulations, reg 8(3).
59 STCW Regulations, reg 14.
60 STCW Regulations, reg 24(4).
61 STCW Regulations, reg 43(2), (4), respectively.
62 STCW Regulations, reg 43(10)–(11).
63 STCW Regulations, reg 9.
64 STCW Regulations, regs 10–13, respectively; also, Third Schedule, in relation to training and certification of officers on high-speed craft, which also contains (at the Appendix) a model type rating certificate.

Further requirements relate to: certificates of proficiency in survival craft rescue boats;[65] training in advanced firefighting;[66] medical first aid and medical care[67] (see Chapter 17); and hovercraft.[68]

Carriage of certificates

24.19 The company and the master must ensure that all original certificates and documents issued under the STCW Convention are carried on board at all time.[69]

Inspection and detention

24.20 CI ships and non-CI ships (when the latter are in a CI port or roadstead) may be inspected to check for compliance with STCW Convention certification and safe manning requirements.[70] CI ships may be detained for a contravention of the Regulations.[71] Non-CI ships may be detained for: breaches of the safe manning provisions; watchkeeping provisions; or a failure to correct a deficiency specified in reg 39(3) (which includes a failure to hold a valid certificate, endorsement or dispensation) where consequently there is a danger to persons, property or the environment.[72]

Offences

24.21 The following offences apply in respect to CI ships only: failure by the company to ensure that each seafarer holds an appropriate certificate and has been trained in accordance with the STCW Regulations, which is punishable, on summary conviction, by a fine of $25,000 or, on indictment, by a fine of $50,000 and (in the case of an individual) to imprisonment for 12 months.[73]

General defence

24.22 In relation to offences under the STCW Regulations, it is a defence for the accused to prove that they took all reasonable steps to avoid commission of the offence; it is for the accused to prove that it was not reasonably practicable to do more than was, in fact, done to satisfy the relevant requirement.[74]

65 STCW Regulations, reg 15.
66 STCW Regulations, reg 16.
67 STCW Regulations, reg 17.
68 STCW Regulations, regs 20–23.
69 STCW Regulations, reg 38.
70 STCW Regulations, reg 39.
71 STCW Regulations, reg 40(a).
72 STCW Regulations, reg 40(b)(i)–(ii).
73 STCW Regulations, reg 43(1).
74 STCW Regulations, reg 43(10)–(11).

Compliance

24.23 DMLC: implement CI requirements as set out in Pt I, point 3, and record details of compliance measures in DMLC, Pt II, point 3.

REGULATION 1.4: RECRUITMENT AND PLACEMENT

24.24 There is no significant presence (if there is at all) of seafarer recruitment and placement services (RPS) in the CI. Therefore, the MLC implementing provisions are very brief and are set out in the Merchant Shipping (Maritime Labour Convention) (Survey and Certification) Regulations, 2014[75] ('S&C Regulations'). The S&C Regulations only set down conditions relating to the RPS which shipowners may use and do not detail any of the obligations which RPS themselves are required to comply with under Standard A1.4 of the MLC.

CI ships

24.25 Shipowners of CI ships must not use a seafarer RPS unless it:

- is based in the CI;
- is based in a country which has ratified the MLC;
- is based in a country to which another country's ratification of the MLC has been extended; or
- it complies with the requirements of MLC, Standard A1.4 on recruitment and placement.[76]

Shipowners who use RPS should retain documentary evidence to show that they recruit from those which fall into one of the acceptable categories listed above, as this is subject to inspection by the MACI (to qualify for issue of an MLCert)[77] and inspections in foreign ports.[78] The particulars of how the shipowner complies should be entered against point 5 of the DMLC, Pt II.[79]

A shipowner's failure to comply amounts to an offence punishable, on summary conviction, by a fine of $20,000 or, on conviction on indictment, by a fine of $100,000.[80] It is a defence for the accused to show that the offence was committed without their knowledge or, where they had such knowledge, that they took all reasonable precautions and exercised all due diligence to avoid the commission of the offence.[81]

75 Supplement No 5 published with Extraordinary Gazette No 64 dated 29 August 2014.
76 S&C Regulations, reg 14.
77 S&C Regulations, reg 9.
78 MLC, Standard A5.2.1, paras 1(a), (2); Appendix A5-III.
79 S&C Regulations, reg 13(1)(b).
80 S&C Regulations, reg 24(4).
81 S&C Regulations, reg 25.

Non-CI ships in CI waters

24.26 Shipowners of non-CI ships (whether or not they are registered with a country which has ratified the MLC) may be inspected against MLC requirements while they are in CI waters, and detained for non-compliance.[82] The MLC requires that, if a shipowner uses an RPS which is situated in a non-MLC state, the shipowner must ensure, as far as practicable, that it meets the requirements set out in Standard A1.4.[83] In the latter case, it would be advisable to request evidence of a recent successful audit carried out by a classification society or other competent organisation.

For a detailed account of national implementation of the MLC provisions on recruitment and placement, see those of the UK in Chapter 6.

Compliance

24.27 DMLC: implement CI requirements as set out in Pt I, point 5, and record details of compliance measures in DMLC, Pt II, point 5.

REGULATION 2.1: SEAFARERS' EMPLOYMENT AGREEMENTS

24.28 The provisions on seafarers' employment agreements (SEAs) are set out in the Merchant Shipping (Maritime Labour Convention) (Seafarer Employment Agreement, Shipowners' Liabilities and Wages) Regulations, 2014,[84] ('SEA Regulations'). As the SEA Regulations cover various areas of MLC implementation, there will be references back to the powers of inspection, detention and statutory defence, as they also apply to those other areas.

Application

24.29 The SEA Regulations apply to: CI ships wherever they may be; and to non-CI ships which do not carry MLC documentation while they are in CI waters; and regulations 24–25 apply to non-CI ships which carry MLC documentation while they are in CI waters.[85]

The following are excluded: pleasure vessels; fishing vessels; warships or naval auxiliaries; or offshore installations whilst on their working stations.[86]

82 S&C Regulations, reg 21–22.
83 MLC, Standard A1.4.9.
84 Supplement No 6 published with Extraordinary Gazette No 64 dated 29 August 2014.
85 SEA Regulations, reg 3(1)–(2).
86 SEA Regulations, reg 3(3)(a)–(d), respectively.

Seafarer's employment agreement

24.30 There must be a SEA between every seafarer working on a ship and the shipowner, which may incorporate other documents such as a collective agreement.[87]

The SEA must include a statement whereby both the shipowner and seafarer confirm: (a) that the shipowner has provided a sufficient opportunity for the seafarer to review and take advice on the terms and conditions of the agreement; (b) that the shipowner has explained the rights and responsibilities of the seafarer under the agreement; and (c) that the seafarer enters into the agreement freely.[88]

The SEA must include the information set out below, which may be met by incorporating another document, such as a collective agreement:[89]

1. The full name, birthplace and date of birth (or age at the time of entering into the agreement) of the seafarer.
2. The name and address of the shipowner.
3. The place where the agreement is entered into.
4. The date on which the agreement is entered into.
5. The capacity in which the seafarer is to be employed or engaged.[90]
6. The amount of the seafarer's wages or the formula used for calculating it.[91]
7. The amount of the paid annual leave or the formula used for calculating it.[92]
8. If the agreement has been made for a definite period, the termination date.
9. If the agreement has been made for an indefinite period, the period of notice of termination required and the circumstances in which such notice may be given.
10. If the agreement has been made for a voyage, the destination port and the period following arrival after which the agreement terminates.
11. The health and social security protection benefits to be provided to the seafarer by the shipowner.[93]
12. The maximum duration of service periods on board following which the seafarer is entitled to repatriation (which must not exceed a period of 12 months minus the number of days' annual leave to which the seafarer is entitled).[94]
13. The seafarer's entitlement to repatriation (including the mode of transport and destination of repatriation) and the circumstances in which the seafarer is required to meet or reimburse the shipowner for the costs of repatriation.[95]

87 SEA Regulations, reg 4.
88 SEA Regulations, reg 5(3)(a)–(b).
89 SEA Regulations, reg 5(1)–(2); Sch 1.
90 See Regulation 1.3; seafarers should be trained and certified accordingly.
91 See Regulation 2.2.
92 See Regulation 2.4.
93 See Regulation 4.5.
94 See Regulation 2.5.
95 See Regulation 2.5.

14. The maximum sum which the shipowner will pay to the seafarer in respect of compensation for any loss of personal property arising from the loss or foundering of the ship.[96]

A model SEA is available on the MACI website.[97]

Notice periods

24.31 The minimum period of notice is seven days, unless the parties agree to a shorter period.[98] The minimum period of notice which the seafarer is required to give to the shipowner must not be greater than that which the shipowner is required to give to the seafarer.[99] The parties may terminate the SEA, without penalty, even though the minimum notice period has not been given, for compassionate reasons or due to serious misconduct.[100]

Documentation

24.32 The shipowner must:

- provide the seafarer with their SEA and any incorporated collective agreement, as soon as is practicable after it has been signed by the seafarer and the shipowner (or the latter's authorised representative – in which case they must be named as such in the DMLC Pt II);[101]
- ensure that a copy of the SEA and any incorporated documents such as a collective agreement (with an English translation if that is not the language of the original) for each seafarer is held on board, to be viewed by them on request (the master may be required to produce these to an inspector of the MACI);[102]
- as soon as is practicable after a SEA has been terminated, provide the seafarer with a record of their employment.[103]

The record of employment must contain: the name, port of registry, gross or registered tonnage and the official number of the ship; description of voyage; capacity in which the seafarer was employed; the date on which employment started; and the date of discharge.[104] It must not contain any reference to the quality of the seafarer's work or to their wages.[105]

96 SEA Regulations, Sch 1; and Regulation 2.6 on compensation for loss and foundering of a ship.
97 Model SEA (click on 'Maritime Labour Convention'): http://cishipping.com/forms [Accessed 9 June 2018].
98 SEA Regulations, reg 6(1)–(2).
99 SEA Regulations, reg 6(3).
100 SEA Regulations, reg 6(4).
101 SEA Regulations, regs 7(1), (5), 8; DMLC Pt I, point 4.
102 SEA Regulations, regs 7(2), (5), 8–9.
103 SEA Regulations, reg 7(3).
104 SEA Regulations, reg 7(4)(a), Sch 2.
105 SEA Regulations, reg 7(4)(b)–(c).

Criminal offences

24.33 A failure to comply with some of the above obligations amounts to a criminal offence by the shipowner or the master.[106] Fines range from $15,000 on summary conviction and $50,000 on conviction on indictment in respect of the shipowner; and $10,000 on summary conviction in respect of the master.[107]

It is a defence to all charges under the SEA Regulations for the accused to show that the offence was committed without their knowledge or, where they had such knowledge, that they took all reasonable precautions and exercised all due diligence to avoid the commission of the offence.[108]

Inspection and detention in connection with matters covered under the SEA Regulations

24.34 A CI ship (and, when it is in CI waters, a non-CI ship) which does not carry MLC documentation may be inspected to check for compliance with the matters covered by the SEA Regulations.[109] The ship may be detained for a serious breach or the latest in a series of repeated breaches of specified requirements, including those on: SEAs; shipowner's obligations to pay seafarers' wages and issue monthly accounts,[110] and to pay interest for late payment of wages;[111] annual leave and shore leave;[112] shipowners' liability to indemnify seafarers due to unemployment resulting from the loss or wreck of the ship;[113] and shipowners' liability towards sick or injured seafarers and the duty to provide related financial security.[114]

A non-CI ship with MLC documentation may, while it is in CI waters, have its MLC documentation reviewed and, where Standard A5.2.1 applies,[115] be subjected to a more detailed inspection in accordance with that standard.[116] Where there are clear grounds for believing that there is a non-compliance with the MLC, which represents a serious or repeated breach of the MLC, the ship is liable to be detained.[117]

106 SEA Regulations, reg 12(1)–(3).
107 SEA Regulations, reg 12(3).
108 SEA Regulations, reg 27.
109 SEA Regulations, reg 22.
110 See MLC, Regulation 2.2.
111 See MLC, Regulation 2.2.
112 See MLC, Regulation 2.4.
113 See MLC, Regulation 2.6.
114 SEA Regulations, reg 23. See MLC, Regulations 4.1 and 4.2.
115 Standard A5.2.1 of the MLC covers port state control and is set out in full in Appendix 1.
116 SEA Regulations, reg 24.
117 SEA Regulations, reg 25.

Future amendments to the MLC

24.35 When the 2018 amendments to the MLC come into force (which is likely to be 26 December 2020) ratifying states will be required to provide that: (a) SEAs continue for the entirety of any period in which a seafarer is held in captivity as a result of an act of piracy or armed robbery at sea; and (b) seafarers' wages, allotments and other entitlements must be fully paid during the entirety of any such period. The full text of the amendments is set out in Appendix 2.

Compliance

24.36 DMLC: implement CI requirements as set out in Pt I, point 4, and record details of compliance measures in DMLC, Pt II, point 4.

REGULATION 2.2: WAGES

24.37 Shipowners must ensure that:

- seafarers are paid in full at no greater than monthly intervals and in accordance with their SEA and any applicable collective agreement;[118] and
- accounts of wages or other remuneration due under the SEA are prepared and delivered to the seafarer periodically at intervals not exceeding one month, and within one month of the SEA terminating.[119]

Except in the case of payments to a self-employed seafarer[120] (on which, see para 24.38 below), the account must contain the following information:

> '(a) name of the seafarer;
>
> (b) the number of the seafarer's current discharge book (if any);
>
> (c) the seafarer's income tax code (if applicable);
>
> (d) the seafarer's national insurance number and the dates on which national insurance contributions commenced and ceased (if applicable);
>
> (e) name of the ship and its official number;
>
> (f) capacity in which the seafarer was employed;
>
> (g) dates when employment commenced and ceased and total period of employment in which wages were earned, showing separately the dates of the beginning and end of any period in which wages were not earned;
>
> (h) sums payable under each allotment note, date when the first payment was due, the intervals between payments, and the total of all such sums; and

118 SEA Regulations, reg 19(1).
119 SEA Regulations, reg 19(2)(a)–(b), respectively.
120 SEA Regulations, reg 19(5).

(i) total amount of gross wages earned with, shown separately and with sufficient detail to indicate how each amount is calculated, the total amounts in respect of–

(i) the wages at the rate provided for in the relevant [SEA];

(ii) overtime;

(iii) leave pay;

(iv) subsistence;

(v) any other earnings during the period of employment;

(vi) deductions, specifying the nature of the deduction and showing the total amount in respect of each deduction;

(vii) total amount deducted from gross wages;

(viii) total amount of net wages; and

(ix) balance of wages.'[121]

Where the accounts include information about amounts which have been determined by reference to a currency exchange rate, they must also include details of the relevant exchange rate and any commission paid.[122]

Self-employed seafarers

24.38 For self-employed seafarers, the accounts must only contain the following information:

'(a) payments due;

(b) payments made (including any not falling within subparagraph (a)); and

(c) any rates of exchange and any commissions paid which are relevant to those payments.'[123]

Allotments

24.39 Seafarers must be allowed to allot part of their wages to be paid directly to a nominated person.[124] Unless the employer or master agrees, allotment payments (which must be paid at regular intervals) need not be paid any more frequently than on a monthly basis, and the seafarer may only allot wages that have already been earned.[125]

121 SEA Regulations, reg 19(3)(a)–(i)(i)–(ix).
122 SEA Regulations, reg 19(4).
123 SEA Regulations, reg 19(5)(a)–(c).
124 SEA Regulations, reg 20(1), (3).
125 SEA Regulations, reg 20(2)(a)–(b), respectively.

Shipowners may recover the costs incurred in making allotment payments, other than those it ordinarily incurs in making payments to the seafarer, but must not levy a charge for providing the service.[126] If it is appropriate or necessary to exchange currency to make an allotment payment, the shipowner must use a reasonable exchange rate.[127]

Interest for late payment

24.40 If wages are not paid on time (in accordance with the SEA), interest at the rate of 20% must be paid from the due date until payment is made.[128] An exception applies where the failure to make payment on the due date, or as soon as practicable thereafter, was due to: a mistake; a reasonable dispute as to liability; the act or default of the seafarer; or any other cause not being the wrongful act or default of the persons liable to make the payment or of their servants or agents.[129]

Offences

24.41 Any shipowner who fails to comply with the provisions on seafarers' wages and accounts, or fails to pay interest for late payment of wages, commits an offence and is liable on summary conviction to a fine of $15,000.[130]

Inspection and detention

24.42 See paragraph 24.28 above which, under the SEA Regulations, also applies to non-compliances with a shipowner's obligations to pay seafarers' wages and issue monthly accounts, and to pay interest for late payment of wages.

Future amendments to the MLC

24.43 See paragraph 24.35 above regarding the 2018 amendments to the MLC, which are likely to come into force on 26 December 2020.

Compliance

24.44 DMLC: implement CI requirements as set out in Pt I, point 14, and record details of compliance measures in DMLC, Pt II, point 14.

126 SEA Regulations, reg 20(4).
127 SEA Regulations, reg 20(5).
128 SEA Regulations, reg 18(1).
129 SEA Regulations, reg 18(2)(a)–(d), respectively.
130 SEA Regulations, reg 21.

REGULATION 2.3: HOURS OF WORK AND HOURS OF REST

24.45 The relevant provisions are contained in the STCW Regulations, as amended by the Merchant Shipping (Certification, Safe Manning, Hours of Work and Watchkeeping) (Amendment) Regulations, 2014[131] ('STCW Amendment Regulations'), which insert a new definition of 'seafarer'[132] and a new reg 30, and introduce CISN 05/2014.[133]

Application and definitions

24.46 On the application of the STCW Regulations, see paragraph 24.3 above.

The STCW Regulations address their obligations to the 'company', the definition of which is set out in para 24.14 above.

General duties

24.47 Subject to the exceptions that apply in emergencies, a general duty is imposed on the company, the master and every employer to ensure, so far as is reasonably practicable, that seafarers do not work more hours than is safe in relation to the safety of the ship and the performance of their duties.[134] Each seafarer must also ensure that, so far as is reasonably practicable, they are properly rested when commencing duty and obtain adequate rest during their rest periods.[135]

Schedule of duties and minimum hours of rest

24.48 The company must produce a schedule of duties and, before doing so, must consult any other employers of the seafarers on board, and seek the views of the master, who must seek the views of the seafarers or their representatives and convey them to the company.[136] The company may arrange for any other employer to produce a schedule of duties, and any other employer which does so will also be subject to the reg 30 duties to which the company is subject.[137] The schedule may only be changed by the company or an employer (who has become subject to the reg 30 duties) by following the same consultation processes, and so long as it remains compliant with the requirements set out below.[138]

131 Supplement No 1 published with Extraordinary Gazette No 68 dated 17 September 2014.
132 STCW Regulations, reg 2(1), as amended by STCW Amendment Regulations, reg 2(a).
133 STCW Regulations, reg 2(1), as amended by STCW Amendment Regulations, reg 2(b); CISN 05/2014 – Recording hours of work and rest on Cayman Islands flagged vessels.
134 STCW Regulations, reg 28.
135 STCW Regulations, reg 29.
136 STCW Regulations, reg 30(1)–(2), (4), as amended by STCW Amendment Regulations, reg 3.
137 STCW Regulations, reg 30(3), as amended.
138 STCW Regulations, reg 30(7)(a)–(c), as amended (the requirements are set out in reg 30(5), as amended).

In preparing the schedule of duties, the company must take into account the nature of the operation and voyages in arranging hours of work at sea and in port,[139] and the schedule must:

- be posted in an easily accessible place and for every position contain the schedule of service at sea and service in port, and the minimum hours of rest required in accordance with Pt 5 of the STCW Regulations or any applicable collective agreement;[140]
- be established using the form in the schedule to CISN 05/2014 or in any other standardised format so long as it contains the same information and, as a minimum, it sets out the hours of work for: seafarers whose work includes regular watchkeeping or ship handling; and the master, chief engineer, chief officer and second engineer officer, so as to provide that they do not work more hours than is safe (as described above);[141]
- specify the maximum period of continuous watchkeeping, the minimum rest period between watches, and the total daily, weekly and monthly hours of work;[142] and
- provide a minimum of ten hours of rest in any 24-hour period (which may be divided into no more than two periods, one of which must be at least six hours in length) and a minimum of 77 hours' rest in any seven-day period.[143]

For these purposes, 'hours of rest' means time outside hours of work and does not include short breaks.[144]

The schedule must be displayed prominently in the crew accommodation and be in the working language of the ship and in English.[145] The guidance states that the schedule may be displayed on an easily accessible computer network.[146] The master must ensure, so far as is reasonably practicable, that the specified hours of work are not exceeded.[147]

Exceptions to minimum hours of rest

24.49 In accordance with the MLC, the MACI may permit exceptions to the minimum hours of rest that are part of a collective agreement, or in connection with which the shipowner (when making its application) can produce evidence that the relevant exception has been agreed by the seafarers or their representatives.[148] The exceptions must, as far as possible, follow the requirements relating to the

139 STCW Regulations, reg 30(6), as amended.
140 STCW Regulations, reg 30(5)(a)(i)–(ii), as amended.
141 STCW Regulations, reg 30(5)(c)(i)(aa)–(bb), as amended.
142 STCW Regulations, reg 30(5)(c)(ii), as amended.
143 STCW Regulations, reg 30(5)(c)(iii)–(iv), as amended.
144 CISN 05/2014, para 2.2.
145 STCW Regulations, reg 30(8), as amended.
146 CISN 05/2014, para 4.5.
147 STCW Regulations, reg 30(9), as amended.
148 CISN 05/2014, para 7.1; MLC, Standard A2.3.13.

minimum hours of rest in the Regulations, but may take account of more frequent or longer leave periods, and the granting of compensatory leave for watchkeeping seafarers or seafarers working on board ships on short voyages.[149]

Records

24.50 The company and the master are responsible for maintaining a copy of the schedule of work and a record of all deviations from its requirements and preserving it for five years (if there ceases to be a company in relation to the ship, the duty remains with the last such company) and make it available for inspection.[150] The master must give every seafarer a copy of the schedule relevant to them, which must be signed by the master (or delegate) and the seafarer.[151]

An individual record of hours of rest must be kept for each seafarer, with any deviations or breaches from the minimum rest hours noted, as well as compensatory rest periods granted.[152] The records must be maintained in English, and each seafarer should receive a copy of their records, generally monthly, which must be endorsed by the master (or designate) and the seafarer.[153] The guidance also sets down standards (including observance of ILO guidelines) under which the records may be kept in electronic format.[154] The MACI does not produce its own form on its website, but the Isle of Man's MLN 2.3 (at Annex II) provides a good example.[155]

A copy of Pts V (hours of work) and VI (watchkeeping) of the STCW Regulations must be carried on board every CI ship.[156]

Emergencies, drills and call out

24.51 The minimum rest periods need not be maintained in case of any emergency, including giving assistance to other ships or persons in distress at sea, or where there is a threat to the safety of the ship, the life of any person or damage to the environment.[157] When the emergency is over, any seafarer who worked during a scheduled rest period must be given an adequate rest period as soon as practicable, and their name and the reason they were required to work must be recorded in the record of deviations on the schedule.[158]

149 CISN 05/2014, para 7.2.
150 STCW Regulations, reg 30(10)(a)–(c), as amended.
151 STCW Regulations, reg 30(10)(d), as amended.
152 CISN 05/2014, paras 5.1–5.2.
153 CISN 05/2014, para 5.3.
154 CISN 05/2014, paras 6.1.1–6.1.5.
155 IOM MLN 2.3, Annex II: Records of hours of rest: www.iomshipregistry.com/media/1331/mln-23-hours-of-work-and-hours-of-rest.pdf [Accessed 12 June 2018].
156 STCW Regulations, reg 32.
157 STCW Regulations, reg 31(1)–(2).
158 STCW Regulations, reg 31(3)–(4).

Musters, fire-fighting and lifeboat drills must be conducted in a way that minimises disturbance of rest periods and does not induce fatigue.[159]

An adequate compensatory rest period must be given to any on-call seafarer if their normal period of rest is disturbed by a call-out to work.[160]

Young seafarers

24.52 Night work for young seafarers under the age of 18 years is a restricted task which may only be carried out when the exception described in paragraph 24.1 above applies.

Inspection and detention

24.53 A CI ship or a non-CI ship may be inspected to assess the ability of the seafarers to maintain the watchkeeping standards required by the STCW Regulations where there are clear grounds for believing that such standards are not being maintained because, while in a CI port or roadstead, the ship was involved in an incident such as a collision, grounding or pollution, etc.[161] If the inspector finds one of a number of specified breached of the STCW Regulations, including inadequately rested seafarers for the first watch at the commencement of a voyage, the master of a CI ship must be notified in writing (for a non-CI ship, a representative of the flag state must be informed).[162] CI ships may be detained for a breach of the STCW Regulations, and the same powers apply on a 'parity of treatment' basis to other ships registered in an STCW state.[163] Non-CI ships which are registered with an MLC state may (while they are in CI waters) have their MLC documentation reviewed, which could lead to a more detailed inspection, resulting in detention for any dangerous, serious or repeated breach of the MLC.[164]

Offences

24.54 Specified non-compliances amount to offences by the company, employer (if it becomes subject to the reg 30 duty – see para 24.48 above), master and seafarers: all are punishable by fines (ranging from level 1 on the standard scale to $50,000), and some are also punishable by imprisonment (for maximum

159 STCW Regulations, reg 30(11), as amended.
160 STCW Regulations, reg 30(12), as amended.
161 STCW Regulations, reg 39(1)(c)(i)–(iv).
162 STCW Regulations, reg 39(2)–(3)(f).
163 STCW Regulations, regs 40–41.
164 Merchant Shipping (Maritime Labour Convention) (Survey and Certification) Regulations 2014, regs 21–22.

periods ranging from six to 12 months).[165] It is a defence for the accused to show that they took all reasonable steps to avoid commission of the offence and (where applicable) prove that it was not reasonably practicable to do more than what was done.[166]

Compliance

24.55 DMLC: implement CI requirements as set out in Pt I, point 6, and record details of compliance measures in DMLC, Pt II, point 6.

REGULATION 2.4: ENTITLEMENT TO LEAVE

24.56 The relevant provisions are set out in the SEA Regulations.

The shipowner must ensure that every seafarer is given paid annual leave of not less than 38 days per annum.[167] The 38 days is derived from the MLC's mandatory two and a half days leave per month and its non-mandatory guideline that public holidays (of which there are eight in the CI) should not be counted as paid annual leave.[168] However, the eight days provided in lieu of public holidays is inclusive of such holidays, and there is no further entitlement on the actual days on which those holidays fall.[169] Annual leave is to accrue at no less than 3.20 days per month, and is to be calculated pro-rata for an incomplete year.[170] Entitlement to paid leave accrues from the moment the seafarer leaves their home to join the ship, until they are repatriated.[171] Any agreement to forgo annual leave for payment (except where the employment is terminated before leave can be taken) is void.[172]

Periods of absence for the following reasons are not to be counted as part of annual leave with pay: incapacity through injury or illness; maternity leave; temporary shore leave; travelling to or from the ship; approved training courses; and compensatory leave following drills, emergencies or other unplanned periods of duty.[173]

Seafarers must be permitted to take their annual leave in the place where they have a substantial connection, which may be their repatriation destination, unless

165 STCW Regulations, reg 43(1)–(3), (6)–(9).
166 STCW Regulations, reg 43(10)–(11).
167 SEA Regulations, reg 10(1). Although the word 'paid' is absent, this is likely to be a drafting error, as this is clearly what the MLC intended (see Standard A2.4.2) and, furthermore, 'annual leave with pay' is referred to in reg 10(5).
168 MLC, Standard A2.4.2; Guideline B2.4.4(a).
169 SEA Regulations, reg 10(4).
170 SEA Regulations, reg 10(2).
171 SEA Regulations, reg 10(6).
172 SEA Regulations, reg 10(3).
173 SEA Regulations, reg 10(5)(a)–(e), respectively.

they consent to take it elsewhere.[174] Recalls from leave are only permitted in cases of emergency and with the seafarer's consent.[175]

The seafarer's entitlement to annual leave, or the formula used for calculating it, must be entered in their SEA (see para 24.30 above).

Shore leave

24.57 The shipowner and the master must allow seafarers to take shore leave to benefit their health and well-being, where consistent with the operational requirements of their positions.[176]

Criminal offences

24.58 A failure to comply with any of the provisions on annual leave amounts to a criminal offence by the shipowner punishable, on summary conviction, by a fine of $15,000 or, on conviction on indictment, by a fine of $50,000.[177]

Inspection and detention

24.59 See paragraph 24.28 above which, under the SEA Regulations, also applies to non-compliances with annual leave and shore leave.

REGULATION 2.5: REPATRIATION

24.60 The provisions are set out in the Merchant Shipping (Maritime Labour Convention) (Repatriation) Regulations, 2014[178] ('Repatriation Regulations').

Application

24.61 The Repatriation Regulations apply to CI ships wherever they may be and (while they are in CI waters) to non-CI ships which do not carry MLC documentation.[179] With regard to non-CI ships which do carry MLC documentation, they are only subject to the inspection and detention powers in regulations 16–17, while they are in CI waters.[180] The following are excluded: pleasure vessels; fishing vessels; warships or naval auxiliaries; and offshore

174 SEA Regulations, reg 10(7).
175 SEA Regulations, reg 10(8).
176 SEA Regulations, reg 11.
177 SEA Regulations, reg 12(1)(a)–(b), respectively.
178 Supplement No 7 published with Extraordinary Gazette No 64 dated 29 August 2014.
179 Repatriation Regulations, reg 3(1).
180 Repatriation Regulations, reg 3(2).

installations whilst on their working stations.[181] The Merchant Shipping (Repatriation) (Cayman Islands) Regulations, 1989, no longer apply to any ship which is now subject to the Repatriation Regulations.[182]

CI SHIPS AND (WHILE THEY ARE IN CI WATERS) NON-CI SHIPS WITHOUT MLC DOCUMENTATION

Duty to repatriate

24.62 Shipowners are responsible for making provision to repatriate seafarers as soon as practicable in circumstances where:

- their SEA expires;
- their SEA is terminated by the shipowner;
- their SEA is terminated by the seafarer in accordance with the terms of the agreement;
- the seafarer is no longer able to carry out their duties under their SEA or cannot be expected to carry them out in the specific circumstances (see below);
- the seafarer has completed the maximum duration of service periods on board, following which the seafarer is entitled to repatriation, as set out in their SEA.[183]

A non-exhaustive list of the 'specific circumstances' (referred to above) is provided and includes: an illness, injury or medical condition which requires the seafarer's repatriation when found medically fit to travel; shipwreck; the shipowner is not able to fulfil its legal or contractual obligations to the seafarer following insolvency, the sale of the ship or a change in the ship's registration; and the ship is bound for a war zone to which the seafarer does not consent to go.[184]

A failure by the shipowner to repatriate a seafarer in the circumstances set out above amounts to an offence punishable. on summary conviction, by a fine of $10,000 and, on indictment, by a fine of $50,000.[185]

Place of repatriation

24.63 This is the place stated in the seafarer's SEA, or any other place subsequently agreed with the shipowner.[186] If the SEA does not specify a destination, the seafarer is entitled to choose any of the following: the place at

181 Repatriation Regulations, reg 3(3)(a)–(d), respectively.
182 Repatriation Regulations, reg 3(4).
183 Repatriation Regulations, reg 4(1)–(5), (7).
184 Repatriation Regulations, reg 4(6)(a)–(d), respectively.
185 SEA Regulations, reg 4(8)(a)–(b), respectively.
186 SEA Regulations, reg 5(1).

which they entered into their SEA; a place agreed with the shipowner; or the seafarer's country of residence.[187]

Limitations on duty to repatriate

24.64 The duty to repatriate ends when: the seafarer is repatriated (having been provided with any necessary relief and maintenance); the shipowner's repatriation arrangements are unsuccessful because of the seafarer's unreasonable conduct; the shipowner is unable to contact the seafarer for a period of three months; the seafarer provides the shipowner with written confirmation that they do not wish to be repatriated; or the seafarer is dead.[188]

Relief and maintenance pending repatriation

24.65 The shipowner must make any necessary provision for the seafarer's relief and maintenance (including food and lodging) pending repatriation, including (but not limited to):

> '(a) clothing;
>
> (b) toiletries and other personal necessaries;
>
> (c) surgical, medical, dental or optical treatment (including the repair or replacement of any appliance) for any condition requiring immediate care;
>
> (d) in cases where legal aid is unavailable or insufficient, reasonable costs for the defence of the seafarer in any criminal proceedings in respect of any act or omission within the scope of the seafarer's employment, being proceedings where neither the employer nor the employer's agent is a party to the prosecution; and
>
> (e) sufficient money to meet any minor ancillary expenses necessarily incurred or likely to be so incurred for the seafarer's relief and maintenance.'[189]

A failure to provide any such necessary relief and maintenance amounts to an offence by the shipowner punishable, on summary conviction, by a fine of $10,000 or, on indictment, by a fine of $25,000.[190]

Prohibition on recovering costs of repatriation from seafarer

24.66 Subject to the following exception, any agreement with the shipowner under which a seafarer agrees to pay for the cost of their repatriation or relief and

187 SEA Regulations, reg 5(2)(a)–(c), respectively.
188 SEA Regulations, reg 6(a)–(e), respectively.
189 Repatriation Regulations, reg 7(1)–(3)(a)–(e), respectively.
190 Repatriation Regulations, reg 7(5)(a)–(b), respectively.

maintenance is prohibited and void.[191] The SEA may provide that the seafarer must reimburse repatriation costs, subject to a maximum of $1,000 if it is terminated because of the seafarer's misconduct (in which case, the costs may be deducted from the seafarer's wages).[192]

Any shipowner who enters into a prohibited agreement commits an offence punishable, on summary conviction, by a fine of $10,000 or, on indictment, by a fine of $15,000.[193]

This prohibition does not affect a shipowner's right to recover the costs of repatriation through third party contractual arrangements[194] (for example, with the employer of the seafarer).

Seafarer property

24.67 Where a repatriated seafarer has left property behind, the master must take charge of it and enter a description of each item in the official log book.[195] The master and the shipowner must ensure that reasonable care is taken of the property and that it is (together with a copy of the entry in the log book) delivered to the seafarer or to the seafarer's next of kin (their last known address will suffice).[196] The seafarer or next of kin is obliged to reimburse the shipowner for the reasonable costs of delivery, if demanded.[197] However, the master may at any time: (a) sell any part of the property which is of a perishable or deteriorating nature (the proceeds of any sale will be the property of the seafarer, and details of the sale must be entered in the official log book); or (b) destroy or otherwise dispose of any part of the property considered a potential risk to the health or safety of any person (details of the destruction must be entered in the official log book).[198]

The Repatriation Regulations

24.68 The shipowner must ensure that a copy of the Repatriation Regulations is carried on board and made available to seafarers, with a translation in the working language of the ship if it is not English.[199] A failure to comply amounts to an offence punishable: (a) on summary conviction, by a fine of $10,000; or (b) on conviction on indictment, by a fine of $15,000.[200]

191 Repatriation Regulations, reg 8(1), (6).
192 Repatriation Regulations, reg 8(2)–(3).
193 Repatriation Regulations, reg 8(5)(a)–(b), respectively.
194 Repatriation Regulations, reg 9.
195 Repatriation Regulations, reg 10(1)–(2).
196 Repatriation Regulations, reg 10(3), (7), (9).
197 Repatriation Regulations, reg 10(9).
198 Repatriation Regulations, reg 10(4)–(6).
199 Repatriation Regulations, reg 11(1)–(2).
200 Repatriation Regulations, reg 11(3)(a)–(b), respectively.

Financial security

24.69 The MLC provisions on financial security for repatriation (together with those on shipowners' liability) were the first Parts of the MLC to be amended. Before the amendments came into force on 18 January 2017, the MLC already required ratifying states to ensure that their ships carried financial security for repatriation.[201] A shipowner must not operate a ship unless there is in force a contract of insurance or other security to cover the repatriation and relief and maintenance obligations[202] (which remains in force).

The amendments introduce much more detailed requirements for the financial security system, as well as further rights for seafarers and liabilities for shipowners. To date, the UK, Gibraltar and the Isle of Man are the only REG members which have enshrined the amendments into statute, and the others have issued shipping notices informing shipowners what they must do to comply with the amendments. MACI has issued CISN 01/2017, which requires that a certificate or other documentary evidence of financial security required by Standard A2.5.2 of the MLC must be carried on board and posted in a conspicuous place where it is available to seafarers.[203]

It is expected that the CI will incorporate the amendments into statute in the near future.

The full text of the MLC amendments on financial security are set out in Appendix 2.

Also, as a guide to implementation, see the UK provisions which are set out in Chapter 11 at paragraphs 11.9 to 11.11.

Offences

24.70 A failure to carry any of the above documents amounts to an offence punishable, on summary conviction, by a fine of $10,000 or, on indictment, by a fine of $15,000.[204] Note that this provision pre-dates the MLC amendments on financial security, and any penalty for a failure to comply with those could well be more severe, which will become apparent when the amendments are incorporated into statute.

201 MLC, Regulation 2.5, para 2.
202 Repatriation Regulations, reg 12(1)–(2).
203 CISN 01/2017 (Rev 1) – Amendments to the Maritime Labour Convention, 2006. Insurance or other financial security, paras 2.1–3.3.
204 Repatriation Regulations, regs 11(3)(a)–(b), 12(3)(a)–(b), respectively.

If the shipowner fails to repatriate

24.71 If the shipowner of a CI ship fails in its duty to repatriate a seafarer, or provide relief and maintenance, the MACI must make provision for the same.[205] In respect of a non-CI ship in CI waters, the MACI may make such provision.[206] In both cases the MACI may recover its costs from the shipowner, as well as the costs of reimbursing another flag state in a case in which it has repatriated seafarers from a CI ship following the shipowner's default.[207]

Inspection and detention

24.72 A CI ship (or, while it is in CI waters, a non-CI ship which does not carry MLC documentation) may be inspected to check for compliance with the Repatriation Regulations.[208] If the inspector has clear grounds for believing that it has not complied with its repatriation duties, the provision of relief and maintenance pending repatriation, or does not carry financial security certification, it is liable to be detained.[209]

A non-CI ship with MLC documentation may, while it is in CI waters, have its MLC documentation reviewed and, where there are grounds under MLC, Standard A5.2.1, be subject to a more detailed inspection.[210] Where there are clear grounds for believing that there is a non-compliance representing a serious or repeated breach of the MLC, the ship is liable to be detained.[211]

Compliance

24.73 DMLC: implement CI requirements as set out in Pt I, point 15 (financial security for repatriation), and record details of compliance measures in DMLC, Pt II, point 15.

REGULATION 2.6: SEAFARER COMPENSATION FOR THE SHIP'S LOSS OR FOUNDERING

24.74 If a seafarer becomes unemployed as a result of their ship being wrecked or lost, the shipowner must pay them the wages that they would otherwise have earned under their SEA; the liability is limited to any period of unemployment until two months after the date of the loss of the ship.[212]

205 Repatriation Regulations, reg 13(1).
206 Repatriation Regulations, reg 13(2).
207 Repatriation Regulations, reg 3(3)(a)–(b), respectively.
208 Repatriation Regulations, reg 14.
209 Repatriation Regulations, reg 15.
210 Repatriation Regulations, reg 16.
211 Repatriation Regulations, reg 17.
212 SEA Regulations, reg 13(1)–(3).

If the wreck or loss of the ship causes the seafarer to suffer injury or loss, the shipowner must pay compensation to the seafarer.[213] Except in relation to personal injury or death, the compensation will be limited to the amount specified (if any) in the SEA (which would include incorporated documents such as a collective agreement).[214]

Any amounts outstanding may be recovered by the seafarer as a civil debt.[215]

Shipowners must provide financial security to cover any liabilities in respect of compensation in the event of death or long-term disability to seafarers arising from occupational injury, illness or hazard.[216] For more details, see paragraphs 24.129 and 24.136 below.

Inspection and detention

24.75 See the provisions set out at paragraph 24.28 above, which also apply to shipowners' liability to indemnify seafarers in connection with losses arising from the loss or wreck of a ship.

Defence

24.76 It is a defence for a person charged with an offence under the Repatriation Regulations to show that it was committed without their knowledge or, where they had such knowledge, that they took all reasonable precautions and exercised all due diligence to avoid the commission of the offence.[217]

REGULATION 2.7: MANNING LEVELS

24.77 The provisions are set out in Pt IV of the STCW Regulations.

However, the requirement for certification, safe manning, hours of work and watchkeeping in respect of pleasure yachts under 3000 GT in commercial use must be in accordance with the relevant provisions of the Code referred to in regulation 4 of the Merchant Shipping (Vessels in Commercial Use for Sport or Pleasure) Regulations, 2002.[218] The current Code is the Large Commercial Yacht Code (LY3).[219] It should be noted that the LY3 Code and the Passenger

213 SEA Regulations, reg 13(4).
214 SEA Regulations, regs 5(2), 13(5).
215 SEA Regulations, reg 13(6).
216 SEA Regulations, reg 14.
217 Repatriation Regulations, reg 19.
218 STCW Regulations, reg 44.
219 LY3 Code: applicable to yachts which are 24 metres and over in load line length, are in commercial use for sport or pleasure, do not carry cargo and do not carry more than 12 passengers.

Yacht Code (PYC) are being merged into the 'Red Ensign Group Yacht Code' (REG YC), which comes into force on 1 January 2019 (see Chapter 15 at para 15.9 for further information). There is also a recently issued manning policy manual for yachts (of 24 metres and over) which are engaged in trade (which is also to serve as guidance for such yachts which are not engaged in trade).[220]

Application

24.78 On the application of the STCW Regulations, see paragraph 24.3 above.

Responsibilities of companies, operators, masters and seafarers

24.79 As regards CI ships, the company or operator must ensure that: every seafarer holds an appropriate certificate in respect of any function they are to perform and has had the training specified in the STCW Regulations in respect of their duties; and all documentation and data on all seafarers' experience, training, medical fitness and competence in their assigned duties is held on board and available for inspection.[221]

The company must provide written instructions to the master, setting out the policies and the procedures to be followed, to ensure that newly joined seafarers are given a reasonable opportunity to become familiar with the shipboard equipment, operating procedures and other arrangements needed for the proper performance of their duties (before being assigned to them).[222] These are to include time allocated for new seafarers on board to become acquainted with the specific equipment they will be using or operating, and ship-specific watchkeeping, safety, environmental protection and emergency procedures and arrangements, and the designation of a knowledgeable crew member who will be responsible for ensuring that an opportunity is provided to each newly employed seafarer to receive essential information in a language they understand.[223] Each seafarer must ensure they take steps to familiarise themselves accordingly.[224]

Safe manning document

24.80 The company must ensure, in respect of every ship of 500 GT or more, that: a safe manning document (SMD) is in force in respect of the ship and the manning of the ship; the SMD is kept on board at all times; and the manning of

220 Manning Policy Manual – Yachts engaged in trade 24m and over (May 2018).
221 STCW Regulations, reg 24(1)–(2).
222 STCW Regulations, reg 24(4).
223 STCW Regulations, reg 24(5).
224 STCW Regulations, reg 24(6).

the ship is maintained at all times to at least the levels specified in the SMD.[225] The master must ensure that the ship does not proceed to sea unless it complies with these requirements.[226] Owners of ships under 500 GT may apply for an SMD on a voluntary basis.

In applying for an SMD, the company must submit proposals as to numbers and grade of personnel, taking into account the guidelines contained in the Fifth Schedule and any additional guidance issued by the MACI.[227] The Schedule contains tables 1–4 which set out guidance for safe manning levels for the deck and engine departments in unlimited trading areas and near-coastal trading areas. The MACI will consider a ship to be safely manned if the crew includes sufficient officers and ratings with the requisite capabilities and abilities set out in paragraph 1, Annex 1 of IMO Resolution A.890(21), taking into account other relevant instruments of the IMO, ILO ITU[228] and WHO, and specified on-board functions (as set out in paragraphs 2–3 of Annex 1).[229] A safe manning application form (for ships and yachts) and guidance are available on the MACI website.[230]

The company must inform the MACI of any changes in circumstances relating to the SMD, so that its validity can be reviewed, or new proposals can be approved.[231]

If the ship falls below SMD levels, due to a seafarer becoming incapacitated because of an accident or illness, or is unable to sail due to disciplinary action, it will be for the master to decide whether the ship should proceed to sea. This is permissible on specific conditions being met, including that the duration of the voyage is no more than 21 days and only to the next port of call; there must be a replacement seafarer at that next port.[232]

Dispensations

24.81 In circumstances of exceptional necessity, and where there does not appear to be any danger to persons, property or the environment, the MACI may issue a dispensation permitting a specified seafarer who does not hold the appropriate certificate to serve in a specified ship for a specified period not exceeding six months (except radio personnel, unless otherwise specified in the Radio Regulations),

225 STCW Regulations, reg 25(1)(a)–(c), respectively.
226 STCW Regulations, reg 25(2).
227 STCW Regulations, reg 25(3)–(4).
228 For example, the Radio Regulations adopted by the World Radiocommunication Conference (Geneva, 1995), as revised – available on the website of the International Telecommunication Union: www.itu.int/pub/R-REG-RR-2016 [Accessed 13 October 2018].
229 STCW Regulations, Fifth Schedule, para 2.1; IMO Resolution A.890(21), Principles of Safe Manning, adopted 25 November 1999.
230 Safe manning application forms, etc: http://cishipping.com/forms [Accessed 17 June 2018].
231 STCW Regulations, reg 25(5).
232 STCW Regulations, reg 25(8)(a)–(f).

provided the seafarer is adequately qualified to fill the vacant post in a safe manner, in accordance with the applicable safe manning requirements.[233]

Inspection and detention

24.82 There are wide powers to inspect CI ships (and, while they are in a CI port or roadstead, non-CI ships), to check for compliance with matters covered by the STCW Convention and the STCW Regulations, including safe manning requirements.[234] Any such ship may be detained for specified breaches of the STCW Regulations, including non-compliance with the provisions set out in reg 25 in relation to the SMD.[235]

Offences

24.83 Specified breaches of the obligations amount to criminal offences punishable as set out below:

- the company – on summary conviction, a fine of $25,000; or, on indictment, a fine of $50,000 and (in the case of an individual) imprisonment for 12 months;
- the master – on summary conviction, a fine of $15,000; or, on indictment, a fine of $25,000 and imprisonment for 12 months;
- seafarer – on summary conviction, a fine not exceeding level 3 on the standard scale.[236]

Defence

24.84 It is a defence for the accused to prove that they took all reasonable steps to avoid the commission of the offence.[237] Where applicable, the onus is on the accused to prove that it was not reasonably practicable to do more than was in fact done to satisfy the relevant duty or requirement.[238]

Compliance

24.85 DMLC: implement CI requirements as set out in Pt I, point 7, and record details of compliance measures in DMLC, Pt II, point 7.

233 STCW Regulations, reg 26.
234 STCW Regulations, reg 39.
235 STCW Regulations, reg 40.
236 STCW Regulations, reg 43(1)–(2), (4).
237 STCW Regulations, reg 43(10).
238 STCW Regulations, reg 43(11).

REGULATION 2.8: CAREER AND SKILL DEVELOPMENT AND OPPORTUNITIES FOR SEAFARERS' EMPLOYMENT

24.86 The MLC requires ratifying states to have national policies to promote employment in the maritime sector, and to encourage career and skill development and greater employment opportunities for domiciled seafarers.[239] According to the MACI, there are no active domiciled seafarers in the CI, consequently there is little by way of implementation. However, in the recent past MACI has, in partnership with the Department of Education, offered maritime scholarships for study in the following disciplines: marine engineering; marine surveying; maritime administration; nautical studies; and naval architecture.[240] The scheme is open to Caymanians or those who hold Caymanian status, and participants must be aged 18 or over.

REGULATION 3.1:ACCOMMODATION AND RECREATIONAL FACILITIES

24.87 The relevant provisions are set out in the Merchant Shipping (Maritime Labour Convention) (Crew Accommodation) Regulations, 2014[241] ('MLC Accommodation Regulations') which came into force on 29 August 2014, set out transitional provisions, the requirement for masters' inspections, and provide powers to authorised persons to inspect ships and enforce compliance, including the power of detention. The detailed technical requirements on crew accommodation and recreational facilities are set out in CISN 03/2014, and closely follow those in Regulation 3.1 and Code of the MLC.[242]

The MLC Accommodation Regulations repeal the Merchant Shipping (Crew Accommodation) Regulations 1988[243] ('1988 Regulations'); however, the transitional provisions in the former apply the latter Regulations to older ships as if they had not been repealed.

Application

24.88 The MLC Accommodation Regulations apply the same standards to CI ships (wherever they may be) as they do to non-CI ships, which do not carry MLC documentation, when they are in CI waters.[244] When non-CI ships, which do carry MLC documentation, are in CI waters, the standards which will be applied are those set out in Regulation 3.1 and Standard A3.1 of the MLC.[245]

239 MLC, Regulation 2.8.1.
240 Maritime scholarship: http://cishipping.com/forms [Accessed 17 June 2018].
241 Supplement No 8 published with Extraordinary Gazette No 64 dated 29 August 2014.
242 CISN 03/2014: MLC, 2006 – Crew accommodation on Cayman Islands flagged vessels.
243 MLC Accommodation Regulations, reg 15.
244 MLC Accommodation Regulations, reg 3(1)(a)–(b), respectively.
245 MLC Accommodation Regulations, regs 3(2)(a)–(b), 10–12.

The following are excluded: pleasure vessels; fishing vessels; warships or naval auxiliaries; or offshore installations whilst on their working stations.[246]

CI SHIPS, AND NON-CI SHIPS WITHOUT MLC DOCUMENTATION WHILE THEY ARE IN CI WATERS

Transitional provisions

24.89 For a ship the keel of which was laid or which was at a similar stage of construction before 11 July 1997: if the crew accommodation has not been substantially reconstructed or altered on or after 11 July 1997, it must comply with Pt II of, and Sch 6 to, the 1988 Regulations.[247] If the crew accommodation has been substantially reconstructed or altered on or after 11 July 1997, but before 29 August 2014, it must comply with the requirements of Pt I of the 1988 Regulations.[248]

For a ship the keel of which was laid or which was at a similar stage of construction on or after 11 July 1997, but before 29 August 2014, if the crew accommodation has not been substantially reconstructed or altered on or after 29 August 2014, it must comply with the requirements of Pt I of the 1988 Regulations.[249]

For ships constructed on or after 29 August 2014 or, if constructed before that date, the crew accommodation has been substantially reconstructed or altered on or after 29 August 2014, the MLC Accommodation Regulations and the requirements set out in CISN 03/2014 apply.[250]

The term 'similar stage of construction' means the stage at which construction identifiable with a specific ship begins, assembly having commenced comprising at least 50 tonnes or 1%of the estimated mass of all structural material, whichever is less.[251]

Exemptions and substantial equivalence

24.90 In terms of flexibility, the MACI has power to issue limited and specific written exemptions to ships of less than 200 GT, provided that any exemption does not result in overall less favourable conditions.[252]

The MACI may issue written approval for the adoption of alternative measures which are 'substantially equivalent' to those set out in CISN 03/2014.[253] There

246 MLC Accommodation Regulations, reg 3(3)(a)–(d), respectively.
247 MLC Accommodation Regulations, reg 16(1)(a).
248 MLC Accommodation Regulations, reg 16(1)(b).
249 MLC Accommodation Regulations, reg 16(2).
250 MLC Accommodation Regulations, reg 6(1).
251 MLC Accommodation Regulations, reg 16(3).
252 MLC Accommodation Regulations, reg 4.
253 MLC Accommodation Regulations, reg 5.

are such provisions on crew accommodation and recreational facilities for yachts which hold a certificate of compliance with the large commercial yacht code (LY3 Code) if they were constructed on or after 20 August 2013 (the date the MLC entered into force internationally).[254] It should be noted that the LY3 Code and the Passenger Yacht Code (PYC) are being merged into the 'Red Ensign Group Yacht Code' (REG YC), which comes into force on 1 January 2019 (see Chapter 15 at para 15.9 for further information and references to the relevant chapters of the Codes which set out the substantially equivalent provisions for yachts, according to their gross tonnage).

Crew accommodation inspections

24.91 The master (or designate) must carry out inspections of the crew accommodation (at intervals not exceeding seven days) to ensure it is cleaned and maintained in accordance with CISN 03/2014; the findings must be recorded in the official log book.[255]

The following non-compliances amount to criminal offences, which are punishable by fines, as shown: the shipowner's failure to comply with CISN 03/2014 (including cleaning and maintenance) or the 1988 Regulations, whichever is applicable (summary: $10,000; indictment: $50,000);[256] the shipowner's failure to comply with a condition or limitation of an exemption or substantial equivalence approval (summary: $10,000; indictment: $25,000);[257] and the master's failure to inspect the crew accommodation at intervals not exceeding seven days or record the findings (summary only: $10,000).[258] It is a defence for the accused to show that they took all reasonable steps to comply with the provision in question.[259]

Powers of inspection and detention

24.92 Authorised persons have power to inspect ships for compliance with the MLC Accommodation Regulations, and power to detain a ship on which there are dangerous, serious or repeated breaches.[260] An 'authorised person' means a person authorised by the MACI to carry out inspections and audits for the purposes of the MLC Accommodation Regulations and includes any surveyor of ships appointed under section 419 of the Merchant Shipping Law (2011 Revision).[261]

254 Large Commercial Yacht Code, applicable to yachts which are 24 metres and over in load line length, are in commercial use for sport or pleasure, do not carry cargo and do not carry more than 12 passengers: https://assets.publishing.service.gov.uk/government/uploads/system/uploads/attachment_data/file/444652/LY3_-_Final_Version.pdf [Accessed 30 May 2018].
255 MLC Accommodation Regulations, reg 6(2)–(3).
256 MLC Accommodation Regulations, reg 7(1)(a)–(b).
257 MLC Accommodation Regulations, reg 7(2)(a)–(b).
258 MLC Accommodation Regulations, reg 7(3).
259 MLC Accommodation Regulations, reg 7(4).
260 MLC Accommodation Regulations, regs 8–9, respectively.
261 MLC Accommodation Regulations, reg 2(1).

NON-CI SHIPS WITH MLC DOCUMENTATION WHILE THEY ARE IN CI WATERS

24.93 When a non-CI ship with MLC documentation is in CI waters and is subject to an inspection, it must comply with the accommodation and recreational facilities requirements, as set out in Regulation 3.1 and Standard A3.1 of the MLC.[262] The master (or designate) must carry out 'frequent inspections'[263] to ensure that the accommodation is clean, decently habitable and maintained in a good state of repair, record the findings and keep them available for review.[264] A failure to comply with these requirements amounts to a criminal offence by the shipowner or master (drafted in the same terms as those applying to CI ships).[265]

Powers of inspection and detention

24.94 A port state inspector may: (a) review the ship's MLCert and DMLC or interim MLCert; and (b) where Standard A5.2.1 of the MLC applies, carry out a more detailed inspection accordingly.[266] MLC, Standard A5.2.1 is set out in Appendix 1, and states the circumstances in which port state control may carry out a more detailed inspection (eg beyond a review of a ship's MLC documentation).[267] Where there are clear grounds for believing that the ship does not comply with the requirements of the MLC, and the non-compliance represents a significant danger to seafarers or a serious or repeated breach of the requirements of the MLC, the ship is liable to be detained.[268]

Compliance

24.95 DMLC: implement CI requirements as set out in Pt I, points 8–9, and record details of compliance measures in DMLC, Pt II, points 8–9.

REGULATION 3.2: FOOD AND CATERING

24.96 The provisions are set out in the Merchant Shipping (Maritime Labour Convention) (Food and Catering) Regulations 2014 ('F&C Regulations'),

262 MLC Accommodation Regulations, regs 10(1), 11(2).

263 The MLC uses the term 'frequent inspections' at Standard A3.1, para 18. It is recommended that such inspections be carried out at intervals not exceeding seven days, as this is what is required of CI ships: MLC Accommodation Regulations, reg 6(3).

264 MLC Accommodation Regulations, reg 10(2)(a)–(b).

265 MLC Accommodation Regulations, reg 10(3)–(5).

266 MLC Accommodation Regulations, reg 11(1)(a)–(b).

267 MLC, Standard A5.2.1.1(a)–(d).

268 MLC Accommodation Regulations, reg 12(1).

which came into force on 29 August 2014, CISN 05/2011[269] and CISN 07/2014.[270]

Application

24.97 The F&C Regulations apply to:

- CI ships, wherever they may be; and non-CI ships without MLC documentation while they are in CI waters;[271] and
- (as regards regulations 13–15) to non-CI ships with MLC documentation while they are in CI waters.[272]

The following are excluded: pleasure vessels; fishing vessels; warships or naval auxiliaries; or offshore installations whilst on their working stations.[273]

CI SHIPS, AND NON-CI SHIPS WITHOUT MLC DOCUMENTATION WHILE THEY ARE IN CI WATERS

Provision of food and drinking water

24.98 The shipowner and master must ensure that food and drinking water are provided, free of charge to seafarers, which:

- are suitable in respect of quantity, nutritive value, quality and variety having regard to the number of seafarers on board and the character, nature and duration of the voyage, and the different religious requirements and cultural practices in relation to food of the seafarers on board;
- do not contain anything which is likely to cause sickness or injury to health or which renders any food or water unpalatable; and
- are otherwise fit for consumption.[274]

Furthermore, the shipowner and the master must ensure that food and drinking water are stored and handled – and the catering department is organised and equipped for the provision of adequate, varied and nutritious meals prepared and served – in hygienic conditions in accordance with the requirements set out in CISN 07/2014.[275]

269 CISN 05/2011 (Rev 6) – Issue of endorsements attesting to the recognition of a certificate of competency.
270 CISN 07/2014 – Requirements and guidance for the provision of food and fresh water and training requirements for catering staff on ships.
271 F&C Regulations, reg 3(1)(a)–(b).
272 F&C Regulations, reg 3(2)(a)–(b).
273 F&C Regulations, reg 3(3)(a)–(d), respectively.
274 F&C Regulations, reg 4(1)–(2).
275 F&C Regulations, reg 5.

In fulfilling the above requirements, the master and shipowner must take account of the following provisions contained in CISN 07/2014: Annex 1, section 1 (design, construction, equipment and maintenance of galley areas); Annex 1, section 7 (stores); and Annex 2 (water supply and maintenance).[276]

Annex 1 in general provides detailed guidance on food safety and hygiene.

Inspections

24.99 The master (or designate), with a member of the catering staff,. must inspect (at least every week) the supplies of food and drinking water and the catering department and its equipment.[277] The master must ensure that the results of any inspections are recorded in the official log book.[278]

Complaints

24.100 There is a specific statutory procedure for complaints about food and drinking water. If at least three seafarers consider that the standards set out above have not been complied with, they may complain to the master, who must investigate the complaint.[279] If the seafarers are dissatisfied with the outcome, they can require the master to make arrangements for them to refer the matter to a 'shipping master' or 'proper officer' for investigation and who will, if appropriate, examine the food or drinking water.[280] If the latter notifies the master in writing that any food or drinking water does not comply with the applicable standards, the master and shipowner must replace or replenish it within a reasonable time, and the master must ensure that any defective food or water is not consumed.[281]

In general, any seafarer may submit a complaint about an alleged non-compliance with the MLC, by way of the on-board or onshore complaints procedures.[282] The specific procedure in the F&C Regulations does not expressly prevent the MLC-derived complaints procedures from being used, which are not contingent on a minimum threshold of three complainants.[283]

276 CISN 07/2014, paras 4.2–4.3.
277 F&C Regulations, 6(1(a)–(b), respectively.
278 F&C Regulations, reg 6(2).
279 F&C Regulations, reg 7(1).
280 F&C Regulations, reg 7(2)–(3).
281 F&C Regulations, reg 7(4)(a)–(b).
282 The MLC on-board and onshore procedures are contained in Regulation 5.1.5 and Standard A5.1.5 and Regulation 5.2.2 and Standard A5.2.2, respectively, and these are reproduced in Appendix 1.
283 MLC, Regulation 5.1.5 and Code (on-board complaint procedures); MLC, Regulation 5.2.2 (onshore seafarer complaint-handling procedures).

Ship's cook

24.101 In respect of a CI ship which ordinarily operates with ten or more seafarers on board, the shipowner and master must ensure that a qualified ship's cook (who must not be under 18 years of age) holding a recognised certificate is carried.[284]

Exceptions

24.102 The MACI may, in circumstances of exceptional necessity, grant a written exemption: (a) until the next port of call; or (b) for a period not exceeding one month, but only if there is a person on board who is trained or instructed in areas including food and personal hygiene and handling and storage of food on board ships, in accordance with the requirements set out in CISN 07/2014.[285]

Furthermore, the MACI may grant written approval of other requirements which it considers are substantially equivalent to the requirement to have a qualified ship's cook on board.[286]

Recognised ship's cook certificates

24.103 The following ship's cook certificates are acceptable:

- limited grandfathering rights to certificates granted or recognised as equivalent under the Merchant Shipping (Certification of Ships' Cooks) Regulations, 2004,[287] which were still in force on 29 August 2014, will remain valid until 29 August 2019;[288]
- certificates issued by an authority in one of the many countries or territories listed in CISN 05/2011, which are those which the MACI considers have standards of competency and training equivalent to STCW Convention standards in the UK;[289]
- furthermore, the MACI has discretion to approve a certificate issued by an authority in a country or territory which is not listed in CISN 05/2011.[290]

The qualifications which the MACI finds acceptable for ship's cooks are set out at paragraphs 6.3.1–6.3.5 of CISN 05/2011.

In addition, ship's cooks intending to serve on large yachts and passenger yachts may apply on a voluntary basis for a 'Recognition of Qualification as a Ship's

284 F&C Regulations, reg 8(1); CISN 07/2014, para 6.1.
285 F&C Regulations, reg 8(2), (4).
286 F&C Regulations, reg 8(3)–(4).
287 The 2004 Regulations were repealed by F&C Regulations, reg 19(2).
288 F&C Regulations, reg 9(1)–(2).
289 F&C Regulations, reg 9(3), CISN 05/2011, paras 1.1, 1.3, 2.1.
290 F&C Regulations, reg 9(4).

Cook' statement, which will be issued to those who can show that they have the necessary qualifications and experience.[291]

Catering staff

24.104 The shipowner and the master must ensure that each member of the catering staff is properly trained or instructed for their position, and in areas including food and personal hygiene, and the handling and storage of food on board a ship, in accordance with the requirements set out in CISN 07/2014.[292]

Powers of inspection and detention

24.105 Authorised persons have power to inspect ships for compliance with the F&C Regulations, and power to detain a ship on which there are dangerous, serious or repeated breaches.[293] There is a right of appeal against detention.[294]

NON-CI SHIPS WITH MLC DOCUMENTATION WHILE THEY ARE IN CI WATERS

24.106 The shipowner and the master must ensure that the ship complies with MLC, Regulation 3.2 and Standard A3.2 on food and catering.[295]

The master (or designate) must carry out frequent inspections in accordance with MLC, Standard A3.2.7, with respect to: supplies of food and drinking water; all spaces and equipment used for its storage and handling; and the galley and other equipment used for the preparation and service of meals.[296] The findings of the inspection must be recorded and kept available for review.[297]

Inspection and detention

24.107 A port state inspector may: (a) review the ship's MLCert and DMLC or interim MLCert; and (b) where Standard A5.2.1 of the MLC applies, carry out a more detailed inspection accordingly.[298] Where there are clear grounds

291 Guidance Note 02/2018 (Rev 1.0) – Recognition of ship's cooks on Cayman Island vessels, para 2.5. The application procedure is set out in paras 3.1–3.3.
292 F&C Regulations, reg 10.
293 F&C Regulations, regs 11–12, respectively.
294 F&C Regulations, reg 17.
295 F&C Regulations, reg 13(1)–(2).
296 F&C Regulations, reg 13(3)(a); MLC, Standard A3.2.7(a)–(c).
297 F&C Regulations, reg 13(3)(b).
298 F&C Regulations, reg 14.

for believing that the ship does not comply with the requirements of the MLC, and the non-compliance represents a significant danger to seafarers or a serious or repeated breach of the requirements of the MLC, the ship is liable to be detained.[299] There is a right of appeal against detention.[300]

Offences

24.108 Many non-compliances amount to offences by the shipowner and master, punishable by fines of $10,000 (on summary conviction) or $50,000 (on indictment).[301] The statutory defences apply.[302]

Compliance

24.109 DMLC: implement CI requirements as set out in Pt I, point 10, and record details of compliance measures in DMLC, Pt II, point 10.

REGULATION 4.1: MEDICAL CARE ON BOARD SHIP AND ASHORE

24.110 The main provisions are set out in the Merchant Shipping (Maritime Labour Convention) (Medical Care) Regulations, 2014[303] ('Medical Care Regulations') and CISN 06/2014.[304]

Application

24.111 The Medical Care Regulations apply to CI ships wherever they may be and (while they are in CI waters) non-CI ships which do not carry MLC documentation.[305] For the purposes of port state control, regulations 14–15 apply to non-CI ships which carry MLC documentation while they are in CI waters.[306] The following are excluded: pleasure vessels; fishing vessels; warships or naval auxiliaries; or offshore installations whilst on their working stations.[307]

299 F&C Regulations, reg 15.
300 F&C Regulations, reg 17.
301 F&C Regulations, reg 16(1)–(2).
302 F&C Regulations, regs 16(3), 18.
303 Supplement No 2 published with Extraordinary Gazette No 64 dated 29 August 2014.
304 CISN 06/2014 – Requirements and guidance on the carriage of medical stores and radio medical advice on Cayman Islands flagged vessels.
305 Medical Care Regulations, reg 3(1)(a)–(b)(i)–(ii).
306 Medical Care Regulations, reg 3(2)(a)–(b)(i)–(ii).
307 Medical Care Regulations, reg 3(3)(a)–(d), respectively.

CI SHIPS WHEREVER THEY MAY BE AND (WHILE THEY ARE IN CI WATERS) NON-CI SHIPS WHICH DO NOT CARRY MLC DOCUMENTATION

Provision of medical care

24.112 Shipowners must provide seafarers with health protection and medical care as comparable as possible to that which is generally available to workers ashore, including prompt access to the necessary medicines, medical equipment and facilities for diagnosis and treatment and to medical information and expertise.[308] The care is to be provided at no cost to the seafarer and is to include measures of a preventive character such as health promotion and health education programmes.[309]

The duty to meet the seafarer's medical expenses reasonably incurred arises when the sickness or injury first occurs during the period commencing with their tour of duty on board and ending when the shipowner's duty to repatriate them ends under the Repatriation Regulations[310] (see para 24.60 onwards above). It also arises if the sickness or injury first occurs after that period but is caused by circumstances or events arising during it.[311] The duty is without prejudice to the shipowner's obligation to provide for relief and maintenance pending repatriation, and the seafarer is not entitled to 'double recovery' to the extent that there is any overlap relating to medical expenses.[312] The duty does not arise if the sickness or injury first arises during a period of leave which is not 'shore leave'[313] (unless it was caused by circumstances during employment, as stated above – see para 24.56 onwards above).

The expenses which the shipowner is liable to meet are those relating to surgical, medical, dental or optical treatment, including the repair or replacement of any appliance, and board and lodging.[314]

The seafarer may recover their expenses against the shipowner as a civil debt, if the latter fails in its obligations.[315]

Limitation of duty

24.113 The duty is limited to expenses incurred during the period of 16 weeks from the day on which the sickness or injury first occurs or, if shorter, the date

308 Medical Care Regulations, reg 4(1).
309 Medical Care Regulations, reg 4(2)(a)–(b), respectively.
310 Medical Care Regulations, reg 5(1)(a), (2).
311 Medical Care Regulations, reg 5(1)(c), (2).
312 Medical Care Regulations, reg 5(4); Repatriation Regulations, reg 7.
313 Medical Care Regulations, reg 5(1)(b).
314 Medical Care Regulations, reg 5(3)(a)–(b).
315 Medical Care Regulations, reg 5(7).

on which a certifying medical practitioner notifies the seafarer that they are permanently unfit to carry out their duties.[316]

All references in the Medical Care Regulations to a 'medical practitioner' means 'a medical practitioner who is entitled to practise in the country or territory in which that practitioner is based and whose qualifications are as equivalent to those required of a practitioner based in the [CI] who is a registered medical practitioner'.[317]

Medical attention in port

24.114 When the ship is in port, the shipowner and master must permit a seafarer to seek medical attention, where reasonably practicable.[318] A failure to comply amounts to an offence punishable, on summary conviction, by a fine of $10,000 or, on conviction on indictment, by a fine of $50,000.[319]

Duty to carry a medical practitioner

24.115 The shipowner must ensure that a medical practitioner is carried on board a ship which has 100 or more persons on board and is engaged on a voyage which is (i) an international voyage lasting more than 72 hours, or (ii) a voyage during which the ship is more than 36 hours' sailing time from a port with adequate medical equipment.[320] A failure to comply amounts to an offence by the shipowner punishable, on summary conviction, by a fine of $10,000 or, on conviction on indictment, by a fine of $50,000.[321]

Other medically trained personnel

24.116 As regards ships which do not require a medical practitioner, the following provisions apply.

A ship that is ordinarily capable of reaching qualified medical care and medical facilities within eight hours must have at least one designated seafarer on board who is competent to provide medical first aid.[322] A failure by the shipowner to comply amounts to an offence punishable, on summary conviction, by a fine of $10,000 or, on conviction on indictment, by a fine of $50,000.[323]

316 Medical Care Regulations, reg 5(5)–(6).
317 Medical Care Regulations, reg 2.
318 Medical Care Regulations, reg 8(1).
319 Medical Care Regulations, reg 8(2)(a)–(b), respectively.
320 Medical Care Regulations, reg 6(1)–(2).
321 Medical Care Regulations, reg 6(3)(a)–(b), respectively.
322 Medical Care Regulations, reg 7(1).
323 Medical Care Regulations, reg 7(4)(a)–(b), respectively.

Any other ship must carry a designated seafarer on board who is in charge of medical care and administering medicine as part of their regular duties and (unless they are a medical doctor) have satisfactorily completed approved training which meets the requirements of the STCW Convention in relation to medical care on board ships.[324] There is no such criminal sanction in relation to a breach of reg 7(2) or (3), which may be a drafting error, taking into account the higher standard it sets in terms of medical care on a voyage further away from medical facilities than a ship which falls into the category described by reg 7(1).

Access to medical advice

24.117 Ships must carry a complete and up-to-date list of radio stations relevant to their area of operation, if equipped with a satellite communication system, and an up-to-date and complete list of Land Earth Stations, in both cases for the purpose of obtaining medical advice.[325] For CI ships the officially designated centres are at the Queen Alexandra Hospital in Portsmouth and the Aberdeen Royal Infirmary.[326] To obtain radio medical advice, masters should first contact HM Coastguard on either MF DSC, VHF DSC, VHF Channel 16 or INMARSAT.[327]

Any seafarer with responsibility for medical care or medical first aid on board must be instructed in the use of the Ship Captain's Medical Guide[328] and the medical section of the most recent edition of the IMO's International Code of Signals, to facilitate understanding of the type of information needed by the advising doctor and any advice received.[329]

Medical report form

24.118 The master, and on-board and onshore medical personnel, must use medical report form 'MRF 3906' or one containing at least the same information.[330] When completed, the form and its contents must be kept confidential and only used to facilitate the treatment of a seafarer; the original must accompany the seafarer ashore for treatment, and afterwards it must be retained on board for at least three years.[331]

324 Medical Care Regulations, reg 7(2)–(3).
325 Medical Care Regulations, reg 9(1).
326 CISN 06/2014 – see generally paras 4.1–4.4.
327 CISN 06/2014, para 4.3.
328 Ship Captain's Medical Guide: www.gov.uk/government/publications/the-ship-captains-medical-guide [Accessed 16 June 2018].
329 Medical Care Regulations, reg 9(2)–(3).
330 Medical Care Regulations, reg 10(1).
331 Medical Care Regulations, reg 10(2); MRF 3906.

Medical supplies and equipment

Ship's hospital

24.119 Ships carrying 15 or more seafarers and engaged on voyages of more than three days' duration must provide separate hospital accommodation and facilities, to be used exclusively for medical purposes.[332]

Medicine chest

24.120 Ships must carry a medicine chest and medical equipment (all of which are subject to inspection)[333] which meet the standards set out in CISN 06/2014.[334] A failure by the shipowner or master to comply amounts to an offence punishable, on summary conviction, by a fine of $10,000 or, on conviction on indictment, by a fine of $50,000.[335]

The medical supplies which ships (to which the Medical Care Regulations apply) are required to carry depend on which category they fall into:

- category A is seagoing vessels with no limitation on length of trips;
- category B is seagoing vessels making trips of less than 150 nautical miles from the nearest port with adequate medical equipment (or less than 175 nautical miles if they remain continuously within range of helicopter rescue services);
- category C is harbour vessels, boats and craft staying very close to shore, or with no cabin accommodation other than a wheelhouse. Lifeboats and life-rafts are also included.[336]

Regarding category C, it is for the master to determine, in relation to each voyage, whether it will remain 'very close to shore'; however, the maximum range of this concept is 60 nautical miles from shore.[337]

The requirements are listed in Schedule 1 (medical supplies) and Schedule 2 (medical equipment) to CISN 06/2014, in columns A, B and C (as applicable).

Further requirements in connection with medical cabinets, relating to storage and security, are set out in CISN 03/2014.[338]

332 CISN 03/2014 – Crew accommodation on Cayman Island flagged vessels, para 27.1, and see paras 27.2–27.17 for specific requirements.
333 The Medical Care Regulations do not specify how frequently inspections should be carried out; however, it is recommended that, in accordance with MLC, Guideline B4.1.1(4), inspections are carried out '… at regular intervals, not exceeding 12 months …'.
334 Medical Care Regulations, reg 11(1)–(2); CISN 06/2014 – Requirements and guidance on the carriage of medical stores and radio medical advice on Cayman Island flagged vessels.
335 Medical Care Regulations, reg 11(3)(a)–(b), respectively.
336 CISN 06/2014, para 3.1.
337 CISN 06/2014, para 3.2.
338 CISN 03/2014, paras 28.1–28.2.

Doctor's bag

24.121 On ships which carry more than 12 passengers with no crew member who is a qualified medical practitioner, a doctor's bag must be carried; the requirements are set out in Schedule 3 to CISN 06/2014.[339] See Chapter 17 regarding the required labelling and security measures.

First aid kits

24.122 Seagoing ships with a crew of more than 10 should carry first aid kits, distributed in appropriate locations on the ship (eg in the galley and engine room). Passenger vessels must carry one first aid kit for every 100 passengers, or fraction thereof, up to a maximum requirement of three kits. A first aid kit is to be included in the doctor's bag.[340]

Medical guides

24.123 Ships in categories A and B must carry copies of the Ship Captain's Medical Guide and CISN 06/2014; those in category C must carry a first aid manual or first aid instructions, in English (and, for lifeboats and life rafts, it must be on waterproof paper).[341]

Precautions against malaria

24.124 Advice is set out in Schedule 6 to CISN 06/2014, which also refers to the Ship Captain's Medical Guide, which contains further advice on preventative measures and treatment.[342] Ships regularly trading in mosquito-infested ports must be fitted with the appropriate devices required by the competent authorities in those ports.[343]

Defence

24.125 In relation to all offences under the Medical Care Regulations, it is a defence for the accused to show that the offence was committed without their knowledge or, where they had such knowledge, that they took all reasonable precautions and exercised all due diligence to avoid the commission of the offence.[344]

339 CISN 06/2014, Sch 3 – additional requirements for passenger ships Doctor's Bag.
340 CISN 06/2014, Sch 4 – first aid kits.
341 CISN 06/2014, Sch 5 – medical guides to be carried.
342 Ship Captain's Medical Guide, ch 6 (communicable diseases), pp 105–107.
343 CISN 03/2014, para 29.1.
344 Medical Care Regulations, reg 17.

Inspection and detention

24.126 Ships may be inspected by the MACI to check for compliance with the Medical Care Regulations.[345] Where there are clear grounds for believing that the ship does not comply with any of the requirements of regs 4 (provision of medical care and preventative measures), 5 (defraying seafarers' medical expenses) and 6 (duty to carry a medical practitioner, where applicable), or there is a significant danger to the safety, health or security of seafarers, the ship is liable to be detained.[346]

NON-CI SHIPS WHICH CARRY MLC DOCUMENTATION (WHILE THEY ARE IN CI WATERS)

24.127 The MACI may review the MLC documentation of such ships and, where MLC, Standard A5.2.1 applies, carry out a more detailed inspection.[347] Where the conditions on the ship, or any non-conformity, fall within MLC, Standard A5.2.1.6, the ship is liable to be detained.[348] See MLC, Regulation 5.2.1 'Inspections in port' which is set out in Appendix 1.

Compliance

24.128 DMLC: implement CI requirements as set out in Pt I, point 12, and record details of compliance measures in DMLC, Pt II, point 12.

REGULATION 4.2: SHIPOWNERS' LIABILITY

24.129 The main provisions are set out in the SEA Regulations.

A shipowner's liabilities arise if a seafarer becomes sick, or suffers injury, which first occurs: during the period starting on the date on which the seafarer's employment agreement (SEA) commences and ends on the date of repatriation, or (where the obligation to repatriate does not arise) the date the SEA terminates; or subsequent to that period but is caused by circumstances or events arising during that period.[349]

While the seafarer remains on the ship

24.130 The shipowner must ensure that any sick or injured seafarer is paid their full wages in accordance with their SEA while they remain on board the ship,

345 Medical Care Regulations, reg 12.
346 Medical Care Regulations, reg 13.
347 Medical Care Regulations, reg 14.
348 Medical Care Regulations, reg 15.
349 SEA Regulations, reg 15(1)(a)–(b), respectively.

until the date on which they are repatriated or, if the obligation to repatriate does not arise, they leave the ship.[350] If the seafarer was paid less than the amounts due (eg by their employer, who will not necessarily be the shipowner), the shipowner must pay to the seafarer any shortfall which would have been due if they had remained fit to work during that period.

After repatriation

24.131 Once the sick or injured seafarer has been repatriated or, if that duty did not arise, they have left the ship, the shipowner must still ensure that the incapacitated seafarer is paid their full wages in accordance with their SEA, as if they had remained fit for work during that period.[351] The duty applies from the day after the seafarer was repatriated until the date the seafarer is fit for work. However, in this scenario, the shipowner may reduce their liability to pay the seafarer during a particular period, by any amounts that the seafarer is entitled to receive in respect of that period under the laws or arrangements in the country to which they have been repatriated.[352] This would include social security benefit, and the shipowner may discount their liability on the basis of actual entitlement; the right to such a discount is not contingent on the seafarer receiving the benefit, so seafarers should be encouraged to make the necessary application. This obligation ends after 16 weeks, commencing on the day following the date of the injury or the first day of the sickness.[353]

Remedy

24.132 The seafarer may recover any outstanding sum due from the shipowner as a civil debt.[354]

Property left behind

24.133 If the seafarer leaves property behind, the same obligations as those set out in reg 10 of the Repatriation Regulations apply.[355] See paragraph 24.67 above.

Exceptions

24.134 The above obligations (except those in relation to a seafarer's property left behind) do not apply in circumstances where:

350 SEA Regulations, reg 15(2)(a)–(b), (6).
351 SEA Regulations, reg 15(3)(a)–(b), (6).
352 SEA Regulations, reg 15(4).
353 SEA Regulations, reg 15(5).
354 SEA Regulations, reg 15(7).
355 SEA Regulations, reg 15(8).

- the injury occurred while the seafarer was not at work;
- the injury or sickness occurred due to the seafarer's wilful misconduct;
- the sickness or incapacity for work existed on the date on which the seafarer entered into their SEA, and was deliberately concealed by the seafarer.[356]

Deceased seafarers

24.135 If a seafarer dies during their engagement on board, the shipowner must meet any reasonable expenses incurred in connection with the seafarer's burial or cremation, unless these are met by a public authority; the seafarer's estate may recover any sums due from the shipowner as a civil debt.[357]

Financial security

24.136 The MLC provisions on financial security for shipowners' liabilities (together with those on repatriation) were the first Parts of the MLC to be amended. Before the amendments came into force on 18 January 2017, the MLC already required ratifying states to ensure that their ships carried financial security for shipowners' liabilities.[358] Consequently, a CI ship is not permitted to proceed to sea, or remain at sea, without having in place a contract of insurance or other security adequate to ensure that the shipowner will be able to meet any liabilities in respect of compensation in the event of death or long-term disability to seafarers arising from occupational injury, illness or hazard.[359]

The amendments introduce much more detailed requirements for the financial security system, as well as further rights for seafarers and liabilities for shipowners. To date, the UK, Gibralter and the Isle of Man are the only REG members which have enshrined the amendments into statute, and the others have issued shipping notices informing shipowners what they must do to comply with the amendments. MACI has issued CISN 01/2017, which requires that shipowners must ensure that there is in force a contract of insurance or other financial security as required by MLC, Standard A4.2.1, which must be carried on board and posted in a conspicuous place where it is available to seafarers.[360]

It is expected that the CI will incorporate the amendments into statute in the near future.

The full text of the MLC amendments on financial security is set out in Appendix 2.

356 SEA Regulations, reg 15(9)(a)–(c), respectively.
357 SEA Regulations, reg 16.
358 MLC, Standard A4.2, para 1(b).
359 SEA Regulations, reg 14.
360 CISN 01/2017 (Rev 1) – Amendments to the Maritime Labour Convention, 2006. Insurance or other financial security, paras 3.1, 3.4 (the latter is erroneously numbered '3.6').

Also, as a guide to implementation, see the UK provisions which are set out in Chapter 18 at paragraphs 18.3 to 18.6.

Offences

24.137 A failure to comply with any of these obligations (except that of meeting the burial expenses of a deceased seafarer) amounts to an offence by the shipowner punishable, on summary conviction, by a fine of $15,000 or, on conviction on indictment, by a fine of $50,000.[361]

Note that this provision pre-dates the MLC amendments on financial security, and any penalty for a failure to comply with those could well be more severe, which will become apparent when the amendments are incorporated into statute.

Inspection and detention

24.138 An authorised inspector may inspect CI ships, and non-CI ships, which do not carry MLC documentation, while they are in CI waters to check for compliance with the SEA Regulations.[362] The ship is liable to be detained where the inspector has clear grounds for believing that there is a breach of any of the obligations set out above (except that relating to the burial or cremation of a deceased seafarer).[363]

As regards non-CI ships, which carry MLC documentation, while they are in CI waters, there is a power to review the ship's MLCert and DMLC and, where MLC, Standard A5.2.1[364] applies, carry out a more detailed inspection.[365] Where there are clear grounds for believing that: (a) the ship does not comply with the requirements of the MLC; and (b) the non-compliance represents a serious or repeated breach of the requirements of the MLC, the ship is liable to be detained.[366]

Compliance

24.139 DMLC: implement CI requirements as set out in Pt I, point 16 (financial security for shipowners' liabilities), and record details of compliance measures in DMLC, Pt II, point 16.

361 SEA Regulations, reg 17(a)–(b), respectively.
362 SEA Regulations, reg 22.
363 SEA Regulations, reg 23.
364 MLC, Standard A5.2.1 is set out in full in Appendix 1.
365 SEA Regulations, reg 24.
366 SEA Regulations, reg 25(1)(a)–(b).

REGULATION 4.3: HEALTH AND SAFETY PROTECTION AND ACCIDENT PREVENTION

24.140 The main provisions are set out in the H&S Regulations. The UK MCA Code of Safe Working Practices for Merchant Seafarers (COSWP) must also be taken into account,[367] as this has been adopted as the published '... guidelines for the management of occupational safety and health on board ships ...', which is required by Regulation 4.3, paragraph 2 of the MLC.

The H&S Regulations apply to:

- CI ships, wherever they may be; and non-CI ships without MLC documentation while they are in CI waters; and
- (as regards regs 25–26 on the inspection and detention of ships, respectively) non-CI ships with MLC documentation while they are in CI waters.[368]

The following are excluded: pleasure vessels; fishing vessels; warships or naval auxiliaries; or offshore installations whilst on their working stations.[369]

The shipowner must ensure that seafarers are provided (at no cost to themselves) with occupational health protection and that they live, work and train on board in a safe and hygienic environment in accordance with the requirements of the H&S Regulations.[370] The measures to be taken in carrying out those obligations closely follow the 'general duties' set out in reg 5 of the UK's Merchant Shipping and Fishing Vessels (Health and Safety at Work) Regulations 1997,[371] which are discussed in Chapter 19.[372] When complying with the H&S Regulations, the shipowner and master must take into account the guidance contained in the COSWP.[373] A failure to comply with these requirements amounts to an offence by the shipowner punishable, on summary conviction, by a fine of $10,000 and, on conviction on indictment, by a fine of $50,000.[374]

The following is intended to be a summary of the key compliance points:

- The shipowner must make a risk assessment (to be reviewed as appropriate) to identify: a seafarer at particular risk in the performance of their duties; the measures required to be taken to comply with the shipowner's health and safety responsibilities; and a record of any significant findings to be kept and

367 H&S Regulations, reg 4(4): COSWP (2015 edition), Amendment 2: https://assets.publishing.service.gov.uk/government/uploads/system/uploads/attachment_data/file/671403/CSWPMS_GOV_UK_2017.pdf [Accessed 3 June 2018].

368 H&S Regulations, reg 3(1)–(2).

369 H&S Regulations, reg 3(3)(a)–(d).

370 H&S Regulations, reg 4(1)–(2).

371 SI 1997/2962.

372 H&S Regulations, reg 4(3)(a)–(i).

373 H&S Regulations, reg 4(4); COSWP, (2015 ed.) Amendments 2: https://assets.publishing.service.gov.uk/government/uploads/system/uploads/attachment_data/file/671403/CSWPMS_GOV_UK_2017.pdf [Accessed 1 June 2018].

374 H&S Regulations, reg 4(5)(a)–(b), respectively.

made available to seafarers.[375] The shipowner must conduct a risk evaluation in relation to the management of occupational health and safety, and refer to any appropriate statistical information from ships and any general statistics provided by the MACI.[376] A failure to comply amounts to an offence by the shipowner punishable, on summary conviction, by a fine of $10,000 and, on conviction on indictment, by a fine of $50,000.[377] The shipowner must carry out its health and safety consultation and co-ordination obligations with self-employed seafarers, and employers of seafarers who are not employed by the shipowner or its representative;[378] those other employers, or self-employed seafarers, must inform the shipowner of any risks to health and safety arising out of or in connection with their activities.[379]

- Every person working on board must: take care for the health and safety of themselves and others who may be affected by their acts or omissions; co-operate with the shipowner or their employer on health and safety compliance; make proper use of protective personal equipment; and not intentionally or recklessly interfere with anything provided for the health and safety of a person on board, etc. Non-compliance with any of those obligations amounts to an offence punishable, on summary conviction, by a fine of $10,000 and, on conviction on indictment, by a fine of $50,000 ($100,000 for the 'misuse' offence).[380]
- A safety officer (who may be the master or designate) must be appointed to: take specific responsibility for implementation of, and compliance with, the ship's occupational health and safety policies and programmes; investigate complaints, accidents and carry out inspections (at least every three months) and maintain records; and ensure that, where there is a safety committee on board, records of its meeting are accessible to seafarers. The safety officer must have at least two years' sea service since attaining the age of 18; if the ship is a tanker, this must include at least six months' service on such a ship.[381] If a safety officer fails to comply with their statutory duties, this amounts to an offence punishable, on summary conviction, by a fine of $10,000 and, on conviction on indictment, by a fine of $50,000.[382]
- The master of a ship with: five or more seafarers must appoint a safety representative, who may be elected by the seafarers on board; and more than 16 seafarers must appoint a safety representative from each department, who may be elected by the seafarers on board, and must include such a representative from the deck and engine departments;[383] a safety representative (who must not be the master) must have at least two years' sea service since attaining the age of 18 and, if the ship is a tanker, this must include at least six months' service on such a ship.[384] Safety representatives have specific powers, including

375 H&S Regulations, reg 5(1)–(3).
376 H&S Regulations, reg 5(4).
377 H&S Regulations, reg 5(5)(a)–(b), respectively.
378 H&S Regulations, reg 6(1)(a)–(c).
379 H&S Regulations, reg 6(2).
380 H&S Regulations, reg 7.
381 H&S Regulations, regs 8(1)–(4), 9(1).
382 H&S Regulations, regs 8(5), 9(2).
383 H&S Regulations, reg 10(1)–(2).
384 H&S Regulations, reg 10(3)–(4).

the right to participate (with the safety officer's agreement) in or carry out investigations, and to make recommendations, and to request, through the safety committee, an investigation into any work which they recommend to the master should be suspended as they believe it may cause an accident, etc.[385] If the master fails to make the above appointments, this amounts to an offence punishable, on summary conviction, by a fine of $10,000 and, on conviction on indictment, by a fine of $50,000.[386]

The 2018 Regulations provide that, on a ship with 'more than five seafarers', the master must appoint a safety committee.[387] However, this is almost certainly a drafting error, as the MLC requires that a safety committee must be appointed on ships on which there are 'five or more seafarers', and the DMLC Pt I, requires '... the holding of regular safety committees on all vessels with five or more seafarers'.[388] The master must chair the safety committee, which must include the safety officer (who could be the master) and every safety representative; every member must be recorded in the official log book.[389] Meetings must be held at intervals not exceeding six weeks, and a record must be kept including that of any representations made, with replies and any resulting action.[390]

- The shipowner and the master must facilitate the work of the safety officer, safety representatives and the safety committee in carrying out their occupational health and safety functions, in accordance with the prescribed duties.[391] A shipowner or master who fails to comply commits an offence punishable, on summary conviction, by fine of $10,000 and, on conviction on indictment, by a fine of $50,000.[392]
- The shipowner must provide seafarers with suitable personal protective equipment (and training on its use), when risks cannot be avoided or sufficiently limited by organisation of work procedures or collective protection measures.[393] A shipowner who fails to comply commits an offence punishable, on summary conviction, by a fine of $10,000 and, on conviction on indictment, by a fine of $100,000.[394]
- The shipowner must take into account employed seafarers' capabilities as regards health and safety and ensure they are provided with adequate and appropriate safety training and instruction, before being assigned to shipboard duties or being exposed to new or increased risks, as prescribed.[395]

There are special obligations in respect of young seafarers (under the age of 18), as set out below:

385 H&S Regulations, reg 11.
386 H&S Regulations, reg 10(5)(a)–(b), respectively.
387 H&S Regulations, reg 12(1).
388 MLC, Standard A4.3.2(d); DMLC Pt I, point 11.
389 H&S Regulations, reg 12(2)–(4).
390 H&S Regulations, reg 12(5).
391 H&S Regulations, reg 13(1)(a)–(j).
392 H&S Regulations, reg 13(2)(a)–(b), respectively.
393 H&S Regulations, reg 14(1)–(8).
394 H&S Regulations, reg 14(9)(a)–(b), respectively.
395 H&S Regulations, reg 15.

- In addition to the general risk assessment (under reg 5), the shipowner must carry out risk assessments to assess the health and safety risk to any young seafarer before they begin work.[396]
- If the specific risk assessment for young seafarers (under reg 16) identifies a risk to the young seafarer's safety, physical or mental health, or they are likely to be required to work at night, the shipowner must carry out a health assessment, before the seafarer begins work and at regular intervals while the work continues.[397] For these purposes, 'night' means a period of at least nine consecutive hours including the period from midnight to 5am.[398]
- There are restricted tasks which must not be carried out by young seafarers without appropriate supervision and instruction (unless they are recognised as fully competent to carry out the task).[399] A 'restricted task is one involving any agents, processes or work specified in Sch 1, or a task identified by the specific risk assessment required for the young seafarer (under reg 16) as presenting a special risk of accident or detrimental effect on the young seafarer's health or physical development.[400]
- There are prescribed prohibited tasks which a young seafarer must not carry out unless they are an indispensable part of their established training programme, in which case the task must be performed under the supervision of a competent person, and carried out so that the young seafarer's health and safety is ensured as far as is reasonably practicable.[401]
- The shipowner must provide guidance on the detrimental effects to the young seafarer's health and well-being from the abuse of alcohol, drugs and other potentially harmful substances, the risk and concerns relating to HIV/AIDS and other health risk-related activities.[402]

A number of criminal offences have been created for non-compliances with the above provisions relating to young seafarers. If the shipowner fails in its obligations under reg 16 (risk assessment for young persons) or 17 (health assessment), it commits an offence punishable in each case, on summary conviction, by a fine of $10,000 and, on conviction on indictment, by a fine of $50,000.[403] If the master commits an offence for any failure to comply with reg 18 (restricted tasks) or 19 (prohibited tasks), both are punishable, on summary conviction, by a fine of $10,000 and, on conviction on indictment, by a fine of $50,000 or $100,000, respectively.[404]

General defence

24.141 It is a defence for a person charged with any offence under the H&S Regulations to show that the offence was committed without their knowledge

396 H&S Regulations, reg 16; Sch 1.
397 H&S Regulations, reg 17(1)–(2), respectively.
398 H&S Regulations, reg 2.
399 H&S Regulations, reg 18.
400 H&S Regulations, reg 18(2)(a)–(b), respectively.
401 H&S Regulations, reg 19.
402 H&S Regulations, reg 20.
403 H&S Regulations, regs 16(4)(a)–(b), 17(3)(a)–(b), respectively.
404 H&S Regulations, regs 18(4)(a)–(b), 19(3)(a)–(b), respectively.

or, where they had such knowledge, they took all reasonable precautions and exercised all due diligence to avoid the commission of the offence.[405]

Detailed guidance on the implementation of health and safety measures can be found in the COSWP, such as: health surveillance (ch 7); personal protective equipment (ch 8); noise, vibration and other physical agent (ch 12); safety officials (ch 13); entering dangerous (enclosed) spaces (ch 15); and hazardous substances and mixtures (ch 21).

Reporting of diseases, accidents and injuries

Occupational diseases

24.142 If a seafarer on a ship suffers from any of the occupational diseases specified in Sch 2, column 1, where the work involved an activity specified in the corresponding entry in column 2, the shipowner must send a report to the MACI; the duty only applies if the shipowner or the master has received a written statement from a medical practitioner diagnosing the disease as one of those specified in Sch 2.[406] The report must be made within seven days of the master or the shipowner receiving the written statement.[407] A failure to comply amounts to an offence by the shipowner punishable, on summary conviction, by a fine of $10,000 and, on conviction on indictment, by a fine of $50,000.[408]

Notifiable diseases

24.143 In addition, there is a requirement to report to the MACI, as soon as confirmed, a diagnosis of a notifiable disease (as listed in Annex 2 to CISN 02/2015).[409]

Any report of an occupational disease or a notifiable disease can be made by email to shipping.master@cishipping.com or by telephone on +44 1489 799 203.[410]

Serious accidents and injuries

24.144 Accidents and injuries must be reported to the MACI, in accordance with CISN 02/2015.[411] These are: any accident resulting in death or serious injury of a seafarer, occasional worker or passenger, whether on board, ashore or elsewhere (to be reported immediately); any accident resulting in a seafarer

405 H&S Regulations, reg 28.
406 H&S Regulations, reg 21(1)–(2).
407 H&S Regulations, reg 21(3)(a)–(b).
408 H&S Regulations, reg 21(4)(a)–(b), respectively.
409 CISN 02/2015 (Rev 1): Mandatory reporting of certain incidents and occurrences on board Cayman Island ships.
410 CISN 02/2015, para 2.8; Annex 1 (contact details).
411 H&S Regulations, reg 22(1).

being unfit to discharge their normal duties for a period in excess of 24 hours (to be reported within seven days); and any accident resulting in a crew member being unfit to discharge their normal duties for a period in excess of 72 hours, including cases where the injuries sustained result in the person leaving the ship (to be reported within 24 hours).[412] These accidents can be reported by email to reporting@cishipping.com or by telephone on +1 345 9498831 or +44 1489 799 203 (the relevant form will then be sent by the MACI for completion).[413]

The MACI must conduct an investigation into any accident or incident resulting in the loss of life of a seafarer or other person on board a ship, the total loss of the ship, or severe damage to the environment.[414]

Inspection and detention

24.145 There are powers to inspect CI ships (and non-CI ships without MLC documentation while they are in CI waters) to check for compliance with the 2018 Regulations, and to detain such a ship for a dangerous, serious or repeated breach of regs 4 (provision of occupational health protection), 5 (risk assessment and evaluation) and 6 (consultation with seafarers not employed by the shipowner).[415]

There are also powers to inspect non-CI ships with MLC documentation (while they are in CI waters) to review the ship's MLC documentation and, where MLC, Standard A5.2.1 applies,[416] carry out a more detailed inspection.[417] There is a power to detain the ship where there are clear grounds to believe that it does not comply with the MLC and that such non-compliance represents a significant danger to seafarers or serious or repeated breach of the MLC.[418]

Amendments to the MLC addressing bullying and harassment

24.146 On 8 January 2019, the 2016 amendments to the Guidelines of Regulation 4.3 of the MLC will come into force, the intention of which is to address the issue of bullying and harassment in a health and safety context. The amendments are set out in Appendix 2. Details of how the CI will implement the amendments have still to be promulgated.

Compliance

24.147 DMLC: implement CI requirements as set out in Pt I, point 11, and record details of compliance measures in DMLC, Pt II, point 11.

412 CISN 02/2015, para 2.2.
413 CISN 02/2015, Annex 1 (contact details).
414 H&S Regulations, reg 22(2)(a)–(c). See also Merchant Shipping Law (2016 Revision), Pt XVIII.
415 H&S Regulations, regs 23–24.
416 MLC, Standard A5.2.1 is set out in full in Appendix 1.
417 H&S Regulations, reg 25 (and reg 25(2) applies reg 23).
418 H&S Regulations, reg 26.

REGULATION 4.4: ACCESS TO SHORE-BASED WELFARE FACILITIES

24.148 The MLC requires ratifying states to promote the development of welfare facilities for the benefit of visiting seafarers.[419] The MACI reports that the majority of visiting seafarers arrive on daytime, short visits for typically 8–10 hours on cruise ships, which remain at anchor. There are no dedicated seafarer welfare facilities in the CI; however, there are no restrictions on visiting seafarers accessing general facilities ashore.

REGULATION 4.5: SOCIAL SECURITY

24.149 The MLC provides that the nine branches to be considered, with a view to achieving progressively comprehensive social security protection, for all seafarers ordinarily resident in the relevant state's territory, are: medical care, sickness benefit, unemployment benefit, old-age benefit, employment injury benefit, family benefit, maternity benefit, invalidity benefit and survivor's benefit, complementing the protection which shipowners are required to provide under MLC, Regulations 4.1 (medical care) and 4.2 (shipowners' liability), and other titles of the MLC.[420] The ILO's website shows that, in accordance with MLC, Standard A4.5(2) and (10), the CI government has specified the following branches of social security as being applicable to seafarers: medical care; old-age benefit; family benefit; and survivor's benefit.[421]

The obligations which the MLC imposes on ratifying states are mainly aimed at resident seafarers and their dependants. Although the MACI reports that there are no serving seafarers resident in the CI, there are retired seafarers domiciled there, who are entitled to the same social security benefits as other members of the population.

Specifically, retired seafarers who first went to sea before 1 January 1985 (and who meet the eligibility criteria) are entitled to free medical care through the government-owned Cayman Islands National Insurance Company (CINICO)[422] and are also entitled to old age benefit of $510 per month; their widows are entitled to the same amount as a survivor's benefit.

Compliance

24.150 Details of the health and social security protection benefits provided by the shipowner to the seafarer should be entered in the SEA.[423]

419 MLC, Regulation 4.4.1.
420 MLC, Standard A4.5(1), (3).
421 See www.ilo.org/dyn/normlex/en/f?p=1000:11300:0::NO::P11300_INSTRUMENT_ID:312331 [Accessed 13 October 2018]. Note that CI's entry appears under that of the UK.
422 Health Insurance Amendment Law, 2003; CINICO: www.cinico.ky/seafarers-veterans#b [Accessed 17 January 2018].
423 SEA Regulations, reg 5(1)–(2), Sch 1, para 11.

INTRODUCTION TO TITLE 5

24.151 The complete Title 5 of the MLC is set out in Appendix 1, which fully explains MLC flag state and port state responsibilities. It has been annotated with references to the ILO Guidelines on flag state control[424] and port state control.[425]

The UK's Title 5 provisions are described in some detail in Chapter 22. Those provisions may be used as a guide to flag state and port state implementation.

A summary of the CI's main provisions in this area is set out below, with references to the main sources, which should be read by those who need to know more detail on the precise requirements.

REGULATION 5.1: FLAG STATE RESPONSIBILITIES

24.152 The main provisions are set out in the S&C Regulations.

All CI ships of 500 GT must be surveyed to confirm that they comply with the CI provisions implementing the MLC, and issued with an MLCert.[426] An intermediate survey and endorsement of the MLCert is required between the second and third anniversaries of the initial survey,[427] and a renewal inspection is required on its expiry.[428]

Ships which have been issued with an MLCert, DMLC or interim MLCert must carry those documents on board, and post them in a conspicuous place on board the ship and where they are available for inspection.[429]

A copy of the MLC must also be kept on board[430] (and should include any amendments). The MLC, as amended, is available on the ILO's website.[431]

Under the MLC, ships which do not meet the mandatory criteria for certification may be put forward for voluntary certification.[432] Ships below 500 GT must

424 Guidelines for flag State inspections under the Maritime Labour Convention, 2006 (published 2009): www.ilo.org/global/standards/maritime-labour-convention/monitoring-implementation-tools/WCMS_101788/lang--en/index.htm [Accessed 6 July 2018].

425 Guidelines for port State control officers carrying out inspections under the Maritime Labour Convention, 2006: www.ilo.org/global/standards/maritime-labour-convention/monitoring-implementation-tools/WCMS_101787/lang--en/index.htm [Accessed 6 July 2018].

426 S&C Regulations, regs 4–5.

427 S&C Regulations, regs 4(3), 7.

428 S&C Regulations, reg 6.

429 S&C Regulations, reg 15(2)–(3).

430 S&C Regulations, reg 15(1)–(3).

431 MLC, 2006, as amended: www.ilo.org/wcmsp5/groups/public/---ed_norm/---normes/documents/normativeinstrument/wcms_554767.pdf [Accessed 13 October 2018].

432 MLC, Regulation 5.1.3, para 2.

still comply with the CI MLC legislation, even if they are not put forward for voluntary certification.

Inspection

24.153 The inspection for the issue of an MLCert will cover the 16 areas as set out in MLC, Appendix A5-I.

An application for an interim MLCert (valid for a maximum period of six months) may be made in respect of a ship being first registered with the MACI, or on a change of flag or ownership, so long as the prescribed conditions are met.[433]

Validity of MLCert

24.154 The MLCert will be valid for a maximum period of five years, on condition that an intermediate inspection is carried out between the second and third anniversaries; a renewal inspection must be carried out for the issue of a new MLCert.[434] However, when the 2016 amendments to the MLC come into force on 8 January 2019, ratifying states will have the power to extend the validity for a further period not exceeding five months, following a successful renewal inspection, where the new MLCert cannot be immediately issued to and made available on board the ship.[435] Details on how the CI will implement this amendment have still to be promulgated. The MLC amendments are set out in Appendix 2.

MLCert and DMLC

24.155 The shipowner must provide the MACI with the information necessary to draw up the DMLC Pt I (which shows the flag state requirement), and the shipowner must complete the DMLC, Pt II (which shows the shipowner's measures to comply with the flag state requirements).[436]

The model MLCert and DMLC, Pt I, with 'substantial equivalences' are available on the MACI website.[437]

On-board complaint procedure (and the right to complain directly to the Shipping Master)

24.156 An on-board complaint procedure (complying with CISN 04/2014) must be made available to seafarers so that they can lodge a complaint alleging

433 S&C Regulations, reg 11.
434 S&C Regulations, regs 6(2)(a)–(c), 12(1), (3)(a).
435 This provision will become MLC, Standard A5.1.3.4.
436 S&C Regulations, reg 13.
437 CI DMLC, Pt 1: http://cishipping.com/forms [Accessed 6 July 2018].

a breach of the requirements of the MLC and for that complaint to be resolved fairly, effectively and expeditiously.[438]

A seafarer may complain directly to the Shipping Master (shipping.master@cishipping.com) at the MACI concerning breaches of the MLC.[439]

Arbitration

24.157 If a shipowner is unhappy with the outcome of a survey, they may ask for the dispute to be referred to a single arbitrator, by serving notice on the MACI within 21 days of the completion of the survey.[440]

Inspection and detention of CI ships

24.158 An authorised officer has power to inspect ships for the purpose of ascertaining if they comply with the S&C Regulations.[441] Where there are clear grounds for believing that a CI ship that is required to have a valid MLCert and DMLC Pts I and II, or an interim MLCert (the requirement applies to ships of 500 GT and above), does not have them, or does not carry them on board, or there is no on-board complaints procedure, the ship is liable to be detained.[442] A detention notice must be served, stating the grounds of detention and the requirements to be complied with before the ship can be released.[443]

When an inspection is conducted under the S&C Regulations, all reasonable efforts must be made to avoid a ship being unreasonably delayed.[444]

REGULATION 5.2: PORT STATE RESPONSIBILITIES

24.159 See also the ILO Guidelines on port state control.[445]

Inspections of non-CI ships

Inspection

24.160 Non-CI MLC ships may be inspected for the purpose of reviewing the ship's MLCert, DMLC, Pt I and II, or the interim MLCert; and, where MLC,

438 S&C Regulations, reg 16. CISN 04/2014 – Requirements and guidance for on-board and on-shore complaint procedures on Cayman Islands flagged vessels.
439 S&C Regulations, reg 16(4).
440 S&C Regulations, reg 17.
441 S&C Regulations, reg 18.
442 S&C Regulations, reg 19(1)–(2).
443 S&C Regulations, reg 19(4).
444 S&C Regulations, reg 18(5).
445 Guidelines for port State control officers carrying out inspections under the Maritime Labour Convention, 2006: www.ilo.org/global/standards/maritime-labour-convention/monitoring-implementation-tools/WCMS_101787/lang--en/index.htm [Accessed 5 July 2018].

Standard A5.2.1 applies, a more detailed inspection may be carried out in accordance with that Standard.[446] Non-CI ships registered with a non-MLC state may also be inspected in accordance with MLC, Standard A5.2.1.[447]

Detention

24.161 Where, following the more detailed inspection, the ship is found not to conform to the requirements of the MLC and:

(a) the conditions on board are hazardous to the safety, health or security of seafarers; or

(b) the non-conformity constitutes a repeated breach of the requirements of the MLC (including seafarers' rights),

the ship is liable to be detained.[448]

An authorised person may permit the ship to proceed to sea for the purpose of proceeding to the nearest appropriate repaid yard.[449]

In implementing MLC responsibilities, all possible efforts must be taken to avoid a ship being unduly detained or delayed.[450]

On-shore seafarer complaint-handling procedures

24.162 The provision permitting a complaint directly to the Shipping Master at the MACI, in accordance with CISN 04/2014, only applies to seafarers serving on CI ships.[451] This does not implement the MLC requirement that seafarers on any MLC ship must have a right to make a complaint when visiting the port of any ILO member state.[452] Even so, such seafarers would be well advised to contact the MACI if they wish to make an on-shore complaint about a non-compliance with the MLC.

OFFENCES

24.163 A failure to comply with any of the main provisions amounts to a criminal offence by the shipowner and master, or by any person in connection with wrongful acts in connection with the MLC certification, punishable by

446 S&C Regulations, reg 21(1).

447 S&C Regulations, reg 21(2). This is an application of the 'no more favourable treatment clause' (set out in MLC, Article V, para 7) towards non-MLC ships.

448 S&C Regulations, reg 22(1).

449 S&C Regulations, reg 22(2).

450 MLC, Standard A5.2.1.8.

451 S&C Regulations, reg 16(4) which, by virtue of reg 3(1)–(2), only applies to CI ships.

452 MLC, Standard A5.2.2.1.

fines.[453] It is a defence for the accused to show that the offence was committed without their knowledge or, where they had such knowledge, that they took all reasonable precautions and exercised all due diligence to avoid the commission of the offence.[454]

Compliance

24.164 CI ships and visiting non-CI ships should ensure that they comply with the 16 areas of inspection, as set out in accordance with Appendices A5-I and A5-III to the MLC, respectively.

453 S&C Regulations, reg 24.
454 S&C Regulations, reg 25.

CHAPTER 25

Gibraltar

INTRODUCTION

25.1 The Gibraltar Maritime Administration (GMA) was established in its present format as a Registry of Ships in 1997. The Registry has experienced steady growth over the last eight years and is an EU Member States' Register.[1]

1 GMA: www.gibraltarship.com/about-us [Accessed 13 October 2018].

Like the UK, Gibraltar's MLC legislation is underpinned by the various EU Directives implementing the Convention into EU law, the main one being Directive 2009/13/EC,[2] which has been followed by others on flag state control, port state control, and amendments to the MLC. The Directives do not add any substantive requirements to those in the MLC; however, they encourage EU member states to ratify the MLC, as they would, in any case, be subject to its provisions. Furthermore, the Directives facilitate enforcement of MLC obligations by virtue of: the availability of infringement proceedings against a member state for any failure to fully implement its MLC obligations as expressed in the Directive; the doctrine of direct effect; and a uniform interpretation across the EU as expressed through any judgments of the Court of Justice of the European Union. It remains to be seen how Brexit will affect the relevance of the EU legal regime to the UK and Gibraltar's MLC laws, and whether any changes need to be made. In any event, the UK has ratified the MLC (and extended it to Gibraltar), so both will remain bound to fully implement its provisions.

The main provisions are set out in the Gibraltar Merchant Shipping (Maritime Labour Convention) Regulations 2013[3] ('2013 Regulations') and a set of Maritime Labour Guidance Notices ('MLNs'). The 2013 Regulations have been amended in 2014,[4] 2015[5] and, more recently, in 2018 to implement the MLC amendments on financial security. MLN 001[6] sets out a current index list. MLN 002 states that implementation of the guidance will be taken as evidence of compliance with the Gibraltar legislation; however, the guidance does not preclude shipowners from demonstrating an equivalent or higher standard as an 'alternative method' of evidence of compliance.[7] Even although the UK and Gibraltar are the only REG members subject to EU law, only the latter relies on some aspects of implementation through express reference to underlying EU Directives with which EEA ships must comply when in Gibraltar waters.

Definitions used in the 2013 Regulations

25.2 The 2013 Regulations set out definitions of key MLC concepts.[8] Those which are referred to throughout are set out below; others relating to specific areas of the MLC will be set out at the relevant sections to which they relate:

2 Council Directive 2009/13/EC of 16 February 2009 implementing the Agreement concluded by the European Community Shipowners' Associations (ECSA) and the European Transport Workers' Federation (ETF) on the Maritime Labour Convention, 2006, and amending Directive 1999/63/EC (OJ L 124/30, 20.5.2009).

3 LN 2013/120.

4 Notice of Corrigendum, LN 2014/159: this replaced a number of erroneous references in regs 34–35 to 'Directive 2009/63/EC' with the correct reference to 'Directive 2009/13/EC'.

5 Gibraltar Merchant Shipping (Maritime Labour Convention) (Amendment) Regulations 2015 (LN 2015/150).

6 MLN 001: Current Index List.

7 MLN 002: Introduction to MLC Notices, paras 5–6.

8 2013 Regulations, reg 2.

"'Gibraltar ship" means a ship registered under the provisions of the Gibraltar Merchant Shipping (Registration) Act 1993;

...

"Maritime Administrator" means the person appointed under section 3 of the Merchant Shipping (Safety, etc.) Act, 1993, or a suitably qualified member of the maritime administrator's staff;

"Member State" means any State within the European Economic Area;

"Member State ship" means a ship, other than a Gibraltar ship, which is registered in and flying the flag of a Member State;

"MLC State" means a State which is a Party to the MLC and in which the MLC has come into force, other than the United Kingdom extending the MLC to Gibraltar;

"MLC ship" means a ship, other than a Gibraltar ship, which–

(a) is registered in an MLC State;

(b) is flying the flag of that State; and

(c) carries a Maritime Labour Certificate to which a Declaration of Maritime Labour Compliance is attached or an interim Maritime Labour Certificate;

"port" and "port of Gibraltar" have the meanings given to them by the Port Act;

"seafarer" means–

(a) any person, including a master, who is employed or engaged or works in any capacity on board a ship; and

(b) in relation to a ship which is not a Gibraltar ship or an MLC flag [sic] ship, includes any person on board that ship who is in a category of persons considered by the competent authority of the flag State of that ship to be a seafarer;

...

"ship" means any ship ordinarily engaged in commercial activities, other than–

(a) a ship which navigates exclusively in inland waters or waters within, or closely adjacent to, sheltered waters or areas where port regulations apply;

(b) a ship engaged in fishing or in similar pursuits;

(c) a ship of traditional build such as a dhow or junk;

(d) a warship;

(e) a naval auxiliary;

"shipowner" means–

(a) in relation to a ship which has a valid Maritime Labour Certificate or valid interim Maritime Labour Certificate, the person identified as the shipowner on that Certificate;

(b) in relation to any other ship, the owner of the ship or, if different, any other organisation or person such as the manager, agent or bareboat charterer, who has assumed the responsibility for the operation of the ship from the owner, and in this definition "responsibility for the operation of the ship" includes the duties and responsibilities imposed on shipowners in accordance with the Agreements forming the Annexes to Directive 1999/63/EC[9] and Directive 2009/13/EC;[10]

"STCW" means the International Convention of Standards of Training, Certification and Watchkeeping for Seafarers, 1978, as amended.'

Determinations of the GMA on definitions and exceptions

25.3 In cases of doubt as to whether a person is a seafarer, or whether a ship is one to which the 2013 Regulations apply, the GMA can make a determination, following consultation with the relevant shipowners' and seafarers' organisations.[11] In the former case, the GMA must also take account of the ILO Resolution on occupational groups[12] (set out in Chapter 1 at para 1.9).

There are also powers for the GMA to approve: different provisions for Gibraltar ships of less than 200 GT in cases where it would not be practicable or reasonable to apply the 2013 Regulations;[13] and other requirements on Gibraltar ships (of any gross tonnage) which are considered to be 'substantially equivalent' measures to those in the 2013 Regulations.[14]

Application

25.4 The 2013 Regulations apply to:

(a) a Gibraltar ship wherever it is;

(b) any other ship in Gibraltar waters (see the definition below) and which is (i) in the Port of Gibraltar; (ii) at an offshore installation; or (iii) anchored off the port or such an installation;

(c) any seafarer on a Gibraltar ship;

(d) a seafarer recruitment organisation operating in Gibraltar.[15]

9 Council Directive 1999/63/EC of 21 June 1999 concerning the Agreement on the organisation of working time of seafarers concluded by the European Community Shipowners' Association (ECSA) and the Federation of Transport Workers' Unions in the European Union (FST) (OJ L 167, 2.7.1999, pp 33–37). The FST is now known as the European Transport Workers' Federation (ETF).

10 See footnote 2 above.

11 2013 Regulations, reg 3(2)–(3).

12 Resolutions adopted by the International Labour Conference at its 94th (Maritime) Session, Resolution VII concerning information on occupational groups and Annex: www.ilo.org/wcmsp5/groups/public/@ed_norm/@normes/documents/publication/wcms_088130.pdf [Accessed 20 March 2018].

13 2013 Regulations, reg 3(4)–(5).

14 2013 Regulations, reg 3(6).

15 2013 Regulations, reg 3(1)(a)–(d).

There is a definition of 'British Gibraltar Territorial Waters', which means 'the area of sea, the sea bed and subsoil within the seaward limits of the territorial sea adjacent to Gibraltar under British sovereignty and which, in accordance with the United Nations Convention on the Law of the Sea 1982, currently extends to three nautical miles and to the median line in the Bay of Gibraltar'.[16] In this chapter, 'British territorial Gibraltar waters' has been abbreviated to 'Gibraltar waters', which should also be understood to include, in relation to a ship, the circumstances referred to in paragraph (b)(i)–(iii) above.

REGULATION 1.1: MINIMUM AGE

Gibraltar ships

25.5 The shipowner, master and employer must ensure that:

(a) no person below the age of 16 is employed, engaged or works on board a ship;

(b) no person below the age of 18 is employed, engaged or works at night on board a ship;

(c) no person below the age of 18 is employed, engaged or works on board a ship on work which is likely to jeopardise their health or safety.[17]

Further to paragraph (a), it should be noted that a ship's cook must be aged at least 18.[18]

'Night' means (a) a period of nine consecutive hours, and (b) includes the period between midnight and 5am.[19]

The GMA may make exceptions to night work in cases where: (a) the effective training of seafarers, in accordance with established programmes and schedules, would otherwise be impaired; or (b) the specific nature of the duty or recognised training programme requires night duties and the GMA has determined, after consultation with the relevant shipowners' and seafarers' organisations, that the work will not be detrimental to the seafarers' health or well-being.[20]

Established training programme(s) means those leading to STCW qualifications and, in most cases, this will be a cadet training scheme.[21]

The MLC provides that seafarers under the age of 18 are prohibited from work which is likely to jeopardise their health or safety.[22] MLN 003 provides detailed

16 2013 Regulations, reg 2(1).
17 2013 Regulations, reg 4(1)(a)–(c).
18 MLN 003: Young Persons, para 3(a).
19 2013 Regulations, reg 4(2)(a)–(b).
20 2013 Regulations, reg 4(3)(a)–(b), (4).
21 MLN 003, para 2(a).
22 MLC, Standard A1.1.4.

guidance[23] on health and safety issues for young seafarers including: risk assessment; health assessment; prohibited and restricted tasks; and a schedule of dangerous agents and processes at work, which closely follows that adopted by the UK (see Chapter 3).

In addition to the general duty of employers and shipowners to ensure that seafarers on Gibraltar ships have regular health assessments,[24] there is a specific duty to ensure this is carried out in respect of young seafarers who work at night; the assessment is to be made before and during night work.[25] If a medical practitioner certifies that a seafarer (of any age) is suffering from health problems due to night work, the shipowner, master and employer must, if possible, transfer the seafarer to other suitable work which does not involve night work.[26]

MLC ships (other than Gibraltar ships)

25.6 The shipowner, master and employer must ensure that, when in Gibraltar waters etc (see application as set out in para 25.4 above):

(a) an EEA MLC ship complies with the requirements of clauses 3–9 and 11 of the Annex to Directive 1999/63/EC,[27] as transposed into the law of the Member State (the Annex was inserted by Directive 2009/13/EC and contains MLC provisions, including the prohibition and exceptions relating to young persons performing night work);

(b) a non-EEA MLC ship complies with MLC, Regulation 1.1 and Standard 1.1 on minimum age, as applied to that ship by its flag state.[28]

Compliance

25.7 DMLC: implement Gibraltar requirements as set out in Pt I, point 1, and record details of compliance measures in DMLC, Pt II, point 1.

REGULATION 1.2: MEDICAL CERTIFICATE

25.8 An obligation is imposed on the shipowner, master and employer to ensure that a seafarer holds a valid medical certificate for the duties they are

23 MLN 006, paras 8(a)–(n), Sch.
24 2013 Regulations, reg 7(1).
25 MLN 003: paras 4(c), 8(k)–(m).
26 2013 Regulations, reg 7(2).
27 Council Directive 1999/63/EC of 21 June 1999 concerning the Agreement on the organisation of working time of seafarers concluded by the European Community Shipowners' Association (ECSA) and the Federation of Transport Workers' Unions in the European Union (FST) (OJ L 167, 2.7.1999, pp 33–37).
28 2013 Regulations, reg 5(a)–(b).

to perform on board.[29] Seafarers are prohibited from working on board without such a certificate.[30]

There are some exceptions: (i) in urgent cases, where a seafarer on board does not hold a valid medical certificate, but has held one for at least 24 months (or, in the case of a seafarer under 18 at the time of issue of the certificate, 12 months) and it has expired no earlier than one month before the seafarer joined the ship, the GMA may grant permission for the seafarer to work on that ship until the first port of call at which it is possible for an application for a certificate to be made and the seafarer to be examined by a medical practitioner; however the period of working without a certificate must not exceed three months;[31] or (ii) a seafarer whose certificate has expired during the course of a voyage may continue to work on board until (a) the first port of call at which it is possible to make an application for a certificate and to be examined by a medical practitioner, or (b) the expiry of three months from the date of expiry of the certificate, whichever is sooner.[32]

Seafarers are to be examined in accordance with the ILO/WHO Guidelines for Conducting Pre-Sea and Periodic Medical Fitness Examinations for Seafarers and other applicable international guidelines published by ILO/IMO/WHO.[33]

Medical certificates will be valid for a maximum period of one year in respect of seafarers under the age of 18, and two years in respect of other seafarers; in both cases, the certification relating to colour vision will be valid for a maximum period of six years.[34]

Due to the low number of seafarers resident in Gibraltar, the GMA does not regulate medical practitioners or issue medical certificates. The GMA will accept medical certificates as set out below:

(1) For seafarers on a Gibraltar ship or an EEA ship, issued in accordance with clause 13 of the Annex to Directive 1999/63/EC (which is the MLC, Regulation 1.2 and Standard A1.2 requirements, as inserted by Annex A to Directive 2009/13/EC); clause 13, para 5, permits certificates issued in accordance with the STCW Convention.[35]

(2) For seafarers on any other ship, issued in accordance with MLC, Regulation 1.2 and Standard A1.2, as transposed into the national laws of the issuing state, or issued in accordance with the STCW Convention.[36]

29 2013 Regulations, reg 6(2).
30 2013 Regulations, reg 6(1).
31 2013 Regulations, reg 6(3).
32 2013 Regulations, reg 6(5)(a)–(b).
33 2013 Regulations, Sch, para 1(c).
34 2013 Regulations, Sch, para 6.
35 2013 Regulations, reg 6(6)(b)(i).
36 2013 Regulations, reg 6(6)(b)(ii).

(3) In respect of a seafarer not covered by the STCW Convention, a certificate which meets the substance of the STCW requirements.[37]

(4) A certificate issued in accordance with Co73 – Medical Examination (Seafarers) Convention, 1946 (No. 73).[38]

(5) A certificate issued in accordance with Administrative Instruction No. STCW-14 (which replaces No. STCW 11). The Administrative Instruction is issued under section 3(5) of the Gibraltar Merchant Shipping (Safety etc) Act 1993 and relates to qualifications and certification required for domestic vessels. The current version offers little by way of guidance on medical certificates but requires that a seafarer who holds an operating certificate for specified vessels must possess a valid Medical Fitness Certificate.[39]

For a certificate to be valid, it must be in English and state that: the seafarer's hearing and sight is satisfactory; colour vision is satisfactory (this only applies to seafarers performing tasks whose performance would be adversely affected by defective colour vision – the guidance states these are generally electricians but may include other seafarers);[40] and the seafarer is not suffering from any medical condition likely to be aggravated by service at sea or to render the seafarer unfit for such service or to endanger the health of other persons on board.[41]

If a seafarer has been refused a medical certificate, or had a restriction imposed on a certificate, they may have the matter reviewed by an independent medical practitioner.[42]

Compliance

25.9 DMLC: implement Gibraltar requirements as set out in Pt I, point 2, and record details of compliance measures in DMLC, Pt II, point 2.

REGULATION 1.3: TRAINING AND QUALIFICATIONS

25.10 A shipowner, master and employer of seafarers must ensure that they are trained, certified as competent or otherwise qualified to perform their duties on the ship; in addition, they must ensure that the seafarer has successfully completed training for personal safety on board.[43] A seafarer is prohibited from working on board a ship unless they meet all of those requirements.[44]

37 2013 Regulations, reg 6(6)(c).

38 2013 Regulations, reg 6(6)(a)(i); MLN 004, para 3.1.3.

39 2013 Regulations, reg 6(6)(a)(ii); Administrative Instruction No. STCW-14; Boatmaster's Certificate, required for the operation of passenger vessels and other vessels under 500 GT within Gibraltar waters; Marine Engine Operator's Certificate, applicable for those operating marine diesel engines of less than 750 KW on domestic and international voyages.

40 MLN 004, para 3.2.2.

41 2013 Regulations, Sch, para 6; MLN 004, paras 3.2.1–3.2.3.

42 2013 Regulations, Sch, paras 4–5.

43 2013 Regulations, reg 8(2)(a)–(b).

44 2013 Regulations, reg 8(1)(a)–(b).

Training and certification in accordance with the mandatory instrument of the IMO will meet the requirements referred to above.[45] The main IMO instrument is the International Convention on Standards of Training, Certification and Watchkeeping for Seafarers, 1978 ('STCW Convention') (as amended, most recently by the Manila amendments of 2010).

The Gibraltar Merchant Shipping (Manning, Training and Certification for Seafarers) (Amendment) Regulations 2014[46] amended those of 2006,[47] to implement Directive 2012/35/EU,[48] which incorporated the Manilla amendments into EU law.

Like the other REG members, except the UK, Gibraltar does not issue its own Certificates of Competency. For the purposes of MLC implementation, MLN 005 provides that the shipowner must ensure that all seafarers are suitably qualified for the safe operation of the ship.[49] Compliance with Administrative Instructions[50] 1–14 (made under the Merchant Shipping (Safety etc) Act 1993) and the UK MCA's MSN 1856[51] and MSN 1857[52] (which replace MGN 91 and MGN 92), which set out the STCW training requirements, is mandatory on Gibraltar ships.[53] Furthermore, officers and ratings should be qualified as set out in the ship's safe manning document ('SMD').

In order to serve as a master or an officer on a Gibraltar ship, the seafarer must hold a Certificate of Competency or a Certificate of Equivalent Competency issued by the UK MCA, an Appropriate Certificate or a Gibraltar endorsement to a recognised Appropriate Certificate.[54] The GMA has published a list of STCW states which it recognises for the purpose of issuing a recognition endorsement under Regulation I/10 of the STCW Convention.[55]

The working language on Gibraltar ships is English, of which officers on board must have an appropriate level of proficiency, commensurate with their permitted

45 2013 Regulations, reg 8(3)(a).
46 LN 2014/112.
47 Gibraltar Merchant Shipping (Manning, Training and Certification for Seafarers) Regulations 2006 (LN 2006/023).
48 Directive 2012/35/EU of the European Parliament and of the Council of 21 November 2012 amending Directive 2008/106/EC on the minimum level of training for seafarers (OJ L 343/78, 14.12.2012).
49 MLN 005: Training and Qualifications, para 1.
50 LN 2004/068.
51 MSN 1856 (M+F) — Training & Certification Guidance: UK Requirements for Master and Deck Officers.
52 MSN 1857 (M+F) — Training & Certification Guidance: UK Requirements for Engineer Officers and Engineer Operators.
53 MLN 005, para 2.
54 Administrative Instruction, No STCW-4, para 2.
55 Gibraltar – Recognised Administrations for STCW: www.gibraltarship.com/seafarers [Accessed 23 March 2018].

functions.[56] Applications for endorsements can be made to: maritime.seafarers@gibraltar.gov.gi.

Since the Gibraltar requirements in this area closely follow those of the UK, see Chapter 5 for more details on STCW training and certification.

Compliance

25.11 DMLC: implement Gibraltar requirements as set out in Pt I, point 3, and record details of compliance measures in DMLC, Pt II, point 3.

REGULATION 1.4: RECRUITMENT AND PLACEMENT

25.12 Gibraltar defines a 'seafarer recruitment service' as a business: (a)(i) whose primary purpose is the recruitment and placement of seafarers; or (ii) which recruits and places a significant number of seafarers; or (b) a public service which recruits and places seafarers and which is operated in an orderly manner that protects and promotes seafarers' employment rights as provided in the MLC.[57] This definition is amplified by MLN 006,[58] which states that the three types of recruitment services at which the various requirements are aimed are: employment agencies ('EA'); employment businesses ('EB'); and placement businesses. The former two are defined as they are for the UK (see Chapter 6), and the latter (which does not find its way into the UK provisions) is defined as:

> '"Placement business" (PB) is a business engaged in working on behalf of a ship-owner and ensures that seafarers from either an EB or EA, or employed directly by a ship-owner, are allocated to and travel to and from ships operated by the ship-owner in line with the ship owner's requirements. While the Gibraltar regulations covered by this MLN [006] do not apply to a PB they may request inspection and certification and the PB would need to show how they comply with the areas for inspection highlighted below.'[59]

A PB is therefore a business which is not strictly involved in the core activities of a recruitment and placement service; its functions are mainly facilitating seafarers' travel to and from ships as required by the shipowner. This is likely to be the reason that the inspection and certifications provisions only apply to PBs on request. However, those provisions are mandatory in their application to EAs and EBs.

To be consistent with the other chapters of this book, from this point onwards, the MLC phrase 'recruitment and placement services' ('RPS') will be used instead of 'seafarer recruitment service'. As regards RPS, the 2013 Regulations and MLN 006 only apply to those operating in Gibraltar.[60]

56 Gibraltar Merchant Shipping (Manning, Training and Certification for Seafarers) Regulations 2006, reg 12A.
57 2013 Regulations, regs 2(1), 10(5).
58 MLN 006: Recruitment and placement.
59 MLN 006, para 5.3.
60 2013 Regulations, reg 3(1)(d); MLN 006, para 2.

Duties of hirers of seafarers

25.13 Shipowners and employers who are seeking seafarers to work on a Gibraltar ship must: (a) use an RPS operating in the territory of an MLC-ratifying state; (b) if using an RPS not operating in the territory of an MLC-ratifying state, ensure that it complies with the requirements of Regulation 1.4 of the MLC; (c) in a case where the RPS is being used to supply seafarers who are Gibraltar nationals to the shipowner of a Gibraltar ship, use a seafarers' organisation operating in Gibraltar; or (d) use an efficient, adequate and accountable system, other than an RPS or seafarers' organisation, to which all seafarers have access without charge.[61]

Shipowners are required to state, in the DMLC, Pt II, point 5, how they recruit seafarers; they should also state, in respect of using RPSs based in a state which has not ratified the MLC, what measures they have taken to ensure that it is compliant with MLC, Standard A1.4.[62]

The role of the GMA

25.14 The GMA must: (a) ensure that any public RPS operating in Gibraltar is operated in an orderly manner that protects and promotes seafarers' employment rights as provided in the MLC; (b) closely supervise any other RPS operating in Gibraltar; (c) ensure that there are procedures for investigating complaints concerning the activities of RPSs operating in Gibraltar or which are used by a shipowner of a Gibraltar ship; and (d) advise Gibraltar nationals on the possible problems of signing on a ship which is not a Gibraltar ship or an MLC ship.[63]

Regulation of seafarer RPSs

25.15 A person who operates a private seafarer RPS in Gibraltar must (a) have a valid 'seafarers' recruitment services certificate' issued by the GMA, and (b) operate the service in accordance with the certificate.[64] Before a certificate can be issued, the GMA must consult with any relevant shipowners' and seafarers' organisations in Gibraltar, and the RPS must:

(a) not use means, mechanisms or lists intended to prevent or deter seafarers from gaining employment for which they are qualified;

(b) not impose fees or other charges, directly or indirectly, on the seafarer, other than the costs of the seafarer obtaining a national statutory medical certificate, the national seafarer's book, a passport or similar personal travel document, but not including the cost of visas which must be borne by the shipowner;

61 2013 Regulations, reg 9(1)(a)–(d).
62 MLN 006, paras 7–8.
63 2013 Regulations, reg 9(2)(a)–(d).
64 2013 Regulations, reg 10(1)(a)–(b).

(c) maintain an up-to-date register of all seafarers recruited or placed through the RPS, and keep the register available for inspection by the GMA;

(d) ensure that seafarers are informed of their rights and duties under their seafarer employment agreements ('SEAs') prior to or in the process of engagement. and that proper arrangements are made for seafarers to examine their SEAs before and after they are signed and for them to receive a copy;

(e) verify that seafarers recruited or placed by the RPS are qualified and hold the documents necessary for the job concerned, and that SEAs are in accordance with applicable laws and regulations and any applicable collective bargaining agreement ('CBA') that forms part of the SEA;

(f) ensure, as far as practicable, that the shipowner has the means to protect seafarers on the ship from being stranded at a foreign port (RPSs should request and retain a copy of the ship's MLC certificate of financial security covering repatriation and abandonment (see para 25.37 onwards below);

(g) examine and respond to any complaint concerning the RPS's activities and inform the GMA of any unresolved complaint;

(h) establish a system of protection, by way of insurance or an equivalent appropriate measure, to compensate a seafarer for monetary loss as a result of (i) a failure of the RPS to meet its obligations to the seafarer, or (ii) a failure of the shipowner under the SEA to meet its obligations to the seafarer;[65]

(i) determine, with due regard to the right to privacy and the need to protect confidentiality, the conditions under which seafarers' personal data may be processed by the RPS, including the collection, storage, combination and communication of such data to third parties;[66]

(j) maintain up-to-date lists of the ships for which the RPS provides seafarers and ensure that there is a means by which the RPS can be contacted in an emergency at all hours.[67]

As regards sub-paragraph (i), RPSs should comply with the Data Protection Act 2004 and Regulation (EU) 2016/679 (GDPR).[68]

Although not a legal requirement, it is recommended that Gibraltar-based RPSs which have seafarer recruitment dealings with RPSs based in a country which has not ratified the MLC take steps to ensure that the latter complies with Standard A1.4 of the MLC.[69]

The GMA will issue the certificate (or a renewal) to a compliant RPS for a period not exceeding five years; it may also suspend or cancel a certificate, and charge

65 2013 Regulations, reg 10(2)(a)–(h)(i)–(ii).

66 MLN 006, para 6.9.

67 MLN 006, para 6.10.

68 Regulation (EU) 2016/679 of the European Parliament and of the Council on the protection of natural persons with regard to the processing of personal data and on the free movement of such data, and repealing Directive 95/46/EC (General Data Protection Regulation) (OJ L119/1 4.5.2016).

69 MLN 006, para 9.

a fee for its issue or renewal.[70] The GMA will carry out annual inspections of seafarer RPSs operating in Gibraltar to ensure compliance.[71]

Compliance

25.16 DMLC: implement Gibraltar requirements as set out in Pt I, point 5, and record details of compliance measures in DMLC, Pt II, point 5.

REGULATION 2.1: SEAFARERS' EMPLOYMENT AGREEMENTS

Seafarers to be issued with a seafarer's employment agreement

25.17 The shipowner, master and employer must ensure that: (a) an employed seafarer has a seafarer's employment agreement ('SEA'); (b) if the seafarer is not an employee, they have evidence of contractual or similar arrangements which provide the seafarer with decent working and living conditions on board the ship as required by the MLC; and (c) the seafarer has a seafarer's employment record.[72]

Seafarers are prohibited from working on a ship without being in possession of a SEA or (for self-employed seafarers) evidence of contractual or similar arrangements which provide the seafarer with decent working and living conditions on board the ship as required by (i) the MLC, and (ii) if the ship is a Gibraltar ship or EEA ship, Directive 2009/13/EC.[73]

The SEA must be signed by the shipowner (or its representative) and the seafarer.[74] A representative signing on behalf of the shipowner may do so by electronic signature, subject to the following conditions:

(a) there must be a formal contract, between the shipowner and the crewing agency or managers, which appoints the crew agency or managers to sign on behalf of the shipowner;

(b) in addition to the signature, the name of the person signing, and their position in the crewing company, must be printed on the SEA;

(c) it must be clear on the SEA that the person signing does so on behalf of the shipowner;

(d) the seafarer's signature must be original (not electronic).[75]

70 2013 Regulations, reg 10(3)–(4).
71 MLN 006, para 3.
72 2013 Regulations, reg 11(2)(a)–(c); MLN 007, paras 17–18(a)–(i).
73 2013 Regulations, reg 11(1)(a)–(b)(i)–(ii); Council Directive 2009/13/EC of 16 February 2009 implementing the Agreement concluded by the European Community Shipowners' Associations (ECSA) and the European Transport Workers' Federation (ETF) on the Maritime Labour Convention, 2006, and amending Directive 1999/63/EC.
74 MLN 007: Seafarers' Employment Agreements, para 5.
75 MLN 029: Seafarers' employment agreements – use of electronic signatures, paras (a)–(d), respectively.

It would also be good practice to state in the DMLC the name and details of the shipowner's authorised representative (which is a requirement under UK implementation).

The shipowner must ensure that each seafarer has the opportunity to examine the SEA and seek advice before signing it, and has been given the necessary facilities to ensure that they have entered into the agreement with a sufficient understanding of their rights and responsibilities.[76] The shipowner must also explain to the seafarer their rights and duties under the SEA, prior to or in the course of engagement.[77]

The SEA must be clear, written in a language the seafarer understands, and be a legally enforceable document, including either a contract of employment or articles of agreement, which:

> '… contains, as a minimum, the following particulars–
>
> (i) the seafarer's full name, date of birth or age, and birthplace,
>
> (ii) the shipowner's name and address,
>
> (iii) the place where and date when the seafarers' employment agreement is entered into,
>
> (iv) the capacity in which the seafarer is to be employed,[78]
>
> (v) the amount of the seafarer's wages or, where applicable, the formula used for calculating that amount,[79]
>
> (vi) the amount of paid annual leave or, where applicable, the formula used for calculating it,[80]
>
> (vii) provisions for termination of the agreement and the conditions thereof, including–
>
> (aa) if the agreement has been made for an indefinite period, the conditions entitling either party to terminate it, as well as the required notice period, which must not be less for the shipowner than for the seafarer,
>
> (bb) if the agreement has been made for a definite period, the date fixed for its expiry, and
>
> (cc) if the agreement has been made for a voyage, the port of destination and the time which has to expire after arrival before the seafarer should be discharged,
>
> (viii) the health and social security protection benefits to be provided to the seafarer by the shipowner,[81] and
>
> (ix) the seafarer's entitlement to repatriation;

76 MLN 007, paras 6–7.
77 MLN 007, para 8.
78 See Regulation 1.3; seafarers should be trained and certified accordingly.
79 See Regulation 2.2.
80 See Regulation 2.4.
81 See Regulation 4.5.

(d) incorporates by reference any collective agreement or workforce agreement applicable to the agreement; and

(e) in relation to–

(i) an MLC ship, contains any other provisions required by the MLC State whose flag that ship flies, and

(ii) any other ship, contains any other provisions as determined by the Maritime Administrator;'[82]

A model SEA is set out, with helpful explanatory notes, at Annex 1 to MLN 007. The use of the model SEA is not mandatory but, if it is adopted, it will amount to evidence of compliance with the 2013 Regulations.[83]

The shipowner, master and employer must ensure that:

(a) the seafarer has a signed original of their SEA and a copy of their seafarers' employment record;

(b) the seafarer can easily obtain on board clear information as to the conditions of their employment;

(c) a copy of any collective agreement or workforce agreement forming all or part of a SEA is available on board;

(d) the following documents are available for review by the GMA: (i) a copy of the standard form of SEA for every seafarer on board; (ii) the information referred to in paragraph (b) above; (iii) a copy in English of the standard form of SEA for every seafarer on board; and (iv) a copy in English of any portions of a collective agreement or workforce agreement referred to in paragraph (c) above, which are subject to port state inspection.[84]

The shipowner must also keep a signed original of the SEA for every seafarer on board any of its ships.[85]

Termination of a SEA

25.18 The minimum notice period to terminate a SEA is seven days, and the notice period must not be less for the shipowner than for the seafarer.[86]

Gibraltar ships

25.19 Early termination of a SEA is only permissible as follows:

(a) the seafarer is terminating the SEA for compassionate or other urgent reasons;

82 2013 Regulations, reg 2(1); MLN 007, paras 12, 15.
83 MLN 007, para 21.
84 2013 Regulations, reg 13(1)(a)–(d)(i)–(iv).
85 2013 Regulations, reg 13(2).
86 MLN 007, para 13.

(b) the termination of the SEA is in accordance with circumstances determined by the GMA as justifying termination at shorter notice or without notice; or

(c) the person terminating the agreement gives a minimum of seven days' notice.[87]

As regards sub-paragraph (a), for those not covered by a collective agreement, the GMA provides guidance on what should amount to compassionate grounds as including the death of next of kin or a nominated beneficiary, spouse, child and, in the case of a single person, a parent, and such grounds should also take account of such a person becoming seriously or dangerously ill; other urgent reasons should include emergency situations which would not be expediently resolved without the seafarer's attendance.[88]

As regards sub-paragraph (b), the GMA has specified the circumstances justifying early termination as follows: as agreed in a collective agreement; the parties agree that a shorter notice period is acceptable; or due to the seafarer's misconduct.[89]

In a case of misconduct, for those not covered by a collective agreement, the shipowner or its representative must inform the seafarer of any applicable disciplinary rules or procedures (these should substantially meet the provisions contained in 'The Code of Conduct for the Merchant Navy').[90]

MLC ships in Gibraltar waters

25.20 Early termination of a SEA is only permissible as follows:

(a) for compassionate or other urgent reasons;

(b) in accordance with the circumstances determined by the flag state as justifying early termination or termination without notice; or

(c) where the person terminating the agreement gives a minimum notice period of seven days or, if longer, the minimum notice period determined by the flag state.[91]

The shipowner, master and employer are prohibited from imposing any penalty on a seafarer for terminating their SEA for compassionate or urgent grounds (this applies to Gibraltar ships and MLC ships).[92]

Seafarer's record of employment

25.21 The shipowner, master and employer must ensure that each seafarer is provided with a seafarer's employment record relating to their employment on

87 2013 Regulations, reg 12(1)(a)–(c), respectively.
88 MLN 007, para 14(c).
89 MLN 007, para 14(a)–(c).
90 MLN 007, para 14(b).
91 2013 Regulations, reg 12(2)(a)–(c), respectively.
92 2013 Regulations, reg 12(3).

board the ship; the seafarer's discharge book may be used for this purpose.[93] The record must be provided in English and, as a minimum, contain the following particulars: (a) seafarer's full name, date of birth or age and birth place; (b) name, port of registry, gross tonnage and IMO number of the ship; (c) description of voyage; (d) capacity in which the seafarer was employed; (e) the date of employment; and (f) the date of discharge.[94] The record must not contain any statement as to the quality of the seafarer's work or as to their wages.[95]

Future amendments to the MLC

25.22 When the 2018 amendments to the MLC come into force (which is likely to be 26 December 2020), ratifying states will be required to provide that: (a) SEAs continue for the entirety of any period in which a seafarer is held in captivity as a result of an act of piracy or armed robbery at sea; and (b) seafarers' wages, allotments and other entitlements must be fully paid during the entirety of any such period. The full text of the amendments is set out in Appendix 2.

Compliance

25.23 DMLC: implement Gibraltar requirements as set out in Pt I, point 4, and record details of compliance measures in DMLC, Pt II, point 4.

REGULATION 2.2: WAGES

25.24 The shipowner and employer must ensure that:

- every seafarer is paid: (a) regularly; (b) at intervals no greater than one month; and (c) in full in accordance with the seafarer's employment agreement ('SEA') and any applicable collective agreement or workforce agreement.[96] Additional payments such as overtime may be paid in the next monthly pay cycle;[97]
- every seafarer is given a monthly account of the payments due and the amounts paid, including: (a) wages; (b) additional payments; (c) if payment has been made in a currency other than that specified in the SEA, the rate of exchange used to calculate the payment; and (d) if payment has been made at a rate of exchange other than that agreed to, the rate of exchange.[98] Details of any allotments or other deductions must also be shown;[99]
- every seafarer is provided with a means to transmit all or part of their wages and additional payments to their family, dependants or legal beneficiaries, and

93 2013 Regulations, reg 11(2)(c); MLN 007, para 19.
94 MLN 007, para 19(a)–(f).
95 MLN 007, para 20.
96 2013 Regulations, reg 14(1)(a)–(c).
97 MLN 008: Seafarer's wages, para 3(a).
98 2013 Regulations, reg 14(2)(a)–(d).
99 MLN 008, para 9(d).

that those means of transmission include: (a) a system enabling the seafarer, at the time of starting work on board the ship or during it, to allot, if the seafarer so desires, a proportion of their wages for remittance at regular intervals to their family by bank transfer or similar means; and (b) a requirement that allotments should be remitted in due time to the nominee.[100] In practice, such payments should be monthly at the same time the seafarer gets paid;[101]

- in respect of using the transmission service referred to above: (a) any charge is reasonable in amount; and (b) the rate of currency exchange is: (i) at the prevailing market rate or official published rate according to the national laws of the flag state; and (ii) not unfavourable to the seafarer.[102] An example of an official published rate is the mid-rate in the Financial Times at the last working day of the month.[103]

For these purposes, 'wages' means the pay, however composed, for the seafarer's normal hours of work including overtime, allowances, paid leave and other remuneration (but excluding bonuses).[104]

Basic pay and overtime

25.25 The guidance provides that, for the purposes of calculating basic pay, the normal working day should not exceed eight hours.[105] For the purposes of calculating overtime, the normal hours of work covered by basic pay must not exceed 48 hours per week (although a collective agreement may provide for different treatment so long as it is not less favourable).[106] Unless prescribed differently in a collective agreement, the overtime rate must be not less than 1.25 times the basic hourly rate.[107] The same principle of enhancement must also be applied to overtime hours within a consolidated or partially consolidated wage.[108]

The master (or authorised person) must keep records (which may be in electronic form) of seafarers' overtime, which must be endorsed by the seafarer at no more than monthly intervals.[109]

For these purposes: 'basic pay or wages' means 'the pay, however composed, for normal hours of work. This does not include payments for overtime worked, bonuses, allowances, paid leave or any other additional remuneration'. 'Consolidated wage' is 'the wage or salary which includes the basic pay and other pay-related benefits. A consolidated wage may include compensation for

100 2013 Regulations, reg 14(3)(a)–(b).
101 MLN 008, para 6.
102 2013 Regulations, reg 14(4)(a)–(b)(i)–(ii).
103 MLN 008, para 6.
104 2013 Regulations, reg 2, as inserted by 2018 Amendment Regulations, reg 3.
105 MLN 008, para 3(b)(i).
106 MLN 008, para 3(b)(ii).
107 MLN 008, para 3(b)(iii).
108 MLN 008, para 3(c)(i)–(ii).
109 MLN 008, para 3(d).

all overtime worked and all other pay-related benefits, or it may include only certain benefits in a partial consolidation'.[110]

Deductions from wages

25.26 The following deductions may be made: those permitted by applicable national laws; those agreed in a collective agreement; those in respect of on-board purchases, phone calls and internet use, cash advances, allotments, contributions to a pension fund, charity, membership body, trade union or friendly society.[111]

No deduction may be made in respect of obtaining or retaining employment.[112] Monetary fines, other than those authorised in a collective agreement, are prohibited.[113]

Future amendments to the MLC

25.27 See paragraph 25.22 above regarding the 2018 amendments to the MLC, which are likely to come into force on 26 December 2020.

Compliance

25.28 DMLC: implement Gibraltar requirements as set out in Pt I, point 14, and record details of compliance measures in DMLC, Pt II, point 14.

REGULATION 2.3: HOURS OF WORK AND HOURS OF REST

Gibraltar ships

25.29 The shipowner, master and employer must ensure that:

(a) the normal working hours' standard for the seafarer is, in principle, based on an eight-hour day, with one day of rest each week and rest on public holidays, and the seafarer's hours of rest are not less than 10 hours in any 24-hour period and 77 hours in any seven-day period.[114] For these purposes, 'hours of rest' means time outside of hours of work and does not include short breaks.[115]

The GMA has power to grant an exemption from those standards, in respect of seafarers on board a ship to which a collective agreement or workforce

110 MLN 008, para 2.
111 MLN 008, para 7(a)–(g).
112 MLN 008, para 8.
113 MLN 008, para 11.
114 2013 Regulations, reg 15(1)(a)–(b).
115 MLN 009: MLC Title 2.3 Hours of work and hours of rest, para 1.2.

agreement applies to those seafarers, which: (a) as far as possible follows those standards; and (b) takes account of more frequent or longer leave periods or the granting of compensatory leave for watchkeeping seafarers or seafarers working on board a ship on short voyages.[116]

The 10-hour minimum rest period may be divided into no more than two periods, one of which must be at least six hours in length, and the interval between those periods must not exceed 14 hours.[117]

(b) musters, fire-fighting and lifeboat drills are conducted in a manner that minimises the disturbances of rest periods and does not induce fatigue; and, if the seafarer's normal period of rest is disturbed by call-outs to work, the seafarer has an adequate compensatory rest period.[118] If there is no collective agreement, workforce agreement or arbitration award regulating these issues, or the GMA considers that the provisions of any such agreement or award are inadequate to ensure that the seafarer has sufficient rest, the GMA may determine the requirements with which the shipowner, master and employer must comply to ensure that the seafarer has sufficient rest.[119]

The master may require seafarers to work any hours necessary for the immediate safety of the ship, persons and cargo on board, or for assisting other ships or persons in distress at sea; any seafarer who has performed work during a scheduled rest period must be given an adequate period of rest as soon as normality is restored.[120]

MLC and other ships

25.30 The provisions in this section apply to MLC ships (other than Gibraltar ships) and 'other ships' (being those which do not fall within the definition of 'MLC ship'),[121] when they are in Gibraltar waters.[122]

The shipowner, master and employer of a seafarer on a ship other than a Gibraltar ship must ensure, in respect of a seafarer's hours of work and hours of rest, that:

(a) if the ship is registered in the EEA, they comply with the requirements of Directive 1999/63/EC,[123] as applied by the Member State in which the ship is registered;

116 2013 Regulations, reg 15(3)(a)–(b).
117 2013 Regulations, reg 15(2).
118 2013 Regulations, reg 15(4)(a)–(b).
119 2013 Regulations, reg 15(5)(a)–(b).
120 2013 Regulations, reg 5 15(6)(a)–(c).
121 2013 Regulations, reg 2(1).
122 2013 Regulations, reg 3(1)(b)(i)–(iii), (c).
123 Council Directive 1999/63/EC of 21 June 1999 concerning the Agreement on the organisation of working time of seafarers concluded by the European Community Shipowners' Association (ECSA) and the Federation of Transport Workers' Unions in the European Union (FST). The latter organisation is now known as the European Transport Workers' Federation (ETF).

(b) if the ship is an MLC ship which is not registered in the EEA, they comply with the requirements of Regulation 2.3 and Standard A2.3 of the MLC, as applied by the ship's flag state;

(c) if the ship is not an MLC ship, they comply with the requirements of Regulation 2.3 and Standard A2.3 of the MLC.[124]

In regard to paragraph (a) above, Directive 1999/63/EC was amended by Annex A to Directive 2009/13/EC[125] to make it consistent with the MLC provisions on hours of work and hours of rest. As regards the application of Directive 1999/63/EC by the relevant Member State, it should be noted that, like the MLC, the Directive obliges the state to choose between a regime of minimum hours of rest or maximum hours of work (the same limits apply for the Directive and the MLC).[126] The minimum hours of rest regime is set out above; the maximum hours of work regime (if adopted) provides that hours of work must not exceed: (a) 14 hours in any 24-hour period; and (b) 72 hours in any seven-day period.

In regard to paragraph (b) above, the relevant provisions are those of the flag state: these should be referenced in point 6 of the ship's Declaration of Maritime Labour Compliance ('DMLC') (Parts I and II).

In regard to paragraph (c) above, ratifying states are required to ensure that visiting ships (of the type to which the MLC applies)[127] which are registered with a non-party state '... do not receive more favourable treatment...' than MLC ships, and therefore Gibraltar will apply the relevant MLC standards to such ships in its waters.[128]

Documentation of seafarers' hours of work

25.31 The shipowner, master and employer must ensure that:

- on Gibraltar ships and other ships in Gibraltar waters:

    (a) a record of each seafarer's daily hours of work or daily hours of rest is maintained, in the working language(s) of the ship and in English, in accordance with the requirements of the flag state;

    Note: a standard model format record of hours of rest, based on ILO guidelines,[129] is published in Annex II to MLN 009, although shipowners

124 2013 Regulations, reg 16(a)–(c).

125 Council Directive 2009/13/EC of 16 February 2009 implementing the Agreement concluded by the European Community Shipowners' Association (ECSA) and the European Transport Workers' Federation (ETF) on the Maritime Labour Convention, 2006, and amending Directive 1999/63/EC.

126 MLC, Standard A2.3.5(a)–(b); Directive 1999/63/EC, Annex clause 5(a)–(b).

127 Fishing vessels, ships of traditional build such as dhows and junks, warships and naval auxiliaries are excluded: MLC Article II(i), para 4.

128 MLC, Article V, para 7; 2013 Regulations, reg 16(c).

129 IMO/ILO Guidelines for the Development of Tables of Seafarers' Shipboard Working Arrangements and Formats of Records of Seafarers' Hours of Work or Hours of Rest: www.imo.org/en/OurWork/HumanElement/VisionPrinciplesGoals/Documents/ILO-IMO-Hours%20of%20rest_1.pdf [Accessed 26 March 2018].

may develop their own format, so long as it shows the necessary information.[130] Shipowners may also use electronic means for facilitating seafarers to record their hours of rest, so long as: the format is based on ILO guidelines; the records are accessible to seafarers and are secure from unauthorised alterations; there is a means for the record to be endorsed by the seafarer and the master; there is a means for the seafarer to obtain a copy of their record; and the system is available for inspection by the GMA inspectors and port state control officers.[131]

(b) the seafarer receives a copy of their record, endorsed by the master (or authorised person) and the seafarer;

Note: each seafarer should receive a copy of their record of hours of rest each month.[132]

(c) a table is posted in an easily accessible place on board which contains, for every seafaring position: (i) the schedule of service at sea and service in port: and (ii) the maximum hours of work or the minimum hours of rest required by the laws, regulations, collective agreements or workforce agreements in force in relation to the ship and the seafarers on board;[133] the table must be in a standardised format and be in the working language(s) of the ship and in English;[134]

Note: a standard model format table of shipboard working arrangements, based on ILO guidelines,[135] is published in Annex I to MLN 009.[136] Shipowners may develop their own, so long as they show the following information: (1) entries for each position/rank of seafarer; (2) schedules of service at sea and in port; and (3) a statement of the minimum hours of rest required.[137] The table may be posted on a computer network if it can be demonstrated that it is available to all seafarers, and it must be available for inspection by the GMA and port state control officers.[138]

- on Gibraltar ships and EEA ships in Gibraltar waters:

(d) a copy of the relevant provisions of the national legislation pertaining to the Annex to Directive 1999/63/EC and any relevant collective agreements or workforce agreements are kept on board and are easily accessible to the seafarers;[139] the competent authority of the flag state is to be provided, on request, with information on the watchkeepers and other night workers on the ship.[140]

On Gibraltar ships, the GMA is required to determine: (a) the procedures for keeping records of seafarers' hours of work or rest, including the intervals at

130 MLN 009, para 10.
131 MLN 009, paras 12.1–12.5.
132 MLN 009, para 11.
133 2013 Regulations, reg 17(1)(a)–(c)(i)–(ii).
134 2013 Regulations, reg 17(2).
135 See footnote 129 above.
136 MLN 009, para 6, Sch I.
137 MLN 009, paras 7.1–7.3.
138 MLN 009, para 8.
139 2013 Regulations, reg 17(1)(d).
140 2013 Regulations, reg 17(1)(e)–(f).

which the information must be recorded; and (b) the format of those records, having taken into account any available international guidelines.[141] The master must examine and endorse the records at appropriate intervals.[142]

Compliance

25.32 DMLC: implement Gibraltar requirements as set out in Pt I, point 6, and record details of compliance measures in DMLC, Pt II, point 6.

REGULATION 2.4: ENTITLEMENT TO LEAVE

Leave accrual

25.33 The shipowner, master and employer of a seafarer on a Gibraltar ship must ensure that: (a) the seafarer takes paid annual leave at a minimum of 2.5 calendar days per month (taken to be 30 days)[143] of employment, and pro-rata for incomplete months; and (b) within the operational requirements of the seafarer's position, the seafarer is granted shore leave to benefit their health and well-being.[144] The GMA may approve alternative minimum standards for the calculation of annual leave set out in a collective agreement or a workforce agreement.[145]

MLC guidance recommends that the flag state's public and customary holidays should not be considered as part of the paid annual leave entitlement.[146] To reflect this, Gibraltar's guidance states that seafarers should be entitled to a further 10 days' paid leave pro-rata for each 12 months of employment.[147] However, this will not apply if an applicable collective agreement includes paid leave entitlement for public holidays.[148]

The service period over which the leave will accrue begins when the seafarer leaves home to join their ship, and continues all the way through to repatriation.[149] However, if the seafarer takes local leave before being repatriated, annual leave will not accrue during that period.[150]

When calculating any pro-rata leave entitlement over a period of less than 30 days, or less than 12 months (as the case may be), fractions of a day should be rounded up to the nearest half-day.[151]

141 2013 Regulations, reg 17(3)(a)–(b).
142 2013 Regulations, reg 17(4).
143 MLN 010: Entitlement to leave, para 2.1.
144 2013 Regulations, reg 18(1)(a)–(b).
145 2013 Regulations, reg 18(4)(a)–(b).
146 MLC, Guideline B2.4.1.4(a).
147 MLN 010, paras 2.1, 2.7.
148 MLN 010, para 2.6.
149 MLN 010, para 2.2.
150 MLN 010, para 2.2.
151 MLN 010, paras 2.3–2.4, 2.7–2.8.

On leaving employment, the shipowner or employer may make a payment to the seafarer, in lieu of any outstanding leave accrued.[152]

Taking of leave

25.34 Seafarers are entitled to take leave in a place where they have a substantial connection, which will normally be their chosen place of repatriation.[153] The time at which leave is to be taken should either be fixed in a collective agreement or agreed between the shipowner and seafarers.[154]

Justified absences from work must not be treated as annual leave.[155] The following are not to be counted as paid annual leave: periods of incapacity from work as a result of illness, injury or maternity; temporary shore leave in respect of seafarers employed under a SEA; compensatory leave of any kind; and time spent travelling to and from the ship.[156]

Leave is to be paid, as a minimum, at the level of basic pay or basic wage.[157] It is prohibited to enter into an agreement with a seafarer under which they forgo their monthly or public holiday leave for pay (except in respect of any outstanding balance on leaving employment).[158] Seafarers cannot be recalled from their monthly accrued leave, but they may be recalled during a public holiday or leave accrued in lieu of public holidays, but only in cases of extreme emergency and with their consent.[159]

Young seafarers

25.35 Seafarers under the age of 18 years must be repatriated at no cost to themselves in order to take leave when they have served for six months (or less, if specified in their SEA or collective agreement), and they have worked on a foreign-going ship which has not returned to their country of residence during that time.[160]

Compliance

25.36 The amount of annual leave entitlement (or the formula used for calculating it) must be entered in the SEA.[161]

152 2013 Regulations, reg 18(2).
153 MLN 010, para 7.1.
154 MLN 010, para 7.2.
155 2013 Regulations, reg 18(3).
156 MLN 010, paras 3.1–3.4.
157 MLN 010, para 4.
158 MLN 010, para 5; 2013 Regulations, reg 13(2).
159 MLN 010, para 6.
160 MLN 010, paras 8.1–8.2.
161 MLN 007, para 12(f).

REGULATION 2.5: REPATRIATION

Gibraltar ships

Entitlement to repatriation

25.37 The provisions on repatriation contained within the 2013 Regulations have been amended by the Gibraltar Merchant Shipping (Maritime Labour Convention) (Amendment) Regulations 2018 ('2018 Amendment Regulations'), as from 12 July 2018. These changes, amongst other things, implement the MLC 2014 amendments on the requirement for ships to carry financial security to cover the costs (and associated expenses) of repatriation of abandoned seafarers.

The shipowner and employer must ensure that a seafarer is repatriated, at no cost to themselves, if: (a) the SEA expires while the seafarer is abroad; (b) the SEA is terminated by the shipowner; (c) the SEA is terminated by the seafarer for justified reasons; (d) the seafarer is no longer able to carry out their duties specified in their SEA; or (e) the seafarer cannot be expected to carry out their duties in the specific circumstances.[162] The relevant circumstances will be those set out in a collective agreement[163] or, if those documents are silent on the issue, the following circumstances:

- illness or injury or other medical condition which requires their repatriation when found medically fit to travel;
- shipwreck;
- the shipowner not being able to continue to fulfil their legal or contractual obligations as an employer of the seafarer by reason of insolvency, sale of ship, change of ship's registration or any other similar reason;
- a ship being bound for a war zone as defined by the UK Warlike Operations Committee or the seafarer's SEA, to which the seafarer does not consent to go;
- termination or interruption of employment in accordance with an industrial award or collective agreement, or termination of employment for any other similar reason;
- compassionate or other urgent reasons (as set out in MLN 007 – see para 25.19 above).[164]

Furthermore, seafarers who have served on the ship for a very long time will be entitled to repatriation, without any other reason, before their length of service reaches 12 months' duration.[165]

The shipowner's duty to repatriate ends where:

(a) the seafarer is repatriated to the destination as provided for in regulation 19A;

162 2013 Regulations, reg 19(1)(a)–(e).
163 MLN 011, paras 6–7.
164 2013 Regulations, reg 19(4)(a); MLN 011, para 8(ii)–(vii).
165 2013 Regulations, reg 19(4)(b); MLN 011, para 9.

(b) the shipowner makes reasonable arrangements for repatriation which are unsuccessful because of the seafarer's unreasonable conduct;

(c) the shipowner has used reasonable endeavours to contact the seafarer for a period of three months or more, but has been unable to make such contact;

(d) the seafarer confirms in writing to the shipowner that repatriation is not required; or

(e) the seafarer is dead.[166]

Prohibition against taking advance payment for repatriation

25.38 The shipowner and employer are prohibited from taking an advance payment from the seafarer towards the cost of repatriation.[167] They are also prohibited from making a deduction from a seafarer's wages towards the costs of repatriation, unless, in the case of a Gibraltar ship, the GMA determines the seafarer to be in serious default of their employment agreement.[168]

Repatriation destination

25.39 A seafarer is entitled to be repatriated to the destination provided for in their SEA, or such other place as may subsequently be agreed with the shipowner if the SEA does not identify a destination.[169] Where there is no such place stated or agreed, the seafarer is entitled to be repatriated to their choice of the following destinations: the place at which they entered into their SEA; or their country of residence.[170]

Mode of transport and other entitlements

25.40 The normal mode of transport is by air, to one of the following destinations: (i) the place where the seafarer entered into the engagement; (ii) the place stipulated by an applicable collective agreement; (iii) the seafarer's country of residence; or (iv) such other place as mutually agreed at the time of engagement.[171]

The shipowner and employer are responsible for the following costs until the seafarer has reached their repatriation destination: (a) transport; (b) accommodation and food; (c) pay; (d) reasonable expenses incurred; (e) transport of 30kg of luggage; and (f) necessary medical treatment.[172] See paragraph 25.43 below on financial security for repatriation in cases of abandonment.

166 2013 Regulations, reg 19B(a)–(e), respectively, as inserted by 2018 Amendment Regulations, reg 5.
167 2013 Regulations, reg 19(2)(a).
168 2013 Regulations, reg 19(2)(b)(i).
169 2013 Regulations, reg 19A(1), as inserted by 2018 Amendment Regulations, reg 5.
170 2013 Regulations, reg 19A(2)(a)–(b), as inserted by 2018 Amendment Regulations, reg 5.
171 MLN 011, paras 10(a)–(b)(i)–(iv).
172 MLN 011, para 10(a)–(f).

Young seafarers

25.41 If it is apparent that a seafarer under the age of 18, on their first foreign-going voyage, is not suited to life at sea, they must be given the opportunity to be repatriated from the first suitable port of call; the body that authorised the seafarer to take up sea-going employment should be notified of the repatriation and the reasons.[173]

Copy of reg 19 to be carried on board

25.42 The shipowner, master and employer must ensure that a copy of reg 19 of the 2013 Regulations (on seafarers' right to repatriation) is carried on board in the working language(s) of the ship and in English, and is available to seafarers on board.[174]

Financial security

25.43 The MLC 2014 amendments on financial security for repatriation (together with those on shipowners' liability) were the first Parts of the MLC to be amended. Before those amendments came into force on 18 January 2017, the MLC already required ratifying states to ensure that their ships carried financial security for repatriation.[175] Consequently, Gibraltar required shipowners of a Gibraltar ship to ensure that there is in force a contract of insurance or other financial security in respect of the liabilities arising from the shipowner's duty to make provision for the repatriation of seafarers in accordance with the 2013 Regulations.[176]

The MLC amendments introduce much more detailed requirements for the financial security system, as well as further rights for seafarers and liabilities for shipowners, which is triggered when a seafarer becomes abandoned. The provisions are now set out in Part VB of the 2013 Regulations, which was inserted by the 2018 Amendment Regulations, which came into force on 12 July 2018.[177] Previously, from 18 January 2017 until 11 July 2018, implementation had been by way of instructions set out in MLN 030.

The full text of the MLC amendments on financial security is set out in Appendix 2, which defines what amounts to 'abandonment', and describes the extent of the liabilities which the financial security must meet, and how they can be accessed. There is also a detailed account of the UK provisions set out in Chapter 11 at paragraphs 11.9 to 11.11. Gibraltar's provisions closely follow those of the MLC

173 MLN 011, paras 12–13.
174 2013 Regulations, reg 19(9); MLN 011, para 16.
175 MLC, Regulation 2.5(2).
176 Repatriation Regulations, reg 19(3).
177 From 18 January 2017 until 12 July 2018, guidance on implementation was set out in MLN 030.

amendments and the UK, which can be used as a guide, so only some of the main compliance points are set out below.

A ship must not be operated unless there is force, in relation to the ship, an 'abandonment security' or 'financial security'.[178] Those concepts are defined as:

- 'abandonment security' means a contract of insurance or other form of security which provides for a seafarer to make an abandonment claim, receive financial assistance, and covers the expenses which the shipowner reasonably considers are adequate to cover the costs of repatriation, and other associated expenses and liabilities, including up to four months' wages;[179]
- 'financial security' must be in accordance with MLC, Standard 2.5.2.3 (which may be in the form of a social security scheme or insurance or a national fund or other similar arrangements).[180]

A failure to comply amounts to an offence by the shipowner, punishable on summary conviction by a fine not exceeding level 4 on the standard scale.[181]

The shipowner must ensure that the abandonment security document (which must be in English or accompanied by an English translation) is carried on board the ship and displayed in a conspicuous place.[182] A failure to carry an abandonment security document amounts to an offence by the shipowner and the master, punishable by a fine not exceeding level 4 on the standard scale.[183]

The requirement to carry financial security for repatriation and shipowners' liability are now entered as the 15th and 16th areas of inspection (respectively) on the Declaration of Maritime Labour Compliance (Pts I and II) ('DMLC').[184] Under the transitional provisions, existing MLC documentation (which does not include any reference to those areas of inspection) will remain valid; however, the revised DMLC Pts I and II must be issued to the ship following its first MLC renewal inspection after 18 January 2017.[185] Shipowners should therefore submit the revised DMLC Pt II to the GMA or delegated recognised organisation at least three months before that inspection.[186]

GMA responsibilities where shipowner fails to repatriate

25.44 If the shipowner and employer fail to repatriate a seafarer from a Gibraltar ship, or the shipowner, employer and flag state fail to repatriate a seafarer from

178 2013 Regulations, reg 32M(1)(a)–(b), as inserted by 2018 Amendment Regulations, reg 7.
179 2013 Regulations, reg 32N, as inserted by 2018 Amendment Regulations, reg 7.
180 2013 Regulations, reg 32N, as inserted by 2018 Amendment Regulations, reg 7.
181 2013 Regulations, reg 32M(2), as inserted by 2018 Amendment Regulations, reg 7.
182 2013 Regulations, reg 32Q(1)–(2), (4), as inserted by 2018 Amendment Regulations, reg 7.
183 2013 Regulations, reg 32Q(3), (5), as inserted by 2018 Amendment Regulations, reg 7.
184 MLC, Appendices A5-I, A5-II and A5-III (as amended).
185 MLN 030.
186 MLN 030.

any other ship in Gibraltar waters or, in the case of a Gibraltar national, from any ship wherever it may be, the GMA must repatriate the seafarer, and has powers to recover the costs from the defaulting parties or the flag state of the ship (which it may detain as security).[187] The GMA's obligation, in respect of a seafarer on board a Gibraltar ship, applies whether or not the seafarer is entitled to receive assistance under the abandonment financial security required under Part VB of the 2013 Regulations.[188]

MLC ships other than Gibraltar ships

25.45 The shipowner and employer are prohibited from taking an advance payment from the seafarer towards the cost of repatriation.[189] They are also prohibited from making a deduction from a seafarer's wages towards the costs of repatriation, unless the seafarer has been found, in accordance with the relevant national laws, regulations, other measures or applicable collective bargaining agreement, to be in serious default of their employment obligations.[190] The ship must also carry financial security provision (as described above) and display it in a conspicuous place on board the ship.[191]

Compliance

25.46 DMLC: implement Gibraltar requirements as set out in Pt I, point 15 (on financial security for repatriation), and record details of compliance measures in DMLC, Pt II, point 15. Details of seafarers' entitlement to repatriation must be entered in their SEA.[192]

REGULATION 2.6: SEAFARER COMPENSATION FOR THE SHIP'S LOSS OR FOUNDERING

25.47 If a ship is lost or founders, the shipowner must pay to the seafarer: (a) basic wages[193] (at the level set in the SEA) for each day the seafarer remains unemployed as a result; and (b) compensation in respect of any resulting personal injury or loss of personal effects.[194]

In respect of paragraph (a) above, the payment is an indemnity against loss during any resulting period of unemployment, and is limited to a maximum of

187 2013 Regulations, reg 19(5)–(8).
188 2013 Regulations, reg 19(5)(a),as amended by 2018 Amendment Regulations, reg 4.
189 2013 Regulations, reg 19(2)(a).
190 2013 Regulations, reg 19(2)(b)(ii).
191 2013 Regulations, regs 32M(1)(a)–(b), 32Q(1)–(2), (4), as amended by 2018 Amendment Regulations, reg 4.
192 MLN 030, para 12(i).
193 Gibraltar's definition of 'basic pay or wages' is set out in para 25.25 above.
194 2013 Regulations, reg 20(1)(a)–(b); MLN 012: Seafarer compensation for the ship's loss or foundering, paras 2(a)–(b), 5.

two months' wages (unless otherwise provided in a collective agreement) or, if shorter, until the date the seafarer would have been otherwise employed on the ship, or remained unemployed.[195]

In respect of paragraph (b) above, the amount payable in respect of loss (other than for personal injury or death) may be limited by a provision in the SEA.[196] Seafarers are to be entitled to adequate compensation for injury arising through the ship's loss or foundering (see MLN 016) and must have in place financial security to cover compensation to seafarers in the event of death or long-term disability due to an occupational injury, illness or hazard (see para 25.70 below).[197]

The above entitlements are without prejudice to any other rights the seafarer may have in respect of losses or injuries arising out of the ship's loss or foundering.[198] If the relevant payment is not made, it may be recovered as a civil debt.[199]

REGULATION 2.7: MANNING LEVELS

Gibraltar ships

25.48 The GMA must ensure that a safe manning document ('SMD') issued to a ship under the Gibraltar Merchant Shipping (Manning, Training and Certification of Seafarers) Regulations 2006[200] ('2006 Regulations') is in compliance with the requirements of MLC, Regulation 2.7 and clause 10 (avoidance or minimisation of excessive hours of work) and clause 12 (ship to be properly resourced and seafarers' hour of work and rest to be complied with) of the Annex to Council Directive 1999/63/EC.[201]

The 2006 Regulations give effect to the IMO's International Convention on Standards of Training, Certification and Watchkeeping for Seafarers, 1978 (as amended) ('STCW Convention'), the STCW Code and related EU Directives. The requirement to carry an SMD applies to Gibraltar ships engaged in international voyages and to other ships of 500 GT and over; it is to be issued by the GMA and must be in compliance with Chapter V of the IMO's International Convention for the Safety of Life at Sea ('SOLAS').[202] Such ships are prohibited

195 2013 Regulations, reg 20(2)(a)(i)–(ii); MLN 012, para 2.
196 2013 Regulations, reg 20(2)(b).
197 MLN 012, para 4; MLN 016: Ship-owners liability.
198 2013 Regulations, reg 20(2)(c).
199 2013 Regulations, reg 20(2)(d).
200 LN 2006/023.
201 2013 Regulations, reg 21(1). Council Directive 1999/63/EC of 21 June 1999 concerning the Agreement on the organisation of working time of seafarers concluded by the European Community Shipowners' Association (ECSA) and the Federation of Transport Workers' Unions in the European Union (FST), OJ L 167/33, 2.7.1999. The FST is now known as the European Transport Workers' Federation (ETF).
202 Administrative Instruction No STCW 1, para 1, under Merchant Shipping (Safety etc) Act 1993 (LN 2004/068); 2006 Regulations, reg 4(1).

from proceeding to sea unless they carry a valid SMD and the ship is manned accordingly, to at least the minimum acceptable standard.[203]

The application to the GMA for an SMD must include detailed particulars of the ship, nature of trade, area of operation and the proposed minimum scale of manning, and will be considered in the light of IMO Assembly Resolution A.1047(27) (which revokes Assembly Resolution A-890).[204] If the GMA is satisfied that the proposed manning meets the requirements for the safe operation of the ship and protection of the marine environment, an SMD will be issued.[205]

Guidance or manning levels for deck and engineer officers, based on ship size, propulsion power and trading areas, are set out in tables 1 and 2 (respectively) in Administrative Instruction No. STCW-1.

Guidance on safe manning is also provided in the LY3 Code for large commercial yachts.[206] It should be noted that the LY3 Code and the Passenger Yacht Code (PYC) are being merged into the 'Red Ensign Group Yacht Code' (REG YC), which comes into force on 1 January 2019.

Other ships in Gibraltar waters

25.49 When they are in Gibraltar waters: (a) EEA registered ships must comply with Directive 1999/63/EC, as applied by flag state; and (b) the 2013 Regulations state that non-EEA ships must comply with MLC, Regulation 2.7 and Standard A2.7, as applied by the flag state.[207] It is submitted that there may be a drafting error here, in that paragraph (b) should be limited to non-EEA 'MLC ships' (rather than non-EEA 'ships') because there will be no flag state implementation of those MLC provisions in non-ratifying states. In any case, ships registered with non-MLC states are subject to inspections on MLC standards, when visiting MLC states.[208]

Compliance

25.50 DMLC: implement Gibraltar requirements as set out in Pt I, point 7, and record details of compliance measures in DMLC, Pt II, point 7.

203 2006 Regulations, reg 4(2)–(3).

204 2006 Regulations, reg 5(1)–(3); IMO Assembly Resolution A.1047(27), adopted on 30 November 2011, Principles on Safe Manning: www.mardep.gov.hk/en/msnote/pdf/msin1332anx1.pdf [Accessed 31 March 2018].

205 2016 Regulations, reg 5(4).

206 LY3 – Large Commercial Yacht Code, pp 134–140.

207 2013 Regulations, reg 21(2)(a)–(b).

208 MLC, Article V, para 7.

REGULATION 2.8: CAREER AND SKILL DEVELOPMENT AND OPPORTUNITIES FOR SEAFARERS' EMPLOYMENT

25.51 Gibraltar's provisions in this area are very basic no doubt due to the fact that few, if any, seafarers reside there. Gibraltar relies on its provisions to recognise and endorse the Certificates of Competency issued to seafarers by maritime administrations in seafarer-supplying countries (see para 25.10 above).

The GMA may: promote employment in the maritime sector; encourage career and skill development and greater employment opportunities for seafarers; and help seafarers strengthen their competencies, qualifications and employment opportunities.[209]

The GMA must, having consulted with shipowners' and seafarers' organisations, establish clear objectives for the vocational guidance, education and training of seafarers whose duties on board ship primarily relate to the safe operation and navigation of the ship, including ongoing training.[210]

A limited number of cadets have been supported in the past by funding provided by the government and local bunkering companies. The GMA and the Port of Gibraltar also take part in the annual careers fairs, which are organised by the Department of Education.[211] The GMA has a careers section on its website, which advertises jobs, although there is currently no information promoting career and skill development.[212]

REGULATION 3.1: ACCOMMODATION AND RECREATIONAL FACILITIES

Gibraltar ships

25.52 The shipowner must ensure that crew accommodation: (a) is decent accommodation, consistent with promoting the seafarers' safety, health and well-being; and (b) if the ship was constructed on or after 20 August 2013,[213] is constructed, equipped, provided and maintained to the minimum standards for on-board accommodation and recreational facilities, amenities and services set out in Regulation 3.1.1 and Standard A3.1 of the MLC, which is implemented through the regulations set out in MLN 013.[214] For these purposes, a ship is constructed on the date when its keel is laid or when it is at a similar stage of construction.[215]

209 2013 Regulations, reg 22(1)(a)–(c).
210 2013 Regulations, reg 22(2).
211 Careers Fair 2017: www.gibraltar.gov.gi/new/sites/default/files/press/2016/Press%20 Releases/541-2016.pdf [Accessed 1 April 2018].
212 GMA careers: www.gibraltarship.com/careers [Accessed 1 April 2018].
213 This is the date that both the MLC and the 2013 Regulations entered into force.
214 2013 Regulations, reg 23(1)(a)–(b); MLN 013: Accommodation and recreational facilities.
215 MLN 013, reg 2.3.

In setting out the applicable standards for crew accommodation and recreational facilities, MLN 013 closely follows Standard A3.1 of the MLC, as do the UK provisions set out in MSN 1844[216] and MGN 481,[217] which may be used as a guide (see Chapter 15). MLN 013 sets out the regulations in its left-hand column and (where applicable) implementation measures which will amount to 'evidence of compliance'.[218]

As regards a ship that was constructed before 20 August 2013, the shipowner must ensure that: (i) it is constructed and equipped[219] with the applicable requirements set out in the ILO Accommodation of Crew Convention (Revised), 1949 (No 92) and the ILO Accommodation of Crews (Supplementary Provisions) Convention, 1970 (No 133) which applied to that ship immediately before that date; and (ii) it is provided and maintained to the minimum standards for on-board accommodation and recreational facilities, amenities and services set out in Regulation 3.1.1 and Standard A3.1 of the MLC.[220]

Inspections and records

25.53 The master (or authorised person) must: (a) ensure that the crew accommodation is cleaned and maintained to conform with the applicable requirements (as set out above); (b) carry out frequent inspections to ensure that the crew accommodation is clean, decently habitable and maintained in a good state of repair; and (c) record the findings of those inspections (with date, time and name and rank of inspecting person) in the official log book and keep them available for review.[221]

Exemptions

25.54 The GMA may exempt a Gibraltar ship of less than 200 GT from some or all of the requirements of reg 23 if the exemption: (a) is reasonable, taking account of the size of the ship and the number of persons on board; (b) does not result in overall facilities less favourable than those which would result if no exemption had been given and relates to Standard A3.1.7(b), 11(d) and 13 of the MLC or, regarding floor area only, Standard A3.1.9(f)

216 MSN 1844(M): MLC, 2006 – Crew Accommodation.

217 MGN 481(M): Amendment 1: MLC, 2006: Crew Accommodation, Supplementary Guidance.

218 MLN 013, Key points, paras 1–4.

219 MLC, Regulation 3.1.2 provides that Standard A3.1 and its associated Code, as far as it relates to ship construction and equipment, only applies to ships constructed on or after the date the MLC came into force for the flag state.

220 2013 Regulations, reg 23(1)(c)(i)–(ii).

221 2013 Regulations, reg 23(2)(a)–(c). MLN 013, reg 19(3)(a)–(c).

and (h)–(l) of the MLC; or (c) is otherwise expressly permitted in Standard A3.1 of the MLC.[222]

MLN 013 indicates the requirements from which an exemption may be sought from the GMA, which will only be permitted in circumstances where an exemption can be justified on clear grounds, and subject to protecting the seafarer's health and safety.[223] A written application must be made by the shipowner, with evidence of having carried out consultation with concerned seafarers' organisations and any response received.[224] There is a standard form on the GMA website for submitting a request for an exemption or an application of a substantial equivalence.[225]

MLC ships other than Gibraltar ships

25.55 When in Gibraltar waters, the shipowner of an MLC ship must ensure that the crew accommodation is constructed, equipped, provided and maintained to the standards for on-board accommodation and recreational facilities set out in Regulation 3.1.1 and Standard A3.1 of the MLC, as implemented by the ship's flag state.[226] The master or authorised person must ensure that the crew accommodation is inspected in accordance with Standard A3.1 of the MLC.[227]

Compliance

25.56 DMLC: implement Gibraltar requirements as set out in Pt I, points 8–9, and record details of compliance measures in DMLC, Pt II, points 8–9.

REGULATION 3.2: FOOD AND CATERING

Gibraltar ships

Provision of food and water

25.57 The shipowner and master must ensure that food and drinking water are provided, free of charge to seafarers, which:

222 2013 Regulations, reg 24(a)–(c). For paragraphs (a) and (b), the scope for flag state exemptions derives from MLC, Standard A3.1(2); for paragraph (c), there are various provisions within Standard A3.1 which provide scope for flag state exemptions; for example, Standard A3.1(9)(a) permits the flag state to grant an exemption from providing individual sleeping room on ships of less than 3000 GT or on special purpose ships. Before granting an exemption, the competent authority must consult with shipowners' and seafarers' organisations.

223 MLN 013, reg 5(2).

224 MLN 013, reg 5(3).

225 Form RA-09-F038 – Request for exemption/substantial equivalence: www.gibraltarship.com/maritime-labour-convention [Accessed 16 October 2018].

226 2013 Regulations, reg 25(1).

227 2013 Regulations, reg 25(2).

(a) are suitable in respect of quantity, nutritional value, quality and variety, taking account of: (i) the number of seafarers on board; (ii) the character, nature and duration of the voyage; and (iii) the different religious requirements and cultural practices in relation to food of the seafarers on board;

(b) do not contain anything which is likely to cause sickness or injury to health or which renders any food or drinking water unpalatable;

(c) are otherwise fit for consumption.[228]

Catering department

25.58 The shipowner and the master must ensure that: the catering department is organised and equipped for the provision of adequate, varied and nutritious meals prepared and served in hygienic conditions; seafarers whose normal duties include work such as the preparation, storage of food and the service of meals, or work in the galley, are properly trained or instructed for their positions; and any person processing food in the galley has been trained or instructed in areas including food and personal hygiene and the handling and storage of food on board ship.[229]

Requirement to carry a ship's cook

25.59 The shipowner and the master must ensure that, in respect of a ship which ordinarily operates with 10 or more seafarers on board, it does not proceed to sea unless a qualified ship's cook is on board.[230] The GMA may grant an exemption from this requirement until the ship's next port of call, or for a period not exceeding one month, but only if there is a person on board who is trained or instructed in areas including food and personal hygiene and the handling and storage of food on board ship.[231]

A ship's cook must: be over the age of 18; have completed a minimum amount of sea service as determined by the GMA (the period is not currently specified in the relevant guidance – MLN 014A);[232] hold a valid certificate of medical fitness; have completed a GMA or MLC State approved or recognised training course, covering practical cookery, food and personal hygiene, food storage, stock control and environmental protection and catering health and safety, or other training as determined by the GMA; and have been issued by the GMA with a 'Certificate of Qualification as a Ships' Cook'.[233] The GMA will accept: a national vocational qualification (NVQ) level II in catering and hospitality; or confirmation of having served as a chef in a professional kitchen, commercial yacht or passenger ship, together with evidence of having completed training

228 2013 Regulations, reg 26(1)(a)–(c), (2)(a).
229 2013 Regulations, reg 26(2)(b)–(d).
230 2013 Regulations, reg 26(4).
231 2013 Regulations, reg 26(5)(a)–(b).
232 MLN 014A: Food and catering.
233 2013 Regulations, reg 26(6)(a)(i)–(v).

in food and personal hygiene, food storage, stock control, and environmental protection and catering health and safety.[234]

Alternatively, it can be a person who: (i) meets the minimum requirements for a ship's cook as set out in Standard A3.2 of the MLC; and (ii) holds a valid certificate issued by an MLC state or a state which has ratified the ILO Certificate of Ships' Cook Convention, 1946 (No 69).[235]

Inspections

25.60 The master (or authorised person) must carry out frequent inspections of: (a) supplies of food and drinking water; (b) all spaces and equipment used for the storage and handling of food and drinking water; and (c) the galley and other equipment for the preparation and service of meals; the findings of the inspections must be recorded and kept available for review.[236] The inspections should be carried out at intervals not exceeding seven days, and the following details should be recorded in the official log book: time and date of inspection; name and rank of the person carrying out the inspection; and any findings.[237]

MLC ships other than Gibraltar ships

25.61 When in Gibraltar waters, the shipowner and master of an MLC ship must ensure that: (a) food and catering on the ship is provided and maintained to the standards for food and catering set out in Regulation 3.2 and Standard A3.2 of the MLC; and (b) that a seafarer is engaged as a ship's cook as required by Regulation 3.2 and Standard A3.2, in both (a) and (b) as implemented by the ship's flag state.[238] The master (or authorised person) must also ensure that frequent documented inspections are carried out in accordance with the requirements of Standard A3.2 of the MLC, as implemented by the ship's flag state.[239]

Further information

25.62 Guidance is set out in MLN 014(A) on: cook and catering staff qualifications; food safety and hygiene, including guidance on diet and nutrition; and water, including its supply, storage and distribution and directions on maintenance of water systems.

234 MLN 014A, paras 3.1, 3.4.
235 2013 Regulations, reg 26(6)(b)(i)–(ii).
236 2013 Regulations, reg 26(3)(a)–(c).
237 MLN 014(A), paras 18.1–18.2.
238 2013 Regulations, reg 27(1)(a)–(b).
239 2013 Regulations, reg 27(2).

Compliance

25.63 DMLC: implement Gibraltar requirements as set out in Pt I, point 10, and record details of compliance measures in DMLC, Pt II, point 10.

REGULATION 4.1: MEDICAL CARE ON BOARD SHIP AND ASHORE

Gibraltar ships

Provision of medical care

25.64 The shipowner, master and employer must ensure that:

(a) seafarers are given health protection and medical care, including essential dental care, which is as comparable as possible to that generally available to workers in Gibraltar, including prompt access to the necessary medicines, medical equipment and facilities for diagnosis and treatment and to medical information and expertise;

(b) seafarers are given the right to visit a qualified medical doctor or dentist without delay in ports of call where applicable;

(c) seafarers are provided with measures of a preventative character such as health promotion and health and education programmes;

(d) seafarers' medical information is kept confidential and only used to facilitate the treatment of seafarers;

(e) a medicine chest, medical equipment and a medical guide are carried on board in accordance with requirements determined by the GMA;

(f) if the ship carries 100 or more persons and is ordinarily engaged on international voyages of more than three days' duration, or the GMA determines so, a qualified medical doctor must be carried on board;

(g) if the ship is not required to carry a qualified medical doctor, at least one seafarer on board has satisfactorily completed training in (i) medical care or (ii) medical first aid, that meets the requirements of the STCW Convention to the level determined by the GMA.[240]

Further to sub-paragraph (g) above, ships that are capable of reaching medical facilities within eight hours should have at least one designated seafarer trained to STCW Section A-VI/4.1 standards; all other ships should have at least one designated seafarer trained to STCW Section A-VI/4.2 standards.[241]

The shipowner and employer must ensure that the medical and dental care described above are provided free of charge to all seafarers, while they are on board ship or landed in a foreign port.[242]

240 2013 Regulations, reg 28(1)(a)–(g), respectively.

241 2013 Regulations, reg 28(3)(d); MLN 015: Medical care on board ship and ashore, para 2.

242 2013 Regulations, reg 28(2).

Vessels must carry appropriate radio equipment to receive medical advice from coast radio stations and shore services. Such advice is available to all ships at sea by contacting HM Coastguard; however, the master should contact the nearest station which can give the best advice.[243]

Shipowners should provide information on preventative measures such as health promotion and health education programmes, such as that provided by the International Seafarers' Welfare and Assistance Network ('ISWAN') and the UK's MCA.[244]

The Gibraltar Merchant Shipping (Medical Stores) Regulations 2000,[245] which implement Council Directive 92/29/EEC,[246] set out the requirements in relation to the carriage of medicines, medical equipment and antidotes. The 2000 Regulations adopt the UK requirements, the latest edition of which is set out in MSN 1768,[247] which are detailed in Chapter 17.

There are also provisions on: the carriage of medical guides (as specified in MSN 1768); inspections of medicines and medical stores at least annually; and offences and powers of detention for non-compliance.[248]

The shipowner should provide guidance for providing assistance to other vessels in distress. Guidance can be found in the International Convention on Maritime Search and Rescue, 1979, and the International Aeronautical and Maritime Search and Rescue ('IAMSAR') Manual; these publications should be carried on board.[249]

The confidential ship master's medical report form should be used to facilitate treatment of sick or injured seafarers, after which it should be filed on the ship's medical log.[250] It may also be helpful to refer to MLN 021: Reporting of Occupational Accidents, Incidents and Diseases.

MLC ships other than Gibraltar ships

25.65 When such ships are in Gibraltar waters, the shipowner, master and employer must ensure that the requirements of Regulation 4.1 and Standard A4.1 of the MLC, as implemented by ship's flag state, are complied with.[251]

243 2013 Regulations, reg 28(3)(e); MLN 015, para 3.
244 MLN 015, para 5: ISWAN's Seafarers' Health Information Programme Shop: https://seafarerswelfare.org/ship-shop; UK MCA: www.gov.uk/government/organisations/maritime-and-coastguard-agency [Accessed 3 April 2018].
245 LN 2000/004.
246 Council Directive 92/29/EEC of 31 March 1992 on the minimum safety and health requirements for improved medical treatment on board vessels, OJ L 113/19, 30.4.92.
247 MSN 1768: Application of the Merchant Shipping and Fishing Vessels (Medical Stores) Regulations 1995 (SI 1995/1802) and the Merchant Shipping and Fishing Vessels (Medical Stores) (Amendment) Regulations 1996 (SI 1996/2821).
248 2000 Regulations, regs 10–11, 13–15.
249 MLN 015, para 14.
250 MLN 015, para 6; Ship Master's Medical Report Form: www.gibraltarship.com/maritime-labour-convention [Accessed 3 April 2018].
251 2013 Regulations, reg 28(4)(a)–(b).

Compliance

25.66 DMLC: implement Gibraltar requirements as set out in Pt I, point 12, and record details of compliance measures in DMLC, Pt II, point 12.

REGULATION 4.2: SHIPOWNERS' LIABILITY

25.67 In this area, the 2013 Regulations have recently been amended by the 2018 Amendment Regulations, which insert reg 29A (on further provisions on a shipowner's liability to meet the wages of a sick or injured seafarer) and Part VA (requirement to carry financial security for shipowner's liability to pay compensation for death or long-term disability of seafarers), the latter of which implements the MLC 2016 amendments (in this area) on financial security.

The shipowner of a Gibraltar ship must:

(a) provide medical care for a seafarer on the ship, including medical treatment and the supply of necessary medicines and therapeutic appliances, in respect of sickness or injury occurring during the commencement of duty until repatriation, or arising from employment during that period;

(b) provide board and lodging away from home until the sick or injured seafarer has recovered, or until the sickness or incapacity has been declared of a permanent character;

(c) where the sickness or injury results in the seafarer's incapacity for work: (i) pay full wages (defined in para 25.24 above) while the seafarer is on board and (if the seafarer is entitled to be repatriated) until repatriation; and (ii) pay wages in full or in part until the seafarer has recovered or is entitled to cash payments from the Government of Gibraltar [see para 25.69 below on reg 29A (introduced by the 2018 Amendment Regulations) which expands on the provisions imposed by reg 29(1)(c)];

(d) in accordance with the laws of Gibraltar, the SEA or a collective agreement, pay compensation in the event of death or long-term disability of a seafarer due to an occupational injury, illness or hazard while the seafarer is employed or engaged in work on the ship, or arising from the same;

(e) meet the costs of burial expenses in the case of the death of a seafarer occurring on board or ashore during their period of engagement;

(f) safeguard any property left on board by a sick, injured or deceased seafarer, and return it to the seafarer or their next of kin.[252]

Limitations and exceptions

25.68 The liabilities of the shipowner in respect of the obligations set out under paragraphs (a)–(c) above is limited to a period of 16 weeks from the date

252 2013 Regulations, reg 29(1)(a)–(f).

of the injury or the commencement of the illness or, in regard to paragraph (c)(i)–(ii), as provided for in a collective agreement.[253] The shipowner should not have to meet the liabilities arising under paragraphs (a)–(b) from any point that the same is assumed by a public authority.[254] Furthermore the shipowner is not liable in respect of the liabilities under paragraphs (a)–(f) if: (i) the injury occurred otherwise than in the service of the ship; (ii) the injury or sickness was due to the wilful misconduct or the sick, injured or deceased seafarer; or (iii) the sickness or infirmity was intentionally concealed when the employment or engagement was entered into.[255]

Regulation 29A

25.69 The new reg 29A is subject to reg 29(1)(c) (set out above) and applies in relation to a seafarer who first suffers sickness or injury during their period of employment (up until repatriation), or that is caused during circumstances or events arising during that period, and results in their incapacity to work; it does not apply if sickness or injury first occurs during a period of leave (other than shore leave).[256] Furthermore, it does not apply in the circumstances set out in paras (i)–(iii) in paragraph 25.68 above.[257]

The shipowner must, during the period of a seafarer's incapacity, pay the difference between any amount of wages received by the seafarer under their SEA during the period of incapacity and the amount they would otherwise have received if they had remained fit for work throughout that period (even if their SEA terminates during that period).[258] This applies whether or not the shipowner is the employer of the seafarer. The obligation is to make good full 'wages' (defined in para 25.24 above) until the seafarer has been repatriated;[259] after repatriation, the obligation is to make good 'basic wages' (defined in para 25.25 above); however, this is limited to a period of 16 weeks commencing on the day following the date of the injury or the first day of the sickness.[260] The obligation of the shipowner to make good the basic wages after repatriation is subject to the seafarer applying for all relevant social security benefits, and the seafarer must (on request) declare any such amounts received to the shipowner, who may reduce any payments otherwise due by that amount.[261]

253 2013 Regulations, reg 29(2)(a)–(b); MLN 016: MLC Title 4.2 Shipowners' Liability, para 7.
254 MLN 016, para 5.
255 2013 Regulations, reg 29(2)(c)(i)–(iii).
256 2013 Regulations, reg 29A(1)(a)–(c), as inserted by 2018 Amendment Regulations, reg 6.
257 2013 Regulations, reg 29A(11)(a)–(c), as inserted by 2018 Amendment Regulations, reg 6.
258 2013 Regulations, reg 29A(1)–(4), as inserted by 2018 Amendment Regulations, reg 6.
259 2013 Regulations, reg 29A(2)(b), (3)(a)–(b), as inserted by 2018 Amendment Regulations, reg 6.
260 2013 Regulations, reg 29A(4)(a)–(b), (5), respectively, as inserted by 2018 Amendment Regulations, reg 6.
261 2013 Regulations, reg 29A(6)–(8), as inserted by 2018 Amendment Regulations, reg 6

The shipowner may recover any amounts overpaid to the seafarer, and the seafarer may recover any amounts outstanding from the shipowner, in both cases as a civil debt.[262]

Financial security

25.70 The MLC 2014 amendments on shipowners' liability (together with those on repatriation) were the first Parts of the MLC to be amended. Before those amendments came into force on 18 January 2017, the MLC already required ratifying states to ensure that their ships carried financial security to assure compensation in the event of the death or long-term disability of seafarers due to an occupational injury, illness or hazard.[263] Consequently, Gibraltar already required shipowners of a Gibraltar ship to ensure that there is in force a contract of insurance or other security to cover such liabilities, including the other liabilities arising under reg 29 (which remains in force).[264]

The MLC amendments introduce much more detailed requirements for the financial security system, as well as further rights for seafarers and obligations for shipowners, in connection with seafarers' 'contractual claims' for compensation for death or long-term disability due to an occupational injury, illness or hazard. Those provisions are now set out in Part VA of the 2013 Regulations, which was inserted by the Gibraltar Merchant Shipping (Maritime Labour Convention) (Amendment) Regulations 2018, which came into force on 12 July 2018. Previously, from 18 January 2017 until 11 July 2018, implementation had been by way of instructions set out in MLN 030.

The full text of the MLC amendments on financial security is set out in Appendix 2, which defines what amounts to 'abandonment', and describes the extent of the liabilities which the financial security must meet, and how they can be accessed. There is also a detailed account of the UK provisions set out in Chapter 11 at paragraphs 11.3 to 11.6. Gibraltar's provisions closely follow those of the MLC amendments and the UK, which can be used as a guide, so only some of the main compliance points are set out below.

A Gibraltar ship (or an MLC ship in Gibraltar waters) must not be operated unless:

(a) a shipowner's security is in force in relation to the ship; or

(b) financial security to assure compensation in the event of death or long-term disability of seafarers due to occupational illness, injury or hazard is provided in relation to the ship in accordance with paragraph 1 of Standard A4.2.1 of

262 2013 Regulations, reg 29A(7)(b), (10), respectively, as inserted by 2018 Amendment Regulations, reg 6.

263 MLC, Standard A4.2.1(1)(b).

264 2013 Regulations, reg 29(3).

the MLC[265] [which relates to compensation as set out in the 'national law, seafarers' employment agreement [(SEA)] or collective agreement'].

A failure to comply amounts to an offence by the shipowner, punishable on summary conviction by a fine not exceeding level 4 on the standard scale.[266]

The shipowner's security provider must pay the claim for contractual compensation within seven days of liability being established, either by agreement, or by order of a court or tribunal (which is not subject to appeal); late payments are subject to 20% interest.[267] A 'claim for contractual compensation' means 'a claim for compensation in the event of death or long-term disability of a seafarer arising from occupational injury, illness or hazard where the compensation payable in respect of the claim is set out in the seafarer's seafarer employment agreement …'.[268] This will include a collective agreement or workforce which is incorporated into the SEA.[269] However, here it makes no reference to compensation payable under 'national law', as required by the MLC.[270]

The shipowner must ensure that, for each shipowner's security that is in force, there is carried on board the ship (in English or accompanied by an English translation) a shipowner's security document.[271] A failure to comply amounts to an offence by the shipowner, punishable on summary conviction by a fine not exceeding level 4 on the standard scale.[272]

The shipowner and the master must ensure that each shipowner's security document that relates to the ship, together with any English translation, is displayed in a conspicuous place on board ship – a failure to comply amounts to an offence by both[273] (the degree of any sanction on conviction is not stated).

The requirement to carry financial security for repatriation and shipowners' liability are now entered as the 15th and 16th areas of inspection (respectively) on the Declaration of Maritime Labour Compliance (Pts I and II) ('DMLC').[274] Under the transitional provisions, existing MLC documentation (which does not include any reference to those areas of inspection) will remain valid; however, the revised DMLC Pts I and II must be issued to the ship following its first MLC renewal inspection after 18 January 2017.[275] Shipowners should therefore submit

265 2013 Regulations, reg 32B(1)(a)–(b), respectively, as inserted by 2018 Amendment Regulations, reg 7. A 'shipowner's security' is defined in reg 32C.
266 2013 Regulations, reg 32B(2), as inserted by 2018 Amendment Regulations, reg 7.
267 2013 Regulations, reg 32D(1)–(3), as inserted by 2018 Amendment Regulations, reg 7.
268 2013 Regulations, reg 32D(4), as inserted by 2018 Amendment Regulations, reg 7.
269 2013 Regulations, reg 2(1)(d).
270 MLC, Standard A4.2.2(1).
271 2013 Regulations, reg 32G(1)–(2), as inserted by 2018 Amendment Regulations, reg 7.
272 2013 Regulations, reg 32G(3), as inserted by 2018 Amendment Regulations, reg 7.
273 2013 Regulations, reg 32G(4), as inserted by 2018 Amendment Regulations, reg 7.
274 MLC, Appendices A5-I, A5-II and A5-III (as amended).
275 MLN 030: Amendments to MLC entering into force on 18 January 2017.

the revised DMLC Pt II to the GMA or delegated recognised organisation at least three months before that inspection.[276]

Compliance

25.71 DMLC: implement Gibraltar requirements as set out in Pt I, point 16 (on financial security for shipowners' liabilities), and record details of compliance measures in DMLC, Pt II, point 16.

REGULATION 4.3: HEALTH AND SAFETY PROTECTION AND ACCIDENT PREVENTION

25.72 In respect of Gibraltar ships, the shipowner, master and employer must ensure that seafarers on board are provided with: (a) occupational health protection; (b) a safe and hygienic environment in which to live, work and train; (c) safety and health protection appropriate to the nature of the seafarer's work; and (d) equivalent protection and prevention services or facilities with regard to the safety and health of seafarers working by day or by night.[277]

The shipowner and employer must comply with the requirements of applicable international and national instruments on the acceptable level of exposure to workforce hazards on board ships, and on the development and implementation of ships' occupational safety and health policies and programmes.[278]

In accordance with the 2013 Regulations, the GMA has published a series of guidelines on compliance with health and safety.[279] These cover the following areas: policies and programmes (MLN 017); vibration (MLN 018); noise (MLN 019); hazardous chemical agents (MLN 020); and reporting of occupational accidents, incidents and diseases (MLN 021). Implementation of the guidelines will be taken as evidence of compliance with the 2013 Regulations, although the shipowner may adopt equivalent or higher standards as an alternative method of compliance.[280]

A summary of the main points for MLC compliance is as follows:

- General duties: the shipowner must ensure that seafarers are provided with occupational health protection and make provision for seafarers to live, work and train on board in a safe and hygienic environment.[281]
- Health and safety measures: the shipowner must take measures such as implementing a general health and safety policy which is to be maintained and revised as appropriate, and made available to seafarers.[282]

276 MLN 030.
277 2013 Regulations, reg 30(1)(a)–(d).
278 2013 Regulations, reg 30(2).
279 2013 Regulations, reg 30(3)(a)–(b).
280 MLN 017: Health and safety policies and programmes, explanatory remark.
281 See MLN 017, paras 1.1.1–1.1.6.
282 See MLN 017, paras 1.2.1–1.2.7.

- Shipowner's duty to consult with other employers: the shipowner has overall responsibility for health and safety and must consult with any other employer of seafarers on board, or with self-employed persons.[283]
- Safety officer to be appointed, who will have specific responsibility for the implementation of, and compliance with, the ship's occupational health and safety policies. The safety officer must have a minimum of two years' sea service since attaining the age of 18 and, if serving on tankers, the two years' sea service must include at least six months on tankers.[284]
- Safety representatives are to be elected or appointed on any ship on which there are five or more seafarers.[285]
- A safety committee is to be appointed by the master on any ship on which there are five or more seafarers, and must include the master as chairman, the safety officer and safety representatives, and the membership must be recorded in the official log book. Meetings must be held at intervals not exceeding six weeks.[286]
- Personal protective equipment (PPE) must be issued, free of charge, to seafarers if a risk cannot be avoided or adequately controlled in any other way. The PPE includes safety helmets, gloves, eye protection, respirators, high-visibility clothing, safety footwear and safety harnesses.[287]
- The shipowner is to ensure that seafarers are provided with adequate and appropriate health and safety training.[288]
- Risk assessments and evaluations are to be carried out, applying the following principles: (i) the avoidance of risks; and (ii) the evaluation and action to minimise unavoidable risks.[289]

  When a risk assessment has identified that there is a potential long-term risk to the seafarer's health, further steps must be taken which may include health surveillance.[290]
- There are special provisions relating to seafarers under the age of 18, including: a mandatory risk assessment (which may adapted from a general risk assessment); prohibited and restricted tasks; health assessment; and health education.[291]

  The risk assessment for young seafarers must be completed before the young seafarer begins work and must pay particular attention to: (a) how the workplace is fitted and laid out; (b) what type of work equipment will be used and how it will be handled; (c) the organisation of processes and activities; (d) the extent of the health and safety training provided or to be provided to the young person concerned; and (e) any risks from agents, processes and work as detailed in the Schedule to MLN 017.[292]

283 See MLN 017, paras 1.3.1–1.3.3.
284 See MLN 017, paras 2.1.1–2.5.1.
285 See MLN 017, paras 2.3.1–2.3.5.
286 See MLN 017, paras 2.4.1–2.4.5.
287 See MLN 017, paras 3.1.1–3.3.2.
288 See MLN 017, paras 4.1.1–4.1.6.
289 See MLN 017, paras 5.1.1–5.3.1.
290 See MLN 017, paras 6.1.1–6.4.1.
291 MLN 017, paras 7.1.1–7.5.1.
292 MLN 017, para 7.1.3(a)–(e).

- The shipowner and master are required to report casualties, accidents, incidents and occupational diseases to the GMA. Detailed guidance is provided in MLN 021 and the report form is available on the GMA website.[293]

For further information see: the UK MCA's Code of Safe Working Practices for Merchant Seafarers (COSWP);[294] and Chapter 19, which sets out a more detailed account of the UK provisions, which may be used as a guide.

Forthcoming amendments to the MLC

25.73 The 2016 amendments to the MLC come into force on 8 January 2019 and will amend Code B of Regulation 4.5 addressing harassment and bullying in a health and safety context. The full text of the amendments is set out in Appendix 2. See also Chapter 19, where a more detailed commentary is provided.

Compliance

25.74 DMLC: implement Gibraltar requirements as set out in Pt I, point 1, and record details of compliance measures in DMLC, Pt II, point 11.

REGULATION 4.4: ACCESS TO SHORE-BASED WELFARE FACILITIES

25.75 The captain of the Port of Gibraltar is required to ensure that shore-based facilities are easily accessible by seafarers, irrespective of nationality, race, colour, sex, religion, political opinion or social origin, and irrespective of the flag state of the ship on which they work.[295] The captain must also promote the development of welfare facilities in Gibraltar and encourage the establishment of welfare boards which regularly review seafarers' welfare facilities and services, to ensure that they are appropriate in the light of changes in the needs of seafarers resulting from technical, operational and other developments in the shipping industry.[296]

There is a port welfare committee in Gibraltar, which is affiliated to the UK's Merchant Navy Welfare Board ('MNWB').[297] In terms of facilities, there are the Mediterranean Mission to Seafarers Flying Angel Club, North Mole and a seafarers' drop-in centre at Gibdock.[298]

293 Report of a case of occupational disease (Form MLC-003): www.gibraltarship.com/maritime-labour-convention [Accessed 5 April 2018].

294 COSWP, 2015 edition – Amendment 2, December 2017: https://assets.publishing.service.gov.uk/government/uploads/system/uploads/attachment_data/file/671403/CSWPMS_GOV_UK_2017.pdf [Accessed 19 October 2018].

295 2013 Regulations, reg 31(a); MLN 022: Access to shore-based welfare facilities.

296 2013 Regulations, reg 31(b)–(c).

297 MLN-MNWB: www.mnwb.org [Accessed 5 April 2018].

298 Gibraltar port welfare facilities: www.gibraltarportwelfare.com/facilities.html [Accessed 5 April 2018].

REGULATION 4.5: SOCIAL SECURITY

25.76 The MLC provides that the nine branches to be considered, with a view to achieving progressively comprehensive social security protection, for all seafarers ordinarily resident in the relevant state's territory, are: medical care; sickness benefit; unemployment benefit; old-age benefit; employment injury benefit; family benefit; maternity benefit; invalidity benefit; and survivor's benefit; complementing the protection which shipowners are required to provide under MLC, Regulations 4.1 (medical care) and 4.2 (shipowners' liability), and other titles of the MLC.[299] The ILO's website shows that, in accordance with MLC, Standard A4.5(2) and (10), the Gibraltar government has specified the following branches of social security as being applicable to seafarers: employment injury benefit; invalidity benefit; and survivors' benefit.[300] The social security benefits apply to:

(a) a person who is domiciled or ordinarily resident in Gibraltar and is employed on board a ship;

(b) a person who is employed on or working on board a Gibraltar ship and is an EU national, other than an EU national who is resident in a Member State in which the shipowner or employer (if different) has a registered office or place of business;

(c) a person who: (i) is employed on or working on board a Gibraltar ship, (ii) is not domiciled in Gibraltar, ordinarily resident in Gibraltar or an EU national, and (iii) does not ordinarily have access to social security provision, or to medical care when in Gibraltar, which satisfies the requirements of the MLC.[301]

A person who works on board a Gibraltar ship must be treated as being in 'insurable employment' for the purposes of the Social Security (Employable Injuries Insurance) Act (No 1952-10), which entitles them to: employment injury benefit; invalidity benefit; and survivor's benefit, if they are injured in an accident arising out of and in the course of their employment.[302] Such a person, and the shipowner, are liable to pay contributions under the 1952 Act.[303] The 1952 Act applies to employment in Gibraltar[304] or, by virtue of the 2013 Regulations, on Gibraltar ships.

A person who falls within paragraph (a), (b) or (c) above must be treated as resident in Gibraltar for the purposes of Pt II of Sch 1 to the Gibraltar Medical (Group Practice Scheme) Regulations (LN. 1973/052).[305] This means that such

299 MLC, Standard A4.5.1.

300 ILO's MLC ratifications website (Gibraltar's entry is shown under that of the UK): www.ilo.org/dyn/normlex/en/f?p=NORMLEXPUB:11300:0::NO::P11300_INSTRUMENT_ID:312331 [Accessed 19 October 2018].

301 2013 Regulations, reg 32(1)(a)–(c)(i)–(iii).

302 2013 Regulations, reg 32(2); 1952 Act, s 10.

303 2013 Regulations, reg 32(3).

304 1952 Act, s 3(1).

305 2013 Regulations, reg 32(4).

a person is entitled to register under the Scheme and have access to medical treatment; fees apply for the registration and care.[306] However, as regards occupational accidents or diseases deriving out of insurable employment, an insured person will be entitled to free medical, surgical and pharmaceutical care at a hospital in Gibraltar.[307]

Under the MLC, Gibraltar is also required to allow seafarers on visiting ships to visit medical facilities ashore, if they are in need of immediate medical treatment.[308] Any costs (subject to some exceptions) are to be met by the shipowner: see Regulations 4.1 and 4.2 above on Gibraltar's provisions on medical care on board ships and ashore, and shipowners' liability, respectively.

Compliance

25.77 Details of the health and social security protection benefits provided to the seafarer should be entered in the SEA.[309]

INTRODUCTION TO TITLE 5

25.78 The complete Title 5 of the MLC is set out at Appendix 1, which fully explains MLC flag state and port state responsibilities. It has been annotated by references to the ILO Guidelines on flag state control[310] and port state control.[311]

The UK's Title 5 provisions are described in some detail at Chapter 22. Those provisions may be used as a guide to flag state implementation and port state enforcement.

Set out below are references to the main Gibraltar provisions, which are contained in the 2013 Regulations. Guidance is also provided in MLN 027[312] and MLN 033.[313]

306 1973 Regulations, regs 4–8.
307 1973 Regulations, reg 3; 1952 Act, s 30.
308 MLC, Regulation 4.1.3.
309 MLN 007, para 12(h).
310 Guidelines for flag State inspections under the Maritime Labour Convention, 2006 (published 2009): www.ilo.org/global/standards/maritime-labour-convention/monitoring-implementation-tools/WCMS_101788/lang--en/index.htm [Accessed 5 July 2018].
311 Guidelines for port State control officers carrying out inspections under the Maritime Labour Convention, 2006: www.ilo.org/global/standards/maritime-labour-convention/monitoring-implementation-tools/WCMS_101787/lang--en/index.htm [Accessed 5 July 2018].
312 MLN 027 – A route to MLC certification (amended 07.08.13).
313 MLN 033 – MLC Title 5.1.3 & 5.1.4: Certification, Inspection & Enforcement.

REGULATION 5.1: FLAG STATE RESPONSIBILITIES

Gibraltar ships

Inspections and issue of MLC documentation

25.79 Gibraltar ships of 500 GT and over which are engaged in international voyages or operating from a foreign port, or other ships at the request of the shipowner, are subject to the following inspections:

- before an MLCert can be issued, an initial inspection;
- a renewal inspection thereafter at intervals not exceeding five years;
- between the second and third anniversary dates of the MLCert, an intermediate inspection.[314]

The purpose of the inspection is to ascertain if the ship meets the standards of the MLC, Directive 1999/63/EC[315] and Directive 2009/13/EC.[316] Gibraltar is the only REG member which expressly makes inspections subject to Directive 2009/13/EC, which do not add any substantive provisions to the MLC, but implement most of the MLC's mandatory Code A into EU law.

The shipowner must: apply to the GMA for a DMLC, Pt I, and notify which Class Society it wishes to carry out the inspection; provide the inspector with the information necessary for the latter to draw up the DMLC, Pt I; and draw up the DMLC, Pt II.[317]

An MLCert must be issued on the date of inspection and will be valid for a period not exceeding five years.[318] However, when the 2016 amendments to the MLC come into force on 8 January 2019, ratifying states will have the power to extend the validity for a further period not exceeding five months, following a successful renewal inspection, where the new MLCert cannot be immediately issued to and made available on board the ship.[319] Details on how Gibraltar will implement this amendment have still to be promulgated. The MLC amendments are set out in Appendix 2.

314 2013 Regulations, regs 33(1)–(2), 34.

315 Council Directive 1999/63/EC concerning the Agreement on the organisation of working time of seafarers concluded by the European Community Shipowners' Associations (ECSA) and the Federation of Transport Workers' Unions in the European Union (FST), OJ 2.7.1999 L 167/33.

316 Council Directive 2009/13/EC of 16 February 2009 implementing the Agreement concluded between the European Community Shipowners' Associations (ECSA) and the European Transport Workers' Federation (ETF) on the Maritime Labour Convention, 2006 and amending Directive 1999/63/EC, OJ 20.5.2009 L 124/30.

317 2013 Regulations, reg 39; MLN 027, para 1. The DMLC, Pts I and II are available on the GMA website: www.gibraltarship.com/maritime-labour-convention [Accessed 7 July 2018].

318 2013 Regulations, reg 38(1).

319 This provision will become MLC, Standard A5.1.3(4).

The GMA may also issue an interim MLCert for a maximum period of six months, in accordance with the circumstances and conditions set out in the MLC.[320] An inspector must record the results of an MLC inspection or verification in the DMLC, Pt I, or make them available to the seafarers on board, inspectors and shipowners' and seafarers' representatives.[321]

The GMA may request another MLC state to carry out an initial, intermediate or renewal inspection against the same standards and issue an MLCert on its behalf.[322] Conversely, the GMA may carry out inspections at the request of another state and issue an MLCert or interim MLCert on behalf of that state.[323]

Appeal

25.80 A shipowner may appeal to the Minister against the decision of the GMA within seven days of the inspection, and the Minister may confirm or cancel the decision made by the GMA.[324] A second appeal may be made to the Supreme Court (on a point of law only) within 21 days of the decision on the first appeal.[325]

Documents to be carried on board

25.81 The shipowner and master must ensure that there is carried on board at all times, and made available to seafarers, inspectors and shipowners' and seafarers' representatives:

- a copy of the MLC (with amendments); and
- where issued, an MLCert with the DMLC, Pts I and II, or an interim MLCert.[326]

The master must ensure that all seafarers have access to a copy of Directive 2009/13/EC, and this may be facilitated electronically.[327]

On-board and onshore complaints procedure

25.82 The shipowner and master must ensure that there is a procedure for seafarers to lodge a complaint alleging breaches of the MLC, and for the complaint to be resolved fairly, effectively and efficiently.[328] A seafarer may complain directly to the GMA.[329] Guidance on the procedure is provided

320 2013 Regulations, reg 36; MLC, Standard A5.1.3, paras 7–8.
321 2013 Regulations, reg 39(5).
322 2013 Regulations, reg 35.
323 2013 Regulations, reg 37.
324 2013 Regulations, reg 40(1)–(2).
325 2013 Regulations, reg 40(3)–(4).
326 2013 Regulations, reg 41.
327 2013 Regulations, reg 43C(6), as inserted by Gibraltar Merchant Shipping (Maritime Labour Convention) (Amendment) Regulations 2015 ('2015 Amendment Regulations'), reg 3.
328 2013 Regulations, regs 42, 43E; reg 43E was inserted by 2015 Amendment Regulations, reg 3.
329 2013 Regulations, reg 42(5).

in MLN 023.[330] Each seafarer on board must be provided with a copy of the procedure.[331]

The contact details[332] to lodge a complaint directly with the GMA are:

- Email: maritime.feedback@gibraltar.gov.gi; telephone no +350 200 79728
- Person in Charge – Senior Surveyor

Inspection and detention of Gibraltar ships

25.83 For the purpose of checking compliance with the 2013 Regulations, an authorised inspector may at all reasonable times go on board a Gibraltar ship and inspect the ship, its equipment and any article and document carried on board.[333] Where there are clear grounds of a contravention of the 2013 Regulations or of a determination, exemption, approval, authorisation or permission granted by the GMA, the ship is liable to be detained.[334]

REGULATION 5.2: PORT STATE RESPONSIBILITIES

25.84 When an MLC ship with MLC documentation is in Gibraltar waters or a Gibraltar port, it must comply with the following requirements of the MLC:

- Standard A5.1.1 – requirement to have a copy of the MLC on board.
- Regulation 5.1.3, paragraphs 3 and 4, and Standard A5.1.3.12 – MLCert and DMLC to be carried.
- Regulation 5.2.2 and Standard A5.2.2 – onshore seafarer complaints handling procedures.[335]

Inspection and detention

Inspection

25.85 MLC ships in Gibraltar waters or a Gibraltar port may be inspected for the purpose of reviewing the ship's MLCert, DMLC, Pt I and II, or the interim MLCert.[336] Where MLC Standard A5.2.1(a), (c) or (d) (set out in Appendix 1) applies, the inspector may carry out a more detailed inspection to ascertain the living and working conditions on board.[337] Where the inspector believes, or it is

330 MLN 023: On board complaint procedures.
331 MLN 023, para 6.
332 MLN 023, para 6a.
333 2013 Regulations, reg 44(1).
334 2013 Regulations, reg 44(2)(a)–(b).
335 2013 Regulations, reg 43(1)(a)–(d), respectively.
336 2013 Regulations, reg 45(1).
337 2013 Regulations, reg 45(2).

alleged, that the working and living condition on board are defective, and the defect could constitute a clear hazard to the safety, health or security of seafarers or a serious breach of the requirements of the MLC, a more detailed inspection may be carried out to ascertain the working and living conditions on board.[338]

Detention

25.86 Where an inspector has clear grounds for believing that the ship does not conform to the requirements of the MLC and the non-compliance represents:

(a) a significant danger to the safety, health or security of seafarers; or

(b) a serious or repeated breach of the requirements of the MLC,

the ship is liable to be detained.[339]

Offences under the 2013 Regulations

25.87 It is an offence for a person to fail, without reasonable cause, to comply with a requirement of the 2013 Regulations,[340] or a determination, exemption, exception, approval, authorisation or permission given by the GMA in accordance with the 2013 Regulations.[341]

If a Gibraltar ship, which requires an MLCert (or where the owner has requested one), proceeds or attempts to proceed to sea or on a voyage or excursion without a valid MLCert and a DMLC, Pts I and II, or a valid interim MLCert, the shipowner and the master commit an offence.[342]

It is also an offence to: intentionally alter an MLCert; make a false MLCert; knowingly or recklessly provide false information in connection with an MLC inspection; lend to another an MLCert; fail to surrender an MLCert; or obstruct the GMA or an inspector in the exercise of their MLC inspection and detention powers.[343]

All offences are punishable by a fine not exceeding level 5 on the standard scale.[344] It is a defence for the accused to show that they took all reasonable steps to comply with the provision in question.[345]

338 2013 Regulations, reg 45(3).
339 2013 Regulations, reg 45(4)(a)–(b).
340 2013 Regulations, reg 46(1).
341 2013 Regulations, reg 46(2).
342 2013 Regulations, reg 46(3).
343 2013 Regulations, reg 46(4)(a)–(f), respectively.
344 2013 Regulations, reg 46.
345 2013 Regulations, reg 46(4).

Chapter 26

Isle of Man

INTRODUCTION

26.1 The Isle of Man Ship Registry[1] (IOMSR) has served the international maritime industry for over 30 years. Its annual report for 2017 shows that it had 1,041 vessels registered with it as follows: 404 merchant vessels; 356 pleasure

1 IOMSR: www.iomshipregistry.com [Accessed 21 October 2018].

yachts; 121 small ships; 64 commercial yachts; 74 fishing vessels; and 22 demise merchant vessels.

The Isle of Man (IOM) provisions are set out in the Merchant Shipping (Maritime Labour Convention) Regulations 2013 ('2013 Regulations'),[2] as amended.[3] The Regulations are supplemented by guidelines set out in a series of Maritime Labour Notices (MLNs), implementation of which will be taken to be evidence of compliance. The guidelines do not preclude the shipowner from demonstrating an equivalent or higher standard as an alternative method of evidence of compliance.

It is the shipowner's responsibility to ensure that its ships are constructed, equipped and operated in accordance with the 2013 Regulations, and to ensure that each seafarer enjoys all the rights set out therein (except those relating to recruitment and placement), even if the obligation is also imposed on another person.[4] A failure of the shipowner to comply with any of the provisions amounts to an offence punishable, on summary conviction, by a fine not exceeding £10,000[5] or, on conviction on information, by imprisonment to a term not exceeding two years and a fine.[6]

The first requirement is that a ship must have a copy of the Maritime Labour Convention, 2006 (MLC) on board.[7]

Definitions used in the 2013 Regulations

26.2 The 2013 Regulations (at reg 4) set out definitions of key MLC concepts. Those which are referred to throughout are set out below; others relating to specific areas of the MLC will be set out in the sections to which they relate:

- 'established training programme' means a training programme leading to an STCW qualification;
- 'foreign ship' means any ship that is not a Manx ship;
- 'large commercial yacht' means a yacht of 24 metres and over in load line length which is in commercial use for sport or pleasure and does not carry cargo or more than 12 passengers;
- 'Manx ship' has the meaning given by section 1 of the Merchant Shipping Registration Act 1991 and includes ships registered under Part IV of that Act (the Demise Charter Register) [in summary, for present purposes, s 1 of the

2 Statutory document (SD) 0234/13.
3 The amending statutes are listed in the explanatory note to the 2013 Regulations.
4 2013 Regulations, reg 5(1)–(2).
5 When the 2013 Regulations came into force, the maximum fines on summary conviction were set at £5,000; these have now been increased to a maximum of £10,000: Interpretation Act 2015, s 55.
6 2013 Regulations, reg 5(3).
7 2013 Regulations, reg 6.

1991 Act states that a Manx ship is one which is registered in the IOM under Parts I, II or III of that Act, or which is wholly owned by one or more qualified persons (set out in s 2)];

- 'pleasure vessel' has the meaning given by regulation 6 of the Merchant Shipping (Pleasure Vessel) Regulations 2003,[8]

  [which means any vessel which at the time it is being used:

  (a) is wholly owned by an individual or individuals, and is used only for the sport or pleasure of the owner or the immediate family or friends of the owner; or

  (b) is owned by a body corporate, and is carrying only such persons as are the employees or officers of the body corporate, or their immediate family or friends; and

  (c) is on a voyage or excursion which is one for which the owner does not receive money or money's worth for or in connection with the operation of the vessel or the carrying of any person other than as a contribution to the direct expenses of the operation of the vessel incurred during the voyage or excursion, and no other payments are made by, on behalf of, or for the benefit of users of the vessel, other than by the owner; or

  (d) is owned by a body corporate but pursuant to a long-term lease agreement, is used only for the sport or pleasure of the lessee, and the immediate friends or family of the lessee, if an individual, or the employees or officers and their immediate friends and family, if a corporate lessee;

  Such lease agreement must specify that:

  (i) the vessel may only be used for private purposes and must not be used for commercial purposes;

  (ii) the vessel must not be sub-leased or chartered; and

  (iii) no other payments are made by, on behalf of, or for the benefit of users of the vessel, other than by the lessee;

  (e) is wholly owned by or on behalf of a members' club formed for the purpose of sport or pleasure, and at the time it is being used, is used only for the sport or pleasure of members of that club or their immediate family, and any charges levied in respect of that use are paid into club funds and applied for the general use of the club, and no other payments are made by, on behalf of, or for the benefit of users of the vessel, other than by the club.]

- 'RO' means any recognised organisation specified in Manx Shipping Notice 020 which is authorised by the Department to undertake the specified function;

- 'seafarer' means any person who is employed or engaged or works in any capacity on board a ship to which these Regulations apply;

- 'shipowner' means the owner of the ship or another organisation or person, such as the manager, agent or bareboat charterer, who has assumed the responsibility for the operation of the ship from the owner and who, on assuming that

8 SD 396/03.

responsibility, has agreed to take over the duties and responsibilities imposed on the shipowner in accordance with the Maritime Labour Convention, regardless of whether any other organisation or person fulfils certain of the duties or responsibilities on behalf of the shipowner;

- 'shipowners' and seafarers' organisations' means the United Kingdom Chamber of Shipping, Nautilus International and the National Union of Rail, Maritime and Transport Workers (RMT);
- 'young seafarer' means a seafarer under the age of 18.

Application

26.3 Unless provided otherwise, the 2013 Regulations apply to all seafarers and all Manx ships wherever they may be.[9] Parts 24 (inspections in port) and 25 (onshore seafarer complaint-handling procedures) apply to a foreign ship calling, in the normal course of its business or for operational reasons, at a port in the IOM.[10] The following ships are excluded: (a) pleasure vessels; (b) ships engaged in fishing or similar pursuits; (c) ships of traditional build, such as dhows and junks; (d) warships or naval auxiliaries; or (e) Manx ships which navigate exclusively within 60 nautical miles of the IOM's coast.[11]

REGULATION 1.1: MINIMUM AGE

26.4 No person may employ or engage a person under the age of 16 to work in any capacity on board a ship, or a seafarer under the age of 18 to work on board a ship if the work is likely to jeopardise their health or safety.[12] Consequently, young seafarers must not carry out 'prohibited tasks' which are those which: (a) are objectively beyond the young seafarer's physical or psychological capacity; (b) involve harmful exposure to agents which are toxic, carcinogenic, cause heritable genetic damage or harm to the unborn child or that in any other way chronically affect human health; or (c) involve harmful exposure to radiation.[13] There are also 'restricted tasks' which young seafarers may only perform under specific conditions.[14]

There is also a prohibition against young seafarers (those under the age of 18) working at night, which is defined as a period of at least nine hours starting no later than midnight and ending no earlier than 5am.[15] Exceptions may be made when: (i) the effective training of the young seafarer concerned is in accordance

9 2013 Regulations, reg 3(1).
10 2013 Regulations, reg 3(2).
11 2013 Regulations, reg 3(3)(a)–(e).
12 2013 Regulations, reg 7(1)–(2), respectively.
13 2013 Regulations, regs 7(3), 115(a)–(c).
14 2013 Regulations, reg 114 (as substituted by Merchant Shipping (Maritime Labour Convention) (Amendment) Regulations 2016 (SD 2016/0328), reg 9), Sch 1.
15 2013 Regulations, reg 35(1); MLN 1.1 (Revision No 1), para 1.

with an established training programme, and schedules would be impaired; or (ii) the specific nature of the duty or a recognised training programme requires the young seafarer to perform duties at night and the Department for Enterprise determines, after consultation with the shipowners' and seafarers' organisations concerned, that the work will not be detrimental to their health.[16] Furthermore, a health assessment must be made before and during night work.[17] An 'established training programme' is one leading to STCW qualifications and, in most cases, this will be a cadet training scheme.[18]

Compliance

26.5 DMLC: implement IOM requirements as set out in Pt I, point 1, and record details of compliance measures in DMLC, Pt II, point 1.

REGULATION 1.2: MEDICAL CERTIFICATE

26.6 Shipowners must ensure that, before commencing work on a ship, a seafarer holds a valid medical certificate (in English) attesting that they are medically fit to perform their duties at sea.[19]

A valid medical certificate is one issued to a seafarer by a qualified medical practitioner in accordance with the requirements of: (a) the MLC; (b) the IMO's International Convention on Standards of Training, Certification and Watchkeeping, 1978 ('STCW Convention'); (c) the ILO's Medical Examination (Seafarers) Convention, 1946 (No 73); or (d) in the case of a seafarer not covered by the STCW Convention, a medical certificate meeting the substance thereof.[20] The latter could apply to a person who is not a watchkeeper, but who comes within the wide definition of 'seafarer' under the MLC.[21]

For a seafarer serving on a ship servicing the oil and gas industry on the UK continental shelf, a valid UK oil and gas medical certificate will suffice.[22]

Unless a shorter period is applicable due to the specific duties to be performed by the seafarer, or is required under the STCW Convention: (a) a medical certificate is valid for a maximum period of two years except that, if the seafarer is under the age of 18, it will be valid for a maximum period of one year; and (b) a certificate of colour vision is valid for a maximum period of six years.[23]

16 2013 Regulations, reg 35(2)(a)–(b); MLN 1.1, para 1.
17 MLN 1.1; para 7.4 sets out information about the health assessment.
18 2013 Regulations, reg 4; MLN 1.1, para 1.
19 2013 Regulations, reg 8(1), (7).
20 2013 Regulations, reg 8(2).
21 MLN 1.2 (Revision 2): Medical certificate, para 3.1.
22 2013 Regulations, reg 8(3).
23 2013 Regulations, reg 8(4)(a)–(b).

If the certificate expires during a voyage, it is to be treated as continuing in force until the next port of call where the seafarer can obtain a medical certificate from a qualified medical practitioner, although this extension is limited to three months.[24]

Where there is an urgent crewing requirement, the IOMSR may permit a seafarer to join a ship and work without a valid medical certificate until the next port of call where the seafarer can obtain a medical certificate from a qualified medical practitioner, provided: (a) the period of permission does not exceed three months; and (b) the seafarer is in possession of a medical certificate which expired not earlier than 30 days before the seafarer joined the ship.[25]

For these purposes, a 'qualified medical practitioner' is one who is recognised by the competent authority of a country which has ratified ILO Convention No 73, the MLC or the STCW Convention as qualified to issue medical certificates under one of those Conventions.[26] The registry does not regulate medical practitioners or issue seafarers' medical certificates; however, seafarers may use UK MCA-approved medical practitioners residing on the Island.[27]

Compliance

26.7 DMLC: implement IOM requirements as set out in Pt I, point 2, and record details of compliance measures in DMLC, Pt II, point 2.

REGULATION 1.3: TRAINING AND QUALIFICATIONS

26.8 The IOM requirements are based on the STCW Convention.

Seafarers must be trained or certified as competent or otherwise qualified to perform their duties; they must also have successfully completed training for personal safety before commencing work on a ship.[28] These requirements are satisfied by training in accordance with: the Merchant Shipping (Manning and Training) Regulations 1996 ('1996 Regulations');[29] the Merchant Shipping (Manning and STCW) Regulations 2014[30] ('2014 Regulations'); and the Merchant Shipping (ISM Code) Regulations 1998[31] (which apply s 6 of the ISM Code on resources and personnel);[32] or, for a seafarer working on a large commercial

24 2013 Regulations, reg 8(5).
25 2013 Regulations, reg 8(6)(a)–(b); MLN 1.2, para 4.3.
26 2013 Regulations, reg 8(8).
27 MLN 1.2 (Revision 1), para 2.
28 2013 Regulations, reg 9(1)–(2).
29 SD 723/96.
30 SD 2014/0238.
31 SD 421/98.
32 2013 Regulations, reg 9(3). MLN 1.3, para 1(b); International Management Code for the safe operation of ships and for pollution prevention (ISM Code).

yacht, training and certification in accordance with the STCW Convention or the IOM's National Annex[33] to the UK MCA's Large Commercial Yacht Code 'LY3 Code'.[34]

The 2014 Regulations implement the STCW Convention's 'Manila amendments' of 2010, and replace most of the 1996 Regulations, although the latter still cover type rating certificates for high-speed craft.[35] The company and the master must ensure that seafarers on Manx ships are trained in accordance with the STCW Convention and:

'(a) hold a certificate of competency in accordance with the requirements of chapters II, III, IV or VII of the Annex to the STCW Convention;

(b) hold a certificate of proficiency in accordance with the requirements of the STCW Convention;

(c) receive refresher and updating training as required by the STCW Convention; and

(d) be familiarised with their specific duties and with all ship arrangements, installations, equipment, procedures and ship characteristics that are relevant to their routine or emergency duties in accordance with the requirements of the STCW Code, Section A-1/14 and taking into account Section B-1/14.'[36]

Before being assigned to any duties on board, a seafarer must receive safety familiarisation and basic training and instruction in accordance with the STCW Code, Section A-VI/1 and meet the standards of competence specified in the STCW Code, Tables A-VI/1-1 to A-VI/1-4.[37]

The IOM does not issue its own CoCs; however, in accordance with STCW Regulation I/10, a master, officer or radio operator must have an IOM endorsement issued by the registry, unless they hold a UK CoC, in which case no endorsement is required.[38] The endorsement may be issued to a seafarer who holds a CoC issued by a recognised 'white list' country specified in Appendix 1 to MSN 051.[39] The application should be made through the shipowner or operator

33 MSN 054: Isle of Man LY3 National Annex, pp 10–13.

34 2013 Regulations, reg 9(4)–(5); MLN 1.3, para 1(c); Large Commercial Yacht Code – Applicable to yachts which are 24 metres and over in load line length, are in commercial use for sport or pleasure, do not carry cargo and do not carry more than 12 passengers: https://assets.publishing.service.gov.uk/government/uploads/system/uploads/attachment_data/file/444652/LY3_-_Final_Version.pdf [Accessed 12 April 2018]. Note that the LY3 Code will be consolidated into the Red Ensign Group Yacht Code, which comes into force on 1 January 2019.

35 2014 Regulations, reg 32, Sch 2, para 10(1)(a)–(h); 1996 Regulations, regs 54–56; MLN 1.3, para 1(d).

36 2014 Regulations, regs 14(1)–(2)(a)–(d), 15(1)(a)–(b); MSN 50: Implementing the STCW Manila Amendments, para 3(a).

37 2014 Regulations, reg 20.

38 2014 Regulations, reg 17(1)–(2).

39 2014 Regulations, reg 17(3).

by hard copy, email or online.[40] The company must maintain documentation and data on the seafarer's experience, training, medical fitness and competency in assigned duties.[41] Any certificate required by the STCW Convention must be kept available in its original form on board the ship on which the holder is serving.[42]

Once the CoC holder has applied for an endorsement, there is a three-month period within which they may serve on an IOM ship while the application is being processed, so long as they hold on board a confirmation of receipt of application.[43] Furthermore, in circumstances of exceptional necessity, and only in accordance with Article 8 of the STCW Convention, a dispensation may be granted to a seafarer (except in the case of a radio officer or radio telephone operator) to serve on a Manx ship without an appropriate CoC.[44]

Foreign ships

26.9 When a foreign ship calls at an IOM port in the normal course of its business or for operational reasons, it may be inspected to ensure compliance with the STCW Convention, with regard to safe manning and certification.[45] In the event of a failure to correct any deficiency which the inspector determines may pose a danger to persons, property or the environment, the ship may be detained.[46]

See also the related topic of manning levels at paragraph 26.53 below, and MSN 052: Minimum Safe Manning Requirements.

Compliance

26.10 DMLC: implement IOM requirements as set out in Pt I, point 3, and record details of compliance measures in DMLC, Pt II, point 3.

REGULATION 1.4: RECRUITMENT AND PLACEMENT

26.11 A seafarer recruitment and placement service (RPS) means 'any person, company, institution, agency or other organisation, in the public or the private sector, which is engaged in recruiting seafarers on behalf of shipowners or placing seafarers with shipowners'.[47]

40 MSN 051, paras 1–2.
41 2014 Regulations, reg 18.
42 2014 Regulations, reg 23.
43 2014 Regulations, reg 17(5)(a)–(c).
44 2014 Regulations, reg 25(1)–(2).
45 2014 Regulations, reg 30.
46 2014 Regulations, reg 31.
47 2013 Regulations, reg 10(2).

There are two types of RPS: an 'employment agency' (EA) which introduces seafarers to and for employment by the shipowner (or another party); and an 'employment business' (EB) which employs seafarers and supplies them to act for and under the control of shipowners.[48]

Businesses which work on behalf of shipowners to ensure that seafarers, whether supplied by an EB, EA or employed directly by the shipowner, are allocated and travel to and from ships operated by the shipowner are classified by the IOM as 'placement businesses' (PBs); the 2013 Regulations do not apply to PBs, but they may request inspection and certification, upon which they would be required to demonstrate compliance.[49]

A private RPS operating on the IOM, whose primary purpose is the recruitment and placement of seafarers, or that recruit and place a significant number of seafarers (for ships registered under any flag), is subject to the obligations listed below. Although the MLC does not make any such distinction, the IOM guidance provides that, due to the more limited role of an EA, the requirements in paragraphs (b), (f), (h), (i) and (j) do not apply to the latter:[50]

> '(a) maintain an up-to-date register of all seafarers recruited or placed through it, to be available for inspection by an inspector;
>
> (b) ensure each seafarer is informed of his or her rights and duties under the employment agreement prior to or in the process of engagement and that proper arrangements are made for the seafarer to examine the employment agreements before and after it is signed and for the seafarer to receive a copy of the agreement;
>
> (c) ensure the seafarer is advised of any particular conditions applicable to the job for which he or she is to be engaged and of the particular shipowner's policies relating to his or her employment;
>
> (d) verify that a seafarer recruited or placed by the service is qualified and holds the documents necessary for the job concerned and that the seafarer's employment agreement is in accordance with any applicable statutory provisions and any applicable collective agreement that forms part of the employment agreement;
>
> (e) maintain, with due regard to the right to privacy and the need to protect confidentiality, full and complete records of the seafarers covered by the recruitment and placement system, which must include but is not limited to the seafarer's: (i) qualifications; (ii) record of employment; (iii) personal data relevant to employment; and (iv) medical data relevant to employment;
>
> (f) make sure, as far as practicable, that the shipowner has the means to protect the seafarer from being stranded in a foreign port;

48 MLN 1.4: Recruitment and placement, key points, pp 1–2.

49 MLN 1.4, key points, p 2.

50 MLN 1.4, key points, p 1; areas on inspection, pp 1–2 (note that the paragraphs referred to above, which denote exceptions for EAs, correspond to those in the 2013 Regulations, not MLN 1.4 which lists the obligations in a different order.

(g) examine and respond to any complaint concerning its activities and advise the [IOMSR] of any unresolved complaint;

(h) establish a system of protection, by way of insurance or an equivalent appropriate measure, to compensate seafarers for monetary loss that may be incurred as a result of the failure of the provider or the relevant shipowner under the seafarer's employment agreement to meet its obligations to the seafarer;

(i) maintain up-to-date lists of the ships for which the service provides seafarers;

(j) ensure there is a means by which the service can be contacted in an emergency at all hours;'[51]

To meet the requirement in paragraph (f) above, the RPS should ensure that the ship to which the seafarer is supplied carries a valid financial security certificate to cover the costs of abandonment (see para 26.46 below).

There is a prohibition against any person using a blacklist, mechanism or other means intended to prevent or deter a seafarer from gaining employment for which they are qualified.[52]

No person may directly or indirectly charge a seafarer for providing them with employment, although a seafarer may be required to pay for the cost of obtaining a medical certificate, a seafarer's discharge book, passport or similar personal travel documents (other than the cost of visas, which must be borne by the shipowner).[53]

An RPS must maintain a certificate of compliance (which will be valid for a maximum period of five years), certifying that it has been inspected and found to meet the requirements of Pt 3 of the 2013 Regulations; an inspection will be carried out by the registry or a recognised organisation.[54] There must also be annual inspections (three months either side of the anniversary date of the certificate) to verify continuing compliance, upon which the certificate must be endorsed.[55] A renewal inspection must take place three months before the expiry of the existing certificate, upon which a new certificate will be issued, valid for five years from the date of expiry of the existing certificate.[56]

The registry may withdraw the certificate if any identified non-compliance is not rectified.[57] A person who fails to comply with the requirements set out above commits an offence and is liable, on summary conviction, to a fine not exceeding £10,000 or, on conviction on information, to imprisonment for a term not exceeding two years and a fine.[58]

51 2013 Regulations, reg 11(1)–(3).
52 2013 Regulations, reg 12.
53 2013 Regulations, reg 13(1)–(2).
54 2013 Regulations, reg 14(1)–(3).
55 2013 Regulations, reg 15(1)–(3).
56 2013 Regulations, reg 16(1)–(3).
57 2013 Regulations, reg 17.
58 2013 Regulations, reg 18, as amended by Interpretation Act 2015, s 55.

Use of RPSs based in non-MLC states

26.12 Any shipowner who uses an RPS based in a non-MLC state must provide information to the IOMSR or recognised organisation regarding the regulation of the service to ensure that it is operated in conformity with the standards required by Pt 3 of the 2013 Regulations.[59] The shipowner must also detail how it complies with this provision under point 5 of the Declaration of Maritime Labour Compliance, Pt 2.[60] Whereas there is no legal requirement for IOM-based RPSs to comply with this in their dealings with RPSs based in non-MLC states, the IOMSR recommends that it is carried out as a matter of good practice, which assists in annual inspections.[61]

Ships registered with non-MLC states

26.13 The MLC requires ratifying states to takes measures, as far as practicable, to advise its national seafarers of the possible problems which may arise if they sign on to a ship registered with a non-MLC state.[62] The IOM has produced MLN 1.4.8, which highlights the problems that seafarers may face on such ships, and good practice dictates that RPSs issue this to relevant seafarers.

Compliance

26.14 DMLC: implement IOM requirements as set out in Pt I, point 5, and record details of compliance measures in DMLC, Pt II, point 5.

REGULATION 2.1: SEAFARERS' EMPLOYMENT AGREEMENTS

Seafarers to be issued with a seafarers' employment agreement

26.15 A shipowner must ensure that:

- an employed seafarer has a clear, written, legally enforceable seafarer's employment agreement ('SEA') (which may incorporate all or part of a collective agreement) signed by both the seafarer and the shipowner or a representative of the shipowner;[63] an employment business employing a seafarer may sign a SEA on behalf of the shipowner, provided that it has evidence that it is authorised to do so;[64]

59 2013 Regulations, reg 10(1).
60 MLN 1.4, p 3.
61 MLN 1.4, p 3.
62 MLC, Standard A1.4.8.
63 2013 Regulations, reg 19(1), (7).
64 MLC Title 2.1: Seafarers' Employment Agreements (Revision No 5), para 5. It is advisable for details of a shipowner's authorised signatories to be entered into the DMLC, Pt II.

- a self-employed seafarer has evidence of contractual or similar arrangements providing the seafarer with decent working and living conditions on board the ship as required by the 2013 Regulations;[65]
- a seafarer is given an opportunity to examine and seek advice on the terms and conditions in their SEA before signing, as well as other facilities as are necessary to ensure that they have freely entered into an agreement with a sufficient understanding of their rights and responsibilities and freely accept them before signing;[66]
- seafarers, including the ship's master, can easily obtain on board: (a) clear information as to their conditions of employment; and (b) a copy of their SEA or evidence of contractual or similar arrangements.[67] This information must also be available in English for inspection purposes.[68]

The shipowner and seafarer concerned must each have a signed original of the SEA, and a copy of the signed original for each seafarer must be made available on board for inspection purposes.[69]

A copy of any applicable collective agreement must be kept on board and, if that agreement and the SEA are not in English, the following must also be made available on board in English: (a) a copy of the standard form of the SEA; and (b) the portions of any applicable collective agreement that are subject to port state inspection in accordance with the MLC.[70]

Contents of a SEA

26.16 The SEA must contain the following particulars:

(a) seafarer's full name, date of birth or age and birthplace;

(b) shipowner's name and address;

(c) place where and date when the SEA is entered into;

(d) capacity in which the seafarer is to be employed;[71]

(e) amount of the seafarer's wages or, if applicable, the formula used for calculating them;[72]

(f) amount of paid leave or, if applicable, the formula used for calculating it;[73]

(g) the termination of the agreement and the conditions of termination, including:

65 2013 Regulations, reg 19(2).
66 2013 Regulations, reg 19(3).
67 2013 Regulations, reg 19(4)(a)–(b).
68 2013 Regulations, reg 19(5).
69 2013 Regulations, reg 19(6).
70 2013 Regulations, reg 19(8)(a)–(b).
71 See Regulation 1.3; seafarers should be trained and certified accordingly.
72 See Regulation 2.2.
73 See Regulation 2.4.

(i) if the SEA has been made for an indefinite period, the conditions entitling either party to terminate it, as well as the required notice period which must not be less for the shipowner than for the seafarer;

(ii) if the SEA has been made for a definite period, the date fixed for its expiry; and

(iii) if the agreement has been made for a voyage, the port of destination and the time which must expire after arrival before the seafarer is discharged;

(h) health and social security protection benefits provided to the seafarer by the shipowner;[74]

(i) seafarer's entitlement to repatriation, including repatriation destination;[75] and

(j) reference to any applicable collective agreement.[76]

A model SEA is contained in Annex 2 to MLN 2.1 which, although not compulsory, will, if used, be evidence of compliance with the 2013 Regulations, if adopted.[77]

Termination provisions

26.17 Subject to the following exceptions, the notice period which each party must give to terminate the SEA must be at least seven days.[78] However, a SEA may be terminated by less than seven days' notice, or without notice, under any terms provided for in a collective agreement or if the seafarer: (a) has been guilty of misconduct; or (b) has need for early termination due to compassionate grounds or other urgent reasons (and, in this case, it must be without penalty unless provided otherwise in a collective agreement).[79]

If there is no collective agreement, the shipowner must have a policy or procedure which allows the parties to come to an agreement on early termination, and any costs to be borne by the seafarer must be subject to written agreement.[80] For seafarers not covered by a collective agreement, the shipowner must inform the seafarer of any disciplinary rules or procedures applicable to the seafarer's employment, which substantially meet the provisions contained in the Code of Conduct for the Merchant Navy.[81]

Where there is no collective agreement outlining reasons for termination on compassionate grounds, the shipowner should provide for this, with such grounds

74 See Regulation 4.5.
75 See Regulation 2.5.
76 2013 Regulations, reg 20(a)–(j).
77 MLN 2.1, para 24.
78 2013 Regulations, reg 21(1).
79 2013 Regulations, reg 21(2)–(3).
80 MLN 2.1, para 17.
81 MLN 2.1, para 18; Code of Conduct for the Merchant Navy (2013): www.alphamarine.ie/assets/PDFs/Code-of-Conduct-for-the-Merchant-Navy.pdf [Accessed 15 April 2018].

including the death or serious illness of next of kin or a nominated beneficiary, or emergency situations arising which cannot be expediently resolved without the seafarer's attendance.[82]

Seafarer's record of employment

26.18 A shipowner must ensure that a seafarer is given a record of their employment on board the ship, which may be a seafarer's discharge book.[83] The record must contain: (a) the seafarer's full name, date of birth or age and birthplace; (b) the name, port of registry, gross tonnage and IMO number of the ship; (c) a description of the voyage; (d) the capacity in which the seafarer was employed; (e) the commencement date of employment; and (f) the date of discharge.[84] The record must be in English and must not contain any statement as to the quality of the seafarer's work or their wages.[85]

Future amendments to the MLC

26.19 When the 2018 amendments to the MLC come into force (which is likely to be 26 December 2020), ratifying states will be required to provide that: (a) SEAs continue for the entirety of any period in which a seafarer is held in captivity as a result of an act of piracy or armed robbery at sea; and (b) seafarers' wages, allotments and other entitlements must be fully paid during the entirety of any such period. These amendments will be inserted as Standard A2.1.7 and A2.2.7 and to Guideline B2.5.1.8. The full text of the amendments is set out in Appendix 2.

Compliance

26.20 DMLC: implement IOM requirements as set out in Pt I, point 4, and record details of compliance measures in DMLC, Pt II, point 4.

REGULATION 2.2: WAGES

Payment of wages and monthly account

26.21 A shipowner must ensure that a seafarer is paid in full at no greater than monthly intervals and in accordance with their SEA and any applicable

82 MLN 2.1, para 19.
83 2013 Regulations, reg 22(1).
84 2013 Regulations, reg 22(2)(a)–(f).
85 2013 Regulations, reg 22(3).

collective agreement, and given a monthly account of the payments due and the amounts paid, including wages, additional payments and any allotments or deductions permitted, as set out below.[86] However, additional payments, such as for overtime worked, may be made in the monthly pay cycle following that in which they accrue.[87]

If payment has been made in a currency or at a rate different from the one agreed upon, the monthly account must state the rate of exchange applied.[88] Wages must be denominated in legal tender and paid directly to the seafarer's designated bank account unless the seafarer requests otherwise in writing.[89] On termination of employment, all wages due to the seafarer must be paid without undue delay, and in any case no later than the date on which the next payment of wages would have fallen, had the employment not been terminated.[90]

Overtime

26.22 The following definitions apply in the context of overtime:

> '*Basic pay* – means the pay, however composed, for normal hours of work; it does not include payments for overtime worked, bonuses, allowances, paid leave or any other additional remuneration.
>
> *Consolidated wage* – means a wage or salary which includes the basic pay and other pay-related benefits, and may include compensation for all overtime hours worked and all other pay-related benefits, or it may include only certain benefits in a partial consolidation.
>
> *Overtime* means – time worked in excess of the normal hours of work.'[91]

Non-consolidated wage

26.23 Where wages include separate compensation for overtime worked: (a) for the purpose of calculating basic pay, the normal hours of work at sea and in port must not exceed eight hours per day; (b) for the purpose of calculating overtime, the normal hours of work covered by basic pay must not exceed 48 hours per week, except that an applicable collective agreement may provide for a different but not less favourable treatment of the seafarer; and (c) the rate of compensation for overtime must not be less than 1.25 times the basic pay per hour, unless an applicable collective agreement provides otherwise.[92]

86 2013 Regulations, reg 23(1)–(2).
87 MLN 2.2, para 3(a).
88 2013 Regulations, reg 23(3).
89 2013 Regulations, reg 24(3).
90 2013 Regulations, reg 28.
91 MLN 2.2, para 2.
92 2013 Regulations, reg 24(1)(a)–(c).

Fully or partial consolidated wage

26.24 In a fully or partially consolidated wage, as regards overtime worked, either within or beyond the hours to which the consolidated pay applies, the hourly rate must not be less than 1.25 times the basic pay.[93]

Records of overtime

26.25 Where separate compensation for overtime is paid (in relation to a non-consolidated wage or a partially consolidated wage), records of all overtime worked must be maintained by the master (or designated person) and endorsed by the seafarer at no greater than monthly intervals.[94] The records may be kept in electronic format.[95]

Allotment of wages

26.26 Shipowners must provide for seafarers to transmit (by bank transfer or similar means) all or part of their earnings directly to nominated family, dependants or legal beneficiaries, at regular intervals.[96] Such payments should be made monthly at the time the seafarer is due to be paid.[97]

Any charge for allotments must be reasonable in amount and the rate of currency exchange must, unless provided otherwise in any applicable collective agreement or SEA, be at the prevailing market rate or the official published rate and not unfavourable to the seafarer.[98] An example of an official published rate is the mid-rate published in the Financial Times at the last day of the month.[99]

Deductions from wages

26.27 Unless provided otherwise in an applicable collective agreement, the shipowner may only make deductions from a seafarer's wage for: (a) on-board purchases; (b) telecommunication calls and internet access; (c) cash advances; (d) allotments; (e) contributions by the seafarer to a pension fund, charity or a contribution in respect of membership of a body to any trade union or any friendly society; and (f) any other sum authorised by law.[100]

93 2013 Regulations, reg 24(2).
94 2013 Regulations, reg 25.
95 MLN 2.2, para 3(d).
96 2013 Regulations, reg 26(1)–(3).
97 MLN 2.2, para 6.
98 2013 Regulations, reg 26(4).
99 MLN 2.2, para 6.
100 2013 Regulations, reg 27(1)–(2)(a)–(f).

No deductions may be made for obtaining or retaining employment.[101] A shipowner is prohibited from imposing monetary fines upon a seafarer, unless provided otherwise in a collective agreement.[102]

Future amendments to the MLC

26.28 See paragraph 26.19 above regarding the 2018 amendments to the MLC, which are likely to come into force on 26 December 2020.

Compliance

26.29 DMLC: implement IOM requirements as set out in Pt I, point 14, and record details of compliance measures in DMLC, Pt II, point 14.

REGULATION 2.3: HOURS OF WORK AND HOURS OF REST

Minimum hours of rest

26.30 The shipowner must ensure that a seafarer is given at least the minimum hours of rest, which must not be less than: (i) 10 hours in any 24-hour period; and (ii) 77 hours in any seven-day period.[103] Hours of rest may be divided into no more than two periods, one of which must be at least six hours in length, and the interval between consecutive periods of rest must not exceed 14 hours.[104] Although the 'Manila amendments' to the STCW Convention allows state parties to derogate from the latter provision, this has not been adopted by the IOM.[105]

For these purposes, 'hours of rest' means time outside hours of work and does not include short breaks of one hour or less or a break for a meal; 'hours of work' means time during which a seafarer is required to do work on account of the ship.[106]

Musters, fire-fighting and lifeboat drills, or other drills prescribed by statute or international instrument must be conducted in a manner that minimises the disturbance of rest periods and does not induce fatigue.[107] When a seafarer is on call, such as when a machinery space is unattended, they must have an adequate compensatory rest period if their normal period of rest is disturbed by call-outs to work.[108]

101 2013 Regulations, reg 27(3).
102 2013 Regulations, reg 27(4).
103 2013 Regulations, reg 29(1)–(2)(a)(i)–(ii).
104 2013 Regulations, reg 29(2)(b).
105 MLN 2.3, para 1.
106 2013 Regulations, reg 4.
107 2013 Regulations, reg 30.
108 2013 Regulations, reg 31.

Table of the shipboard working arrangements

26.31 A table with the shipboard working arrangements must be posted on board, in an easily accessible place, and for every position it must contain: (a) the schedule of service at sea and service in port; and (b) the minimum hours of rest required in accordance with the 2013 Regulations (as set out above) or any applicable collective agreement.[109]

The table must be in English and be in: (a) the form prescribed in Annex I to MLN 2.3; or (b) any other standardised format, provided it contains the same information as stated in MLN 2.3.[110]

The table may be posted on a computer network that is demonstrably available to all seafarers on board.[111]

Record of hours of rest

26.32 The shipowner must ensure that records of daily hours of rest (in English) are maintained, retained for a period of three years and made available for inspection purposes.[112] The record must be maintained: (a) using the form prescribed at Annex II to MLN 2.3; or (b) in any other standardised format, provided it contains the same information as stated in MLN 2.3.[113] Each seafarer must be given a copy of their record on a monthly basis, which must be endorsed by the master (or authorised person) and by the seafarer.[114] Any breaches of or deviations from the hours of rest must be shown, as well as any compensatory rest periods given in lieu or in advance of any unavoidable minor deviations.[115]

Records may be kept in electronic format, provided that: they are based on the ILO guidelines; each seafarer can access their record and it is secure from unauthorised alterations; there is a means of endorsement by the seafarer and the master; the seafarer can obtain a copy of their record; and the system must be available for inspection by IOMSR inspectors and port state control officers.[116]

Young seafarers

26.33 Subject to the general requirement of all seafarers to work during an emergency, while at sea and in port the following provisions apply to all young

109 2013 Regulations, reg 32(1)(a)–(b).
110 2013 Regulations, reg 32(2)–(3); MLN 2.3, para 3.
111 MLN 2.3, para 3.
112 2013 Regulations, reg 33(1).
113 2013 Regulations, reg 33(1)–(3); MLN 2.3, para 4.
114 2013 Regulations, reg 33(4).
115 MLN 2.3, para 4.
116 MLN 2.3, paras 5.1–5.5.

seafarers: (a) working hours must not exceed eight hours per day and 40 hours per week, and overtime may be worked only if unavoidable for safety reasons; (b) sufficient time must be allowed for all meals, and a break of at least one hour for the main meal of the day must be assured; and (c) a 15-minute rest period as soon as possible following each two hours of continuous work must be allowed.[117]

Exceptionally, those provisions need not be applied when: (a) they are impracticable for young seafarers in the deck, engine room or catering departments who are assigned to watch keeping duties or working on a rostered shift-work system; or (b) the effective training of a young seafarer in accordance with established programmes and schedules would be impaired.[118] Any such exceptions must be recorded, with reasons, and signed by the master.[119]

Subject to the following exception, a young seafarer must not work at night (which must include a period of at least nine hours, starting no later than midnight and ending no earlier than 5am).[120] An exception to strict compliance with the night work restriction may be made when: (a) the effective training of the young seafarer concerned in accordance with established training programmes and schedules would be impaired; or (b) the specific nature of the duty or a recognised training programme requires that the young seafarer concerned perform duties at night and the IOMSR determines, after consultation with the shipowners' and seafarers' organisations concerned, that the work will not be detrimental to the young person's health.[121]

Emergencies

26.34 The master may require any seafarer (including young seafarers) to perform any hours of work necessary for the immediate safety of the ship, persons on board or cargo, or for the purpose of giving assistance to other ships or persons in distress at sea.[122] The master must ensure that any seafarer who has performed work in a scheduled rest period is provided with an adequate period of rest as soon as practicable after the normal situation has been restored.[123]

Exceptions

26.35 The IOMSR has a power to authorise or register collective agreements permitting exceptions to the minimum hours of rest.[124] Any such exception

117 2013 Regulations, reg 34(1)(a)–(c).
118 2013 Regulations, reg 34(2)(a)–(b).
119 2013 Regulations, reg 34(3).
120 2013 Regulations, reg 35(1).
121 2013 Regulations, reg 35(2)(a)–(b).
122 2013 Regulations, reg 36(1)–(2).
123 2013 Regulations, reg 36(3).
124 2013 Regulations, reg 37(1).

must, as far as possible, follow the minimum hours of rest set out above, but may take account of more frequent or longer leave periods, or the granting of compensatory leave for a watchkeeping seafarer, or a seafarer working on board a ship on short voyages.[125]

Master's responsibility

26.36 In addition to the shipowner's duty to ensure compliance with the above requirements, the master must ensure that: (a) watchkeeping officers and ratings are sufficiently rested before taking up any watchkeeping duties; (b) the watchkeeping arrangements are adequate for the maintenance of a safe watch at all times; and (c) the ship does not sail from any port unless those seafarers who will be in charge of a watch immediately after sailing have received rest sufficient to allow them to maintain a safe watch.[126]

A failure to comply with this provision amounts to an offence by the master punishable, on summary conviction, by a fine not exceeding £10,000 or, on conviction on information, by imprisonment for a term not exceeding two years and a fine.[127]

Compliance

26.37 DMLC: implement IOM requirements as set out in Pt I, point 6, and record details of compliance measures in DMLC, Pt II, point 6.

REGULATION 2.4: ENTITLEMENT TO LEAVE

Entitlement to paid leave

26.38 Unless provided otherwise by a collective agreement, seafarers on a Manx ship must be given paid: (a) annual leave calculated on the basis of a minimum of 2.5 days per 30 days of service period; and (b) public holiday leave calculated on the basis of a minimum of 10 days per 12 months of service period.[128] However, a seafarer who derives paid public holiday leave from a collective agreement is not entitled to the paid public holiday leave under the 2013 Regulations in addition, but still must be granted a minimum of 10 days' paid public holiday leave by virtue of any such agreement.[129] For any service periods of less than 30 days or less than 12 months respectively, the leave entitlement must be calculated on a

125 2013 Regulations, reg 37(2).
126 2013 Regulations, reg 38(1)(a)–(c).
127 2013 Regulations, reg 38(2), as amended by Interpretation Act 2015, s 55.
128 2013 Regulations, reg 39(4)(a)–(b).
129 MLN 2.4, para 2.

pro-rata basis, with any fraction of a day being rounded up to the nearest half day.[130] Any agreement to forgo leave with pay is prohibited.[131]

The following provisions only apply to annual leave and public holiday leave derived under the 2013 Regulations, and not to any additional leave.[132]

For the purpose of calculating leave entitlement, the service period must: (a) include the period of time from when a seafarer commences travel to a vessel up until the time of repatriation in accordance their SEA; and (b) be calculated in days and any part of a day must be counted as a full day.[133] However, any paid leave taken during the service period is not to be counted as part of the service period for the purpose of accruing leave.[134]

The level of pay during leave for a seafarer on a non-consolidated wage must be at least the rate of the seafarer's basic pay as stated in their SEA; for a seafarer on a consolidated wage, pay must be made at least at the rate of the consolidated wage, as stated in their SEA. See the definitions of 'basic pay' and 'consolidated wage' in paragraph 26.22 above .[135]

Taking of leave

26.39 A seafarer is entitled to take annual leave in the place with which they have a substantial connection, which will usually be their repatriation destination.[136] The seafarer must not be required, without their consent, to take annual leave in any other place, except as may be provided in their SEA.[137] The time at which leave is to be taken must, unless stated in an applicable collective agreement or arbitration award, be determined by the shipowner after consultation (and, as far as possible, be in agreement) with the seafarer or their representative.[138]

Specified absences not to be counted as paid leave

26.40 Absences for the following reasons must not be counted as paid leave: (a) periods of incapacity for work resulting from illness, injury or maternity; (b) temporary shore leave granted to a seafarer while serving under a SEA; (c) compensatory leave of any kind; (d) travel time to and from the ship; and (e) time spent awaiting repatriation.[139]

130 2013 Regulations, reg 39(5).
131 2013 Regulations, reg 43.
132 2013 Regulations, reg 39(3).
133 2013 Regulations, reg 40(1)(a)–(b).
134 MLN 2.4, para 2.
135 2013 Regulations, reg 41.
136 2013 Regulations, reg 42(1).
137 2013 Regulations, reg 42(2).
138 2013 Regulations, reg 42(3).
139 2013 Regulations, reg 44(a)–(e).

Recalls from leave

26.41 It is prohibited to recall to a ship a seafarer taking annual leave.[140] A seafarer taking public holiday leave may be recalled, but only in cases of extreme emergency and with the seafarer's consent.[141]

Shore leave

26.42 The shipowner must ensure that seafarers are granted shore leave to benefit their health and well-being, subject to the operational requirements of their position.[142] As stated above, temporary shore leave should not be counted as paid leave.

Young seafarers

26.43 Any young seafarer (under the age of 18) who has served six months (or less, if provided for in a collective agreement or their SEA) without leave, on a ship that has not returned to the seafarer's country of residence in that time, must be offered the opportunity of repatriation, at no expense to the seafarer, to the place of original engagement in their country of residence for the purpose of taking any leave earned during the voyage.[143]

Compliance

26.44 Details of seafarers' annual leave (or the method used for calculating it) must be entered in their SEAs.[144]

REGULATION 2.5: REPATRIATION

26.45 A seafarer has the right to be repatriated, at no cost to themselves, in the following circumstances:

(a) if their SEA expires when the seafarer is anywhere other than the repatriation destination stated therein;

(b) upon the expiry of the notice period, given in accordance with the SEA, by the seafarer or the shipowner;[145]

(c) if the SEA is terminated by the shipowner;

140 2013 Regulations, reg 45(1).
141 2013 Regulations, reg 45(2).
142 2013 Regulations, regs 39(2), 44(b).
143 2013 Regulations, reg 46; MLN 2.4, para 8.
144 2013 Regulations, reg 20(f).
145 IOM guidance advises that the right to repatriation is lost in a case where the seafarer leaves the ship, having refused to work their full notice period: MLN 2.5: Repatriation, para 13.

(d) if the SEA is terminated by the seafarer when they are no longer able to carry out their duties under the SEA, or cannot be expected to carry them out in the following circumstances:

  (i) in the event of illness or injury or other medical condition which requires the seafarer to be repatriated when found medically fit to travel;

  (ii) in the event of shipwreck;

  (iii) in the event of the shipowner not being able to continue to fulfil its legal or contractual obligations as an employer of the seafarer by reason of insolvency, sale of ship, change of ship's registration or any other similar reason;

  (iv) in the event of a ship being bound for a war zone as defined by the UK Warlike Operations Committee or by the SEA, to which the seafarer does not consent to go;

  (v) in the event of termination or interruption of employment, in accordance with an industrial award or any applicable collective agreement, or termination of employment for any other similar reason; or

  (vi) if the seafarer terminates their SEA for compassionate grounds or other urgent reasons.[146]

Furthermore, the maximum duration of service on board, following which a seafarer is entitled to repatriation, must be less than 12 months.[147]

A copy of Pt 8 of the 2013 Regulations on repatriation must be carried on board and made available to seafarers.[148]

The IOMSR is also required to facilitate repatriation of a seafarer on a ship in an IOM port and the boarding of their replacement.[149] Furthermore, the IOMSR must not refuse a seafarer's repatriation because of the financial circumstances of the shipowner or the latter's inability or unwillingness to replace a seafarer.[150]

Financial security

26.46 The MLC 2014 amendments on financial security for repatriation of abandoned seafarers (together with those on shipowners' liability) were the first Parts of the MLC to be amended, coming into force on 18 January 2017.

The Merchant Shipping (Maritime Labour Convention) (Amendment) Regulations 2016[151] ('2016 Amendment Regulations') insert reg 57A into the 2013 Regulations, setting out the shipowner's duty to provide financial security

146 2013 Regulations, reg 48(a)–(d)(i)–(iv).
147 2013 Regulations, reg 49.
148 2013 Regulations, reg 57.
149 2013 Regulations, reg 56(6)(a)–(b), respectively.
150 2013 Regulations, reg 56(7).
151 SD 2016/0328.

for repatriation and associated expenses. All Manx ships, to which the 2013 Regulations apply, are required to carry a certificate or other documentary evidence of financial security (which must be in English or accompanied by an English translation) and post a copy in a conspicuous place on board.[152] The financial security system may be in the form of a social security scheme, insurance or a national fund, but must not be in the form of self-insurance.[153]

The full text of the MLC amendments on financial security is set out in Appendix 2, which defines what amounts to 'abandonment', and describes the extent of the liabilities which the financial security must meet, and how they can be accessed. These include: adequate food, accommodation, drinking water, essential fuel for survival on board, necessary medical care, and up to four months arrears of wages.[154]

There is also a detailed account of the UK provisions set out in Chapter 11 at paragraphs 11.9 to 11.11. The IOM's provisions closely follow those of the MLC amendments and the UK, which can be used as a guide to compliance.

Responsibility for arranging repatriation

26.47 The shipowner is responsible for arranging repatriation, which should normally be by air.[155]

There is a prohibition against requiring a seafarer to make an advance payment towards the cost of repatriation or recovering the cost from the seafarer's wages or other entitlements, except if: (i) permitted by any applicable collective agreement; and (ii) the seafarer has been found, in accordance with any applicable collective agreement, to be in serious default of his or her employment obligations.[156]

Although the shipowner is ultimately responsible towards the seafarer for the costs of repatriation, there is no prohibition against the former seeking recovery of such costs under any third party contractual arrangements, where they exist.[157]

Where the shipowner fails in its duty to repatriate a seafarer, the following applies:

(a) if the seafarer is on a Manx ship and is not entitled to receive assistance under the abandonment financial security, the IOMSR must arrange repatriation; if the seafarer is on a Manx ship and is entitled to receive assistance under the abandonment financial security, the IOMSR may arrange repatriation;

152 2013 Regulations, reg 57A(7)(a)–(b), respectively, as inserted by the 2016 Amendment Regulations.
153 2013 Regulations, reg 57A(2)–(3), as inserted by 2016 Amendment Regulations, reg 5(3).
154 2013 Regulations, reg 57A(6), (10), as inserted by 2016 Amendment Regulations, reg 5(3).
155 2013 Regulations, reg 50.
156 2013 Regulations, reg 53(a)–(b)(i)–(ii).
157 2013 Regulations, reg 55.

(b) if a Manx seafarer is on a foreign ship to which the MLC applies, the IOMSR may arrange repatriation.[158]

In such circumstances, the IOMSR is entitled to recover the costs from the shipowner, and has powers to detain its ships for this purpose.[159]

Repatriation destination

26.48 The destinations to which a seafarer is to be repatriated must be one of: (a) the place at which the seafarer agreed to enter into the engagement; (b) the place stipulated by any applicable collective agreement; (c) the seafarer's country of residence; or (d) another place as may be mutually agreed at the time of engagement.[160]

Repatriation costs

26.49 The shipowner must cover the costs of repatriation, until the seafarer concerned is landed at the repatriation destination stated in their SEA, including: passage; accommodation and food; pay; minor ancillary costs connected with the seafarer's relief and maintenance; transportation of 30kg of luggage; and necessary medical treatment until the seafarer is fit to travel.[161] As stated above, a ship must carry financial security to cover these expenses.[162]

Young seafarers

26.50 Seafarers under the age of 18 must be given the opportunity of being repatriated from the first suitable port (at no expense to themselves) if, during their first foreign-going voyage, it becomes apparent they are unsuited to life at sea; in such cases, notification (with reasons) must be given to the authority which issued the papers enabling the young seafarer to take up seagoing employment.[163]

Compliance

26.51 DMLC: implement IOM requirements as set out in Pt I, point 15 (on financial security for repatriation), and record details of compliance measures in DMLC, Pt II, point 15.

158 2013 Regulations, reg 56(1)–(1A) (as substituted by 2016 Amendment Regulations, reg 5(2)), (4).
159 2013 Regulations, reg 56(2)–(3).
160 2013 Regulations, reg 51(a)–(d).
161 2013 Regulations, reg 52(1)–(2)(a)–(f).
162 2013 Regulations, reg 57A, as inserted by 2016 Amendment Regulations, reg 5(3).
163 2013 Regulations, reg 54(1)–(2).

Details of seafarers' entitlement to repatriation, including the destination, must be entered in their SEAs.[164]

REGULATION 2.6: SEAFARER COMPENSATION FOR THE SHIP'S LOSS OR FOUNDERING

26.52 The shipowner must provide a seafarer with adequate compensation in the case of injury or loss, including loss of wages (in accordance with their SEA), for each day of unemployment arising from the ship's loss or foundering.[165]

Unless an applicable collective agreement provides otherwise, the shipowner may limit the compensation for unemployment to two months' basic pay or consolidated wages (whichever applies to the seafarer concerned).[166] No limitation is placed on compensation for injury or any other losses. Such other losses could include personal effects, and 'adequate compensation' is regarded as the industry average based on Protection and Indemnity (P&I) and any collective bargaining agreement allowances.[167]

The above entitlements are without prejudice to any other rights the seafarer may have arising from the ship's loss or foundering.[168]

REGULATION 2.7: MANNING LEVELS

26.53 A ship must have a sufficient number of seafarers on board to ensure that it is operated safely, efficiently and with due regard to security.[169] The manning must be adequate, in terms of size and qualifications, to ensure the safety and security of the ship and its personnel under all operating conditions, and be in accordance with the safe manning document ('SMD').[170]

The detailed requirements are set out in the 2014 Regulations;[171] Part 2 (minimum safe manning) applies to Manx ships of 200 GT or over, engaged on international voyages or operating from a port or between ports in another country;[172] however, the following are excluded: (a) fishing vessels; (b) pleasure vessels; (c) wooden ships of primitive build; (d) warships, naval auxiliaries or other ships owned or operated by a state and engaged only on governmental non-commercial service; and (e) ships not propelled by mechanical means.[173] It is the duty of the

164 2013 Regulations, reg 20(i).
165 2013 Regulations, reg 58(1)–(3), (5).
166 2013 Regulations, reg 58(4).
167 MLN 2.6, para 5.
168 2013 Regulations, reg 59.
169 2013 Regulations, reg 60(1).
170 2013 Regulations, reg 60(2)(a)–(b), respectively.
171 2013 Regulations, reg 60(3).
172 2014 Regulations, reg 3(1)(a)–(b).
173 2014 Regulations, reg 3(2)(a)–(e).

company to ensure compliance with the above provisions, otherwise it (and other defaulting parties, such as a director, manager, secretary, etc) commits an offence and will be liable, on summary conviction, to a fine not exceeding £10,000 or, on conviction on information, to imprisonment for a term not exceeding two years and a fine.[174] It is a defence for the accused to show that they took all reasonable steps to avoid the commission of the offence.[175]

A ship must not proceed to sea without the appropriate SMD; breach of this requirement amounts to an offence by the master punishable, on summary conviction, by a fine not exceeding £10,000 or, on conviction on information, by imprisonment for a term not exceeding two years and a fine.[176] For these purposes, an SMD means: (a) for a ship of 500 GT or over, the SMD required by SOLAS Chapter V, regulation 14; or (b) for a ship of 200 GT or over but less than 500 GT, a Manx minimum safe manning document, issued by the IOMSR.[177] In exceptional circumstances, the IOMSR may grant a written exemption from the requirement to be manned in accordance with the SMD (but not from the requirement to carry an SMD) for a period not exceeding 21 days.[178]

To obtain an SMD, a proposal has to be submitted and approved by the IOMSR, taking into account MSN 052,[179] which sets out the relevant requirements and provides guidance on minimum safe manning scales for deck department, engine room, radio officer and ship's cook, etc.[180] In developing the guidelines, account has been taken of Annex 2 to IMO Resolution A.1047(27).[181]

If any change is to be made to a ship's operational area, construction, machinery, equipment, operation or maintenance which affects its minimum safe manning, a new SMD must first be obtained.[182]

Commercial vessels and pleasure vessels

Vessels in commercial use for sport or pleasure

26.54 These are covered by the Merchant Shipping (Vessels in Commercial use for Sport or Pleasure) Regulations 2014 ('Commercial SP Regulations').[183]

174 2014 Regulations, regs 5 (as amended by Interpretation Act 2015, s 55), 6(2)–(5); the 'company' (defined in reg 4(1)) is, in most cases, likely to be the same person as the MLC 'shipowner', as defined in MLC, Article II, para 1(j).
175 2014 Regulations, reg 6(1).
176 2014 Regulations, reg 8, as amended by Interpretation Act 2015, s 55.
177 2014 Regulations, reg 7.
178 2014 Regulations, reg 8(3)–(4).
179 MSN 052: Minimum Safe Manning Requirements.
180 2014 Regulations, reg 9; MSN 052.
181 IMO Resolution A.1047(27): Principles of Minimum Safe Manning, adopted 30 November 2011.
182 2014 Regulations, reg 10.
183 SD 2014/0415.

26.55 *Isle of Man*

These apply to a Manx vessel of 24 metres or over in load line length used for sport or pleasure which is not a pleasure vessel; they do not apply to a vessel carrying more than 12 passengers.[184] Such vessels must comply with the Large Commercial Yacht Code (LY3 Code), including the IOM's National Annex (MSN 054) thereto.[185] Note that the LY3 Code is being merged into the Red Ensign Group Yacht Code (see para 26.62 below). The legislation listed in Sch 1 to the Commercial SP Regulations (which includes the 2014 STCW Regulations referred to in para 26.53 above) does not apply to such a vessel if it has been examined and certified under s 28 of the LY3 Code.[186]

Pleasure vessels

26.55 Although the MLC does not apply to pleasure vessels, as they are not 'ordinarily engaged in commercial activities', this brief summary has been provided for the sake of completeness.[187] The definition of a 'pleasure vessel' has been set out at paragraph 26.1 above, which describes the various private purposes for which it may be used and still fall within that definition.

The manning requirements for Manx pleasure vessels of 24 metres in load line length and above are set out in MSN 033,[188] although there is no certification regime (like the SMD) applying to them.[189] Such a vessel must not proceed to sea unless it is manned in accordance with MSN 033; a breach amounts to an offence by the master punishable, on summary conviction, by a fine not exceeding £10,000 or, on conviction on information, to imprisonment for a term not exceeding two years and a fine.[190]

The manning scales for yachts up to 3000 GT are provided in the Appendix to MSN 033; any requirement for deviations must be submitted to and agreed by the IOMSR.

Manning requirements in respect of yachts over 3000 GT will be considered on a case-by-case basis.

Foreign ships

26.56 A foreign ship visiting a IOM port may be inspected to verify that the manning and certificates of the seafarers serving on board are in conformity with the applicable safe manning requirements of the ship's flag state.[191] If those

184 Commercial SP Regulations, reg 3.
185 Commercial SP Regulations, reg 7(1)–(2)(a); MSN 054: Isle of Man LY3 National Annex.
186 Commercial SP Regulations, reg 7(4), Sch 1.
187 MLC, Article II(4).
188 MSN 033: Pleasure Vessel Manning.
189 MSN 033, introduction.
190 2014 Regulations, reg 12, as amended by Interpretation Act 2015, s 55.
191 2014 Regulations, reg 30(1)(b).

requirements are not met, the ship may be detained if the inspector determines that it poses a danger to persons, property or the environment.[192]

Compliance

26.57 DMLC: implement IOM requirements as set out in Pt I, point 7, and record details of compliance measures in DMLC, Pt II, point 7.

REGULATION 2.8: CAREER AND SKILL DEVELOPMENT AND OPPORTUNITIES FOR SEAFARERS' EMPLOYMENT

26.58 The MLC requires ratifying states to have policies to promote employment in the maritime sector and to encourage career and skill development and greater employment opportunities for seafarers domiciled in its territory.[193]

The IOM's Department for Enterprise (of which the IOMSR is part), in conjunction with the UK's Maritime Education Foundation, provides limited funding for IOM resident cadets. Recent additional funding from those bodies, in collaboration with V.Group, has led to an increase in cadetships with the latter.[194]

REGULATION 3.1: ACCOMMODATION AND RECREATIONAL FACILITIES

26.59 Manx ships registered with the IOMSR must provide and maintain decent accommodation and recreational facilities for seafarers working or living on board, or both, consistent with promoting the seafarers' health and well-being.[195]

The provisions on accommodation and recreational facilities are set out in detail in Pt 11 of the 2013 Regulations and in MLN 3.1.[196] These closely follow the provisions set out in MLC, Regulation 3.1 and Code, although reference should be made to the IOM provisions as the authoritative standards applying to Manx ships.

Part 11 also contains the transitional provisions, as the MLC standards on construction and equipment do not apply to ships constructed before

192 2014 Regulations, regs 30(3)(b), 31(1).

193 MLC, Regulation 2.8.1.

194 See www.mynewsdesk.com/uk/v-group-limited/pressreleases/isle-of-man-government-funds-five-manx-vgroup-cadets-in-conjunction-with-the-maritime-education-foundation-1882060 [Accessed 18 May 2018].

195 2013 Regulations, reg 62(1).

196 MLN 3.1: Accommodation and recreational facilities.

the Convention came into force for the flag state concerned[197] (which, in the case of the IOM, is 7 August 2014).[198] However, the other provisions on accommodation and recreational facilities do apply to ships constructed before that date.

Transitional provisions

26.60 The transitional provisions are set out below. For these purposes, a ship, including a large commercial yacht, is deemed to have been constructed on the date its keel is laid or when it is at a similar stage of construction.[199] A 'similar stage of construction' means 'the stage at which construction identifiable with a specific ship begins, and assembly of that ship has commenced comprising at least 50 tonnes or 1% of the estimated mass of all structural material, whichever is less'.[200]

Ships (except large commercial yachts)

26.61 For ships constructed before the MLC came into force for the IOM (7 August 2014), the relevant requirements are: for construction and equipment, those set out in the UK's Merchant Shipping (Crew Accommodation) Regulations 1978,[201] as applied by the IOM;[202] and, for recreational facilities, those set out in reg 75 of the 2013 Regulations.[203]

For ships constructed on or after 7 August 2014, Pt 11 of the 2013 Regulations applies.

Large commercial yachts

26.62 Large yachts are those which are 24 metres and over in load line length, and the relevant Large Yacht Code applies to yachts which are in commercial use for sport or pleasure, do not carry cargo and do not carry more than 12 passengers.

For large commercial yachts constructed before 20 August 2013 (the date when the MLC came into force internationally), the relevant requirements for construction

197 MLC, Regulation 3.1.2.
198 Which is the date 12 months after the UK extended the MLC to the IOM.
199 2013 Regulations, reg 62(5).
200 2013 Regulations, reg 61.
201 SI 1978/795.
202 As applied by the Merchant Shipping (Masters and Seamen) (Application) Order 1980 (GC 168/80).
203 2013 Regulations, regs 61, 62(2).

and equipment are as set out in s 21 of LY1[204] or LY2[205] as is applicable to the yacht; for recreational facilities, reg 75 of the 2013 Regulations applies.[206]

For large commercial yachts constructed on or after 20 August 2013, the relevant requirements for construction and equipment are set out in s 21, 21A or 21B of LY3;[207] for recreational facilities, reg 75 of the 2013 Regulations applies.[208]

See Chapter 15 for more information on how LY3, and its 'substantial equivalences', applies to commercial yachts. Note too that the LY3 Code and the Passenger Yacht Code (PYC) are being merged into the 'Red Ensign Group Yacht Code'[209] (REG YC), which comes into force on 1 January 2019.

Health and safety

26.63 To ensure that accommodation for seafarers is safe and decent, in light of the specific needs of the seafarers, ships must also comply with the following health and safety provisions of the 2013 Regulations: Pt 15 (policies and programmes); Pt 16 (vibration); Pt 17 (noise); and Pt 18 (hazardous chemical agents).[210]

Substantial alterations

26.64 Before making any substantial alterations to seafarer accommodation, the shipowner must submit the relevant plans for approval to the IOMSR or recognised organisation; in cases of doubt, the IOMSR will decide if the proposals are 'substantial'.[211]

Exemptions and variations

26.65 The MLC permits flag states to authorise exemptions or variations, particularly in relation to ships of less than 200 GT, less than 3000 GT or

204 Code of Practice for Safety of Large Commercial Sailing & Motor Vessels, 1997: www.cishipping.com/sites/default/files/others/Large%20Yacht%20Code%20%28LY1%29%20%281997%29.pdf [Accessed 18 May 2018].

205 Large Commercial Yacht Code, as set out is MSN 1792 (M), 2007: https://assets.publishing.service.gov.uk/government/uploads/system/uploads/attachment_data/file/295047/msn_1792_edition_2.pdf [Accessed 18 May 2018].

206 2013 Regulations, regs 61, 62(3).

207 Large Commercial Yacht Code, 2012: https://assets.publishing.service.gov.uk/government/uploads/system/uploads/attachment_data/file/444652/LY3_-_Final_Version.pdf [Accessed 18 May 2018].

208 2013 Regulations, reg 61, 62(4).

209 REG YC (January 2019): www.redensigngroup.org/media/2343/reg-yc_january_2019_edition_-_part_b.pdf [Accessed 22 October 2018].

210 2013 Regulations, reg 63(a).

211 2013 Regulations, reg 64.

special purpose ships; a written application must be made for authorisation to the IOMSR.[212]

Inspections

26.66 Inspections must be carried out by the master (or designate), accompanied by at least one other seafarer, at intervals not exceeding seven days to ensure that the seafarer accommodation is clean, decently habitable and maintained in a good state of repair.[213] The results must be recorded in the official log book, be available for review and state: the time and date of the inspection; the name and rank of persons making the inspection; and any findings.[214]

Compliance

26.67 DMLC: implement IOM requirements as set out in Pt I, points 8–9, and record details of compliance measures in DMLC, Pt II, points 8–9.

REGULATION 3.2: FOOD AND CATERING

26.68 The general requirements are that seafarers must have access to good quality food and drinking water provided under hygienic conditions as set out in Pt 12 of the 2013 Regulations.[215] The food and drinking water must be of appropriate quality, nutritional value, variety and quantity which adequately covers the requirements of the ship, having regard to the number of seafarers on board, religious requirements and cultural practices as they pertain to food and the duration and nature of the voyage.[216]

The shipowner must ensure that water provided to the ship does not contain anything which is likely to cause sickness or injury to health or which renders any water unpalatable. In addition, a supply of hot, fresh water and cold drinking water should be provided to any sink, hand wash basin or other washing facilities in a galley.[217] The food must be provided free of charge[218] and the guidance also states that water must be provided free of charge.[219]

212 2013 Regulations, regs 65–66.
213 2013 Regulations, reg 79(1)–(2).
214 2013 Regulations, reg 79(3)(a)–(c), respectively.
215 2013 Regulations, reg 80(1). Guidance on food safety, hygiene, diet and nutrition is set out in MLN 3.2, Pt 2.
216 2013 Regulations, reg 80(2).
217 MLN 3.2, Pt 3, para 6.1; see also Pt 3 for guidance on water, its storage, distribution and directions on maintenance of water systems.
218 2013 Regulations, reg 81.
219 MLN 3.2, key points; para 4.2.

A copy of the UK MCA's 'Code of Safe Working Practices for Merchant Seafarers' must be carried on board; and chapter 23 of the Code contains guidance on 'Food preparation and handling in the Catering Department'.[220]

Catering

26.69 The organisation and equipment of the catering department must permit the provision of adequate, varied and nutritious meals prepared and served in hygienic conditions.[221] Catering staff must be properly trained or instructed for their positions.[222]

Ships' cooks

26.70 A fully qualified cook must be engaged on ships with a prescribed manning of six or more seafarers, if engaged in voyages of more than three days, or more than 36 hours from a safe port.[223] It is prohibited to employ a cook unless they have been trained and qualified (as recognised by the IOMSR) and are competent and have completed training related to practical cookery, food and personal hygiene, food storage, stock control, environmental protection and catering health and safety.[224] In addition, ship's cooks must not be under 18 years old.[225]

Recognised cooks' qualifications include: (1) a National Vocational Qualification (NVQ) Level II in catering and hospitality; (2) a certificate of qualification issued by an MLC state; (3) a certificate of qualification issued by a country that has ratified the ILO Certification of Ships' Cooks Convention, 1946 (No 69); (4) confirmation of having served as a chef in a professional kitchen, commercial yacht or passenger ship and evidence of having completed training in food and personal hygiene, food storage, stock control, and environmental protection and catering health and safety; or (5) confirmation of having served as a ship's cook before the MLC was extended by the UK to the IOM (7 August 2013) and evidence of having completed training in food and personal hygiene, food storage, stock control, and environmental protection and catering health and safety.[226]

For a ship that is not required to carry a fully qualified cook, the person engaged to perform the duties of a cook, and anyone processing food in the galley, must

220 The latest is the 2015 edition, Amendment 1, published in 2017: https://assets.publishing.service.gov.uk/government/uploads/system/uploads/attachment_data/file/671403/CSWPMS_GOV_UK_2017.pdf [Accessed 20 May 2018].
221 2013 Regulations, reg 82(1).
222 2013 Regulations, reg 82(2).
223 2013 Regulations, reg 83(1).
224 2013 Regulations, reg 83(2)–(3).
225 2013 Regulations, reg 83(6).
226 MLN 3.2, paras 1.3.1–1.3.5.

have evidence showing that they have been trained or instructed in areas including food and personal hygiene, handling and storage of food on board ship.[227]

Dispensation

26.71 In cases of exceptional necessity, the IOMSR may issue a dispensation permitting a non-fully qualified cook to serve on a specific ship for a specified period, until the next convenient port of call or for a period not exceeding 30 days, provided that the person is trained or instructed in areas including food and personal hygiene, handling and storage of food on board ship.[228]

Inspections

26.72 Inspections must be carried out by the master (or designate), and at least one other seafarer involved in catering, at intervals not exceeding seven days with respect to: supplies of food and drinking water; all spaces and equipment used for the storage and handling of food and drinking water; and the galley and other equipment used for the preparation and service of meals.[229] The results must be recorded in the official log book, and state: the time and date of the inspection; the name and rank of persons making the inspection; and any findings.[230]

Compliance

26.73 DMLC: implement IOM requirements as set out in Pt I, point 10, and record details of compliance measures in DMLC, Pt II, point 10.

REGULATION 4.1: MEDICAL CARE ON BOARD SHIP AND ASHORE

Access to medical care on board and ashore

26.74 Seafarers have the right to: be covered by adequate measures for the protection of their health, including essential dental care and must have access to prompt and adequate medical care on board and ashore; and be given health protection and medical care as comparable as possible to that which is generally available to workers ashore, including prompt access to the necessary medicines, medical equipment and facilities for diagnosis and treatment and to medical information and expertise.[231] This protection and care must be provided at no cost to the seafarer; it must include measures of a preventive character such as health

227 2013 Regulations, reg 83(4); MLN 3.2, paras 1.4–1.5.
228 2013 Regulations, reg 83(5).
229 2013 Regulations, reg 84(1)(a)–(c), (2).
230 2013 Regulations, reg 84(3)(a)–(c), respectively.
231 2013 Regulations, reg 85(1)(a)–(b), respectively.

promotion and health education programmes.[232] Information can be obtained about occupational accidents, diseases, and fatalities through the IOMSR annual report, flag state and industry publications, to benefit from the lessons learned from such incidents.[233]

Shipowners must ensure that seafarers have the right, at no cost to themselves, to visit a qualified medical doctor or dentist without delay in ports of call, where practicable.[234] The practicability relates to the availability of such services, not the convenience of the ship's schedule.[235] It is also the responsibility of the master to ensure a seafarer can exercise this right; failure to comply amounts to an offence by the master punishable, on summary conviction, by a fine not exceeding £10,000 or, on conviction on information, by imprisonment for a term not exceeding two years and a fine.[236]

Medical doctor and medically trained personnel on board

26.75 The requirement depends on which one of the three categories the ship falls into:

(i) ships which carry 100 or more persons, and are ordinarily engaged on international voyages of more than three days' duration, must carry a qualified medical doctor;[237]

(ii) ships which do not meet the criteria in paragraph (i), and are ordinarily capable of reaching qualified medical care and medical facilities within eight hours, must carry at least one designated seafarer who is competent to provide medical first aid and who (if not a medical doctor) has completed training in accordance with the STCW Convention (Section A-VI/4.1);[238]

(iii) ships which do not fall within paragraph (i) or (ii) must carry at least one designated seafarer who is in charge of medical care and administering medicine as part of their regular duties, and who (if not a medical doctor) has completed training in accordance with the STCW Convention (Section A-VI/4.2).[239]

Access to medical advice

26.76 For the purpose of obtaining medical advice, ships must carry a complete and up-to-date list of radio stations relevant to their area of operation; those which have a satellite communication system must carry an up-to-date and complete list of coast earth stations.[240]

232 2013 Regulations, reg 85(2)(a)–(b), respectively.
233 MLN 4.1, para 1.3.
234 2013 Regulations, reg 86(1)–(2).
235 MLN 4.1, para 1.6.
236 2013 Regulations, reg 86(3)–(4), respectively, as amended by Interpretation Act 2015, s 55.
237 2013 Regulations, reg 87(1).
238 2013 Regulations, reg 87(2)–(3); MLN 4.1, para 1.1.2.
239 2013 Regulations, reg 87(4)–(5); MLN 4.1, para 1.1.3.
240 2013 Regulations, reg 88(1).

Seafarers with responsibility for medical care or medical first aid must be instructed in the use of the ship's medical guide and the medical section of the most recent edition of the IMO's International Code of Signals,[241] so that they are familiar with the type of information needed by the advising doctor, and understand the advice received.[242]

Radio medical advice is available to all ships at sea by contacting HM Coastguard. Advice is provided by two UK designated centres at Aberdeen Royal Infirmary and Queen Alexandra Hospital, Portsmouth, but initial contact should be made with the Coastguard.[243]

The shipowner should provide guidance for rendering aid to other ships in distress. Guidance can be obtained from the IMO's International Convention on Maritime Search and Rescue, 1979,[244] as amended, and the International Aeronautical and Maritime Search and Rescue (IAMSAR) Manual, which should be carried on board.[245]

Medical report form

26.77 The master, on-shore and on-board medical personnel must use either the IOMSR medical report form MR001 as set out in MLN 4.1, or a different form which, as a minimum, contains the same information.[246] The completed form must be kept confidential and only be used to facilitate the treatment of a seafarer.[247]

The following should also be carried: patient health status form, to be used when a seafarer requires medical evacuation (form MR002); and the report of a case of occupational disease to the IOMSR (form OD001), the information in which must also be kept confidential.[248]

Medical care facilities

26.78 Ships must carry a medicine chest, medical equipment and a medical guide, all of which are subject to inspection by the IOMSR or recognised organisation.[249] Compliance with the provisions of the Merchant Shipping (Medical Stores) Regulations 2015[250] ('Medical Stores Regulations') meets these requirements.

241 The latest edition is that of 2005.
242 2013 Regulations, reg 88(2)–(3).
243 MLN 4.1, para 1.2.
244 Adopted 27 April 1979, Hamburg.
245 MLN 4.1, para 1.7.
246 2013 Regulations, reg 89(1)(a)–(b), respectively; Form MR001 is set out in MLN 4.1, Appendix 4.
247 2013 Regulations, reg 89(2).
248 MLN 4.1, para 1.5; Form MR002 is at Appendix 5 and Form OD001 is at Appendix 6.
249 2013 Regulations, reg 90(1).
250 SD 2015/0055; 2013 Regulations, reg 90(2).

The shipowner and the master are responsible for ensuring that the ship is equipped and operated in accordance with the Medical Stores Regulations; a failure to do so amounts to an offence (by the shipowner, master, and other defaulting parties, such as a director, manager, secretary, etc) punishable, on conviction on information, by imprisonment for not more than two years, a fine, or both; or, on summary conviction, by a fine not exceeding £10,000.[251] It is a defence for the accused to show that they took all reasonable steps to avoid the commission of the offence.[252]

The Medical Stores Regulations and MLN 4.1 are extremely detailed; however, the main requirements are:

- a ship which operates no more than 30 nautical miles from the nearest port with adequate medical facilities must carry medical stores of Category C;
- a ship which operates more than 30 nautical miles, but less than 150 nautical miles from the nearest port with adequate medical facilities, must carry medical stores of Category B;
- all other ships must carry medical stores of Category A.[253]

Categories A, B and C medical stores must contain the medicines and equipment in the quantities prescribed in MLN 4.1, unless a qualified medical doctor or pharmacist advises, taking into account the nature of the voyage, on any variations (in which case, written evidence of the advice should be kept).[254]

Additional requirements apply to ships transporting dangerous goods, including the compulsory carriage of a copy of the up-to-date Medical First Aid Guide for Use in Accidents Involving Dangerous Goods (MFAG).[255] Furthermore, ro-ro passenger ships not normally carrying a medical doctor must carry an emergency medical kit or bag (Doctor's Bag) containing the contents specified in the Annex to MSC/Circular 1042.[256]

All ships of: (a) less than 500 GT must carry one first aid kit; and (b) 500 GT or more must carry three first aid kits; the first aid kits must be portable and be stored and equipped in accordance with the requirements of MLN 4.1.[257] For ships of 500 GT or more, kits must be kept in the galley and the engine room, and the other must be in an easily accessible place such as the hospital or on the bridge.[258]

251 Medical Stores Regulations, regs 5 (as amended by Interpretation Act 2015, s 55), 6.
252 Medical Stores Regulations, reg 6(1).
253 Medical Stores Regulations, reg 8(1)–(3), respectively.
254 Medical Stores Regulations, reg 8(4)–(5); MLN 4.1, para 2.2.
255 Medical Stores Regulations, reg 9; MFAG is the Chemicals Supplement to the International Medical Guide for Ships, published by the WHO.
256 Medical Stores Regulations, reg 10; MLN 4.1, para 2.5; IMO MSC/Circ. 1042 'List of contents of the "emergency medical kit/bag" and medical consideration for its use on ro-ro passenger ships not normally carrying a medical doctor'.
257 Medical Stores Regulations, reg 11.
258 MLN 4.1, para 2.3(a).

All ships must carry a copy of the International Medical Guide for Ships published by WHO, or the Ship Captain's Medical Guide published by the UK's MCA.[259]

A medical stores inventory must be maintained on board the ship by the master (or authorised person), and updated each time an item is purchased, disposed of, or used.[260]

There are further provisions on: the storage of medicines and their disposal when expired;[261] controlled drugs;[262] and precautions against malaria.[263]

It is not a statutory requirement to carry an automated external defibrillator but, if carried, it should be maintained in accordance with the manufacturer's instructions, and training should be provided to designated persons.[264]

Annual inspections must be carried out by the master, a medical doctor or a qualified pharmacist.[265]

Compliance

26.79 DMLC: implement IOM requirements as set out in Pt I, point 12, and record details of compliance measures in DMLC, Pt II, point 12.

REGULATION 4.2: SHIPOWNERS' LIABILITY

26.80 The shipowner must provide:

- a seafarer with material assistance and support with respect to the financial consequences of sickness, injury or death occurring while they are serving under their SEA, or arising from employment;[266]
- a financial security system to assure compensation in the event of death or long-term disability of a seafarer due to an occupational injury, illness or hazard.[267]

The entitlements described below are without prejudice to any other remedies the seafarer may pursue.[268]

259 Medical Stores Regulations, reg 13(a)–(b), respectively.
260 Medical Stores Regulations, reg 14.
261 Medical Stores Regulations, regs 15–16; MLN 4.1, paras 2.7–2.8, respectively.
262 MLN 4.1, s 3.
263 MLN 4.1, s 4.
264 MLN 4.1, para 2.11.
265 Medical Stores Regulations, reg 17.
266 2013 Regulations, reg 92.
267 2013 Regulations, reg 93.
268 2013 Regulations, reg 98.

Health protection and medical care

26.81 The shipowner is responsible for the health protection and medical care of all seafarers working on board and must: (a) bear the costs for a seafarer in respect of sickness and injury occurring during the service period (as defined below), or (if occurring after the service period) arising from their employment during the service period; and (b) defray the expense of medical care, including medical treatment, the supply of the necessary medicines, therapeutic appliances and board and lodging away from home until the sick or injured seafarer has recovered or until the sickness or incapacity has been declared of a permanent character.[269]

The 'service period' starts when the seafarer commences travel to their vessel and ends when they are repatriated.[270]

The shipowner's liability to defray the expenses listed in paragraph (b) above may be limited to a period of not less than 16 weeks from the day of the injury or the commencement of the sickness.[271]

The shipowner (or its representative) must safeguard any property left on board by a sick, injured or deceased seafarer, and return it to the seafarer or their next of kin.[272]

Payment of wages

26.82 Where the sickness or injury results in incapacity for work, the shipowner must pay the seafarer:

(a) full wages as long as they remain on board or until they have been repatriated; and

(b) from the time they are repatriated until recovery, their basic pay or consolidated wage, unless an applicable collective agreement provides for other arrangements.[273]

For these purposes, 'full wages' means 'consolidated wages at the rate stated in the SEA for a seafarer on a consolidated wage or for a seafarer on a non-consolidated wage means pay, however composed for the normal hours of work plus any guaranteed overtime, allowances and paid leave at the rate stated in the SEA; it does not include bonuses';[274] 'basic pay' is that for normal hours of work; it does not include payments for guaranteed overtime, bonuses, allowances, paid leave or any other additional remuneration.[275]

269 2013 Regulations, reg 94(1)(a)–(b).
270 2013 Regulations, reg 91.
271 2013 Regulations, reg 94(2).
272 2013 Regulations, reg 94(3).
273 2013 Regulations, reg 95(1)(a)–(b), respectively.
274 2013 Regulations, reg 91.
275 MLN 4.2: Shipowners' liability, definitions.

The amounts payable under paragraph (b) above may be reduced by any sums that the seafarer is entitled to receive in respect of that period in accordance with: (a) any IOM statutory sickness or incapacity benefits; or (b) any laws or arrangements in the country to which they are repatriated.[276]

The shipowner's liability to pay basic pay or consolidated pay for a seafarer no longer on board is limited to a period of 16 weeks from the day of the injury or the commencement of the sickness.[277]

Burial costs

26.83 The shipowner must meet burial expenses in respect of a seafarer who dies on board or ashore during the service period.[278]

Exceptions and limitations to liability

26.84 A shipowner is not liable to bear the costs of a sick, injured or deceased seafarer: if the condition is due to the wilful misconduct of the seafarer; if the condition was intentionally concealed when entering into the engagement; to the extent that the expenses are met by public authorities; and from the time the seafarer can claim equivalent medical benefits under a scheme of compulsory sickness insurance, compulsory accident insurance or worker's compensation for accidents.[279]

Financial security

26.85 The MLC 2014 amendments on shipowners' liability (together with those on repatriation) were the first Parts of the MLC to be amended. Before those amendments came into force on 18 January 2017, the MLC already required ratifying states to ensure that their ships carried financial security to assure compensation in the event of the death or long-term disability of seafarers due to an occupational injury, illness or hazard,[280] which had been implemented by the IOM (and remains in force).[281] However, the MLC amendments introduce much more detailed requirements for the financial security system, as well as further rights for seafarers and obligations for shipowners, in connection with seafarers' 'contractual claims' for compensation for death or long-term disability due to an occupational injury, illness or hazard.

276 2013 Regulations, reg 95(2)(a)–(b), respectively.
277 2013 Regulations, reg 95(3).
278 2013 Regulations, reg 97; MLN 4.2, para 7.
279 2013 Regulations, reg 96(1)–(3).
280 MLC, Standard A4.2.1.1(b).
281 2013 Regulations, reg 93(1), as amended by 2016 Amendment Regulations, reg 8(3)(a).

The full text of the MLC amendments on financial security is set out in Appendix 2. There is also a detailed account of the UK provisions set out in Chapter 18 at paragraphs 18.3 to 18.6. The IOM provisions closely follow those of the MLC and the UK, which can be used as a guide, so only some of the main compliance points are set out below.

The 2013 Regulations have been updated by the 2016 Amendment Regulations to reflect the changes, by the insertion of regs 93(2)–(3), 93A–93B.

Shipowners must provide a financial security system to assure compensation for contractual claims in the event of death or long-term disability of a seafarer due to an occupational injury, illness or hazard.[282] This may be in the form of a social security scheme, insurance or national fund, but must not be a form of self-insurance.[283] Shipowners must put in place arrangements to receive, deal with and impartially settle contractual claims expeditiously and fairly.[284] A 'contractual claim' means 'any claim which relates to death or long-term disability of a seafarer due to an occupational injury, illness or hazard as set out in [Part 14 of the 2013 Regulations], the seafarers' employment agreement or collective agreement'.[285]

A certificate or other documentary evidence of financial security must be carried on board the ship, a copy of which must be posted in a conspicuous place, where it is available to seafarers.[286] It must be in English (or accompanied by an English translation) and contain the information set out in Appendix A4-I to the MLC.[287]

Compliance

26.86 DMLC: implement IOM requirements as set out in Pt I, point 16 (on financial security for shipowners' liability), and record details of compliance measures in DMLC, Pt II, point 16.

REGULATION 4.3: HEALTH AND SAFETY PROTECTION AND ACCIDENT PREVENTION

26.87 The detailed provisions on health and safety are set out in the following Parts of the 2013 Regulations and MLNs: policies and programmes – Pt 15 and MLN 4.3(A); vibration – Pt 16 and MLN 4.3(B); noise – Pt 17 and MLN 4.3(C); hazardous chemical agents – Pt 18 and MLN 4.3(D); and reporting of accidents,

282 2013 Regulations, regs 93(1), 93A(1), as inserted by 2016 Amendment Regulations, reg 8(4).
283 2013 Regulations, reg 93(2)–(3), as inserted by 2016 Amendment Regulations, reg 8(3)(b)–(c), respectively.
284 2013 Regulations, reg 93B, as inserted by the 2016 Amendment Regulations.
285 2013 Regulations, reg 91, as inserted by 2016 Amendment Regulations, reg 8(2).
286 2013 Regulations, reg 93A(4)(a)–(b), as inserted by 2016 Amendment Regulations, reg 8(4).
287 2013 Regulations, reg 93A(6)(a)–(b), as inserted by 2016 Amendment Regulations, reg 8(4).

incidents and occupational disease – Pt 19 and MLN 4.3(E), to which reference should be made for the precise requirements and guidance to achieve full compliance.

More generally, the shipowner must ensure that seafarers are provided (at no cost to themselves) with occupational health protection and that they live, work and train on board in a safe and hygienic environment in accordance with the requirements of Pts 15–18 of the 2013 Regulations.[288] The measures to be taken in carrying out those obligations closely follow the 'general duties' set out in reg 5 of the UK's Merchant Shipping and Fishing Vessels (Health and Safety at Work Regulations) 1997,[289] which are set out in Chapter 19 at paragraphs 19.8 to 19.19.

The following is intended to be a summary of the key compliance points:

- The shipowner must maintain and revise, as appropriate, a written statement of general policy with respect to health and safety, and make it available to seafarers, with any revisions.[290]
- The shipowner must make a risk assessment (to be reviewed as appropriate) to identify: a seafarer at particular risk in the performance of their duties; the measures required to be taken to comply with the shipowner's health and safety responsibilities; and a record of any significant findings to be kept and made available to seafarers.[291]
- The shipowner must conduct a risk evaluation in relation to management of occupational health and safety, and refer to any appropriate statistical information from ships and any general statistics provided by the IOMSR.[292]
- The shipowner must carry out its health and safety consultation and co-ordination obligations with self-employed seafarers, and employers of seafarers who are not employed by the shipowner or its representative;[293] those other employers, or self-employed seafarers, must inform the shipowner of any risks to health and safety arising out of or in connection with their activities.[294]
- Every person working on board must: take care for the health and safety of themselves and others who may be affected by their acts or omissions; co-operate with the shipowner or their employer on health and safety compliance; make proper use of protective personal equipment; not intentionally or recklessly interfere with anything provided for the health and safety of a person on board, etc.[295] Non-compliance with any of the obligations amounts to an offence punishable, on summary conviction, by a fine not exceeding £10,000 or, on conviction on information, by imprisonment for a term not exceeding two years and a fine.[296]

288 2013 Regulations, reg 100(1)–(2).
289 SI 1997/2962.
290 2013 Regulations, reg 100(3)(c).
291 2013 Regulations, reg 101(1)–(3).
292 2013 Regulations, reg 101(4).
293 2013 Regulations, reg 102(1)(a)–(c).
294 2013 Regulations, reg 102(2).
295 2013 Regulations, reg 103(1)(a)–(e), (3).
296 2013 Regulations, reg 103(2) (as amended by Interpretation Act 2015, s 55), (4).

- A safety officer (who may be the master or designate) must be appointed to: take specific responsibility for implementation and compliance with the ship's occupational health and safety policies and programmes; investigate complaints, accidents and carry out inspections (at least every three months) and maintain records; and ensure that, where there is a safety committee on board, records of its meeting are accessible to seafarers.[297] The safety officer must have at least two years' sea service since attaining the age of 18; if the ship is a tanker, this must include at least six months' service on such a ship.[298] If a safety officer fails to comply with their statutory duties, this amounts to an offence punishable, on summary conviction, by a fine not exceeding £10,000 or, on conviction on information, by imprisonment for a term not exceeding two years and a fine.[299]

- A ship with five or more seafarers must elect or appoint a safety representative; a ship with 16 or more seafarers must elect or appoint a safety representative from each department, including the deck and engine departments.[300] Safety representatives have specific powers, including the right to participate (with the safety officer's agreement) in, or carry out, investigations, and to make recommendations; and to request, through the safety committee, an investigation into any work which they recommend to the master should be suspended as they believe it may cause an accident, etc.[301] A safety representative (who must not be the master) must have at least two years' sea service since attaining the age of 18 and, if the ship is a tanker, this must include at least six months' service on such a ship.[302]

- On a ship with five or more seafarers, the master must appoint and chair a safety committee, which must include the safety officer (who could be the master) and every safety representative; every member must be recorded in the official log book.[303] Meetings must be held at intervals not exceeding six weeks and a record must be kept including that of any representations made, with replies and any resulting action.[304]

- The shipowner and the master must facilitate the work of the safety officer, safety representatives and the safety committee in carrying out their occupational health and safety functions, in accordance with the prescribed duties.[305]

- The shipowner must provide seafarers with suitable personal protective equipment (and training on its use), when risks cannot be avoided or sufficiently limited by organisation of work procedures or collective protection measures.[306]

297 2013 Regulations, regs 104–105.
298 2013 Regulations, reg 104(2).
299 2013 Regulations, reg 104(5) (as amended by Interpretation Act 2015, s 55).
300 2013 Regulations, reg 106(1)–(2).
301 2013 Regulations, reg 107.
302 2013 Regulations, reg 106(3)–(4).
303 2013 Regulations, reg 108(1)–(4).
304 2013 Regulations, reg 108(5).
305 2013 Regulations, reg 109(a)–(j).
306 2013 Regulations, reg 110.

- The shipowner must take into account employed seafarers' capabilities as regards health and safety and ensure they are provided with adequate and appropriate safety training and instruction, before being assigned to shipboard duties or being exposed to new or increased risks, as prescribed.[307]

Further measures apply to specific areas of risk, such as:

- The shipowner must carry out a specific risk assessments to assess the level of mechanical vibration, noise and, if hazardous chemical agents are present, any risk to the health and safety of seafarers on board; measures must be taken to eliminate any risk at source or, if this is not reasonably practicable, reduce the risk to a level that is as low as reasonably practicable.[308]

Young seafarers

26.88 There are special obligations in respect of young seafarers (under the age of 18) as follows: the requirement for a specific risk assessment and health assessment;[309] restricted tasks;[310] prohibited tasks;[311] and health education.[312]

Reporting requirements

26.89 There are also requirements to report, to the IOMSR, occupational diseases within seven days of the master receiving written notification from a registered medical practitioner,[313] and accidents, casualties and incidents, in accordance with the Merchant Shipping (Accident Reporting and Investigation) Regulations 2001.[314]

Amendments to the MLC addressing bullying and harassment

26.90 On 8 January 2019, the 2016 amendments to the Guidelines of Regulation 4.3 of the MLC will come into force, the intention of which is to address the issue of bullying and harassment in a health and safety context. The amendments are set out in Appendix 2. Details of how the IOM will implement the amendments have still to be promulgated.

307 2013 Regulations, reg 111.
308 2013 Regulations, regs 117–124 (vibration), 125–134 (noise) and 135–144 (hazardous chemical agents). Detailed guidance on compliance is set out in: MLN 4.3(B) – Vibration; MLN 4.3(C) – Noise; and MLN 4.3(D) – Hazardous chemical agents.
309 2013 Regulations, regs 112–113, respectively.
310 2013 Regulations, reg 114, as amended.
311 2013 Regulations, reg 115.
312 2013 Regulations, reg 116.
313 2013 Regulations, reg 145, Sch 3. Guidance is set out in MLN 4.3 – Reporting of Occupational Accidents, Incidents and Diseases; this contains Form OD001, which should be used, or another containing at least the same information.
314 SD 815/01; 2013 Regulations, reg 146.

Compliance

26.91 DMLC: implement IOM requirements as set out in Pt I, point 11, and record details of compliance measures in DMLC, Pt II, point 11.

REGULATION 4.4: ACCESS TO SHORE-BASED WELFARE FACILITIES

26.92 Due to the low volume of shipping traffic and trading patterns (most ships calling at an IOM port are from the UK or Ireland), the IOM considers that there are no ports in which it is 'appropriate'[315] to establish seafarer welfare facilities.[316] However, seafarers visiting the IOM have access to all public recreational facilities, places of worship and voluntary organisations.[317]

REGULATION 4.5: SOCIAL SECURITY

26.93 Ratifying states are required to ensure that all seafarers and, to the extent provided for in national laws, their dependants have access to social security protection in accordance with the MLC Code[318] (without prejudice to any more favourable conditions which apply nationally).[319] Such states are required to take steps, according to their national circumstances, individually and through international cooperation, to achieve progressively comprehensive social security protection for seafarers.[320] Furthermore, states are required to ensure that seafarers who are subject to their social security legislation and, again to the extent provided for by their national law, their dependants are entitled to social security protection which is no less favourable than that enjoyed by shore workers.[321]

The nine branches to be considered, with a view to achieving progressively comprehensive social security protection for all seafarers ordinarily resident in an MLC state's territory, are extended by the IOM to resident seafarers (in many cases, by the IOM applying UK statutes) as follows: medical care,[322]

315 Ratifying states are required to promote and develop welfare facilities in appropriate ports: MLC, Standard 4.4.2.

316 MLN 4.4 – Access to shore-based welfare facilities, para 1.

317 MLN 4.4, para 2.

318 At some points the MLC Code distinguishes between, on the one hand, seafarers who are ordinarily resident in the state's territory (Standard A4.5.3) and, on the other, those who are serving on a ship registered with the state (Standard A4.5.5).

319 MLC, Regulation 4.5.1. Under Article 19, para 8, of the ILO Constitution, the adoption of any Convention or Recommendation, or the ratification of any Convention by a member, cannot be deemed to affect any law, award, custom or agreement, which ensures more favourable conditions to the workers concerned.

320 MLC, Regulation 4.5.2.

321 MLC, Regulation 4.5.3.

322 National Health Service Act 2001; National Health Services (Overseas Visitors) Regulations 2011 (SD 44/11).

sickness benefit,[323] unemployment benefit,[324] old-age benefit,[325] employment injury benefit,[326] family benefit,[327] maternity benefit,[328] invalidity benefit[329] and survivor's benefit,[330] complementing the protection which shipowners are required to provide under MLC, Regulations 4.1 (medical care) and 4.2 (shipowners' liability), and other titles of the MLC.[331]

The application of these social security benefits has been notified to the ILO in accordance with Standard A4.5(2) and (10).[332]

Compliance

26.94 Details of the health and social security protection benefits provided to the seafarer should be entered in the SEA.[333]

323 Social Security (Incapacity for Work) Act 1994 (applied by GC 508/94); Social Security Contributions and Benefits Act 1992 (applied by GC 505/94); Social Security (Incapacity Benefit) Regulations 1994 (SI 1994/2946) (applied by SD 123/95).

324 Jobseekers Act 1995 (applied by SD 8/96); Jobseeker's Allowance Regulations 1996 (SI 1996/207) (applied by SD 634/96); Social Security (Mariner's Benefit) Regulations 1975 (SI 1975/529) (applied by GC 156/75).

325 Social Security Contributions and Benefits Act 1992 (applied by GC 505/94); Social Security (Contributions) Regulations 2001 (SI 2001/1004) (applied by SD 374/02). Persons reaching state pension age on or after 6 April 2019 will qualify for the new Manx state pension under the Pensions Act 2014 (as applied to the IOM). Those reaching state pension age before that date will continue to qualify for the state retirement pension under the Social Security Contributions and Benefits Act 1992 (as applied by the IOM).

326 Social Security Contributions and Benefits Act 1992 (applied by GC 505/94); Social Security (Industrial Injuries) (Mariners' Benefits) Regulations 1975 (SI 1975/470) (applied by GC 156/75).

327 Social Security Contributions and Benefits Act 1992 (applied by GC 505/94); Child Benefit (General) Regulations 2006 (SI 2006/223) (applied by SD 30/07); Paternity Allowance and Adoption Allowance (General) Regulations 2002 (SI 2002/2822) (applied by SD 43/04); Paternity Allowance (Persons Abroad and Mariners) Regulations 2002 (SI 2002/2821) (applied by SD 43/04); Employed Person's Allowance (General) Regulations 2011 (SD 431/11); Paternity Allowance (Adoption) (Adoptions from Overseas) (Persons Abroad and Mariners) Regulations 2003 (SI 2003/1193) (applied by SD 43/04); Paternity Allowance (Adoption) and Adoption Allowance (Adoptions from Overseas) (No 2) Regulations 2003 (SI 2003/1194) (applied by SD 43/04).

328 Social Security Contributions and Benefits Act 1992 (applied by GC 505/94); Social Security (Maternity Allowance) Regulations 1987 (SI 1987/416) (applied by GC 108/88); Social Security (Maternity Allowance) (Work Abroad) Regulations 1987 (SI 1987/417) (applied by GC 108/99).

329 Social Security Contributions and Benefits Act 1992 (applied by GC 505/94); Employed Person's Allowance (General) Regulations 2011 (SD 431/11).

330 Social Security Contributions and Benefits Act 1992 (applied by GC 505/94). Note that survivors whose spouses or civil partners died on or after 6 April 2017 will qualify for bereavement support payment instead of the earlier bereavement benefit: Pensions Act 2014 (applied by SD 2018/0076); Bereavement Support Payment Regulations 2017 (SI 2017/410) (applied by SD 2017/0140).

331 MLC, Standards A4.5.1, A4.5.3.

332 ILO MLC ratifications page listing social security benefits: www.ilo.org/dyn/normlex/en/f?p=NORMLEXPUB:11300:0::NO::P11300_INSTRUMENT_ID:312331 [Accessed 28 June 2018].

333 2013 Regulations, reg 20(h).

INTRODUCTION TO TITLE 5

26.95 The complete Title 5 of the MLC is set out at Appendix 1, which fully explains MLC flag state and port state responsibilities. It has been annotated with references to the ILO Guidelines on flag state control[334] and port state control.[335]

The UK's Title 5 provisions are described in some detail in Chapter 22. Those provisions may be used as a guide to flag state implementation and port state enforcement.

Set out below is a summary of the main IOM provisions, with references to the key sources, for the benefit of those who need to refer to the precise requirements.

REGULATION 5.1: FLAG STATE RESPONSIBILITIES

26.96 The main provisions are set out in the 2013 Regulations. Guidance is also provided in the relevant MLN.[336]

Inspections and MLC certification

Mandatory certification

26.97 All ships of 500 GT and over which are engaged in international voyages, or operating from a port in another country, or between ports in another country, are required to be inspected for compliance with the 2013 Regulations, for the issue of an MLCert and DMLC.[337] The DMLC, Pt I, will be drawn up by the IOMSR and will list the 16 areas of inspection; the shipowner must complete Pt II, showing the measures that it has implemented to ensure ongoing compliance with the 2013 Regulations.[338]

Voluntary certification

26.98 The owner of a ship not meeting the above criteria may voluntarily put the ship forward for inspection and the issue of an MLCert.[339] If such a ship is

334 Guidelines for flag state inspections under the Maritime Labour Convention, 2006 (published 2009): www.ilo.org/global/standards/maritime-labour-convention/monitoring-implementation-tools/WCMS_101788/lang--en/index.htm [Accessed 5 July 2018].

335 Guidelines for port state control officers carrying out inspections under the Maritime Labour Convention, 2006: www.ilo.org/global/standards/maritime-labour-convention/monitoring-implementation-tools/WCMS_101787/lang--en/index.htm [Accessed 5 July 2018].

336 MLN 5.1.3 & 5.1.4 – Certification, Inspection and Enforcement (Review 2, issued 21 November 2017).

337 2013 Regulations, regs 147–148, 150 (as amended by 2016 Amendment Regulations, reg 10(a)-(b)).

338 2013 Regulations, reg 154.

339 2013 Regulations, reg 147(2). For the provisions on the mandatory (and voluntary) requirements to carry an MLCert and DMLC, see 2013 Regulations, Pt 20. For the provisions on flag state inspection and enforcement, see 2013 Regulations, Pt 22.

not put forward for voluntary inspection, it still must maintain a DMLC, Pts I and II, with Pt II showing how ongoing compliance with the 2013 Regulations is met, albeit that no MLCert is issued.[340] The DMLC will be valid for a maximum period of five years.[341] The IOM is the only REG member which requires ships, which are not required to be certified and are not put forward for voluntary certification, to maintain a DMLC. Shipowners would be as well to opt for voluntary certification, as an MLCert is taken to be prima facie evidence of compliance with the MLC.[342]

Interim certification

26.99 An interim MLCert (valid for a maximum period of six months) may be applied for in the case of new-builds, change of flag or ownership, so long as the prescribed conditions are met.[343]

The model DMLC Pt II is available on the IOMSR website.[344]

Validity of MLCert

26.100 The MLCert will be valid for a maximum period of five years, on condition that an intermediate inspection is carried out between the second and third anniversaries; a new renewal inspection must be carried out for the issue of a new MLCert.[345] However, when the 2016 amendments to the MLC come into force on 8 January 2019, MLC states will have the power to extend the validity for a further period not exceeding five months, following a successful renewal inspection, where the new MLCert cannot be immediately issued to, and made available on board, the ship.[346] Details on how the IOM will implement this amendment have still to be promulgated. The MLC amendments are set out in Appendix 2.

Documents to be carried

26.101 A valid MLCert, DMLC and copies of any inspections or verifications must be posted in a conspicuous place on board that is accessible to seafarers, authorised persons in port states and shipowners' and seafarers' representatives.[347]

A copy of the MLC must also be carried on board.[348]

340 For the provisions on the requirement to carry a DMLC only, in relation to ships which are neither mandatorily required to carry an MLCert nor have been voluntarily put forward for the issue of an MLCert, see 2013 Regulations, Pt 21.
341 2013 Regulations, reg 160(3), as inserted by 2016 Amendment Regulations, reg 11(2).
342 2013 Regulations, reg 149(1); MLC, Standard A5.2.1.2.
343 2013 Regulations, reg 153.
344 DMLC Pt II: www.iomshipregistry.com/media/1577/dmlc-part-ii.pdf [Accessed 7 July 2018].
345 2013 Regulations, regs 149, 151–152.
346 This provision will become MLC, Standard A5.1.3.4.
347 2013 Regulations, regs 155, 166.
348 MLC, Standard A5.1.1.2.

On-board complaint procedure

26.102 An on-board complaint procedure must be made available to seafarers (and they must be given a copy of it) so that they can lodge a complaint alleging a breach of the requirements of the 2013 Regulations and for that complaint to be resolved fairly, effectively and expeditiously.[349] The procedure must seek to resolve the complaint at the lowest level possible, but in all cases the seafarer must have a right to complain directly to the master and, if the seafarer considers it necessary, to the Department for Enterprise and other appropriate external authorities.[350]

Guidance on the procedure and its content is set out in MLN 5.1.5 and Annex.[351]

The IOMSR's preferred method of receiving complaints is by e-mail (marine.mlc@gov.im) or the seafarer can write to: Principal Surveyor, Department for Enterprise Isle of Man Ship Registry, St Georges Court, Upper Church Street, Douglas, Isle of Man IM1 1EX British Isles.[352]

REGULATION 5.2: PORT STATE RESPONSIBILITIES

26.103 See also the ILO Guidelines on port state control.[353]

Inspection

26.104 A foreign ship in an IOM port may be subject to inspection by an authorised officer to review compliance with the relevant requirements of the Articles, Regulations and Part A of the Code to the MLC (including seafarers' rights) relating to the working and living conditions of seafarers on the ship.[354]

A valid MLCert and DMLC are accepted as prima facie evidence of compliance with the requirements, so the inspection must be limited to a review of the documentation.[355] However, a more detailed inspection may be carried out where: the ship is not registered with an MLC state; or in the case of ship carrying MLC documentation, one of the circumstances in MLC, Standard A5.2.1(a)–(d) applies (these are set out in Appendix 1).

349 2013 Regulations, Pt 23; MLC, Regulation 5.1.5 and associated Code.
350 2013 Regulations, reg 178(b).
351 MLN 5.1.5 – On board complaint procedures.
352 MLN 5.1.5.
353 Guidelines for port state control officers carrying out inspections under the Maritime Labour Convention, 2006: www.ilo.org/global/standards/maritime-labour-convention/monitoring-implementation-tools/WCMS_101787/lang--en/index.htm [Accessed 5 July 2018].
354 2013 Regulations, reg 180. For the provisions on inspections in port, see 2013 Regulations, Pt 24.
355 2013 Regulations, reg 181.

In such cases, a more detailed inspection may be carried out to ascertain the working and living conditions on board the ship.[356]

A more detailed inspection may also be carried out where the working and living conditions believed or alleged to be defective could constitute a clear hazard to the safety, health or security of a seafarer, or if the authorised officer has grounds to believe that any deficiencies constitute a serious breach of the relevant requirements of the Articles, Regulations and Part A of the Code to the MLC (including seafarers' rights).[357]

If, following a more detailed inspection, the ship is found not to conform to the relevant requirements of the Articles, Regulations and Part A of the Code to the MLC, and:

(a) the conditions on board are clearly hazardous to the safety, health or security of a seafarer; or

(b) the deficiency constitutes a serious or repeated breach of the requirements (including seafarers' rights),

an authorised officer may detain the ship until any deficiencies that fall within sub-paragraph (a) or (b) above have been rectified or until the authorised officer has accepted a plan of action to rectify the deficiency and is satisfied that the plan will be implemented in an expeditious manner.[358]

All reasonable efforts must be made to avoid a ship being unreasonably detained or delayed.[359]

Onshore complaint procedure

26.105 A seafarer on a foreign MLC ship in an IOM port has the right to report a breach of the requirements of the MLC (including seafarers' rights), in order to facilitate a prompt means of redress.[360] See the generic procedure as set out in MLC, Regulation 5.2.2 and Code (set out in Appendix 1. The contact details for lodging a complaint with the Department for Enterprise are shown at paragraph 26.102 above.

Offences

26.106 The Parts of the 2013 Regulations which implement Title 5 of the MLC create offences for various non-compliances, some of which are set out below.

356 2013 Regulations, reg 182(2)(a)–(d), (4).
357 2013 Regulations, reg 182(3).
358 2013 Regulations, reg 184(3).
359 2013 Regulations, reg 172.
360 2013 Regulations, regs 185–188. The on-shore complaints procedures are set out in 2013 Regulations, Pt 25.

If a Manx ship proceeds, or attempts to proceed, to sea without a valid MLCert (with appended DMLC) or interim MLCert, the master commits an offence.[361] This only applies to ships for which the issue of an MLCert is mandatory and also to other ships which the owner has volunteered for the issue of an MLCert.[362]

In regard to ships for which the carriage of an MLCert is not mandatory and a voluntary request for an MLCert has not been made, it is an offence by the master if the ship proceeds, or attempts to proceed, to sea without a valid DMLC.[363]

It is also an offence:

- to wilfully obstruct an inspector in the exercise of their powers under Parts 20 and 21 of the 2013 Regulations;[364] or
- to take adverse action against a seafarer for lodging a complaint that is not manifestly vexatious or maliciously made.[365]

All of the offences set out above are punishable, on summary conviction, by a fine not exceeding £10,000 or, on conviction on information, by imprisonment for a term not exceeding two years and a fine.[366] If the commission of any of those offences is due to the default of another person, that person is also guilty, and proceedings may be brought against the former, whether or not they are taken against the latter.[367] It is a defence for the person charged to show that they took all reasonable steps to avoid the commission of the offence.[368]

361 2013 Regulations, reg 158.
362 2013 Regulations, reg 147.
363 2013 Regulations, reg 169.
364 2013 Regulations, reg 171(4).
365 2013 Regulations, reg 176(1)–(2).
366 2013 Regulations, regs 158(2), 169(2), 171(4) and 176(2); all of those sub-regs were amended by Interpretation Act 2015, s 55.
367 2013 Regulations, reg 173(3).
368 2013 Regulations, reg 173(2).

PART VIII

Appendices

APPENDIX 1

Title 5: Compliance and Enforcement

INTRODUCTION

A1.1 Due to the generic style of implementing Title 5, it has been decided to reproduce it in full, rather than to set out every aspect of that of each REG member which is subject to the MLC. The Regulations and Standards are mandatory; the Guidelines are non-mandatory, however, flag states must give due consideration to implementing their responsibilities in the manner set out in the Guidelines.[1] The Title 5 provisions have been annotated with references, including to the relevant parts of the Guidelines for flag state inspections under the Maritime Labour Convention, 2006[2] (FSC Guidelines) and Guidelines for port state control officers carrying out inspections under the Maritime Labour Convention, 2006[3] (PSC Guidelines).

The ILO has recently indicated that work will begin to update these guidelines to reflect the amendments that have been made to the MLC.[4]

The FSC Guidelines have been developed to assist flag state administrations to effectively implement their responsibilities with respect to the ship inspection and certification duties under the MLC.[5] However, the flag state's own national laws or regulations, or collective bargaining agreements or other measures implementing the MLC, 2006, should be viewed as the authoritative statement of the requirements in the flag state.[6]

The relevant domestic legislation, merchant shipping notices and key documents for the REG members are listed after the sections on flag state control and port state control respectively.

1 MLC, Article VI, paras 1–2.

2 Guidelines for flag State inspections under the Maritime Labour Convention, 2006, adopted by the Tripartite Expert Meeting, Geneva 15–19 September 2008: www.ilo.org/wcmsp5/groups/public/@ed_norm/@normes/documents/meetingdocument/wcms_099068.pdf [Accessed 5 May 2018].

3 Guidelines for port State control officers carrying out inspections under the Maritime Labour Convention, 2006, adopted September 2008, Geneva: www.ilo.org/wcmsp5/groups/public/---ed_norm/---normes/documents/publication/wcms_101787.pdf [Accessed 5 May 2018].

4 Resolution concerning amendments to the ILO flag State inspection and port State control guidelines to reflect amendments to the Code of the Maritime Labour Convention, 2006, STCMLC/2018, 23–27 April, Geneva.

5 FSC Guidelines, para 1.

6 FSC Guidelines, para 4.

The EU has also enacted limited aspects of Title 5.1 into Directive 2013/54/EU.[7]

TEXT OF TITLE 5

A1.2

'TITLE 5. COMPLIANCE AND ENFORCEMENT

1. The Regulations in this Title specify each Member's responsibility to fully implement and enforce the principles and rights set out in the Articles of this Convention as well as the particular obligations provided for under its Titles 1, 2, 3 and 4.
2. Paragraphs 3 and 4 of Article VI, which permit the implementation of Part A of the Code through substantially equivalent provisions, do not apply to Part A of the Code in this Title.
3. In accordance with paragraph 2 of Article VI, each Member shall implement its responsibilities under the Regulations in the manner set out in the corresponding Standards of Part A of the Code, giving due consideration to the corresponding Guidelines in Part B of the Code.
4. The provisions of this Title shall be implemented bearing in mind that seafarers and shipowners, like all other persons, are equal before the law and are entitled to the equal protection of the law and shall not be subject to discrimination in their access to courts, tribunals or other dispute resolution mechanisms. The provisions of this Title do not determine legal jurisdiction or a legal venue.

Regulation 5.1 – Flag State responsibilities

Purpose: To ensure that each Member implements its responsibilities under this Convention with respect to ships that fly its flag

Regulation 5.1.1 – General principles

1. Each Member is responsible for ensuring implementation of its obligations under this Convention on ships that fly its flag.
2. Each Member shall establish an effective system for the inspection and certification of maritime labour conditions, in accordance with Regulations 5.1.3 and 5.1.4 ensuring that the working and living conditions for seafarers on ships that fly its flag meet, and continue to meet, the standards in this Convention.
3. In establishing an effective system for the inspection and certification of maritime labour conditions, a Member may, where appropriate, authorize public institutions or other organizations (including those of another Member, if the latter agrees) which it recognizes as competent and independent to carry out inspections or to issue certificates or to do both. In all cases, the Member shall remain fully responsible for the inspection and

7 Directive 2013/54/EU of the European Parliament and of the Council of 20 November 2013 concerning certain flag State responsibilities for compliance with and enforcement of the Maritime Labour Convention, 2006, OJ L 329/1, 10.12.2013.

certification of the working and living conditions of the seafarers concerned on ships that fly its flag.

4. A maritime labour certificate, complemented by a declaration of maritime labour compliance, shall constitute prima facie evidence that the ship has been duly inspected by the Member whose flag it flies and that the requirements of this Convention relating to working and living conditions of the seafarers have been met to the extent so certified.

5. Information about the system referred to in paragraph 2 of this Regulation, including the method used for assessing its effectiveness, shall be included in the Member's reports to the International Labour Office pursuant to article 22 of the Constitution.

Standard A5.1.1 – General principles

1. Each Member shall establish clear objectives and standards covering the administration of its inspection and certification systems, as well as adequate overall procedures for its assessment of the extent to which those objectives and standards are being attained.

2. Each Member shall require all ships that fly its flag to have a copy of this Convention available on board.

Guideline B5.1.1 – General principles

1. The competent authority[8] should make appropriate arrangements to promote effective cooperation between public institutions and other organizations, referred to in Regulations 5.1.1 and 5.1.2, concerned with seafarers' shipboard working and living conditions.

2. In order to better ensure cooperation between inspectors and shipowners, seafarers and their respective organizations, and to maintain or improve seafarers' working and living conditions, the competent authority should consult the representatives of such organizations at regular intervals as to the best means of attaining these ends. The manner of such consultation should be determined by the competent authority after consulting with shipowners' and seafarers' organizations.

Regulation 5.1.2 – Authorization of recognized organizations

1. The public institutions or other organizations referred to in paragraph 3 of Regulation 5.1.1 ("recognized organizations") shall have been recognized by the competent authority as meeting the requirements in the Code regarding competency and independence. The inspection or certification functions which the recognized organizations may be authorized to carry out shall come within the scope of the activities that are expressly mentioned in the Code as being carried out by the competent authority or a recognized organization.

2. The reports referred to in paragraph 5 of Regulation 5.1.1 shall contain information regarding any recognized organization, the extent of

8 The 'competent authority' means 'the minister, government department or other authority having power to issue and enforce regulations, orders or other instructions having the force of law in respect of the subject matter of the provision concerned': Article II, para 1(a).

authorizations given and the arrangements made by the Member to ensure that the authorized activities are carried out completely and effectively.

Standard A5.1.2 – Authorization of recognized organizations

1. For the purpose of recognition in accordance with paragraph 1 of Regulation 5.1.2, the competent authority shall review the competency and independence of the organization concerned and determine whether the organization has demonstrated, to the extent necessary for carrying out the activities covered by the authorization conferred on it, that the organization:

    (a) has the necessary expertise in the relevant aspects of this Convention and an appropriate knowledge of ship operations, including the minimum requirements for seafarers to work on a ship, conditions of employment, accommodation, recreational facilities, food and catering, accident prevention, health protection, medical care, welfare and social security protection;

    (b) has the ability to maintain and update the expertise of its personnel;

    (c) has the necessary knowledge of the requirements of this Convention as well as of applicable national laws and regulations and relevant international instruments; and

    (d) is of the appropriate size, structure, experience and capability commensurate with the type and degree of authorization.

2. Any authorizations granted with respect to inspections shall, as a minimum, empower the recognized organization to require the rectification of deficiencies that it identifies in seafarers' working and living conditions and to carry out inspections in this regard at the request of a port State.

3. Each Member shall establish:

    (a) a system to ensure the adequacy of work performed by recognized organizations, which includes information on all applicable national laws and regulations and relevant international instruments; and

    (b) procedures for communication with and oversight of such organizations.

4. Each Member shall provide the International Labour Office with a current list of any recognized organizations authorized to act on its behalf and it shall keep this list up to date. The list shall specify the functions that the recognized organizations have been authorized to carry out. The Office shall make the list publicly available.

Guideline B5.1.2 – Authorization of recognized organizations

1. The organization seeking recognition should demonstrate the technical, administrative and managerial competence and capacity to ensure the provision of timely service of satisfactory quality.

2. In evaluating the capability of an organization, the competent authority should determine whether the organization:

    (a) has adequate technical, managerial and support staff;

    (b) has sufficient qualified professional staff to provide the required service, representing an adequate geographical coverage;

(c) has proven ability to provide a timely service of satisfactory quality; and

(d) is independent and accountable in its operations.

3. The competent authority should conclude a written agreement with any organization that it recognizes for purposes of an authorization. The agreement should include the following elements:

(a) scope of application;

(b) purpose;

(c) general conditions;

(d) the execution of functions under authorization;

(e) legal basis of the functions under authorization;

(f) reporting to the competent authority;

(g) specification of the authorization from the competent authority to the recognized organization; and

(h) the competent authority's supervision of activities delegated to the recognized organization.

4. Each Member should require the recognized organizations to develop a system for qualification of staff employed by them as inspectors to ensure the timely updating of their knowledge and expertise.

5. Each Member should require the recognized organizations to maintain records of the services performed by them such that they are able to demonstrate achievement of the required standards in the items covered by the services.

6. In establishing the oversight procedures referred to in Standard A5.1.2, paragraph 3(b), each Member should take into account the *Guidelines for the Authorization of Organizations Acting on Behalf of the Administration*, adopted in the framework of the International Maritime Organization.[9]

Regulation 5.1.3 – Maritime labour certificate and declaration of maritime labour compliance

1. This Regulation applies to ships of:

(a) 500 gross tonnage or over, engaged in international voyages; and

(b) 500 gross tonnage or over, flying the flag of a Member and operating from a port, or between ports, in another country.

For the purpose of this Regulation, "international voyage" means a voyage from a country to a port outside such a country.

9 The IMO has issued updated guidance in the form of the Annex to the Code for Recognised Organizations (RO Code), Resolution MSC.349(92), adopted on 21 June 2013: www.imo.org/en/KnowledgeCentre/IndexofIMOResolutions/Maritime-Safety-Committee-(MSC)/Documents/MSC.349(92).pdf [Accessed 5 May 2018].

2. This Regulation also applies to any ship that flies the flag of a Member and is not covered by paragraph 1 of this Regulation, at the request of the shipowner to the Member concerned.[10]

3. Each Member shall require ships that fly its flag to carry and maintain a maritime labour certificate certifying that the working and living conditions of seafarers on the ship, including measures for ongoing compliance to be included in the declaration of maritime labour compliance referred to in paragraph 4 of this Regulation, have been inspected and meet the requirements of national laws or regulations or other measures implementing this Convention.

4. Each Member shall require ships that fly its flag to carry and maintain a declaration of maritime labour compliance stating the national requirements implementing this Convention for the working and living conditions for seafarers and setting out the measures adopted by the shipowner to ensure compliance with the requirements on the ship or ships concerned.

5. The maritime labour certificate and the declaration of maritime labour compliance shall conform to the model prescribed by the Code.[11]

6. Where the competent authority of the Member or a recognized organization duly authorized for this purpose has ascertained through inspection that a ship that flies the Member's flag meets or continues to meet the standards of this Convention, it shall issue or renew a maritime labour certificate to that effect and maintain a publicly available record of that certificate.

7. Detailed requirements for the maritime labour certificate and the declaration of maritime labour compliance, including a list of the matters that must be inspected and approved, are set out in Part A of the Code.

Standard A5.1.3 – Maritime labour certificate and declaration of maritime labour compliance

1. The maritime labour certificate shall be issued to a ship by the competent authority, or by a recognized organization duly authorized for this purpose, for a period which shall not exceed five years.[12] A list of matters that must be inspected and found to meet national laws and regulations or other measures implementing the requirements of this Convention regarding

10 It should be noted that ships which do not fall within Regulation 5.1.3, para 1, are still subject to the MLC, and the flag state must verify compliance for all the same requirements as a certified ship: FSC Guidelines, paras 19, 23. Although ships that are not certified will not have a DMLC, inspectors may still find it useful to refer to the national provisions in the DMLC, Part I, as a basic checklist for the matters it covers: FSC Guidelines, para 68.

11 Parts I and II of the declaration of maritime labour compliance, set out at Appendix A5-II to the MLC, have been amended to incorporate areas of inspection 15 and 16 on financial security for repatriation and shipowners' liability respectively, the requirements for which came into force on 18 January 2017. See Appendix 2 of this book for the full text of the amendments.

12 The 2016 amendments to the MLC come into force on 8 January 2019, under which the validity of a maritime labour certificate may be extended by up to a period not exceeding five months where, following a renewal inspection, a new certificate cannot be immediately issued. See Appendix 2 of this book for the full text of the amendments.

the working and living conditions of seafarers on ships before a maritime labour certificate can be issued is found in Appendix A5-I.[13]

2. The validity of the maritime labour certificate shall be subject to an intermediate inspection by the competent authority, or by a recognized organization duly authorized for this purpose, to ensure continuing compliance with the national requirements implementing this Convention. If only one intermediate inspection is carried out and the period of validity of the certificate is five years, it shall take place between the second and third anniversary dates of the certificate. Anniversary date means the day and month of each year which will correspond to the date of expiry of the maritime labour certificate. The scope and depth of the intermediate inspection shall be equal to an inspection for renewal of the certificate. The certificate shall be endorsed following satisfactory intermediate inspection.

3. Notwithstanding paragraph 1 of this Standard, when the renewal inspection has been completed within three months before the expiry of the existing maritime labour certificate, the new maritime labour certificate shall be valid from the date of completion of the renewal inspection for a period not exceeding five years from the date of expiry of the existing certificate.

4. When the renewal inspection is completed more than three months before the expiry date of the existing maritime labour certificate, the new maritime labour certificate shall be valid for a period not exceeding five years starting from the date of completion of the renewal inspection.

5. A maritime labour certificate may be issued on an interim basis:

   (a) to new ships on delivery;

   (b) when a ship changes flag; or

   (c) when a shipowner assumes responsibility for the operation of a ship which is new to that shipowner.

6. An interim maritime labour certificate may be issued for a period not exceeding six months by the competent authority or a recognized organization duly authorized for this purpose.

7. An interim maritime labour certificate may only be issued following verification that:

   (a) the ship has been inspected, as far as reasonable and practicable, for the matters listed in Appendix A5-I, taking into account verification of items under subparagraphs (b), (c) and (d) of this paragraph;

   (b) the shipowner has demonstrated to the competent authority or recognized organization that the ship has adequate procedures to comply with this Convention;

   (c) the master is familiar with the requirements of this Convention and the responsibilities for implementation; and

13 The 2014 amendments to the MLC amended Appendix A5-I on 17 January 2017 to include financial security for repatriation and shipowners' liability, as further areas of inspection. See Appendix 2 of this book for the full text of the amendments.

(d) relevant information has been submitted to the competent authority or recognized organization to produce a declaration of maritime labour compliance.

8. A full inspection in accordance with paragraph 1 of this Standard shall be carried out prior to expiry of the interim certificate to enable issue of the full-term maritime labour certificate. No further interim certificate may be issued following the initial six months referred to in paragraph 6 of this Standard. A declaration of maritime labour compliance need not be issued for the period of validity of the interim certificate.

9. The maritime labour certificate, the interim maritime labour certificate and the declaration of maritime labour compliance shall be drawn up in the form corresponding to the models given in Appendix A5-II.[14]

10. The declaration of maritime labour compliance shall be attached to the maritime labour certificate. It shall have two parts:

(a) Part I shall be drawn up by the competent authority which shall: (i) identify the list of matters to be inspected in accordance with paragraph 1 of this Standard; (ii) identify the national requirements embodying the relevant provisions of this Convention by providing a reference to the relevant national legal provisions as well as, to the extent necessary, concise information on the main content of the national requirements; (iii) refer to ship-type specific requirements under national legislation; (iv) record any substantially equivalent provisions adopted pursuant to paragraph 3 of Article VI; and (v) clearly indicate any exemption granted by the competent authority as provided in Title 3; and

(b) Part II shall be drawn up by the shipowner and shall identify the measures adopted to ensure ongoing compliance with the national requirements between inspections and the measures proposed to ensure that there is continuous improvement.

The competent authority or recognized organization duly authorized for this purpose shall certify Part II and shall issue the declaration of maritime labour compliance.

11. The results of all subsequent inspections or other verifications carried out with respect to the ship concerned and any significant deficiencies found during any such verification shall be recorded, together with the date when the deficiencies were found to have been remedied. This record, accompanied by an English-language translation where it is not in English, shall, in accordance with national laws or regulations, be inscribed upon or appended to the declaration of maritime labour compliance or made available in some other way to seafarers, flag State inspectors, authorized officers in port States and shipowners' and seafarers' representatives.

12. A current valid maritime labour certificate and declaration of maritime labour compliance, accompanied by an English-language translation where

14 The 2014 amendments to the MLC amended Appendix A5-II on 17 January 2017 to include financial security for repatriation and shipowners' liability, as further areas of inspection. See Appendix 2 of this book for the full text of the amendments.

it is not in English, shall be carried on the ship and a copy shall be posted in a conspicuous place on board where it is available to the seafarers. A copy shall be made available in accordance with national laws and regulations, upon request, to seafarers, flag State inspectors, authorized officers in port States, and shipowners' and seafarers' representatives.

13. The requirement for an English-language translation in paragraphs 11 and 12 of this Standard does not apply in the case of a ship not engaged in an international voyage.

14. A certificate issued under paragraph 1 or 5 of this Standard shall cease to be valid in any of the following cases:

    (a) if the relevant inspections are not completed within the periods specified under paragraph 2 of this Standard;

    (b) if the certificate is not endorsed in accordance with paragraph 2 of this Standard;

    (c) when a ship changes flag;

    (d) when a shipowner ceases to assume the responsibility for the operation of a ship; and

    (e) when substantial changes have been made to the structure or equipment covered in Title 3.

15. In the case referred to in paragraph 14(c), (d) or (e) of this Standard, a new certificate shall only be issued when the competent authority or recognized organization issuing the new certificate is fully satisfied that the ship is in compliance with the requirements of this Standard.

16. A maritime labour certificate shall be withdrawn by the competent authority or the recognized organization duly authorized for this purpose by the flag State, if there is evidence that the ship concerned does not comply with the requirements of this Convention and any required corrective action has not been taken.

17. When considering whether a maritime labour certificate should be withdrawn in accordance with paragraph 16 of this Standard, the competent authority or the recognized organization shall take into account the seriousness or the frequency of the deficiencies.

Guideline B5.1.3 – Maritime labour certificate and declaration of maritime labour compliance

1. The statement of national requirements in Part I of the declaration of maritime labour compliance should include or be accompanied by references to the legislative provisions relating to seafarers' working and living conditions in each of the matters listed in Appendix A5-I. Where national legislation precisely follows the requirements stated in this Convention, a reference may be all that is necessary. Where a provision of the Convention is implemented through substantial equivalence as provided under Article VI, paragraph 3, this provision should be identified and a concise explanation should be provided. Where an exemption is granted by the competent authority as provided in Title 3, the particular provision or provisions concerned should be clearly indicated.

2. The measures referred to in Part II of the declaration of maritime labour compliance, drawn up by the shipowner, should, in particular, indicate the occasions on which ongoing compliance with particular national requirements will be verified, the persons responsible for verification, the records to be taken, as well as the procedures to be followed where non-compliance is noted. Part II may take a number of forms. It could make reference to other more comprehensive documentation covering policies and procedures relating to other aspects of the maritime sector, for example documents required by the *International Safety Management (ISM) Code* or the information required by Regulation 5 of the SOLAS Convention, Chapter XI-1 relating to the ship's Continuous Synopsis Record.

3. The measures to ensure ongoing compliance should include general international requirements for the shipowner and master to keep themselves informed of the latest advances in technology and scientific findings concerning workplace design, taking into account the inherent dangers of seafarers' work, and to inform the seafarers' representatives accordingly, thereby guaranteeing a better level of protection of the seafarers' working and living conditions on board.

4. The declaration of maritime labour compliance should, above all, be drafted in clear terms designed to help all persons concerned, such as flag State inspectors, authorized officers in port States and seafarers, to check that the requirements are being properly implemented.

5. An example of the kind of information that might be contained in a declaration of maritime labour compliance is given in Appendix B5-I.

6. When a ship changes flag as referred to in Standard A5.1.3, paragraph 14(c), and where both States concerned have ratified this Convention, the Member whose flag the ship was formerly entitled to fly should, as soon as possible, transmit to the competent authority of the other Member copies of the maritime labour certificate and the declaration of maritime labour compliance carried by the ship before the change of flag and, if applicable, copies of the relevant inspection reports if the competent authority so requests within three months after the change of flag has taken place.

Regulation 5.1.4 – Inspection and enforcement

1. Each Member shall verify, through an effective and coordinated system of regular inspections, monitoring and other control measures, that ships that fly its flag comply with the requirements of this Convention as implemented in national laws and regulations.

2. Detailed requirements regarding the inspection and enforcement system referred to in paragraph 1 of this Regulation are set out in Part A of the Code.

Standard A5.1.4 – Inspection and enforcement

1. Each Member shall maintain a system of inspection of the conditions for seafarers on ships that fly its flag which shall include verification that the measures relating to working and living conditions as set out in the

declaration of maritime labour compliance, where applicable, are being followed, and that the requirements of this Convention are met.[15]

2. The competent authority shall appoint a sufficient number of qualified inspectors to fulfil its responsibilities under paragraph 1 of this Standard. Where recognized organizations have been authorized to carry out inspections, the Member shall require that personnel carrying out the inspection are qualified to undertake these duties and shall provide them with the necessary legal authority to perform their duties.

3. Adequate provision shall be made to ensure that the inspectors have the training, competence, terms of reference, powers, status and independence necessary or desirable so as to enable them to carry out the verification and ensure the compliance referred to in paragraph 1 of this Standard.

4. Inspections shall take place at the intervals required by Standard A5.1.3, where applicable. The interval shall in no case exceed three years.

5. If a Member receives a complaint[16] which it does not consider manifestly unfounded or obtains evidence that a ship that flies its flag does not conform to the requirements of this Convention or that there are serious deficiencies in the implementation of the measures set out in the declaration of maritime labour compliance, the Member shall take the steps necessary to investigate the matter and ensure that action is taken to remedy any deficiencies found.

6. Adequate rules shall be provided and effectively enforced by each Member in order to guarantee that inspectors have the status and conditions of service to ensure that they are independent of changes of government and of improper external influences.

7. Inspectors, issued with clear guidelines as to the tasks to be performed and provided with proper credentials, shall be empowered:

   (a) to board a ship that flies the Member's flag;

   (b) to carry out any examination, test or inquiry which they may consider necessary in order to satisfy themselves that the standards are being strictly observed; and

   (c) to require that any deficiency is remedied and, where they have grounds to believe that deficiencies constitute a serious breach of the requirements of this Convention (including seafarers' rights), or represent a significant danger to seafarers' safety, health or security, to prohibit a ship from leaving port until necessary actions are taken.

8. Any action taken pursuant to paragraph 7(c) of this Standard shall be subject to any right of appeal to a judicial or administrative authority.

9. Inspectors shall have the discretion to give advice instead of instituting or recommending proceedings when there is no clear breach of the requirements of this Convention that endangers the safety, health or

15 A flag state inspector must also be aware of any national determinations, substantial equivalences, exemptions and variations: FSC Guidelines, para 75.

16 Such a complaint could be from various sources, for instance, it could be from a seafarer raising a complaint through the on-board complaints procedure (see Regulation 5.1.5 and Code) or indirectly through their trade union.

security of the seafarers concerned and where there is no prior history of similar breaches.

10. Inspectors shall treat as confidential the source of any grievance or complaint alleging a danger or deficiency in relation to seafarers' working and living conditions or a violation of laws and regulations and give no intimation to the shipowner, the shipowner's representative or the operator of the ship that an inspection was made as a consequence of such a grievance or complaint.

11. Inspectors shall not be entrusted with duties which might, because of their number or nature, interfere with effective inspection or prejudice in any way their authority or impartiality in their relations with shipowners, seafarers or other interested parties. In particular, inspectors shall:

    (a) be prohibited from having any direct or indirect interest in any operation which they are called upon to inspect; and

    (b) subject to appropriate sanctions or disciplinary measures, not reveal, even after leaving service, any commercial secrets or confidential working processes or information of a personal nature which may come to their knowledge in the course of their duties.

12. Inspectors shall submit a report of each inspection to the competent authority. One copy of the report in English or in the working language of the ship shall be furnished to the master of the ship and another copy shall be posted on the ship's notice board for the information of the seafarers and, upon request, sent to their representatives.

13. The competent authority of each Member shall maintain records of inspections of the conditions for seafarers on ships that fly its flag. It shall publish an annual report on inspection activities within a reasonable time, not exceeding six months, after the end of the year.

14. In the case of an investigation pursuant to a major incident, the report shall be submitted to the competent authority as soon as practicable, but not later than one month following the conclusion of the investigation.[17]

15. When an inspection is conducted or when measures are taken under this Standard, all reasonable efforts shall be made to avoid a ship being unreasonably detained or delayed.

16. Compensation shall be payable in accordance with national laws and regulations for any loss or damage suffered as a result of the wrongful exercise of the inspectors' powers. The burden of proof in each case shall be on the complainant.

17. Adequate penalties and other corrective measures for breaches of the requirements of this Convention (including seafarers' rights) and for obstructing inspectors in the performance of their duties shall be provided for and effectively enforced by each Member.

17 Investigations and reports are produced by the Marine Accident Investigation Branch (MAIB) in respect of serious incidents in which a UK ship is involved: www.gov.uk/government/organisations/marine-accident-investigation-branch [Accessed 6 May 2018].

Guideline B5.1.4 – Inspection and enforcement

1. The competent authority and any other service or authority wholly or partly concerned with the inspection of seafarers' working and living conditions should have the resources necessary to fulfil their functions. In particular:

   (a) each Member should take the necessary measures so that duly qualified technical experts and specialists may be called upon, as needed, to assist in the work of inspectors; and

   (b) inspectors should be provided with conveniently situated premises, equipment and means of transport adequate for the efficient performance of their duties.

2. The competent authority should develop a compliance and enforcement policy to ensure consistency and otherwise guide inspection and enforcement activities related to this Convention. Copies of this policy should be provided to all inspectors and relevant law-enforcement officials and should be made available to the public and shipowners and seafarers.

3. The competent authority should establish simple procedures to enable it to receive information in confidence concerning possible breaches of the requirements of this Convention (including seafarers' rights) presented by seafarers directly or by representatives of the seafarers, and permit inspectors to investigate such matters promptly, including:

   (a) enabling masters, seafarers or representatives of the seafarers to request an inspection when they consider it necessary; and

   (b) supplying technical information and advice to shipowners and seafarers and organizations concerned as to the most effective means of complying with the requirements of this Convention and of bringing about a continual improvement in seafarers' on-board conditions.

4. Inspectors should be fully trained and sufficient in numbers to secure the efficient discharge of their duties with due regard to:

   (a) the importance of the duties which the inspectors have to perform, in particular the number, nature and size of ships subject to inspection and the number and complexity of the legal provisions to be enforced;

   (b) the resources placed at the disposal of the inspectors; and

   (c) the practical conditions under which inspections must be carried out in order to be effective.

5. Subject to any conditions for recruitment to the public service which may be prescribed by national laws and regulations, inspectors should have qualifications and adequate training to perform their duties and where possible should have a maritime education or experience as a seafarer. They should have adequate knowledge of seafarers' working and living conditions and of the English language.

6. Measures should be taken to provide inspectors with appropriate further training during their employment.

7. All inspectors should have a clear understanding of the circumstances in which an inspection should be carried out, the scope of the inspection to be

carried out in the various circumstances referred to and the general method of inspection.

8. Inspectors provided with proper credentials under the national law should at a minimum be empowered:

   (a) to board ships freely and without previous notice; however, when commencing the ship inspection, inspectors should provide notification of their presence to the master or person in charge and, where appropriate, to the seafarers or their representatives;

   (b) to question the master, seafarer or any other person, including the shipowner or the shipowner's representative, on any matter concerning the application of the requirements under laws and regulations, in the presence of any witness that the person may have requested;

   (c) to require the production of any books, log books, registers, certificates or other documents or information directly related to matters subject to inspection, in order to verify compliance with the national laws and regulations implementing this Convention;

   (d) to enforce the posting of notices required under the national laws and regulations implementing this Convention;

   (e) to take or remove, for the purpose of analysis, samples of products, cargo, drinking water, provisions, materials and substances used or handled;

   (f) following an inspection, to bring immediately to the attention of the shipowner, the operator of the ship or the master, deficiencies which may affect the health and safety of those on board ship;

   (g) to alert the competent authority and, if applicable, the recognized organization to any deficiency or abuse not specifically covered by existing laws or regulations and submit proposals to them for the improvement of the laws or regulations; and

   (h) to notify the competent authority of any occupational injuries or diseases affecting seafarers in such cases and in such manner as may be prescribed by laws and regulations.

9. When a sample referred to in paragraph 8(e) of this Guideline is being taken or removed, the shipowner or the shipowner's representative, and where appropriate a seafarer, should be notified or should be present at the time the sample is taken or removed. The quantity of such a sample should be properly recorded by the inspector.

10. The annual report published by the competent authority of each Member, in respect of ships that fly its flag, should contain:

   (a) a list of laws and regulations in force relevant to seafarers' working and living conditions and any amendments which have come into effect during the year;

   (b) details of the organization of the system of inspection;

   (c) statistics of ships or other premises subject to inspection and of ships and other premises actually inspected;

(d) statistics on all seafarers subject to its national laws and regulations;

(e) statistics and information on violations of legislation, penalties imposed and cases of detention of ships; and

(f) statistics on reported occupational injuries and diseases affecting seafarers.

Regulation 5.1.5 – On-board complaint procedures

1. Each Member shall require that ships that fly its flag have on-board procedures for the fair, effective and expeditious handling of seafarer complaints alleging breaches of the requirements of this Convention (including seafarers' rights).

2. Each Member shall prohibit and penalize any kind of victimization of a seafarer for filing a complaint.

3. The provisions in this Regulation and related sections of the Code are without prejudice to a seafarer's right to seek redress through whatever legal means the seafarer considers appropriate.

Standard A5.1.5 – On-board complaint procedures

1. Without prejudice to any wider scope that may be given in national laws or regulations or collective agreements, the on-board procedures may be used by seafarers to lodge complaints relating to any matter that is alleged to constitute a breach of the requirements of this Convention (including seafarers' rights).

2. Each Member shall ensure that, in its laws or regulations, appropriate on-board complaint procedures are in place to meet the requirements of Regulation 5.1.5. Such procedures shall seek to resolve complaints at the lowest level possible. However, in all cases, seafarers shall have a right to complain directly to the master and, where they consider it necessary, to appropriate external authorities.

3. The on-board complaint procedures shall include the right of the seafarer to be accompanied or represented during the complaints procedure, as well as safeguards against the possibility of victimization of seafarers for filing complaints. The term "victimization" covers any adverse action taken by any person with respect to a seafarer for lodging a complaint which is not manifestly vexatious or maliciously made.

4. In addition to a copy of their seafarers' employment agreement, all seafarers shall be provided with a copy of the on-board complaint procedures applicable on the ship. This shall include contact information for the competent authority in the flag State and, where different, in the seafarers' country of residence, and the name of a person or persons on board the ship who can, on a confidential basis, provide seafarers with impartial advice on their complaint and otherwise assist them in following the complaint procedures available to them on board the ship.

Guideline B5.1.5 – On-board complaint procedures

1. Subject to any relevant provisions of an applicable collective agreement, the competent authority should, in close consultation with shipowners' and seafarers' organizations, develop a model for fair, expeditious and well-

documented on-board complaint-handling procedures for all ships that fly the Member's flag. In developing these procedures the following matters should be considered:

(a) many complaints may relate specifically to those individuals to whom the complaint is to be made or even to the master of the ship. In all cases seafarers should also be able to complain directly to the master and to make a complaint externally; and

(b) in order to help avoid problems of victimization of seafarers making complaints about matters under this Convention, the procedures should encourage the nomination of a person on board who can advise seafarers on the procedures available to them and, if requested by the complainant seafarer, also attend any meetings or hearings into the subject matter of the complaint.

2. At a minimum the procedures discussed during the consultative process referred to in paragraph 1 of this Guideline should include the following:

(a) complaints should be addressed to the head of the department of the seafarer lodging the complaint or to the seafarer's superior officer;

(b) the head of department or superior officer should then attempt to resolve the matter within prescribed time limits appropriate to the seriousness of the issues involved;

(c) if the head of department or superior officer cannot resolve the complaint to the satisfaction of the seafarer, the latter may refer it to the master, who should handle the matter personally;

(d) seafarers should at all times have the right to be accompanied and to be represented by another seafarer of their choice on board the ship concerned;

(e) all complaints and the decisions on them should be recorded and a copy provided to the seafarer concerned;

(f) if a complaint cannot be resolved on board, the matter should be referred ashore to the shipowner, who should be given an appropriate time limit for resolving the matter, where appropriate, in consultation with the seafarers concerned or any person they may appoint as their representative; and

(g) in all cases seafarers should have a right to file their complaints directly with the master and the shipowner and competent authorities.

Regulation 5.1.6 – Marine casualties

1. Each Member shall hold an official inquiry into any serious marine casualty, leading to injury or loss of life, that involves a ship that flies its flag. The final report of an inquiry shall normally be made public.[18]

18 The UK's Merchant Shipping Act 1995, Pt XI, makes provisions for accident investigations and inquiries. The Marine Accident and Investigation Branch (MAIB) carries out investigations into serious accidents involving UK ships, or foreign ships in UK territorial waters, under the Merchant Shipping (Accident Reporting and Investigation) Regulations 2012 (SI 2012/1743).

2. Members shall cooperate with each other to facilitate the investigation of serious marine casualties referred to in paragraph 1 of this Regulation.

Standard A5.1.6 – Marine casualties

(No provisions)

Guideline B5.1.6 – Marine casualties

(No provisions)

Regulation 5.2 – Port State responsibilities

Purpose: To enable each Member to implement its responsibilities under this Convention regarding international cooperation in the implementation and enforcement of the Convention standards on foreign ships

Regulation 5.2.1 – Inspections in port

1. Every foreign ship calling, in the normal course of its business or for operational reasons, in the port of a Member may be the subject of inspection in accordance with paragraph 4 of Article V[19] for the purpose of reviewing compliance with the requirements of this Convention (including seafarers' rights) relating to the working and living conditions of seafarers on the ship.

2. Each Member shall accept the maritime labour certificate and the declaration of maritime labour compliance required under Regulation 5.1.3 as prima facie evidence of compliance with the requirements of this Convention (including seafarers' rights). Accordingly, the inspection in its ports shall, except in the circumstances specified in the Code, be limited to a review of the certificate and declaration.[20]

3. Inspections in a port shall be carried out by authorized officers in accordance with the provisions of the Code and other applicable international arrangements governing port State control inspections in the Member.[21] Any such inspection shall be limited to verifying that the matter inspected

19 Article V, para 4 provides that 'A ship to which this Convention applies may, in accordance with international law, be inspected by a Member other than the flag State, when the ship is in one of its ports, to determine whether the ship is in compliance with the requirements of this Convention'. It is not only ships registered with ratifying states which are subject to such inspections, but also those which are registered with non-ratifying states, which must not '... receive more favourable treatment ...' than the former (Article V, para 7).

20 The document review is concerned with ascertaining the existence of, and verifying the completeness of, the maritime labour certificate, declaration of maritime labour compliance (Pts I and II) or, where appropriate, the interim maritime labour certificate. If the documents are not complete, the PSCO may determine or consider whether to carry out a more detailed inspection. See PSC Guidelines, paras 52–76.

21 Other international arrangements include: the IMO Procedures for Port State Control (Resolution A.787(19), as amended by the Annex to IMO Resolution A.882(21); ILO MLC PSC Guidelines; the Paris MOU on Port State Control, which covers the waters of the European coastal states and the North Atlantic basin from North America to Europe: www.parismou.org/about-us/organisation [Accessed 11 May 2018]; many of the MLC provisions on port state control have also been implemented into EU law by Directive 2013/38/EU of the European Parliament and of the Council of 12 August 2013 amending Directive 2009/16/EC on port State control, OJ L 218/1, 14.8.2013. There is also the Tokyo MOU on Port State Control, which covers the Asia-Pacific region: www.tokyo-mou.org [Accessed 11 May 2018].

is in conformity with the relevant requirements set out in the Articles and Regulations of this Convention and in Part A only of the Code.

4. Inspections that may be carried out in accordance with this Regulation shall be based on an effective port State inspection and monitoring system to help ensure that the working and living conditions for seafarers on ships entering a port of the Member concerned meet the requirements of this Convention (including seafarers' rights).

5. Information about the system referred to in paragraph 4 of this Regulation, including the method used for assessing its effectiveness, shall be included in the Member's reports pursuant to article 22 of the Constitution.[22]

Standard A5.2.1 – Inspections in port

1. Where an authorized officer, having come on board to carry out an inspection and requested, where applicable, the maritime labour certificate and the declaration of maritime labour compliance, finds that:

   (a) the required documents are not produced or maintained or are falsely maintained or that the documents produced do not contain the information required by this Convention or are otherwise invalid;[23] or

   (b) there are clear grounds for believing that the working and living conditions on the ship do not conform to the requirements of this Convention;[24] or

   (c) there are reasonable grounds to believe that the ship has changed flag for the purpose of avoiding compliance with this Convention;[25] or

   (d) there is a complaint alleging that specific working and living conditions on the ship do not conform to the requirements of this Convention;[26]

   a more detailed inspection may be carried out to ascertain the working and living conditions on board the ship. Such inspection shall in any case be carried out where the working and living conditions believed or alleged to be defective could constitute a clear hazard to the safety, health or security of seafarers or where the authorized officer has grounds to believe that any deficiencies constitute a serious breach of the requirements of this Convention (including seafarers' rights).

2. Where a more detailed inspection is carried out on a foreign ship in the port of a Member by authorized officers in the circumstances set out in

22 Article 22 of the ILO Constitution requires each ILO Member to make an annual report to the ILO on its implementation provisions of Conventions to which it is a party.

23 See PSC Guidelines, paras 52–76.

24 Such grounds may arise during the review of the maritime labour certificate, or the DMLC Pts I and II, or during the preparations for inspections, general impressions, visual observations when on board or during the investigation of a complaint: see PSC Guidelines, paras 67–72.

25 See PSC Guidelines, paras 73–74.

26 In respect of a complaint submitted as part of a PSC inspection, see PSC Guidelines, paras 77–83; in respect of a complaint made by way of the onshore complaints procedure, see PSC Guidelines, paras 109–117.

subparagraph (a), (b) or (c) of paragraph 1 of this Standard, it shall in principle cover the matters listed in Appendix A5-III.[27]

3. In the case of a complaint under paragraph 1(d) of this Standard, the inspection shall generally be limited to matters within the scope of the complaint, although a complaint, or its investigation, may provide clear grounds for a detailed inspection in accordance with paragraph 1(b) of this Standard. For the purpose of paragraph 1(d) of this Standard, "complaint" means information submitted by a seafarer, a professional body, an association, a trade union or, generally, any person with an interest in the safety of the ship, including an interest in safety or health hazards to seafarers on board.[28]

4. Where, following a more detailed inspection, the working and living conditions on the ship are found not to conform to the requirements of this Convention, the authorized officer shall forthwith bring the deficiencies to the attention of the master of the ship, with required deadlines for their rectification.[29] In the event that such deficiencies are considered by the authorized officer to be significant, or if they relate to a complaint made in accordance with paragraph 3 of this Standard, the authorized officer shall bring the deficiencies to the attention of the appropriate seafarers' and shipowners' organizations in the Member in which the inspection is carried out, and may:

   (a) notify a representative of the flag State;

   (b) provide the competent authorities of the next port of call with the relevant information.

5. The Member in which the inspection is carried out shall have the right to transmit a copy of the officer's report, which must be accompanied by any reply received from the competent authorities of the flag State within the prescribed deadline, to the Director-General of the International Labour Office with a view to such action as may be considered appropriate and expedient in order to ensure that a record is kept of such information and that it is brought to the attention of parties which might be interested in availing themselves of relevant recourse procedures.

27 Appendix A5-III sets out the 16 areas of inspection. The PSC Guidelines state: '[para 84] For an authoritative statement of requirements on any issue, reference should be made to the text of the MLC, 2006, and – in so far as they are outlined in a valid Maritime Labour Certificate and attached DMLC – to the national laws or regulations or collective bargaining agreements or other measures implementing the MLC, 2006, that are applicable to the ship concerned. [parat85] Where a ship is not carrying a Maritime Labour Certificate and DMLC (because it is a ship for which certification is not mandatory (Regulation 5.1.3, paragraph 1) and has not requested a certificate or it is a ship of a non-ratifying State), PSCOs will need to use their professional judgement when evaluating compliance with the specific requirements of the MLC, 2006' (see generally paras 84–88). For practical examples of: basic requirements across the original 14 areas of inspection (note that there are now 16); sources of information to verify compliance; examples of deficiencies and non-conformities, see PSC Guidelines, pp 39–64.

28 The complaint could be made through the onshore seafarer complaint-handling procedures, established under MLC, Regulation 5.2.2 and Code, set out below.

29 For guidance on action to be taken by a PSCO when non-conformities or deficiencies are found, see PSC Guidelines, paras 89–108.

6. Where, following a more detailed inspection by an authorized officer, the ship is found not to conform to the requirements of this Convention and:

   (a) the conditions on board are clearly hazardous to the safety, health or security of seafarers;[30] or

   (b) the non-conformity constitutes a serious or repeated breach of the requirements of this Convention (including seafarers' rights);[31]

   the authorized officer shall take steps to ensure that the ship shall not proceed to sea until any non-conformities that fall within the scope of subparagraph (a) or (b) of this paragraph have been rectified, or until the authorized officer has accepted a plan of action to rectify such non-conformities and is satisfied that the plan will be implemented in an expeditious manner. If the ship is prevented from sailing, the authorized officer shall forthwith notify the flag State accordingly and invite a representative of the flag State to be present, if possible, requesting the flag State to reply within a prescribed deadline. The authorized officer shall also inform forthwith the appropriate shipowners' and seafarers' organizations in the port State in which the inspection was carried out.

7. Each Member shall ensure that its authorized officers are given guidance, of the kind indicated in Part B of the Code, as to the kinds of circumstances justifying detention of a ship under paragraph 6 of this Standard.[32]

8. When implementing their responsibilities under this Standard, each Member shall make all possible efforts to avoid a ship being unduly detained or delayed. If a ship is found to be unduly detained or delayed, compensation shall be paid for any loss or damage suffered. The burden of proof in each case shall be on the complainant.

Guideline B5.2.1 – Inspections in port

1. The competent authority should develop an inspection policy for authorized officers carrying out inspections under Regulation 5.2.1. The objective of the policy should be to ensure consistency and to otherwise guide inspection and enforcement activities related to the requirements of this Convention (including seafarers' rights). Copies of this policy should be provided to all authorized officers and should be available to the public and shipowners and seafarers.

30 The PSC Guidelines, at pp 60–63, provide an overview of the MLC provisions on health and safety protection and accident prevention, as well as examples of deficiencies.

31 The PSC Guidelines, at para 98, provide examples of circumstances which could (in the absence of an agreement to a proposed rectification plan) warrant the detention of a ship, either because they are repeated or because of the seriousness of a single instance.

32 The PSC Guidelines, at paras 98–100, provide examples of circumstances that may require detention of the ship. However, the applicable guidelines in the port state concerned will be paramount. The Paris MOU carried out a concentrated inspection campaign (CIC) to ascertain MLC compliance between 1 September 2016 and 30 November 2016. The resulting report shows that a total of 3,674 inspections were performed with the CIC questionnaire on ships targeted for inspection, and 42 ships were detained, representing 1.1% of the total. The principal grounds of detentions were linked with deficiencies in connection with: wages; seafarers' employment agreements; and complaints procedures: www.parismou.org/system/files/Public%20final%20report%20of%20the%202016%20CIC%20on%20Maritime%20Labour%20Convention%202006.pdf [Accessed 20 July 2018].

2. When developing a policy relating to the circumstances warranting a detention of the ship under Standard A5.2.1, paragraph 6, the competent authority should consider that, with respect to the breaches referred to in Standard A5.2.1, paragraph 6(b), the seriousness could be due to the nature of the deficiency concerned. This would be particularly relevant in the case of the violation of fundamental rights and principles or seafarers' employment and social rights under Articles III and IV.[33] For example, the employment of a person who is under age should be considered as a serious breach even if there is only one such person on board. In other cases, the number of different defects found during a particular inspection should be taken into account: for example, several instances of defects relating to accommodation or food and catering which do not threaten safety or health might be needed before they should be considered as constituting a serious breach.

3. Members should cooperate with each other to the maximum extent possible in the adoption of internationally agreed guidelines on inspection policies, especially those relating to the circumstances warranting the detention of a ship.

Regulation 5.2.2 – Onshore seafarer complaint-handling procedures

1. Each Member shall ensure that seafarers on ships calling at a port in the Member's territory who allege a breach of the requirements of this Convention (including seafarers' rights) have the right to report such a complaint in order to facilitate a prompt and practical means of redress.

Standard A5.2.2 – Onshore seafarer complaint-handling procedures

1. A complaint by a seafarer alleging a breach of the requirements of this Convention (including seafarers' rights) may be reported to an authorized officer in the port at which the seafarer's ship has called. In such cases, the authorized officer shall undertake an initial investigation.

2. Where appropriate, given the nature of the complaint, the initial investigation shall include consideration of whether the on-board complaint procedures provided under Regulation 5.1.5 have been explored. The authorized officer may also conduct a more detailed inspection in accordance with Standard A5.2.1.

3. The authorized officer shall, where appropriate, seek to promote a resolution of the complaint at the ship-board level.

4. In the event that the investigation or the inspection provided under this Standard reveals a non-conformity that falls within the scope of paragraph 6 of Standard A5.2.1, the provisions of that paragraph shall be applied.

5. Where the provisions of paragraph 4 of this Standard do not apply, and the complaint has not been resolved at the ship-board level, the authorized officer shall forthwith notify the flag State, seeking, within a prescribed deadline, advice and a corrective plan of action.

6. Where the complaint has not been resolved following action taken in accordance with paragraph 5 of this Standard, the port State shall transmit a copy of the authorized officer's report to the Director-General. The

33 The text of Articles III and IV is set out in Chapter 1 at paragraph 1.12.

report must be accompanied by any reply received within the prescribed deadline from the competent authority of the flag State. The appropriate shipowners' and seafarers' organizations in the port State shall be similarly informed. In addition, statistics and information regarding complaints that have been resolved shall be regularly submitted by the port State to the Director-General. Both such submissions are provided in order that, on the basis of such action as may be considered appropriate and expedient, a record is kept of such information and is brought to the attention of parties, including shipowners' and seafarers' organizations, which might be interested in availing themselves of relevant recourse procedures.

7. Appropriate steps shall be taken to safeguard the confidentiality of complaints made by seafarers.

Guideline B5.2.2 – Onshore seafarer complaint-handling procedures

1. Where a complaint referred to in Standard A5.2.2 is dealt with by an authorized officer, the officer should first check whether the complaint is of a general nature which concerns all seafarers on the ship, or a category of them, or whether it relates only to the individual case of the seafarer concerned.

2. If the complaint is of a general nature, consideration should be given to undertaking a more detailed inspection in accordance with Standard A5.2.1.

3. If the complaint relates to an individual case, an examination of the results of any on-board complaint procedures for the resolution of the complaint concerned should be undertaken. If such procedures have not been explored, the authorized officer should suggest that the complainant take advantage of any such procedures available. There should be good reasons for considering a complaint before any on-board complaint procedures have been explored. These would include the inadequacy of, or undue delay in, the internal procedures or the complainant's fear of reprisal for lodging a complaint.

4. In any investigation of a complaint, the authorized officer should give the master, the shipowner and any other person involved in the complaint a proper opportunity to make known their views.

5. In the event that the flag State demonstrates, in response to the notification by the port State in accordance with paragraph 5 of Standard A5.2.2, that it will handle the matter, and that it has in place effective procedures for this purpose and has submitted an acceptable plan of action, the authorized officer may refrain from any further involvement with the complaint.

Regulation 5.3 – Labour-supplying responsibilities

Purpose: To ensure that each Member implements its responsibilities under this Convention as pertaining to seafarer recruitment and placement and the social protection of its seafarers

1. Without prejudice to the principle of each Member's responsibility for the working and living conditions of seafarers on ships that fly its flag, the Member also has a responsibility to ensure the implementation of the requirements of this Convention regarding the recruitment and placement of seafarers as well as the social security protection of seafarers that are its

nationals or are resident or are otherwise domiciled in its territory, to the extent that such responsibility is provided for in this Convention.

2. Detailed requirements for the implementation of paragraph 1 of this Regulation are found in the Code.[34]

3. Each Member shall establish an effective inspection and monitoring system for enforcing its labour-supplying responsibilities under this Convention.

4. Information about the system referred to in paragraph 3 of this Regulation, including the method used for assessing its effectiveness, shall be included in the Member's reports pursuant to article 22 of the Constitution.

Standard A5.3 – Labour-supplying responsibilities

1. Each Member shall enforce the requirements of this Convention applicable to the operation and practice of seafarer recruitment and placement services established on its territory through a system of inspection and monitoring and legal proceedings for breaches of licensing and other operational requirements provided for in Standard A1.4.

Guideline B5.3 – Labour-supplying responsibilities

1. Private seafarer recruitment and placement services established in the Member's territory and securing the services of a seafarer for a shipowner, wherever located, should be required to assume obligations to ensure the proper fulfilment by shipowners of the terms of their employment agreements concluded with seafarers.[35]

34 Standard A1.4 (recruitment and placement) and Standard A4.5 (social security).

35 It is in the interests of recruitment and placement services (RPS) to take such steps, as they are required to establish a system of protection, by way of insurance or other appropriate measure, to compensate seafarers for monetary loss as a result of the failure by the RPS or the shipowner to meet their contractual obligations to seafarers (Standard A1.4.5(c)(vi)). RPSs must also ensure that shipowners have the means to protect seafarers from being stranded in a foreign port (Standard A1.4.5(c)(iv)); it is therefore advisable to ensure that the shipowner provides a copy of their financial security certificate for repatriation.

APPENDIX A2-I

Evidence of financial security under Regulation 2.5, paragraph 2

The certificate or other documentary evidence referred to in Standard A2.5.2, paragraph 7, shall include the following information:

(a) name of the ship;

(b) port of registry of the ship;

(c) call sign of the ship;

(d) IMO number of the ship;

(e) name and address of the provider or providers of the financial security;

(f) contact details of the persons or entity responsible for handling seafarers' requests for relief;

(g) name of the shipowner;

(h) period of validity of the financial security; and

(i) an attestation from the financial security provider that the financial security meets the requirements of Standard A2.5.2.

APPENDIX A4-I

Evidence of financial security under Regulation 4.2

The certificate or other documentary evidence of financial security required under Standard A4.2.1, paragraph 14, shall include the following information:

(a) name of the ship;

(b) port of registry of the ship;

(c) call sign of the ship;

(d) IMO number of the ship;

(e) name and address of the provider or providers of the financial security;

(f) contact details of the persons or entity responsible for handling seafarers' contractual claims;

(g) name of the shipowner;

(h) period of validity of the financial security; and

(i) an attestation from the financial security provider that the financial security meets the requirements of Standard A4.2.1.

APPENDIX B4-I

Model Receipt and Release Form

referred to in Guideline B4.2.2

Ship (name, port of registry and IMO number): ....

Incident (date and place): ....

Seafarer/legal heir and/or dependant: ....

Shipowner: ....

I, [Seafarer] [Seafarer's legal heir and/or dependant]* hereby acknowledge receipt of the sum of [currency and amount] in satisfaction of the Shipowner's obligation to pay contractual compensation for personal injury and/or death under the terms and conditions of [my] [the Seafarer's]* employment and I hereby release the Shipowner from their obligations under the said terms and conditions.

The payment is made without admission of liability of any claims and is accepted without prejudice to [my] [the Seafarer's legal heir and/or dependant's]* right to pursue any claim at law in respect of negligence, tort, breach of statutory duty or any other legal redress available and arising out of the above incident.

Dated: ....

Seafarer/legal heir and/or dependant: ....

Signed: ....

For acknowledgement:

Shipowner/Shipowner representative:

Signed: ....

Financial security provider:

Signed: ....

* Delete as appropriate.

APPENDIX A5-I

The working and living conditions of seafarers that must be inspected and approved by the flag State before certifying a ship in accordance with Standard A5.1.3, paragraph 1:

Minimum age

Medical certification

Qualifications of seafarers

Seafarers' employment agreements

Use of any licensed or certified or regulated private recruitment and placement service

Hours of work or rest

Manning levels for the ship

Accommodation

On-board recreational facilities

Food and catering

Health and safety and accident prevention

On-board medical care

On-board complaint procedures

Payment of wages

Financial security for repatriation

Financial security relating to shipowners' liability

APPENDIX A5-II

Maritime Labour Certificate

(Note: This Certificate shall have a Declaration of Maritime Labour Compliance attached)

Issued under the provisions of Article V and Title 5 of the Maritime Labour Convention, 2006 (referred to below as "the Convention")

under the authority of the Government of:

....

(full designation of the State whose flag the ship is entitled to fly)

by ....

(full designation and address of the competent authority or recognized organization duly authorized under the provisions of the Convention)

Particulars of the ship

Name of ship ....

Distinctive number or letters ....

Port of registry ....

Date of registry ....

Gross tonnage[36] ....

IMO number ....

Type of ship ....

Name and address of the shipowner[37] ....

....

....

This is to certify:

1. That this ship has been inspected and verified to be in compliance with the requirements of the Convention, and the provisions of the attached Declaration of Maritime Labour Compliance.

2. That the seafarers' working and living conditions specified in Appendix A5-I of the Convention were found to correspond to the abovementioned country's national requirements implementing the Convention. These

36 For ships covered by the tonnage measurement interim scheme adopted by the IMO, the gross tonnage is that which is included in the **REMARKS** column of the International Tonnage Certificate (1969). See Article II(1)(c) of the Convention.

37 *Shipowner* means the owner of the ship or another organization or person, such as the manager, agent or bareboat charterer, who has assumed the responsibility for the operation of the ship from the owner and who, on assuming such responsibility, has agreed to take over the duties and responsibilities imposed on shipowners in accordance with this Convention, regardless of whether any other organizations or persons fulfil certain of the duties or responsibilities on behalf of the shipowner. See Article II(1)(j) of the Convention.

national requirements are summarized in the Declaration of Maritime Labour Compliance, Part I.

This Certificate is valid until .... subject to inspections in accordance with Standards A5.1.3 and A5.1.4 of the Convention.

This Certificate is valid only when the Declaration of Maritime Labour Compliance issued

at .... on .... is attached.

Completion date of the inspection on which this Certificate is based was ....

....

Issued at .... on ....

Signature of the duly authorized official issuing the Certificate

(Seal or stamp of issuing authority, as appropriate)

Endorsements for mandatory intermediate inspection and, if required, any additional inspection

This is to certify that the ship was inspected in accordance with Standards A5.1.3 and A5.1.4 of the Convention and that the seafarers' working and living conditions specified in Appendix A5-I of the Convention were found to correspond to the abovementioned country's national requirements implementing the Convention.

Intermediate inspection:	Signed ....
(to be completed between the second and third anniversary dates)	(Signature of authorized official)
	....
	Place ....
	Date ....
	(Seal or stamp of the authority, as appropriate)

Additional endorsements (if required)

This is to certify that the ship was the subject of an additional inspection for the purpose of verifying that the ship continued to be in compliance with the national requirements implementing the Convention, as required by Standard A3.1, paragraph 3, of the Convention (re-registration or substantial alteration of accommodation) or for other reasons.

Additional inspection:	Signed ....
(if required)	(Signature of authorized official)
	....
	Place ....
	Date ....
	(Seal or stamp of the authority, as appropriate)

Additional inspection:	Signed ....
(if required)	(Signature of authorized official)
	....
	Place ....
	Date ....
	(Seal or stamp of the authority, as appropriate)
Additional inspection:	Signed ....
(if required)	(Signature of authorized official)
	....
	Place ....
	Date ....
	(Seal or stamp of the authority, as appropriate)

Maritime Labour Convention, 2006

Declaration of Maritime Labour Compliance – Part I

(Note: This Declaration must be attached to the ship's Maritime Labour Certificate)

Issued under the authority of: .... *(insert name of competent authority as defined in Article II, paragraph 1(a), of the Convention)*

With respect to the provisions of the Maritime Labour Convention, 2006, the following referenced ship:

Name of ship	IMO number	Gross tonnage

is maintained in accordance with Standard A5.1.3 of the Convention.

The undersigned declares, on behalf of the abovementioned competent authority, that:

(a) the provisions of the Maritime Labour Convention are fully embodied in the national requirements referred to below;

(b) these national requirements are contained in the national provisions referenced below; explanations concerning the content of those provisions are provided where necessary;

(c) the details of any substantial equivalencies under Article VI, paragraphs 3 and 4, are provided <under the corresponding national requirement listed below> <in the section provided for this purpose below> *(strike out the statement which is not applicable);*

(d) any exemptions granted by the competent authority in accordance with Title 3 are clearly indicated in the section provided for this purpose below; and

(e) any ship-type specific requirements under national legislation are also referenced under the requirements concerned.

1. Minimum age (Regulation 1.1)
2. Medical certification (Regulation 1.2)
3. Qualifications of seafarers (Regulation 1.3)
4. Seafarers' employment agreements (Regulation 2.1)
5. Use of any licensed or certified or regulated private recruitment and placement service (Regulation 1.4)
6. Hours of work or rest (Regulation 2.3)
7. Manning levels for the ship (Regulation 2.7)
8. Accommodation (Regulation 3.1)
9. On-board recreational facilities (Regulation 3.1))
10. Food and catering (Regulation 3.2)
11. Health and safety and accident prevention (Regulation 4.3)

12. On-board medical care (Regulation 4.1)
13. On-board complaint procedures (Regulation 5.1.5)
14. Payment of wages (Regulation 2.2)
15. Financial security for repatriation (Regulation 2.5)
16. Financial security relating to shipowners' liability (Regulation 4.2)

Name: ....
Title: ....
Signature: ....
Place ....
Date ....
(Seal or stamp of the authority, as appropriate)

Substantial equivalencies

(Note: Strike out the statement which is not applicable)

The following substantial equivalencies, as provided under Article VI, paragraphs 3 and 4, of the Convention, except where stated above, are noted *(insert description if applicable):*

No equivalency has been granted.

Name: ....
Title: ....
Signature: ....
Place ....
Date ....
(Seal or stamp of the authority, as appropriate)

Exemptions

(Note: Strike out the statement which is not applicable)

The following exemptions granted by the competent authority as provided in Title 3 of the Convention are noted:

No exemption has been granted.

Name: ....
Title: ....
Signature: ....
Place ....
Date ....
(Seal or stamp of the authority, as appropriate)

Declaration of Maritime Labour Compliance – Part II

Measures adopted to ensure ongoing compliance between inspections

The following measures have been drawn up by the shipowner, named in the Maritime Labour Certificate to which this Declaration is attached, to ensure ongoing compliance between inspections:

(State below the measures drawn up to ensure compliance with each of the items in Part I)

1. Minimum age (Regulation 1.1) ☐

   ....

2. Medical certification (Regulation 1.2) ☐

   ....

3. Qualifications or seafarers (Regulation 1.3) ☐

   ....

4. Seafarers' employment agreements (Regulation 2.1) ☐

   ....

5. Use of any licensed or certified or regulated private recruitment and placement service (Regulation 1.4) ☐

   ....

6. Hours of work or rest (Regulation 2.3) ☐

   ....

7. Manning levels for the ship (Regulation 2.7) ☐

   ....

8. Accommodation (Regulation 3.1) ☐

   ....

9. On-board recreational facilities (Regulation 3.1) ☐

   ....

10. Food and catering (Regulation 3.2) ☐

    ....

11. Health and safety and accident prevention (Regulation 4.3) ☐

    ....

12. On-board medical care (Regulation 4.1) ☐

    ....

13. On-board complaint procedures (Regulation 5.1.5) ☐

    ....

14. Payment of wages (Regulation 2.2) ☐

    ....

15. Financial security for repatriation (Regulation 2.5) ☐

    ....

16. Financial security relating to shipowners' liability (Regulation 4.2) ☐

    ....

A1.2 *Title 5: Compliance and Enforcement*

I hereby certify that the above measures have been drawn up to ensure ongoing compliance, between inspections, with the requirements listed in Part I.

Name of shipowner:[38] ....

....

Company address: ....

....

Name of the authorized signatory:

....

Title: ....

....

Signature of the authorized signatory:

....

Date: ....

(Stamp or seal of the shipowner[1])

The above measures have been reviewed by *(insert name of competent authority or duly recognized organization)* and, following inspection of the ship, have been determined as meeting the purposes set out under Standard A5.1.3, paragraph 10(b), regarding measures to ensure initial and ongoing compliance with the requirements set out in Part I of this Declaration.

Name: ....

Title: ....

Address: ....

....

....

Signature: ....

Place ....

Date ....

(Seal or stamp of the authority, as appropriate)

38 *Shipowner* means the owner of the ship or another organization or person, such as the manager, agent or bareboat charterer, who has assumed the responsibility for the operation of the ship from the owner and who, on assuming such responsibility, has agreed to take over the duties and responsibilities imposed on shipowners in accordance with this Convention, regardless of whether any other organizations or persons fulfil certain of the duties or responsibilities on behalf of the shipowner. See Article II(1)(j) of the Convention.

Interim Maritime Labour Certificate

Issued under the provisions of Article V and Title 5 of the Maritime Labour Convention, 2006 (referred to below as "the Convention")

under the authority of the Government of:

....

(full designation of the State whose flag the ship is entitled to fly)

by ....

(full designation and address of the competent authority or recognized organization duly authorized under the provisions of the Convention)

Particulars of the ship

Name of ship ....

Distinctive number or letters ....

Port of registry ....

Date of registry ....

Gross tonnage[39] ....

IMO number ....

Type of ship ....

Name and address of the shipowner[40] ....

This is to certify, for the purposes of Standard A5.1.3, paragraph 7, of the Convention, that:

(a) this ship has been inspected, as far as reasonable and practicable, for the matters listed in Appendix A5-I to the Convention, taking into account verification of items under (b), (c) and (d) below;

(b) the shipowner has demonstrated to the competent authority or recognized organization that the ship has adequate procedures to comply with the Convention;

(c) the master is familiar with the requirements of the Convention and the responsibilities for implementation; and

(d) relevant information has been submitted to the competent authority or recognized organization to produce a Declaration of Maritime Labour Compliance.

39 For ships covered by the tonnage measurement interim scheme adopted by the **IMO,** the gross tonnage is that which is included in the **REMARKS** column of the International Tonnage Certificate (1969). See Article II(1)(c) of the Convention.

40 *Shipowner* means the owner of the ship or another organization or person , such as the manager, agent or bareboat charterer, who has assumed the responsibility for the operation of the ship from the owner and who, on assuming such responsibility, has agreed to take over the duties and responsibilities imposed on shipowners in accordance with this Convention , regardless of whether any other organizations or persons fulfil certain of the duties or responsibilities on behalf of the shipowner. See Article II(1)(j) of the Convention.

A1.2 *Title 5: Compliance and Enforcement*

This Certificate is valid until .... subject to inspections in accordance with Standards A5.1.3 and A5.1.4.

Completion date of the inspection referred to under (a) above was..................

Issued at .... on ....

Signature of the duly authorized official
issuing the interim certificate ....

(Seal or stamp of issuing authority, as appropriate)

APPENDIX A5-III

General areas that are subject to a detailed inspection by an authorized officer in a port of a Member carrying out a port State inspection pursuant to Standard A5.2.1:

Minimum age

Medical certification

Qualifications of seafarers

Seafarers' employment agreements

Use of any licensed or certified or regulated private recruitment and placement service

Hours of work or rest

Manning levels for the ship

Accommodation

On-board recreational facilities

Food and catering

Health and safety and accident prevention

On-board medical care

On-board complaint procedures

Payment of wages

Financial security for repatriation

Financial security relating to shipowners' liability

APPENDIX B5-I – EXAMPLE OF A NATIONAL DECLARATION

See Guideline B5.1.3, paragraph 5

Maritime Labour Convention, 2006

Declaration of Maritime Labour Compliance – Part I

(Note: This Declaration must be attached to the ship's Maritime Labour Certificate)

Issued under the authority of: **The Ministry of Maritime Transport of Xxxxxx**

With respect to the provisions of the Maritime Labour Convention, 2006, the following referenced ship:

Name of ship	**IMO number**	**Gross tonnage**
M.S. EXAMPLE	12345	1,000

is maintained in accordance with Standard A5.1.3 of the Convention.

The undersigned declares, on behalf of the abovementioned competent authority, that:

(a) the provisions of the Maritime Labour Convention are fully embodied in the national requirements referred to below;

(b) these national requirements are contained in the national provisions referenced below; explanations concerning the content of those provisions are provided where necessary;

(c) the details of any substantial equivalencies under Article VI, paragraphs 3 and 4, are provided <under the corresponding national requirement listed below> <in the section provided for this purpose below> *(strike out the statement which is not applicable);*

(d) any exemptions granted by the competent authority in accordance with Title 3 are clearly indicated in the section provided for this purpose below; and

(e) any ship-type specific requirements under national legislation are also referenced under the requirements concerned.

1. Minimum age (Regulation 1.1)

Shipping Law, No. 123 of 1905, as amended ("Law"), Chapter X; Shipping Regulations ("Regulations"), 2006, Rules 1111-1222.

Minimum ages are those referred to in the Convention

"Night" means 9 p.m. to 6 a.m. unless the Ministry of Maritime Transport ("Ministry") approves a different period.

Examples of hazardous work restricted to 18-year-olds or over are listed in Schedule A hereto. In the case of cargo ships, no one under 18 may work in the areas marked on the ship's plan (to be attached to this Declaration) as "hazardous area".

2. Medical certification (Regulation 1.2)

Law, Chapter XI; Regulations, Rules 1223-1233.

Medical certificates shall conform to the STCW requirements, where applicable; in other cases, the STCW requirements are applied with any necessary adjustments.

Qualified opticians on list approved by Ministry may issue certificates concerning eyesight.

Medical examinations follow the /LO/WHO Guidelines referred to in Guideline Bl.2.1

....

....

Declaration of Maritime Labour Compliance – Part II

Measures adopted to ensure ongoing compliance between inspections

The following measures have been drawn up by the shipowner, named in the Maritime Labour Certificate to which this Declaration is attached, to ensure ongoing compliance between inspections:

(State below the measures drawn up to ensure compliance with each of the items in Part I)

1. Minimum age (Regulation 1.1)

   Date of birth of each seafarer is noted against his/her name on the crew list.

   The list is checked at the beginning of each voyage by the master or officer acting on his or her behalf ("competent officer"), who records the date of such verification.

   Each seafarer under 18 receives, at the time of engagement, a note prohibiting him/ her from performing night work or the work specifically listed as hazardous (see Part I, section 1, above) and any other hazardous work, and requiring him/her to consult the competent officer in case of doubt. A copy of the note, with the seafarer's signature under "received and read and the date of signature, is kept by the competent officer.

2. Medical certification (Regulation 1.2)

   The medical certificates are kept in strict confidence by the competent officer, together with a list, prepared under the competent officer's responsibility and stating for each seafarer on board: the functions of the seafarer, the date of the current medical certificate(s) and the health status noted on the certificate concerned.

   In any case of possible doubt as to whether the seafarer is medically fit for a particular function or functions, the competent officer consults the seafarer's doctor or another qualified practitioner and records a summary of the practitioner's conclusions, as well as the practitioner's name and telephone number and the date of the consultation.

   ....

   ....,

APPENDIX 2

In Force and Future Amendments to the MLC

INTRODUCTION

A2.1 The Special Tripartite Committee (STC), established by Article XIII of the MLC, has met three times (in 2014, 2016 and 2018) to consider amendments to the Code, under the procedure set out in Article XV. The 2014 amendments on financial security for repatriation and shipowners' liability are already in force; the dates for entry into force of the other amendments are set out below. The annotations in the footnotes have been inserted by the author.

2014 AMENDMENTS

A2.2 In 2014 the STC agreed the first set of amendments to the MLC to Standards A2.5 and A4.2 (on financial security for repatriation and shipowners' liability respectively) and these came into force on 18 January 2017.[1] There is a consolidated version of the MLC, incorporating these amendments, now available.[2]

The requirement for financial security for repatriation was introduced in the context of a significant number of seafarers being abandoned in foreign ports. This led to the establishment of the joint IMO/ILO database on reported incidents of abandoned seafarers (hosted by the ILO), which is regularly updated and contains details of resolved, unresolved, disputed and inactive cases.[3]

A resolution was also agreed to the effect that maritime labour certificates and declarations of maritime labour compliance would remain valid until the next renewal inspection following entry into force of the amendments, even though they would not contain references to the new inspection points 15 and 16 on financial

1 Amendments of 2014 to the Maritime Labour Convention, 2006, approved by the Conference at its one hundred and third session, Geneva, 11 June 2014: www.ilo.org/wcmsp5/groups/public/---ed_norm/---relconf/documents/meetingdocument/wcms_248905.pdf [Accessed 5 May 2018].

2 MLC, 2006, as amended: www.ilo.org/wcmsp5/groups/public/---ed_norm/---normes/documents/normativeinstrument/wcms_554767.pdf [Accessed 7 May 2018].

3 IMO/ILO Joint data base on reported incidents of abandoned seafarers: www.ilo.org/dyn/seafarers/seafarersBrowse.Home?p_lang=en [Accessed 11 May 2018].

security. However, ships registered with ratifying states have been required to carry the requisite financial security certificates since 18 January 2017.[4]

Financial security for repatriation

A2.3 Before the amendments came into force, Regulation 2.5.2 already required shipowners to have in place financial security to ensure that seafarers were repatriated. The amendments introduced more specific provisions, including: a definition of 'abandonment'; a list of the liabilities which the financial security must cover, including a minimum of four months' wages; and a new Appendix A2-I setting out the information which the certificate of financial security must contain. The amendments also set out the types of financial security that will be acceptable; it will often be a certificate issued by the ship's P&I Club.

'TEXT OF THE AMENDMENTS OF 2014 TO THE MARITIME LABOUR CONVENTION, 2006

Amendments to the Code implementing Regulations 2.5 and 4.2 and appendices of the Maritime Labour Convention, 2006 (MLC, 2006), adopted by the Special Tripartite Committee on 11 April 2014

I. Amendments to the Code implementing Regulation 2.5 – Repatriation of the MLC, 2006 (and appendices)

A. Amendments relating to Standard A2.5

In the present heading, "Standard A2.5 – Repatriation", replace "A2.5" by "A2.5.1".

Following paragraph 9 of the present Standard A2.5, add the following heading and text:

Standard A2.5.2 – Financial security

1. In implementation of Regulation 2.5, paragraph 2, this Standard establishes requirements to ensure the provision of an expeditious and effective financial security system to assist seafarers in the event of their abandonment.

2. For the purposes of this Standard, a seafarer shall be deemed to have been abandoned where, in violation of the requirements of this Convention or the terms of the seafarers' employment agreement, the shipowner:

   (a) fails to cover the cost of the seafarer's repatriation; or

   (b) has left the seafarer without the necessary maintenance and support; or

   (c) has otherwise unilaterally severed their ties with the seafarer including failure to pay contractual wages for a period of at least two months.

4 Resolution on the transitional measures relating to the entry into force of the amendments to the Maritime Labour Convention, 2006, concerning financial security requirements in respect of abandonment of seafarers and for shipowners' liability, paras 1-5: www.ilo.org/wcmsp5/groups/public/---ed_norm/---normes/documents/genericdocument/wcms_360943.pdf [Accessed 10 May 2018].

3. Each Member shall ensure that a financial security system meeting the requirements of this Standard is in place for ships flying its flag. The financial security system may be in the form of a social security scheme or insurance or a national fund or other similar arrangements. Its form shall be determined by the Member after consultation with the shipowners' and seafarers' organizations concerned.

4. The financial security system shall provide direct access, sufficient coverage and expedited financial assistance, in accordance with this Standard, to any abandoned seafarer on a ship flying the flag of the Member.

5. For the purposes of paragraph 2(b) of this Standard, necessary maintenance and support of seafarers shall include: adequate food, accommodation, drinking water supplies, essential fuel for survival on board the ship and necessary medical care.

6. Each Member shall require that ships that fly its flag, and to which paragraph 1 or 2 of Regulation 5.1.3 applies,[5] carry on board a certificate or other documentary evidence of financial security issued by the financial security provider. A copy shall be posted in a conspicuous place on board where it is available to the seafarers. Where more than one financial security provider provides cover, the document provided by each provider shall be carried on board.

7. The certificate or other documentary evidence of financial security shall contain the information required in Appendix A2-I. It shall be in English or accompanied by an English translation.

8. Assistance provided by the financial security system shall be granted promptly upon request made by the seafarer or the seafarer's nominated representative and supported by the necessary justification of entitlement in accordance with paragraph 2 above.[6]

9. Having regard to Regulations 2.2[7] and 2.5,[8] assistance provided by the financial security system shall be sufficient to cover the following:

5 The requirement to carry a certificate of financial security for repatriation only applies to ships which are mandatorily required to carry a maritime labour certificate and those voluntarily put forward for certification; however, other ships are still required to have in place 'an expeditious and effective financial security system' (Standard A2.5.2.1), even if they are not required to carry a financial security certificate. It should be noted that, in respect of financial security for shipowners' liabilities, all ships to which the MLC applies are required to carry 'a certificate or other documentary evidence of financial security' (Standard A4.2.1.11), even if they are not required to carry a maritime labour certificate.

6 The seafarers' employment agreement must set out the repatriation entitlements (Standard A2.1.4(i)) and details of wages (Standard A2.1.4(e)); seafarers are entitled to a monthly account of wages due (Standard A2.2.2); and ships must carry a copy of the flag state's repatriation provisions (Standard A2.5.1.9).

7 Regulation 2.2 provides: 'All seafarers shall be paid for their work regularly and in full in accordance with their employment agreements'; and the associated Code sets out the detailed provisions on payment of wages.

8 Regulation 2.5.1 provides that seafarers must have the right to repatriation at no cost to themselves; and Regulation 2.5.2 establishes the original requirement to provide financial security to ensure that seafarers are duly repatriated.

(a) outstanding wages and other entitlements due from the shipowner to the seafarer under their employment agreement, the relevant collective bargaining agreement or the national law of the flag State,[9] limited to four months of any such outstanding wages and four months of any such outstanding entitlements;

(b) all expenses reasonably incurred by the seafarer, including the cost of repatriation referred to in paragraph 10; and

(c) the essential needs of the seafarer including such items as: adequate food, clothing where necessary, accommodation, drinking water supplies, essential fuel for survival on board the ship, necessary medical care and any other reasonable costs or charges from the act or omission constituting the abandonment until the seafarer's arrival at home.

10. The cost of repatriation shall cover travel by appropriate and expeditious means, normally by air, and include provision for food and accommodation of the seafarer from the time of leaving the ship until arrival at the seafarer's home, necessary medical care, passage and transport of personal effects and any other reasonable costs or charges arising from the abandonment.

11. The financial security shall not cease before the end of the period of validity of the financial security unless the financial security provider has given prior notification of at least 30 days to the competent authority of the flag State.

12. If the provider of insurance or other financial security has made any payment to any seafarer in accordance with this Standard, such provider shall, up to the amount it has paid and in accordance with the applicable law, acquire by subrogation, assignment or otherwise, the rights which the seafarer would have enjoyed.[10]

13. Nothing in this Standard shall prejudice any right of recourse of the insurer or provider of financial security against third parties.

14. The provisions in this Standard are not intended to be exclusive or to prejudice any other rights, claims or remedies that may also be available to compensate seafarers who are abandoned. National laws and regulations may provide that any amounts payable under this Standard can be offset against amounts received from other sources arising from any rights, claims or remedies that may be the subject of compensation under the present Standard.

B. Amendments relating to Guideline B2.5

At the end of the present Guideline B2.5, add the following heading and text:

Guideline B2.5.3 – Financial security

1. In implementation of paragraph 8 of Standard A2.5.2, if time is needed to check the validity of certain aspects of the request of the seafarer or the

9 Any additional national law entitlements should be set out in the seafarers' employment agreement (Standard A2.1.4(k)) and at point 14 of the declaration of maritime labour compliance (Part I) (see MLC, Appendix A5-II).

10 The financial security provider may decide to arrest the relevant ship, to recover any monies it has paid to seafarers, by enforcing a maritime lien.

seafarer's nominated representative, this should not prevent the seafarer from immediately receiving such part of the assistance requested as is recognized as justified.

C. Amendment to include a new appendix

Before Appendix A5-I, add the following appendix:

Appendix A2-I – Evidence of financial security under Regulation 2.5, paragraph 2

The certificate or other documentary evidence referred to in Standard A2.5.2, paragraph 7, shall include the following information:

(a) name of the ship;

(b) port of registry of the ship;

(c) call sign of the ship;

(d) IMO number of the ship;

(e) name and address of the provider or providers of the financial security;

(f) contact details of the persons or entity responsible for handling seafarers' requests for relief;

(g) name of the shipowner;

(h) period of validity of the financial security; and

(i) an attestation from the financial security provider that the financial security meets the requirements of Standard A2.5.2.

D. Amendments relating to Appendices A5-I, A5-II and A5-III

At the end of Appendix A5-I, add the following item:

Financial security for repatriation[11]

In Appendix A5-II, after item 14 under the heading Declaration of Maritime Labour Compliance – Part I, add the following item:

15. Financial security for repatriation (Regulation 2.5)[12]

In Appendix A5-II, after item 14 under the heading Declaration of Maritime Labour Compliance – Part II, add the following item:

15. Financial security for repatriation (Regulation 2.5)[13]

At the end of Appendix A5-III, add the following area:

Financial security for repatriation[14]

11 This makes the financial security certificate subject to flag state inspection for the purposes of issuance or maintenance of a maritime labour certificate.

12 This requires the flag state to set out its national requirements in respect of financial security for repatriation.

13 This requires the shipowner to set out how it meets the flag state requirements to carry a financial security certificate.

14 This makes compliance with the flag state's requirements on the carriage of a financial security certificate subject to a detailed inspection by port state control in a foreign country.

II. Amendments to the Code implementing Regulation 4.2 – Shipowners' liability of the MLC, 2006 (and appendices)

A. Amendments relating to Standard A4.2

In the present heading, "Standard A4.2 – Shipowners' liability", replace "A4.2" by "A4.2.1".

Following paragraph 7 of the present Standard A4.2, add the following text:

8. National laws and regulations shall provide that the system of financial security to assure compensation as provided by paragraph 1(b) of this Standard for contractual claims, as defined in Standard A4.2.2, meet the following minimum requirements:

   (a) the contractual compensation, where set out in the seafarer's employment agreement and without prejudice to subparagraph (c) of this paragraph, shall be paid in full and without delay;

   (b) there shall be no pressure to accept a payment less than the contractual amount;

   (c) where the nature of the long-term disability of a seafarer makes it difficult to assess the full compensation to which the seafarer may be entitled, an interim payment or payments shall be made to the seafarer so as to avoid undue hardship;

   (d) in accordance with Regulation 4.2, paragraph 2, the seafarer shall receive payment without prejudice to other legal rights, but such payment may be offset by the shipowner against any damages resulting from any other claim made by the seafarer against the shipowner and arising from the same incident;[15] and

   (e) the claim for contractual compensation may be brought directly by the seafarer concerned, or their next of kin, or a representative of the seafarer or designated beneficiary.

9. National laws and regulations shall ensure that seafarers receive prior notification if a shipowner's financial security is to be cancelled or terminated.[16]

10. National laws and regulations shall ensure that the competent authority of the flag State is notified by the provider of the financial security if a shipowner's financial security is cancelled or terminated.

11. Each Member shall require that ships that fly its flag carry on board a certificate or other documentary evidence of financial security issued by the financial security provider.[17] A copy shall be posted in a conspicuous place on board where it is available to the seafarers. Where more than one financial security provider provides cover, the document provided by each provider shall be carried on board.

15 This could be a claim in negligence for personal injury.

16 There is no equivalent requirement contained in the financial security provisions for repatriation.

17 All ships to which the MLC applies must carry a certificate of financial security for shipowner's liability. See footnote 5 above, regarding the position with certificates of financial security for repatriation.

12. The financial security shall not cease before the end of the period of validity of the financial security unless the financial security provider has given prior notification of at least 30 days to the competent authority of the flag State.

13. The financial security shall provide for the payment of all contractual claims covered by it which arise during the period for which the document is valid.

14. The certificate or other documentary evidence of financial security shall contain the information required in Appendix A4-I. It shall be in English or accompanied by an English translation.

Add the following heading and text following the present Standard A4.2:

Standard A4.2.2 – Treatment of contractual claims

1. For the purposes of Standard A4.2.1, paragraph 8, and the present Standard, the term "contractual claim" means any claim which relates to death or long-term disability of seafarers due to an occupational injury, illness or hazard as set out in national law, the seafarers' employment agreement or collective agreement.[18]

2. The system of financial security, as provided for in Standard A4.2.1, paragraph 1(b), may be in the form of a social security scheme or insurance or fund or other similar arrangements.[19] Its form shall be determined by the Member after consultation with the shipowners' and seafarers' organizations concerned.

3. National laws and regulations shall ensure that effective arrangements are in place to receive, deal with and impartially settle contractual claims relating to compensation referred to in Standard A4.2.1, paragraph 8, through expeditious and fair procedures.

B. Amendments relating to Guideline B4.2

In the present heading, "Guideline B4.2 – Shipowners' liability", replace "B4.2" by "B4.2.1".

In paragraph 1 of the present Guideline B4.2, replace "Standard A4.2" by "Standard A4.2.1".

Following paragraph 3 of the present Guideline B4.2, add the following heading and text:

Guideline B4.2.2 – Treatment of contractual claims

1. National laws or regulations should provide that the parties to the payment of a contractual claim may use the Model Receipt and Release Form set out in Appendix B4-I.

18 The collective bargaining agreements of the International Transport Workers' Federation (ITF) provide for death in service benefits and detailed scales of compensation for personal injuries: www.itfseafarers.org/itf_agreements.cfm [Accessed 10 May 2018].

19 In many cases, financial security is provided by the P&I Club, which issues the appropriate certificate.

C. Amendment to include new appendices

After Appendix A2-I, add the following appendix:

Appendix A4-I
Evidence of financial security under Regulation 4.2

The certificate or other documentary evidence of financial security required under Standard A4.2.1, paragraph 14, shall include the following information:

(a) name of the ship;

(b) port of registry of the ship;

(c) call sign of the ship;

(d) IMO number of the ship;

(e) name and address of the provider or providers of the financial security;

(f) contact details of the persons or entity responsible for handling seafarers' contractual claims;

(g) name of the shipowner;

(h) period of validity of the financial security; and

(i) an attestation from the financial security provider that the financial security meets the requirements of Standard A4.2.1.

After Appendix A4-I, add the following appendix:

Appendix B4-I – Model Receipt and Release Form

referred to in Guideline B4.2.2

Ship (name, port of registry and IMO number): ....

Incident (date and place): ....

Seafarer/legal heir and/or dependant: ....

Shipowner: ....

I, [Seafarer] [Seafarer's legal heir and/or dependant]* hereby acknowledge receipt of the sum of [currency and amount] in satisfaction of the Shipowner's obligation to pay contractual compensation for personal injury and/or death under the terms and conditions of [my] [the Seafarer's]* employment and I hereby release the Shipowner from their obligations under the said terms and conditions.

The payment is made without admission of liability of any claims and is accepted without prejudice to [my] [the Seafarer's legal heir and/or dependant's]* right to pursue any claim at law in respect of negligence, tort, breach of statutory duty or any other legal redress available and arising out of the above incident.

Dated: ....

Seafarer/legal heir and/or dependant: ....

Signed: ....

For acknowledgement:

Shipowner/Shipowner representative:

Signed: ....

Financial security provider:

Signed: ....

* Delete as appropriate.

D. Amendments relating to Appendices A5-I, A5-II and A5-III

At the end of Appendix A5-I, add the following item:

Financial security relating to shipowners' liability[20]

In Appendix A5-II, as the last item under the heading Declaration of Maritime Labour Compliance – Part I, add the following item:

16. Financial security relating to shipowners' liability (Regulation 4.2)[21]

In Appendix A5-II, as the last item under the heading Declaration of Maritime Labour Compliance – Part II, add the following item:

16. Financial security relating to shipowners' liability (Regulation 4.2)[22]

At the end of Appendix A5-III, add the following area:

Financial security relating to shipowners' liability'[23]

2016 AMENDMENTS

A2.4 In April 2016, the STC agreed amendments to the MLC, which were approved by the International Labour Conference (ILC) in June that year.[24] They come into force on 8 January 2019.

The amendments will: (i) introduce recommendations into Guideline 4.3 (health and safety protection and accident prevention) aimed at addressing the problems arising out of harassment and bullying on board; and (ii) amend Standard A5.1.3 to permit ratifying states to extend the validity of existing maritime labour certificates where, following a successful renewal inspection, a new certificate

20 This makes the financial security certificate subject to flag state inspection for the purposes of issuance or maintenance of a maritime labour certificate.

21 This requires the flag state to set out its national requirements in respect of financial security for shipowners' liabilities.

22 This requires the shipowner to set out how it meets the flag state requirements to carry a financial security certificate.

23 This makes compliance with the flag state's requirements on the carriage of a financial security certificate subject to a detailed inspection by port state control in a foreign country.

24 Amendments of 2016 to the Code of the Maritime Labour Convention, 2006 approved by the Conference at its one hundred and fifth session, Geneva, 9 June 2016: www.ilo.org/wcmsp5/groups/public/---ed_norm/---relconf/documents/meetingdocument/wcms_502375.pdf [Accessed 10 May 2018].

cannot be immediately issued and made available on board the ship to which it relates.

'AMENDMENTS OF 2016 TO THE MARITIME LABOUR CONVENTION, 2006

Amendments to the Code relating to Regulation 4.3 of the MLC, 2006

Guideline B4.3.1 – Provisions on occupational accidents, injuries and diseases

At the end of paragraph 1,[25] add the following text:

Account should also be taken of the latest version of the *Guidance on eliminating shipboard harassment and bullying*[26] jointly published by the International Chamber of Shipping and the International Transport Workers' Federation.

In paragraph 4, move "and" from the end of subparagraph (b) to the end of subparagraph (c). Add the following new subparagraph:

(d) harassment and bullying.[27]

Guideline B4.3.6 – Investigations

In paragraph 2, move "and" from the end of subparagraph (e) to the end of subparagraph (f). Add the following new subparagraph:

(g) problems arising from harassment and bullying.[28]

Amendments to the Code relating to Regulation 5.1 of the MLC, 2006

Standard A5.1.3 – Maritime labour certificate and declaration of maritime labour compliance

Move the text of the current paragraph 4 to the end of paragraph 3.

Replace the current paragraph 4 with the following:

Notwithstanding paragraph 1 of this Standard,[29] where, after a renewal inspection completed prior to the expiry of a maritime labour certificate, the ship is found to continue to meet national laws and regulations or other measures implementing the requirements of this Convention, but a new certificate cannot immediately be issued to and made available on board that ship, the competent authority, or the recognized organization duly authorized for this purpose, may extend the validity

25 MLC Guideline B4.3.1.1 provides that, in the context of Standard A4.3 on health and safety protection and accident prevention, account should be taken of relevant international standards and guidelines.

26 ICS/ITF Guidance on eliminating shipboard harassment and bullying (21 January 2016): www.itfglobal.org/media/1279810/harassment-guide.pdf [Accessed 10 May 2018].

27 This adds 'harassment and bullying' to the matters which the competent should take account of in regard to its implications for health and safety. The list already includes: emergency and accident response; the effects of drug and alcohol dependency; and HIV/AIDS protection and prevention (Guideline B4.3.1.4, paras (a)–(c) respectively).

28 This adds 'problems arising from harassment and bullying' to the list of matters which the competent authority should require to be considered in the context of investigations into the causes and circumstances of serious occupational accidents, injuries and diseases (see also Guideline B4.3.6.1).

29 Standard A5.1.3.1 provides that the validity of a maritime labour certificate must not exceed five years.

of the certificate for a further period not exceeding five months from the expiry date of the existing certificate, and endorse the certificate accordingly. The new certificate shall be valid for a period not exceeding five years starting from the date provided for in paragraph 3 of this Standard.[30]

Appendix A5–II
Maritime Labour Certificate

Add the following text to the end of the model form for the maritime labour certificate:

Extension after renewal inspection (if required)

This is to certify that, following a renewal inspection, the ship was found to continue to be in compliance with national laws and regulations or other measures implementing the requirements of this Convention, and that the present certificate is hereby extended, in accordance with paragraph 4 of Standard A5.1.3, until .... (not more than five months after the expiry date of the existing certificate) to allow for the new certificate to be issued to and made available on board the ship.

Completion date of the renewal inspection on which this extension is based was:

....

Signed: ....

(Signature of authorized official)

Place: ....

Date: ....

(Seal or stamp of the authority, as appropriate)'

2018 AMENDMENTS

A2.5 The STC met again in April 2018 to discuss proposals for amendments to ensure payment of seafarers' wages during the entire period that they were kept in captivity as a result of an act of piracy or armed robbery, including the provision of financial security to cover such liabilities. This matter had also been on the agenda at the 2016 STC and, although agreement was not reached, the matter was delegated to a working group to examine the issue and prepare further proposals.

The 2018 STC agreed to amendments to require that a seafarer's employment agreement will continue to have effect during the entire period of captivity and that wages and other entitlements must be paid during that time.[31] There

30 Which is the date of expiry of the existing certificate.

31 Third Meeting of the Special Tripartite Committee established by the Governing Body in accordance with Article XIII of the Maritime Labour Convention, 2006, as amended (MLC, 2006): www.ilo.org/wcmsp5/groups/public/---ed_norm/---normes/documents/meetingdocument/wcms_627161.pdf [Accessed 11 May 2018].

was no agreement to introduce a requirement for specific financial security to be obtained. However, if a shipowner unilaterally severs its ties with captured seafarers, including failing to pay their wages for two months, this will amount to abandonment, so the latter may rely on the financial security for repatriation (agreed at the 2014 STC), which must cover a minimum of four months' wages and other contractual entitlements during that period.

In accordance with Article XV of the MLC, the 2018 amendments are expected to come into force on 26 December 2020.

'TEXT OF THE AMENDMENTS ADOPTED ON 27 APRIL 2018

Amendments to the Code of the MLC, 2006, relating to Regulation 2.1

Standard A2.1 – Seafarers' employment agreements

Insert new paragraph 7:

7. Each Member shall require that a seafarer's employment agreement shall continue to have effect while a seafarer is held captive on or off the ship as a result of acts of piracy or armed robbery against ships, regardless of whether the date fixed for its expiry has passed or either party has given notice to suspend or terminate it. For the purpose of this paragraph, the term:

   (a) piracy shall have the same meaning as in the United Nations Convention on the Law of the Sea, 1982;[32]

   (b) armed robbery against ships means any illegal act of violence or detention or any act of depredation, or threat thereof, other than an act of piracy, committed for private ends and directed against a ship or against persons or property on board such a ship, within a State's internal waters, archipelagic waters and territorial sea, or any act of inciting or of intentionally facilitating an act described above.[33]

Amendments to the Code of the MLC, 2006, relating to Regulation 2.2

Standard A2.2 – Wages

Insert a new paragraph 7:

7. Where a seafarer is held captive on or off the ship as a result of acts of piracy or armed robbery against ships, wages and other entitlements under the seafarers' employment agreement, relevant collective bargaining agreement or applicable national laws, including the remittance of any allotments as provided in paragraph 4 of this Standard, shall continue

32 Under Article 101(a)(i)–(ii) of UNCLOS, to amount to piracy, the illegal act of violence or detention, or any act of depredation, must take place on the high seas or outside the jurisdiction of any state. For a discussion on the definitions of 'piracy' and 'armed robbery at sea', see Petrig, A, 'Piracy', in Rothwell, D, et al, *The Oxford Handbook of the Law of the Sea* (OUP, Oxford, 2017), 846–851, ch 37. For a brief discourse on the definition of 'piracy', see Professor Malcolm Forster, 'Somali Piracy – An Affront to International Law', in Clarke, M, *Maritime Law Evolving* (Hart Publishing Ltd), 5–7.

33 This definition is taken from paras 2.2.1–2.2.2 of the Annex to IMO Resolution A.1025(26), Code of Practice for the investigation of crimes of piracy and armed robbery against ships, 18 January 2010.

to be paid during the entire period of captivity and until the seafarer is released and duly repatriated in accordance with Standard A2.5.1 or, where the seafarer dies while in captivity, until the date of death as determined in accordance with applicable national laws or regulations. The terms piracy and armed robbery against ships shall have the same meaning as in Standard A2.1, paragraph 7.

Amendments to the Code of the MLC, 2006, relating to Regulation 2.5 – Repatriation

Guideline B2.5.1 – Entitlement

Replace paragraph 8 by the following:

8. The entitlement to repatriation may lapse if the seafarers concerned do not claim it within a reasonable period of time to be defined by national laws or regulations or collective agreements, except where they are held captive on or off the ship as a result of acts of piracy or armed robbery against ships. The terms piracy and armed robbery against ships shall have the same meaning as in Standard A2.1, paragraph 7.'[34]

34 The original para 8 simply stated that: 'The entitlement to repatriation may lapse if the seafarers concerned do not claim it within a reasonable period of time to be defined by national laws or regulations or collective agreements'.

APPENDIX 3

Resources

BIBLIOGRAPHY

Abel, A, 'The Maritime Labour Convention 2006 in the European Union', in Lavelle, J, *The Maritime Labour Convention 2006, International Labour Law Redefined* (Informa Law from Routledge, Abingdon, Oxon)

Aldous, G and Nelson, L, *Work Accidents at Sea* (2nd edition, 9 Gough Square, London)

Baatz, Y, *Maritime Law* (4th edition, Informa Law from Routledge, 2018, Abingdon, Oxon), 368–372, contributed by Filippo Lorenzon

Berlingieri, F, *Berlingieri on Arrest of Ships*, Volume II (Informa Law from Routledge, 6th edition, Abingdon, Oxon)

Churchill, R and Lowe, A, *The Law of the Sea* (Manchester University Press, Manchester, 3rd edition, 2017)

Egan, M and Smith, M, *Employment Agencies, Recruitment Agencies and Agency Workers* (Lexis Nexis, Bristol 2017)

Forster, M, 'Somali Piracy – An Affront to International Law', in Clarke, M, *Maritime Law Evolving* (Hart Publishing Ltd)

Lavelle, J, *The Maritime Labour Convention, 2006, International Labour Law Redefined* (Informa Law from Routledge, Abingdon, Oxon)

Lorenzon, F and Coles, R, *The Law of Yachts and Yachting* (Informa Law from Routledge, 2nd edition, Abingdon, Oxon, 2018)

McConnell, ML, Devlin, D and Doumbia-Henry, C, *The Maritime Labour Convention, 2006: A Legal Primer to an Emerging International Regime* (1st edn, Martinus Nijhoff)

Petrig, A, 'Piracy', in Rothwell, D, et al, *The Oxford Handbook of the Law of the Sea* (OUP, Oxford, 2017)

Syreloglou S, et al, *The UK maritime sectors beyond Brexit – A report on the impact of Brexit on UK shipping, maritime legal services, fisheries and trade by the Institute of Maritime Law and the Southampton Marine and Maritime Institute of the University of Southampton*

Tolley's Employment Handbook (32nd edn, Lexis Nexis, 2018)

USEFUL WEBSITES

General

Human Rights at Sea – contains links to research on seafarers' human rights and labour rights:

- www.humanrightsatsea.org/#about

International Labour Organisation – this section of the ILO website contains a host of material about the MLC, including reports of meetings, monitoring and implementation tools, and a list of ratifying states. There is also a link to the MLC, as amended to include the 2014 amendments on financial security:

- www.ilo.org/global/standards/maritime-labour-convention/lang--en/index.htm

International Seafarers' Welfare and Assistance Network (ISWAN) – this organisation works to promote the welfare of seafarers around the globe, including areas connected with the MLC, such as health and welfare:

- www.seafarerswelfare.org

Nautilus International – a general guide to the MLC:

- www.nautilusint.org/en/news-insight/resources/advice-and-guidance/a-guide-to-the-maritime-labour-convention-2006/

Seafarers' Rights International – an animated guide to the MLC and much information on issues such as abandonment of seafarers, and ship arrest to recover outstanding wages through the enforcement of a maritime lien:

- seafarersrights.org/seafarers-subjects/maritime-labour-convention-mlc/

Red Ensign Group

UK Maritime and Coastguard Agency – access to MLC statutes, MSNs and MGNs:

- www.gov.uk/guidance/mlc-2006-titles-1-to-5-regulations-guidance-and-information

Bermuda Shipping and Maritime Authority – access to MLC legislation, shipping notes and guidance notes:

- www.bermudashipping.bm

Cayman Islands Shipping Registry – access to MLC shipping notes and guidance notes. A fee must be paid to access legislation:

- www.cishipping.com

Gibraltar Shipping Registry – access to MLC legislation, notices and forms:

- www.gibraltarship.com

Isle of Man Ship Registry – access to MLC legislation, notices, guidance and forms:

- www.iomshipregistry.com

Index

All references are to paragraph number.